4.4BSD
User's
Supplementary Documents
(USD)

Now in its twentieth year, the USENIX Association, the UNIX and Advanced Computing Systems professional and technical organization, is a not-for-profit membership association of individuals and institutions with an interest in UNIX and UNIX-like systems, and, by extension, C++, X windows, and other advanced tools and technologies.

USENIX and its members are dedicated to:

- fostering innovation and communicating research and technological developments,
- sharing ideas and experience relevant to UNIX, UNIX-related, and advanced computing systems, and
- providing a neutral forum for the exercise of critical thought and airing of technical issues.

USENIX publishes a journal (**Computing Systems**), a newsletter (*;login:*), Proceedings from its frequent Conferences and Symposia, and a Book Series.

SAGE, The Systems Administrators Guild, a Special Technical Group with the USENIX Association, is dedicated to the advancement of system administration as a profession.

SAGE brings together systems managers and administrators to:

- propagate knowledge of good professional practice,
- recruit talented individuals to the profession,
- recognize individuals who attain professional excellence,
- foster technical development and share solutions to technical problems, and
- communicate in an organized voice with users, management, and vendors on system administration topics.

4.4BSD
User's
Supplementary Documents
(USD)

Berkeley Software Distribution

April, 1994

Computer Systems Research Group
University of California at Berkeley

A USENIX Association Book
O'Reilly & Associates, Inc.
103 Morris Street, Suite A
Sebastopol, CA 94572

Contents

Introduction   ix

Getting Started

Unix for Beginners – Second Edition   tabbed 1

    An introduction to the most basic uses of the system.

Learn – Computer–Aided Instruction on UNIX (Second Edition)   tabbed 2

    Describes a computer-aided instruction program that walks new users through the basics of files, the editor, and document prepararation software.

Basic Utilities

An Introduction to the UNIX Shell   tabbed 3

    Steve Bourne's introduction to the capabilities of *sh,* a command interpreter especially popular for writing shell scripts.

An Introduction to the C shell   tabbed 4

    This introduction to *csh,* (a command interpreter popular for interactive work) describes many commonly used UNIX commands, assumes little prior knowledge of UNIX, and has a glossary useful for beginners.

DC – An Interactive Desk Calculator   tabbed 5

    A super HP calculator, if you do not need floating point.

BC – An Arbitrary Precision Desk-Calculator Language   tabbed 6

    A front end for DC that provides infix notation, control flow, and built–in functions.

Communicating with the World

Mail Reference Manual   tabbed 7

    Complete details on one of the programs for sending and reading your mail.

The Rand MH Message Handling System   tabbed 8

This system for managing your computer mail uses lots of small programs, instead of
one large one.

Text Editing

A Tutorial Introduction to the Unix Text Editor   tabbed 9

An easy way to get started with the line editor, *ed.*

Advanced Editing on Unix   tabbed 10

The next step.

An Introduction to Display Editing with Vi   tabbed 11

The document to learn to use the *vi* screen editor.

Ex Reference Manual (Version 3.7)   tabbed 12

The final reference for the *ex* editor.

Vi Reference Manual   tabbed 13

The definitive reference for the *nvi* editor.

Jove Manual for UNIX Users   tabbed 14

Jove is a small, self-documenting, customizable display editor, based on EMACS. A
plausible alternative to *vi.*

SED – A Non-interactive Text Editor   tabbed 15

Describes a one-pass variant of *ed* useful as a filter for processing large files.

AWK – A Pattern Scanning and Processing Language (Second Edition)   tabbed 16

A program for data selection and transformation.

Document Preparation

Typing Documents on UNIX: Using the −ms Macros with Troff and Nroff   tabbed 17

Describes and gives examples of the basic use of the typesetting tools and ''-ms'', a
frequently used package of formatting requests that make it easier to lay out most
documents.

A Revised Version of −ms   tabbed 18
    A brief description of the Berkeley revisions made to the −ms formatting macros for nroff and troff.

Writing Papers with *nroff* using −me   tabbed 19
    Another popular macro package for *nroff.*

−me Reference Manual   tabbed 20
    The final word on −me.

NROFF/TROFF User´s Manual   tabbed 21
    Extremely detailed information about these document formatting programs.

A TROFF Tutorial   tabbed 22
    An introduction to the most basic uses of *troff* for those who really want to know such things, or want to write their own macros.

A System for Typesetting Mathematics   tabbed 23
    Describes *eqn,* an easy-to-learn language for high-quality mathematical typesetting.

Typesetting Mathematics − User´s Guide (Second Edition)   tabbed 24
    More details about how to use *eqn.*

Tbl − A Program to Format Tables   tabbed 25
    A program for easily typesetting tabular material.

Refer − A Bibliography System   tabbed 26
    An introduction to one set of tools used to maintain bibliographic databases. The major program, *refer,* is used to automatically retrieve and format the references based on document citations.

Some Applications of Inverted Indexes on the UNIX System   tabbed 27
    Mike Lesk's paper describes the *refer* programs in a somewhat larger context.

BIB − A Program for Formatting Bibliographies   tabbed 28
    This is an alternative to *refer* for expanding citations in documents.

Writing Tools − The STYLE and DICTION Programs   tabbed 29
    These are programs which can help you understand and improve your writing style.

Amusements

A Guide to the Dungeons of Doom   tabbed 30

An introduction to the popular game of *rogue*, a fantasy game which is one of the biggest known users of VAX cycles.

Star Trek   tabbed 31

You are the Captain of the Starship Enterprise. Wipe out the Klingons and save the Federation.

List of Documents   inside back cover

Introduction

The documentation for 4.4BSD is in a format similar to the one used for the 4.2BSD and 4.3BSD manuals. It is divided into three sets; each set consists of one or more volumes. The abbreviations for the volume names are listed in square brackets; the abbreviations for the manual sections are listed in parenthesis.

> I. User's Documents
>> User's Reference Manual [URM]
>>> Commands (1)
>>> Games (6)
>>> Macro packages and language conventions (7)
>> User's Supplementary Documents [USD]
>>> Getting Started
>>> Basic Utilities
>>> Communicating with the World
>>> Text Editing
>>> Document Preparation
>>> Amusements
>
> II. Programmer's Documents
>> Programmer's Reference Manual [PRM]
>>> System calls (2)
>>> Subroutines (3)
>>> Special files (4)
>>> File formats and conventions (5)
>> Programmer's Supplementary Documents [PSD]
>>> Documents of Historic Interest
>>> Languages in common use
>>> Programming Tools
>>> Programming Libraries
>>> General Reference
>
> III. System Manager's Manual [SMM]
>> Maintenance commands (8)
>> System Installation and Administration

References to individual documents are given as "volume:document", thus USD:1 refers to the first document in the "User's Supplementary Documents". References to manual pages are given as "*name*(section)" thus *sh*(1) refers to the shell manual entry in section 1.

The manual pages give descriptions of the features of the 4.4BSD system, as developed at the University of California at Berkeley. They do not attempt to provide perspective or tutorial information about the 4.4BSD operating system, its facilities, or its implementation. Various documents on those topics are contained in the "UNIX User's Supplementary Documents" (USD), the "UNIX Programmer's Supplementary Documents" (PSD), and "UNIX System Manager's Manual" (SMM). In particular, for an overview see "The UNIX Time-Sharing System" (PSD:1) by Ritchie and Thompson; for a tutorial see "UNIX for Beginners" (USD:1) by Kernighan, and for an guide to the new features of this latest version, see "Berkeley Software Architecture Manual (4.4 Edition)" (PSD:5).

Within the area it surveys, this volume attempts to be timely, complete and concise. Where the latter two objectives conflict, the obvious is often left unsaid in favor of brevity. It is intended that each program be described as it is, not as it should be. Inevitably, this means that various sections will soon be out of date.

Commands are programs intended to be invoked directly by the user, in contrast to subroutines, that are intended to be called by the user's programs. User commands are described in URM section 1. Commands generally reside in directory */bin* (for *bin*ary programs). Some programs also reside in */usr/bin*, to save space in */bin*. These directories are searched automatically by the command interpreters. Additional directories that may be of interest include */usr/ contrib/ bin,* which has contributed software */usr/ old/ bin,* which has old but sometimes still useful software and */usr/ local/ bin,* which contains software local to your site.

Games have been relegated to URM section 6 and */usr/ games,* to keep them from contaminating the more staid information of URM section 1.

Miscellaneous collection of information necessary for writing in various specialized languages such as character codes, macro packages for typesetting, etc is contained in URM section 7.

System calls are entries into the BSD kernel. The system call interface is identical to a C language procedure call; the equivalent C procedures are described in PRM section 2.

An assortment of subroutines is available; they are described in PRM section 3. The primary libraries in which they are kept are described in *intro*(3). The functions are described in terms of C.

PRM section 4 discusses the characteristics of each system "file" that refers to an I/O device. The names in this section refer to the HP300 device names for the hardware, instead of the names of the special files themselves.

The file formats and conventions (PRM section 5) documents the structure of particular kinds of files; for example, the form of the output of the loader and assembler is given. Excluded are files used by only one command, for example the assembler's intermediate files.

Commands and procedures intended for use primarily by the system administrator are described in SMM section 8. The files described here are almost all kept in the directory */ etc.* The system administration binaries reside in */ sbin,* and */ usr/ sbin.*

Each section consists of independent entries of a page or so each. The name of the entry is in the upper corners of its pages, together with the section number. Entries within each section are alphabetized. The page numbers of each entry start at 1; it is infeasible to number consecutively the pages of a document like this that is republished in many variant forms.

All entries are based on a common format; not all subsections always appear.

The *name* subsection lists the exact names of the commands and subroutines covered under the entry and gives a short description of their purpose.

The *synopsis* summarizes the use of the program being described. A few conventions are used, particularly in the Commands subsection:

Boldface words are considered literals, and are typed just as they appear.

Square brackets [ ] around an argument show that the argument is optional. When an argument is given as "name", it always refers to a file name.

Ellipses "..." are used to show that the previous argument-prototype may be repeated.

A final convention is used by the commands themselves. An argument beginning with a minus sign "−" usually means that it is an option-specifying argument, even if it appears in a position where a file name could appear. Therefore, it is unwise to have files whose names begin with "−".

The *description* subsection discusses in detail the subject at hand.

The *files* subsection gives the names of files that are built into the program.

A *see also* subsection gives pointers to related information.

A *diagnostics* subsection discusses the diagnostic indications that may be produced. Messages that are intended to be self-explanatory are not listed.

The *bugs* subsection gives known bugs and sometimes deficiencies. Occasionally the suggested fix is also described.

At the beginning of URM, PRM, and SSM is a List of Manual Pages, organized by section and alphabetically within each section, and a Permuted Index derived from that List. Within each index entry, the title of the writeup to which it refers is followed by the appropriate section number in parentheses. This fact is important because there is considerable name duplication among the sections, arising principally from commands that exist only to exercise a particular system call. Finally, there is a list of documents on the inside back cover of each volume.

1

UNIX For Beginners — Second Edition

Brian W. Kernighan

AT&T Bell Laboratories
Murray Hill, New Jersey 07974

(Updated for 4.3BSD by Mark Seiden)

ABSTRACT

This paper is meant to help new users get started on the UNIX† operating system. It includes:

- basics needed for day-to-day use of the system — typing commands, correcting typing mistakes, logging in and out, mail, inter-terminal communication, the file system, printing files, redirecting I/O, pipes, and the shell.

- document preparation — a brief discussion of the major formatting programs and macro packages, hints on preparing documents, and capsule descriptions of some supporting software.

- UNIX programming — using the editor, programming the shell, programming in C, other languages and tools.

- An annotated UNIX bibliography.

INTRODUCTION

From the user's point of view, the UNIX operating system is easy to learn and use, and presents few of the usual impediments to getting the job done. It is hard, however, for the beginner to know where to start, and how to make the best use of the facilities available. The purpose of this introduction is to help new users get used to the main ideas of the UNIX system and start making effective use of it quickly.

You should have a couple of other documents with you for easy reference as you read this one. The most important is *The UNIX Programmer's Manual*; it's often easier to tell you to read about something in the manual than to repeat its contents here. The other useful document is *A Tutorial Introduction to the UNIX Text Editor,* which will tell you how to use the editor to get text — programs, data, documents — into the computer.

A word of warning: the UNIX system has become quite popular, and there are several major variants in widespread use. Of course details also change with time. So although the basic structure of UNIX and how to use it is common to all versions, there will certainly be a few things which are different on your system from what is described here. We

have tried to minimize the problem, but be aware of it. In cases of doubt, this paper describes Version 7 UNIX.

This paper has five sections:

1. Getting Started: How to log in, how to type, what to do about mistakes in typing, how to log out. Some of this is dependent on which system you log into (phone numbers, for example) and what terminal you use, so this section must necessarily be supplemented by local information.

2. Day-to-day Use: Things you need every day to use the system effectively: generally useful commands; the file system.

3. Document Preparation: Preparing manuscripts is one of the most common uses for UNIX systems. This section contains advice, but not extensive instructions on any of the formatting tools.

4. Writing Programs: UNIX is an excellent system for developing programs. This section talks about some of the tools, but again is not a tutorial in any of the programming languages provided by the system.

5. A UNIX Reading List. An annotated bibliography of documents that new users should be aware of.

---

† UNIX is a registered trademark of AT&T Bell Laboratories in the USA and other countries.

I. GETTING STARTED

Logging In

You must have a UNIX login name, which you can get from whoever administers your system. You also need to know the phone number, unless your system uses permanently connected terminals. The UNIX system is capable of dealing with a wide variety of terminals: Terminet 300's; Execuport, TI and similar portables; video (CRT) terminals like the HP2640, etc.; high-priced graphics terminals like the Tektronix 4014; plotting terminals like those from GSI and DASI; and even the venerable Teletype in its various forms. But note: UNIX is strongly oriented towards devices with *lower case*. If your terminal produces only upper case (e.g., model 33 Teletype, some video and portable terminals), life will be so difficult that you should look for another terminal.

Be sure to set the switches appropriately on your device. Switches that might need to be adjusted include the speed, upper/lower case mode, full duplex, even parity, and any others that local wisdom advises. Establish a connection using whatever magic is needed for your terminal; this may involve dialing a telephone call or merely flipping a switch. In either case, UNIX should type "**login:**" at you. If it types garbage, you may be at the wrong speed; check the switches. If that fails, push the "break" or "interrupt" key a few times, slowly. If that fails to produce a login message, consult a guru.

When you get a **login:** message, type your login name *in lower case*. Follow it by a RETURN; the system will not do anything until you type a RETURN. If a password is required, you will be asked for it, and (if possible) printing will be turned off while you type it. Don't forget RETURN.

The culmination of your login efforts is a "prompt character," a single character that indicates that the system is ready to accept commands from you. The prompt character is usually a dollar sign **$** or a percent sign **%**. (You may also get a message of the day just before the prompt character, or a notification that you have mail.)

Typing Commands

Once you've seen the prompt character, you can type commands, which are requests that the system do something. Try typing

     date

followed by RETURN. You should get back something like

     Mon Jan 16 14:17:10 EST 1978

Don't forget the RETURN after the command, or nothing will happen. If you think you're being ignored, type a RETURN; something should happen. RETURN won't be mentioned again, but don't forget it — it has to be there at the end of each line.

Another command you might try is **who**, which tells you everyone who is currently logged in:

     who

gives something like

mb	**tty01**	**Jan 16**	**09:11**
ski	**tty05**	**Jan 16**	**09:33**
gam	**tty11**	**Jan 16**	**13:07**

The time is when the user logged in; "ttyxx" is the system's idea of what terminal the user is on.

If you make a mistake typing the command name, and refer to a non-existent command, you will be told. For example, if you type

     whom

you will be told

     whom: not found

Of course, if you inadvertently type the name of some other command, it will run, with more or less mysterious results.

Strange Terminal Behavior

Sometimes you can get into a state where your terminal acts strangely. For example, each letter may be typed twice, or the RETURN may not cause a line feed or a return to the left margin. You can often fix this by logging out and logging back in.†
Or you can read the description of the command **stty** in section 1 of the manual. To get intelligent treatment of tab characters (which are much used in UNIX) if your terminal doesn't have tabs, type the command

     stty −tabs

and the system will convert each tab into the right number of blanks for you. If your terminal does have computer-settable tabs, the command **tabs** will set the stops correctly for you.

Mistakes in Typing

If you make a typing mistake, and see it before RETURN has been typed, there are two ways to recover. The sharp-character **#** erases the last character typed; in fact successive uses of **#** erase characters back to the beginning of the line (but not beyond). So if you type badly, you can correct as you go:

     dd#atte##e

is the same as **date**.‡

---

† In Berkeley Unix, the command "reset<control-j>" will often reset a terminal apparently in a strange state because a fullscreen editor crashed.

‡ Many installations set the erase character for display terminals to the delete or backspace key. "stty all" tells you what it actually is.

1

The at-sign **@** erases all of the characters typed so far on the current input line, so if the line is irretrievably fouled up, type an **@** and start the line over.

What if you must enter a sharp or at-sign as part of the text? If you precede either **#** or **@** by a backslash ****, it loses its erase meaning. So to enter a sharp or at-sign in something, type **\#** or **\@**. The system will always echo a newline at you after your at-sign, even if preceded by a backslash. Don't worry — the at-sign has been recorded.

To erase a backslash, you have to type two sharps or two at-signs, as in **\#\#**. The backslash is used extensively in UNIX to indicate that the following character is in some way special.

Read-ahead

UNIX has full read-ahead, which means that you can type as fast as you want, whenever you want, even when some command is typing at you. If you type during output, your input characters will appear intermixed with the output characters, but they will be stored away and interpreted in the correct order. So you can type several commands one after another without waiting for the first to finish or even begin.

Stopping a Program

You can stop most programs by typing the character "DEL" (perhaps called "delete" or "rubout" on your terminal). The "interrupt" or "break" key found on most terminals can also be used.† In a few programs, like the text editor, DEL stops whatever the program is doing but leaves you in that program. Hanging up the phone will stop most programs.‡

Logging Out

The easiest way to log out is to hang up the phone. You can also type

> **login**

and let someone else use the terminal you were on.* It is usually not sufficient just to turn off the terminal. Most UNIX systems do not use a time-out mechanism, so you'll be there forever unless you hang up.

Mail

When you log in, you may sometimes get the message

> **You have mail.**

UNIX provides a postal system so you can communicate with other users of the system. To read your mail, type the command

> **mail**

Your mail will be printed, one message at a time, most recent message first.‡ After each message, **mail** waits for you to say what to do with it. The two basic responses are **d**, which deletes the message, and RETURN, which does not (so it will still be there the next time you read your mailbox). Other responses are described in the manual. (Earlier versions of **mail** do not process one message at a time, but are otherwise similar.)

How do you send mail to someone else? Suppose it is to go to "joe" (assuming "joe" is someone's login name). The easiest way is this:

> **mail joe**
> *now type in the text of the letter*
> *on as many lines as you like ...*
> *After the last line of the letter*
> *type the character "control–d",*
> *that is, hold down "control" and type*
> *a letter "d".*

And that's it. The "control-d" sequence, often called "EOF" for end-of-file, is used throughout the system to mark the end of input from a terminal, so you might as well get used to it.

For practice, send mail to yourself. (This isn't as strange as it might sound — mail to oneself is a handy reminder mechanism.)

There are other ways to send mail — you can send a previously prepared letter, and you can mail to a number of people all at once. For more details see **mail**(1). (The notation **mail**(1) means the command **mail** in section 1 of the *UNIX Programmer's Manual*.)

Writing to other users†

At some point, out of the blue will come a message like

> **Message from joe tty07...**

accompanied by a startling beep. It means that Joe wants to talk to you, but unless you take explicit action you won't be able to talk back. To respond, type the command

> **write joe**

This establishes a two-way communication path. Now whatever Joe types on his terminal will appear on yours and vice versa. The path is slow, rather like talking to the moon. (If you are in the middle of something, you have to get to a state where you can type a command. Normally, whatever program you are running has to terminate or be terminated.

---

† In Berkeley Unix, "control–c" is the usual way to stop programs. "stty all" tells you the value of your "intr" key.
‡ If you use the c shell, programs running in the background continue running even if you hang up.
* "control–d" and "logout" are other alternatives.

‡ The Berkeley mail program lists the headers of some number of un-read pieces of mail in the order of their receipt.
† Although "write" works on Berkeley UNIX, there is a much nicer way of communicating using display-terminals — "talk" splits the screen into two sections, and both of you can type simultaneously (see talk(1)).

1

If you're editing, you can escape temporarily from the editor — read the editor tutorial.)

A protocol is needed to keep what you type from getting garbled up with what Joe types. Typically it's like this:

>Joe types **write smith** and waits.
>Smith types **write joe** and waits.
>Joe now types his message (as many lines as he likes). When he's ready for a reply, he signals it by typing (**o**), which stands for "over".
>Now Smith types a reply, also terminated by (**o**).
>This cycle repeats until someone gets tired; he then signals his intent to quit with (**oo**), for "over and out".
>To terminate the conversation, each side must type a "control-d" character alone on a line. ("Delete" also works.) When the other person types his "control-d", you will get the message **EOF** on your terminal.

If you write to someone who isn't logged in, or who doesn't want to be disturbed, you'll be told. If the target is logged in but doesn't answer after a decent interval, simply type "control-d".

On-line Manual

The *UNIX Programmer's Manual* is typically kept on-line. If you get stuck on something, and can't find an expert to assist you, you can print on your terminal some manual section that might help. This is also useful for getting the most up-to-date information on a command. To print a manual section, type "man command-name". Thus to read up on the **who** command, type

>**man who**

and, of course,

>**man man**

tells all about the **man** command.

Computer Aided Instruction

Your UNIX system may have available a program called **learn**, which provides computer aided instruction on the file system and basic commands, the editor, document preparation, and even C programming. Try typing the command

>**learn**

If **learn** exists on your system, it will tell you what to do from there. s.

II. DAY-TO-DAY USE

Creating Files — The Editor

If you have to type a paper or a letter or a program, how do you get the information stored in the machine? Most of these tasks are done with the UNIX "text editor" **ed**. Since **ed** is thoroughly documented in **ed**(1) and

explained in *A Tutorial Introduction to the UNIX Text Editor,* we won't spend any time here describing how to use it. All we want it for right now is to make some *files.* (A file is just a collection of information stored in the machine, a simplistic but adequate definition.)

To create a file called **junk** with some text in it, do the following:

>**ed junk**   (invokes the text editor)
>**a**   (command to "ed", to add text)
>*now type in*
>*whatever text you want ...*
>**.**   (signals the end of adding text)

The "**.**" that signals the end of adding text must be at the beginning of a line by itself. Don't forget it, for until it is typed, no other **ed** commands will be recognized — everything you type will be treated as text to be added.

At this point you can do various editing operations on the text you typed in, such as correcting spelling mistakes, rearranging paragraphs and the like. Finally, you must write the information you have typed into a file with the editor command **w**:

>**w**

ed will respond with the number of characters it wrote into the file **junk**.

Until the **w** command, nothing is stored permanently, so if you hang up and go home the information is lost.† But after **w** the information is there permanently; you can re-access it any time by typing

>**ed junk**

Type a **q** command to quit the editor. (If you try to quit without writing, **ed** will print a **?** to remind you. A second **q** gets you out regardless.)

Now create a second file called **temp** in the same manner. You should now have two files, **junk** and **temp**.

What files are out there?

The **ls** (for "list") command lists the names (not contents) of any of the files that UNIX knows about. If you type

>**ls**

the response will be

>**junk**
>**temp**

which are indeed the two files just created. The names are sorted into alphabetical order automatically, but other variations are possible. For example, the command

>**ls −t**

causes the files to be listed in the order in which they were

---

† This is not strictly true — if you hang up while editing, the data you were working on is saved in a file called **ed.hup**, which you can continue with at your next session.

last changed, most recent first. The –l option gives a ''long'' listing:

ls –l

will produce something like

–rw–rw–rw– 1 bwk   41 Jul 22 2:56 junk
–rw–rw–rw– 1 bwk   78 Jul 22 2:57 temp

The date and time are of the last change to the file. The 41 and 78 are the number of characters (which should agree with the numbers you got from **ed**). **bwk** is the owner of the file, that is, the person who created it. The **–rw–rw–rw–** tells who has permission to read and write the file, in this case everyone.

Options can be combined: **ls –lt** gives the same thing as **ls –l**, but sorted into time order. You can also name the files you're interested in, and **ls** will list the information about them only. More details can be found in **ls**(1).

The use of optional arguments that begin with a minus sign, like –t and –lt, is a common convention for UNIX programs. In general, if a program accepts such optional arguments, they precede any filename arguments. It is also vital that you separate the various arguments with spaces: **ls–l** is not the same as **ls –l**.

Printing Files

Now that you've got a file of text, how do you print it so people can look at it? There are a host of programs that do that, probably more than are needed.

One simple thing is to use the editor, since printing is often done just before making changes anyway. You can say

ed junk
1,$p

ed will reply with the count of the characters in **junk** and then print all the lines in the file. After you learn how to use the editor, you can be selective about the parts you print.

There are times when it's not feasible to use the editor for printing. For example, there is a limit on how big a file **ed** can handle (several thousand lines). Secondly, it will only print one file at a time, and sometimes you want to print several, one after another. So here are a couple of alternatives.

First is **cat**, the simplest of all the printing programs. **cat** simply prints on the terminal the contents of all the files named in a list. Thus

cat junk

prints one file, and

cat junk temp

prints two. The files are simply concatenated (hence the name ''cat'') onto the terminal.

pr produces formatted printouts of files. As with **cat**, **pr** prints all the files named in a list. The difference is that it produces headings with date, time, page number and file name at the top of each page, and extra lines to skip over the fold in the paper. Thus,

pr junk temp

will print **junk** neatly, then skip to the top of a new page and print **temp** neatly.

pr can also produce multi-column output:

pr –3 junk

prints **junk** in 3-column format. You can use any reasonable number in place of ''3'' and **pr** will do its best. **pr** has other capabilities as well; see **pr**(1).

It should be noted that **pr** is *not* a formatting program in the sense of shuffling lines around and justifying margins. The true formatters are **nroff** and **troff**, which we will get to in the section on document preparation.

There are also programs that print files on a high-speed printer. Look in your manual under **opr** and **lpr**. Which to use depends on what equipment is attached to your machine.

Shuffling Files About

Now that you have some files in the file system and some experience in printing them, you can try bigger things. For example, you can move a file from one place to another (which amounts to giving it a new name), like this:

mv junk precious

This means that what used to be ''junk'' is now ''precious''. If you do an **ls** command now, you will get

precious
temp

Beware that if you move a file to another one that already exists, the already existing contents are lost forever.

If you want to make a *copy* of a file (that is, to have two versions of something), you can use the **cp** command:

cp precious temp1

makes a duplicate copy of **precious** in **temp1**.

Finally, when you get tired of creating and moving files, there is a command to remove files from the file system, called **rm**.

rm temp temp1

will remove both of the files named.

You will get a warning message if one of the named files wasn't there, but otherwise **rm**, like most UNIX commands, does its work silently. There is no prompting or chatter, and error messages are occasionally curt. This terseness is sometimes disconcerting to newcomers, but experienced users find it desirable.

What's in a Filename

So far we have used filenames without ever saying what's a legal name, so it's time for a couple of rules. First,

1

filenames are limited to 14 characters, which is enough to be descriptive.† Second, although you can use almost any character in a filename, common sense says you should stick to ones that are visible, and that you should probably avoid characters that might be used with other meanings. We have already seen, for example, that in the **ls** command, **ls −t** means to list in time order. So if you had a file whose name was **−t**, you would have a tough time listing it by name. Besides the minus sign, there are other characters which have special meaning. To avoid pitfalls, you would do well to use only letters, numbers and the period until you're familiar with the situation.

On to some more positive suggestions. Suppose you're typing a large document like a book. Logically this divides into many small pieces, like chapters and perhaps sections. Physically it must be divided too, for **ed** will not handle really big files. Thus you should type the document as a number of files. You might have a separate file for each chapter, called

        chap1
        chap2
        etc...

Or, if each chapter were broken into several files, you might have

        chap1.1
        chap1.2
        chap1.3
        ...
        chap2.1
        chap2.2
        ...

You can now tell at a glance where a particular file fits into the whole.

There are advantages to a systematic naming convention which are not obvious to the novice UNIX user. What if you wanted to print the whole book? You could say

        pr chap1.1 chap1.2 chap1.3 ......

but you would get tired pretty fast, and would probably even make mistakes. Fortunately, there is a shortcut. You can say

        pr chap*

The * means "anything at all," so this translates into "print all files whose names begin with **chap**", listed in alphabetical order.

This shorthand notation is not a property of the **pr** command, by the way. It is system-wide, a service of the program that interprets commands (the "shell," **sh**(1)). Using that fact, you can see how to list the names of the files in the book:

        ls chap*

_____
† In 4.2 BSD the limit was extended to 255 characters.

produces

        chap1.1
        chap1.2
        chap1.3
        ...

The * is not limited to the last position in a filename — it can be anywhere and can occur several times. Thus

        rm *junk* *temp*

removes all files that contain **junk** or **temp** as any part of their name. As a special case, * by itself matches every filename, so

        pr *

prints all your files (alphabetical order), and

        rm *

removes _all files_. (You had better be _very_ sure that's what you wanted to say!)

The * is not the only pattern-matching feature available. Suppose you want to print only chapters 1 through 4 and 9. Then you can say

        pr chap[12349]*

The [...] means to match any of the characters inside the brackets. A range of consecutive letters or digits can be abbreviated, so you can also do this with

        pr chap[1–49]*

Letters can also be used within brackets: [a–z] matches any character in the range **a** through **z**.

The ? pattern matches any single character, so

        ls ?

lists all files which have single-character names, and

        ls −l chap?.1

lists information about the first file of each chapter (**chap1.1**, **chap2.1**, etc.).

Of these niceties, * is certainly the most useful, and you should get used to it. The others are frills, but worth knowing.

If you should ever have to turn off the special meaning of *, ?, etc., enclose the entire argument in single quotes, as in

        ls '?'

We'll see some more examples of this shortly.

What's in a Filename, Continued

When you first made that file called **junk**, how did the system know that there wasn't another **junk** somewhere else, especially since the person in the next office is also reading this tutorial? The answer is that generally each user has a private _directory_, which contains only the files that belong to him. When you log in, you are "in" your direc-

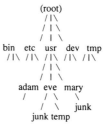

tory. Unless you take special action, when you create a new file, it is made in the directory that you are currently in; this is most often your own directory, and thus the file is unrelated to any other file of the same name that might exist in someone else's directory.

The set of all files is organized into a (usually big) tree, with your files located several branches into the tree. It is possible for you to "walk" around this tree, and to find any file in the system, by starting at the root of the tree and walking along the proper set of branches. Conversely, you can start where you are and walk toward the root.

Let's try the latter first. The basic tools is the command **pwd** ("print working directory"), which prints the name of the directory you are currently in.

Although the details will vary according to the system you are on, if you give the command **pwd**, it will print something like

/usr/your-name

This says that you are currently in the directory **your-name**, which is in turn in the directory **/usr**, which is in turn in the root directory called by convention just **/**. (Even if it's not called **/usr** on your system, you will get something analogous. Make the corresponding mental adjustment and read on.)

If you now type

ls /usr/your-name

you should get exactly the same list of file names as you get from a plain **ls**: with no arguments, **ls** lists the contents of the current directory; given the name of a directory, it lists the contents of that directory.

Next, try

ls /usr

This should print a long series of names, among which is your own login name **your-name**. On many systems, **usr** is a directory that contains the directories of all the normal users of the system, like you.

The next step is to try

ls /

You should get a response something like this (although again the details may be different):

       bin
       dev
       etc
       lib
       tmp
       usr

This is a collection of the basic directories of files that the system knows about; we are at the root of the tree.

Now try

cat /usr/your-name/junk

(if **junk** is still around in your directory). The name

/usr/your-name/junk

is called the **pathname** of the file that you normally think of as "junk". "Pathname" has an obvious meaning: it represents the full name of the path you have to follow from the root through the tree of directories to get to a particular file. It is a universal rule in the UNIX system that anywhere you can use an ordinary filename, you can use a pathname.

Here is a picture which may make this clearer:

```
                        (root)
                        / | \
                       /  |  \
                      /   |   \
                bin  etc  usr  dev  tmp
               / | \  / | \  / | \  / | \  / | \
                          /   |   \
                         /    |    \
                      adam   eve   mary
                      /    /  \      \
                     /    /    \    junk
                  junk temp
```

Notice that Mary's **junk** is unrelated to Eve's.

This isn't too exciting if all the files of interest are in your own directory, but if you work with someone else or on several projects concurrently, it becomes handy indeed. For example, your friends can print your book by saying

pr /usr/your-name/chap*

Similarly, you can find out what files your neighbor has by saying

ls /usr/neighbor-name

or make your own copy of one of his files by

cp /usr/your-neighbor/his-file yourfile

If your neighbor doesn't want you poking around in his files, or vice versa, privacy can be arranged. Each file and directory has read-write-execute permissions for the owner, a group, and everyone else, which can be set to control access. See **ls**(1) and **chmod**(1) for details. As a matter of observed fact, most users most of the time find openness of more benefit than privacy.

As a final experiment with pathnames, try

ls /bin /usr/bin

Do some of the names look familiar? When you run a program, by typing its name after the prompt character, the system simply looks for a file of that name. It normally looks first in your directory (where it typically doesn't find it), then in **/bin** and finally in **/usr/bin**. There is nothing magic about commands like **cat** or **ls**, except that they have been collected into a couple of places to be easy to find and administer.

What if you work regularly with someone else on common information in his directory? You could just log in as your friend each time you want to, but you can also say "I want to work on his files instead of my own". This is done

1

by changing the directory that you are currently in:

cd /usr/your-friend

(On some systems, **cd** is spelled **chdir**.) Now when you use a filename in something like **cat** or **pr**, it refers to the file in your friend's directory. Changing directories doesn't affect any permissions associated with a file — if you couldn't access a file from your own directory, changing to another directory won't alter that fact. Of course, if you forget what directory you're in, type

pwd

to find out.

It is usually convenient to arrange your own files so that all the files related to one thing are in a directory separate from other projects. For example, when you write your book, you might want to keep all the text in a directory called **book**. So make one with

mkdir book

then go to it with

cd book

then start typing chapters. The book is now found in (presumably)

/usr/your-name/book

To remove the directory **book**, type

rm book/*
rmdir book

The first command removes all files from the directory; the second removes the empty directory.

You can go up one level in the tree of files by saying

cd ..

"**..**" is the name of the parent of whatever directory you are currently in. For completeness, "**.**" is an alternate name for the directory you are in.

Using Files instead of the Terminal

Most of the commands we have seen so far produce output on the terminal; some, like the editor, also take their input from the terminal. It is universal in UNIX systems that the terminal can be replaced by a file for either or both of input and output. As one example,

ls

makes a list of files on your terminal. But if you say

ls >filelist

a list of your files will be placed in the file **filelist** (which will be created if it doesn't already exist, or overwritten if it does). The symbol > means "put the output on the following file, rather than on the terminal." Nothing is produced on the terminal. As another example, you could combine several files into one by capturing the output of **cat** in a file:

cat f1 f2 f3 >temp

The symbol >> operates very much like > does, except that it means "add to the end of." That is,

cat f1 f2 f3 >>temp

means to concatenate **f1**, **f2** and **f3** to the end of whatever is already in **temp**, instead of overwriting the existing contents. As with >, if **temp** doesn't exist, it will be created for you.

In a similar way, the symbol < means to take the input for a program from the following file, instead of from the terminal. Thus, you could make up a script of commonly used editing commands and put them into a file called **script**. Then you can run the script on a file by saying

ed file <script

As another example, you can use **ed** to prepare a letter in file **let**, then send it to several people with

mail adam eve mary joe <let

Pipes

One of the novel contributions of the UNIX system is the idea of a *pipe*. A pipe is simply a way to connect the output of one program to the input of another program, so the two run as a sequence of processes — a pipeline.

For example,

pr f g h

will print the files **f**, **g**, and **h**, beginning each on a new page. Suppose you want them run together instead. You could say

cat f g h >temp
pr <temp
rm temp

but this is more work than necessary. Clearly what we want is to take the output of **cat** and connect it to the input of **pr**. So let us use a pipe:

cat f g h | pr

The vertical bar | means to take the output from **cat**, which would normally have gone to the terminal, and put it into **pr** to be neatly formatted.

There are many other examples of pipes. For example,

ls | pr −3

prints a list of your files in three columns. The program **wc** counts the number of lines, words and characters in its input, and as we saw earlier, **who** prints a list of currently-logged on people, one per line. Thus

who | wc

tells how many people are logged on. And of course

ls | wc

counts your files.

Any program that reads from the terminal can read from a pipe instead; any program that writes on the terminal can drive a pipe. You can have as many elements in a pipeline as you wish.

Many UNIX programs are written so that they will take their input from one or more files if file arguments are given; if no arguments are given they will read from the terminal, and thus can be used in pipelines. **pr** is one example:

pr –3 a b c

prints files **a**, **b** and **c** in order in three columns. But in

cat a b c | pr –3

pr prints the information coming down the pipeline, still in three columns.

The Shell

We have already mentioned once or twice the mysterious "shell," which is in fact **sh**(1).† The shell is the program that interprets what you type as commands and arguments. It also looks after translating *, etc., into lists of filenames, and <, >, and | into changes of input and output streams.

The shell has other capabilities too. For example, you can run two programs with one command line by separating the commands with a semicolon; the shell recognizes the semicolon and breaks the line into two commands. Thus

date; who

does both commands before returning with a prompt character.

You can also have more than one program running *simultaneously* if you wish. For example, if you are doing something time-consuming, like the editor script of an earlier section, and you don't want to wait around for the results before starting something else, you can say

ed file <script &

The ampersand at the end of a command line says "start this command running, then take further commands from the terminal immediately," that is, don't wait for it to complete. Thus the script will begin, but you can do something else at the same time. Of course, to keep the output from interfering with what you're doing on the terminal, it would be better to say

ed file <script >script.out &

which saves the output lines in a file called **script.out**.

When you initiate a command with **&**, the system replies with a number called the process number, which

---
† On Berkeley Unix systems, the usual shell for interactive use is the c shell, **csh**(1).

identifies the command in case you later want to stop it. If you do, you can say

kill process-number

If you forget the process number, the command **ps** will tell you about everything you have running. (If you are desperate, **kill 0** will kill all your processes.) And if you're curious about other people, **ps a** will tell you about *all* programs that are currently running.

You can say

(command-1; command-2; command-3) &

to start three commands in the background, or you can start a background pipeline with

command-1 | command-2 &

Just as you can tell the editor or some similar program to take its input from a file instead of from the terminal, you can tell the shell to read a file to get commands. (Why not? The shell, after all, is just a program, albeit a clever one.) For instance, suppose you want to set tabs on your terminal, and find out the date and who's on the system every time you log in. Then you can put the three necessary commands (**tabs, date, who**) into a file, let's call it **startup**, and then run it with

sh startup

This says to run the shell with the file **startup** as input. The effect is as if you had typed the contents of **startup** on the terminal.

If this is to be a regular thing, you can eliminate the need to type **sh**: simply type, once only, the command

chmod +x startup

and thereafter you need only say

startup

to run the sequence of commands. The **chmod**(1) command marks the file executable; the shell recognizes this and runs it as a sequence of commands.

If you want **startup** to run automatically every time you log in, create a file in your login directory called **.profile**, and place in it the line **startup**. When the shell first gains control when you log in, it looks for the **.profile** file and does whatever commands it finds in it.† We'll get back to the shell in the section on programming.

III. DOCUMENT PREPARATION

UNIX systems are used extensively for document preparation. There are two major formatting programs, that is, programs that produce a text with justified right margins, automatic page numbering and titling, automatic hyphenation, and the like. **nroff** is designed to produce output on terminals and line-printers. **troff** (pronounced "tee-roff")

---
† The c shell instead reads a file called **.login**

instead drives a phototypesetter, which produces very high quality output on photographic paper. This paper was formatted with **troff**.

Formatting Packages

The basic idea of **nroff** and **troff** is that the text to be formatted contains within it "formatting commands" that indicate in detail how the formatted text is to look. For example, there might be commands that specify how long lines are, whether to use single or double spacing, and what running titles to use on each page.

Because **nroff** and **troff** are relatively hard to learn to use effectively, several "packages" of canned formatting requests are available to let you specify paragraphs, running titles, footnotes, multi-column output, and so on, with little effort and without having to learn **nroff** and **troff**. These packages take a modest effort to learn, but the rewards for using them are so great that it is time well spent.

In this section, we will provide a hasty look at the "manuscript" package known as **−ms**. Formatting requests typically consist of a period and two upper-case letters, such as **.TL**, which is used to introduce a title, or **.PP** to begin a new paragraph.

A document is typed so it looks something like this:

```
.TL
title of document
.AU
author name
.SH
section heading
.PP
paragraph ...
.PP
another paragraph ...
.SH
another section heading
.PP
etc.
```

The lines that begin with a period are the formatting requests. For example, **.PP** calls for starting a new paragraph. The precise meaning of **.PP** depends on what output device is being used (typesetter or terminal, for instance), and on what publication the document will appear in. For example, **−ms** normally assumes that a paragraph is preceded by a space (one line in **nroff**, ½ line in **troff**), and the first word is indented. These rules can be changed if you like, but they are changed by changing the interpretation of **.PP**, not by re-typing the document.

To actually produce a document in standard format using **−ms**, use the command

troff −ms files ...

for the typesetter, and

nroff −ms files ...

for a terminal. The **−ms** argument tells **troff** and **nroff** to use the manuscript package of formatting requests.

There are several similar packages; check with a local expert to determine which ones are in common use on your machine.

Supporting Tools

In addition to the basic formatters, there is a host of supporting programs that help with document preparation. The list in the next few paragraphs is far from complete, so browse through the manual and check with people around you for other possibilities.

eqn and **neqn** let you integrate mathematics into the text of a document, in an easy-to-learn language that closely resembles the way you would speak it aloud. For example, the **eqn** input

$$\text{sum from i=0 to n x sub i }\tilde{}=\tilde{}\text{ pi over 2}$$

produces the output

The program **tbl** provides an analogous service for preparing tabular material; it does all the computations necessary to align complicated columns with elements of varying widths.

refer prepares bibliographic citations from a data base, in whatever style is defined by the formatting package. It looks after all the details of numbering references in sequence, filling in page and volume numbers, getting the author's initials and the journal name right, and so on.

spell and **typo** detect possible spelling mistakes in a document.† **spell** works by comparing the words in your document to a dictionary, printing those that are not in the dictionary. It knows enough about English spelling to detect plurals and the like, so it does a very good job. **typo** looks for words which are "unusual", and prints those. Spelling mistakes tend to be more unusual, and thus show up early when the most unusual words are printed first.

grep looks through a set of files for lines that contain a particular text pattern (rather like the editor's context search does, but on a bunch of files). For example,

grep 'ing$' chap*

will find all lines that end with the letters **ing** in the files **chap***. (It is almost always a good practice to put single quotes around the pattern you're searching for, in case it contains characters like * or $ that have a special meaning to the shell.) **grep** is often useful for finding out in which of a set of files the misspelled words detected by **spell** are actually located.

diff prints a list of the differences between two files, so you can compare two versions of something automatically (which certainly beats proofreading by hand).

wc counts the words, lines and characters in a set of files. **tr** translates characters into other characters; for example it will convert upper to lower case and vice versa.

---

† "typo" is not provided with Berkeley Unix.

1

This translates upper into lower:

tr A–Z a–z <input >output

sort sorts files in a variety of ways; **cref** makes cross-references; **ptx** makes a permuted index (keyword-in-context listing). **sed** provides many of the editing facilities of **ed**, but can apply them to arbitrarily long inputs. **awk** provides the ability to do both pattern matching and numeric computations, and to conveniently process fields within lines. These programs are for more advanced users, and they are not limited to document preparation. Put them on your list of things to learn about.

Most of these programs are either independently documented (like **eqn** and **tbl**), or are sufficiently simple that the description in the *UNIX Programmer's Manual* is adequate explanation.

Hints for Preparing Documents

Most documents go through several versions (always more than you expected) before they are finally finished. Accordingly, you should do whatever possible to make the job of changing them easy.

First, when you do the purely mechanical operations of typing, type so that subsequent editing will be easy. Start each sentence on a new line. Make lines short, and break lines at natural places, such as after commas and semicolons, rather than randomly. Since most people change documents by rewriting phrases and adding, deleting and rearranging sentences, these precautions simplify any editing you have to do later.

Keep the individual files of a document down to modest size, perhaps ten to fifteen thousand characters. Larger files edit more slowly, and of course if you make a dumb mistake it's better to have clobbered a small file than a big one. Split into files at natural boundaries in the document, for the same reasons that you start each sentence on a new line.

The second aspect of making change easy is to not commit yourself to formatting details too early. One of the advantages of formatting packages like –**ms** is that they permit you to delay decisions to the last possible moment. Indeed, until a document is printed, it is not even decided whether it will be typeset or put on a line printer.

As a rule of thumb, for all but the most trivial jobs, you should type a document in terms of a set of requests like **.PP**, and then define them appropriately, either by using one of the canned packages (the better way) or by defining your own **nroff** and **troff** commands. As long as you have entered the text in some systematic way, it can always be cleaned up and re-formatted by a judicious combination of editing commands and request definitions.

IV. PROGRAMMING

There will be no attempt made to teach any of the programming languages available but a few words of advice are in order. One of the reasons why the UNIX system is a productive programming environment is that there is already a rich set of tools available, and facilities like pipes, I/O redirection, and the capabilities of the shell often make it possible to do a job by pasting together programs that already exist instead of writing from scratch.

The Shell

The pipe mechanism lets you fabricate quite complicated operations out of spare parts that already exist. For example, the first draft of the **spell** program was (roughly)

```
cat ...      collect the files
| tr ...     put each word on a new line
| tr ...     delete punctuation, etc.
| sort       into dictionary order
| uniq       discard duplicates
| comm       print words in text
             but not in dictionary
```

More pieces have been added subsequently, but this goes a long way for such a small effort.

The editor can be made to do things that would normally require special programs on other systems. For example, to list the first and last lines of each of a set of files, such as a book, you could laboriously type

```
ed
e chap1.1
1p
$p
e chap1.2
1p
$p
etc.
```

But you can do the job much more easily. One way is to type

ls chap* >temp

to get the list of filenames into a file. Then edit this file to make the necessary series of editing commands (using the global commands of **ed**), and write it into **script**. Now the command

ed <script

will produce the same output as the laborious hand typing. Alternately (and more easily), you can use the fact that the shell will perform loops, repeating a set of commands over and over again for a set of arguments:

```
for i in chap*
do
      ed $i <script
done
```

This sets the shell variable **i** to each file name in turn, then does the command. You can type this command at the terminal, or put it in a file for later execution.

1

Programming the Shell

An option often overlooked by newcomers is that the shell is itself a programming language, with variables, control flow (**if-else**, **while**, **for**, **case**), subroutines, and interrupt handling. Since there are many building-block programs, you can sometimes avoid writing a new program merely by piecing together some of the building blocks with shell command files.

We will not go into any details here; examples and rules can be found in *An Introduction to the UNIX Shell*, by S. R. Bourne.

Programming in C

If you are undertaking anything substantial, C is the only reasonable choice of programming language: everything in the UNIX system is tuned to it. The system itself is written in C, as are most of the programs that run on it. It is also a easy language to use once you get started. C is introduced and fully described in *The C Programming Language* by B. W. Kernighan and D. M. Ritchie (Prentice-Hall, 1978). Several sections of the manual describe the system interfaces, that is, how you do I/O and similar functions. Read *UNIX Programming* for more complicated things.

Most input and output in C is best handled with the standard I/O library, which provides a set of I/O functions that exist in compatible form on most machines that have C compilers. In general, it's wisest to confine the system interactions in a program to the facilities provided by this library.

C programs that don't depend too much on special features of UNIX (such as pipes) can be moved to other computers that have C compilers. The list of such machines grows daily; in addition to the original PDP-11, it currently includes at least Honeywell 6000, IBM 370 and PC families, Interdata 8/32, Data General Nova and Eclipse, HP 2100, Harris /7, Motorola 68000 family (including machines like Sun Microsystems and Apple Macintosh), VAX 11 family, SEL 86, and Zilog Z80. Calls to the standard I/O library will work on all of these machines.

There are a number of supporting programs that go with C. **lint** checks C programs for potential portability problems, and detects errors such as mismatched argument types and uninitialized variables.

For larger programs (anything whose source is on more than one file) **make** allows you to specify the dependencies among the source files and the processing steps needed to make a new version; it then checks the times that the pieces were last changed and does the minimal amount of recompiling to create a consistent updated version.

The debugger **adb** is useful for digging through the dead bodies of C programs, but is rather hard to learn to use effectively. The most effective debugging tool is still careful thought, coupled with judiciously placed print statements.†

---
† The "dbx" debugger, supplied starting with 4.2BSD, has extensive facilities for high-level debugging of C programs and is much easier to

The C compiler provides a limited instrumentation service, so you can find out where programs spend their time and what parts are worth optimizing. Compile the routines with the −**p** option; after the test run, use **prof** to print an execution profile. The command **time** will give you the gross run-time statistics of a program, but they are not super accurate or reproducible.

Other Languages

If you *have* to use Fortran, there are two possibilities. You might consider Ratfor, which gives you the decent control structures and free-form input that characterize C, yet lets you write code that is still portable to other environments. Bear in mind that UNIX Fortran tends to produce large and relatively slow-running programs. Furthermore, supporting software like **adb**, **prof**, etc., are all virtually useless with Fortran programs. There may also be a Fortran 77 compiler on your system. If so, this is a viable alternative to Ratfor, and has the non-trivial advantage that it is compatible with C and related programs. (The Ratfor processor and C tools can be used with Fortran 77 too.)

If your application requires you to translate a language into a set of actions or another language, you are in effect building a compiler, though probably a small one. In that case, you should be using the **yacc** compiler-compiler, which helps you develop a compiler quickly. The **lex** lexical analyzer generator does the same job for the simpler languages that can be expressed as regular expressions. It can be used by itself, or as a front end to recognize inputs for a **yacc**-based program. Both **yacc** and **lex** require some sophistication to use, but the initial effort of learning them can be repaid many times over in programs that are easy to change later on.

Most UNIX systems also make available other languages, such as Algol 68, APL, Basic, Lisp, Pascal, and Snobol. Whether these are useful depends largely on the local environment: if someone cares about the language and has worked on it, it may be in good shape. If not, the odds are strong that it will be more trouble than it's worth.

V. UNIX READING LIST

General:

K. L. Thompson and D. M. Ritchie, *The UNIX Programmer's Manual*, Bell Laboratories, 1978 (PS2:3)‡ Lists commands, system routines and interfaces, file formats, and some of the maintenance procedures. You can't live without this, although you will probably only need to read section 1.

D. M. Ritchie and K. L. Thompson, ''The UNIX Time-sharing System,'' CACM, July 1974. (PS2:1)‡ An overview

---
use than "adb".
† These documents (previously in Volume 2 of the Bell Labs Unix distribution) are provided among the "User Supplementary" Documents for 4.3BSD, available from the Usenix Association.
‡ These are among the "Programmer Supplementary" Documents for 4.3BSD. PS1 is Volume 1, PS2 is Volume 2.

1

of the system, for people interested in operating systems. Worth reading by anyone who programs. Contains a remarkable number of one-sentence observations on how to do things right.

The Bell System Technical Journal (BSTJ) Special Issue on UNIX, July/August, 1978, contains many papers describing recent developments, and some retrospective material.

The 2nd International Conference on Software Engineering (October, 1976) contains several papers describing the use of the Programmer's Workbench (PWB) version of UNIX.

Document Preparation:

B. W. Kernighan, "A Tutorial Introduction to the UNIX Text Editor" (USD:12) and "Advanced Editing on UNIX," (USD:13) Bell Laboratories, 1978.† Beginners need the introduction; the advanced material will help you get the most out of the editor.

M. E. Lesk, "Typing Documents on UNIX," Bell Laboratories, 1978. (USD:20)† Describes the −**ms** macro package, which isolates the novice from the vagaries of **nroff** and **troff**, and takes care of most formatting situations. If this specific package isn't available on your system, something similar probably is. The most likely alternative is the PWB/UNIX macro package −**mm**; see your local guru if you use PWB/UNIX.*

B. W. Kernighan and L. L. Cherry, "A System for Typesetting Mathematics," Bell Laboratories Computing Science Tech. Rep. 17. (USD:26)†

M. E. Lesk, "Tbl — A Program to Format Tables," Bell Laboratories CSTR 49, 1976. (USD:28)†

J. F. Ossanna, Jr., "NROFF/TROFF User's Manual," Bell Laboratories CSTR 54, 1976. (USD:24)† **troff** is the basic formatter used by −**ms**, **eqn** and **tbl**. The reference manual is indispensable if you are going to write or maintain these or similar programs. But start with:

B. W. Kernighan, "A TROFF Tutorial," Bell Laboratories, 1976. (USD:25)† An attempt to unravel the intricacies of **troff**.

Programming:

B. W. Kernighan and D. M. Ritchie, *The C Programming Language,* Prentice-Hall, 1978. Contains a tutorial introduction, complete discussions of all language features, and the reference manual.

B. W. Kernighan and R. Pike, *The Unix Programming Environment,* Prentice-Hall, 1984. Contains many examples of C programs which use the system interfaces, and explanations of "why".

B. W. Kernighan and D. M. Ritchie, "UNIX Programming," Bell Laboratories, 1978. (PS2:3)‡ Describes how to interface with the system from C programs: I/O calls, signals, processes.

S. R. Bourne, "An Introduction to the UNIX Shell," Bell Laboratories, 1978. (USD:3)† An introduction and reference manual for the Version 7 shell. Mandatory reading if you intend to make effective use of the programming power of this shell.

S. C. Johnson, "Yacc — Yet Another Compiler-Compiler," Bell Laboratories CSTR 32, 1978. (PS1:15)‡

M. E. Lesk, "Lex — A Lexical Analyzer Generator," Bell Laboratories CSTR 39, 1975. (PS1:16)‡

S. C. Johnson, "Lint, a C Program Checker," Bell Laboratories CSTR 65, 1977. (PS1:9)‡

S. I. Feldman, "MAKE — A Program for Maintaining Computer Programs," Bell Laboratories CSTR 57, 1977. (PS1:12)‡

J. F. Maranzano and S. R. Bourne, "A Tutorial Introduction to ADB," Bell Laboratories CSTR 62, 1977. (PS1:10)‡ An introduction to a powerful but complex debugging tool.

S. I. Feldman and P. J. Weinberger, "A Portable Fortran 77 Compiler," Bell Laboratories, 1978. (PS1:2)‡ A full Fortran 77 for UNIX systems.

---

*The macro package -me is additionally available on Berkeley Unix Systems. -mm is typically not available.

LEARN — Computer-Aided Instruction on UNIX
(Second Edition)

Brian W. Kernighan

Michael E. Lesk

ABSTRACT

This paper describes the second version of the *learn* program for interpreting CAI scripts on the UNIX† operating system, and a set of scripts that provide a computerized introduction to the system.

Six current scripts cover basic commands and file handling, the editor, additional file handling commands, the *eqn* program for mathematical typing, the "–ms" package of formatting macros, and an introduction to the C programming language. These scripts now include a total of about 530 lessons.

Many users from a wide variety of backgrounds have used *learn* to acquire basic UNIX skills. Most usage involves the first two scripts, an introduction to UNIX files and commands, and the UNIX editor.

The second version of *learn* is about four times faster than the previous one in CPU utilization, and much faster in perceived time because of better overlap of computing and printing. It also requires less file space than the first version. Many of the lessons have been revised; new material has been added to reflect changes and enhancements in UNIX itself. Script-writing is also easier because of revisions to the script language.

1. Introduction.

Learn is a driver for CAI scripts. It is intended to permit the easy composition of lessons and lesson fragments to teach people computer skills. Since it is teaching the same system on which it is implemented, it makes direct use of UNIX facilities to create a controlled UNIX environment. The system includes two main parts: (1) a driver that interprets the lesson scripts; and (2) the lesson scripts themselves. At present there are seven scripts:

— basic file handling commands

— the UNIX text editors *ed* and *vi*

— advanced file handling

— the *eqn* language for typing mathematics

— the "ms" macro package for document formatting

— the C programming language

The purported advantages of CAI scripts for training in computer skills include the following:

(a) students are forced to perform the exercises that are in fact the basis of training in any case;

(b) students receive immediate feedback and confirmation of progress;

---

† UNIX is a registered trademark of AT&T Bell Laboratories in the USA and other countries.

(c)   students may progress at their own rate;

(d)   no schedule requirements are imposed; students may study at any time convenient for them;

(e)   the lessons may be improved individually and the improvements are immediately available to new users;

(f)   since the student has access to a computer for the CAI script there is a place to do exercises;

(g)   the use of high technology will improve student motivation and the interest of their management.

Opposed to this, of course, is the absence of anyone to whom the student may direct questions. If CAI is used without a "counselor" or other assistance, it should properly be compared to a textbook, lecture series, or taped course, rather than to a seminar. CAI has been used for many years in a variety of educational areas.[1, 2, 3] The use of a computer to teach computer use itself, however, offers unique advantages. The skills developed to get through the script are exactly those needed to use the computer; there is no waste effort.

The scripts written so far are based on some familiar assumptions about education; these assumptions are outlined in the next section. The remaining sections describe the operation of the script driver and the particular scripts now available. The driver puts few restrictions on the script writer, but the current scripts are of a rather rigid and stereotyped form in accordance with the theory in the next section and practical limitations.

2. Educational Assumptions and Design.

First, the way to teach people how to do something is to have them do it. Scripts should not contain long pieces of explanation; they should instead frequently ask the student to do some task. So teaching is always by example: the typical script fragment shows a small example of some technique and then asks the user to either repeat that example or produce a variation on it. All are intended to be easy enough that most students will get most questions right, reinforcing the desired behavior.

Most lessons fall into one of three types. The simplest presents a lesson and asks for a yes or no answer to a question. The student is given a chance to experiment before replying. The script checks for the correct reply. Problems of this form are sparingly used.

The second type asks for a word or number as an answer. For example a lesson on files might say

How many files are there in the current directory? Type "answer N", where N is the number of files.

The student is expected to respond (perhaps after experimenting) with

answer 17

or whatever. Surprisingly often, however, the idea of a substitutable argument (i.e., replacing N by 17) is difficult for non-programmer students, so the first few such lessons need real care.

The third type of lesson is open-ended — a task is set for the student, appropriate parts of the input or output are monitored, and the student types *ready* when the task is done. Figure 1 shows a sample dialog that illustrates the last of these, using two lessons about the *cat* (concatenate, i.e., print) command taken from early in the script that teaches file handling. Most *learn* lessons are of this form.

After each correct response the computer congratulates the student and indicates the lesson number that has just been completed, permitting the student to restart the script after that lesson. If the answer is wrong, the student is offered a chance to repeat the lesson. The "speed" rating of the student (explained in section 5) is given after the lesson number when the lesson is completed successfully; it is printed only for the aid of script authors checking out possible errors in the lessons.

It is assumed that there is no foolproof way to determine if the student truly "understands" what he or she is doing; accordingly, the current *learn* scripts only measure performance, not comprehension. If the student can perform a given task, that is deemed to be "learning."[4]

The main point of using the computer is that what the student does is checked for correctness immediately. Unlike many CAI scripts, however, these scripts provide few facilities for dealing with wrong answers. In practice, if most of the answers are not right the script is a failure; the universal solution

2

Figure 1: Sample dialog from basic files script

(Student responses in italics; '$' is the prompt)

A file can be printed on your terminal
by using the "cat" command. Just say
"cat file" where "file" is the file name.
For example, there is a file named
"food" in this directory. List it
by saying "cat food"; then type "ready".
$ *cat food*
  this is the file
  named food.
$ *ready*

Good. Lesson 3.3a (1)

Of course, you can print any file with "cat".
In particular, it is common to first use
"ls" to find the name of a file and then "cat"
to print it. Note the difference between
"ls", which tells you the name of the file,
and "cat", which tells you the contents.
One file in the current directory is named for
a President. Print the file, then type "ready".
$ *cat President*
cat: can't open President
$ *ready*

Sorry, that's not right. Do you want to try again? *yes*
Try the problem again.
$ *ls*
.ocopy
X1
roosevelt
$ *cat roosevelt*
  this file is named roosevelt
  and contains three lines of
  text.
$ *ready*

Good. Lesson 3.3b (0)

The "cat" command can also print several files
at once. In fact, it is named "cat" as an abbreviation
for "concatenate"....

to student error is to provide a new, easier script. Anticipating possible wrong answers is an endless job, and it is really easier as well as better to provide a simpler script.

Along with this goes the assumption that anything can be taught to anybody if it can be broken into sufficiently small pieces. Anything not absorbed in a single chunk is just subdivided.

2

To avoid boring the faster students, however, an effort is made in the files and editor scripts to pro-vide three tracks of different difficulty. The fastest sequence of lessons is aimed at roughly the bulk and speed of a typical tutorial manual and should be adequate for review and for well-prepared students. The next track is intended for most users and is roughly twice as long. Typically, for example, the fast track might present an idea and ask for a variation on the example shown; the normal track will first ask the stu-dent to repeat the example that was shown before attempting a variation. The third and slowest track, which is often three or four times the length of the fast track, is intended to be adequate for anyone. (The lessons of Figure 1 are from the third track.) The multiple tracks also mean that a student repeating a course is unlikely to hit the same series of lessons; this makes it profitable for a shaky user to back up and try again, and many students have done so.

The tracks are not completely distinct, however. Depending on the number of correct answers the student has given for the last few lessons, the program may switch tracks. The driver is actually capable of following an arbitrary directed graph of lesson sequences, as discussed in section 5. Some more structured arrangement, however, is used in all current scripts to aid the script writer in organizing the material into lessons. It is sufficiently difficult to write lessons that the three-track theory is not followed very closely except in the files and editor scripts. Accordingly, in some cases, the fast track is produced merely by skip-ping lessons from the slower track. In others, there is essentially only one track.

The main reason for using the *learn* program rather than simply writing the same material as a work-book is not the selection of tracks, but actual hands-on experience. Learning by doing is much more effec-tive than pencil and paper exercises.

Learn also provides a mechanical check on performance. The first version in fact would not let the student proceed unless it received correct answers to the questions it set and it would not tell a student the right answer. This somewhat Draconian approach has been moderated in version 2. Lessons are some-times badly worded or even just plain wrong; in such cases, the student has no recourse. But if a student is simply unable to complete one lesson, that should not prevent access to the rest. Accordingly, the current version of *learn* allows the student to skip a lesson that he cannot pass; a ''no'' answer to the ''Do you want to try again?'' question in Figure 1 will pass to the next lesson. It is still true that *learn* will not tell the student the right answer.

Of course, there are valid objections to the assumptions above. In particular, some students may object to not understanding what they are doing; and the procedure of smashing everything into small pieces may provoke the retort ''you can't cross a ditch in two jumps.'' Since writing CAI scripts is consid-erably more tedious than ordinary manuals, however, it is safe to assume that there will always be alterna-tives to the scripts as a way of learning. In fact, for a reference manual of 3 or 4 pages it would not be surprising to have a tutorial manual of 20 pages and a (multi-track) script of 100 pages. Thus the reference manual will exist long before the scripts.

3. Scripts.

As mentioned above, the present scripts try at most to follow a three-track theory. Thus little of the potential complexity of the possible directed graph is employed, since care must be taken in lesson con-struction to see that every necessary fact is presented in every possible path through the units. In addition, it is desirable that every unit have alternate successors to deal with student errors.

In most existing courses, the first few lessons are devoted to checking prerequisites. For example, before the student is allowed to proceed through the editor script the script verifies that the student under-stands files and is able to type. It is felt that the sooner lack of student preparation is detected, the easier it will be on the student. Anyone proceeding through the scripts should be getting mostly correct answers; otherwise, the system will be unsatisfactory both because the wrong habits are being learned and because the scripts make little effort to deal with wrong answers. Unprepared students should not be encouraged to continue with scripts.

There are some preliminary items which the student must know before any scripts can be tried. In particular, the student must know how to connect to a UNIX system, set the terminal properly, log in, and execute simple commands (e.g., *learn* itself). In addition, the character erase and line kill conventions (# and @) should be known. It is hard to see how this much could be taught by computer-aided instruction,

2

since a student who does not know these basic skills will not be able to run the learning program. A brief description on paper is provided (see Appendix A), although assistance will be needed for the first few minutes. This assistance, however, need not be highly skilled.

The first script in the current set deals with files. It assumes the basic knowledge above and teaches the student about the *ls*, *cat*, *mv*, *rm*, *cp* and *diff* commands. It also deals with the abbreviation characters *, ?, and [ ] in file names. It does not cover pipes or I/O redirection, nor does it present the many options on the *ls* command.

This script contains 31 lessons in the fast track; two are intended as prerequisite checks, seven are review exercises. There are a total of 75 lessons in all three tracks, and the instructional passages typed at the student to begin each lesson total 4,476 words. The average lesson thus begins with a 60-word message. In general, the fast track lessons have somewhat longer introductions, and the slow tracks somewhat shorter ones. The longest message is 144 words and the shortest 14.

The second script trains students in the use of the UNIX context editor *ed*, a sophisticated editor using regular expressions for searching.[5] All editor features except encryption, mark names and ';' in addressing are covered. The fast track contains 2 prerequisite checks, 93 lessons, and a review lesson. It is supplemented by 146 additional lessons in other tracks.

A comparison of sizes may be of interest. The *ed* description in the reference manual is 2,572 words long. The *ed* tutorial[6] is 6,138 words long. The fast track through the *ed* script is 7,407 words of explanatory messages, and the total *ed* script, 242 lessons, has 15,615 words. The average *ed* lesson is thus also about 60 words; the largest is 171 words and the smallest 10. The original *ed* script represents about three man-weeks of effort.

The advanced file handling script deals with *ls* options, I/O diversion, pipes, and supporting programs like *pr*, *wc*, *tail*, *spell* and *grep*. (The basic file handling script is a prerequisite.) It is not as refined as the first two scripts; this is reflected at least partly in the fact that it provides much less of a full three-track sequence than they do. On the other hand, since it is perceived as "advanced," it is hoped that the student will have somewhat more sophistication and be better able to cope with it at a reasonably high level of performance.

A fourth script covers the *eqn* language for typing mathematics. This script must be run on a terminal capable of printing mathematics, for instance the DASI 300 and similar Diablo-based terminals, or the nearly extinct Model 37 teletype. Again, this script is relatively short of tracks: of 76 lessons, only 17 are in the second track and 2 in the third track. Most of these provide additional practice for students who are having trouble in the first track.

The *−ms* script for formatting macros is a short one-track only script. The macro package it describes is no longer the standard, so this script will undoubtedly be superseded in the future. Furthermore, the linear style of a single learn script is somewhat inappropriate for the macros, since the macro package is composed of many independent features, and few users need all of them. It would be better to have a selection of short lesson sequences dealing with the features independently.

The script on C is in a state of transition. It was originally designed to follow a tutorial on C, but that document has since become obsolete. The current script has been partially converted to follow the order of presentation in *The C Programming Language*,[7] but this job is not complete. The C script was never intended to teach C; rather it is supposed to be a series of exercises for which the computer provides checking and (upon success) a suggested solution.

This combination of scripts covers much of the material which any UNIX user will need to know to make effective use of the system. With enlargement of the advanced files course to include more on the command interpreter, there will be a relatively complete introduction to UNIX available via *learn*. Although we make no pretense that *learn* will replace other instructional materials, it should provide a useful supplement to existing tutorials and reference manuals.

4. Experience with Students.

Learn has been installed on many different UNIX systems. Most of the usage is on the first two scripts, so these are more thoroughly debugged and polished. As a (random) sample of user experience, the *learn* program has been used at Bell Labs at Indian Hill for 10,500 lessons in a four month period.

About 3600 of these are in the files script, 4100 in the editor, and 1400 in advanced files. The passing rate is about 80%, that is, about 4 lessons are passed for every one failed. There have been 86 distinct users of the files script, and 58 of the editor. On our system at Murray Hill, there have been nearly 2000 lessons over two weeks that include Christmas and New Year. Users have ranged in age from six up.

It is difficult to characterize typical sessions with the scripts; many instances exist of someone doing one or two lessons and then logging out, as do instances of someone pausing in a script for twenty minutes or more. In the earlier version of *learn*, the average session in the files course took 32 minutes and covered 23 lessons. The distribution is quite broad and skewed, however; the longest session was 130 minutes and there were five sessions shorter than five minutes. The average lesson took about 80 seconds. These numbers are roughly typical for non-programmers; a UNIX expert can do the scripts at approximately 30 seconds per lesson, most of which is the system printing.

At present working through a section of the middle of the files script took about 1.4 seconds of processor time per lesson, and a system expert typing quickly took 15 seconds of real time per lesson. A novice would probably take at least a minute. Thus a UNIX system could support ten students working simultaneously with some spare capacity.

5. The Script Interpreter.

The *learn* program itself merely interprets scripts. It provides facilities for the script writer to capture student responses and their effects, and simplifies the job of passing control to and recovering control from the student. This section describes the operation and usage of the driver program, and indicates what is required to produce a new script. Readers only interested in the existing scripts may skip this section.

The file structure used by *learn* is shown in Figure 2. There is one parent directory (named *lib*) containing the script data. Within this directory are subdirectories, one for each subject in which a course is available, one for logging (named *log*), and one in which user sub-directories are created (named *play*). The subject directory contains master copies of all lessons, plus any supporting material for that subject. In a given subdirectory, each lesson is a single text file. Lessons are usually named systematically; the file that contains lesson *n* is called *Ln*.

```
        Figure 2:  Directory structure for learn

lib

        play
                        student1
                                        files for student1...
                        student2
                                        files for student2...

        files
                        L0.1a          lessons for files course
                        L0.1b
                        ...

        editor
                        ...

        (other courses)

        log
```

When *learn* is executed, it makes a private directory for the user to work in, within the *learn* portion of the file system. A fresh copy of all the files used in each lesson (mostly data for the student to operate upon) is made each time a student starts a lesson, so the script writer may assume that everything is reinitialized each time a lesson is entered. The student directory is deleted after each session; any permanent records must be kept elsewhere.

The script writer must provide certain basic items in each lesson:

(1)   the text of the lesson;

(2)   the set-up commands to be executed before the user gets control;

(3)   the data, if any, which the user is supposed to edit, transform, or otherwise process;

(4)   the evaluating commands to be executed after the user has finished the lesson, to decide whether the
       answer is right; and

(5)   a list of possible successor lessons.

Learn tries to minimize the work of bookkeeping and installation, so that most of the effort involved in
script production is in planning lessons, writing tutorial paragraphs, and coding tests of student performance.

The basic sequence of events is as follows. First, *learn* creates the working directory. Then, for
each lesson, *learn* reads the script for the lesson and processes it a line at a time. The lines in the script
are: (1) commands to the script interpreter to print something, to create a files, to test something, etc.; (2)
text to be printed or put in a file; (3) other lines, which are sent to the shell to be executed. One line in each
lesson turns control over to the user; the user can run any UNIX commands. The user mode terminates
when the user types *yes*, *no*, *ready*, or *answer*. At this point, the user's work is tested; if the lesson is
passed, a new lesson is selected, and if not the old one is repeated.

Let us illustrate this with the script for the second lesson of Figure 1; this is shown in Figure 3.

Figure 3: Sample Lesson

#print
Of course, you can print any file with "cat".
In particular, it is common to first use
"ls" to find the name of a file and then "cat"
to print it. Note the difference between
"ls", which tells you the name of the files,
and "cat", which tells you the contents.
One file in the current directory is named for
a President. Print the file, then type "ready".
#create roosevelt
  this file is named roosevelt
  and contains three lines of
  text.
#copyout
#user
#uncopyout
tail −3 .ocopy >X1
#cmp X1 roosevelt
#log
#next
3.2b 2

Lines which begin with # are commands to the *learn* script interpreter. For example,

    #print

causes printing of any text that follows, up to the next line that begins with a sharp.

#print file

prints the contents of *file*; it is the same as *cat file* but has less overhead. Both forms of *#print* have the added property that if a lesson is failed, the *#print* will not be executed the second time through; this avoids annoying the student by repeating the preamble to a lesson.

#create filename

creates a file of the specified name, and copies any subsequent text up to a # to the file. This is used for creating and initializing working files and reference data for the lessons.

#user

gives control to the student; each line he or she types is passed to the shell for execution. The *#user* mode is terminated when the student types one of *yes*, *no*, *ready* or *answer*. At that time, the driver resumes interpretation of the script.

#copyin
#uncopyin

Anything the student types between these commands is copied onto a file called *.copy*. This lets the script writer interrogate the student's responses upon regaining control.

#copyout
#uncopyout

Between these commands, any material typed at the student by any program is copied to the file *.ocopy*. This lets the script writer interrogate the effect of what the student typed, which true believers in the performance theory of learning usually prefer to the student's actual input.

#pipe
#unpipe

Normally the student input and the script commands are fed to the UNIX command interpreter (the "shell") one line at a time. This won't do if, for example, a sequence of editor commands is provided, since the input to the editor must be handed to the editor, not to the shell. Accordingly, the material between *#pipe* and *#unpipe* commands is fed continuously through a pipe so that such sequences work. If *copyout* is also desired the *copyout* brackets must include the *pipe* brackets.

There are several commands for setting status after the student has attempted the lesson.

#cmp file1 file2

is an in-line implementation of *cmp*, which compares two files for identity.

#match stuff

The last line of the student's input is compared to *stuff*, and the success or fail status is set according to it. Extraneous things like the word *answer* are stripped before the comparison is made. There may be several *#match* lines; this provides a convenient mechanism for handling multiple "right" answers. Any text up to a # on subsequent lines after a successful *#match* is printed; this is illustrated in Figure 4, another sample lesson.

#bad stuff

This is similar to *#match*, except that it corresponds to specific failure answers; this can be used to produce hints for particular wrong answers that have been anticipated by the script writer.

#succeed
#fail

print a message upon success or failure (as determined by some previous mechanism).

When the student types one of the "commands" *yes*, *no*, *ready*, or *answer*, the driver terminates the *#user* command, and evaluation of the student's work can begin. This can be done either by the built-in commands above, such as *#match* and *#cmp*, or by status returned by normal UNIX commands, typically *grep* and *test*. The last command should return status true (0) if the task was done successfully and false (non-zero) otherwise; this status return tells the driver whether or not the student has successfully passed the lesson.

Figure 4: Another Sample Lesson

```
#print
What command will move the current line
to the end of the file?  Type
"answer COMMAND", where COMMAND is the command.
#copyin
#user
#uncopyin
#match m$
#match .m$
"m$" is easier.
#log
#next
63.1d 10
```

Performance can be logged:

#log file

writes the date, lesson, user name and speed rating, and a success/failure indication on *file*. The command

#log

by itself writes the logging information in the logging directory within the *learn* hierarchy, and is the normal form.

#next

is followed by a few lines, each with a successor lesson name and an optional speed rating on it. A typical set might read

    25.1a 10
    25.2a 5
    25.3a 2

indicating that unit 25.1a is a suitable follow-on lesson for students with a speed rating of 10 units, 25.2a for student with speed near 5, and 25.3a for speed near 2. Speed ratings are maintained for each session with a student; the rating is increased by one each time the student gets a lesson right and decreased by four each time the student gets a lesson wrong. Thus the driver tries to maintain a level such that the users get 80% right answers. The maximum rating is limited to 10 and the minimum to 0. The initial rating is zero unless the student specifies a different rating when starting a session.

If the student passes a lesson, a new lesson is selected and the process repeats. If the student fails, a false status is returned and the program reverts to the previous lesson and tries another alternative. If it can not find another alternative, it skips forward a lesson. *bye* , bye, which causes a graceful exit from the *learn* system. Hanging up is the usual novice's way out.

The lessons may form an arbitrary directed graph, although the present program imposes a limitation on cycles in that it will not present a lesson twice in the same session. If the student is unable to answer one of the exercises correctly, the driver searches for a previous lesson with a set of alternatives as successors (following the *#next* line). From the previous lesson with alternatives one route was taken earlier; the program simply tries a different one.

It is perfectly possible to write sophisticated scripts that evaluate the student's speed of response, or try to estimate the elegance of the answer, or provide detailed analysis of wrong answers. Lesson writing is so tedious already, however, that most of these abilities are likely to go unused.

The driver program depends heavily on features of UNIX that are not available on many other operating systems. These include the ease of manipulating files and directories, file redirection, the ability to use the command interpreter as just another program (even in a pipeline), command status testing and branching, the ability to catch signals like interrupts, and of course the pipeline mechanism itself. Although some parts of *learn* might be transferable to other systems, some generality will probably be lost.

A bit of history: The first version of *learn* had fewer built-in words in the driver program, and made more use of the facilities of UNIX. For example, file comparison was done by creating a *cmp* process, rather than comparing the two files within *learn*. Lessons were not stored as text files, but as archives. There was no concept of the in-line document; even *#print* had to be followed by a file name. Thus the initialization for each lesson was to extract the archive into the working directory (typically 4-8 files), then *#print* the lesson text.

The combination of such things made *learn* slower. The new version is about 4 or 5 times faster. Furthermore, it appears even faster to the user because in a typical lesson, the printing of the message comes first, and file setup with *#create* can be overlapped with the printng, so that when the program finishes printing, it is really ready for the user to type at it.

It is also a great advantage to the script maintainer that lessons are now just ordinary text files. They can be edited without any difficulty, and UNIX text manipulation tools can be applied to them. The result has been that there is much less resistance to going in and fixing substandard lessons.

6. Conclusions

The following observations can be made about secretaries, typists, and other non-programmers who have used *learn*:

(a)   A novice must have assistance with the mechanics of communicating with the computer to get through to the first lesson or two; once the first few lessons are passed people can proceed on their own.

(b)   The terminology used in the first few lessons is obscure to those inexperienced with computers. It would help if there were a low level reference card for UNIX to supplement the existing programmer oriented bulky manual and bulky reference card.

(c)   The concept of ''substitutable argument'' is hard to grasp, and requires help.

(d)   They enjoy the system for the most part. Motivation matters a great deal, however.

It takes an hour or two for a novice to get through the script on file handling. The total time for a reasonably intelligent and motivated novice to proceed from ignorance to a reasonable ability to create new files and manipulate old ones seems to be a few days, with perhaps half of each day spent on the machine.

The normal way of proceeding has been to have students in the same room with someone who knows UNIX and the scripts. Thus the student is not brought to a halt by difficult questions. The burden on the counselor, however, is much lower than that on a teacher of a course. Ideally, the students should be encouraged to proceed with instruction immediately prior to their actual use of the computer. They should exercise the scripts on the same computer and the same kind of terminal that they will later use for their real work, and their first few jobs for the computer should be relatively easy ones. Also, both training and initial work should take place on days when the UNIX hardware and software are working reliably. Rarely is all of this possible, but the closer one comes the better the result. For example, if it is known that the hardware is shaky one day, it is better to attempt to reschedule training for another one. Students are very frustrated by machine downtime; when nothing is happening, it takes some sophistication and experience to distinguish an infinite loop, a slow but functioning program, a program waiting for the user, and a broken machine.*

One disadvantage of training with *learn* is that students come to depend completely on the CAI system, and do not try to read manuals or use other learning aids. This is unfortunate, not only because of the increased demands for completeness and accuracy of the scripts, but because the scripts do not cover all of the UNIX system. New users should have manuals (appropriate for their level) and read them; the scripts ought to be altered to recommend suitable documents and urge students to read them.

---

* We have even known an expert programmer to decide the computer was broken when he had simply left his terminal in local mode. Novices have great difficulties with such problems.

There are several other difficulties which are clearly evident. From the student's viewpoint, the most serious is that lessons still crop up which simply can't be passed. Sometimes this is due to poor explanations, but just as often it is some error in the lesson itself — a botched setup, a missing file, an invalid test for correctness, or some system facility that doesn't work on the local system in the same way it did on the development system. It takes knowledge and a certain healthy arrogance on the part of the user to recognize that the fault is not his or hers, but the script writer's. Permitting the student to get on with the next lesson regardless this somewhat, and the logging facilities make it easy to watch for lessons that no one can pass, but it is still a problem.

The biggest problem with the previous *learn* was speed (or lack thereof) — it was often excruciatingly slow and made a significant drain on the system. The current version so far does not seem to have that difficulty, although some scripts, notably *eqn*, are intrinsically slow. *eqn*, for example, must do a lot of work even to print its introductions, let alone check the student responses, but delay is perceptible in all scripts from time to time.

Another potential problem is that it is possible to break *learn* inadvertently, by pushing interrupt at the wrong time, or by removing critical files, or any number of similar slips. The defenses against such problems have steadily been improved, to the point where most students should not notice difficulties. Of course, it will always be possible to break *learn* maliciously, but this is not likely to be a problem.

One area is more fundamental — some UNIX commands are sufficiently global in their effect that *learn* currently does not allow them to be executed at all. The most obvious is *cd*, which changes to another directory. The prospect of a student who is learning about directories inadvertently moving to some random directory and removing files has deterred us from even writing lessons on *cd*, but ultimately lessons on such topics probably should be added.

7. Acknowledgments

We are grateful to all those who have tried *learn,* for we have benefited greatly from their suggestions and criticisms. In particular, M. E. Bittrich, J. L. Blue, S. I. Feldman, P. A. Fox, and M. J. McAlpin have provided substantial feedback. Conversations with E. Z. Rothkopf also provided many of the ideas in the system. We are also indebted to Don Jackowski for serving as a guinea pig for the second version, and to Tom Plum for his efforts to improve the C script.

References

1.   D.L. Bitzer and D. Skaperdas, "The Economics of a Large Scale Computer Based Educational System: Plato IV," in *Computer Assisted Instruction, Testing and Guidance*, ed. Wayne Holtzman, pp. 17-29, Harper and Row, New York, 1970.

2.   D.C. Gray, J.P. Hulskamp, J.H. Kumm, S. Lichtenstein, and N.E. Nimmervoll, "COALA - A Minicomputer CAI System," *IEEE Trans. Education*, vol. E-20(1), pp. 73-77, Feb. 1977.

3.   P. Suppes, "On Using Computers to Individualize Instruction," in *The Computer in American Education*, ed. D.D. Bushnell and D.W. Allen, pp. 11-24, John Wiley, New York, 1967.

4.   B.F. Skinner, "Why We Need Teaching Machines," *Harv. Educ. Review*, vol. 31, pp. 377-398, 1961. Reprinted in *Educational Technology,* ed. J.P. DeCecco, Holt Rinehart & Winston (New York, 1964)

5.   K. Thompson and D. M. Ritchie, *UNIX Programmer's Manual,* Bell Laboratories, 1978. See section *ed* (1).

6.   B.W. Kernighan, *A Tutorial Introduction to the UNIX text editor*, 1974. Bell Laboratories internal memorandum

7.   B. W. Kernighan and D. M. Ritchie, *The C Programming Language,* Prentice-Hall, Englewood Cliffs, New Jersey, 1978.

An Introduction to the UNIX Shell

S. R. Bourne

Murray Hill, NJ

(Updated for 4.3BSD by Mark Seiden)

ABSTRACT

The *shell‡* is a command programming language that provides an interface to the UNIX†
operating system. Its features include control-flow primitives, parameter passing, variables and string substitution. Constructs such as *while, if then else, case* and *for* are
available. Two-way communication is possible between the *shell* and commands.
String-valued parameters, typically file names or flags, may be passed to a command. A
return code is set by commands that may be used to determine control-flow, and the standard output from a command may be used as shell input.

The *shell* can modify the environment in which commands run. Input and output can be
redirected to files, and processes that communicate through 'pipes' can be invoked.
Commands are found by searching directories in the file system in a sequence that can be
defined by the user. Commands can be read either from the terminal or from a file, which
allows command procedures to be stored for later use.

1.0 Introduction

The shell is both a command language and a programming language that provides an interface to the UNIX
operating system. This memorandum describes, with examples, the UNIX shell. The first section covers
most of the everyday requirements of terminal users. Some familiarity with UNIX is an advantage when
reading this section; see, for example, "UNIX for beginners".[1] Section 2 describes those features of the
shell primarily intended for use within shell procedures. These include the control-flow primitives and
string-valued variables provided by the shell. A knowledge of a programming language would be a help
when reading this section. The last section describes the more advanced features of the shell. References
of the form "see *pipe* (2)" are to a section of the UNIX manual.[2]

1.1 Simple commands

Simple commands consist of one or more words separated by blanks. The first word is the name of the
command to be executed; any remaining words are passed as arguments to the command. For example,

        who

is a command that prints the names of users logged in. The command

        ls −l

prints a list of files in the current directory. The argument *−l* tells *ls* to print status information, size and the
creation date for each file.

---

‡ This paper describes sh(1). If it's the c shell (csh) you're interested in, a good place to begin is William Joy's paper "An
Introduction to the C shell" (USD:4).
† UNIX is a registered trademark of AT&T Bell Laboratories in the USA and other countries.

1.2 Background commands

To execute a command the shell normally creates a new *process* and waits for it to finish. A command may be run without waiting for it to finish. For example,

> cc pgm.c &

calls the C compiler to compile the file *pgm.c*. The trailing **&** is an operator that instructs the shell not to wait for the command to finish. To help keep track of such a process the shell reports its process number following its creation. A list of currently active processes may be obtained using the *ps* command.

1.3 Input output redirection

Most commands produce output on the standard output that is initially connected to the terminal. This output may be sent to a file by writing, for example,

> ls –l >file

The notation >*file* is interpreted by the shell and is not passed as an argument to *ls*. If *file* does not exist then the shell creates it; otherwise the original contents of *file* are replaced with the output from *ls*. Output may be appended to a file using the notation

> ls –l ≫file

In this case *file* is also created if it does not already exist.

The standard input of a command may be taken from a file instead of the terminal by writing, for example,

> wc <file

The command *wc* reads its standard input (in this case redirected from *file*) and prints the number of characters, words and lines found. If only the number of lines is required then

> wc –l <file

could be used.

1.4 Pipelines and filters

The standard output of one command may be connected to the standard input of another by writing the 'pipe' operator, indicated by |, as in,

> ls –l | wc

Two commands connected in this way constitute a *pipeline* and the overall effect is the same as

> ls –l >file; wc <file

except that no *file* is used. Instead the two processes are connected by a pipe (see *pipe* (2)) and are run in parallel. Pipes are unidirectional and synchronization is achieved by halting *wc* when there is nothing to read and halting *ls* when the pipe is full.

A *filter* is a command that reads its standard input, transforms it in some way, and prints the result as output. One such filter, *grep,* selects from its input those lines that contain some specified string. For example,

> ls | grep old

prints those lines, if any, of the output from *ls* that contain the string *old.* Another useful filter is *sort.* For example,

> who | sort

will print an alphabetically sorted list of logged in users.

A pipeline may consist of more than two commands, for example,

        ls | grep old | wc –l

prints the number of file names in the current directory containing the string *old.*

1.5 File name generation

Many commands accept arguments which are file names. For example,

        ls –l main.c

prints information relating to the file *main.c* .

The shell provides a mechanism for generating a list of file names that match a pattern. For example,

        ls –l *.c

generates, as arguments to *ls,* all file names in the current directory that end in *.c* . The character * is a pattern that will match any string including the null string. In general *patterns* are specified as follows.

      *   Matches any string of characters including the null string.

      ?   Matches any single character.

      [...]   Matches any one of the characters enclosed. A pair of characters separated by a minus will match any character lexically between the pair.

For example,

        [a–z]*

matches all names in the current directory beginning with one of the letters *a* through *z*.

        /usr/fred/test/?

matches all names in the directory **/usr/fred/test** that consist of a single character. If no file name is found that matches the pattern then the pattern is passed, unchanged, as an argument.

This mechanism is useful both to save typing and to select names according to some pattern. It may also be used to find files. For example,

        echo /usr/fred/*/core

finds and prints the names of all *core* files in sub-directories of **/usr/fred** . (*echo* is a standard UNIX command that prints its arguments, separated by blanks.) This last feature can be expensive, requiring a scan of all sub-directories of **/usr/fred** .

There is one exception to the general rules given for patterns. The character '.' at the start of a file name must be explicitly matched.

        echo *

will therefore echo all file names in the current directory not beginning with '.' .

        echo .*

will echo all those file names that begin with '.' . This avoids inadvertent matching of the names '.' and '..' which mean 'the current directory' and 'the parent directory' respectively. (Notice that *ls* suppresses information for the files '.' and '..' .)

1.6 Quoting

Characters that have a special meaning to the shell, such as < > * ? | **&** , are called metacharacters. A complete list of metacharacters is given in appendix B.

Any character preceded by a \ is *quoted* and loses its special meaning, if any. The \ is elided so that

> echo \?

will echo a single **?**, and

> echo \\

will echo a single ****. To allow long strings to be continued over more than one line the sequence **\newline** is ignored.

\ is convenient for quoting single characters. When more than one character needs quoting the above mechanism is clumsy and error prone. A string of characters may be quoted by enclosing the string between single quotes. For example,

> echo xx´****´xx

will echo

> xx****xx

The quoted string may not contain a single quote but may contain newlines, which are preserved. This quoting mechanism is the most simple and is recommended for casual use.

A third quoting mechanism using double quotes is also available that prevents interpretation of some but not all metacharacters. Discussion of the details is deferred to section 3.4.

1.7 Prompting

When the shell is used from a terminal it will issue a prompt before reading a command. By default this prompt is '**$** '. It may be changed by saying, for example,

> PS1=yesdear

that sets the prompt to be the string *yesdear*. If a newline is typed and further input is needed then the shell will issue the prompt '**>** '. Sometimes this can be caused by mistyping a quote mark. If it is unexpected then an interrupt (DEL) will return the shell to read another command. This prompt may be changed by saying, for example,

> PS2=more

1.8 The shell and login

Following *login* (1) the shell is called to read and execute commands typed at the terminal. If the user's login directory contains the file **.profile** then it is assumed to contain commands and is read by the shell before reading any commands from the terminal.

1.9 Summary

- **ls**
  Print the names of files in the current directory.
- **ls >file**
  Put the output from *ls* into *file*.
- **ls | wc –l**
  Print the number of files in the current directory.
- **ls | grep old**
  Print those file names containing the string *old*.
- **ls | grep old | wc –l**
  Print the number of files whose name contains the string *old*.

- **cc pgm.c &**
  Run *cc* in the background.

2.0 Shell procedures

The shell may be used to read and execute commands contained in a file. For example,

        sh file [args ...]

calls the shell to read commands from *file*. Such a file is called a *command procedure* or *shell procedure*. Arguments may be supplied with the call and are referred to in *file* using the positional parameters **$1, $2,** **....** For example, if the file *wg* contains

        who | grep $1

then

        sh wg fred

is equivalent to

        who | grep fred

UNIX files have three independent attributes, *read, write* and *execute.* The UNIX command *chmod* (1) may be used to make a file executable. For example,

        chmod +x wg

will ensure that the file *wg* has execute status. Following this, the command

        wg fred

is equivalent to

        sh wg fred

This allows shell procedures and programs to be used interchangeably. In either case a new process is created to run the command.

As well as providing names for the positional parameters, the number of positional parameters in the call is available as **$#**. The name of the file being executed is available as **$0**.

A special shell parameter **$*** is used to substitute for all positional parameters except **$0**. A typical use of this is to provide some default arguments, as in,

        nroff −T450 −ms $*

which simply prepends some arguments to those already given.

2.1 Control flow - for

A frequent use of shell procedures is to loop through the arguments (**$1, $2, ...**) executing commands once for each argument. An example of such a procedure is *tel* that searches the file **/usr/lib/telnos** that contains lines of the form

        ...
        fred mh0123
        bert mh0789
        ...

The text of *tel* is

        for i
        do grep $i /usr/lib/telnos; done

The command

        tel fred

prints those lines in **/usr/lib/telnos** that contain the string *fred*.

        tel fred bert

prints those lines containing *fred* followed by those for *bert*.

The **for** loop notation is recognized by the shell and has the general form

        for *name* **in** *w1 w2 ...*
        do *command-list*
        done

A *command-list* is a sequence of one or more simple commands separated or terminated by a newline or semicolon. Furthermore, reserved words like **do** and **done** are only recognized following a newline or semicolon. *name* is a shell variable that is set to the words *w1 w2 ...* in turn each time the *command-list* following **do** is executed. If **in** *w1 w2 ...* is omitted then the loop is executed once for each positional parameter; that is, **in** *$*$* is assumed.

Another example of the use of the **for** loop is the *create* command whose text is

        for i do >$i; done

The command

        create alpha beta

ensures that two empty files *alpha* and *beta* exist and are empty. The notation >*file* may be used on its own to create or clear the contents of a file. Notice also that a semicolon (or newline) is required before **done.**

2.2 Control flow - case

A multiple way branch is provided for by the **case** notation. For example,

        case $# in
           1)   cat ≫$1 ;;
           2)   cat ≫$2 <$1 ;;
           ∗)   echo ´usage: append [from] to´ ;;
        esac

is an *append* command. When called with one argument as

        append file

$# is the string *1* and the standard input is copied onto the end of *file* using the *cat* command.

        append file1 file2

appends the contents of *file1* onto *file2*. If the number of arguments supplied to *append* is other than 1 or 2 then a message is printed indicating proper usage.

The general form of the **case** command is

        case *word* **in**
          pattern) *command-list* **;;**
          ...
        esac

The shell attempts to match *word* with each *pattern*, in the order in which the patterns appear. If a match is found the associated *command-list* is executed and execution of the **case** is complete. Since ∗ is the pattern that matches any string it can be used for the default case.

A word of caution: no check is made to ensure that only one pattern matches the case argument. The first match found defines the set of commands to be executed.

In the example below the commands following the second ∗ will never be executed.

```
case $# in
    *) ... ;;
    *) ... ;;
esac
```

Another example of the use of the **case** construction is to distinguish between different forms of an argument. The following example is a fragment of a *cc* command.

```
for i
do case $i in
        -[ocs])   ... ;;
        -*) echo
        *.c)/lib/c0 $i ... ;;
        *)  echo
    esac
done
```

To allow the same commands to be associated with more than one pattern the **case** command provides for alternative patterns separated by a | . For example,

```
case $i in
    -x|-y)...
esac
```

is equivalent to

```
case $i in
    -[xy]) ...
esac
```

The usual quoting conventions apply so that

```
case $i in
    \?)   ...
esac
```

will match the character **?** .

2.3 Here documents

The shell procedure *tel* in section 2.1 uses the file **/usr/lib/telnos** to supply the data for *grep*. An alternative is to include this data within the shell procedure as a *here* document, as in,

```
for i
do grep $i <<!
    ...
    fred mh0123
    bert mh0789
    ...
!
done
```

In this example the shell takes the lines between <<! and ! as the standard input for *grep*. The string ! is arbitrary, the document being terminated by a line that consists of the string following << .

Parameters are substituted in the document before it is made available to *grep* as illustrated by the following procedure called *edg* .

```
ed $3 ≪%
g/$1/s//$2/g
w
%
```

The call

```
edg string1 string2 file
```

is then equivalent to the command

```
ed file ≪%
g/string1/s//string2/g
w
%
```

and changes all occurrences of *string1* in *file* to *string2* . Substitution can be prevented using \ to quote the special character **$** as in

```
ed $3 ≪+
1,\$s/$1/$2/g
w
+
```

(This version of *edg* is equivalent to the first except that *ed* will print a **?** if there are no occurrences of the string **$1** .) Substitution within a *here* document may be prevented entirely by quoting the terminating string, for example,

```
grep $i ≪\#
...
#
```

The document is presented without modification to *grep*. If parameter substitution is not required in a *here* document this latter form is more efficient.

2.4 Shell variables

The shell provides string-valued variables. Variable names begin with a letter and consist of letters, digits and underscores. Variables may be given values by writing, for example,

```
user=fred box=m000 acct=mh0000
```

which assigns values to the variables **user, box** and **acct.** A variable may be set to the null string by saying, for example,

```
null=
```

The value of a variable is substituted by preceding its name with **$** ; for example,

```
echo $user
```

will echo *fred.*

Variables may be used interactively to provide abbreviations for frequently used strings. For example,

```
b=/usr/fred/bin
mv pgm $b
```

will move the file *pgm* from the current directory to the directory **/usr/fred/bin** .

A more general notation is available for parameter (or variable) substitution, as in,

> echo ${user}

which is equivalent to

> echo $user

and is used when the parameter name is followed by a letter or digit. For example,

> tmp=/tmp/ps
> ps a >${tmp}a

will direct the output of *ps* to the file **/tmp/psa,** whereas,

> ps a >$tmpa

would cause the value of the variable **tmpa** to be substituted.

Except for **$?** the following are set initially by the shell. **$?** is set after executing each command.

$?   The exit status (return code) of the last command executed as a decimal string. Most commands return a zero exit status if they complete successfully, otherwise a non-zero exit status is returned. Testing the value of return codes is dealt with later under **if** and **while** commands.

$#   The number of positional parameters (in decimal). Used, for example, in the *append* command to check the number of parameters.

$$ The process number of this shell (in decimal). Since process numbers are unique among all existing processes, this string is frequently used to generate unique temporary file names. For example,

> ps a >/tmp/ps$$
> ...
> rm /tmp/ps$$

$!   The process number of the last process run in the background (in decimal).

$–   The current shell flags, such as –**x** and –**v**.

Some variables have a special meaning to the shell and should be avoided for general use.

$MAIL   When used interactively the shell looks at the file specified by this variable before it issues a prompt. If the specified file has been modified since it was last looked at the shell prints the message *you have mail* before prompting for the next command. This variable is typically set in the file **.profile,** in the user's login directory. For example,

> MAIL=/usr/spool/mail/fred

$HOME   The default argument for the *cd* command. The current directory is used to resolve file name references that do not begin with a **/,** and is changed using the *cd* command. For example,

> cd /usr/fred/bin

makes the current directory **/usr/fred/bin .**

> cat wn

will print on the terminal the file *wn* in this directory. The command *cd* with no argument is equivalent to

> cd $HOME

This variable is also typically set in the the user's login profile.

3

$PATH   A list of directories that contain commands (the *search path*). Each time a command is executed by the shell a list of directories is searched for an executable file. If **$PATH** is not set then the current directory, **/bin**, and **/usr/bin** are searched by default. Otherwise **$PATH** consists of directory names separated by **:**. For example,

> PATH=:/usr/fred/bin:/bin:/usr/bin

specifies that the current directory (the null string before the first **:**), **/usr/fred/bin**, **/bin** and **/usr/bin** are to be searched in that order. In this way individual users can have their own 'private' commands that are accessible independently of the current directory. If the command name contains a **/** then this directory search is not used; a single attempt is made to execute the command.

$PS1   The primary shell prompt string, by default, '**$** '.

$PS2   The shell prompt when further input is needed, by default, '**>** '.

$IFS   The set of characters used by *blank interpretation* (see section 3.4).

2.5 The test command

The *test* command, although not part of the shell, is intended for use by shell programs. For example,

> test −f file

returns zero exit status if *file* exists and non-zero exit status otherwise. In general *test* evaluates a predicate and returns the result as its exit status. Some of the more frequently used *test* arguments are given here, see *test* (1) for a complete specification.

test s	true if the argument *s* is not the null string
test −f file	true if *file* exists
test −r file	true if *file* is readable
test −w file	true if *file* is writable
test −d file	true if *file* is a directory

2.6 Control flow - while

The actions of the **for** loop and the **case** branch are determined by data available to the shell. A **while** or **until** loop and an **if then else** branch are also provided whose actions are determined by the exit status returned by commands. A **while** loop has the general form

> **while** *command-list₁*
> **do** *command-list₂*
> **done**

The value tested by the **while** command is the exit status of the last simple command following **while.** Each time round the loop *command-list₁* is executed; if a zero exit status is returned then *command-list₂* is executed; otherwise, the loop terminates. For example,

> while test $1
> do ...
>   shift
> done

is equivalent to

> for i
> do ...
> done

shift is a shell command that renames the positional parameters **$2, $3, ...** as **$1, $2, ...** and loses **$1** .

Another kind of use for the **while/until** loop is to wait until some external event occurs and then run some commands. In an **until** loop the termination condition is reversed. For example,

> until test −f file
> do sleep 300; done
> *commands*

will loop until *file* exists. Each time round the loop it waits for 5 minutes before trying again. (Presumably another process will eventually create the file.)

2.7 Control flow - if

Also available is a general conditional branch of the form,

> **if** *command-list*
> **then** *command-list*
> **else** *command-list*
> **fi**

that tests the value returned by the last simple command following **if.**

The **if** command may be used in conjunction with the *test* command to test for the existence of a file as in

> if test −f file
> then *process file*
> else *do something else*
> fi

An example of the use of **if, case** and **for** constructions is given in section 2.10.

A multiple test **if** command of the form

> if ...
> then ...
> else if ...
>   then ...
>   else if ...
>   ...
>   fi
>   fi
> fi

may be written using an extension of the **if** notation as,

> if ...
> then ...
> elif ...
> then ...
> elif ...
> ...
> fi

The following example is the *touch* command which changes the 'last modified' time for a list of files. The command may be used in conjunction with *make* (1) to force recompilation of a list of files.

```
flag=
for i
do case $i in
        −c) flag=N ;;
        *)  if test −f $i
            then   ln $i junk$$; rm junk$$
            elif test $flag
            then   echo file \`$i\` does not exist
            else   >$i
            fi
    esac
done
```

The −c flag is used in this command to force subsequent files to be created if they do not already exist. Otherwise, if the file does not exist, an error message is printed. The shell variable *flag* is set to some non-null string if the −c argument is encountered. The commands

```
ln ...; rm ...
```

make a link to the file and then remove it thus causing the last modified date to be updated.

The sequence

```
if command1
then   command2
fi
```

may be written

```
command1 && command2
```

Conversely,

```
command1 || command2
```

executes *command2* only if *command1* fails. In each case the value returned is that of the last simple command executed.

2.8 Command grouping

Commands may be grouped in two ways,

```
{ command-list ; }
```

and

```
( command-list )
```

In the first *command-list* is simply executed. The second form executes *command-list* as a separate process. For example,

```
(cd x; rm junk )
```

executes *rm junk* in the directory **x** without changing the current directory of the invoking shell.

The commands

```
cd x; rm junk
```

have the same effect but leave the invoking shell in the directory **x.**

2.9 Debugging shell procedures

The shell provides two tracing mechanisms to help when debugging shell procedures. The first is invoked within the procedure as

    set −v

(v for verbose) and causes lines of the procedure to be printed as they are read. It is useful to help isolate syntax errors. It may be invoked without modifying the procedure by saying

    sh −v proc ...

where *proc* is the name of the shell procedure. This flag may be used in conjunction with the −n flag which prevents execution of subsequent commands. (Note that saying *set −n* at a terminal will render the terminal useless until an end-of-file is typed.)

The command

    set −x

will produce an execution trace. Following parameter substitution each command is printed as it is executed. (Try these at the terminal to see what effect they have.) Both flags may be turned off by saying

    set −

and the current setting of the shell flags is available as $−.

2.10 The man command

```
            cd /usr/man

            : 'colon is the comment command'
            : 'default is nroff ($N), section 1 ($s)'
            N=n s=1

            for i
            do case $i in

                    [1−9]*)   s=$i ;;

                    −t) N=t ;;

                    −n) N=n ;;

                    −*) echo unknown flag \'$i\' ;;

                    *)   if test −f man$s/$i.$s
                         then   ${N}roff man0/${N}aa man$s/$i.$s
                         else   : 'look through all manual sections'
                                found=no
                                for j in 1 2 3 4 5 6 7 8 9
                                do if test −f man$j/$i.$j
                                   then man $j $i
                                        found=yes
                                   fi
                                done
                                case $found in
                                    no) echo '$i: manual page not found'
                                esac
                         fi
            esac
            done
```

Figure 1. A version of the man command

The preceding is the *man* command which is used to diplay sections of the UNIX manual on your terminal. It is called, for example, as

        man sh
        man –t ed
        man 2 fork

In the first the manual section for *sh* is displayed.. Since no section is specified, section 1 is used. The second example will typeset (**–t** option) the manual section for *ed*. The last prints the *fork* manual page from section 2, which covers system calls.

3.0 Keyword parameters

Shell variables may be given values by assignment or when a shell procedure is invoked. An argument to a shell procedure of the form *name=value* that precedes the command name causes *value* to be assigned to *name* before execution of the procedure begins. The value of *name* in the invoking shell is not affected. For example,

        user=fred command

will execute *command* with **user** set to *fred*. The **–k** flag causes arguments of the form *name=value* to be interpreted in this way anywhere in the argument list. Such *names* are sometimes called keyword parameters. If any arguments remain they are available as positional parameters **$1, $2, ...**

The *set* command may also be used to set positional parameters from within a procedure. For example,

        set – *

will set **$1** to the first file name in the current directory, **$2** to the next, and so on. Note that the first argument, –, ensures correct treatment when the first file name begins with a – .

3.1 Parameter transmission

When a shell procedure is invoked both positional and keyword parameters may be supplied with the call. Keyword parameters are also made available implicitly to a shell procedure by specifying in advance that such parameters are to be exported. For example,

        export user box

marks the variables **user** and **box** for export. When a shell procedure is invoked copies are made of all exportable variables for use within the invoked procedure. Modification of such variables within the procedure does not affect the values in the invoking shell. It is generally true of a shell procedure that it may not modify the state of its caller without explicit request on the part of the caller. (Shared file descriptors are an exception to this rule.)

Names whose value is intended to remain constant may be declared *readonly*. The form of this command is the same as that of the *export* command,

        readonly name . . .

Subsequent attempts to set readonly variables are illegal.

3.2 Parameter substitution

If a shell parameter is not set then the null string is substituted for it. For example, if the variable **d** is not set

        echo $d

or

        echo ${d}

will echo nothing. A default string may be given as in

        echo ${d−.}

which will echo the value of the variable **d** if it is set and '.' otherwise. The default string is evaluated using the usual quoting conventions so that

        echo ${d−´∗´}

will echo ∗ if the variable **d** is not set. Similarly

        echo ${d−$1}

will echo the value of **d** if it is set and the value (if any) of **$1** otherwise. A variable may be assigned a default value using the notation

        echo ${d=.}

which substitutes the same string as

        echo ${d−.}

and if **d** were not previously set then it will be set to the string '.'. (The notation ${...=...} is not available for positional parameters.)

If there is no sensible default then the notation

        echo ${d?message}

will echo the value of the variable **d** if it has one, otherwise *message* is printed by the shell and execution of the shell procedure is abandoned. If *message* is absent then a standard message is printed. A shell procedure that requires some parameters to be set might start as follows.

        : ${user?} ${acct?} ${bin?}
        ...

Colon (:) is a command that is built in to the shell and does nothing once its arguments have been evaluated. If any of the variables **user, acct** or **bin** are not set then the shell will abandon execution of the procedure.

3.3 Command substitution

The standard output from a command can be substituted in a similar way to parameters. The command *pwd* prints on its standard output the name of the current directory. For example, if the current directory is **/usr/fred/bin** then the command

        d=`pwd`

is equivalent to

        d=/usr/fred/bin

The entire string between grave accents (`...`) is taken as the command to be executed and is replaced with the output from the command. The command is written using the usual quoting conventions except that a ` must be escaped using a \.

For example,

> ls `echo "$1"`

is equivalent to

> ls $1

Command substitution occurs in all contexts where parameter substitution occurs (including *here* documents) and the treatment of the resulting text is the same in both cases. This mechanism allows string processing commands to be used within shell procedures. An example of such a command is *basename* which
removes a specified suffix from a string. For example,

> basename main.c .c

will print the string *main* . Its use is illustrated by the following fragment from a *cc* command.

```
case $A in
    ...
    *.c)    B=`basename $A .c`
    ...
esac
```

that sets **B** to the part of **$A** with the suffix **.c** stripped.

Here are some composite examples.

- **for i in `ls –t`; do ...**
  The variable **i** is set to the names of files in time order, most recent first.
- **set `date`; echo $6 $2 $3, $4**
  will print, e.g., *1977 Nov 1, 23:59:59*

3.4 Evaluation and quoting

The shell is a macro processor that provides parameter substitution, command substitution and file name
generation for the arguments to commands. This section discusses the order in which these evaluations
occur and the effects of the various quoting mechanisms.

Commands are parsed initially according to the grammar given in appendix A. Before a command is executed the following substitutions occur.

- parameter substitution, e.g. **$user**
- command substitution, e.g. **`pwd`**

  Only one evaluation occurs so that if, for example, the value of the variable **X** is the string *$y*
  then

  > echo $X

  will echo *$y* .

- blank interpretation

  Following the above substitutions the resulting characters are broken into non-blank words
  (*blank interpretation*). For this purpose 'blanks' are the characters of the string **$IFS**. By
  default, this string consists of blank, tab and newline. The null string is not regarded as a word
  unless it is quoted. For example,

  > echo ''

  will pass on the null string as the first argument to *echo*, whereas

  > echo $null

  will call *echo* with no arguments if the variable **null** is not set or set to the null string.

- file name generation

  Each word is then scanned for the file pattern characters *****, **?** and **[...]** and an alphabetical list of file names is generated to replace the word. Each such file name is a separate argument.

The evaluations just described also occur in the list of words associated with a **for** loop. Only substitution occurs in the *word* used for a **case** branch.

As well as the quoting mechanisms described earlier using **** and ´...´ a third quoting mechanism is provided using double quotes. Within double quotes parameter and command substitution occurs but file name generation and the interpretation of blanks does not. The following characters have a special meaning within double quotes and may be quoted using ****.

> **$**   parameter substitution
> `   command substitution
> "   ends the quoted string
> \   quotes the special characters **$** ` " \

For example,

>   echo "$x"

will pass the value of the variable **x** as a single argument to *echo*. Similarly,

>   echo "$*"

will pass the positional parameters as a single argument and is equivalent to

>   echo "$1 $2 ..."

The notation **$@** is the same as **$*** except when it is quoted.

>   echo "$@"

will pass the positional parameters, unevaluated, to *echo* and is equivalent to

>   echo "$1" "$2" ...

The following table gives, for each quoting mechanism, the shell metacharacters that are evaluated.

				metacharacter		
	\	$	*	`	"	´
´	n	n	n	n	n	t
`	y	n	n	t	n	n
"	y	y	n	y	t	n

t	terminator
y	interpreted
n	not interpreted

Figure 2. Quoting mechanisms

In cases where more than one evaluation of a string is required the built-in command *eval* may be used. For example, if the variable **X** has the value *$y*, and if **y** has the value *pqr* then

>   eval echo $X

will echo the string *pqr*.

In general the *eval* command evaluates its arguments (as do all commands) and treats the result as input to the shell. The input is read and the resulting command(s) executed.

For example,

>   wg=´eval who | grep´
> $wg fred

is equivalent to

>   who | grep fred

In this example, *eval* is required since there is no interpretation of metacharacters, such as **|**, **following
substitution.**

3.5 Error handling

The treatment of errors detected by the shell depends on the type of error and on whether the shell is being
used interactively. An interactive shell is one whose input and output are connected to a terminal (as determined by *gtty* (2)). A shell invoked with the **−i** flag is also interactive.

Execution of a command (see also 3.7) may fail for any of the following reasons.

- Input output redirection may fail. For example, if a file does not exist or cannot be created.
- The command itself does not exist or cannot be executed.
- The command terminates abnormally, for example, with a "bus error" or "memory fault". See Figure
  2 below for a complete list of UNIX signals.
- The command terminates normally but returns a non-zero exit status.

In all of these cases the shell will go on to execute the next command. Except for the last case an error
message will be printed by the shell. All remaining errors cause the shell to exit from a command procedure. An interactive shell will return to read another command from the terminal. Such errors include
the following.

- Syntax errors. e.g., if ... then ... done
- A signal such as interrupt. The shell waits for the current command, if any, to finish execution and
  then either exits or returns to the terminal.
- Failure of any of the built-in commands such as *cd*.

The shell flag **−e** causes the shell to terminate if any error is detected.

1	hangup
2	interrupt
3*	quit
4*	illegal instruction
5*	trace trap
6*	IOT instruction
7*	EMT instruction
8*	floating point exception
9	kill (cannot be caught or ignored)
10*	bus error
11*	segmentation violation
12*	bad argument to system call
13	write on a pipe with no one to read it
14	alarm clock
15	software termination (from *kill* (1))

Figure 3. UNIX signals†

Those signals marked with an asterisk produce a core dump if not caught. However, the shell itself ignores
quit which is the only external signal that can cause a dump.

---

† Additional signals have been added in Berkeley Unix. See sigvec(2) or signal(3C) for an up-to-date list.

The signals in this list of potential interest to shell programs are 1, 2, 3, 14 and 15.

3.6 Fault handling

Shell procedures normally terminate when an interrupt is received from the terminal. The *trap* command is used if some cleaning up is required, such as removing temporary files. For example,

> trap ´rm /tmp/ps$$; exit´ 2

sets a trap for signal 2 (terminal interrupt), and if this signal is received will execute the commands

> rm /tmp/ps$$; exit

exit is another built-in command that terminates execution of a shell procedure. The *exit* is required; otherwise, after the trap has been taken, the shell will resume executing the procedure at the place where it was interrupted.

UNIX signals can be handled in one of three ways. They can be ignored, in which case the signal is never sent to the process. They can be caught, in which case the process must decide what action to take when the signal is received. Lastly, they can be left to cause termination of the process without it having to take any further action. If a signal is being ignored on entry to the shell procedure, for example, by invoking it in the background (see 3.7) then *trap* commands (and the signal) are ignored.

The use of *trap* is illustrated by this modified version of the *touch* command (Figure 4). The cleanup action is to remove the file **junk$$**.

```
            flag=
            trap ´rm −f junk$$; exit´ 1 2 3 15
            for i
            do case $i in
                    −c)  flag=N ;;
                    ∗)  if test −f $i
                        then   ln $i junk$$; rm junk$$
                        elif test $flag
                        then   echo file \´$i\´ does not exist
                        else   >$i
                        fi
                esac
            done
```

Figure 4. The touch command

The *trap* command appears before the creation of the temporary file; otherwise it would be possible for the process to die without removing the file.

Since there is no signal 0 in UNIX it is used by the shell to indicate the commands to be executed on exit from the shell procedure.

A procedure may, itself, elect to ignore signals by specifying the null string as the argument to trap. The following fragment is taken from the *nohup* command.

> trap ´´ 1 2 3 15

which causes *hangup, interrupt, quit* and *kill* to be ignored both by the procedure and by invoked commands.

Traps may be reset by saying

> trap 2 3

which resets the traps for signals 2 and 3 to their default values.

A list of the current values of traps may be obtained by writing

    trap

The procedure *scan* (Figure 5) is an example of the use of *trap* where there is no exit in the trap command. *scan* takes each directory in the current directory, prompts with its name, and then executes commands typed at the terminal until an end of file or an interrupt is received. Interrupts are ignored while executing the requested commands but cause termination when *scan* is waiting for input.

```
        d=`pwd`
        for i in *
        do if test -d $d/$i
            then cd $d/$i
                while echo "$i:"
                        trap exit 2
                        read x
                do trap : 2; eval $x; done
            fi
        done
```

Figure 5. The scan command

read x is a built-in command that reads one line from the standard input and places the result in the variable **x**. It returns a non-zero exit status if either an end-of-file is read or an interrupt is received.

3.7 Command execution

To run a command (other than a built-in) the shell first creates a new process using the system call *fork*. The execution environment for the command includes input, output and the states of signals, and is established in the child process before the command is executed. The built-in command *exec* is used in the rare cases when no fork is required and simply replaces the shell with a new command. For example, a simple version of the *nohup* command looks like

    trap ´´ 1 2 3 15
    exec $*

The *trap* turns off the signals specified so that they are ignored by subsequently created commands and *exec* replaces the shell by the command specified.

Most forms of input output redirection have already been described. In the following *word* is only subject to parameter and command substitution. No file name generation or blank interpretation takes place so that, for example,

    echo ... >*.c

will write its output into a file whose name is ***.c**. Input output specifications are evaluated left to right as they appear in the command.

> *word*	The standard output (file descriptor 1) is sent to the file *word* which is created if it does not already exist.
>> *word*	The standard output is sent to file *word*. If the file exists then output is appended (by seeking to the end); otherwise the file is created.
< *word*	The standard input (file descriptor 0) is taken from the file *word*.
<< *word*	The standard input is taken from the lines of shell input that follow up to but not including a line consisting only of *word*. If *word* is quoted then no interpretation of the document occurs. If *word* is not quoted then parameter and command substitution occur and \ is used to quote the characters \ $ ` and the first character of *word*. In the latter case **\newline** is ignored (c.f. quoted strings).

>& *digit*   The file descriptor *digit* is duplicated using the system call *dup* (2) and the result is used as the standard output.

<& *digit*   The standard input is duplicated from file descriptor *digit.*

<&–   The standard input is closed.

>&–   The standard output is closed.

Any of the above may be preceded by a digit in which case the file descriptor created is that specified by the digit instead of the default 0 or 1. For example,

> ... 2>file

runs a command with message output (file descriptor 2) directed to *file.*

> ... 2>&1

runs a command with its standard output and message output merged. (Strictly speaking file descriptor 2 is created by duplicating file descriptor 1 but the effect is usually to merge the two streams.)

The environment for a command run in the background such as

> list *.c | lpr &

is modified in two ways. Firstly, the default standard input for such a command is the empty file **/dev/null**. This prevents two processes (the shell and the command), which are running in parallel, from trying to read the same input. Chaos would ensue if this were not the case. For example,

> ed file &

would allow both the editor and the shell to read from the same input at the same time.

The other modification to the environment of a background command is to turn off the QUIT and INTER-RUPT signals so that they are ignored by the command. This allows these signals to be used at the terminal without causing background commands to terminate. For this reason the UNIX convention for a signal is that if it is set to 1 (ignored) then it is never changed even for a short time. Note that the shell command *trap* has no effect for an ignored signal.

3.8 Invoking the shell

The following flags are interpreted by the shell when it is invoked. If the first character of argument zero is a minus, then commands are read from the file **.profile**.

–**c** *string*
> If the –**c** flag is present then commands are read from *string*.

–**s**   If the –**s** flag is present or if no arguments remain then commands are read from the standard input. Shell output is written to file descriptor 2.

–**i**   If the –**i** flag is present or if the shell input and output are attached to a terminal (as told by *gtty*) then this shell is *interactive*. In this case TERMINATE is ignored (so that **kill 0** does not kill an interactive shell) and INTERRUPT is caught and ignored (so that **wait** is interruptable). In all cases QUIT is ignored by the shell.

Acknowledgements

The design of the shell is based in part on the original UNIX shell[3] and the PWB/UNIX shell,[4] some features having been taken from both. Similarities also exist with the command interpreters of the Cambridge Multiple Access System[5] and of CTSS.[6]

I would like to thank Dennis Ritchie and John Mashey for many discussions during the design of the shell. I am also grateful to the members of the Computing Science Research Center and to Joe Maranzano for their comments on drafts of this document.

References

1.   B. W. Kernighan, *UNIX for Beginners*, 1978.

2.   K. Thompson and D. M. Ritchie, *UNIX Programmer's Manual,* Bell Laboratories, 1978. Seventh Edition.

3.   K. Thompson, "The UNIX Command Language," in *Structured Programming—Infotech State of the Art Report*, pp. 375-384, Infotech International Ltd., Nicholson House, Maidenhead, Berkshire, England, March 1975.

4.   J. R. Mashey, *PWB/UNIX Shell Tutorial*, September 30, 1977.

5.   D. F. Hartley (Ed.), *The Cambridge Multiple Access System – Users Reference Manual,* University Mathematical Laboratory, Cambridge, England, 1968.

6.   P. A. Crisman (Ed.), *The Compatible Time-Sharing System,* M.I.T. Press, Cambridge, Mass., 1965.

3

Appendix A - Grammar

item: *word*
               input-output
               name = value

simple-command: item
               simple-command item

command: *simple-command*
               (command-list)
               { command-list }
               for *name* **do** *command-list* **done**
               for *name* **in** *word* **...** **do** *command-list* **done**
               while *command-list* **do** *command-list* **done**
               until *command-list* **do** *command-list* **done**
               case *word* **in** *case-part* **... esac**
               if *command-list* **then** *command-list else-part* **fi**

pipeline: *command*
               pipeline | command

andor: *pipeline*
               andor **&&** *pipeline*
               andor **| |** *pipeline*

command-list: *andor*
               command-list **;**
               command-list **&**
               command-list **;** *andor*
               command-list **&** *andor*

input-output: **>** *file*
               < *file*
               ≫ *word*
               ≪ *word*

file: *word*
               & *digit*
               & –

case-part: *pattern*) *command-list* **;;**

pattern: *word*
               pattern | word

else-part: **elif** *command-list* **then** *command-list else-part*
               else *command-list*
               empty

empty:

word: a sequence of non-blank characters

name: a sequence of letters, digits or underscores starting with a letter

digit: **0 1 2 3 4 5 6 7 8 9**

3

Appendix B - Meta-characters and Reserved Words

a) syntactic

| | pipe symbol
&& 'andf' symbol
| | 'orf' symbol
; command separator
;; case delimiter
& background commands
( ) command grouping
< input redirection
« input from a here document
> output creation
» output append

b) patterns

* match any character(s) including none
? match any single character
[...] match any of the enclosed characters

c) substitution

${...} substitute shell variable
`...` substitute command output

d) quoting

\ quote the next character
'...' quote the enclosed characters except for '
"..." quote the enclosed characters except for **$ ` \ "**

e) reserved words

if then else elif fi
case in esac
for while until do done
{ }

An Introduction to the C shell

William Joy
(revised for 4.3BSD by Mark Seiden)

Computer Science Division
Department of Electrical Engineering and Computer Science
University of California, Berkeley
Berkeley, California 94720

ABSTRACT

Csh is a new command language interpreter for UNIX† systems. It incorporates good features of other shells and a *history* mechanism similar to the *redo* of INTERLISP. While incorporating many features of other shells which make writing shell programs (shell scripts) easier, most of the features unique to *csh* are designed more for the interactive UNIX user.

UNIX users who have read a general introduction to the system will find a valuable basic explanation of the shell here. Simple terminal interaction with *csh* is possible after reading just the first section of this document. The second section describes the shell's capabilities which you can explore after you have begun to become acquainted with the shell. Later sections introduce features which are useful, but not necessary for all users of the shell.

Additional information includes an appendix listing special characters of the shell and a glossary of terms and commands introduced in this manual.

4

Introduction

A *shell* is a command language interpreter. *Csh* is the name of one particular command interpreter on UNIX. The primary purpose of *csh* is to translate command lines typed at a terminal into system actions, such as invocation of other programs. *Csh* is a user program just like any you might write. Hopefully, *csh* will be a very useful program for you in interacting with the UNIX system.

In addition to this document, you will want to refer to a copy of the UNIX User Reference Manual. The *csh* documentation in section 1 of the manual provides a full description of all features of the shell and is the definitive reference for questions about the shell.

Many words in this document are shown in *italics*. These are important words; names of commands, and words which have special meaning in discussing the shell and UNIX. Many of the words are defined in a glossary at the end of this document. If you don't know what is meant by a word, you should look for it in the glossary.

Acknowledgements

Numerous people have provided good input about previous versions of *csh* and aided in its debugging and in the debugging of its documentation. I would especially like to thank Michael Ubell who made the crucial observation that history commands could be done well over the word structure of input text, and implemented a prototype history mechanism in an older version of the shell. Eric Allman has also provided a large number of useful comments on the shell, helping to unify those concepts which are present

---

† UNIX is a registered trademark of AT&T Bell Laboratories in the USA and other countries.

and to identify and eliminate useless and marginally useful features. Mike O'Brien suggested the pathname hashing mechanism which speeds command execution. Jim Kulp added the job control and directory
stack primitives and added their documentation to this introduction.

1. Terminal usage of the shell

1.1. The basic notion of commands

A *shell* in UNIX acts mostly as a medium through which other *programs* are invoked. While it has a
set of *builtin* functions which it performs directly, most commands cause execution of programs that are, in
fact, external to the shell. The shell is thus distinguished from the command interpreters of other systems
both by the fact that it is just a user program, and by the fact that it is used almost exclusively as a mechanism for invoking other programs.

Commands in the UNIX system consist of a list of strings or *words* interpreted as a *command name*
followed by *arguments*. Thus the command

      mail bill

consists of two words. The first word *mail* names the command to be executed, in this case the mail program which sends messages to other users. The shell uses the name of the command in attempting to execute it for you. It will look in a number of *directories* for a file with the name *mail* which is expected to
contain the mail program.

The rest of the words of the command are given as *arguments* to the command itself when it is executed. In this case we specified also the argument *bill* which is interpreted by the *mail* program to be the
name of a user to whom mail is to be sent. In normal terminal usage we might use the *mail* command as
follows.

      % mail bill
      I have a question about the csh documentation.
      My document seems to be missing page 5.
      Does a page five exist?
          Bill
      EOT
      %

Here we typed a message to send to *bill* and ended this message with a ^D which sent an end-of-file
to the mail program. (Here and throughout this document, the notation ''^*x*'' is to be read ''control-*x*'' and
represents the striking of the *x* key while the control key is held down.) The mail program then echoed the
characters 'EOT' and transmitted our message. The characters '% ' were printed before and after the mail
command by the shell to indicate that input was needed.

After typing the '% ' prompt the shell was reading command input from our terminal. We typed a
complete command 'mail bill'. The shell then executed the *mail* program with argument *bill* and went
dormant waiting for it to complete. The mail program then read input from our terminal until we signalled
an end-of-file via typing a ^D after which the shell noticed that mail had completed and signaled us that it
was ready to read from the terminal again by printing another '% ' prompt.

This is the essential pattern of all interaction with UNIX through the shell. A complete command is
typed at the terminal, the shell executes the command and when this execution completes, it prompts for a
new command. If you run the editor for an hour, the shell will patiently wait for you to finish editing and
obediently prompt you again whenever you finish editing.

An example of a useful command you can execute now is the *tset* command, which sets the default
erase and *kill* characters on your terminal – the erase character erases the last character you typed and the
kill character erases the entire line you have entered so far. By default, the erase character is the delete key
(equivalent to '^?') and the kill character is '^U'. Some people prefer to make the erase character the

backspace key (equivalent to '^H'). You can make this be true by typing

>   tset −e

which tells the program *tset* to set the erase character to tset's default setting for this character (a back-space).

1.2. Flag arguments

A useful notion in UNIX is that of a *flag* argument. While many arguments to commands specify file names or user names, some arguments rather specify an optional capability of the command which you wish to invoke. By convention, such arguments begin with the character '−' (hyphen). Thus the command

>   ls

will produce a list of the files in the current *working directory*. The option −s is the size option, and

>   ls −s

causes *ls* to also give, for each file the size of the file in blocks of 512 characters. The manual section for each command in the UNIX reference manual gives the available options for each command. The *ls* command has a large number of useful and interesting options. Most other commands have either no options or only one or two options. It is hard to remember options of commands which are not used very frequently, so most UNIX utilities perform only one or two functions rather than having a large number of hard to remember options.

1.3. Output to files

Commands that normally read input or write output on the terminal can also be executed with this input and/or output done to a file.

Thus suppose we wish to save the current date in a file called 'now'. The command

>   date

will print the current date on our terminal. This is because our terminal is the default *standard output* for the date command and the date command prints the date on its standard output. The shell lets us *redirect* the *standard output* of a command through a notation using the *metacharacter* '>' and the name of the file where output is to be placed. Thus the command

>   date > now

runs the *date* command such that its standard output is the file 'now' rather than the terminal. Thus this command places the current date and time into the file 'now'. It is important to know that the *date* command was unaware that its output was going to a file rather than to the terminal. The shell performed this *redirection* before the command began executing.

One other thing to note here is that the file 'now' need not have existed before the *date* command was executed; the shell would have created the file if it did not exist. And if the file did exist? If it had existed previously these previous contents would have been discarded! A shell option *noclobber* exists to prevent this from happening accidentally; it is discussed in section 2.2.

The system normally keeps files which you create with '>' and all other files. Thus the default is for files to be permanent. If you wish to create a file which will be removed automatically, you can begin its name with a '#' character, this 'scratch' character denotes the fact that the file will be a scratch file.* The system will remove such files after a couple of days, or sooner if file space becomes very tight. Thus, in running the *date* command above, we don't really want to save the output forever, so we would more

---

*Note that if your erase character is a '#', you will have to precede the '#' with a '\'. The fact that the '#' character is the old (pre-CRT) standard erase character means that it seldom appears in a file name, and allows this convention to be used for scratch files. If you are using a CRT, your erase character should be a ^H, as we demonstrated in section 1.1 how this could be set up.

likely do

> date > #now

1.4. Metacharacters in the shell

The shell has a large number of special characters (like '>') which indicate special functions. We say that these notations have *syntactic* and *semantic* meaning to the shell. In general, most characters which are neither letters nor digits have special meaning to the shell. We shall shortly learn a means of *quotation* which allows us to use *metacharacters* without the shell treating them in any special way.

Metacharacters normally have effect only when the shell is reading our input. We need not worry about placing shell metacharacters in a letter we are sending via *mail,* or when we are typing in text or data to some other program. Note that the shell is only reading input when it has prompted with '% ' (although we can type our input even before it prompts).

1.5. Input from files; pipelines

We learned above how to *redirect* the *standard output* of a command to a file. It is also possible to redirect the *standard input* of a command from a file. This is not often necessary since most commands will read from a file whose name is given as an argument. We can give the command

> sort < data

to run the *sort* command with standard input, where the command normally reads its input, from the file 'data'. We would more likely say

> sort data

letting the *sort* command open the file 'data' for input itself since this is less to type.

We should note that if we just typed

> sort

then the sort program would sort lines from its *standard input.* Since we did not *redirect* the standard input, it would sort lines as we typed them on the terminal until we typed a ˆD to indicate an end-of-file.

A most useful capability is the ability to combine the standard output of one command with the standard input of another, i.e. to run the commands in a sequence known as a *pipeline.* For instance the command

> ls −s

normally produces a list of the files in our directory with the size of each in blocks of 512 characters. If we are interested in learning which of our files is largest we may wish to have this sorted by size rather than by name, which is the default way in which *ls* sorts. We could look at the many options of *ls* to see if there was an option to do this but would eventually discover that there is not. Instead we can use a couple of simple options of the *sort* command, combining it with *ls* to get what we want.

The −*n* option of sort specifies a numeric sort rather than an alphabetic sort. Thus

> ls −s | sort −n

specifies that the output of the *ls* command run with the option −*s* is to be *piped* to the command *sort* run with the numeric sort option. This would give us a sorted list of our files by size, but with the smallest first. We could then use the −*r* reverse sort option and the *head* command in combination with the previous command doing

> ls −s | sort −n −r | head −5

Here we have taken a list of our files sorted alphabetically, each with the size in blocks. We have run this to the standard input of the *sort* command asking it to sort numerically in reverse order (largest first). This output has then been run into the command *head* which gives us the first few lines. In this case we have asked *head* for the first 5 lines. Thus this command gives us the names and sizes of our 5 largest files.

The notation introduced above is called the *pipe* mechanism. Commands separated by '|' characters are connected together by the shell and the standard output of each is run into the standard input of the next. The leftmost command in a pipeline will normally take its standard input from the terminal and the rightmost will place its standard output on the terminal. Other examples of pipelines will be given later when we discuss the history mechanism; one important use of pipes which is illustrated there is in the routing of information to the line printer.

1.6. Filenames

Many commands to be executed will need the names of files as arguments. UNIX *pathnames* consist of a number of *components* separated by '/'. Each component except the last names a directory in which the next component resides, in effect specifying the *path* of directories to follow to reach the file. Thus the pathname

    /etc/motd

specifies a file in the directory 'etc' which is a subdirectory of the *root* directory '/'. Within this directory the file named is 'motd' which stands for 'message of the day'. A *pathname* that begins with a slash is said to be an *absolute* pathname since it is specified from the absolute top of the entire directory hierarchy of the system (the *root*). *Pathnames* which do not begin with '/' are interpreted as starting in the current *working directory*, which is, by default, your *home* directory and can be changed dynamically by the *cd* change directory command. Such pathnames are said to be *relative* to the working directory since they are found by starting in the working directory and descending to lower levels of directories for each *component* of the pathname. If the pathname contains no slashes at all then the file is contained in the working directory itself and the pathname is merely the name of the file in this directory. Absolute pathnames have no relation to the working directory.

Most filenames consist of a number of alphanumeric characters and '.'s (periods). In fact, all printing characters except '/' (slash) may appear in filenames. It is inconvenient to have most non-alphabetic characters in filenames because many of these have special meaning to the shell. The character '.' (period) is not a shell-metacharacter and is often used to separate the *extension* of a file name from the base of the name. Thus

    prog.c prog.o prog.errs prog.output

are four related files. They share a *base* portion of a name (a base portion being that part of the name that is left when a trailing '.' and following characters which are not '.' are stripped off). The file 'prog.c' might be the source for a C program, the file 'prog.o' the corresponding object file, the file 'prog.errs' the errors resulting from a compilation of the program and the file 'prog.output' the output of a run of the program.

If we wished to refer to all four of these files in a command, we could use the notation

    prog.*

This expression is expanded by the shell, before the command to which it is an argument is executed, into a list of names which begin with 'prog.'. The character '*' here matches any sequence (including the empty sequence) of characters in a file name. The names which match are alphabetically sorted and placed in the *argument list* of the command. Thus the command

    echo prog.*

will echo the names

    prog.c prog.errs prog.o prog.output

Note that the names are in sorted order here, and a different order than we listed them above. The *echo* command receives four words as arguments, even though we only typed one word as as argument directly. The four words were generated by *filename expansion* of the one input word.

Other notations for *filename expansion* are also available. The character '?' matches any single character in a filename. Thus

> echo ? ?? ???

will echo a line of filenames; first those with one character names, then those with two character names, and finally those with three character names. The names of each length will be independently sorted.

Another mechanism consists of a sequence of characters between '[' and ']'. This metasequence matches any single character from the enclosed set. Thus

> prog.[co]

will match

> prog.c prog.o

in the example above. We can also place two characters around a '−' in this notation to denote a range. Thus

> chap.[1−5]

might match files

> chap.1 chap.2 chap.3 chap.4 chap.5

if they existed. This is shorthand for

> chap.[12345]

and otherwise equivalent.

An important point to note is that if a list of argument words to a command (an *argument list)* contains filename expansion syntax, and if this filename expansion syntax fails to match any existing file names, then the shell considers this to be an error and prints a diagnostic

> No match.

and does not execute the command.

Another very important point is that files with the character '.' at the beginning are treated specially. Neither '*' or '?' or the '[' ']' mechanism will match it. This prevents accidental matching of the filenames '.' and '..' in the working directory which have special meaning to the system, as well as other files such as *.cshrc* which are not normally visible. We will discuss the special role of the file *.cshrc* later.

Another filename expansion mechanism gives access to the pathname of the *home* directory of other users. This notation consists of the character '~' (tilde) followed by another user's login name. For instance the word '~bill' would map to the pathname '/usr/bill' if the home directory for 'bill' was '/usr/bill'. Since, on large systems, users may have login directories scattered over many different disk volumes with different prefix directory names, this notation provides a convenient way of accessing the files of other users.

A special case of this notation consists of a '~' alone, e.g. '~/mbox'. This notation is expanded by the shell into the file 'mbox' in your *home* directory, i.e. into '/usr/bill/mbox' for me on Ernie Co-vax, the UCB Computer Science Department VAX machine, where this document was prepared. This can be very useful if you have used *cd* to change to another directory and have found a file you wish to copy using *cp*. If I give the command

> cp thatfile ~

the shell will expand this command to

> cp thatfile /usr/bill

since my home directory is /usr/bill.

There also exists a mechanism using the characters '{' and '}' for abbreviating a set of words which have common parts but cannot be abbreviated by the above mechanisms because they are not files, are the names of files which do not yet exist, are not thus conveniently described. This mechanism will be described much later, in section 4.2, as it is used less frequently.

1.7. Quotation

We have already seen a number of metacharacters used by the shell. These metacharacters pose a problem in that we cannot use them directly as parts of words. Thus the command

    echo *

will not echo the character '*'. It will either echo an sorted list of filenames in the current *working directory*, or print the message 'No match' if there are no files in the working directory.

The recommended mechanism for placing characters which are neither numbers, digits, '/', '.' or '–' in an argument word to a command is to enclose it with single quotation characters '´', i.e.

    echo ´*´

There is one special character '!' which is used by the *history* mechanism of the shell and which cannot be *escaped* by placing it within '´' characters. It and the character '´' itself can be preceded by a single '\' to prevent their special meaning. Thus

    echo \´\!

prints

    ´!

These two mechanisms suffice to place any printing character into a word which is an argument to a shell command. They can be combined, as in

    echo \´´*´

which prints

    ´*

since the first '\' escaped the first '´' and the '*' was enclosed between '´' characters.

1.8. Terminating commands

When you are executing a command and the shell is waiting for it to complete there are several ways to force it to stop. For instance if you type the command

    cat /etc/passwd

the system will print a copy of a list of all users of the system on your terminal. This is likely to continue for several minutes unless you stop it. You can send an INTERRUPT *signal* to the *cat* command by typing ^C on your terminal.* Since *cat* does not take any precautions to avoid or otherwise handle this signal the INTERRUPT will cause it to terminate. The shell notices that *cat* has terminated and prompts you again with '% '. If you hit INTERRUPT again, the shell will just repeat its prompt since it handles INTERRUPT signals and chooses to continue to execute commands rather than terminating like *cat* did, which would have the effect of logging you out.

Another way in which many programs terminate is when they get an end-of-file from their standard input. Thus the *mail* program in the first example above was terminated when we typed a ^D which generates an end-of-file from the standard input. The shell also terminates when it gets an end-of-file printing 'logout'; UNIX then logs you off the system. Since this means that typing too many ^D's can accidentally log us off, the shell has a mechanism for preventing this. This *ignoreeof* option will be discussed in section 2.2.

---

*On some older Unix systems the DEL or RUBOUT key has the same effect. "stty all" will tell you the INTR key value.

If a command has its standard input redirected from a file, then it will normally terminate when it reaches the end of this file. Thus if we execute

    mail bill < prepared.text

the mail command will terminate without our typing a ^D. This is because it read to the end-of-file of our file 'prepared.text' in which we placed a message for 'bill' with an editor program. We could also have done

    cat prepared.text | mail bill

since the *cat* command would then have written the text through the pipe to the standard input of the mail command. When the *cat* command completed it would have terminated, closing down the pipeline and the *mail* command would have received an end-of-file from it and terminated. Using a pipe here is more complicated than redirecting input so we would more likely use the first form. These commands could also have been stopped by sending an INTERRUPT.

Another possibility for stopping a command is to suspend its execution temporarily, with the possibility of continuing execution later. This is done by sending a STOP signal via typing a ^Z. This signal causes all commands running on the terminal (usually one but more if a pipeline is executing) to become suspended. The shell notices that the command(s) have been suspended, types 'Stopped' and then prompts for a new command. The previously executing command has been suspended, but otherwise unaffected by the STOP signal. Any other commands can be executed while the original command remains suspended. The suspended command can be continued using the *fg* command with no arguments. The shell will then retype the command to remind you which command is being continued, and cause the command to resume execution. Unless any input files in use by the suspended command have been changed in the meantime, the suspension has no effect whatsoever on the execution of the command. This feature can be very useful during editing, when you need to look at another file before continuing. An example of command suspension follows.

    % mail harold
    Someone just copied a big file into my directory and its name is
    ^Z
    Stopped
    % ls
    funnyfile
    prog.c
    prog.o
    % jobs
    [1] + Stopped   mail harold
    % fg
    mail harold
    funnyfile. Do you know who did it?
    EOT
    %

In this example someone was sending a message to Harold and forgot the name of the file he wanted to mention. The mail command was suspended by typing ^Z. When the shell noticed that the mail program was suspended, it typed 'Stopped' and prompted for a new command. Then the *ls* command was typed to find out the name of the file. The *jobs* command was run to find out which command was suspended. At this time the *fg* command was typed to continue execution of the mail program. Input to the mail program was then continued and ended with a ^D which indicated the end of the message at which time the mail program typed EOT. The *jobs* command will show which commands are suspended. The ^Z should only be typed at the beginning of a line since everything typed on the current line is discarded when a signal is sent from the keyboard. This also happens on INTERRUPT, and QUIT signals. More information on suspending jobs and controlling them is given in section 2.6.

If you write or run programs which are not fully debugged then it may be necessary to stop them somewhat ungracefully. This can be done by sending them a QUIT signal, sent by typing a ^\. This will usually provoke the shell to produce a message like:

>   Quit (Core dumped)

indicating that a file 'core' has been created containing information about the running program's state when it terminated due to the QUIT signal. You can examine this file yourself, or forward information to the maintainer of the program telling him/her where the *core file* is.

If you run background commands (as explained in section 2.6) then these commands will ignore INTERRUPT and QUIT signals at the terminal. To stop them you must use the *kill* command. See section 2.6 for an example.

If you want to examine the output of a command without having it move off the screen as the output of the

>   cat /etc/passwd

command will, you can use the command

>   more /etc/passwd

The *more* program pauses after each complete screenful and types '—More—' at which point you can hit a space to get another screenful, a return to get another line, a '?' to get some help on other commands, or a 'q' to end the *more* program. You can also use more as a filter, i.e.

>   cat /etc/passwd | more

works just like the more simple more command above.

For stopping output of commands not involving *more* you can use the ^S key to stop the typeout. The typeout will resume when you hit ^Q or any other key, but ^Q is normally used because it only restarts the output and does not become input to the program which is running. This works well on low-speed terminals, but at 9600 baud it is hard to type ^S and ^Q fast enough to paginate the output nicely, and a program like *more* is usually used.

An additional possibility is to use the ^O flush output character; when this character is typed, all output from the current command is thrown away (quickly) until the next input read occurs or until the next shell prompt. This can be used to allow a command to complete without having to suffer through the output on a slow terminal; ^O is a toggle, so flushing can be turned off by typing ^O again while output is being flushed.

1.9. What now?

We have so far seen a number of mechanisms of the shell and learned a lot about the way in which it operates. The remaining sections will go yet further into the internals of the shell, but you will surely want to try using the shell before you go any further. To try it you can log in to UNIX and type the following command to the system:

>   chsh myname /bin/csh

Here 'myname' should be replaced by the name you typed to the system prompt of 'login:' to get onto the system. Thus I would use 'chsh bill /bin/csh'. **You only have to do this once; it takes effect at next login.** You are now ready to try using *csh*.

Before you do the 'chsh' command, the shell you are using when you log into the system is '/bin/sh'. In fact, much of the above discussion is applicable to '/bin/sh'. The next section will introduce many features particular to *csh* so you should change your shell to *csh* before you begin reading it.

2. Details on the shell for terminal users

2.1. Shell startup and termination

When you login, the shell is started by the system in your *home* directory and begins by reading commands from a file *.cshrc* in this directory. All shells which you may start during your terminal session will read from this file. We will later see what kinds of commands are usefully placed there. For now we need not have this file and the shell does not complain about its absence.

A *login shell*, executed after you login to the system, will, after it reads commands from *.cshrc,* read commands from a file *.login* also in your home directory. This file contains commands which you wish to do each time you login to the UNIX system. My *.login* file looks something like:

```
set ignoreeof
set mail=(/usr/spool/mail/bill)
echo "${prompt}users" ; users
alias ts \
        'set noglob ; eval `tset −s −m dialup:c100rv4pna −m plugboard:?hp2621nl *`';
ts; stty intr ^C kill ^U crt
set time=15 history=10
msgs −f
if (−e $mail) then
        echo "${prompt}mail"
        mail
endif
```

This file contains several commands to be executed by UNIX each time I login. The first is a *set* command which is interpreted directly by the shell. It sets the shell variable *ignoreeof* which causes the shell to not log me off if I hit ^D. Rather, I use the *logout* command to log off of the system. By setting the *mail* variable, I ask the shell to watch for incoming mail to me. Every 5 minutes the shell looks for this file and tells me if more mail has arrived there. An alternative to this is to put the command

        biff y

in place of this *set;* this will cause me to be notified immediately when mail arrives, and to be shown the first few lines of the new message.

Next I set the shell variable 'time' to '15' causing the shell to automatically print out statistics lines for commands which execute for at least 15 seconds of CPU time. The variable 'history' is set to 10 indicating that I want the shell to remember the last 10 commands I type in its *history list*, (described later).

I create an *alias* ''ts'' which executes a *tset*(1) command setting up the modes of the terminal. The parameters to *tset* indicate the kinds of terminal which I usually use when not on a hardwired port. I then execute ''ts'' and also use the *stty* command to change the interrupt character to ^C and the line kill character to ^U.

I then run the 'msgs' program, which provides me with any system messages which I have not seen before; the '−f' option here prevents it from telling me anything if there are no new messages. Finally, if my mailbox file exists, then I run the 'mail' program to process my mail.

When the 'mail' and 'msgs' programs finish, the shell will finish processing my *.login* file and begin reading commands from the terminal, prompting for each with '% '. When I log off (by giving the *logout* command) the shell will print 'logout' and execute commands from the file '.logout' if it exists in my home directory. After that the shell will terminate and UNIX will log me off the system. If the system is not going down, I will receive a new login message. In any case, after the 'logout' message the shell is committed to terminating and will take no further input from my terminal.

2.2. Shell variables

The shell maintains a set of *variables.* We saw above the variables *history* and *time* which had values '10' and '15'. In fact, each shell variable has as value an array of zero or more *strings*. Shell variables may be assigned values by the set command. It has several forms, the most useful of which was given above and is

        set name=value

Shell variables may be used to store values which are to be used in commands later through a substitution mechanism. The shell variables most commonly referenced are, however, those which the shell itself refers to. By changing the values of these variables one can directly affect the behavior of the shell.

One of the most important variables is the variable *path*. This variable contains a sequence of directory names where the shell searches for commands. The *set* command with no arguments shows the value of all variables currently defined (we usually say *set)* in the shell. The default value for path will be shown by *set* to be

```
% set
argv      ()
cwd       /usr/bill
home      /usr/bill
path      (. /usr/ucb /bin /usr/bin)
prompt    %
shell     /bin/csh
status    0
term      c100rv4pna
user      bill
%
```

This output indicates that the variable path points to the current directory '.' and then '/usr/ucb', '/bin' and '/usr/bin'. Commands which you may write might be in '.' (usually one of your directories). Commands developed at Berkeley, live in '/usr/ucb' while commands developed at Bell Laboratories live in '/bin' and '/usr/bin'.

A number of locally developed programs on the system live in the directory '/usr/local'. If we wish that all shells which we invoke to have access to these new programs we can place the command

        set path=(. /usr/ucb /bin /usr/bin /usr/local)

in our file *.cshrc* in our home directory. Try doing this and then logging out and back in and do

        set

again to see that the value assigned to *path* has changed.

One thing you should be aware of is that the shell examines each directory which you insert into your path and determines which commands are contained there. Except for the current directory '.', which the shell treats specially, this means that if commands are added to a directory in your search path after you have started the shell, they will not necessarily be found by the shell. If you wish to use a command which has been added in this way, you should give the command

        rehash

to the shell, which will cause it to recompute its internal table of command locations, so that it will find the newly added command. Since the shell has to look in the current directory '.' on each command, placing it at the end of the path specification usually works equivalently and reduces overhead.

Other useful built in variables are the variable *home* which shows your home directory, *cwd* which contains your current working directory, the variable *ignoreeof* which can be set in your *.login* file to tell the shell not to exit when it receives an end-of-file from a terminal (as described above). The variable 'ignoreeof' is one of several variables which the shell does not care about the value of, only whether they are *set* or *unset.* Thus to set this variable you simply do

        set ignoreeof

and to unset it do

_____

† Another directory that might interest you is /usr/new, which contains many useful user-contributed programs provided with Berkeley Unix.

    unset ignoreeof

These give the variable 'ignoreeof' no value, but none is desired or required.

    Finally, some other built-in shell variables of use are the variables *noclobber* and *mail*. The metasyntax

> filename

which redirects the standard output of a command will overwrite and destroy the previous contents of the named file. In this way you may accidentally overwrite a file which is valuable. If you would prefer that the shell not overwrite files in this way you can

    set noclobber

in your *.login* file. Then trying to do

    date > now

would cause a diagnostic if 'now' existed already. You could type

    date >! now

if you really wanted to overwrite the contents of 'now'. The '>!' is a special metasyntax indicating that clobbering the file is ok.†

2.3. The shell's history list

    The shell can maintain a *history list* into which it places the words of previous commands. It is possible to use a notation to reuse commands or words from commands in forming new commands. This mechanism can be used to repeat previous commands or to correct minor typing mistakes in commands.

    The following figure gives a sample session involving typical usage of the history mechanism of the shell. In this example we have a very simple C program which has a bug (or two) in it in the file 'bug.c', which we 'cat' out on our terminal. We then try to run the C compiler on it, referring to the file again as '!$', meaning the last argument to the previous command. Here the '!' is the history mechanism invocation metacharacter, and the '$' stands for the last argument, by analogy to '$' in the editor which stands for the end of the line. The shell echoed the command, as it would have been typed without use of the history mechanism, and then executed it. The compilation yielded error diagnostics so we now run the editor on the file we were trying to compile, fix the bug, and run the C compiler again, this time referring to this command simply as '!c', which repeats the last command which started with the letter 'c'. If there were other commands starting with 'c' done recently we could have said '!cc' or even '!cc:p' which would have printed the last command starting with 'cc' without executing it.

    After this recompilation, we ran the resulting 'a.out' file, and then noting that there still was a bug, ran the editor again. After fixing the program we ran the C compiler again, but tacked onto the command an extra '–o bug' telling the compiler to place the resultant binary in the file 'bug' rather than 'a.out'. In general, the history mechanisms may be used anywhere in the formation of new commands and other characters may be placed before and after the substituted commands.

    We then ran the 'size' command to see how large the binary program images we have created were, and then an 'ls –l' command with the same argument list, denoting the argument list '*'. Finally we ran the program 'bug' to see that its output is indeed correct.

    To make a numbered listing of the program we ran the 'num' command on the file 'bug.c'. In order to compress out blank lines in the output of 'num' we ran the output through the filter 'ssp', but misspelled it as spp. To correct this we used a shell substitute, placing the old text and new text between '^' characters. This is similar to the substitute command in the editor. Finally, we repeated the same command with '!!', but sent its output to the line printer.

---

†The space between the '!' and the word 'now' is critical here, as '!now' would be an invocation of the *history* mechanism, and have a totally different effect.

```
% cat bug.c
main()

{
     printf("hello);
}
% cc !$
cc bug.c
"bug.c", line 4: newline in string or char constant
"bug.c", line 5: syntax error
% ed !$
ed bug.c
29
4s/);/"&/p
     printf("hello");
w
30
q
% !c
cc bug.c
% a.out
hello% !e
ed bug.c
30
4s/lo/lo\\n/p
     printf("hello\n");
w
32
q
% !c −o bug
cc bug.c −o bug
% size a.out bug
a.out: 2784+364+1028 = 4176b = 0x1050b
bug: 2784+364+1028 = 4176b = 0x1050b
% ls −l !*
ls −l a.out bug
−rwxr−xr−x 1 bill       3932 Dec 19 09:41 a.out
−rwxr−xr−x 1 bill       3932 Dec 19 09:42 bug
% bug
hello
% num bug.c | spp
spp: Command not found.
% ^spp^ssp
num bug.c | ssp
   1   main()
   3   {
   4        printf("hello\n");
   5   }
% !! | lpr
num bug.c | ssp | lpr
%
```

There are other mechanisms available for repeating commands. The *history* command prints out a number of previous commands with numbers by which they can be referenced. There is a way to refer to a previous command by searching for a string which appeared in it, and there are other, less useful, ways to select arguments to include in a new command. A complete description of all these mechanisms is given in the C shell manual pages in the UNIX Programmer's Manual.

2.4. Aliases

The shell has an *alias* mechanism which can be used to make transformations on input commands. This mechanism can be used to simplify the commands you type, to supply default arguments to commands, or to perform transformations on commands and their arguments. The alias facility is similar to a macro facility. Some of the features obtained by aliasing can be obtained also using shell command files, but these take place in another instance of the shell and cannot directly affect the current shells environment or involve commands such as *cd* which must be done in the current shell.

As an example, suppose that there is a new version of the mail program on the system called 'newmail' you wish to use, rather than the standard mail program which is called 'mail'. If you place the shell command

        alias mail newmail

in your *.cshrc* file, the shell will transform an input line of the form

        mail bill

into a call on 'newmail'. More generally, suppose we wish the command 'ls' to always show sizes of files, that is to always do '−s'. We can do

        alias ls ls −s

or even

        alias dir ls −s

creating a new command syntax 'dir' which does an 'ls −s'. If we say

        dir ˜bill

then the shell will translate this to

        ls −s /mnt/bill

Thus the *alias* mechanism can be used to provide short names for commands, to provide default arguments, and to define new short commands in terms of other commands. It is also possible to define aliases which contain multiple commands or pipelines, showing where the arguments to the original command are to be substituted using the facilities of the history mechanism. Thus the definition

        alias cd ´cd \!* ; ls ´

would do an *ls* command after each change directory *cd* command. We enclosed the entire alias definition in '´' characters to prevent most substitutions from occurring and the character ';' from being recognized as a metacharacter. The '!' here is escaped with a '\' to prevent it from being interpreted when the alias command is typed in. The '\!*' here substitutes the entire argument list to the pre-aliasing *cd* command, without giving an error if there were no arguments. The ';' separating commands is used here to indicate that one command is to be done and then the next. Similarly the definition

        alias whois ´grep \!ˆ /etc/passwd´

defines a command which looks up its first argument in the password file.

Warning: The shell currently reads the *.cshrc* file each time it starts up. If you place a large number of commands there, shells will tend to start slowly. A mechanism for saving the shell environment after reading the *.cshrc* file and quickly restoring it is under development, but for now you should try to limit the number of aliases you have to a reasonable number... 10 or 15 is reasonable, 50 or 60 will cause a

2.5. More redirection; >> and >&

There are a few more notations useful to the terminal user which have not been introduced yet.

In addition to the standard output, commands also have a *diagnostic output* which is normally directed to the terminal even when the standard output is redirected to a file or a pipe. It is occasionally desirable to direct the diagnostic output along with the standard output. For instance if you want to redirect the output of a long running command into a file and wish to have a record of any error diagnostic it produces you can do

        command >& file

The '>&' here tells the shell to route both the diagnostic output and the standard output into 'file'. Similarly you can give the command

        command |& lpr

to route both standard and diagnostic output through the pipe to the line printer daemon *lpr*.‡

Finally, it is possible to use the form

        command >> file

to place output at the end of an existing file.†

2.6. Jobs; Background, Foreground, or Suspended

When one or more commands are typed together as a pipeline or as a sequence of commands separated by semicolons, a single *job* is created by the shell consisting of these commands together as a unit. Single commands without pipes or semicolons create the simplest jobs. Usually, every line typed to the shell creates a job. Some lines that create jobs (one per line) are

        sort < data
        ls −s | sort −n | head −5
        mail harold

If the metacharacter '&' is typed at the end of the commands, then the job is started as a *background* job. This means that the shell does not wait for it to complete but immediately prompts and is ready for another command. The job runs *in the background* at the same time that normal jobs, called *foreground* jobs, continue to be read and executed by the shell one at a time. Thus

        du > usage &

would run the *du* program, which reports on the disk usage of your working directory (as well as any directories below it), put the output into the file 'usage' and return immediately with a prompt for the next command without out waiting for *du* to finish. The *du* program would continue executing in the background until it finished, even though you can type and execute more commands in the mean time. When a background job terminates, a message is typed by the shell just before the next prompt telling you that the job has completed. In the following example the *du* job finishes sometime during the execution of the *mail* command and its completion is reported just before the prompt after the *mail* job is finished.

---

‡ A command of the form
        command >&! file
exists, and is used when *noclobber* is set and *file* already exists.
† If *noclobber* is set, then an error will result if *file* does not exist, otherwise the shell will create *file* if it doesn't exist. A form
        command >>! file
makes it not be an error for file to not exist when *noclobber* is set.

```
% du > usage &
[1] 503
% mail bill
How do you know when a background job is finished?
EOT
[1] – Done                      du > usage
%
```

If the job did not terminate normally the 'Done' message might say something else like 'Killed'. If you want the terminations of background jobs to be reported at the time they occur (possibly interrupting the output of other foreground jobs), you can set the *notify* variable. In the previous example this would mean that the 'Done' message might have come right in the middle of the message to Bill. Background jobs are unaffected by any signals from the keyboard like the STOP, INTERRUPT, or QUIT signals mentioned earlier.

Jobs are recorded in a table inside the shell until they terminate. In this table, the shell remembers the command names, arguments and the *process numbers* of all commands in the job as well as the working directory where the job was started. Each job in the table is either running *in the foreground* with the shell waiting for it to terminate, running *in the background,* or *suspended.* Only one job can be running in the foreground at one time, but several jobs can be suspended or running in the background at once. As each job is started, it is assigned a small identifying number called the *job number* which can be used later to refer to the job in the commands described below. Job numbers remain the same until the job terminates and then are re-used.

When a job is started in the backgound using '&', its number, as well as the process numbers of all its (top level) commands, is typed by the shell before prompting you for another command. For example,

```
% ls –s | sort –n > usage &
[2] 2034 2035
%
```

runs the 'ls' program with the '–s' options, pipes this output into the 'sort' program with the '–n' option which puts its output into the file 'usage'. Since the '&' was at the end of the line, these two programs were started together as a background job. After starting the job, the shell prints the job number in brackets (2 in this case) followed by the process number of each program started in the job. Then the shell immediates prompts for a new command, leaving the job running simultaneously.

As mentioned in section 1.8, foreground jobs become *suspended* by typing ˆZ which sends a STOP signal to the currently running foreground job. A background job can become suspended by using the *stop* command described below. When jobs are suspended they merely stop any further progress until started again, either in the foreground or the backgound. The shell notices when a job becomes stopped and reports this fact, much like it reports the termination of background jobs. For foreground jobs this looks like

```
% du > usage
ˆZ
Stopped
%
```

'Stopped' message is typed by the shell when it notices that the *du* program stopped. For background jobs, using the *stop* command, it is

```
% sort usage &
[1] 2345
% stop %1
[1] + Stopped (signal)         sort usage
%
```

Suspending foreground jobs can be very useful when you need to temporarily change what you are doing (execute other commands) and then return to the suspended job. Also, foreground jobs can be suspended and then continued as background jobs using the *bg* command, allowing you to continue other work and stop waiting for the foreground job to finish. Thus

```
% du > usage
^Z
Stopped
% bg
[1] du > usage &
%
```

starts 'du' in the foreground, stops it before it finishes, then continues it in the background allowing more
foreground commands to be executed. This is especially helpful when a foreground job ends up taking
longer than you expected and you wish you had started it in the backgound in the beginning.

All *job control* commands can take an argument that identifies a particular job. All job name arguments begin with the character '%', since some of the job control commands also accept process numbers
(printed by the *ps* command.) The default job (when no argument is given) is called the *current* job and is
identified by a '+' in the output of the *jobs* command, which shows you which jobs you have. When only
one job is stopped or running in the background (the usual case) it is always the current job thus no argument is needed. If a job is stopped while running in the foreground it becomes the *current* job and the
existing current job becomes the *previous* job – identified by a '–' in the output of *jobs*. When the current
job terminates, the previous job becomes the current job. When given, the argument is either '%–' (indicating the previous job); '%#', where # is the job number; '%pref' where pref is some unique prefix of the
command name and arguments of one of the jobs; or '%?' followed by some string found in only one of the
jobs.

The *jobs* command types the table of jobs, giving the job number, commands and status ('Stopped'
or 'Running') of each backgound or suspended job. With the '–l' option the process numbers are also
typed.

```
% du > usage &
[1] 3398
% ls −s | sort −n > myfile &
[2] 3405
% mail bill
^Z
Stopped
% jobs
[1] − Running          du > usage
[2]   Running          ls −s | sort −n > myfile
[3] + Stopped          mail bill
% fg %ls
ls −s | sort −n > myfile
% more myfile
```

The *fg* command runs a suspended or background job in the foreground. It is used to restart a previously suspended job or change a background job to run in the foreground (allowing signals or input from
the terminal). In the above example we used *fg* to change the 'ls' job from the background to the foreground since we wanted to wait for it to finish before looking at its output file. The *bg* command runs a
suspended job in the background. It is usually used after stopping the currently running foreground job
with the STOP signal. The combination of the STOP signal and the *bg* command changes a foreground job
into a background job. The *stop* command suspends a background job.

The *kill* command terminates a background or suspended job immediately. In addition to jobs, it
may be given process numbers as arguments, as printed by *ps*. Thus, in the example above, the running *du*
command could have been terminated by the command

```
% kill %1
[1]  Terminated              du > usage
%
```

The *notify* command (not the variable mentioned earlier) indicates that the termination of a specific job should be reported at the time it finishes instead of waiting for the next prompt.

If a job running in the background tries to read input from the terminal it is automatically stopped. When such a job is then run in the foreground, input can be given to the job. If desired, the job can be run in the background again until it requests input again. This is illustrated in the following sequence where the 's' command in the text editor might take a long time.

```
% ed bigfile
120000
1,$s/thisword/thatword/
~Z
Stopped
% bg
[1] ed bigfile &
%
 . . . some foreground commands
[1] Stopped (tty input)       ed bigfile
% fg
ed bigfile
w
120000
q
%
```

So after the 's' command was issued, the 'ed' job was stopped with ~Z and then put in the background using *bg*. Some time later when the 's' command was finished, *ed* tried to read another command and was stopped because jobs in the backgound cannot read from the terminal. The *fg* command returned the 'ed' job to the foreground where it could once again accept commands from the terminal.

The command

    stty tostop

causes all background jobs run on your terminal to stop when they are about to write output to the terminal. This prevents messages from background jobs from interrupting foreground job output and allows you to run a job in the background without losing terminal output. It also can be used for interactive programs that sometimes have long periods without interaction. Thus each time it outputs a prompt for more input it will stop before the prompt. It can then be run in the foreground using *fg*, more input can be given and, if necessary stopped and returned to the background. This *stty* command might be a good thing to put in your *.login* file if you do not like output from background jobs interrupting your work. It also can reduce the need for redirecting the output of background jobs if the output is not very big:

```
% stty tostop
% wc hugefile &
[1] 10387
% ed text
. . . some time later
q
[1] Stopped (tty output)          wc hugefile
% fg wc
wc hugefile
    13371   30123   302577
% stty −tostop
```

Thus after some time the 'wc' command, which counts the lines, words and characters in a file, had one line of output. When it tried to write this to the terminal it stopped. By restarting it in the foreground we allowed it to write on the terminal exactly when we were ready to look at its output. Programs which attempt to change the mode of the terminal will also block, whether or not *tostop* is set, when they are not in the foreground, as it would be very unpleasant to have a background job change the state of the terminal.

Since the *jobs* command only prints jobs started in the currently executing shell, it knows nothing about background jobs started in other login sessions or within shell files. The *ps* can be used in this case to find out about background jobs not started in the current shell.

2.7. Working Directories

As mentioned in section 1.6, the shell is always in a particular *working directory*. The 'change directory' command *chdir* (its short form *cd* may also be used) changes the working directory of the shell, that is, changes the directory you are located in.

It is useful to make a directory for each project you wish to work on and to place all files related to that project in that directory. The 'make directory' command, *mkdir,* creates a new directory. The *pwd* ('print working directory') command reports the absolute pathname of the working directory of the shell, that is, the directory you are located in. Thus in the example below:

```
% pwd
/usr/bill
% mkdir newpaper
% chdir newpaper
% pwd
/usr/bill/newpaper
%
```

the user has created and moved to the directory *newpaper.* where, for example, he might place a group of related files.

No matter where you have moved to in a directory hierarchy, you can return to your 'home' login directory by doing just

```
cd
```

with no arguments. The name '..' always means the directory above the current one in the hierarchy, thus

```
cd ..
```

changes the shell's working directory to the one directly above the current one. The name '..' can be used in any pathname, thus,

```
cd ../programs
```

means change to the directory 'programs' contained in the directory above the current one. If you have several directories for different projects under, say, your home directory, this shorthand notation permits you to switch easily between them.

The shell always remembers the pathname of its current working directory in the variable *cwd*. The shell can also be requested to remember the previous directory when you change to a new working directory. If the 'push directory' command *pushd* is used in place of the *cd* command, the shell saves the name of the current working directory on a *directory stack* before changing to the new one. You can see this list at any time by typing the 'directories' command *dirs*.

```
% pushd newpaper/references
˜/newpaper/references ˜
% pushd /usr/lib/tmac
/usr/lib/tmac ˜/newpaper/references ˜
% dirs
/usr/lib/tmac ˜/newpaper/references ˜
% popd
˜/newpaper/references ˜
% popd
˜
%
```

The list is printed in a horizontal line, reading left to right, with a tilde (˜) as shorthand for your home directory—in this case '/usr/bill'. The directory stack is printed whenever there is more than one entry on it and it changes. It is also printed by a *dirs* command. *Dirs* is usually faster and more informative than *pwd* since it shows the current working directory as well as any other directories remembered in the stack.

The *pushd* command with no argument alternates the current directory with the first directory in the list. The 'pop directory' *popd* command without an argument returns you to the directory you were in prior to the current one, discarding the previous current directory from the stack (forgetting it). Typing *popd* several times in a series takes you backward through the directories you had been in (changed to) by *pushd* command. There are other options to *pushd* and *popd* to manipulate the contents of the directory stack and to change to directories not at the top of the stack; see the *csh* manual page for details.

Since the shell remembers the working directory in which each job was started, it warns you when you might be confused by restarting a job in the foreground which has a different working directory than the current working directory of the shell. Thus if you start a background job, then change the shell's working directory and then cause the background job to run in the foreground, the shell warns you that the working directory of the currently running foreground job is different from that of the shell.

```
% dirs –l
/mnt/bill
% cd myproject
% dirs
˜/myproject
% ed prog.c
1143
˜Z
Stopped
% cd ..
% ls
myproject
textfile
% fg
ed prog.c (wd: ˜/myproject)
```

This way the shell warns you when there is an implied change of working directory, even though no cd command was issued. In the above example the 'ed' job was still in '/mnt/bill/project' even though the shell had changed to '/mnt/bill'. A similar warning is given when such a foreground job terminates or is suspended (using the STOP signal) since the return to the shell again implies a change of working directory.

```
% fg
ed prog.c (wd: ~/myproject)
. . . after some editing
q
(wd now: ~)
%
```

These messages are sometimes confusing if you use programs that change their own working directories, since the shell only remembers which directory a job is started in, and assumes it stays there. The '–l' option of *jobs* will type the working directory of suspended or background jobs when it is different from the current working directory of the shell.

2.8. Useful built-in commands

We now give a few of the useful built-in commands of the shell describing how they are used.

The *alias* command described above is used to assign new aliases and to show the existing aliases. With no arguments it prints the current aliases. It may also be given only one argument such as

    alias ls

to show the current alias for, e.g., 'ls'.

The *echo* command prints its arguments. It is often used in *shell scripts* or as an interactive command to see what filename expansions will produce.

The *history* command will show the contents of the history list. The numbers given with the history events can be used to reference previous events which are difficult to reference using the contextual mechanisms introduced above. There is also a shell variable called *prompt*. By placing a '!' character in its value the shell will there substitute the number of the current command in the history list. You can use this number to refer to this command in a history substitution. Thus you could

    set prompt=\! % ´

Note that the '!' character had to be *escaped* here even within '´' characters.

The *limit* command is used to restrict use of resources. With no arguments it prints the current limitations:

cputime	unlimited
filesize	unlimited
datasize	5616 kbytes
stacksize	512 kbytes
coredumpsize	unlimited

Limits can be set, e.g.:

    limit coredumpsize 128k

Most reasonable units abbreviations will work; see the *csh* manual page for more details.

The *logout* command can be used to terminate a login shell which has *ignoreeof* set.

The *rehash* command causes the shell to recompute a table of where commands are located. This is necessary if you add a command to a directory in the current shell's search path and wish the shell to find it, since otherwise the hashing algorithm may tell the shell that the command wasn't in that directory when the hash table was computed.

The *repeat* command can be used to repeat a command several times. Thus to make 5 copies of the file *one* in the file *five* you could do

    repeat 5 cat one >> five

The *setenv* command can be used to set variables in the environment. Thus

    setenv TERM adm3a

will set the value of the environment variable TERM to 'adm3a'. A user program *printenv* exists which will print out the environment. It might then show:

```
% printenv
HOME=/usr/bill
SHELL=/bin/csh
PATH=:/usr/ucb:/bin:/usr/bin:/usr/local
TERM=adm3a
USER=bill
%
```

The *source* command can be used to force the current shell to read commands from a file. Thus

    source .cshrc

can be used after editing in a change to the *.cshrc* file which you wish to take effect right away.

The *time* command can be used to cause a command to be timed no matter how much CPU time it takes. Thus

```
% time cp /etc/rc /usr/bill/rc
0.0u 0.1s 0:01 8% 2+1k 3+2io 1pf+0w
% time wc /etc/rc /usr/bill/rc
    52   178   1347 /etc/rc
    52   178   1347 /usr/bill/rc
   104   356   2694 total
0.1u 0.1s 0:00 13% 3+3k 5+3io 7pf+0w
%
```

indicates that the *cp* command used a negligible amount of user time (u) and about 1/10th of a system time (s); the elapsed time was 1 second (0:01), there was an average memory usage of 2k bytes of program space and 1k bytes of data space over the cpu time involved (2+1k); the program did three disk reads and two disk writes (3+2io), and took one page fault and was not swapped (1pf+0w). The word count command *wc* on the other hand used 0.1 seconds of user time and 0.1 seconds of system time in less than a second of elapsed time. The percentage '13%' indicates that over the period when it was active the command 'wc' used an average of 13 percent of the available CPU cycles of the machine.

The *unalias* and *unset* commands can be used to remove aliases and variable definitions from the shell, and *unsetenv* removes variables from the environment.

2.9. What else?

This concludes the basic discussion of the shell for terminal users. There are more features of the shell to be discussed here, and all features of the shell are discussed in its manual pages. One useful feature which is discussed later is the *foreach* built-in command which can be used to run the same command sequence with a number of different arguments.

If you intend to use UNIX a lot you you should look through the rest of this document and the csh manual pages (section1) to become familiar with the other facilities which are available to you.

3. Shell control structures and command scripts

3.1. Introduction

It is possible to place commands in files and to cause shells to be invoked to read and execute commands from these files, which are called *shell scripts*. We here detail those features of the shell useful to the writers of such scripts.

3.2. Make

It is important to first note what shell scripts are *not* useful for. There is a program called *make* which is very useful for maintaining a group of related files or performing sets of operations on related files. For instance a large program consisting of one or more files can have its dependencies described in a *makefile* which contains definitions of the commands used to create these different files when changes occur. Definitions of the means for printing listings, cleaning up the directory in which the files reside, and installing the resultant programs are easily, and most appropriately placed in this *makefile*. This format is superior and preferable to maintaining a group of shell procedures to maintain these files.

Similarly when working on a document a *makefile* may be created which defines how different versions of the document are to be created and which options of *nroff* or *troff* are appropriate.

3.3. Invocation and the argv variable

A *csh* command script may be interpreted by saying

    % csh script ...

where *script* is the name of the file containing a group of *csh* commands and '...' is replaced by a sequence of arguments. The shell places these arguments in the variable *argv* and then begins to read commands from the script. These parameters are then available through the same mechanisms which are used to reference any other shell variables.

If you make the file 'script' executable by doing

    chmod 755 script

and place a shell comment at the beginning of the shell script (i.e. begin the file with a '#' character) then a '/bin/csh' will automatically be invoked to execute 'script' when you type

    script

If the file does not begin with a '#' then the standard shell '/bin/sh' will be used to execute it. This allows you to convert your older shell scripts to use *csh* at your convenience.

3.4. Variable substitution

After each input line is broken into words and history substitutions are done on it, the input line is parsed into distinct commands. Before each command is executed a mechanism know as *variable substitution* is done on these words. Keyed by the character '$' this substitution replaces the names of variables by their values. Thus

    echo $argv

when placed in a command script would cause the current value of the variable *argv* to be echoed to the output of the shell script. It is an error for *argv* to be unset at this point.

A number of notations are provided for accessing components and attributes of variables. The notation

    $?name

expands to '1' if name is *set* or to '0' if name is not *set*. It is the fundamental mechanism used for checking whether particular variables have been assigned values. All other forms of reference to undefined variables cause errors.

The notation

    $#name

expands to the number of elements in the variable *name*.

Thus

> % set argv=(a b c)
> % echo $?argv
> 1
> % echo $#argv
> 3
> % unset argv
> % echo $?argv
> 0
> % echo $argv
> Undefined variable: argv.
> %

It is also possible to access the components of a variable which has several values. Thus

> $argv[1]

gives the first component of *argv* or in the example above 'a'. Similarly

> $argv[$#argv]

would give 'c', and

> $argv[1–2]

would give 'a b'. Other notations useful in shell scripts are

> $*n*

where *n* is an integer as a shorthand for

> $argv[*n*]

the *n th* parameter and

> $*

which is a shorthand for

> $argv

The form

> $$

expands to the process number of the current shell. Since this process number is unique in the system it can be used in generation of unique temporary file names. The form

> $<

is quite special and is replaced by the next line of input read from the shell's standard input (not the script it is reading). This is useful for writing shell scripts that are interactive, reading commands from the termi-nal, or even writing a shell script that acts as a filter, reading lines from its input file. Thus the sequence

> echo 'yes or no?\c'
> set a=($<)

would write out the prompt 'yes or no?' without a newline and then read the answer into the variable 'a'. In this case '$#a' would be '0' if either a blank line or end-of-file (^D) was typed.

One minor difference between '$*n* ' and '$argv[*n*]' should be noted here. The form '$argv[*n*]' will yield an error if *n* is not in the range '1–$#argv' while '$n' will never yield an out of range subscript error. This is for compatibility with the way older shells handled parameters.

Another important point is that it is never an error to give a subrange of the form 'n–'; if there are less than *n* components of the given variable then no words are substituted. A range of the form 'm–n' likewise returns an empty vector without giving an error when *m* exceeds the number of elements of the given variable, provided the subscript *n* is in range.

3.5. Expressions

In order for interesting shell scripts to be constructed it must be possible to evaluate expressions in the shell based on the values of variables. In fact, all the arithmetic operations of the language C are available in the shell with the same precedence that they have in C. In particular, the operations '==' and '!=' compare strings and the operators '&&' and '| |' implement the boolean and/or operations. The special operators '=~' and '!~' are similar to '==' and '!=' except that the string on the right side can have pattern matching characters (like *, ? or []) and the test is whether the string on the left matches the pattern on the right.

The shell also allows file enquiries of the form

    −? filename

where '?' is replace by a number of single characters. For instance the expression primitive

    −e filename

tell whether the file 'filename' exists. Other primitives test for read, write and execute access to the file, whether it is a directory, or has non-zero length.

It is possible to test whether a command terminates normally, by a primitive of the form '{ command }' which returns true, i.e. '1' if the command succeeds exiting normally with exit status 0, or '0' if the command terminates abnormally or with exit status non-zero. If more detailed information about the execution status of a command is required, it can be executed and the variable '$status' examined in the next command. Since '$status' is set by every command, it is very transient. It can be saved if it is inconvenient to use it only in the single immediately following command.

For a full list of expression components available see the manual section for the shell.

3.6. Sample shell script

A sample shell script which makes use of the expression mechanism of the shell and some of its control structure follows:

```
% cat copyc
#
# Copyc copies those C programs in the specified list
# to the directory ~/backup if they differ from the files
# already in ~/backup
#
set noglob
foreach i ($argv)
        if ($i !~ *.c) continue  # not a .c file so do nothing

        if (! −r ~/backup/$i:t) then
            echo $i:t not in backup... not cp\´ed
            continue
        endif

        cmp −s $i ~/backup/$i:t # to set $status

        if ($status != 0) then
            echo new backup of $i
            cp $i ~/backup/$i:t
        endif
    end
```

This script makes use of the *foreach* command, which causes the shell to execute the commands between the *foreach* and the matching *end* for each of the values given between '(' and ')' with the named variable, in this case 'i' set to successive values in the list. Within this loop we may use the command *break* to stop executing the loop and *continue* to prematurely terminate one iteration and begin the next. After the *foreach* loop the iteration variable (*i* in this case) has the value at the last iteration.

We set the variable *noglob* here to prevent filename expansion of the members of *argv*. This is a good idea, in general, if the arguments to a shell script are filenames which have already been expanded or if the arguments may contain filename expansion metacharacters. It is also possible to quote each use of a '$' variable expansion, but this is harder and less reliable.

The other control construct used here is a statement of the form

    if (expression) **then**
        command
         ...
    endif

The placement of the keywords here is **not** flexible due to the current implementation of the shell.†

The shell does have another form of the if statement of the form

    if (expression) **command**

which can be written

    if (expression) \
        command

Here we have escaped the newline for the sake of appearance. The command must not involve '|', '&' or ';' and must not be another control command. The second form requires the final '\' to **immediately** precede the end-of-line.

The more general *if* statements above also admit a sequence of *else–if* pairs followed by a single *else* and an *endif*, e.g.:

    if (expression) **then**
        commands
    else if (expression) **then**
        commands
    ...

    else
        commands
    endif

Another important mechanism used in shell scripts is the ':' modifier. We can use the modifier ':r' here to extract a root of a filename or ':e' to extract the *extension*.

---

†The following two formats are not currently acceptable to the shell:

    if (expression)   **# Won't work!**
    then
            command
            ...
    endif

and

    if (expression) **then** command **endif**   **# Won't work**

Thus if the variable *i* has the value '/mnt/foo.bar' then

```
% echo $i $i:r $i:e
/mnt/foo.bar /mnt/foo bar
%
```

shows how the ':r' modifier strips off the trailing '.bar' and the the ':e' modifier leaves only the 'bar'. Other modifiers will take off the last component of a pathname leaving the head ':h' or all but the last component of a pathname leaving the tail ':t'. These modifiers are fully described in the *csh* manual pages in the User's Reference Manual. It is also possible to use the *command substitution* mechanism described in the next major section to perform modifications on strings to then reenter the shell's environment. Since each usage of this mechanism involves the creation of a new process, it is much more expensive to use than the ':' modification mechanism.‡ Finally, we note that the character '#' lexically introduces a shell comment in shell scripts (but not from the terminal). All subsequent characters on the input line after a '#' are discarded by the shell. This character can be quoted using ''' or '\' to place it in an argument word.

3.7. Other control structures

The shell also has control structures *while* and *switch* similar to those of C. These take the forms

```
while ( expression )
        commands
end
```

and

```
switch ( word )

case str1:
        commands
        breaksw

    ...

case strn:
        commands
        breaksw

default:
        commands
        breaksw

endsw
```

For details see the manual section for *csh*. C programmers should note that we use *breaksw* to exit from a *switch* while *break* exits a *while* or *foreach* loop. A common mistake to make in *csh* scripts is to use *break* rather than *breaksw* in switches.

---

‡ It is also important to note that the current implementation of the shell limits the number of ':' modifiers on a '$' substitution to 1. Thus

```
% echo $i $i:h:t
/a/b/c /a/b:t
%
```

does not do what one would expect.

Finally, *csh* allows a *goto* statement, with labels looking like they do in C, i.e.:

loop:
>   commands
>   **goto** loop

3.8. Supplying input to commands

Commands run from shell scripts receive by default the standard input of the shell which is running the script. This is different from previous shells running under UNIX. It allows shell scripts to fully participate in pipelines, but mandates extra notation for commands which are to take inline data.

Thus we need a metanotation for supplying inline data to commands in shell scripts. As an example, consider this script which runs the editor to delete leading blanks from the lines in each argument file:

```
% cat deblank
# deblank — remove leading blanks
foreach i ($argv)
ed – $i << 'EOF'
1,$s/^[ ]*//
w
q
'EOF'
end
%
```

The notation '<< 'EOF'' means that the standard input for the *ed* command is to come from the text in the shell script file up to the next line consisting of exactly ''EOF''. The fact that the 'EOF' is enclosed in ''' characters, i.e. quoted, causes the shell to not perform variable substitution on the intervening lines. In general, if any part of the word following the '<<' which the shell uses to terminate the text to be given to the command is quoted then these substitutions will not be performed. In this case since we used the form '1,$' in our editor script we needed to insure that this '$' was not variable substituted. We could also have insured this by preceding the '$' here with a '\', i.e.:

1,\$s/^[ ]*//

but quoting the 'EOF' terminator is a more reliable way of achieving the same thing.

3.9. Catching interrupts

If our shell script creates temporary files, we may wish to catch interruptions of the shell script so that we can clean up these files. We can then do

onintr label

where *label* is a label in our program. If an interrupt is received the shell will do a 'goto label' and we can remove the temporary files and then do an *exit* command (which is built in to the shell) to exit from the shell script. If we wish to exit with a non-zero status we can do

exit(1)

e.g. to exit with status '1'.

3.10. What else?

There are other features of the shell useful to writers of shell procedures. The *verbose* and *echo* options and the related −*v* and −*x* command line options can be used to help trace the actions of the shell. The −*n* option causes the shell only to read commands and not to execute them and may sometimes be of use.

One other thing to note is that *csh* will not execute shell scripts which do not begin with the character '#', that is shell scripts that do not begin with a comment. Similarly, the '/bin/sh' on your system may

well defer to 'csh' to interpret shell scripts which begin with '#'. This allows shell scripts for both shells to
live in harmony.

There is also another quotation mechanism using '"' which allows only some of the expansion
mechanisms we have so far discussed to occur on the quoted string and serves to make this string into a
single word as '´' does.

4. Other, less commonly used, shell features

4.1. Loops at the terminal; variables as vectors

It is occasionally useful to use the *foreach* control structure at the terminal to aid in performing a
number of similar commands. For instance, there were at one point three shells in use on the Cory UNIX
system at Cory Hall, '/bin/sh', '/bin/nsh', and '/bin/csh'. To count the number of persons using each shell
one could have issued the commands

```
% grep −c csh$ /etc/passwd
27
% grep −c nsh$ /etc/passwd
128
% grep −c −v sh$ /etc/passwd
430
%
```

Since these commands are very similar we can use *foreach* to do this more easily.

```
% foreach i (´sh$´ ´csh$´ ´−v sh$´)
? grep −c $i /etc/passwd
? end
27
128
430
%
```

Note here that the shell prompts for input with '? ' when reading the body of the loop.

Very useful with loops are variables which contain lists of filenames or other words. You can, for
example, do

```
% set a=(`ls`)
% echo $a
csh.n csh.rm
% ls
csh.n
csh.rm
% echo $#a
2
%
```

The *set* command here gave the variable *a* a list of all the filenames in the current directory as value. We
can then iterate over these names to perform any chosen function.

The output of a command within '`' characters is converted by the shell to a list of words. You can
also place the '`' quoted string within '"' characters to take each (non-empty) line as a component of the
variable; preventing the lines from being split into words at blanks and tabs. A modifier ':x' exists which
can be used later to expand each component of the variable into another variable splitting it into separate
words at embedded blanks and tabs.

4.2. Braces { ... } in argument expansion

Another form of filename expansion, alluded to before involves the characters '{' and '}'. These characters specify that the contained strings, separated by ',' are to be consecutively substituted into the containing characters and the results expanded left to right. Thus

A{str1,str2,...strn}B

expands to

Astr1B Astr2B ... AstrnB

This expansion occurs before the other filename expansions, and may be applied recursively (i.e. nested). The results of each expanded string are sorted separately, left to right order being preserved. The resulting filenames are not required to exist if no other expansion mechanisms are used. This means that this mechanism can be used to generate arguments which are not filenames, but which have common parts.

A typical use of this would be

mkdir ~/{hdrs,retrofit,csh}

to make subdirectories 'hdrs', 'retrofit' and 'csh' in your home directory. This mechanism is most useful when the common prefix is longer than in this example, i.e.

chown root /usr/{ucb/{ex,edit},lib/{ex?.?*,how_ex}}

4.3. Command substitution

A command enclosed in '`' characters is replaced, just before filenames are expanded, by the output from that command. Thus it is possible to do

set pwd=`pwd`

to save the current directory in the variable *pwd* or to do

ex `grep –l TRACE *.c`

to run the editor *ex* supplying as arguments those files whose names end in '.c' which have the string 'TRACE' in them.*

4.4. Other details not covered here

In particular circumstances it may be necessary to know the exact nature and order of different substitutions performed by the shell. The exact meaning of certain combinations of quotations is also occasionally important. These are detailed fully in its manual section.

The shell has a number of command line option flags mostly of use in writing UNIX programs, and debugging shell scripts. See the csh(1) manual section for a list of these options.

Appendix – Special characters

The following table lists the special characters of *csh* and the UNIX system, giving for each the section(s) in which it is discussed. A number of these characters also have special meaning in expressions. See the *csh* manual section for a complete list.

---

*Command expansion also occurs in input redirected with '<<' and within '"' quotations. Refer to the shell manual section for full details.

Syntactic metacharacters

;	2.4	separates commands to be executed sequentially
|	1.5	separates commands in a pipeline
( )	2.2,3.6	brackets expressions and variable values
&	2.5	follows commands to be executed without waiting for completion

Filename metacharacters

/	1.6	separates components of a file's pathname
?	1.6	expansion character matching any single character
*	1.6	expansion character matching any sequence of characters
[ ]	1.6	expansion sequence matching any single character from a set
~	1.6	used at the beginning of a filename to indicate home directories
{ }	4.2	used to specify groups of arguments with common parts

Quotation metacharacters

\	1.7	prevents meta-meaning of following single character
'	1.7	prevents meta-meaning of a group of characters
"	4.3	like ', but allows variable and command expansion

Input/output metacharacters

<	1.5	indicates redirected input
>	1.3	indicates redirected output

Expansion/substitution metacharacters

$	3.4	indicates variable substitution
!	2.3	indicates history substitution
:	3.6	precedes substitution modifiers
^	2.3	used in special forms of history substitution
`	4.3	indicates command substitution

Other metacharacters

#	1.3,3.6	begins scratch file names; indicates shell comments
−	1.2	prefixes option (flag) arguments to commands
%	2.6	prefixes job name specifications

Glossary

This glossary lists the most important terms introduced in the introduction to the shell and gives references to sections of the shell document for further information about them. References of the form 'pr (1)' indicate that the command *pr* is in the UNIX User Reference manual in section 1. You can look at an online copy of its manual page by doing

     man 1 pr

References of the form (2.5) indicate that more information can be found in section 2.5 of this manual.

.   Your current directory has the name '.' as well as the name printed by the command *pwd;* see also *dirs.* The current directory '.' is usually the first *component* of the search path contained in the variable *path*, thus commands which are in '.' are found first (2.2). The character '.' is also used in separating *components* of filenames (1.6). The character '.' at the beginning of a *component* of a *pathname* is treated specially and not matched by the *filename expansion* metacharacters '?', '*', and '[' ']' pairs (1.6).

..   Each directory has a file '..' in it which is a reference to its parent directory. After
                      changing into the directory with *chdir*, i.e.

                              chdir paper

                      you can return to the parent directory by doing

                              chdir ..

                      The current directory is printed by *pwd* (2.7).

a.out   Compilers which create executable images create them, by default, in the file *a.out.* for
                      historical reasons (2.3).

absolute pathname
                      A *pathname* which begins with a '/' is *absolute* since it specifies the *path* of directories
                      from the beginning of the entire directory system – called the *root* directory. *Pathname*s
                      which are not *absolute* are called *relative* (see definition of *relative pathname*) (1.6).

alias   An *alias* specifies a shorter or different name for a UNIX command, or a transformation
                      on a command to be performed in the shell. The shell has a command *alias* which
                      establishes *aliases* and can print their current values. The command *unalias* is used to
                      remove *aliases* (2.4).

argument   Commands in UNIX receive a list of *argument* words. Thus the command

                              echo a b c

                      consists of the *command name* 'echo' and three *argument* words 'a', 'b' and 'c'. The
                      set of *arguments* after the *command name* is said to be the *argument list* of the com-
                      mand (1.1).

argv   The list of arguments to a command written in the shell language (a shell script or shell
                      procedure) is stored in a variable called *argv* within the shell. This name is taken from
                      the conventional name in the C programming language (3.4).

background   Commands started without waiting for them to complete are called *background* com-
                      mands (2.6).

base   A filename is sometimes thought of as consisting of a *base* part, before any '.' character,
                      and an *extension* – the part after the '.'. See *filename* and *extension* (1.6) and basename
                      (1).

bg   The *bg* command causes a *suspended* job to continue execution in the *background*
                      (2.6).

bin   A directory containing binaries of programs and shell scripts to be executed is typically
                      called a *bin* directory. The standard system *bin* directories are '/bin' containing the
                      most heavily used commands and '/usr/bin' which contains most other user programs.
                      Programs developed at UC Berkeley live in '/usr/ucb', while locally written programs
                      live in '/usr/local'. Games are kept in the directory '/usr/games'. You can place
                      binaries in any directory. If you wish to execute them often, the name of the directories
                      should be a *component* of the variable *path*.

break   *Break* is a builtin command used to exit from loops within the control structure of the
                      shell (3.7).

breaksw   The *breaksw* builtin command is used to exit from a *switch* control structure, like a
                      break exits from loops (3.7).

builtin   A command executed directly by the shell is called a *builtin* command. Most com-
                      mands in UNIX are not built into the shell, but rather exist as files in *bin* directories.
                      These commands are accessible because the directories in which they reside are named
                      in the *path* variable.

case
: A *case* command is used as a label in a *switch* statement in the shell's control structure, similar to that of the language C. Details are given in the shell documentation 'csh (1)' (3.7).

cat
: The *cat* program catenates a list of specified files on the *standard output*. It is usually used to look at the contents of a single file on the terminal, to 'cat a file' (1.8, 2.3).

cd
: The *cd* command is used to change the *working directory*. With no arguments, *cd* changes your *working directory* to be your *home* directory (2.4, 2.7).

chdir
: The *chdir* command is a synonym for *cd*. *Cd* is usually used because it is easier to type.

chsh
: The *chsh* command is used to change the shell which you use on UNIX. By default, you use an different version of the shell which resides in '/bin/sh'. You can change your shell to '/bin/csh' by doing

>   chsh your-login-name /bin/csh

Thus I would do

>   chsh bill /bin/csh

It is only necessary to do this once. The next time you log in to UNIX after doing this command, you will be using *csh* rather than the shell in '/bin/sh' (1.9).

cmp
: *Cmp* is a program which compares files. It is usually used on binary files, or to see if two files are identical (3.6). For comparing text files the program *diff*, described in 'diff (1)' is used.

command
: A function performed by the system, either by the shell (a builtin *command*) or by a program residing in a file in a directory within the UNIX system, is called a *command* (1.1).

command name
: When a command is issued, it consists of a *command name*, which is the first word of the command, followed by arguments. The convention on UNIX is that the first word of a command names the function to be performed (1.1).

command substitution
: The replacement of a command enclosed in '`' characters by the text output by that command is called *command substitution* (4.3).

component
: A part of a *pathname* between '/' characters is called a *component* of that *pathname*. A variable which has multiple strings as value is said to have several *component*s; each string is a *component* of the variable.

continue
: A builtin command which causes execution of the enclosing *foreach* or *while* loop to cycle prematurely. Similar to the *continue* command in the programming language C (3.6).

control-
: Certain special characters, called *control* characters, are produced by holding down the CONTROL key on your terminal and simultaneously pressing another character, much like the SHIFT key is used to produce upper case characters. Thus *control-*c is produced by holding down the CONTROL key while pressing the 'c' key. Usually UNIX prints an caret (^) followed by the corresponding letter when you type a *control* character (e.g. '^C' for *control-*c (1.8).

core dump
: When a program terminates abnormally, the system places an image of its current state in a file named 'core'. This *core dump* can be examined with the system debugger 'adb (1)' or 'sdb (1)' in order to determine what went wrong with the program (1.8). If the shell produces a message of the form

>   Illegal instruction (core dumped)

(where 'Illegal instruction' is only one of several possible messages), you should report this to the author of the program or a system administrator, saving the 'core' file.

cp
: The *cp* (copy) program is used to copy the contents of one file into another file. It is one of the most commonly used UNIX commands (1.6).

csh
: The name of the shell program that this document describes.

.cshrc
: The file *.cshrc* in your *home* directory is read by each shell as it begins execution. It is usually used to change the setting of the variable *path* and to set *alias* parameters which are to take effect globally (2.1).

cwd
: The *cwd* variable in the shell holds the *absolute pathname* of the current *working directory*. It is changed by the shell whenever your current *working directory* changes and should not be changed otherwise (2.2).

date
: The *date* command prints the current date and time (1.3).

debugging
: *Debugging* is the process of correcting mistakes in programs and shell scripts. The shell has several options and variables which may be used to aid in shell *debugging* (4.4).

default:
: The label *default:* is used within shell *switch* statements, as it is in the C language to label the code to be executed if none of the *case* labels matches the value switched on (3.7).

DELETE
: The DELETE or RUBOUT key on the terminal normally causes an interrupt to be sent to the current job. Many users change the interrupt character to be ^C.

detached
: A command that continues running in the *background* after you logout is said to be *detached*.

diagnostic
: An error message produced by a program is often referred to as a *diagnostic*. Most error messages are not written to the *standard output*, since that is often directed away from the terminal (1.3, 1.5). Error messsages are instead written to the *diagnostic output* which may be directed away from the terminal, but usually is not. Thus *diagnostics* will usually appear on the terminal (2.5).

directory
: A structure which contains files. At any time you are in one particular *directory* whose names can be printed by the command *pwd*. The *chdir* command will change you to another *directory*, and make the files in that *directory* visible. The *directory* in which you are when you first login is your *home* directory (1.1, 2.7).

directory stack
: The shell saves the names of previous *working directories* in the *directory stack* when you change your current *working directory* via the *pushd* command. The *directory stack* can be printed by using the *dirs* command, which includes your current *working directory* as the first directory name on the left (2.7).

dirs
: The *dirs* command prints the shell's *directory stack* (2.7).

du
: The *du* command is a program (described in 'du (1)') which prints the number of disk blocks is all directories below and including your current *working directory* (2.6).

echo
: The *echo* command prints its arguments (1.6, 3.6).

else
: The *else* command is part of the 'if-then-else-endif' control command construct (3.6).

endif
: If an *if* statement is ended with the word *then*, all lines following the *if* up to a line starting with the word *endif* or *else* are executed if the condition between parentheses after the *if* is true (3.6).

EOF
: An *end-of-file* is generated by the terminal by a control-d, and whenever a command reads to the end of a file which it has been given as input. Commands receiving input from a *pipe* receive an *end-of-file* when the command sending them input completes. Most commands terminate when they receive an *end-of-file*. The shell has an option to ignore *end-of-file* from a terminal input which may help you keep from logging out accidentally by typing too many control-d's (1.1, 1.8, 3.8).

escape
: A character '\' used to prevent the special meaning of a metacharacter is said to *escape* the character from its special meaning. Thus

    echo *

will echo the character '*' while just

    echo *

will echo the names of the file in the current directory. In this example, \ *escape*s '*' (1.7). There is also a non-printing character called *escape*, usually labelled ESC or ALT-MODE on terminal keyboards. Some older UNIX systems use this character to indicate that output is to be *suspended*. Most systems use control-s to stop the output and control-q to start it.

/etc/passwd   This file contains information about the accounts currently on the system. It consists of a line for each account with fields separated by ':' characters (1.8). You can look at this file by saying

    cat /etc/passwd

The commands *finger* and *grep* are often used to search for information in this file. See 'finger (1)', 'passwd(5)', and 'grep (1)' for more details.

exit   The *exit* command is used to force termination of a shell script, and is built into the shell (3.9).

exit status   A command which discovers a problem may reflect this back to the command (such as a shell) which invoked (executed) it. It does this by returning a non-zero number as its *exit status*, a status of zero being considered 'normal termination'. The *exit* command can be used to force a shell command script to give a non-zero *exit status* (3.6).

expansion   The replacement of strings in the shell input which contain metacharacters by other strings is referred to as the process of *expansion*. Thus the replacement of the word '*' by a sorted list of files in the current directory is a 'filename expansion'. Similarly the replacement of the characters '!!' by the text of the last command is a 'history expansion'. *Expansions* are also referred to as *substitutions* (1.6, 3.4, 4.2).

expressions   *Expressions* are used in the shell to control the conditional structures used in the writing of shell scripts and in calculating values for these scripts. The operators available in shell *expressions* are those of the language C (3.5).

extension   Filenames often consist of a *base* name and an *extension* separated by the character '.'. By convention, groups of related files often share the same *root* name. Thus if 'prog.c' were a C program, then the object file for this program would be stored in 'prog.o'. Similarly a paper written with the '−me' nroff macro package might be stored in 'paper.me' while a formatted version of this paper might be kept in 'paper.out' and a list of spelling errors in 'paper.errs' (1.6).

fg   The *job control* command *fg* is used to run a *background* or *suspended* job in the *foreground* (1.8, 2.6).

filename   Each file in UNIX has a name consisting of up to 14 characters and not including the character '/' which is used in *pathname* building. Most *filenames* do not begin with the character '.', and contain only letters and digits with perhaps a '.' separating the *base* portion of the *filename* from an *extension* (1.6).

filename expansion
    Filename expansion uses the metacharacters '*', '?' and '[' and ']' to provide a convenient mechanism for naming files. Using *filename expansion* it is easy to name all the files in the current directory, or all files which have a common *root* name. Other *filename expansion* mechanisms use the metacharacter '~' and allow files in other users' directories to be named easily (1.6, 4.2).

flag   Many UNIX commands accept arguments which are not the names of files or other users but are used to modify the action of the commands. These are referred to as *flag* options, and by convention consist of one or more letters preceded by the character '−'

(1.2). Thus the *ls* (list files) command has an option '−s' to list the sizes of files. This is specified

     ls −s

foreach   The *foreach* command is used in shell scripts and at the terminal to specify repetition of a sequence of commands while the value of a certain shell variable ranges through a specified list (3.6, 4.1).

foreground   When commands are executing in the normal way such that the shell is waiting for them to finish before prompting for another command they are said to be *foreground jobs* or *running in the foreground*. This is as opposed to *background*. *Foreground* jobs can be stopped by signals from the terminal caused by typing different control characters at the keyboard (1.8, 2.6).

goto   The shell has a command *goto* used in shell scripts to transfer control to a given label (3.7).

grep   The *grep* command searches through a list of argument files for a specified string. Thus

       grep bill /etc/passwd

will print each line in the file */etc/passwd* which contains the string 'bill'. Actually, *grep* scans for *regular expressions* in the sense of the editors 'ed (1)' and 'ex (1)'. *Grep* stands for 'globally find *regular expression* and print' (2.4).

head   The *head* command prints the first few lines of one or more files. If you have a bunch of files containing text which you are wondering about it is sometimes useful to run *head* with these files as arguments. This will usually show enough of what is in these files to let you decide which you are interested in (1.5).
Head is also used to describe the part of a *pathname* before and including the last '/' character. The *tail* of a *pathname* is the part after the last '/'. The ':h' and ':t' modifiers allow the *head* or *tail* of a *pathname* stored in a shell variable to be used (3.6).

history   The *history* mechanism of the shell allows previous commands to be repeated, possibly after modification to correct typing mistakes or to change the meaning of the command. The shell has a *history list* where these commands are kept, and a *history* variable which controls how large this list is (2.3).

home directory

Each user has a *home directory*, which is given in your entry in the password file, */etc/passwd*. This is the directory which you are placed in when you first login. The *cd* or *chdir* command with no arguments takes you back to this directory, whose name is recorded in the shell variable *home*. You can also access the *home directories* of other users in forming filenames using a *filename expansion* notation and the character '˜' (1.6).

if   A conditional command within the shell, the *if* command is used in shell command scripts to make decisions about what course of action to take next (3.6).

ignoreeof   Normally, your shell will exit, printing 'logout' if you type a control-d at a prompt of '% '. This is the way you usually log off the system. You can *set* the *ignoreeof* variable if you wish in your *.login* file and then use the command *logout* to logout. This is useful if you sometimes accidentally type too many control-d characters, logging yourself off (2.2).

input   Many commands on UNIX take information from the terminal or from files which they then act on. This information is called *input*. Commands normally read for *input* from their *standard input* which is, by default, the terminal. This *standard input* can be redirected from a file using a shell metanotation with the character '<'. Many commands will also read from a file specified as argument. Commands placed in *pipelines* will read from the output of the previous command in the *pipeline*. The leftmost command in a *pipeline* reads from the terminal if you neither redirect its *input* nor give it a filename to use as *standard input*. Special mechanisms exist for supplying input to commands in shell scripts (1.5, 3.8).

interrupt
An *interrupt* is a signal to a program that is generated by typing ˆC. (On older versions of UNIX the RUBOUT or DELETE key were used for this purpose.) It causes most programs to stop execution. Certain programs, such as the shell and the editors, handle an *interrupt* in special ways, usually by stopping what they are doing and prompting for another command. While the shell is executing another command and waiting for it to finish, the shell does not listen to *interrupts*. The shell often wakes up when you hit *interrupt* because many commands die when they receive an *interrupt* (1.8, 3.9).

job
One or more commands typed on the same input line separated by 'l' or ';' characters are run together and are called a *job*. Simple commands run by themselves without any 'l' or ';' characters are the simplest *jobs*. *Jobs* are classified as *foreground*, *background*, or *suspended* (2.6).

job control
The builtin functions that control the execution of jobs are called *job control* commands. These are *bg, fg, stop, kill* (2.6).

job number
When each job is started it is assigned a small number called a *job number* which is printed next to the job in the output of the *jobs* command. This number, preceded by a '%' character, can be used as an argument to *job control* commands to indicate a specific job (2.6).

jobs
The *jobs* command prints a table showing jobs that are either running in the *background* or are *suspended* (2.6).

kill
A command which sends a signal to a job causing it to terminate (2.6).

.login
The file *.login* in your *home* directory is read by the shell each time you login to UNIX and the commands there are executed. There are a number of commands which are usefully placed here, especially *set* commands to the shell itself (2.1).

login shell
The shell that is started on your terminal when you login is called your *login shell*. It is different from other shells which you may run (e.g. on shell scripts) in that it reads the *.login* file before reading commands from the terminal and it reads the *.logout* file after you logout (2.1).

logout
The *logout* command causes a login shell to exit. Normally, a login shell will exit when you hit control-d generating an *end-of-file*, but if you have set *ignoreeof* in you *.login* file then this will not work and you must use *logout* to log off the UNIX system (2.8).

.logout
When you log off of UNIX the shell will execute commands from the file *.logout* in your *home* directory after it prints 'logout'.

lpr
The command *lpr* is the line printer daemon. The standard input of *lpr* spooled and printed on the UNIX line printer. You can also give *lpr* a list of filenames as arguments to be printed. It is most common to use *lpr* as the last component of a *pipeline* (2.3).

ls
The *ls* (list files) command is one of the most commonly used UNIX commands. With no argument filenames it prints the names of the files in the current directory. It has a number of useful *flag* arguments, and can also be given the names of directories as arguments, in which case it lists the names of the files in these directories (1.2).

mail
The *mail* program is used to send and receive messages from other UNIX users (1.1, 2.1), whether they are logged on or not.

make
The *make* command is used to maintain one or more related files and to organize functions to be performed on these files. In many ways *make* is easier to use, and more helpful than shell command scripts (3.2).

makefile
The file containing commands for *make* is called *makefile* or *Makefile* (3.2).

manual
The *manual* often referred to is the 'UNIX manual'. It contains 8 numbered sections with a description of each UNIX program (section 1), system call (section 2), subroutine

(section 3), device (section 4), special data structure (section 5), game (section 6), miscellaneous item (section 7) and system administration program (section 8). There are also supplementary documents (tutorials and reference guides) for individual programs which require explanation in more detail. An online version of the *manual* is accessible through the *man* command. Its documentation can be obtained online via

     man man

If you can't decide what manual page to look in, try the *apropos* (1) command. The supplementary documents are in subdirectories of /usr/doc.

metacharacter

Many characters which are neither letters nor digits have special meaning either to the shell or to UNIX. These characters are called *metacharacters*. If it is necessary to place these characters in arguments to commands without them having their special meaning then they must be *quoted*. An example of a *metacharacter* is the character '>' which is used to indicate placement of output into a file. For the purposes of the *history* mechanism, most unquoted *metacharacters* form separate words (1.4). The appendix to this user's manual lists the *metacharacters* in groups by their function.

mkdir

The *mkdir* command is used to create a new directory.

modifier

Substitutions with the *history* mechanism, keyed by the character '!' or of variables using the metacharacter '$', are often subjected to modifications, indicated by placing the character ':' after the substitution and following this with the *modifier* itself. The *command substitution* mechanism can also be used to perform modification in a similar way, but this notation is less clear (3.6).

more

The program *more* writes a file on your terminal allowing you to control how much text is displayed at a time. *More* can move through the file screenful by screenful, line by line, search forward for a string, or start again at the beginning of the file. It is generally the easiest way of viewing a file (1.8).

noclobber

The shell has a variable *noclobber* which may be set in the file *.login* to prevent accidental destruction of files by the '>' output redirection metasyntax of the shell (2.2, 2.5).

noglob

The shell variable *noglob* is set to suppress the *filename expansion* of arguments containing the metacharacters '~', '*', '?', '[' and ']' (3.6).

notify

The *notify* command tells the shell to report on the termination of a specific *background job* at the exact time it occurs as opposed to waiting until just before the next prompt to report the termination. The *notify* variable, if set, causes the shell to always report the termination of *background* jobs exactly when they occur (2.6).

onintr

The *onintr* command is built into the shell and is used to control the action of a shell command script when an *interrupt* signal is received (3.9).

output

Many commands in UNIX result in some lines of text which are called their *output*. This *output* is usually placed on what is known as the *standard output* which is normally connected to the user's terminal. The shell has a syntax using the metacharacter '>' for redirecting the *standard output* of a command to a file (1.3). Using the *pipe* mechanism and the metacharacter '|' it is also possible for the *standard output* of one command to become the *standard input* of another command (1.5). Certain commands such as the line printer daemon *p* do not place their results on the *standard output* but rather in more useful places such as on the line printer (2.3). Similarly the *write* command places its output on another user's terminal rather than its *standard output* (2.3). Commands also have a *diagnostic output* where they write their error messages. Normally these go to the terminal even if the *standard output* has been sent to a file or another command, but it is possible to direct error diagnostics along with *standard output* using a special metanotation (2.5).

path
: The shell has a variable *path* which gives the names of the directories in which it searches for the commands which it is given. It always checks first to see if the command it is given is built into the shell. If it is, then it need not search for the command as it can do it internally. If the command is not builtin, then the shell searches for a file with the name given in each of the directories in the *path* variable, left to right. Since the normal definition of the *path* variable is

   path   (. /usr/ucb /bin /usr/bin)

the shell normally looks in the current directory, and then in the standard system directories '/usr/ucb', '/bin' and '/usr/bin' for the named command (2.2). If the command cannot be found the shell will print an error diagnostic. Scripts of shell commands will be executed using another shell to interpret them if they have 'execute' permission set. This is normally true because a command of the form

   chmod 755 script

was executed to turn this execute permission on (3.3). If you add new commands to a directory in the *path*, you should issue the command *rehash* (2.2).

pathname
: A list of names, separated by '/' characters, forms a *pathname*. Each *component*, between successive '/' characters, names a directory in which the next *component* file resides. *Pathnames* which begin with the character '/' are interpreted relative to the *root* directory in the filesystem. Other *pathnames* are interpreted relative to the current directory as reported by *pwd*. The last component of a *pathname* may name a directory, but usually names a file.

pipeline
: A group of commands which are connected together, the *standard output* of each connected to the *standard input* of the next, is called a *pipeline*. The *pipe* mechanism used to connect these commands is indicated by the shell metacharacter 'I' (1.5, 2.3).

popd
: The *popd* command changes the shell's *working directory* to the directory you most recently left using the *pushd* command. It returns to the directory without having to type its name, forgetting the name of the current *working directory* before doing so (2.7).

port
: The part of a computer system to which each terminal is connected is called a *port*. Usually the system has a fixed number of *ports*, some of which are connected to telephone lines for dial-up access, and some of which are permanently wired directly to specific terminals.

pr
: The *pr* command is used to prepare listings of the contents of files with headers giving the name of the file and the date and time at which the file was last modified (2.3).

printenv
: The *printenv* command is used to print the current setting of variables in the environment (2.8).

process
: An instance of a running program is called a *process* (2.6). UNIX assigns each *process* a unique number when it is started – called the *process number*. *Process numbers* can be used to stop individual *processes* using the *kill* or *stop* commands when the *processes* are part of a detached *background* job.

program
: Usually synonymous with *command*; a binary file or shell command script which performs a useful function is often called a *program*.

prompt
: Many programs will print a *prompt* on the terminal when they expect input. Thus the editor 'ex (1)' will print a ':' when it expects input. The shell *prompts* for input with '% ' and occasionally with '? ' when reading commands from the terminal (1.1). The shell has a variable *prompt* which may be set to a different value to change the shell's main *prompt*. This is mostly used when debugging the shell (2.8).

4

pushd   The *pushd* command, which means 'push directory', changes the shell's *working directory* and also remembers the current *working directory* before the change is made, allowing you to return to the same directory via the *popd* command later without retyping its name (2.7).

ps   The *ps* command is used to show the processes you are currently running. Each process is shown with its unique process number, an indication of the terminal name it is attached to, an indication of the state of the process (whether it is running, stopped, awaiting some event (sleeping), and whether it is swapped out), and the amount of CPU time it has used so far. The command is identified by printing some of the words used when it was invoked (2.6). Shells, such as the *csh* you use to run the *ps* command, are not normally shown in the output.

pwd   The *pwd* command prints the full *pathname* of the current *working directory*. The *dirs* builtin command is usually a better and faster choice.

quit   The *quit* signal, generated by a control-\, is used to terminate programs which are behaving unreasonably. It normally produces a core image file (1.8).

quotation   The process by which metacharacters are prevented their special meaning, usually by using the character '´' in pairs, or by using the character '\', is referred to as *quotation* (1.7).

redirection   The routing of input or output from or to a file is known as *redirection* of input or output (1.3).

rehash   The *rehash* command tells the shell to rebuild its internal table of which commands are found in which directories in your *path*. This is necessary when a new program is installed in one of these directories (2.8).

relative pathname
                A *pathname* which does not begin with a '/' is called a *relative pathname* since it is interpreted *relative* to the current *working directory*. The first *component* of such a *pathname* refers to some file or directory in the *working directory*, and subsequent *components* between '/' characters refer to directories below the *working directory*. *Pathnames* that are not *relative* are called *absolute pathnames* (1.6).

repeat   The *repeat* command iterates another command a specified number of times.

root   The directory that is at the top of the entire directory structure is called the *root* directory since it is the 'root' of the entire tree structure of directories. The name used in *pathnames* to indicate the *root* is '/'. *Pathnames* starting with '/' are said to be *absolute* since they start at the *root* directory. *Root* is also used as the part of a *pathname* that is left after removing the *extension*. See *filename* for a further explanation (1.6).

RUBOUT   The RUBOUT or DELETE key is often used to erase the previously typed character; some users prefer the BACKSPACE for this purpose. On older versions of UNIX this key served as the INTR character.

scratch file   Files whose names begin with a '#' are referred to as *scratch files*, since they are automatically removed by the system after a couple of days of non-use, or more frequently if disk space becomes tight (1.3).

script   Sequences of shell commands placed in a file are called shell command *scripts*. It is often possible to perform simple tasks using these *scripts* without writing a program in a language such as C, by using the shell to selectively run other programs (3.3, 3.10).

set   The builtin *set* command is used to assign new values to shell variables and to show the values of the current variables. Many shell variables have special meaning to the shell itself. Thus by using the *set* command the behavior of the shell can be affected (2.1).

setenv   Variables in the environment 'environ (5)' can be changed by using the *setenv* builtin command (2.8). The *printenv* command can be used to print the value of the variables in the environment.

shell	A *shell* is a command language interpreter. It is possible to write and run your own *shell*, as *shells* are no different than any other programs as far as the system is concerned. This manual deals with the details of one particular *shell*, called *csh*.
shell script	See *script* (3.3, 3.10).
signal	A *signal* in UNIX is a short message that is sent to a running program which causes something to happen to that process. *Signals* are sent either by typing special *control* characters on the keyboard or by using the *kill* or *stop* commands (1.8, 2.6).
sort	The *sort* program sorts a sequence of lines in ways that can be controlled by argument *flags* (1.5).
source	The *source* command causes the shell to read commands from a specified file. It is most useful for reading files such as *.cshrc* after changing them (2.8).
special character	See *metacharacters* and the appendix to this manual.
standard	We refer often to the *standard input* and *standard output* of commands. See *input* and *output* (1.3, 3.8).
status	A command normally returns a *status* when it finishes. By convention a *status* of zero indicates that the command succeeded. Commands may return non-zero *status* to indicate that some abnormal event has occurred. The shell variable *status* is set to the *status* returned by the last command. It is most useful in shell commmand scripts (3.6).
stop	The *stop* command causes a *background* job to become *suspended* (2.6).
string	A sequential group of characters taken together is called a *string*. *Strings* can contain any printable characters (2.2).
stty	The *stty* program changes certain parameters inside UNIX which determine how your terminal is handled. See 'stty (1)' for a complete description (2.6).
substitution	The shell implements a number of *substitutions* where sequences indicated by metacharacters are replaced by other sequences. Notable examples of this are history *substitution* keyed by the metacharacter '!' and variable *substitution* indicated by '$'. We also refer to *substitutions* as *expansions* (3.4).
suspended	A job becomes *suspended* after a STOP signal is sent to it, either by typing a *control*-z at the terminal (for *foreground* jobs) or by using the *stop* command (for *background* jobs). When *suspended*, a job temporarily stops running until it is restarted by either the *fg* or *bg* command (2.6).
switch	The *switch* command of the shell allows the shell to select one of a number of sequences of commands based on an argument string. It is similar to the *switch* statement in the language C (3.7).
termination	When a command which is being executed finishes we say it undergoes *termination* or *terminates*. Commands normally terminate when they read an *end-of-file* from their *standard input*. It is also possible to terminate commands by sending them an *interrupt* or *quit* signal (1.8). The *kill* program terminates specified jobs (2.6).
then	The *then* command is part of the shell's 'if-then-else-endif' control construct used in command scripts (3.6).
time	The *time* command can be used to measure the amount of CPU and real time consumed by a specified command as well as the amount of disk i/o, memory utilized, and number of page faults and swaps taken by the command (2.1, 2.8).
tset	The *tset* program is used to set standard erase and kill characters and to tell the system what kind of terminal you are using. It is often invoked in a *.login* file (2.1).
tty	The word *tty* is a historical abbreviation for 'teletype' which is frequently used in UNIX to indicate the *port* to which a given terminal is connected. The *tty* command will print the name of the *tty* or *port* to which your terminal is presently connected.

4

unalias   The *unalias* command removes aliases (2.8).

UNIX   UNIX is an operating system on which *csh* runs. UNIX provides facilities which allow
                   csh to invoke other programs such as editors and text formatters which you may wish to
                   use.

unset   The *unset* command removes the definitions of shell variables (2.2, 2.8).

variable expansion

                   See *variables* and *expansion* (2.2, 3.4).

variables   *Variables* in *csh* hold one or more strings as value. The most common use of *variables*
                   is in controlling the behavior of the shell. See *path*, *noclobber*, and *ignoreeof* for
                   examples. *Variables* such as *argv* are also used in writing shell programs (shell com-
                   mand scripts) (2.2).

verbose   The *verbose* shell variable can be set to cause commands to be echoed after they are his-
                   tory expanded. This is often useful in debugging shell scripts. The *verbose* variable is
                   set by the shell's −*v* command line option (3.10).

wc   The *wc* program calculates the number of characters, words, and lines in the files whose
                   names are given as arguments (2.6).

while   The *while* builtin control construct is used in shell command scripts (3.7).

word   A sequence of characters which forms an argument to a command is called a *word*.
                   Many characters which are neither letters, digits, '−', '.' nor '/' form *words* all by them-
                   selves even if they are not surrounded by blanks. Any sequence of characters may be
                   made into a *word* by surrounding it with '´' characters except for the characters '´' and
                   '!' which require special treatment (1.1). This process of placing special characters in
                   words without their special meaning is called *quoting*.

working directory

                   At any given time you are in one particular directory, called your *working directory*.
                   This directory's name is printed by the *pwd* command and the files listed by *ls* are the
                   ones in this directory. You can change *working directories* using *chdir*.

write   The *write* command is an obsolete way of communicating with other users who are
                   logged in to UNIX (you have to take turns typing). If you are both using display termi-
                   nals, use *talk*(1), which is much more pleasant.

DC – An Interactive Desk Calculator

Robert Morris

Lorinda Cherry

ABSTRACT

DC is an interactive desk calculator program implemented on the UNIX† time-sharing system to do arbitrary-precision integer arithmetic. It has provision for manipulating scaled fixed-point numbers and for input and output in bases other than decimal.

The size of numbers that can be manipulated is limited only by available core storage. On typical implementations of UNIX, the size of numbers that can be handled varies from several hundred digits on the smallest systems to several thousand on the largest.

DC is an arbitrary precision arithmetic package implemented on the UNIX time-sharing system in the form of an interactive desk calculator. It works like a stacking calculator using reverse Polish notation. Ordinarily DC operates on decimal integers, but one may specify an input base, output base, and a number of fractional digits to be maintained.

A language called BC [1] has been developed which accepts programs written in the familiar style of higher-level programming languages and compiles output which is interpreted by DC. Some of the commands described below were designed for the compiler interface and are not easy for a human user to manipulate.

Numbers that are typed into DC are put on a push-down stack. DC commands work by taking the top number or two off the stack, performing the desired operation, and pushing the result on the stack. If an argument is given, input is taken from that file until its end, then from the standard input.

SYNOPTIC DESCRIPTION

Here we describe the DC commands that are intended for use by people. The additional commands that are intended to be invoked by compiled output are described in the detailed description.

Any number of commands are permitted on a line. Blanks and new-line characters are ignored except within numbers and in places where a register name is expected.

The following constructions are recognized:

number

The value of the number is pushed onto the main stack. A number is an unbroken string of the digits 0-9 and the capital letters A–F which are treated as digits with values 10–15 respectively. The number may be preceded by an underscore to input a negative number. Numbers may contain decimal points.

---

† UNIX is a registered trademark of AT&T Bell Laboratories in the USA and other countries.

+ – * % ^

> The top two values on the stack are added (+), subtracted (–), multiplied (*), divided (/), remaindered (%), or exponentiated (^). The two entries are popped off the stack; the result is pushed on the stack in their place. The result of a division is an integer truncated toward zero. See the detailed description below for the treatment of numbers with decimal points. An exponent must not have any digits after the decimal point.

s*x*

> The top of the main stack is popped and stored into a register named x, where x may be any character. If the s is capitalized, x is treated as a stack and the value is pushed onto it. Any character, even blank or new-line, is a valid register name.

l*x*

> The value in register x is pushed onto the stack. The register x is not altered. If the l is capitalized, register x is treated as a stack and its top value is popped onto the main stack.

All registers start with empty value which is treated as a zero by the command l and is treated as an error by the command **L**.

d

> The top value on the stack is duplicated.

p

> The top value on the stack is printed. The top value remains unchanged.

f

> All values on the stack and in registers are printed.

x

> treats the top element of the stack as a character string, removes it from the stack, and executes it as a string of DC commands.

[...]

> puts the bracketed character string onto the top of the stack.

q

> exits the program. If executing a string, the recursion level is popped by two. If **q** is capitalized, the top value on the stack is popped and the string execution level is popped by that value.

<*x* >*x* =*x* !<*x* !>*x* !=*x*

> The top two elements of the stack are popped and compared. Register x is executed if they obey the stated relation. Exclamation point is negation.

v

> replaces the top element on the stack by its square root. The square root of an integer is truncated to an integer. For the treatment of numbers with decimal points, see the detailed description below.

!

> interprets the rest of the line as a UNIX command. Control returns to DC when the UNIX command terminates.

c

All values on the stack are popped; the stack becomes empty.

i

The top value on the stack is popped and used as the number radix for further input. If **i** is capitalized, the value of the input base is pushed onto the stack. No mechanism has been provided for the input of arbitrary numbers in bases less than 1 or greater than 16.

o

The top value on the stack is popped and used as the number radix for further output. If **o** is capitalized, the value of the output base is pushed onto the stack.

k

The top of the stack is popped, and that value is used as a scale factor that influences the number of decimal places that are maintained during multiplication, division, and exponentiation. The scale factor must be greater than or equal to zero and less than 100. If **k** is capitalized, the value of the scale factor is pushed onto the stack.

z

The value of the stack level is pushed onto the stack.

?

A line of input is taken from the input source (usually the console) and executed.

DETAILED DESCRIPTION

Internal Representation of Numbers

Numbers are stored internally using a dynamic storage allocator. Numbers are kept in the form of a string of digits to the base 100 stored one digit per byte (centennial digits). The string is stored with the low-order digit at the beginning of the string. For example, the representation of 157 is 57,1. After any arithmetic operation on a number, care is taken that all digits are in the range 0–99 and that the number has no leading zeros. The number zero is represented by the empty string.

Negative numbers are represented in the 100's complement notation, which is analogous to two's complement notation for binary numbers. The high order digit of a negative number is always −1 and all other digits are in the range 0–99. The digit preceding the high order −1 digit is never a 99. The representation of −157 is 43,98,−1. We shall call this the canonical form of a number. The advantage of this kind of representation of negative numbers is ease of addition. When addition is performed digit by digit, the result is formally correct. The result need only be modified, if necessary, to put it into canonical form.

Because the largest valid digit is 99 and the byte can hold numbers twice that large, addition can be carried out and the handling of carries done later when that is convenient, as it sometimes is.

An additional byte is stored with each number beyond the high order digit to indicate the number of assumed decimal digits after the decimal point. The representation of .001 is 1,*3* where the scale has been italicized to emphasize the fact that it is not the high order digit. The value of this extra byte is called the **scale factor** of the number.

The Allocator

DC uses a dynamic string storage allocator for all of its internal storage. All reading and writing of numbers internally is done through the allocator. Associated with each string in the allocator is a four-word header containing pointers to the beginning of the string, the end of the string, the next place to write, and the next place to read. Communication between the allocator and DC is done via pointers to these headers.

The allocator initially has one large string on a list of free strings. All headers except the one point-ing to this string are on a list of free headers. Requests for strings are made by size. The size of the string actually supplied is the next higher power of 2. When a request for a string is made, the allocator first checks the free list to see if there is a string of the desired size. If none is found, the allocator finds the next larger free string and splits it repeatedly until it has a string of the right size. Left-over strings are put on the free list. If there are no larger strings, the allocator tries to coalesce smaller free strings into larger ones. Since all strings are the result of splitting large strings, each string has a neighbor that is next to it in core and, if free, can be combined with it to make a string twice as long. This is an implementation of the 'buddy system' of allocation described in [2].

Failing to find a string of the proper length after coalescing, the allocator asks the system for more space. The amount of space on the system is the only limitation on the size and number of strings in DC. If at any time in the process of trying to allocate a string, the allocator runs out of headers, it also asks the system for more space.

There are routines in the allocator for reading, writing, copying, rewinding, forward-spacing, and backspacing strings. All string manipulation is done using these routines.

The reading and writing routines increment the read pointer or write pointer so that the characters of a string are read or written in succession by a series of read or write calls. The write pointer is interpreted as the end of the information-containing portion of a string and a call to read beyond that point returns an end-of-string indication. An attempt to write beyond the end of a string causes the allocator to allocate a larger space and then copy the old string into the larger block.

Internal Arithmetic

All arithmetic operations are done on integers. The operands (or operand) needed for the operation are popped from the main stack and their scale factors stripped off. Zeros are added or digits removed as necessary to get a properly scaled result from the internal arithmetic routine. For example, if the scale of the operands is different and decimal alignment is required, as it is for addition, zeros are appended to the operand with the smaller scale. After performing the required arithmetic operation, the proper scale factor is appended to the end of the number before it is pushed on the stack.

A register called **scale** plays a part in the results of most arithmetic operations. **scale** is the bound on the number of decimal places retained in arithmetic computations. **scale** may be set to the number on the top of the stack truncated to an integer with the **k** command. **K** may be used to push the value of **scale** on the stack. **scale** must be greater than or equal to 0 and less than 100. The descriptions of the individual arithmetic operations will include the exact effect of **scale** on the computations.

Addition and Subtraction

The scales of the two numbers are compared and trailing zeros are supplied to the number with the lower scale to give both numbers the same scale. The number with the smaller scale is multiplied by 10 if the difference of the scales is odd. The scale of the result is then set to the larger of the scales of the two operands.

Subtraction is performed by negating the number to be subtracted and proceeding as in addition.

Finally, the addition is performed digit by digit from the low order end of the number. The carries are propagated in the usual way. The resulting number is brought into canonical form, which may require stripping of leading zeros, or for negative numbers replacing the high-order configuration 99,–1 by the digit –1. In any case, digits which are not in the range 0–99 must be brought into that range, propagating any carries or borrows that result.

Multiplication

The scales are removed from the two operands and saved. The operands are both made positive. Then multiplication is performed in a digit by digit manner that exactly mimics the hand method of multi-plying. The first number is multiplied by each digit of the second number, beginning with its low order digit. The intermediate products are accumulated into a partial sum which becomes the final product. The product is put into the canonical form and its sign is computed from the signs of the original operands.

The scale of the result is set equal to the sum of the scales of the two operands. If that scale is larger than the internal register **scale** and also larger than both of the scales of the two operands, then the scale of the result is set equal to the largest of these three last quantities.

Division

The scales are removed from the two operands. Zeros are appended or digits removed from the dividend to make the scale of the result of the integer division equal to the internal quantity **scale**. The signs are removed and saved.

Division is performed much as it would be done by hand. The difference of the lengths of the two numbers is computed. If the divisor is longer than the dividend, zero is returned. Otherwise the top digit of the divisor is divided into the top two digits of the dividend. The result is used as the first (high-order) digit of the quotient. It may turn out be one unit too low, but if it is, the next trial quotient will be larger than 99 and this will be adjusted at the end of the process. The trial digit is multiplied by the divisor and the result subtracted from the dividend and the process is repeated to get additional quotient digits until the remaining dividend is smaller than the divisor. At the end, the digits of the quotient are put into the canonical form, with propagation of carry as needed. The sign is set from the sign of the operands.

Remainder

The division routine is called and division is performed exactly as described. The quantity returned is the remains of the dividend at the end of the divide process. Since division truncates toward zero, remainders have the same sign as the dividend. The scale of the remainder is set to the maximum of the scale of the dividend and the scale of the quotient plus the scale of the divisor.

Square Root

The scale is stripped from the operand. Zeros are added if necessary to make the integer result have a scale that is the larger of the internal quantity **scale** and the scale of the operand.

The method used to compute sqrt(y) is Newton's method with successive approximations by the rule

The initial guess is found by taking the integer square root of the top two digits.

Exponentiation

Only exponents with zero scale factor are handled. If the exponent is zero, then the result is 1. If the exponent is negative, then it is made positive and the base is divided into one. The scale of the base is removed.

The integer exponent is viewed as a binary number. The base is repeatedly squared and the result is obtained as a product of those powers of the base that correspond to the positions of the one-bits in the binary representation of the exponent. Enough digits of the result are removed to make the scale of the result the same as if the indicated multiplication had been performed.

Input Conversion and Base

Numbers are converted to the internal representation as they are read in. The scale stored with a number is simply the number of fractional digits input. Negative numbers are indicated by preceding the number with a _ (an underscore). The hexadecimal digits A–F correspond to the numbers 10–15 regardless of input base. The **i** command can be used to change the base of the input numbers. This command pops the stack, truncates the resulting number to an integer, and uses it as the input base for all further input. The input base is initialized to 10 but may, for example be changed to 8 or 16 to do octal or hexadecimal to decimal conversions. The command **I** will push the value of the input base on the stack.

Output Commands

The command **p** causes the top of the stack to be printed. It does not remove the top of the stack. All of the stack and internal registers can be output by typing the command **f**. The **o** command can be used to change the output base. This command uses the top of the stack, truncated to an integer as the base for all further output. The output base in initialized to 10. It will work correctly for any base. The command **O** pushes the value of the output base on the stack.

Output Format and Base

The input and output bases only affect the interpretation of numbers on input and output; they have no effect on arithmetic computations. Large numbers are output with 70 characters per line; a \ indicates a continued line. All choices of input and output bases work correctly, although not all are useful. A particularly useful output base is 100000, which has the effect of grouping digits in fives. Bases of 8 and 16 can be used for decimal-octal or decimal-hexadecimal conversions.

Internal Registers

Numbers or strings may be stored in internal registers or loaded on the stack from registers with the commands s and l. The command sx pops the top of the stack and stores the result in register **x**. x can be any character. lx puts the contents of register **x** on the top of the stack. The l command has no effect on the contents of register x. The s command, however, is destructive.

Stack Commands

The command **c** clears the stack. The command **d** pushes a duplicate of the number on the top of the stack on the stack. The command **z** pushes the stack size on the stack. The command **X** replaces the number on the top of the stack with its scale factor. The command **Z** replaces the top of the stack with its length.

Subroutine Definitions and Calls

Enclosing a string in [ ] pushes the ascii string on the stack. The **q** command quits or in executing a string, pops the recursion levels by two.

Internal Registers – Programming DC

The load and store commands together with [ ] to store strings, **x** to execute and the testing commands '<', '>', '=', '!<', '!>', '!=' can be used to program DC. The **x** command assumes the top of the stack is an string of DC commands and executes it. The testing commands compare the top two elements on the stack and if the relation holds, execute the register that follows the relation. For example, to print the numbers 0-9,

```
[lip1+ si li10>a]sa
0si lax
```

Push-Down Registers and Arrays

These commands were designed for used by a compiler, not by people. They involve push-down registers and arrays. In addition to the stack that commands work on, DC can be thought of as having individual stacks for each register. These registers are operated on by the commands S and L. Sx pushes the top value of the main stack onto the stack for the register x. Lx pops the stack for register x and puts the result on the main stack. The commands s and l also work on registers but not as push-down stacks. l doesn't effect the top of the register stack, and s destroys what was there before.

The commands to work on arrays are : and ;. :x pops the stack and uses this value as an index into the array x. The next element on the stack is stored at this index in x. An index must be greater than or equal to 0 and less than 2048. ;x is the command to load the main stack from the array x. The value on the top of the stack is the index into the array x of the value to be loaded.

Miscellaneous Commands

The command **!** interprets the rest of the line as a UNIX command and passes it to UNIX to execute. One other compiler command is **Q**. This command uses the top of the stack as the number of levels of recursion to skip.

DESIGN CHOICES

The real reason for the use of a dynamic storage allocator was that a general purpose program could be (and in fact has been) used for a variety of other tasks. The allocator has some value for input and for compiling (i.e. the bracket [...] commands) where it cannot be known in advance how long a string will be. The result was that at a modest cost in execution time, all considerations of string allocation and sizes of strings were removed from the remainder of the program and debugging was made easier. The allocation method used wastes approximately 25% of available space.

The choice of 100 as a base for internal arithmetic seemingly has no compelling advantage. Yet the base cannot exceed 127 because of hardware limitations and at the cost of 5% in space, debugging was made a great deal easier and decimal output was made much faster.

The reason for a stack-type arithmetic design was to permit all DC commands from addition to subroutine execution to be implemented in essentially the same way. The result was a considerable degree of logical separation of the final program into modules with very little communication between modules.

The rationale for the lack of interaction between the scale and the bases was to provide an understandable means of proceeding after a change of base or scale when numbers had already been entered. An earlier implementation which had global notions of scale and base did not work out well. If the value of **scale** were to be interpreted in the current input or output base, then a change of base or scale in the midst of a computation would cause great confusion in the interpretation of the results. The current scheme has the advantage that the value of the input and output bases are only used for input and output, respectively, and they are ignored in all other operations. The value of scale is not used for any essential purpose by any part of the program and it is used only to prevent the number of decimal places resulting from the arithmetic operations from growing beyond all bounds.

The design rationale for the choices for the scales of the results of arithmetic were that in no case should any significant digits be thrown away if, on appearances, the user actually wanted them. Thus, if the user wants to add the numbers 1.5 and 3.517, it seemed reasonable to give him the result 5.017 without requiring him to unnecessarily specify his rather obvious requirements for precision.

On the other hand, multiplication and exponentiation produce results with many more digits than their operands and it seemed reasonable to give as a minimum the number of decimal places in the operands but not to give more than that number of digits unless the user asked for them by specifying a value for **scale**. Square root can be handled in just the same way as multiplication. The operation of division gives arbitrarily many decimal places and there is simply no way to guess how many places the user wants. In this case only, the user must specify a **scale** to get any decimal places at all.

The scale of remainder was chosen to make it possible to recreate the dividend from the quotient and remainder. This is easy to implement; no digits are thrown away.

References

[1]   L. L. Cherry, R. Morris, *BC – An Arbitrary Precision Desk-Calculator Language.*

[2]   K. C. Knowlton, *A Fast Storage Allocator,* Comm. ACM **8**, pp. 623-625 (Oct. 1965).

BC – An Arbitrary Precision Desk-Calculator Language

Lorinda Cherry

Robert Morris

ABSTRACT

BC is a language and a compiler for doing arbitrary precision arithmetic on the PDP-11 under the UNIX† time-sharing system. The output of the compiler is interpreted and executed by a collection of routines which can input, output, and do arithmetic on indefinitely large integers and on scaled fixed-point numbers.

These routines are themselves based on a dynamic storage allocator. Overflow does not occur until all available core storage is exhausted.

The language has a complete control structure as well as immediate-mode operation. Functions can be defined and saved for later execution.

Two five hundred-digit numbers can be multiplied to give a thousand digit result in about ten seconds.

A small collection of library functions is also available, including sin, cos, arctan, log, exponential, and Bessel functions of integer order.

Some of the uses of this compiler are

– to do computation with large integers,

– to do computation accurate to many decimal places,

– conversion of numbers from one base to another base.

Introduction

BC is a language and a compiler for doing arbitrary precision arithmetic on the UNIX time-sharing system [1]. The compiler was written to make conveniently available a collection of routines (called DC [5]) which are capable of doing arithmetic on integers of arbitrary size. The compiler is by no means intended to provide a complete programming language. It is a minimal language facility.

There is a scaling provision that permits the use of decimal point notation. Provision is made for input and output in bases other than decimal. Numbers can be converted from decimal to octal by simply setting the output base to equal 8.

The actual limit on the number of digits that can be handled depends on the amount of storage available on the machine. Manipulation of numbers with many hundreds of digits is possible even on the smallest versions of UNIX.

The syntax of BC has been deliberately selected to agree substantially with the C language [2]. Those who are familiar with C will find few surprises in this language.

---

† UNIX is a registered trademark of AT&T Bell Laboratories in the USA and other countries.

6

Simple Computations with Integers

The simplest kind of statement is an arithmetic expression on a line by itself. For instance, if you type in the line:

142857 + 285714

the program responds immediately with the line

428571

The operators $-$, $*$, $/$, %, and ^ can also be used; they indicate subtraction, multiplication, division, remaindering, and exponentiation, respectively. Division of integers produces an integer result truncated toward zero. Division by zero produces an error comment.

Any term in an expression may be prefixed by a minus sign to indicate that it is to be negated (the 'unary' minus sign). The expression

7+–3

is interpreted to mean that -3 is to be added to 7.

More complex expressions with several operators and with parentheses are interpreted just as in Fortran, with ^ having the greatest binding power, then $*$ and % and $/$, and finally + and $-$. Contents of parentheses are evaluated before material outside the parentheses. Exponentiations are performed from right to left and the other operators from left to right. The two expressions

a^b^c and a^(b^c)

are equivalent, as are the two expressions

a*b*c and (a*b)*c

BC shares with Fortran and C the undesirable convention that

a/b*c is equivalent to **(a/b)*c**

Internal storage registers to hold numbers have single lower-case letter names. The value of an expression can be assigned to a register in the usual way. The statement

x = x + 3

has the effect of increasing by three the value of the contents of the register named x. When, as in this case, the outermost operator is an =, the assignment is performed but the result is not printed. Only 26 of these named storage registers are available.

There is a built-in square root function whose result is truncated to an integer (but see scaling below). The lines

x = sqrt(191)
x

produce the printed result

13

Bases

There are special internal quantities, called 'ibase' and 'obase'. The contents of 'ibase', initially set to 10, determines the base used for interpreting numbers read in. For example, the lines

ibase = 8
11

will produce the output line

    9

and you are all set up to do octal to decimal conversions. Beware, however of trying to change the input base back to decimal by typing

    ibase = 10

Because the number 10 is interpreted as octal, this statement will have no effect. For those who deal in hexadecimal notation, the characters A–F are permitted in numbers (no matter what base is in effect) and are interpreted as digits having values 10–15 respectively. The statement

    ibase = A

will change you back to decimal input base no matter what the current input base is. Negative and large positive input bases are permitted but useless. No mechanism has been provided for the input of arbitrary numbers in bases less than 1 and greater than 16.

    The contents of 'obase', initially set to 10, are used as the base for output numbers. The lines

    obase = 16
    1000

will produce the output line

    3E8

which is to be interpreted as a 3-digit hexadecimal number. Very large output bases are permitted, and they are sometimes useful. For example, large numbers can be output in groups of five digits by setting 'obase' to 100000. Strange (i.e. 1, 0, or negative) output bases are handled appropriately.

    Very large numbers are split across lines with 70 characters per line. Lines which are continued end with \. Decimal output conversion is practically instantaneous, but output of very large numbers (i.e., more than 100 digits) with other bases is rather slow. Non-decimal output conversion of a one hundred digit number takes about three seconds.

    It is best to remember that 'ibase' and 'obase' have no effect whatever on the course of internal computation or on the evaluation of expressions, but only affect input and output conversion, respectively.

Scaling

    A third special internal quantity called 'scale' is used to determine the scale of calculated quantities. Numbers may have up to 99 decimal digits after the decimal point. This fractional part is retained in further computations. We refer to the number of digits after the decimal point of a number as its scale.

    When two scaled numbers are combined by means of one of the arithmetic operations, the result has a scale determined by the following rules. For addition and subtraction, the scale of the result is the larger of the scales of the two operands. In this case, there is never any truncation of the result. For multiplications, the scale of the result is never less than the maximum of the two scales of the operands, never more than the sum of the scales of the operands and, subject to those two restrictions, the scale of the result is set equal to the contents of the internal quantity 'scale'. The scale of a quotient is the contents of the internal quantity 'scale'. The scale of a remainder is the sum of the scales of the quotient and the divisor. The result of an exponentiation is scaled as if the implied multiplications were performed. An exponent must be an integer. The scale of a square root is set to the maximum of the scale of the argument and the contents of 'scale'.

    All of the internal operations are actually carried out in terms of integers, with digits being discarded when necessary. In every case where digits are discarded, truncation and not rounding is performed.

    The contents of 'scale' must be no greater than 99 and no less than 0. It is initially set to 0. In case you need more than 99 fraction digits, you may arrange your own scaling.

    The internal quantities 'scale', 'ibase', and 'obase' can be used in expressions just like other variables. The line

scale = scale + 1

increases the value of 'scale' by one, and the line

scale

causes the current value of 'scale' to be printed.

The value of 'scale' retains its meaning as a number of decimal digits to be retained in internal computation even when 'ibase' or 'obase' are not equal to 10. The internal computations (which are still conducted in decimal, regardless of the bases) are performed to the specified number of decimal digits, never hexadecimal or octal or any other kind of digits.

Functions

The name of a function is a single lower-case letter. Function names are permitted to collide with simple variable names. Twenty-six different defined functions are permitted in addition to the twenty-six variable names. The line

define a(x){

begins the definition of a function with one argument. This line must be followed by one or more statements, which make up the body of the function, ending with a right brace }. Return of control from a function occurs when a return statement is executed or when the end of the function is reached. The return statement can take either of the two forms

return
return(x)

In the first case, the value of the function is 0, and in the second, the value of the expression in parentheses.

Variables used in the function can be declared as automatic by a statement of the form

auto x,y,z

There can be only one 'auto' statement in a function and it must be the first statement in the definition. These automatic variables are allocated space and initialized to zero on entry to the function and thrown away on return. The values of any variables with the same names outside the function are not disturbed. Functions may be called recursively and the automatic variables at each level of call are protected. The parameters named in a function definition are treated in the same way as the automatic variables of that function with the single exception that they are given a value on entry to the function. An example of a function definition is

```
define a(x,y){
       auto z
       z = x*y
       return(z)
}
```

The value of this function, when called, will be the product of its two arguments.

A function is called by the appearance of its name followed by a string of arguments enclosed in parentheses and separated by commas. The result is unpredictable if the wrong number of arguments is used.

Functions with no arguments are defined and called using parentheses with nothing between them: b().

If the function *a* above has been defined, then the line

a(7,3.14)

would cause the result 21.98 to be printed and the line

x = a(a(3,4),5)

would cause the value of x to become 60.

Subscripted Variables

A single lower-case letter variable name followed by an expression in brackets is called a subscripted variable (an array element). The variable name is called the array name and the expression in brackets is called the subscript. Only one-dimensional arrays are permitted. The names of arrays are permitted to collide with the names of simple variables and function names. Any fractional part of a subscript is discarded before use. Subscripts must be greater than or equal to zero and less than or equal to 2047.

Subscripted variables may be freely used in expressions, in function calls, and in return statements.

An array name may be used as an argument to a function, or may be declared as automatic in a function definition by the use of empty brackets:

f(a[ ])
define f(a[ ])
auto a[ ]

When an array name is so used, the whole contents of the array are copied for the use of the function, and thrown away on exit from the function. Array names which refer to whole arrays cannot be used in any other contexts.

Control Statements

The 'if', the 'while', and the 'for' statements may be used to alter the flow within programs or to cause iteration. The range of each of them is a statement or a compound statement consisting of a collection of statements enclosed in braces. They are written in the following way

if(relation) statement
while(relation) statement
for(expression1; relation; expression2) statement

or

if(relation) {statements}
while(relation) {statements}
for(expression1; relation; expression2) {statements}

A relation in one of the control statements is an expression of the form

x>y

where two expressions are related by one of the six relational operators <, >, <=, >=, ==, or !=. The relation == stands for 'equal to' and != stands for 'not equal to'. The meaning of the remaining relational operators is clear.

BEWARE of using = instead of == in a relational. Unfortunately, both of them are legal, so you will not get a diagnostic message, but = really will not do a comparison.

The 'if' statement causes execution of its range if and only if the relation is true. Then control passes to the next statement in sequence.

The 'while' statement causes execution of its range repeatedly as long as the relation is true. The relation is tested before each execution of its range and if the relation is false, control passes to the next statement beyond the range of the while.

The 'for' statement begins by executing 'expression1'. Then the relation is tested and, if true, the statements in the range of the 'for' are executed. Then 'expression2' is executed. The relation is tested, and so on. The typical use of the 'for' statement is for a controlled iteration, as in the statement

```
for(i=1; i<=10; i=i+1) i
```

which will print the integers from 1 to 10. Here are some examples of the use of the control statements.

```
define f(n){
auto i, x
x=1
for(i=1; i<=n; i=i+1) x=x*i
return(x)
}
```

The line

```
        f(a)
```

will print *a* factorial if *a* is a positive integer. Here is the definition of a function which will compute values of the binomial coefficient (m and n are assumed to be positive integers).

```
define b(n,m){
auto x, j
x=1
for(j=1; j<=m; j=j+1) x=x*(n–j+1)/j
return(x)
}
```

The following function computes values of the exponential function by summing the appropriate series without regard for possible truncation errors:

```
scale = 20
define e(x){
        auto a, b, c, d, n
        a = 1
        b = 1
        c = 1
        d = 0
        n = 1
        while(1==1){
                a = a*x
                b = b*n
                c = c + a/b
                n = n + 1
                if(c==d) return(c)
                d = c
        }
}
```

Some Details

There are some language features that every user should know about even if he will not use them.

Normally statements are typed one to a line. It is also permissible to type several statements on a line separated by semicolons.

If an assignment statement is parenthesized, it then has a value and it can be used anywhere that an expression can. For example, the line

```
(x=y+17)
```

not only makes the indicated assignment, but also prints the resulting value.

Here is an example of a use of the value of an assignment statement even when it is not parenthesized.

x = a[i=i+1]

causes a value to be assigned to x and also increments i before it is used as a subscript.

The following constructs work in BC in exactly the same manner as they do in the C language. Consult the appendix or the C manuals [2] for their exact workings.

x=y=z is the same as	**x=(y=z)**
x =+ y	**x = x+y**
x =− y	**x = x−y**
x =* y	**x = x*y**
x =/ y	**x = x/y**
x =% y	**x = x%y**
x =^ y	**x = x^y**
x++	**(x=x+1)−1**
x—	**(x=x−1)+1**
++x	**x = x+1**
—x	**x = x−1**

Even if you don't intend to use the constructs, if you type one inadvertently, something correct but unexpected may happen.

WARNING! In some of these constructions, spaces are significant. There is a real difference between **x =− y and x= −y.** The first replaces x by x−y and the second by −y.

Three Important Things

1. To exit a BC program, type 'quit'.

2. There is a comment convention identical to that of C and of PL/I. Comments begin with '/*' and ⟨ end with '*/'.

3. There is a library of math functions which may be obtained by typing at command level

bc –l

This command will load a set of library functions which, at the time of writing, consists of sine (named 's'), cosine ('c'), arctangent ('a'), natural logarithm ('l'), exponential ('e') and Bessel functions of integer order ('j(n,x)'). Doubtless more functions will be added in time. The library sets the scale to 20. You can reset it to something else if you like. The design of these mathematical library routines is discussed elsewhere [3].

If you type

bc file ...

BC will read and execute the named file or files before accepting commands from the keyboard. In this way, you may load your favorite programs and function definitions.

Acknowledgement

The compiler is written in YACC [4]; its original version was written by S. C. Johnson.

References

[1]   K. Thompson and D. M. Ritchie, *UNIX Programmer's Manual,* Bell Laboratories, 1978.

[2]   B. W. Kernighan and D. M. Ritchie, *The C Programming Language,* Prentice-Hall, 1978.

[3]   R. Morris, *A Library of Reference Standard Mathematical Subroutines,* Bell Laboratories internal memorandum, 1975.

6

[4]   S. C. Johnson, *YACC — Yet Another Compiler-Compiler*. Bell Laboratories Computing Science
       Technical Report #32, 1978.

[5]   R. Morris and L. L. Cherry, *DC – An Interactive Desk Calculator*.

Appendix

1. Notation

In the following pages syntactic categories are in *italics*; literals are in **bold**; material in brackets [ ] is optional.

2. Tokens

Tokens consist of keywords, identifiers, constants, operators, and separators. Token separators may be blanks, tabs or comments. Newline characters or semicolons separate statements.

2.1. Comments

Comments are introduced by the characters /* and terminated by */.

2.2. Identifiers

There are three kinds of identifiers – ordinary identifiers, array identifiers and function identifiers. All three types consist of single lower-case letters. Array identifiers are followed by square brackets, possibly enclosing an expression describing a subscript. Arrays are singly dimensioned and may contain up to 2048 elements. Indexing begins at zero so an array may be indexed from 0 to 2047. Subscripts are truncated to integers. Function identifiers are followed by parentheses, possibly enclosing arguments. The three types of identifiers do not conflict; a program can have a variable named **x**, an array named **x** and a function named **x**, all of which are separate and distinct.

2.3. Keywords

The following are reserved keywords:

ibase	**if**
obase	**break**
scale	**define**
sqrt	**auto**
length	**return**
while	**quit**
for	

2.4. Constants

Constants consist of arbitrarily long numbers with an optional decimal point. The hexadecimal digits A–F are also recognized as digits with values 10–15, respectively.

3. Expressions

The value of an expression is printed unless the main operator is an assignment. Precedence is the same as the order of presentation here, with highest appearing first. Left or right associativity, where applicable, is discussed with each operator.

3.1. Primitive expressions

3.1.1. Named expressions

Named expressions are places where values are stored. Simply stated, named expressions are legal on the left side of an assignment. The value of a named expression is the value stored in the place named.

3.1.1.1. *identifiers*

Simple identifiers are named expressions. They have an initial value of zero.

3.1.1.2. *array-name* [*expression*]

Array elements are named expressions. They have an initial value of zero.

3.1.1.3. scale, ibase and **obase**

The internal registers **scale, ibase** and **obase** are all named expressions. **scale** is the number of digits after the decimal point to be retained in arithmetic operations. **scale** has an initial value of zero. **ibase** and **obase** are the input and output number radix respectively. Both **ibase** and **obase** have initial values of 10.

3.1.2. Function calls

3.1.2.1. *function-name* ([*expression* [, *expression* . . .]])

A function call consists of a function name followed by parentheses containing a comma-separated list of expressions, which are the function arguments. A whole array passed as an argument is specified by the array name followed by empty square brackets. All function arguments are passed by value. As a result, changes made to the formal parameters have no effect on the actual arguments. If the function terminates by executing a return statement, the value of the function is the value of the expression in the parentheses of the return statement or is zero if no expression is provided or if there is no return statement.

3.1.2.2. sqrt (*expression*)

The result is the square root of the expression. The result is truncated in the least significant decimal place. The scale of the result is the scale of the expression or the value of **scale,** whichever is larger.

3.1.2.3. length (*expression*)

The result is the total number of significant decimal digits in the expression. The scale of the result is zero.

3.1.2.4. scale (*expression*)

The result is the scale of the expression. The scale of the result is zero.

3.1.3. Constants

Constants are primitive expressions.

3.1.4. Parentheses

An expression surrounded by parentheses is a primitive expression. The parentheses are used to alter the normal precedence.

3.2. Unary operators

The unary operators bind right to left.

3.2.1. − *expression*

The result is the negative of the expression.

3.2.2. ++ *named-expression*

The named expression is incremented by one. The result is the value of the named expression after incrementing.

6

3.2.3. — *named-expression*

The named expression is decremented by one. The result is the value of the named expression after decrementing.

3.2.4. *named-expression* ++

The named expression is incremented by one. The result is the value of the named expression before incrementing.

3.2.5. *named-expression* —

The named expression is decremented by one. The result is the value of the named expression before decrementing.

3.3. Exponentiation operator

The exponentiation operator binds right to left.

3.3.1. *expression ^ expression*

The result is the first expression raised to the power of the second expression. The second expression must be an integer. If a is the scale of the left expression and b is the absolute value of the right expression, then the scale of the result is:

$$\min(a{\times}b, \max(\textbf{scale}, a))$$

3.4. Multiplicative operators

The operators $*, /, \%$ bind left to right.

3.4.1. *expression * expression*

The result is the product of the two expressions. If a and b are the scales of the two expressions, then the scale of the result is:

$$\min(a{+}b, \max(\textbf{scale}, a, b))$$

3.4.2. *expression / expression*

The result is the quotient of the two expressions. The scale of the result is the value of **scale**.

3.4.3. *expression % expression*

The % operator produces the remainder of the division of the two expressions. More precisely, $a\%b$ is $a{-}a/b*b$.

The scale of the result is the sum of the scale of the divisor and the value of **scale**

3.5. Additive operators

The additive operators bind left to right.

3.5.1. *expression + expression*

The result is the sum of the two expressions. The scale of the result is the maximun of the scales of the expressions.

3.5.2. *expression – expression*

The result is the difference of the two expressions. The scale of the result is the maximum of the scales of the expressions.

3.6. assignment operators

The assignment operators bind right to left.

3.6.1. *named-expression = expression*

This expression results in assigning the value of the expression on the right to the named expression on the left.

3.6.2. *named-expression =+ expression*

3.6.3. *named-expression =– expression*

3.6.4. *named-expression =* expression*

3.6.5. *named-expression =/ expression*

3.6.6. *named-expression =% expression*

3.6.7. *named-expression =^ expression*

The result of the above expressions is equivalent to "named expression = named expression OP expression", where OP is the operator after the = sign.

4. Relations

Unlike all other operators, the relational operators are only valid as the object of an **if**, **while**, or inside a **for** statement.

4.1. *expression < expression*

4.2. *expression > expression*

4.3. *expression <= expression*

4.4. *expression >= expression*

4.5. *expression == expression*

4.6. *expression != expression*

5. Storage classes

There are only two storage classes in BC, global and automatic (local). Only identifiers that are to be local to a function need be declared with the **auto** command. The arguments to a function are local to the function. All other identifiers are assumed to be global and available to all functions. All identifiers, global and local, have initial values of zero. Identifiers declared as **auto** are allocated on entry to the function and released on returning from the function. They therefore do not retain values between function calls. **auto** arrays are specified by the array name followed by empty square brackets.

Automatic variables in BC do not work in exactly the same way as in either C or PL/I. On entry to a function, the old values of the names that appear as parameters and as automatic variables are pushed onto a stack. Until return is made from the function, reference to these names refers only to the new values.

6. Statements

Statements must be separated by semicolon or newline. Except where altered by control statements, execution is sequential.

6

6.1. Expression statements

When a statement is an expression, unless the main operator is an assignment, the value of the expression is printed, followed by a newline character.

6.2. Compound statements

Statements may be grouped together and used when one statement is expected by surrounding them with { }.

6.3. Quoted string statements

"any string"

This statement prints the string inside the quotes.

6.4. If statements

if (*relation*) *statement*

The substatement is executed if the relation is true.

6.5. While statements

while (*relation*) *statement*

The statement is executed while the relation is true. The test occurs before each execution of the statement.

6.6. For statements

for (*expression*; *relation*; *expression*) *statement*

The for statement is the same as
first-expression
while (*relation*) **{**
    statement
    last-expression
}
All three expressions must be present.

6.7. Break statements

break

break causes termination of a **for** or **while** statement.

6.8. Auto statements

auto *identifier* [*,identifier*]

The auto statement causes the values of the identifiers to be pushed down. The identifiers can be ordinary identifiers or array identifiers. Array identifiers are specified by following the array name by empty square brackets. The auto statement must be the first statement in a function definition.

6.9. Define statements

define([*parameter* [*,parameter* ...]]) **{**
    statements **}**

The define statement defines a function. The parameters may be ordinary identifiers or array names. Array names must be followed by empty square brackets.

6.10. Return statements

return

return(*expression*)

The return statement causes termination of a function, popping of its auto variables, and specifies the result of the function. The first form is equivalent to **return(0)**. The result of the function is the result of the expression in parentheses.

6.11. Quit

The quit statement stops execution of a BC program and returns control to UNIX when it is first encountered. Because it is not treated as an executable statement, it cannot be used in a function definition or in an **if, for,** or **while** statement.

6

MAIL REFERENCE MANUAL

Kurt Shoens

Revised by

Craig Leres and *Mark Andrews*

Version 5.5

May 17, 1994

1. Introduction

   Mail provides a simple and friendly environment for sending and receiving mail. It divides incoming mail into its constituent messages and allows the user to deal with them in any order. In addition, it provides a set of *ed*-like commands for manipulating messages and sending mail. *Mail* offers the user simple editing capabilities to ease the composition of outgoing messages, as well as providing the ability to define and send to names which address groups of users. Finally, *Mail* is able to send and receive messages across such networks as the ARPANET, UUCP, and Berkeley network.

   This document describes how to use the *Mail* program to send and receive messages. The reader is not assumed to be familiar with other message handling systems, but should be familiar with the UNIX[1] shell, the text editor, and some of the common UNIX commands. "The UNIX Programmer's Manual," "An Introduction to Csh," and "Text Editing with Ex and Vi" can be consulted for more information on these topics.

   Here is how messages are handled: the mail system accepts incoming *messages* for you from other people and collects them in a file, called your *system mailbox*. When you login, the system notifies you if there are any messages waiting in your system mailbox. If you are a *csh* user, you will be notified when new mail arrives if you inform the shell of the location of your mailbox. On version 7 systems, your system mailbox is located in the directory /usr/spool/mail in a file with your login name. If your login name is "sam," then you can make *csh* notify you of new mail by including the following line in your .cshrc file:

   set mail=/usr/spool/mail/sam

When you read your mail using *Mail*, it reads your system mailbox and separates that file into the individual messages that have been sent to you. You can then read, reply to, delete, or save these messages. Each message is marked with its author and the date they sent it.

2. Common usage

   The *Mail* command has two distinct usages, according to whether one wants to send or receive mail. Sending mail is simple: to send a message to a user whose login name is, say, "root," use the shell command:

   % Mail root

---

[1] UNIX is a trademark of Bell Laboratories.

then type your message. When you reach the end of the message, type an EOT (control–d) at the beginning of a line, which will cause *Mail* to echo "EOT" and return you to the Shell. When the user you sent mail to next logs in, he will receive the message:

> You have mail.

to alert him to the existence of your message.

If, while you are composing the message you decide that you do not wish to send it after all, you can abort the letter with a RUBOUT. Typing a single RUBOUT causes *Mail* to print

> (Interrupt -- one more to kill letter)

Typing a second RUBOUT causes *Mail* to save your partial letter on the file "dead.letter" in your home directory and abort the letter. Once you have sent mail to someone, there is no way to undo the act, so be careful.

The message your recipient reads will consist of the message you typed, preceded by a line telling who sent the message (your login name) and the date and time it was sent.

If you want to send the same message to several other people, you can list their login names on the command line. Thus,

> % Mail sam bob john
> Tuition fees are due next Friday. Don't forget!!
> <Control–d>
> EOT
> %

will send the reminder to sam, bob, and john.

If, when you log in, you see the message,

> You have mail.

you can read the mail by typing simply:

> % Mail

Mail will respond by typing its version number and date and then listing the messages you have waiting. Then it will type a prompt and await your command. The messages are assigned numbers starting with 1 — you refer to the messages with these numbers. *Mail* keeps track of which messages are *new* (have been sent since you last read your mail) and *read* (have been read by you). New messages have an **N** next to them in the header listing and old, but unread messages have a **U** next to them. *Mail* keeps track of new/old and read/unread messages by putting a header field called "Status" into your messages.

To look at a specific message, use the **type** command, which may be abbreviated to simply **t**. For example, if you had the following messages:

> N 1 root   Wed Sep 21 09:21 "Tuition fees"
> N 2 sam   Tue Sep 20 22:55

you could examine the first message by giving the command:

> type 1

which might cause *Mail* to respond with, for example:

> Message 1:
> From root Wed Sep 21 09:21:45 1978
> Subject: Tuition fees
> Status: R
>
> Tuition fees are due next Wednesday. Don't forget!!

Many *Mail* commands that operate on messages take a message number as an argument like the **type** command. For these commands, there is a notion of a current message. When you enter the *Mail* program, the current message is initially the first one. Thus, you can often omit the message number and use, for example,

  t

to type the current message. As a further shorthand, you can type a message by simply giving its message number. Hence,

  1

would type the first message.

  Frequently, it is useful to read the messages in your mailbox in order, one after another. You can read the next message in *Mail* by simply typing a newline. As a special case, you can type a newline as your first command to *Mail* to type the first message.

  If, after typing a message, you wish to immediately send a reply, you can do so with the **reply** command. **Reply**, like **type**, takes a message number as an argument. *Mail* then begins a message addressed to the user who sent you the message. You may then type in your letter in reply, followed by a <control-d> at the beginning of a line, as before. *Mail* will type EOT, then type the ampersand prompt to indicate its readiness to accept another command. In our example, if, after typing the first message, you wished to reply to it, you might give the command:

  reply

Mail responds by typing:

  To: root
  Subject: Re: Tuition fees

and waiting for you to enter your letter. You are now in the message collection mode described at the beginning of this section and *Mail* will gather up your message up to a control–d. Note that it copies the subject header from the original message. This is useful in that correspondence about a particular matter will tend to retain the same subject heading, making it easy to recognize. If there are other header fields in the message, the information found will also be used. For example, if the letter had a ''To:'' header listing several recipients, *Mail* would arrange to send your replay to the same people as well. Similarly, if the original message contained a ''Cc:'' (carbon copies to) field, *Mail* would send your reply to *those* users, too. *Mail* is careful, though, not too send the message to *you*, even if you appear in the ''To:'' or ''Cc:'' field, unless you ask to be included explicitly. See section 4 for more details.

  After typing in your letter, the dialog with *Mail* might look like the following:

  reply
  To: root
  Subject: Tuition fees

  Thanks for the reminder
  EOT
  &

  The **reply** command is especially useful for sustaining extended conversations over the message system, with other ''listening'' users receiving copies of the conversation. The **reply** command can be abbreviated to **r**.

  Sometimes you will receive a message that has been sent to several people and wish to reply *only* to the person who sent it. **Reply** with a capital **R** replies to a message, but sends a copy to the sender only.

  If you wish, while reading your mail, to send a message to someone, but not as a reply to one of your messages, you can send the message directly with the **mail** command, which takes as arguments the names of the recipients you wish to send to. For example, to send a message to ''frank,'' you would do:

  mail frank
  This is to confirm our meeting next Friday at 4.
  EOT
  &

The **mail** command can be abbreviated to **m**.

7

Normally, each message you receive is saved in the file *mbox* in your login directory at the time you leave *Mail*. Often, however, you will not want to save a particular message you have received because it is only of passing interest. To avoid saving a message in *mbox* you can delete it using the **delete** command. In our example,

      delete 1

will prevent *Mail* from saving message 1 (from root) in *mbox*. In addition to not saving deleted messages, *Mail* will not let you type them, either. The effect is to make the message disappear altogether, along with its number. The **delete** command can be abbreviated to simply **d**.

Many features of *Mail* can be tailored to your liking with the **set** command. The **set** command has two forms, depending on whether you are setting a *binary* option or a *valued* option. Binary options are either on or off. For example, the "ask" option informs *Mail* that each time you send a message, you want it to prompt you for a subject header, to be included in the message. To set the "ask" option, you would type

      set ask

Another useful *Mail* option is "hold." Unless told otherwise, *Mail* moves the messages from your system mailbox to the file *mbox* in your home directory when you leave *Mail*. If you want *Mail* to keep your letters in the system mailbox instead, you can set the "hold" option.

Valued options are values which *Mail* uses to adapt to your tastes. For example, the "SHELL" option tells *Mail* which shell you like to use, and is specified by

      set SHELL=/bin/csh

for example. Note that no spaces are allowed in "SHELL=/bin/csh." A complete list of the *Mail* options appears in section 5.

Another important valued option is "crt." If you use a fast video terminal, you will find that when you print long messages, they fly by too quickly for you to read them. With the "crt" option, you can make *Mail* print any message larger than a given number of lines by sending it through a paging program. This program is specified by the valued option **PAGER**. If **PAGER** is not set, a default paginator is used. For example, most CRT users with 24-line screens should do:

      set crt=24

to paginate messages that will not fit on their screens. In the default state, *more* (default paginator) prints a screenful of information, then types --More--. Type a space to see the next screenful.

Another adaptation to user needs that *Mail* provides is that of *aliases*. An alias is simply a name which stands for one or more real user names. *Mail* sent to an alias is really sent to the list of real users associated with it. For example, an alias can be defined for the members of a project, so that you can send mail to the whole project by sending mail to just a single name. The **alias** command in *Mail* defines an alias. Suppose that the users in a project are named Sam, Sally, Steve, and Susan. To define an alias called "project" for them, you would use the *Mail* command:

      alias project sam sally steve susan

The **alias** command can also be used to provide a convenient name for someone whose user name is inconvenient. For example, if a user named "Bob Anderson" had the login name "anderson,"" you might want to use:

      alias bob anderson

so that you could send mail to the shorter name, "bob."

While the **alias** and **set** commands allow you to customize *Mail*, they have the drawback that they must be retyped each time you enter *Mail*. To make them more convenient to use, *Mail* always looks for two files when it is invoked. It first reads a system wide file "/usr/lib/Mail.rc," then a user specific file, ".mailrc," which is found in the user's home directory. The system wide file is maintained by the system administrator and contains **set** commands that are applicable to all users of the system. The ".mailrc" file is usually used by each user to set options the way he likes and define individual aliases. For example, my .mailrc file looks like this:

      set ask nosave SHELL=/bin/csh

As you can see, it is possible to set many options in the same **set** command. The ''nosave'' option is described in section 5.

Mail aliasing is implemented at the system-wide level by the mail delivery system *sendmail.* These aliases are stored in the file /usr/lib/aliases and are accessible to all users of the system. The lines in /usr/lib/aliases are of the form:

     alias: name$_1$, name$_2$, name$_3$

where *alias* is the mailing list name and the *name$_i$* are the members of the list. Long lists can be continued onto the next line by starting the next line with a space or tab. Remember that you must execute the shell command *newaliases* after editing /usr/lib/aliases since the delivery system uses an indexed file created by *newaliases.*

We have seen that *Mail* can be invoked with command line arguments which are people to send the message to, or with no arguments to read mail. Specifying the –**f** flag on the command line causes *Mail* to read messages from a file other than your system mailbox. For example, if you have a collection of messages in the file ''letters'' you can use *Mail* to read them with:

     % Mail –f letters

You can use all the *Mail* commands described in this document to examine, modify, or delete messages from your ''letters'' file, which will be rewritten when you leave *Mail* with the **quit** command described below.

Since mail that you read is saved in the file *mbox* in your home directory by default, you can read *mbox* in your home directory by using simply

     % Mail –f

Normally, messages that you examine using the **type** command are saved in the file ''mbox'' in your home directory if you leave *Mail* with the **quit** command described below. If you wish to retain a message in your system mailbox you can use the **preserve** command to tell *Mail* to leave it there. The **preserve** command accepts a list of message numbers, just like **type** and may be abbreviated to **pre**.

Messages in your system mailbox that you do not examine are normally retained in your system mailbox automatically. If you wish to have such a message saved in *mbox* without reading it, you may use the **mbox** command to have them so saved. For example,

     mbox 2

in our example would cause the second message (from sam) to be saved in *mbox* when the **quit** command is executed. **Mbox** is also the way to direct messages to your *mbox* file if you have set the ''hold'' option described above. **Mbox** can be abbreviated to **mb**.

When you have perused all the messages of interest, you can leave *Mail* with the **quit** command, which saves the messages you have typed but not deleted in the file *mbox* in your login directory. Deleted messages are discarded irretrievably, and messages left untouched are preserved in your system mailbox so that you will see them the next time you type:

     % Mail

The **quit** command can be abbreviated to simply **q**.

If you wish for some reason to leave *Mail* quickly without altering either your system mailbox or *mbox*, you can type the **x** command (short for **exit**), which will immediately return you to the Shell without changing anything.

If, instead, you want to execute a Shell command without leaving *Mail*, you can type the command preceded by an exclamation point, just as in the text editor. Thus, for instance:

     !date

will print the current date without leaving *Mail.*

Finally, the **help** command is available to print out a brief summary of the *Mail* commands, using only the single character command abbreviations.

3. Maintaining folders

Mail includes a simple facility for maintaining groups of messages together in folders. This section describes this facility.

To use the folder facility, you must tell *Mail* where you wish to keep your folders. Each folder of messages will be a single file. For convenience, all of your folders are kept in a single directory of your choosing. To tell *Mail* where your folder directory is, put a line of the form

      set folder=letters

in your *.mailrc* file. If, as in the example above, your folder directory does not begin with a '/,' *Mail* will assume that your folder directory is to be found starting from your home directory. Thus, if your home directory is **/usr/person** the above example told *Mail* to find your folder directory in **/usr/person/letters**.

Anywhere a file name is expected, you can use a folder name, preceded with '+.' For example, to put a message into a folder with the **save** command, you can use:

      save +classwork

to save the current message in the *classwork* folder. If the *classwork* folder does not yet exist, it will be created. Note that messages which are saved with the **save** command are automatically removed from your system mailbox.

In order to make a copy of a message in a folder without causing that message to be removed from your system mailbox, use the **copy** command, which is identical in all other respects to the **save** command. For example,

      copy +classwork

copies the current message into the *classwork* folder and leaves a copy in your system mailbox.

The **folder** command can be used to direct *Mail* to the contents of a different folder. For example,

      folder +classwork

directs *Mail* to read the contents of the *classwork* folder. All of the commands that you can use on your system mailbox are also applicable to folders, including **type, delete,** and **reply**. To inquire which folder you are currently editing, use simply:

      folder

To list your current set of folders, use the **folders** command.

To start *Mail* reading one of your folders, you can use the **−f** option described in section 2. For example:

      % Mail −f +classwork

will cause *Mail* to read your *classwork* folder without looking at your system mailbox.

4. More about sending mail

4.1. Tilde escapes

While typing in a message to be sent to others, it is often useful to be able to invoke the text editor on the partial message, print the message, execute a shell command, or do some other auxiliary function. *Mail* provides these capabilities through *tilde escapes*, which consist of a tilde (˜) at the beginning of a line, followed by a single character which indicates the function to be performed. For example, to print the text of the message so far, use:

      ˜p

which will print a line of dashes, the recipients of your message, and the text of the message so far. Since *Mail* requires two consecutive RUBOUT's to abort a letter, you can use a single RUBOUT to abort the output of ˜p or any other ˜ escape without killing your letter.

If you are dissatisfied with the message as it stands, you can invoke the text editor on it using the escape

      ˜e

which causes the message to be copied into a temporary file and an instance of the editor to be spawned. After modifying the message to your satisfaction, write it out and quit the editor. *Mail* will respond by typing

(continue)

after which you may continue typing text which will be appended to your message, or type <control-d> to end the message. A standard text editor is provided by *Mail*. You can override this default by setting the valued option ''EDITOR'' to something else. For example, you might prefer:

set EDITOR=/usr/ucb/ex

Many systems offer a screen editor as an alternative to the standard text editor, such as the *vi* editor from UC Berkeley. To use the screen, or *visual* editor, on your current message, you can use the escape,

~v

~v works like ~e, except that the screen editor is invoked instead. A default screen editor is defined by *Mail*. If it does not suit you, you can set the valued option ''VISUAL'' to the path name of a different editor.

It is often useful to be able to include the contents of some file in your message; the escape

~r filename

is provided for this purpose, and causes the named file to be appended to your current message. *Mail* complains if the file doesn't exist or can't be read. If the read is successful, the number of lines and characters appended to your message is printed, after which you may continue appending text. The filename may contain shell metacharacters like * and ? which are expanded according to the conventions of your shell.

As a special case of ~r, the escape

~d

reads in the file ''dead.letter'' in your home directory. This is often useful since *Mail* copies the text of your message there when you abort a message with RUBOUT.

To save the current text of your message on a file you may use the

~w filename

escape. *Mail* will print out the number of lines and characters written to the file, after which you may continue appending text to your message. Shell metacharacters may be used in the filename, as in ~r and are expanded with the conventions of your shell.

If you are sending mail from within *Mail's* command mode you can read a message sent to you into the message you are constructing with the escape:

~m 4

which will read message 4 into the current message, shifted right by one tab stop. You can name any non-deleted message, or list of messages. Messages can also be forwarded without shifting by a tab stop with ~f. This is the usual way to forward a message.

If, in the process of composing a message, you decide to add additional people to the list of message recipients, you can do so with the escape

~t name1 name2 ...

You may name as few or many additional recipients as you wish. Note that the users originally on the recipient list will still receive the message; you cannot remove someone from the recipient list with ~t.

If you wish, you can associate a subject with your message by using the escape

~s Arbitrary string of text

which replaces any previous subject with ''Arbitrary string of text.'' The subject, if given, is sent near the top of the message prefixed with ''Subject:'' You can see what the message will look like by using ~p.

For political reasons, one occasionally prefers to list certain people as recipients of carbon copies of a message rather than direct recipients. The escape

~c name1 name2 ...

7

adds the named people to the ''Cc:'' list, similar to ˜t. Again, you can execute ˜p to see what the message will look like.

The escape

   ˜b name1 name2 ...

adds the named people to the ''Cc:'' list, but does not make the names visible in the ''Cc:'' line (''blind'' carbon copy).

The recipients of the message together constitute the ''To:'' field, the subject the ''Subject:'' field, and the carbon copies the ''Cc:'' field. If you wish to edit these in ways impossible with the ˜t, ˜s, ˜c and ˜b escapes, you can use the escape

   ˜h

which prints ''To:'' followed by the current list of recipients and leaves the cursor (or printhead) at the end of the line. If you type in ordinary characters, they are appended to the end of the current list of recipients. You can also use your erase character to erase back into the list of recipients, or your kill character to erase them altogether. Thus, for example, if your erase and kill characters are the standard (on printing terminals) # and @ symbols,

   ˜h
   To: root kurt####bill

would change the initial recipients ''root kurt'' to ''root bill.'' When you type a newline, *Mail* advances to the ''Subject:'' field, where the same rules apply. Another newline brings you to the ''Cc:'' field, which may be edited in the same fashion. Another newline brings you to the ''Bcc:'' (''blind'' carbon copy) field, which follows the same rules as the ''Cc:'' field. Another newline leaves you appending text to the end of your message. You can use ˜p to print the current text of the header fields and the body of the message.

To effect a temporary escape to the shell, the escape

   ˜!command

is used, which executes *command* and returns you to mailing mode without altering the text of your message. If you wish, instead, to filter the body of your message through a shell command, then you can use

   ˜|command

which pipes your message through the command and uses the output as the new text of your message. If the command produces no output, *Mail* assumes that something is amiss and retains the old version of your message. A frequently-used filter is the command *fmt*, designed to format outgoing mail.

To effect a temporary escape to *Mail* command mode instead, you can use the

   ˜:Mail command

escape. This is especially useful for retyping the message you are replying to, using, for example:

   ˜:t

It is also useful for setting options and modifying aliases.

If you wish abort the current message, you can use the escape

   ˜q

This will terminate the current message and return you to the shell (or *Mail* if you were using the **mail** command). If the **save** option is set, the message will be copied to the file ''dead.letter'' in your home directory.

If you wish (for some reason) to send a message that contains a line beginning with a tilde, you must double it. Thus, for example,

   ˜˜This line begins with a tilde.

sends the line

   ˜This line begins with a tilde.

Finally, the escape

~?

prints out a brief summary of the available tilde escapes.

On some terminals (particularly ones with no lower case) tilde's are difficult to type. *Mail* allows you to change the escape character with the "escape" option. For example, I set

set escape=]

and use a right bracket instead of a tilde. If I ever need to send a line beginning with right bracket, I double it, just as for ~. Changing the escape character removes the special meaning of ~.

4.2. Network access

This section describes how to send mail to people on other machines. Recall that sending to a plain login name sends mail to that person on your machine. If your machine is directly (or sometimes, even, indirectly) connected to the Arpanet, you can send messages to people on the Arpanet using a name of the form

name@host.domain

where *name* is the login name of the person you're trying to reach, *host* is the name of the machine on the Arpanet, and *domain* is the higher-level scope within which the hostname is known, e.g. EDU (for educational institutions), COM (for commercial entities), GOV (for governmental agencies), ARPA for many other things, BITNET or CSNET for those networks.

If your recipient logs in on a machine connected to yours by UUCP (the Bell Laboratories supplied network that communicates over telephone lines), sending mail can be a bit more complicated. You must know the list of machines through which your message must travel to arrive at his site. So, if his machine is directly connected to yours, you can send mail to him using the syntax:

host!name

where, again, *host* is the name of the machine and *name* is the login name. If your message must go through an intermediary machine first, you must use the syntax:

intermediary!host!name

and so on. It is actually a feature of UUCP that the map of all the systems in the network is not known anywhere (except where people decide to write it down for convenience). Talk to your system administrator about good ways to get places; the *uuname* command will tell you systems whose names are recognized, but not which ones are frequently called or well-connected.

When you use the **reply** command to respond to a letter, there is a problem of figuring out the names of the users in the "To:" and "Cc:" lists *relative to the current machine*. If the original letter was sent to you by someone on the local machine, then this problem does not exist, but if the message came from a remote machine, the problem must be dealt with. *Mail* uses a heuristic to build the correct name for each user relative to the local machine. So, when you **reply** to remote mail, the names in the "To:" and "Cc:" lists may change somewhat.

4.3. Special recipients

As described previously, you can send mail to either user names or **alias** names. It is also possible to send messages directly to files or to programs, using special conventions. If a recipient name has a '/' in it or begins with a '+', it is assumed to be the path name of a file into which to send the message. If the file already exists, the message is appended to the end of the file. If you want to name a file in your current directory (ie, one for which a '/' would not usually be needed) you can precede the name with './' So, to send mail to the file "memo" in the current directory, you can give the command:

% Mail ./memo

If the name begins with a '+,' it is expanded into the full path name of the folder name in your folder directory. This ability to send mail to files can be used for a variety of purposes, such as maintaining a journal and keeping a record of mail sent to a certain group of users. The second example can be done automatically by including the full pathname of the record file in the **alias** command for the group. Using our previous **alias** example, you might give the command:

    alias project sam sally steve susan /usr/project/mail_record

Then, all mail sent to "project" would be saved on the file ''/usr/project/mail_record'' as well as being sent to the members of the project. This file can be examined using *Mail –f*.

It is sometimes useful to send mail directly to a program, for example one might write a project bill-board program and want to access it using *Mail*. To send messages to the billboard program, one can send mail to the special name 'Ibillboard' for example. *Mail* treats recipient names that begin with a 'I' as a pro-gram to send the mail to. An **alias** can be set up to reference a 'I' prefaced name if desired. *Caveats*: the shell treats 'I' specially, so it must be quoted on the command line. Also, the 'I program' must be presented as a single argument to mail. The safest course is to surround the entire name with double quotes. This also applies to usage in the **alias** command. For example, if we wanted to alias 'rmsgs' to 'rmsgs –s' we would need to say:

    alias rmsgs "I rmsgs -s"

5. Additional features

This section describes some additional commands useful for reading your mail, setting options, and handling lists of messages.

5.1. Message lists

Several *Mail* commands accept a list of messages as an argument. Along with **type** and **delete**, described in section 2, there is the **from** command, which prints the message headers associated with the message list passed to it. The **from** command is particularly useful in conjunction with some of the mes-sage list features described below.

A *message list* consists of a list of message numbers, ranges, and names, separated by spaces or tabs. Message numbers may be either decimal numbers, which directly specify messages, or one of the special characters ''↑'' ''.'' or ''$'' to specify the first relevant, current, or last relevant message, respectively. *Relevant* here means, for most commands ''not deleted'' and ''deleted'' for the **undelete** command.

A range of messages consists of two message numbers (of the form described in the previous para-graph) separated by a dash. Thus, to print the first four messages, use

    type 1–4

and to print all the messages from the current message to the last message, use

    type .–$

A *name* is a user name. The user names given in the message list are collected together and each message selected by other means is checked to make sure it was sent by one of the named users. If the message consists entirely of user names, then every message sent by one of those users that is *relevant* (in the sense described earlier) is selected. Thus, to print every message sent to you by ''root,'' do

    type root

As a shorthand notation, you can specify simply ''*'' to get every *relevant* (same sense) message. Thus,

    type *

prints all undeleted messages,

    delete *

deletes all undeleted messages, and

    undelete *

undeletes all deleted messages.

You can search for the presence of a word in subject lines with **/**. For example, to print the headers of all messages that contain the word "PASCAL," do:

        from /pascal

Note that subject searching ignores upper/lower case differences.

5.2. List of commands

This section describes all the *Mail* commands available when receiving mail.

–   The – command goes to the previous message and prints it. The – command may be given a decimal number *n* as an argument, in which case the *n*th previous message is gone to and printed.

?   Prints a brief summary of commands.

!   Used to preface a command to be executed by the shell.

Print

Like **print**, but also print out ignored header fields. See also **print**, **ignore** and **retain**. **Print** can be abbreviated to **P**.

Reply or **Respond**

Note the capital **R** in the name. Frame a reply to a one or more messages. The reply (or replies if you are using this on multiple messages) will be sent ONLY to the person who sent you the message (respectively, the set of people who sent the messages you are replying to). You can add people using the ~t, ~c and ~b tilde escapes. The subject in your reply is formed by prefacing the subject in the original message with "Re:" unless it already began thus. If the original message included a "reply-to" header field, the reply will go *only* to the recipient named by "reply-to." You type in your message using the same conventions available to you through the **mail** command. The **Reply** command is especially useful for replying to messages that were sent to enormous distribution groups when you really just want to send a message to the originator. Use it often. **Reply** (and **Respond**) can be abbreviated to **R**.

Type

Identical to the **Print** command. **Type** can be abbreviated to **T**.

alias Define a name to stand for a set of other names. This is used when you want to send messages to a certain group of people and want to avoid retyping their names. For example

        alias project john sue willie kathryn

creates an alias *project* which expands to the four people John, Sue, Willie, and Kathryn. If no arguments are given, all currently-defined aliases are printed. If one argument is given, that alias is printed (if it exists). **Alias** can be abbreviated to **a**.

alternates

If you have accounts on several machines, you may find it convenient to use the /usr/lib/aliases on all the machines except one to direct your mail to a single account. The **alternates** command is used to inform *Mail* that each of these other addresses is really *you*. *Alternates* takes a list of user names and remembers that they are all actually you. When you **reply** to messages that were sent to one of these alternate names, *Mail* will not bother to send a copy of the message to this other address (which would simply be directed back to you by the alias mechanism). If *alternates* is given no argument, it lists the current set of alternate names. **Alternates** is usually used in the .mailrc file. **Alternates** can be abbreviated to **alt**.

chdir

The **chdir** command allows you to change your current directory. **Chdir** takes a single argument, which is taken to be the pathname of the directory to change to. If no argument is given, **chdir** changes to your home directory. **Chdir** can be abbreviated to **c**.

copy

The **copy** command does the same thing that **save** does, except that it does not mark the messages it is used on for deletion when you quit. **Copy** can be abbreviated to **co**.

delete

> Deletes a list of messages. Deleted messages can be reclaimed with the **undelete** command. **Delete** can be abbreviated to **d**.

dp or **dt**

> These commands delete the current message and print the next message. They are useful for quickly reading and disposing of mail. If there is no next message, *mail* says "at EOF."

edit To edit individual messages using the text editor, the **edit** command is provided. The **edit** command takes a list of messages as described under the **type** command and processes each by writing it into the file Message*x* where *x* is the message number being edited and executing the text editor on it. When you have edited the message to your satisfaction, write the message out and quit, upon which *Mail* will read the message back and remove the file. **Edit** can be abbreviated to **e**.

else Marks the end of the then-part of an **if** statement and the beginning of the part to take effect if the condition of the **if** statement is false.

endif

> Marks the end of an **if** statement.

exit or **xit**

> Leave *Mail* without updating the system mailbox or the file your were reading. Thus, if you accidentally delete several messages, you can use **exit** to avoid scrambling your mailbox. **Exit** can be abbreviated to **ex** or **x**.

file The same as **folder**. **File** can be abbreviated to **fi**.

folders

> List the names of the folders in your folder directory.

folder

> The **folder** command switches to a new mail file or folder. With no arguments, it tells you which file you are currently reading. If you give it an argument, it will write out changes (such as deletions) you have made in the current file and read the new file. Some special conventions are recognized for the name:

Name	Meaning
#	Previous file read
%	Your system mailbox
%name	*Name*'s system mailbox
&	Your ~/mbox file
+folder	A file in your folder directory

> **Folder** can be abbreviated to **fo**.

from

> The **from** command takes a list of messages and prints out the header lines for each one; hence
>
> > from joe
>
> is the easy way to display all the message headers from "joe." **From** can be abbreviated to **f**.

headers

> When you start up *Mail* to read your mail, it lists the message headers that you have. These headers tell you who each message is from, when they were received, how many lines and characters each message is, and the "Subject:" header field of each message, if present. In addition, *Mail* tags the message header of each message that has been the object of the **preserve** command with a "P." Messages that have been **saved** or **written** are flagged with a "*." Finally, **deleted** messages are not printed at all. If you wish to reprint the current list of message headers, you can do so with the **headers** command. The **headers** command (and thus the initial header listing) only lists the first so many message headers. The number of headers listed depends on the speed of your terminal. This can be overridden by specifying the number of headers you want with the *window* option. *Mail* maintains a notion of the current "window" into your messages for the purposes of printing headers. Use the **z** command to move forward and back a window. You can move *Mail's* notion of the

current window directly to a particular message by using, for example,

> headers 40

to move *Mail's* attention to the messages around message 40. If a "+" argument is given, then the next screenful of message headers is printed, and if a "−" argument is given, the previous screenful of message headers is printed. **Headers** can be abbreviated to **h**.

help   Print a brief and usually out of date help message about the commands in *Mail*. The *man* page for *mail* is usually more up-to-date than either the help message or this manual. It is also a synonym for **?**.

hold   Arrange to hold a list of messages in the system mailbox, instead of moving them to the file *mbox* in your home directory. If you set the binary option *hold*, this will happen by default. It does not override the **delete** command. **Hold** can be abbreviated to **ho**.

if   Commands in your ".mailrc" file can be executed conditionally depending on whether you are sending or receiving mail with the **if** command. For example, you can do:

> if receive
> > *commands...*
> endif

An **else** form is also available:

> if send
> > *commands...*
> else
> > *commands...*
> endif

Note that the only allowed conditions are **receive** and **send**.

ignore

> **N.B.:** *Ignore* has been superseded by *retain*.
>
> Add the list of header fields named to the *ignore list*. Header fields in the ignore list are not printed on your terminal when you print a message. This allows you to suppress printing of certain machine-generated header fields, such as *Via* which are not usually of interest. The **Type** and **Print** commands can be used to print a message in its entirety, including ignored fields. If **ignore** is executed with no arguments, it lists the current set of ignored fields.

list   List the valid *Mail* commands. **List** can be abbreviated to **l**.

mail   Send mail to one or more people. If you have the *ask* option set, *Mail* will prompt you for a subject to your message. Then you can type in your message, using tilde escapes as described in section 4 to edit, print, or modify your message. To signal your satisfaction with the message and send it, type control-d at the beginning of a line, or a . alone on a line if you set the option *dot*. To abort the message, type two interrupt characters (RUBOUT by default) in a row or use the ˜q escape. The **mail** command can be abbreviated to **m**.

mbox

> Indicate that a list of messages be sent to *mbox* in your home directory when you quit. This is the default action for messages if you do *not* have the *hold* option set.

next or **+**

> The **next** command goes to the next message and types it. If given a message list, **next** goes to the first such message and types it. Thus,
>
> > next root
>
> goes to the next message sent by "root" and types it. The **next** command can be abbreviated to simply a newline, which means that one can go to and type a message by simply giving its message number or one of the magic characters "ˆ" "." or "$". Thus,
>
> > .
>
> prints the current message and

4

prints message 4, as described previously. **Next** can be abbreviated to **n**.

preserve
> Same as **hold**. Cause a list of messages to be held in your system mailbox when you quit. **Preserve** can be abbreviated to **pre**.

print
> Print the specified messages. If the **crt** variable is set, messages longer than the number of lines it indicates are paged through the command specified by the **PAGER** variable. The **print** command can be abbreviated to **p**.

quit   Terminates the session, saving all undeleted, unsaved and unwritten messages in the user's *mbox* file in their login directory (messages marked as having been read), preserving all messages marked with **hold** or **preserve** or never referenced in their system mailbox. Any messages that were deleted, saved, written or saved to *mbox* are removed from their system mailbox. If new mail has arrived during the session, the message ''You have new mail'' is given. If given while editing a mailbox file with the −**f** flag, then the edit file is rewritten. A return to the Shell is effected, unless the rewrite of edit file fails, in which case the user can escape with the **exit** command. **Quit** can be abbreviated to **q**.

reply or **respond**
> Frame a reply to a single message. The reply will be sent to the person who sent you the message (to which you are replying), plus all the people who received the original message, except you. You can add people using the ˜**t**, ˜**c** and ˜**b** tilde escapes. The subject in your reply is formed by prefacing the subject in the original message with ''Re:'' unless it already began thus. If the original message included a ''reply-to'' header field, the reply will go *only* to the recipient named by ''reply-to.'' You type in your message using the same conventions available to you through the **mail** command. The **reply** (and **respond**) command can be abbreviated to **r**.

retain
> Add the list of header fields named to the *retained list*. Only the header fields in the retain list are shown on your terminal when you print a message. All other header fields are suppressed. The **Type** and **Print** commands can be used to print a message in its entirety. If **retain** is executed with no arguments, it lists the current set of retained fields.

save   It is often useful to be able to save messages on related topics in a file. The **save** command gives you the ability to do this. The **save** command takes as an argument a list of message numbers, followed by the name of the file in which to save the messages. The messages are appended to the named file, thus allowing one to keep several messages in the file, stored in the order they were put there. The filename in quotes, followed by the line count and character count is echoed on the user's terminal. An example of the **save** command relative to our running example is:

> s 1 2 tuitionmail

Saved messages are not automatically saved in *mbox* at quit time, nor are they selected by the **next** command described above, unless explicitly specified. **Save** can be abbreviated to **s**.

set   Set an option or give an option a value. Used to customize *Mail*. Section 5.3 contains a list of the options. Options can be *binary*, in which case they are *on* or *off*, or *valued*. To set a binary option *option on*, do

> set option

To give the valued option *option* the value *value*, do

> set option=value

There must be no space before or after the ''='' sign. If no arguments are given, all variable values are printed. Several options can be specified in a single **set** command. **Set** can be abbreviated to **se**.

shell   The **shell** command allows you to escape to the shell. **Shell** invokes an interactive shell and allows you to type commands to it. When you leave the shell, you will return to *Mail*. The shell used is a default assumed by *Mail*; you can override this default by setting the valued option ''SHELL,'' eg:

> set SHELL=/bin/csh

Shell can be abbreviated to **sh**.

size Takes a message list and prints out the size in characters of each message.

source

> The **source** command reads *mail* commands from a file. It is useful when you are trying to fix your ''.mailrc'' file and you need to re-read it. **Source** can be abbreviated to **so**.

top The **top** command takes a message list and prints the first five lines of each addressed message. If you wish, you can change the number of lines that **top** prints out by setting the valued option ''top-lines.'' On a CRT terminal,

> set toplines=10

> might be preferred. **Top** can be abbreviated to **to**.

type Same as **print**. Takes a message list and types out each message on the terminal. The **type** command can be abbreviated to **t**.

undelete

> Takes a message list and marks each message as *not* being deleted. **Undelete** can be abbreviated to **u**.

unread

> Takes a message list and marks each message as *not* having been read. **Unread** can be abbreviated to **U**.

unset

> Takes a list of option names and discards their remembered values; the inverse of **set** .

visual

> It is often useful to be able to invoke one of two editors, based on the type of terminal one is using. To invoke a display oriented editor, you can use the **visual** command. The operation of the **visual** command is otherwise identical to that of the **edit** command.

> Both the **edit** and **visual** commands assume some default text editors. These default editors can be overridden by the valued options ''EDITOR'' and ''VISUAL'' for the standard and screen editors. You might want to do:

> set EDITOR=/usr/ucb/ex VISUAL=/usr/ucb/vi

> **Visual** can be abbreviated to **v**.

write

> The **save** command always writes the entire message, including the headers, into the file. If you want to write just the message itself, you can use the **write** command. The **write** command has the same syntax as the **save** command, and can be abbreviated to simply **w**. Thus, we could write the second message by doing:

> w 2 file.c

> As suggested by this example, the **write** command is useful for such tasks as sending and receiving source program text over the message system. The filename in quotes, followed by the line count and character count is echoed on the user's terminal.

z *Mail* presents message headers in windowfuls as described under the **headers** command. You can move *Mail's* attention forward to the next window by giving the

> z+

> command. Analogously, you can move to the previous window with:

> z−

5.3. Custom options

> Throughout this manual, we have seen examples of binary and valued options. This section describes each of the options in alphabetical order, including some that you have not seen yet. To avoid confusion, please note that the options are either all lower case letters or all upper case letters. When I start a sentence such as: ''Ask'' causes *Mail* to prompt you for a subject header, I am only capitalizing ''ask'' as a courtesy to English.

7

EDITOR
> The valued option "EDITOR" defines the pathname of the text editor to be used in the **edit** command and ˜e. If not defined, a standard editor is used.

PAGER
> Pathname of the program to use for paginating output when it exceeds *crt* lines. A default paginator is used if this option is not defined.

SHELL
> The valued option "SHELL" gives the path name of your shell. This shell is used for the **!** command and ˜! escape. In addition, this shell expands file names with shell metacharacters like * and ? in them.

VISUAL
> The valued option "VISUAL" defines the pathname of the screen editor to be used in the **visual** command and ˜v escape. A standard screen editor is used if you do not define one.

append
> The "append" option is binary and causes messages saved in *mbox* to be appended to the end rather than prepended. Normally, *Mail* will put messages in *mbox* in the same order that the system puts messages in your system mailbox. By setting "append," you are requesting that *mbox* be appended to regardless. It is in any event quicker to append.

ask "Ask" is a binary option which causes *Mail* to prompt you for the subject of each message you send. If you respond with simply a newline, no subject field will be sent.

askcc
> "Askcc" is a binary option which causes you to be prompted for additional carbon copy recipients at the end of each message. Responding with a newline shows your satisfaction with the current list.

autoprint
> "Autoprint" is a binary option which causes the **delete** command to behave like **dp** — thus, after deleting a message, the next one will be typed automatically. This is useful when quickly scanning and deleting messages in your mailbox.

crt The valued option is used as a threshold to determine how long a message must be before **PAGER** is used to read it.

debug
> The binary option "debug" causes debugging information to be displayed. Use of this option is the same as using the –**d** command line flag.

dot "Dot" is a binary option which, if set, causes *Mail* to interpret a period alone on a line as the terminator of the message you are sending.

escape
> To allow you to change the escape character used when sending mail, you can set the valued option "escape." Only the first character of the "escape" option is used, and it must be doubled if it is to appear as the first character of a line of your message. If you change your escape character, then ˜ loses all its special meaning, and need no longer be doubled at the beginning of a line.

folder
> The name of the directory to use for storing folders of messages. If this name begins with a '/' *Mail* considers it to be an absolute pathname; otherwise, the folder directory is found relative to your home directory.

hold The binary option "hold" causes messages that have been read but not manually dealt with to be held in the system mailbox. This prevents such messages from being automatically swept into your *mbox* file.

ignore
> The binary option "ignore" causes RUBOUT characters from your terminal to be ignored and echoed as @'s while you are sending mail. RUBOUT characters retain their original meaning in *Mail* command mode. Setting the "ignore" option is equivalent to supplying the –**i** flag on the command line as described in section 6.

ignoreeof

An option related to "dot" is "ignoreeof" which makes *Mail* refuse to accept a control–d as the end of a message. "Ignoreeof" also applies to *Mail* command mode.

keep

The "keep" option causes *Mail* to truncate your system mailbox instead of deleting it when it is empty. This is useful if you elect to protect your mailbox, which you would do with the shell command:

chmod 600 /usr/spool/mail/yourname

where *yourname* is your login name. If you do not do this, anyone can probably read your mail, although people usually don't.

keepsave

When you **save** a message, *Mail* usually discards it when you **quit**. To retain all saved messages, set the "keepsave" option.

metoo

When sending mail to an alias, *Mail* makes sure that if you are included in the alias, that mail will not be sent to you. This is useful if a single alias is being used by all members of the group. If however, you wish to receive a copy of all the messages you send to the alias, you can set the binary option "metoo."

noheader

The binary option "noheader" suppresses the printing of the version and headers when *Mail* is first invoked. Setting this option is the same as using –N on the command line.

nosave

Normally, when you abort a message with two RUBOUTs, *Mail* copies the partial letter to the file "dead.letter" in your home directory. Setting the binary option "nosave" prevents this.

Replyall

Reverses the sense of *reply* and *Reply* commands.

quiet

The binary option "quiet" suppresses the printing of the version when *Mail* is first invoked, as well as printing the for example "Message 4:" from the **type** command.

record

If you love to keep records, then the valued option "record" can be set to the name of a file to save your outgoing mail. Each new message you send is appended to the end of the file.

screen

When *Mail* initially prints the message headers, it determines the number to print by looking at the speed of your terminal. The faster your terminal, the more it prints. The valued option "screen" overrides this calculation and specifies how many message headers you want printed. This number is also used for scrolling with the **z** command.

sendmail

To use an alternate mail delivery system, set the "sendmail" option to the full pathname of the program to use. Note: this is not for everyone! Most people should use the default delivery system.

toplines

The valued option "toplines" defines the number of lines that the "top" command will print out instead of the default five lines.

verbose

The binary option "verbose" causes *Mail* to invoke sendmail with the –v flag, which causes it to go into verbose mode and announce expansion of aliases, etc. Setting the "verbose" option is equivalent to invoking *Mail* with the –v flag as described in section 6.

6. Command line options

This section describes command line options for *Mail* and what they are used for.

7

–N   Suppress the initial printing of headers.

–d   Turn on debugging information. Not of general interest.

–f file

> Show the messages in *file* instead of your system mailbox. If *file* is omitted, *Mail* reads *mbox* in your home directory.

–i   Ignore tty interrupt signals. Useful on noisy phone lines, which generate spurious RUBOUT or DELETE characters. It's usually more effective to change your interrupt character to control–c, for which see the *stty* shell command.

–n   Inhibit reading of /usr/lib/Mail.rc. Not generally useful, since /usr/lib/Mail.rc is usually empty.

–s string

> Used for sending mail. *String* is used as the subject of the message being composed. If *string* contains blanks, you must surround it with quote marks.

–u name

> Read *names's* mail instead of your own. Unwitting others often neglect to protect their mailboxes, but discretion is advised. Essentially, –**u user** is a shorthand way of doing –**f /usr/spool/mail/user**.

–v   Use the –**v** flag when invoking sendmail. This feature may also be enabled by setting the the option "verbose".

The following command line flags are also recognized, but are intended for use by programs invoking *Mail* and not for people.

–T file

> Arrange to print on *file* the contents of the *article-id* fields of all messages that were either read or deleted. –**T** is for the *readnews* program and should NOT be used for reading your mail.

–h number

> Pass on hop count information. *Mail* will take the number, increment it, and pass it with –**h** to the mail delivery system. –**h** only has effect when sending mail and is used for network mail forwarding.

–r name

> Used for network mail forwarding: interpret *name* as the sender of the message. The *name* and –**r** are simply sent along to the mail delivery system. Also, *Mail* will wait for the message to be sent and return the exit status. Also restricts formatting of message.

Note that –**h** and –**r**, which are for network mail forwarding, are not used in practice since mail forwarding is now handled separately. They may disappear soon.

7. Format of messages

This section describes the format of messages. Messages begin with a *from* line, which consists of the word "From" followed by a user name, followed by anything, followed by a date in the format returned by the *ctime* library routine described in section 3 of the Unix Programmer's Manual. A possible *ctime* format date is:

> Tue Dec 1 10:58:23 1981

The *ctime* date may be optionally followed by a single space and a time zone indication, which should be three capital letters, such as PDT.

Following the *from* line are zero or more *header field* lines. Each header field line is of the form:

> name: information

Name can be anything, but only certain header fields are recognized as having any meaning. The recognized header fields are: *article-id, bcc, cc, from, reply-to, sender, subject,* and *to*. Other header fields are also significant to other systems; see, for example, the current Arpanet message standard for much more information on this topic. A header field can be continued onto following lines by making the first character on the following line a space or tab character.

If any headers are present, they must be followed by a blank line. The part that follows is called the *body* of the message, and must be ASCII text, not containing null characters. Each line in the message body must be no longer than 512 characters and terminated with an ASCII newline character. If binary data must be passed through the mail system, it is suggested that this data be encoded in a system which encodes six bits into a printable character (i.e.: uuencode). For example, one could use the upper and lower case letters, the digits, and the characters comma and period to make up the 64 characters. Then, one can send a 16-bit binary number as three characters. These characters should be packed into lines, preferably lines about 70 characters long as long lines are transmitted more efficiently.

The message delivery system always adds a blank line to the end of each message. This blank line must not be deleted.

The UUCP message delivery system sometimes adds a blank line to the end of a message each time it is forwarded through a machine.

It should be noted that some network transport protocols enforce limits to the lengths of messages.

8. Glossary

This section contains the definitions of a few phrases peculiar to *Mail*.

alias   An alternative name for a person or list of people.

flag   An option, given on the command line of *Mail*, prefaced with a −. For example, −f is a flag.

header field
At the beginning of a message, a line which contains information that is part of the structure of the message. Popular header fields include *to*, *cc*, and *subject*.

mail   A collection of messages. Often used in the phrase, ''Have you read your mail?''

mailbox
The place where your mail is stored, typically in the directory /usr/spool/mail.

message
A single letter from someone, initially stored in your *mailbox*.

message list
A string used in *Mail* command mode to describe a sequence of messages.

option
A piece of special purpose information used to tailor *Mail* to your taste. Options are specified with the **set** command.

9. Summary of commands, options, and escapes

This section gives a quick summary of the *Mail* commands, binary and valued options, and tilde escapes.

The following table describes the commands:

Command	*Description*
+	Same as **next**
-	Back up to previous message
?	Print brief summary of *Mail* commands
!	Single command escape to shell
Print	Type message with ignored fields
Reply	Reply to author of message only
Respond	Same as **Reply**
Type	Type message with ignored fields
alias	Define an alias as a set of user names
alternates	List other names you are known by
chdir	Change working directory, home by default
copy	Copy a message to a file or folder

7

delete	Delete a list of messages
dp	Same as **dt**
dt	Delete current message, type next message
edit	Edit a list of messages
else	Start of else part of conditional; see **if**
endif	End of conditional statement; see **if**
exit	Leave mail without changing anything
file	Interrogate/change current mail file
folder	Same as **file**
folders	List the folders in your folder directory
from	List headers of a list of messages
headers	List current window of messages
help	Same as **?**
hold	Same as **preserve**
if	Conditional execution of *Mail* commands
ignore	Set/examine list of ignored header fields
list	List valid *Mail* commands
local	List other names for the local host
mail	Send mail to specified names
mbox	Arrange to save a list of messages in *mbox*
next	Go to next message and type it
preserve	Arrange to leave list of messages in system mailbox
print	Print messages
quit	Leave *Mail*; update system mailbox, *mbox* as appropriate
reply	Compose a reply to a message
respond	Same as **reply**
retain	Supersedes **ignore**
save	Append messages, headers included, on a file
set	Set binary or valued options
shell	Invoke an interactive shell
size	Prints out size of message list
source	Read *mail* commands from a file
top	Print first so many (5 by default) lines of list of messages
type	Same as **print**
undelete	Undelete list of messages
unread	Marks list of messages as not been read
unset	Undo the operation of a **set**
visual	Invoke visual editor on a list of messages
write	Append messages to a file, don't include headers
xit	Same as **exit**
z	Scroll to next/previous screenful of headers

7

The following table describes the options. Each option is shown as being either a binary or valued option.

Option	Type	Description
EDITOR	*valued*	Pathname of editor for ˜e and **edit**
PAGER	*valued*	Pathname of paginator for **Print, print, Type** and **type**
SHELL	*valued*	Pathname of shell for **shell**, ˜! and **!**
VISUAL	*valued*	Pathname of screen editor for ˜v, **visual**
append	*binary*	Always append messages to end of *mbox*
ask	*binary*	Prompt user for Subject: field when sending
askcc	*binary*	Prompt user for additional Cc's at end of message
autoprint	*binary*	Print next message after **delete**
crt	*valued*	Minimum number of lines before using **PAGER**
debug	*binary*	Print out debugging information
dot	*binary*	Accept . alone on line to terminate message input
escape	*valued*	Escape character to be used instead of ˜
folder	*valued*	Directory to store folders in
hold	*binary*	Hold messages in system mailbox by default
ignore	*binary*	Ignore RUBOUT while sending mail
ignoreeof	*binary*	Don't terminate letters/command input with ↑**D**
keep	*binary*	Don't unlink system mailbox when empty
keepsave	*binary*	Don't delete **save**d messages by default
metoo	*binary*	Include sending user in aliases
noheader	*binary*	Suppress initial printing of version and headers
nosave	*binary*	Don't save partial letter in *dead.letter*
quiet	*binary*	Suppress printing of *Mail* version and message numbers
record	*valued*	File to save all outgoing mail in
screen	*valued*	Size of window of message headers for **z**, etc.
sendmail	*valued*	Choose alternate mail delivery system
toplines	*valued*	Number of lines to print in **top**
verbose	*binary*	Invoke sendmail with the −**v** flag

The following table summarizes the tilde escapes available while sending mail.

Escape	Arguments	Description
˜!	*command*	Execute shell command
˜b	*name ...*	Add names to "blind" Cc: list
˜c	*name ...*	Add names to Cc: field
˜d		Read *dead.letter* into message
˜e		Invoke text editor on partial message
˜f	*messages*	Read named messages
˜h		Edit the header fields
˜m	*messages*	Read named messages, right shift by tab
˜p		Print message entered so far
˜q		Abort entry of letter; like RUBOUT
˜r	*filename*	Read file into message
˜s	*string*	Set Subject: field to *string*
˜t	*name ...*	Add names to To: field
˜v		Invoke screen editor on message
˜w	*filename*	Write message on file
˜|	*command*	Pipe message through *command*
˜:	*Mail command*	Execute a *Mail* command
˜˜	*string*	Quote a ˜ in front of *string*

7

The following table shows the command line flags that *Mail* accepts:

Flag	Description
−N	Suppress the initial printing of headers
−T *file*	Article-id's of read/deleted messages to *file*
−d	Turn on debugging
−f *file*	Show messages in *file* or 7/*mbox*
−h *number*	Pass on hop count for mail forwarding
−i	Ignore tty interrupt signals
−n	Inhibit reading of /usr/lib/Mail.rc
−r *name*	Pass on *name* for mail forwarding
−s *string*	Use *string* as subject in outgoing mail
−u *name*	Read *name's* mail instead of your own
−v	Invoke sendmail with the −**v** flag

Notes: −**T**, −**d**, −**h**, and −**r** are not for human use.

7

THE RAND MH MESSAGE HANDLING SYSTEM: USER'S MANUAL

UCI Version

Marshall T. Rose
John L. Romine

Based on the original manual by
Borden, Gaines, and Shapiro

May 18, 1994
6.8.3 #6[UCI]

8

CONTENTS

READ THIS i

FOREWORD iii

ACKNOWLEDGMENTS iv

PREFACE v

SUMMARY vi

Section

1. INTRODUCTION 1

2. OVERVIEW 3

3. TUTORIAL 5

4. DETAILED DESCRIPTION 7

      THE USER PROFILE 7

      MESSAGE NAMING 9

      OTHER MH CONVENTIONS 10

      MH COMMANDS 11

              ALI 12

              ANNO 13

              BBC 14

              BBOARDS 16

              BURST 18

              COMP 20

              DIST 22

              FOLDER 24

              FORW 27

              INC 31

              MARK 33

              MHL 35

              MHMAIL 39

               MHN 40

              MHOOK 54

               MHPARAM 56

               MHPATH 57

               MSGCHK 59

               MSH 60

8

NEXT 63

PACKF 64

PICK 65

PREV 69

PROMPTER 70

RCVSTORE 72

REFILE 74

REPL 76

RMF 79

RMM 80

SCAN 81

SEND 83

SHOW 86

SLOCAL 88

SORTM 92

VMH 94

WHATNOW 96

WHOM 98

MORE DETAILS 99

MH-ALIAS 100

MH-FORMAT 103

MH-MAIL 110

MH-PROFILE 113

MH-SEQUENCE 119

AP 122

CONFLICT 124

DP 125

FMTDUMP 126

INSTALL-MH 127

POST 128

5. REPORTING PROBLEMS 130

6. ADVANCED FEATURES 131

USER–DEFINED SEQUENCES 131

Pick and User–Defined Sequences 131

Mark and User–Defined Sequences 132

Public and Private User–Defined Sequences 132

Sequence Negation 132

The Previous Sequence 133

The Unseen Sequence 133

COMPOSITION OF MAIL 134

The Draft Folder 134

What Happens if the Draft Exists 135

The Push Option at What now? Level 136

8

Options at What now? Level 136

Digests 136

FOLDER HANDLING 137

Relative Folder Addressing 138

The Folder–Stack 138

Appendix

A. Command Summary 139

B. Message Name BNF 143

REFERENCES 144

8

READ THIS

Although the *MH* system was originally developed by the RAND Corporation, and is now in the public domain, the RAND Corporation assumes no responsibility for *MH* or this particular version of *MH*.

In addition, the Regents of the University of California issue the following **disclaimer** in regard to the UCI version of *MH*:

> "Although each program has been tested by its contributor, no warranty, express or implied, is made by the contributor or the University of California, as to the accuracy and functioning of the program and related program material, nor shall the fact of distribution constitute any such warranty, and no responsibility is assumed by the contributor or the University of California in connection herewith."

This version of *MH* is in the public domain, and as such, there are no real restrictions on its use. The *MH* source code and documentation have no licensing restrictions whatsoever. As a courtesy, the authors ask only that you provide appropriate credit to the RAND Corporation and the University of California for having developed the software.

MH is a software package that is supported neither by the RAND Corporation nor the University of California. However, since we do use the software ourselves and plan to continue using (and improving) *MH*, bug reports and their associated fixes should be reported back to us so that we may include them in future releases. The current computer mailbox for *MH* is **Bug–MH@ICS.UCI.EDU** (in the ARPA Internet), and **...!ucbvax!ucivax!bug–mh** (UUCP). Presently, there are two Internet discussion groups, **MH–Users@ICS.UCI.EDU** and **MH–Workers@ICS.UCI.EDU**. **MH–Workers** is for people discussing code changes to *MH*. **MH-Users** is for general discussion about how to use *MH*. **MH–Users** is bi-directionally gatewayed into USENET as **comp.mail.mh**.

HOW TO GET MH

Since you probably already have *MH*, you may not need to read this unless you suspect you have an old version. There are two ways to get the latest release:

1. If you can FTP to the ARPA Internet, use anonymous FTP to ics.uci.edu [128.195.1.1] and retrieve the file pub/mh/mh-6.8.tar.Z. This is a tar image after being run through the compress program (approximately 1.8MB). There should also be a **README** file in that directory which tells what the current release of *MH* is, and how to get updates.

This tar file is also available on louie.udel.edu [128.175.1.3] in portal/mh-6.8.tar.Z. You may also find MH on various other hosts; to make sure you get the latest version and don't waste your time re-fixing bugs, it's best to get it from either ics.uci.edu or louie.udel.edu.

2. You can send $75 US to the address below. This covers the cost of a 6250 BPI 9-track magtape, handling, and shipping. In addition, you'll get a laser-printed hard-copy of the entire MH documentation set. Be sure to include your USPS address with your check. Checks must be drawn on U.S. funds and should be made payable to:

Regents of the University of California

8

The distribution address is:

>   Computing Support Group
>   Attn: MH distribution
>   Department of Information and Computer Science
>   University of California, Irvine
>   Irvine, CA 92717
>   714/856-7554

If you just want the hard-copies of the documentation, you still have to pay the $75. The tar image has the documentation source (the manual is in roff format, but the rest are in TeX format). Postscript formatted versions of the TeX papers are available, as are crude tty-conversions of those papers.

8

FOREWORD

This document describes the RAND *MH* Message Handling System. Its primary purpose is to serve as a user's manual. It has been heavily based on a previous version of the manual, prepared by Bruce Borden, Stockton Gaines, and Norman Shapiro.

MH is a particularly novel system, and thus it is often more prone to change than other pieces of production software. As such, some specific points in this manual may not be correct in the future. In all cases, the on–line sections of this manual, available through the UNIX[1] *man* command, should present the most current information.

When reading this document as a user's manual, certain sections are more interesting than others. The Preface and Summary are not particularly interesting to those interested in learning *MH*. The Introduction is slightly more interesting, as it touches upon the organization of the remainder of this document. The most useful sections are the Overview, Tutorial, and Detailed Description. The Overview should be read by all *MH* users, regardless of their expertise (beginning, novice, advanced, or hacker). The Tutorial should be read by all beginning and novice *MH* users, as it presents a nice description of the *MH* system. The Detailed Description should be read by the day–to–day user of *MH*, as it spells out all of the realities of the *MH* system. The Advanced Features section discusses some powerful *MH* capabilities for advanced users. Appendix A is particularly useful for novices, as it summarizes the invocation syntax of all the *MH* commands.

There are also several other documents which may be useful to you: *The RAND MH Message Handling System: Tutorial*, which is a tutorial for *MH*; *The RAND MH Message Handling System: The UCI BBoards Facility*, which describes the BBoards handling under *MH*; *MH.5: How to process 200 messages a day and still get some real work done*, which was presented at the 1985 Summer Usenix Conference and Exhibition in Portland, Oregon; *MH: A Multifarious User Agent*, which has been accepted for publication by Computer Networks; *MZnet: Mail Service for Personal Micro–Computer Systems*, which was presented at the First International Symposium on Computer Message Systems in Nottingham, U.K.; and, *Design of the TTI Prototype Trusted Mail Agent*, which describes a proprietary "trusted" mail system built on *MH*. There are also documents, mostly specific to U.C. Irvine which you may find interesting: *MH for Beginners*, and *MH for MM Users*. All of these documents exist in the *mh.6* distribution sent to your site. There's also a document, *Changes to the RAND MH Message Handling System: MH.6*, which describes user–visible changes made to *MH* since the last major release.

This manual is very large, as it describes a large, powerful system in gruesome detail. The important thing to remember is:

DON'T PANIC[2]

As explained in the tutorial, you really need to know only 5 commands to handle most of your mail.

Very advanced users may wish to consult *The RAND MH Message Handling System: Administrator's Guide*, which is also present in the *mh.6* distribution sent to your site.

---

[1] UNIX is a trademark of AT&T Bell Laboratories.

[2] Note the large, *friendly* letters.

8

ACKNOWLEDGMENTS

The *MH* system described herein is based on the original RAND *MH* system. It has been extensively developed (perhaps too much so) by Marshall T. Rose and John L. Romine at the University of California, Irvine. Einar A. Stefferud, Jerry N. Sweet, and Terry P. Domae provided numerous suggestions to improve the UCI version of *MH*. Of course, a large number of people have helped *MH* along. The list of ''*MH* immortals'' is too long to list here. However, Van Jacobson deserves a special acknowledgement for his tireless work in improving the performance of *MH*. Some programs have been speeded-up by a factor of 10 or 20. All of users of *MH*, everywhere, owe a special thanks to Van. For this release, numerous *MH–Workers* sent in fixes and other changes. A handful of courageous *MH–Workers* volunteered to beta–test these changes; their help is particularly appreciated.

This manual is based on the original *MH* manual written at RAND by Bruce Borden, Stockton Gaines, and Norman Shapiro.

PREFACE

This report describes a system for dealing with messages transmitted on a computer. Such messages might originate with other users of the same computer or might come from an outside source through a network to which the user's computer is connected. Such computer-based message systems are becoming increasingly widely used, both within and outside the Department of Defense.

The message handling system *MH* was developed for two reasons. One was to investigate some research ideas concerning how a message system might take advantage of the architecture of the UNIX time-sharing operating system for Digital Equipment Corporation PDP-11 and VAX computers, and the special features of UNIX's command-level interface with the user (the "shell"). The other reason was to provide a better and more adaptable base than that of conventional designs on which to build a command and control message system. The effort has succeeded in both regards, although this report mainly describes the message system itself and how it fits in with UNIX.

The present report should be of interest to three groups of readers. First, it is a complete reference manual for the users of *MH*. Second, it should be of interest to those who have a general knowledge of computer-based message systems, both in civilian and military applications. Finally, it should be of interest to those who build large subsystems that interface with users, since it illustrates a new approach to such interfaces.

The original *MH* system was developed by Bruce Borden, using an approach suggested by Stockton Gaines and Norman Shapiro. Valuable assistance was provided by Phyllis Kantar in the later stages of the system's implementation. Several colleagues contributed to the ideas included in this system, particularly Robert Anderson and David Crocker. In addition, valuable experience in message systems, and a valuable source of ideas, was available to us in the form of a previous message system for UNIX called MS, designed at RAND by David Crocker.

This report was originally prepared as part of the RAND project entitled "Data Automation Research", sponsored by Project AIR FORCE.

8

SUMMARY

Electronic communication of text messages is becoming commonplace. Computer-based message systems–software packages that provide tools for dealing with messages–are used in many contexts. In particular, message systems are becoming increasingly important in command and control and intelligence applications.

This report describes a message handling system called *MH*. This system provides the user with tools to compose, send, receive, store, retrieve, forward, and reply to messages. *MH* has been built on the UNIX time-sharing system, a popular operating system developed for the DEC PDP-11 and VAX classes of computers.

A complete description of *MH* is given for users of the system. For those who do not intend to use the system, this description gives a general idea of what a message system is like. The system involves some new ideas about how large subsystems can be constructed.

The interesting and unusual features of *MH* include the following: The user command interface to *MH* is the UNIX "shell" (the standard UNIX command interpreter). Each separable component of message handling, such as message composition or message display, is a separate command. Each program is driven from and updates a private user environment, which is stored as a file between program invocations. This private environment also contains information to "custom tailor" *MH* to the individual's tastes. *MH* stores each message as a separate file under UNIX, and it utilizes the tree-structured UNIX file system to organize groups of files within separate directories or "folders". All of the UNIX facilities for dealing with files and directories, such as renaming, copying, deleting, cataloging, off-line printing, etc., are applicable to messages and directories of messages (folders). Thus, important capabilities needed in a message system are available in *MH* without the need (often seen in other message systems) for code that duplicates the facilities of the supporting operating system. It also allows users familiar with the shell to use *MH* with minimal effort.

1. INTRODUCTION

Although people can travel cross-country in hours and can reach others by telephone in seconds, communications still depend heavily upon paper, most of which is distributed through the mails.

There are several major reasons for this continued dependence on written documents. First, a written document may be proofread and corrected prior to its distribution, giving the author complete control over his words. Thus, a written document is better than a telephone conversation in this respect. Second, a carefully written document is far less likely to be misinterpreted or poorly translated than a phone conversation. Third, a signature offers reasonable verification of authorship, which cannot be provided with media such as telegrams.

However, the need for <u>fast</u>, accurate, and reproducible document distribution is obvious. One solution in widespread use is the telefax. Another that is rapidly gaining popularity is electronic mail. Electronic mail is similar to telefax in that the data to be sent are digitized, transmitted via phone lines, and turned back into a document at the receiver. The advantage of electronic mail is in its compression factor. Whereas a telefax must scan a page in very fine lines and send all of the black and white information, electronic mail assigns characters fixed codes which can be transmitted as a few bits of information. Telefax presently has the advantage of being able to transmit an arbitrary page, including pictures, but electronic mail is beginning to deal with this problem. Electronic mail also integrates well with current directions in office automation, allowing documents prepared with sophisticated equipment at one site to be quickly transferred and printed at another site.

Currently, most electronic mail is intraorganizational, with mail transfer remaining within one computer. As computer networking becomes more common, however, it is becoming more feasible to communicate with anyone whose computer can be linked to your own via a network.

The pioneering efforts on general-purpose electronic mail were by organizations using the DoD ARPAnet[1]. The capability to send messages between computers existed before the ARPAnet was developed, but it was used only in limited ways. With the advent of the ARPAnet, tools began to be developed which made it convenient for individuals or organizations to distribute messages over broad geographic areas, using diverse computer facilities. The interest and activity in message systems has now reached such proportions that steps have been taken within the DoD to coordinate and unify the development of military message systems. The use of electronic mail is expected to increase dramatically in the next few years. The utility of such systems in the command and control and intelligence environments is clear, and applications in these areas will probably lead the way. As the costs for sending and handling electronic messages continue their rapid decrease, such uses can be expected to spread rapidly into other areas and, of course, will not be limited to the DoD.

A message system provides tools that help users (individuals or organizations) deal with messages in various ways. Messages must be composed, sent, received, stored, retrieved, forwarded, and replied to. Today's best interactive computer systems provide a variety of word-processing and information handling capabilities. The message handling facilities should be well integrated with the rest of the system, so as to be a graceful extension of overall system capability.

The message system described in this report, *MH*, provides most of the features that can be found in other message systems and also incorporates some new ones. It has been built on the UNIX time-sharing system[2], a popular operating system for the DEC PDP-11[1] and

8

VAX-11 classes of computers. A "secure" operating system similar to UNIX is currently being developed[3], and that system will also run *MH*.

This report provides a complete description of *MH* and thus may serve as a user's manual, although parts of the report will be of interest to non-users as well. Sections 2 and 3, the Overview and Tutorial, present the key ideas of *MH* and will give those not familiar with message systems an idea of what such systems are like.

MH consists of a set of commands which use some special files and conventions. The final section is divided into three parts. The first part covers the information a user needs to know in addition to the commands. Then, each of the *MH* commands is described in detail. Finally, other obscure details are revealed. A summary of the commands is given in Appendix A, and the syntax of message sequences is given in Appendix B.

A novel approach has been taken in the design of *MH*. Instead of creating a large sub-system that appears as a single command to the user (such as MS[4]), *MH* is a collection of separate commands which are run as separate programs. The file and directory system of UNIX are used directly. Messages are stored as individual files (datasets), and collections of them are grouped into directories. In contrast, most other message systems store messages in a complicated data structure within a monolithic file. With the *MH* approach, UNIX commands can be interleaved with commands invoking the functions of the message handler. Conversely, existing UNIX commands can be used in connection with messages. For example, all the usual UNIX editing, text-formatting, and printing facilities can be applied directly to individual messages. MH, therefore, consists of a relatively small amount of new code; it makes extensive use of other UNIX software to provide the capabilities found in other message systems.

---

[1] PDP and VAX are trademarks of Digital Equipment Corporation.

8

2. OVERVIEW

There are three main aspects of *MH* : the way messages are stored (the message database), the user's profile (which directs how certain actions of the message handler take place), and the commands for dealing with messages.

Under *MH*, each message is stored as a separate file. A user can take any action with a message that he could with an ordinary file in UNIX. A UNIX directory in which messages are stored is called a folder. Each folder contains some standard entries to support the message-handling functions. The messages in a folder have numerical names. These folders (directories) are entries in a particular directory path, described in the user profile, through which *MH* can find message folders. Using the UNIX "link" facility, it is possible for one copy of a message to be "filed" in more than one folder, providing a message index facility. Also, using the UNIX tree-structured file system, it is possible to have a folder within a folder, nested arbitrarily deep, and have the full power of the *MH* commands available.

Each user of *MH* has a user profile, a file in his **$HOME** (initial login) directory called *.mh_profile*. This profile contains several pieces of information used by the *MH* commands: a path name to the directory that contains the message folders and parameters that tailor *MH* commands to the individual user's requirements. There is also another file, called the user context, which contains information concerning which folder the user last referenced (the "current" folder). It also contains most of the necessary state information concerning how the user is dealing with his messages, enabling *MH* to be implemented as a set of individual UNIX commands, in contrast to the usual approach of a monolithic subsystem.

In *MH*, incoming mail is appended to the end of a file in a system spooling area for the user. This area is called the mail drop directory, and the file is called the user's mail drop. Normally when the user logins in, s/he is informed of new mail (or the *MH* program *msgchk* may be run). The user adds the new messages to his/her collection of *MH* messages by invoking the command *inc*. The *inc* (incorporate) command adds the new messages to a folder called "inbox", assigning them names which are consecutive integers starting with the next highest integer available in inbox. *inc* also produces a *scan* summary of the messages thus incorporated. A folder can be compacted into a single file, for easy storage, by using the *packf* command. Also, messages within a folder can be sorted by date and time with the *sortm* command.

There are four commands for examining the messages in a folder: *show*, *prev*, *next*, and *scan*. The *show* command displays a message in a folder, *prev* displays the message preceding the current message, and *next* displays the message following the current message. *MH* lets the user choose the program that displays individual messages. A special program, *mhl*, can be used to display messages according to the user's preferences. The *scan* command summarizes the messages in a folder, normally producing one line per message, showing who the message is from, the date, the subject, etc.

The user may move a message from one folder to another with the command *refile*. Messages may be removed from a folder by means of the command *rmm*. In addition, a user may query what the current folder is and may specify that a new folder become the current folder, through the command *folder*. All folders may be summarized with the *folders* command. A message folder (or subfolder) may be removed by means of the command *rmf*.

A set of messages based on content may be selected by use of the command *pick*. This command searches through messages in a folder and selects those that match a given set of criteria. These messages are then bound to a "sequence" name for use with other *MH* commands. The *mark* command manipulates these sequences.

There are five commands enabling the user to create new messages and send them: *comp, dist, forw, repl,* and *send.* The *comp* command provides the facility for the user to compose a new message; *dist* redistributes mail to additional addressees; *forw* enables the user to forward messages; and *repl* facilitates the generation of a reply to an incoming message. The last three commands may optionally annotate the original message. Messages may be arbitrarily annotated with the *anno* command. Once a draft has been constructed by one of the four above composition programs, a user–specifiable program is run to query the user as to the disposition of the draft prior to sending. *MH* provides the simple *whatnow* program to start users off. If a message is not sent directly by one of these commands, it may be sent at a later time using the command *send.* *MH* allows the use of any UNIX editor when composing a message. For rapid entry, a special editor, *prompter*, is provided. For programs, a special mail-sending program, *mhmail*, is provided.

MH supports a personal aliasing facility which gives users the capability to considerably shorten address typein and use meaningful names for addresses. The *ali* program can be used to query *MH* as to the expansion of a list of aliases. After composing a message, but prior to sending, the *whom* command can be used to determine exactly who a message would go to.

MH provides a natural interface for telling the user's shell the names of *MH* messages and folders. The *mhpath* program achieves this capability.

Finally, *MH* supports the UCI BBoards facility. *bbc* can be used to query the status of a group of BBoards, while *msh* can be used to read them. The *burst* command can be used to "shred" digests of messages into individual messages.

All of the elements summarized above are described in more detail in the following sections. Many of the normal facilities of UNIX provide additional capabilities for dealing with messages in various ways. For example, it is possible to print messages on the line-printer without requiring any additional code within *MH* . Using standard UNIX facilities, any terminal output can be redirected to a file for repeated or future viewing. In general, the flexibility and capabilities of the UNIX interface with the user are preserved as a result of the integration of *MH* into the UNIX structure.

8

3. TUTORIAL

This tutorial provides a brief introduction to the *MH* commands. It should be sufficient to allow the user to read his mail, do some simple manipulations of it, and create and send messages.

A message has two major pieces: the header and the body. The body consists of the text of the message (whatever you care to type in). It follows the header and is separated from it by an empty line. (When you compose a message, the form that appears on your terminal shows a line of dashes after the header. This is for convenience and is replaced by an empty line when the message is sent.) The header is composed of several components, including the subject of the message and the person to whom it is addressed. Each component starts with a name and a colon; components must not start with a blank. The text of the component may take more than one line, but each continuation line must start with a blank. Messages typically have "To:", "cc:", and "Subject:" components. When composing a message, you should include the "To:" and "Subject:" components; the "cc:" (for people you want to send copies to) is not necessary.

The basic *MH* commands are *inc*, *scan*, *show*, *next*, *prev*, *rmm*, *comp*, and *repl*. These are described below.

inc

When you get the message "You have mail", type the command *inc*. You will get a "scan listing" such as:

    7+   7/13 Cas   revival of measurement work
    8   10/ 9 Norm   NBS people and publications
    9   11/26 To:norm question «Are there any functions

This shows the messages you received since the last time you executed this command (*inc* adds these new messages to your inbox folder). You can see this list again, plus a list of any other messages you have, by using the *scan* command.

scan

The scan listing shows the message number, followed by the date and the sender. (If you are the sender, the addressee in the "To:" component is displayed. You may send yourself a message by including your name among the "To:" or "cc:" addressees.) It also shows the message's subject; if the subject is short, the first part of the body of the message is included after the characters «.

show

This command shows the current message, that is, the first one of the new messages after an *inc*. If the message is not specified by name (number), it is generally the last message referred to by an *MH* command. For example,

    show 5   will show message 5.

You can use the show command to copy a message or print a message.

show > *x* will copy the message to file x.
show | *lpr* will print the message, using the *lpr* command.
next   will show the message that follows the current message.
prev   will show the message previous to the current message.
rmm   will remove the current message.
rmm 3   will remove message 3.

comp

   The *comp* command puts you in the editor to write or edit a message. Fill in or delete the "To:", "cc:", and "Subject:" fields, as appropriate, and type the body of the message. Then exit normally from the editor. You will be asked "What now?". Type a carriage return to see the options. Typing **send** will cause the message to be sent; typing **quit** will cause an exit from *comp*, with the message draft saved.

   If you quit without sending the message, it will be saved in a file called <name>/Mail/draft (where <name> is your **$HOME** directory). You can resume editing the message later with "comp −use"; or you can send the message later, using the *send* command.

comp −editor prompter

   This command uses a different editor and is useful for preparing "quick and dirty" messages. It prompts you for each component of the header. Type the information for that component, or type a carriage return to omit the component. After that, type the body of the message. Backspacing is the only form of editing allowed with this editor. When the body is complete, type a carriage return followed by <EOT> (usually <CTRL-D>). This completes the initial preparation of the message; from then on, use the same procedures as with *comp* (above).

repl
repl n

   This command makes up an initial message form with a header that is appropriate for replying to an existing message. The message being answered is the current message if no message number is mentioned, or n if a number is specified. After the header is completed, you can finish the message as in *comp* (above).

   This is enough information to get you going using *MH*. There are more commands, and the commands described here have more features. Subsequent sections explain *MH* in complete detail. The system is quite powerful if you want to use its sophisticated features, but the foregoing commands suffice for sending and receiving messages.

   There are numerous additional capabilities you may wish to explore. For example, the *pick* command will select a subset of messages based on specified criteria such as sender and/or subject. Groups of messages may be designated, as described in Sec. IV, under **Message Naming**. The file *.mh_profile* can be used to tailor your use of the message system to your needs and preferences, as described in Sec. IV, under **The User Profile**. In general, you may learn additional features of the system selectively, according to your requirements, by studying the relevant sections of this manual. There is no need to learn all the details of the system at once.

8

4. DETAILED DESCRIPTION

This section describes the *MH* system in detail, including the components of the user profile, the conventions for message naming, and some of the other *MH* conventions. Readers who are generally familiar with computer systems will be able to follow the principal ideas, although some details may be meaningful only to those familiar with UNIX.

THE USER PROFILE

The first time an *MH* command is issued by a new user, the system prompts for a "Path" and creates an *MH* "profile".

Each *MH* user has a profile which contains tailoring information for each individual program. Other profile entries control the *MH* path (where folders and special files are kept), folder and message protections, editor selection, and default arguments for each *MH* program. Each user of *MH* also has a context file which contains current state information for the *MH* package (the location of the context file is kept in the user's *MH* directory, or may be named in the user profile). When a folder becomes the current folder, it is recorded in the user's context. (Other state information is kept in the context file, see the manual entry for *mh–profile* (5) for more details.) In general, the term "profile entry" refer to entries in either the profile or context file. Users of *MH* needn't worry about the distinction, *MH* handles these things automatically.

The *MH* profile is stored in the file *.mh_profile* in the user's **$HOME** directory[1]. It has the format of a message without any body. That is, each profile entry is on one line, with a keyword followed by a colon (:) followed by text particular to the keyword.
⇒ *This file must not have blank lines.*
The keywords may have any combination of upper and lower case. (See the information of *mh–mail* later on in this manual for a description of message formats.)

For the average *MH* user, the only profile entry of importance is "Path". Path specifies a directory in which *MH* folders and certain files such as "draft" are found. The argument to this keyword must be a legal UNIX path that names an existing directory. If this path is not absolute (i.e., does not begin with a **/**), it will be presumed to start from the user's **$HOME** directory. All folder and message references within *MH* will relate to this path unless full path names are used.

Message protection defaults to 644, and folder protection to 711. These may be changed by profile entries "Msg-Protect" and "Folder-Protect", respectively. The argument to these keywords is an octal number which is used as the UNIX file mode[2].

When an *MH* program starts running, it looks through the user's profile for an entry with a keyword matching the program's name. For example, when *comp* is run, it looks for a "comp" profile entry. If one is found, the text of the profile entry is used as the default switch setting until all defaults are overridden by explicit switches passed to the program as arguments. Thus the profile entry "comp: –form standard.list" would direct *comp* to use the file "standard.list" as the message skeleton. If an explicit form switch is given to the *comp* command, it will override the switch obtained from the profile.

---

[1] By defining the envariable **$MH**, you can specify an alternate profile to be used by *MH* commands.

[2] See *chmod* (1) in the *UNIX Programmer's Manual* [5].

In UNIX, a program may exist under several names, either by linking or aliasing. The actual invocation name is used by an *MH* program when scanning for its profile defaults[3]. Thus, each *MH* program may have several names by which it can be invoked, and each name may have a different set of default switches. For example, if *comp* is invoked by the name *icomp*, the profile entry ''icomp'' will control the default switches for this invocation of the *comp* program. This provides a powerful definitional facility for commonly used switch settings.

The default editor for editing within *comp*, *repl*, *forw*, and *dist*, is usually *prompter*, but might be something else at your site, such as */usr/ucb/ex* or */bin/e*. A different editor may be used by specifying the profile entry ''Editor: ''. The argument to ''Editor'' is the name of an executable program or shell command file which can be found via the user's $PATH defined search path, excluding the current directory. The ''Editor:'' profile specification may in turn be overridden by a '–editor <editor>' profile switch associated with *comp*, *repl*, *forw*, or *dist*. Finally, an explicit editor switch specified with any of these four commands will have ultimate precedence.

During message composition, more than one editor may be used. For example, one editor (such as *prompter*) may be used initially, and a second editor may be invoked later to revise the message being composed (see the discussion of *comp* in Section 5 for details). A profile entry ''<lasteditor>–next: <editor>'' specifies the name of the editor to be used after a particular editor. Thus ''comp: –e prompter'' causes the initial text to be collected by *prompter*, and the profile entry ''prompter–next: ed'' names ed as the editor to be invoked for the next round of editing.

Some of the *MH* commands, such as *show*, can be used on message folders owned by others, if those folders are readable. However, you cannot write in someone else's folder. All the *MH* command actions not requiring write permission may be used with a ''read-only'' folder.

Table 1 lists examples of some of the currently defined profile entries, typical arguments, and the programs that reference the entries.

---

[3] Unfortunately, the shell does not preserve aliasing information when calling a program, hence if a program is invoked by an alias different than its name, the program will examine the profile entry for it's name, not the alias that the user invoked it as. The correct solution is to create a (soft) link in your *$HOME/bin* directory to the *MH* program of your choice. By giving this link a different name, you can use an alternate set of defaults for the command.

8

Table 1

PROFILE COMPONENTS

| | *MH* Programs that |
Keyword and Argument	use Component
Path: Mail	All
Current-Folder: inbox	Most
Editor: /usr/ucb/ex	*comp, dist, forw, repl*
Inbox: inbox	*inc, rmf*
Msg–Protect: 644	*inc*
Folder–Protect: 711	*inc, pick, refile*
<program>: default switches	All
prompter–next: ed	*comp, dist, forw, repl*

Path <u>should</u> be present. Current–Folder is maintained automatically by many *MH* commands (see the **Context** sections of the individual commands in Sec. IV). All other entries are optional, defaulting to the values described above.

MESSAGE NAMING

Messages may be referred to explicitly or implicitly when using *MH* commands. A formal syntax of message names is given in Appendix B, but the following description should be sufficient for most *MH* users. Some details of message naming that apply only to certain commands are included in the description of those commands.

Most of the *MH* commands accept arguments specifying one or more folders, and one or more messages to operate on. The use of the word "msg" as an argument to a command means that exactly one message name may be specified. A message name may be a number, such as 1, 33, or 234, or it may be one of the "reserved" message names: first, last, prev, next, and cur. (As a shorthand, a period (.) is equivalent to cur.) The meanings of these names are straightforward: "first" is the first message in the folder; "last" is the last message in the folder; "prev" is the message numerically previous to the current message; "next" is the message numerically following the current message; "cur" (or ".") is the current message in the folder. In addition, *MH* supports user–defined–sequences; see the description of the *mark* command for more information.

The default in commands that take a "msg" argument is always "cur".

The word "msgs" indicates that several messages may be specified. Such a specification consists of several message designations separated by spaces. A message designation is either a message name or a message range. A message range is a specification of the form name1–name2 or name1:n, where name1 and name2 are message names and n is an integer. The first form designates all the messages from name1 to name2 inclusive; this must be a non-empty range. The second form specifies up to n messages, starting with name1 if name1 is a number, or first, cur, or next, and ending with name1 if name1 is last or prev. This interpretation of n is overridden if n is preceded by a plus sign or a minus sign; +n always means up to n messages starting with name1, and –n always means up to n messages ending with name1. Repeated specifications of the same message have the same effect as a single specification of the message. Examples of specifications are:

8

        1 5 7–11 22
        first 6 8 next
        first–10
        last:5

The message name "all" is a shorthand for "first–last", indicating all of the messages in the folder.

In commands that accept "msgs" arguments, the default is either cur or all, depending on which makes more sense.

In all of the *MH* commands, a plus sign preceding an argument indicates a folder name. Thus, "+inbox" is the name of the user's standard inbox. If an explicit folder argument is given to an *MH* command, it will become the current folder (that is, the "Current-Folder:" entry in the user's profile will be changed to this folder). In the case of the *refile* command, which can have multiple output folders, a new source folder (other than the default current folder) is specified by '–src +folder'.

OTHER MH CONVENTIONS

One very powerful feature of *MH* is that the *MH* commands may be issued from any current directory, and the proper path to the appropriate folder(s) will be taken from the user's profile. If the *MH* path is not appropriate for a specific folder or file, the automatic prepending of the *MH* path can be avoided by beginning a folder or file name with */*, or with *J* or *.J* component. Thus any specific absolute path may be specified along with any path relative to the current working directory.

Arguments to the various programs may be given in any order, with the exception of a few switches whose arguments must follow immediately, such as '–src +folder' for *refile*.

Whenever an *MH* command prompts the user, the valid options will be listed in response to a <RETURN>. (The first of the listed options is the default if end-of-file is encountered, such as from a command file.) A valid response is any *unique* abbreviation of one of the listed options.

Standard UNIX documentation conventions are used in this report to describe *MH* command syntax. Arguments enclosed in brackets ([ ]) are optional; exactly one of the arguments enclosed within braces ({ }) must be specified, and all other arguments are required. The use of ellipsis dots (...) indicates zero or more repetitions of the previous item. For example, "+folder ..." would indicate that one or more "+folder" arguments is required and "[+folder ...]" indicates that 0 or more "+folder" arguments may be given.

MH departs from UNIX standards by using switches that consist of more than one character, e.g. '–header'. To minimize typing, only a unique abbreviation of a switch need be typed; thus, for '–header', '–hea' is probably sufficient, depending on the other switches the command accepts. Each *MH* program accepts the switch '–help' (which **must** be spelled out fully) and produces a syntax description and a list of switches. In the list of switches, parentheses indicate required characters. For example, all '–help' switches will appear as "–(help)", indicating that no abbreviation is accepted. Furthermore, the '–help' switch tells the version of the *MH* program you invoked.

Many *MH* switches have both on and off forms, such as '–format' and '–noformat'. In many of the descriptions which follow, only one form is defined; the other form, often used to nullify profile switch settings, is assumed to be the opposite.

8

MH COMMANDS

The *MH* package comprises several programs:

ali (1)	– list mail aliases
anno (1)	– annotate messages
bbc (1)	– check on BBoards
bboards (1)	– the UCI BBoards facility
burst (1)	– explode digests into messages
comp (1)	– compose a message
dist (1)	– redistribute a message to additional addresses
folder (1)	– set/list current folder/message
folders (1)	– list all folders
forw (1)	– forward messages
inc (1)	– incorporate new mail
mark (1)	– mark messages
mhl (1)	– produce formatted listings of MH messages
mhmail (1)	– send or read mail
mhook (1)	– MH receive–mail hooks
mhparam (1)	– print MH profile components
mhpath (1)	– print full pathnames of MH messages and folders
msgchk (1)	– check for messages
msh (1)	– MH shell (and BBoard reader)
next (1)	– show the next message
packf (1)	– compress a folder into a single file
pick (1)	– select messages by content
prev (1)	– show the previous message
prompter (1)	– prompting editor front end
rcvstore (1)	– incorporate new mail asynchronously
refile (1)	– file messages in other folders
repl (1)	– reply to a message
rmf (1)	– remove folder
rmm (1)	– remove messages
scan (1)	– produce a one line per message scan listing
send (1)	– send a message
show (1)	– show (list) messages
slocal (1)	– special local mail delivery
sortm (1)	– sort messages
vmh (1)	– visual front–end to MH
whatnow (1)	– prompting front–end for send
whom (1)	– report to whom a message would go

These programs are described below. The form of the descriptions conforms to the standard form for the description of UNIX commands.

8

NAME
    ali – list mail aliases

SYNOPSIS
    ali [–alias aliasfile] [–list] [–nolist] [–normalize] [–nonormalize] [–user] [–nouser] aliases ... [–help]

DESCRIPTION

Ali searches the named mail alias files for each of the given *aliases*. It creates a list of addresses for those *aliases*, and writes that list on standard output. If the '–list' option is specified, each address appears on a separate line; otherwise, the addresses are separated by commas and printed on as few lines as possible.

The '–user' option directs *ali* to perform its processing in an inverted fashion: instead of listing the addresses that each given alias expands to, *ali* will list the aliases that expand to each given address. If the '–normalize' switch is given, *ali* will try to track down the official hostname of the address.

The files specified by the profile entry ''Aliasfile:'' and any additional alias files given by the '–alias aliasfile' switch will be read. Each *alias* is processed as described in *mh–alias* (5).

Files

$HOME/.mh_profile	The user profile
/etc/passwd	List of users
/etc/group	List of groups

Profile Components

Path:	To determine the user's MH directory
Aliasfile:	For a default alias file

See Also
    mh–alias(5)

Defaults
    '–alias /usr/contrib/mh-6.8/lib/MailAliases'
    '–nolist'
    '–nonormalize'
    '–nouser'

Context
    None

Bugs

The '–user' option with '–nonormalize' is not entirely accurate, as it does not replace local nicknames for hosts with their official site names.

NAME

anno – annotate messages

SYNOPSIS

anno [+folder] [msgs] [–component field] [–inplace] [–noinplace] [–date] [–nodate] [–text body] [–help]

DESCRIPTION

Anno annotates the specified messages in the named folder using the field and body. Annotation is optionally performed by *dist*, *forw*, and *repl*, to keep track of your distribution of, forwarding of, and replies to a
message. By using *anno*, you can perform arbitrary annotations of your own. Each message selected will
be annotated with the lines

> field: date
> field: body

The '–nodate' switch inhibits the date annotation, leaving only the body annotation. The '–inplace' switch
causes annotation to be done in place in order to preserve links to the annotated message.

The field specified should be a valid 822-style message field name, which means that it should consist of
alphanumerics (or dashes) only. The body specified is arbitrary text.

If a '–component field' is not specified when *anno* is invoked, *anno* will prompt the user for the name of
field for the annotation.

Files

$HOME/.mh_profile   The user profile

Profile Components

Path: To determine the user's MH directory
Current–Folder: To find the default current folder

See Also

dist (1), forw (1), repl (1)

Defaults

'+folder' defaults to the current folder
'msgs' defaults to cur
'–noinplace'
'–date'

Context

If a folder is given, it will become the current folder. The first message annotated will become the current
message.

NAME
    bbc – check on BBoards

SYNOPSIS
    bbc [bboards ...] [–topics] [–check] [–read] [–quiet] [–verbose] [–archive] [–noarchive] [–protocol]
         [–noprotocol] [–mshproc program] [switches for *mshproc*] [–rcfile rcfile] [–norcfile]
         [–file BBoardsfile] [–user BBoardsuser] [–host host] [–help]

DESCRIPTION

    bbc is a BBoard reading/checking program that interfaces to the BBoard channel.

    The *bbc* program has three action switches which direct its operation:

    The '–read' switch invokes the *msh* program on the named *BBoards*. If you also specify the '–archive'
    switch, then *bbc* will invoke the *msh* program on the archives of the named *BBoards*. If no *BBoards* are
    given on the command line, and you specified '–archive', *bbc* will not read your 'bboards' profile entry,
    but will read the archives of the "system" *BBoard* instead.

    The '–check' switch types out status information for the named *BBoards*. *bbc* can print one of several
    messages depending on the status of both the BBoard and the user's reading habits. As with each of these
    messages, the number given is the item number of the last item placed in the BBoard. This number (which
    is marked in the messages as the "BBoard–Id") is ever increasing. Hence, when *bbc* says "n items", it
    really means that the highest BBoard–Id is "n". There may, or may not actually be "n" items in the
    BBoard. Some common messages are:

> **BBoard — n items unseen**
> This message tells how many items the user has not yet seen. When invoked with the
> '–quiet' switch, this is the only informative line that *bbc* will possibly print out.

> **BBoard — empty**
> The BBoard is empty.

> **BBoard — n items (none seen)**
> The BBoard has items in it, but the user hasn't seen any.

> **BBoard — n items (all seen)**
> The BBoard is non–empty, and the user has seen everything in it.

> **BBoard — n items seen out of m**
> The BBoard has at most m–n items that the user has not seen.

    The '–topics' switch directs *bbc* to print three items about the named *BBoards*: it's official name, the
    number of items present, and the date and time of the last update. If no *BBoards* are named, then all
    BBoards are listed. If the '–verbose' switch is given, more information is output.

    The '–quiet' switch specifies that *bbc* should be silent if no *BBoards* are found with new information. The
    '–verbose' switch specifies that *bbc* is to consider you to be interested in *BBoards* that you've already seen
    everything in.

    To override the default *mshproc* and the profile entry, use the '–mshproc program' switch. Any arguments
    not understood by *bbc* are passed to this program. The '–protocol' switch tells *bbc* that your *mshproc*
    knows about the special *bbc* protocol for reporting back information. *msh* (1), the default *mshproc*, knows
    all about this.

8

The '–file BBoardsfile' switch tells *bbc* to use a non–standard *BBoards* file when performing its calculations. Similarly, the '–user BBoardsuser' switch tells *bbc* to use a non–standard username. Both of these
switches are useful for debugging a new *BBoards* or *POP* file.

If the local host is configured as an NNTP BBoards client, or if the '–host host' switch is given, then *bbc*
will query the NNTP service host as to the status of the BBoards. For NNTP BBoards clients, the
'–user user' and the '–rpop' switches are ignored.

The *.bbrc* file in the user's **$HOME** directory is used to keep track of what messages have been read. The
'–rcfile rcfile' switch overrides the use of *.bbrc* for this purpose. If the value given to the switch is not
absolute, (i.e., does not begin with a **/**), it will be presumed to start from the current working directory. If
this switch is not given (or the '–norcfile' switch is given), then *bbc* consults the envariable **$MHBBRC**,
and honors it similarly.

Files

$HOME/.mh_profile	The user profile
$HOME/.bbrc	BBoard ''current'' message information

Profile Components

Path:	To determine the user's MH directory
bboards:	To specify interesting BBoards
mshproc:	Program to read a given BBoard

See Also

bbl(1), bboards(1), msh(1)

Defaults

'–read'
'–noarchive'
'–protocol'
'bboards' defaults to ''system''
'–file /usr/spool/bboards/BBoards'
'–user bboards'

Context

None

Bugs

The '–user' switch takes effect only if followed by the '–file' switch.

NAME
          bboards – the UCI BBoards facility

SYNOPSIS
          bbc [–check] [–read] bboards ... [–help]

DESCRIPTION

          The home directory of *bboards* is where the BBoard system is kept. This documentation describes some of
          the nuances of the BBoard system.

          Note that if your system is configured to use the Network News Transfer Protocol (**NNTP**) to read
          BBoards, (your system does seem to be configured this way), then there is no local bboards setup; instead,
          bbc opens an **NNTP** connection to the local server.

          BBoards, BBoard–IDs
          A BBoard is just a file containing a group of messages relating to the same topic. These files live
          in the ˜bboards home directory. Each message in a BBoard file has in its header the line
          ''BBoard-Id: n'', where ''n'' is an ascending decimal number. This id-number is unique for each
          message in a BBoards file. It should NOT be confused with the message number of a message,
          which can change as messages are removed from the BBoard.

          BBoard Handling
          To read BBoards, use the *bbc* and *msh* programs. The *msh* command is a monolithic program
          which contains all the functionality of *MH* in a single program. The '–check' switch to *bbc* lets
          you check on the status of BBoards, and the '–read' switch tells *bbc* to invoke *msh* to read those
          BBoards.

          Creating a BBoard
          Both public, and private BBoards are supported. Contact the mail address *PostMaster* if you'd
          like to have a BBoard created.

          BBoard addresses
          Each BBoard has associated with it 4 addresses, these are (for the ficticious BBoard called
          ''hacks''):
                    hacks : The Internet wide distribution list.
                    dist-hacks : The local BBoard.
                    hacks-request : The people responsible for the BBoard at the Internet level.
                    local-hacks-request : The people responsible for the BBoard locally.

Files
          $HOME/.mh_profile   The user profile
          $HOME/.bbrc   BBoard information

Profile Components
          Path: To determine the user's MH directory
          bboards: To specify interesting BBoards
          mshproc: Program to read a given BBoard

See Also
          bbc(1), bbl(1), bbleader(1), msh(1)

Defaults
          The default bboard is ''system''

8

Context
    None

NAME

burst – explode digests into messages

SYNOPSIS

burst [+folder] [msgs] [–inplace] [–noinplace] [–quiet] [–noquiet] [–verbose] [–noverbose] [–help]

DESCRIPTION

Burst considers the specified messages in the named folder to be Internet digests, and explodes them in that folder.

If '–inplace' is given, each digest is replaced by the "table of contents" for the digest (the original digest is removed). *Burst* then renumbers all of the messages following the digest in the folder to make room for each of the messages contained within the digest. These messages are placed immediately after the digest.

If '–noinplace' is given, each digest is preserved, no table of contents is produced, and the messages contained within the digest are placed at the end of the folder. Other messages are not tampered with in any way.

The '–quiet' switch directs *burst* to be silent about reporting messages that are not in digest format.

The '–verbose' switch directs *burst* to tell the user the general actions that it is taking to explode the digest.

It turns out that *burst* works equally well on forwarded messages and blind–carbon–copies as on Internet digests, provided that the former two were generated by *forw* or *send*.

Files

     $HOME/.mh_profile   The user profile

Profile Components

     Path: To determine the user's MH directory
     Current–Folder: To find the default current folder
     Msg–Protect: To set mode when creating a new message

See Also

Proposed Standard for Message Encapsulation (aka RFC–934),
inc(1), msh(1), pack(1)

Defaults

'+folder' defaults to the current folder
'msgs' defaults to cur
'–noinplace'
'–noquiet'
'–noverbose'

Context

If a folder is given, it will become the current folder. If '–inplace' is given, then the first message burst becomes the current message. This leaves the context ready for a *show* of the table of contents of the digest, and a *next* to see the first message of the digest. If '–noinplace' is given, then the first message extracted from the first digest burst becomes the current message. This leaves the context in a similar, but not identical, state to the context achieved when using '–inplace'.

Bugs

The *burst* program enforces a limit on the number of messages which may be *burst* from a single message. This number is on the order of 1000 messages. There is usually no limit on the number of messages which may reside in the folder after the *burst*ing.

Although *burst* uses a sophisticated algorithm to determine where one encapsulated message ends and another begins, not all digestifying programs use an encapsulation algorithm. In degenerate cases, this usually results in *burst* finding an encapsulation boundary prematurely and splitting a single encapsulated message into two or more messages. These erroneous digestifying programs should be fixed.

Furthermore, any text which appears after the last encapsulated message is not placed in a seperate message by *burst*. In the case of digestified messages, this text is usally an ''End of digest'' string. As a result of this possibly un–friendly behavior on the part of *burst*, note that when the '–inplace' option is used, this trailing information is lost. In practice, this is not a problem since correspondents usually place remarks in text prior to the first encapsulated message, and this information is not lost.

NAME

       comp – compose a message

SYNOPSIS

       comp [+folder] [msg] [–draftfolder +folder] [–draftmessage msg] [–nodraftfolder] [–editor editor]
            [–noedit] [–file file] [–form formfile] [–use] [–nouse] [–whatnowproc program]
            [–nowhatnowproc] [–help]

DESCRIPTION

       Comp is used to create a new message to be mailed. It copies a message form to the draft being composed and then invokes an editor on the draft (unless '–noedit' is given, in which case the initial edit is suppressed).

       The default message form contains the following elements:

            To:
            cc:
            Subject:

       If the file named ''components'' exists in the user's MH directory, it will be used instead of this form. The file specified by '–form formfile' will be used if given. You also start *comp* using the contents of an existing message as the form. If you supply either a '+folder' or 'msg' argument, that message will be used as the form. You may not supply both a '–form formfile' and a '+folder' or 'msg' argument. The line of dashes or a blank line must be left between the header and the body of the message for the message to be identified properly when it is sent (see *send* (1)). The switch '–use' directs *comp* to continue editing an already started message. That is, if a *comp* (or *dist*, *repl*, or *forw*) is terminated without sending the draft, the draft can be edited again via ''comp –use''.

       If the draft already exists, *comp* will ask you as to the disposition of the draft. A reply of **quit** will abort *comp*, leaving the draft intact; **replace** will replace the existing draft with the appropriate form; **list** will display the draft; **use** will use the draft for further composition; and **refile +folder** will file the draft in the given folder, and give you a new draft with the appropriate form. (The '+folder' argument to **refile** is required.)

       The '–draftfolder +folder' and '–draftmessage msg' switches invoke the *MH* draft folder facility. This is an advanced (and highly useful) feature. Consult the **Advanced Features** section of the *MH* manual for more information.

       The '–file file' switch says to use the named file as the message draft.

       The '–editor editor' switch indicates the editor to use for the initial edit. Upon exiting from the editor, *comp* will invoke the *whatnow* program. See *whatnow* (1) for a discussion of available options. The invocation of this program can be inhibited by using the '–nowhatnowproc' switch. (In truth of fact, it is the *whatnow* program which starts the initial edit. Hence, '–nowhatnowproc' will prevent any edit from occurring.)

Files

/usr/contrib/mh-6.8/lib/components	The message skeleton
or <mh–dir>/components	Rather than the standard skeleton
$HOME/.mh_profile	The user profile
<mh–dir>/draft	The draft file

8

Profile Components

Path:	To determine the user's MH directory	
Draft–Folder:	To find the default draft–folder	
Editor:	To override the default editor	
Msg–Protect:	To set mode when creating a new message (draft)	
fileproc:	Program to refile the message	
whatnowproc:	Program to ask the ''What now?'' questions	

See Also

dist(1), forw(1), repl(1), send(1), whatnow(1), mh-profile(5)

Defaults

'+folder' defaults to the current folder
'msg' defaults to the current message
'–nodraftfolder'
'–nouse'

Context

None

Bugs

If *whatnowproc* is *whatnow*, then *comp* uses a built–in *whatnow*, it does not actually run the *whatnow* program. Hence, if you define your own *whatnowproc*, don't call it *whatnow* since *comp* won't run it.

NAME

       dist – redistribute a message to additional addresses

SYNOPSIS

       dist [+folder] [msg] [–annotate] [–noannotate] [–draftfolder +folder] [–draftmessage msg] [–nodraftfolder]
           [–editor editor] [–noedit] [–form formfile] [–inplace] [–noinplace] [–whatnowproc program]
           [–nowhatnowproc] [–help]

DESCRIPTION

       Dist is similar to *forw*. It prepares the specified message for redistribution to addresses that (presumably)
       are not on the original address list.

       The default message form contains the following elements:

           Resent-To:
           Resent-cc:

       If the file named ''distcomps'' exists in the user's MH directory, it will be used instead of this form. In
       either case, the file specified by '–form formfile' will be used if given. The form used will be prepended to
       the message being resent.

       If the draft already exists, *dist* will ask you as to the disposition of the draft. A reply of **quit** will abort *dist*,
       leaving the draft intact; **replace** will replace the existing draft with a blank skeleton; and **list** will display
       the draft.

       Only those addresses in ''Resent–To:'', ''Resent–cc:'', and ''Resent–Bcc:'' will be sent. Also, a
       ''Resent–Fcc: folder'' will be honored (see *send* (1)). Note that with *dist*, the draft should contain only
       ''Resent–xxx:'' fields and no body. The headers and the body of the original message are copied to the
       draft when the message is sent. Use care in constructing the headers for the redistribution.

       If the '–annotate' switch is given, the message being distributed will be annotated with the lines:

          Resent: date
          Resent: addrs

       where each address list contains as many lines as required. This annotation will be done only if the mes-
       sage is sent directly from *dist*. If the message is not sent immediately from *dist*, ''comp –use'' may be
       used to re–edit and send the constructed message, but the annotations won't take place. The '–inplace'
       switch causes annotation to be done in place in order to preserve links to the annotated message.

       See *comp* (1) for a description of the '–editor' and '–noedit' switches. Note that while in the editor, the
       message being resent is available through a link named ''@'' (assuming the default *whatnowproc*). In
       addition, the actual pathname of the message is stored in the envariable **$editalt**, and the pathname of the
       folder containing the message is stored in the envariable **$mhfolder**.

       The '–draftfolder +folder' and '–draftmessage msg' switches invoke the *MH* draft folder facility. This is
       an advanced (and highly useful) feature. Consult the **Advanced Features** section of the *MH* manual for
       more information.

       Upon exiting from the editor, *dist* will invoke the *whatnow* program. See *whatnow* (1) for a discussion of
       available options. The invocation of this program can be inhibited by using the '–nowhatnowproc' switch.
       (In truth of fact, it is the *whatnow* program which starts the initial edit. Hence, '–nowhatnowproc' will
       prevent any edit from occurring.)

8

Files

/usr/contrib/mh-6.8/lib/distcomps	The message skeleton
or <mh–dir>/distcomps	Rather than the standard skeleton
$HOME/.mh_profile	The user profile
<mh–dir>/draft	The draft file

Profile Components

Path:	To determine the user's MH directory
Current–Folder:	To find the default current folder
Draft–Folder:	To find the default draft–folder
Editor:	To override the default editor
fileproc:	Program to refile the message
whatnowproc:	Program to ask the ''What now?'' questions

See Also

comp(1), forw(1), repl(1), send(1), whatnow(1)

Defaults

'+folder' defaults to the current folder
'msg' defaults to cur
'–noannotate'
'–nodraftfolder'
'–noinplace'

Context

If a folder is given, it will become the current folder. The message distributed will become the current message.

History

Dist originally used headers of the form ''Distribute–xxx:'' instead of ''Resent–xxx:''. In order to conform with the ARPA Internet standard, RFC–822, the ''Resent–xxx:'' form is now used. *Dist* will recognize ''Distribute–xxx:'' type headers and automatically convert them to ''Resent–xxx:''.

Bugs

Dist does not *rigorously* check the message being distributed for adherence to the transport standard, but *post* called by *send* does. The *post* program will balk (and rightly so) at poorly formatted messages, and *dist* won't correct things for you.

If *whatnowproc* is *whatnow*, then *dist* uses a built–in *whatnow*, it does not actually run the *whatnow* program. Hence, if you define your own *whatnowproc*, don't call it *whatnow* since *dist* won't run it.

If your current working directory is not writable, the link named ''@'' is not available.

NAME
>   folder, folders – set/list current folder/message

SYNOPSIS
>   folder [+folder] [msg] [–all] [–create] [–nocreate] [–print] [–fast] [–nofast] [–header] [–noheader]
>   [–recurse] [–norecurse] [–total] [–nototal] [–list] [–nolist] [–push] [–pop] [–pack] [–nopack]
>   [–verbose] [–noverbose] [–help]
>
>   folders

DESCRIPTION

Since the *MH* environment is the shell, it is easy to lose track of the current folder from day to day. When *folder* is given the '–print' switch (the default), *folder* will list the current folder, the number of messages in it, the range of the messages (low–high), and the current message within the folder, and will flag extra files if they exist. An example of this summary is:

>   inbox+   has 16 messages (3– 22); cur= 5.

If a '+folder' and/or 'msg' are specified, they will become the current folder and/or message. By comparison, when a '+folder' argument is given, this corresponds to a "cd" operation in the *shell*; when no '+folder' argument is given, this corresponds roughly to a "pwd" operation in the *shell*.

If the specified (or default) folder doesn't exist, the default action is to query the user as to whether the folder should be created; when standard input is not a tty, the answer to the query is assumed to be "yes".

Specifying '–create' will cause *folder* to create new folders without any query. (This is the easy way to create an empty folder for use later.) Specifying '–nocreate' will cause *folder* to exit without creating a non-existant folder.

Multiple Folders

Specifying '–all' will produce a summary line for each top-level folder in the user's MH directory, sorted alphabetically. (If *folder* is invoked by a name ending with "s" (e.g., *folders*), '–all' is assumed). Specifying '–recurse' with '–all' will also produce a line for all sub-folders. These folders are all preceded by the read–only folders, which occur as "atr–cur–" entries in the user's *MH* context. For example,

>   Folder   # of messages (range) cur msg (other files)
>   /fsd/rs/m/tacc   has 35 messages (1– 35); cur= 23.
>   /rnd/phyl/Mail/EP has 82 messages (1–108); cur= 82.
>   ff   has no messages.
>   inbox+   has 16 messages (3– 22); cur= 5.
>   mh   has 76 messages (1– 76); cur= 70.
>   notes   has 2 messages (1– 2); cur= 1.
>   ucom   has 124 messages (1–124); cur= 6; (others).
>   TOTAL= 339 messages in 7 folders

The "+" after inbox indicates that it is the current folder. The "(others)" indicates that the folder 'ucom' has files which aren't messages. These files may either be sub–folders, or files that don't belong under the MH file naming scheme.

The header is output if either a '–all' or a '–header' switch is specified; it is suppressed by '–noheader'. A '–total' switch will produce only the summary line.

If '–fast' is given, only the folder name (or names in the case of '–all') will be listed. (This is faster because the folders need not be read.)

If a '+folder' is given along with the '−all' switch, *folder* will, in addition to setting the current folder, list the top−level folders for the current folder (with '−norecurse') or list all sub-folders under the current folder recursively (with '−recurse'). In this case, if a 'msg' is also supplied, it will become the current message of '+folder'.

The '−recurse' switch lists each folder recursively, so use of this option effectively defeats the speed enhancement of the '−fast' option, since each folder must be searched for subfolders. Nevertheless, the combination of these options is useful.

Compacting a Folder

The '−pack' switch will compress the message names in the designated folders, removing holes in message numbering. The '−verbose' switch directs *folder* to tell the user the general actions that it is taking to compress the folder.

The Folder Stack

The '−push' switch directs *folder* to push the current folder onto the *folder−stack*, and make the '+folder' argument the current folder. If '+folder' is not given, the current folder and the top of the *folder−stack* are exchanged. This corresponds to the "pushd" operation in the *CShell*.

The '−pop' switch directs *folder* to discard the top of the *folder−stack*, after setting the current folder to that value. No '+folder' argument is allowed. This corresponds to the "popd" operation in the *CShell*. The '−push' switch and the '−pop' switch are mutually exclusive: the last occurrence of either one over-rides any previous occurrence of the other. Both of these switches also set '−list' by default.

The '−list' switch directs *folder* to list the contents of the *folder−stack*. No '+folder' argument is allowed. After a successful '−push' or '−pop', the '−list' action is taken, unless a '−nolist' switch follows them on the command line. This corresponds to the "dirs" operation in the *CShell*. The '−push', '−pop', and '−list' switches turn off '−print'.

Files
$HOME/.mh_profile   The user profile

Profile Components
Path: To determine the user's MH directory
Current−Folder: To find the default current folder
Folder−Protect: To set mode when creating a new folder
Folder−Stack: To determine the folder stack

See Also
refile(1), mhpath(1)

Defaults

    '+folder' defaults to the current folder

    'msg' defaults to none

    '–nofast'

    '–noheader'

    '–nototal'

    '–nopack'

    '–norecurse'

    '–noverbose'

    '–print' is the default if no '–list', '–push', or '–pop' is specified

    '–list' is the default if '–push', or '–pop' is specified

Context

    If '+folder' and/or 'msg' are given, they will become the current folder and/or message.

History

    In previous versions of *MH*, the '–fast' switch prevented context changes from occurring for the current folder. This is no longer the case: if '+folder' is given, then *folder* will always change the current folder to that.

Bugs

    '–all' forces '–header' and '–total'.

    There is no way to restore the default behavior (to ask the user whether to create a non-existant folder) after '–create' or '–nocreate' is given.

NAME

   forw – forward messages

SYNOPSIS

   forw [+folder] [msgs] [–annotate] [–noannotate] [–draftfolder +folder] [–draftmessage msg]
         [–nodraftfolder] [–editor editor] [–noedit] [–filter filterfile] [–form formfile] [–format]
         [–noformat] [–inplace] [–noinplace] [–mime] [–nomime] [–whatnowproc program]
         [–nowhatnowproc] [–help]

   forw [+folder] [msgs] [–digest list] [–issue number] [–volume number] [other switches for *forw*] [–help]

DESCRIPTION

   Forw may be used to prepare a message containing other messages. It constructs the new message from
   the components file or '–form formfile' (see *comp*), with a body composed of the message(s) to be forwarded. An editor is invoked as in *comp*, and after editing is complete, the user is prompted before the
   message is sent.

   The default message form contains the following elements:

        To:
        cc:
        Subject:

   If the file named ''forwcomps'' exists in the user's MH directory, it will be used instead of this form. In
   either case, the file specified by '–form formfile' will be used if given.

   If the draft already exists, *forw* will ask you as to the disposition of the draft. A reply of **quit** will abort
   forw, leaving the draft intact; **replace** will replace the existing draft with a blank skeleton; and **list** will
   display the draft.

   If the '–annotate' switch is given, each message being forwarded will be annotated with the lines

      Forwarded: date
      Forwarded: addrs

   where each address list contains as many lines as required. This annotation will be done only if the message is sent directly from *forw*. If the message is not sent immediately from *forw*, ''comp –use'' may be
   used to re–edit and send the constructed message, but the annotations won't take place. The '–inplace'
   switch causes annotation to be done in place in order to preserve links to the annotated message.

   See *comp* (1) for a description of the '–editor' and '–noedit' switches.

   Although *forw* uses the '–form formfile' switch to direct it how to construct the beginning of the draft, the
   '–filter filterfile', '–format', and '–noformat' switches direct *forw* as to how each forwarded message
   should be formatted in the body of the draft. If '–noformat' is specified, then each forwarded message is
   output exactly as it appears. If '–format' or '–filter filterfile' is specified, then each forwarded message is
   filtered (re–formatted) prior to being output to the body of the draft. The filter file for *forw* should be a
   standard form file for *mhl*, as *forw* will invoke *mhl* to format the forwarded messages. The default message
   filter (what you get with '–format') is:

8

```
width=80,overflowtext=,overflowoffset=10
leftadjust,compress,compwidth=9
Date:formatfield="%<(nodate{text})%{text}%|%(tws{text})%>"
From:
To:
cc:
Subject:
:
body:nocomponent,overflowoffset=0,noleftadjust,nocompress
```

If the file named "mhl.forward" exists in the user's MH directory, it will be used instead of this form. In either case, the file specified by '–filter filterfile' will be used if given. To summarize: '–noformat' will reproduce each forwarded message exactly, '–format' will use *mhl* and a default filterfile, "mhl.forward", to format each forwarded message, and '–filter filterfile' will use the named filterfile to format each forwarded message with *mhl*.

Each forwarded message is separated with an encapsulation delimiter and dashes in the first column of the forwarded messages will be prepended with '– ' so that when received, the message is suitable for bursting by *burst* (1). This follows the Internet RFC–934 guidelines.

For users of *prompter* (1), by specifying prompter's '-prepend' switch in the .mh_profile file, any commentary text is entered before the forwarded messages. (A major win!)

To use the MIME rules for encapsulation, specify the '–mime' switch. This directs *forw* to generate an *mhn* composition file. Note that MH will not invoke *mhn* automatically, unless you add this line to your .mh_profile file:

```
automhnproc: mhn
```

Otherwise, you must specifically give the command

```
What now? edit mhn
```

prior to sending the draft.

To automate this somewhat, create a link to *prompter* called *rapid* and put these lines in your .mh_profile file:

```
forw: -editor rapid -mime
rapid: -rapid
rapid-next: mhn
```

Then, you can simply do:

```
forw msgs
To: mailbox
cc:
Subject: whatever

--------Enter initial text

blah, blah, blah.
<CTRL-D>
--------
```

8

What now? *edit*
What now? *send*

The *edit* command invokes *mhn* automatically.

The '–draftfolder +folder' and '–draftmessage msg' switches invoke the *MH* draft folder facility. This is an advanced (and highly useful) feature. Consult the **Advanced Features** section of the *MH* manual for more information.

Upon exiting from the editor, *forw* will invoke the *whatnow* program. See *whatnow* (1) for a discussion of available options. The invocation of this program can be inhibited by using the '–nowhatnowproc' switch. (In truth of fact, it is the *whatnow* program which starts the initial edit. Hence, '–nowhatnowproc' will prevent any edit from occurring.)

The '–digest list', '–issue number', and '–volume number' switches implement a digest facility for *MH*. Specifying these switches enables and/or overloads the following escapes:

Type	Escape	Returns	Description
component	*digest*	string	Argument to '–digest'
function	*cur*	integer	Argument to '–volume'
function	*msg*	integer	Argument to '–issue'

Consult the **Advanced Features** section of the *MH* User's Manual for more information on making digests.

Files

/usr/contrib/mh-6.8/lib/forwcomps	The message skeleton
or <mh–dir>/forwcomps	Rather than the standard skeleton
/usr/contrib/mh-6.8/lib/digestcomps	The message skeleton if '–digest' is given
or <mh–dir>/digestcomps	Rather than the standard skeleton
/usr/contrib/mh-6.8/lib/mhl.forward	The message filter
or <mh–dir>/mhl.forward	Rather than the standard filter
$HOME/.mh_profile	The user profile
<mh–dir>/draft	The draft file

Profile Components

Path:	To determine the user's MH directory
Current–Folder:	To find the default current folder
Draft–Folder:	To find the default draft–folder
Editor:	To override the default editor
Msg–Protect:	To set mode when creating a new message (draft)
fileproc:	Program to refile the message
mhlproc:	Program to filter messages being forwarded
whatnowproc:	Program to ask the "What now?" questions

See Also

Proposed Standard for Message Encapsulation (aka RFC–934),
comp(1), dist(1), repl(1), send(1), whatnow(1), mh–format(5)

Defaults

'+folder' defaults to the current folder
'msgs' defaults to cur
'−noannotate'
'−nodraftfolder'
'−noformat'
'−noinplace'
'−nomime'

Context

If a folder is given, it will become the current folder. The first message forwarded will become the current message.

Bugs

If *whatnowproc* is *whatnow*, then *forw* uses a built−in *whatnow*, it does not actually run the *whatnow* program. Hence, if you define your own *whatnowproc*, don't call it *whatnow* since *forw* won't run it.

When *forw* is told to annotate the messages it forwards, it doesn't actually annotate them until the draft is successfully sent. If from the *whatnowproc*, you *push* instead of *send*, it's possible to confuse *forw* by re−ordering the file (e.g., by using 'folder −pack') before the message is successfully sent. *Dist* and *repl* don't have this problem.

To avoid prepending the leading dash characters in forwarded messages, there is a '−nodashmunging' option. See the ''Hidden Features'' section of the *MH Administrator's Guide* for more details.

NAME

    inc – incorporate new mail

SYNOPSIS

    inc [+folder] [–audit audit–file] [–noaudit] [–changecur] [–nochangecur] [–form formatfile]
        [–format string] [–file name] [–silent] [–nosilent] [–truncate] [–notruncate] [–width columns]
        [–host host] [–user user] [–apop] [–noapop] [–rpop] [–norpop] [–pack file] [–nopack] [–help]

DESCRIPTION

    Inc incorporates mail from the user's incoming mail drop into an *MH* folder. If '+folder' isn't specified, a folder in the user's *MH* directory will be used, either that specified by the "Inbox:" entry in the user's profile, or the folder named "inbox". The new messages being incorporated are assigned numbers starting with the next highest number in the folder. If the specified (or default) folder doesn't exist, the user will be queried prior to its creation. As the messages are processed, a *scan* listing of the new mail is produced.

    If the user's profile contains a "Msg–Protect: nnn" entry, it will be used as the protection on the newly created messages, otherwise the *MH* default of 0644 will be used. During all operations on messages, this initially assigned protection will be preserved for each message, so *chmod*(1) may be used to set a protection on an individual message, and its protection will be preserved thereafter.

    If the switch '–audit audit–file' is specified (usually as a default switch in the profile), then *inc* will append a header line and a line per message to the end of the specified audit–file with the format:

        ≪inc≫ date
            <scan line for first message>
            <scan line for second message>
                <etc.>

    This is useful for keeping track of volume and source of incoming mail. Eventually, *repl, forw, comp*, and *dist* may also produce audits to this (or another) file, perhaps with "Message–Id:" information to keep an exact correspondence history. "Audit–file" will be in the user's MH directory unless a full path is specified.

    Inc will incorporate even improperly formatted messages into the user's MH folder, inserting a blank line prior to the offending component and printing a comment identifying the bad message.

    In all cases, the user's mail drop will be zeroed, unless the '–notruncate' switch is given.

    If the profile entry "Unseen–Sequence" is present and non–empty, then *inc* will add each of the newly incorporated messages to each sequence named by the profile entry. This is similar to the "Previous–Sequence" profile entry supported by all *MH* commands which take 'msgs' or 'msg' arguments. Note that *inc* will not zero each sequence prior to adding messages.

    The interpretation of the '–form formatfile', '–format string', and '–width columns' switches is the same as in *scan* (1).

    By using the '–file name' switch, one can direct *inc* to incorporate messages from a file other than the user's maildrop. Note that the name file will NOT be zeroed, unless the '–truncate' switch is given.

    If the envariable **$MAILDROP** is set, then *inc* uses it as the location of the user's maildrop instead of the default (the '-file name' switch still overrides this, however). If this envariable is not set, then *inc* will consult the profile entry "MailDrop" for this information. If the value found is not absolute, then it is interpreted relative to the user's *MH* directory. If the value is not found, then *inc* will look in the standard system location for the user's maildrop.

8

The '−silent' switch directs *inc* to be quiet and not ask any questions at all. This is useful for putting *inc* in the background and going on to other things.

If the local host is configured as a POP client, or if the '−host host' switch is given, then *inc* will query the POP service host as to the status of mail waiting. If the '−user user' switch is not given, then the current username is used. Normally, *inc* will prompt for a password to use. However, if the '−apop' switch is given, *inc* will generate authentication credentials to provide for origin authentication and replay protection, but which do not involve sending a password in the clear over the network. Otherwise, if the '−rpop' switch is given, then *inc* will try to use a "trusted" connection (ala the BSD r-commands).

If *inc* uses POP, then the '−pack file' switch is considered. If given, then *inc* simply uses the POP to *packf* (1) the user's maildrop from the POP service host to the named file. This switch is provided for those users who prefer to use *msh* to read their maildrops.

Files

$HOME/.mh_profile	The user profile
/usr/contrib/mh-6.8/lib/mtstailor	tailor file
/var/mail/$USER	Location of mail drop

Profile Components

Path:	To determine the user's MH directory
Alternate−Mailboxes:	To determine the user's mailboxes
Inbox:	To determine the inbox, default "inbox"
Folder−Protect:	To set mode when creating a new folder
Msg−Protect:	To set mode when creating a new message and audit−file
Unseen−Sequence:	To name sequences denoting unseen messages

See Also

Post Office Protocol - version 3 (aka RFC−1081),
mhmail(1), scan(1), mh−mail(5), post(8)

Defaults

'+folder' defaulted by "Inbox" above
'−noaudit'
'−changecur'
'−format' defaulted as described above
'−nosilent'
'−truncate' if '−file name' not given, '−notruncate' otherwise
'−width' defaulted to the width of the terminal
'−nopack'
'−rpop'

Context

The folder into which messages are being incorporated will become the current folder. The first message incorporated will become the current message, unless the '−nochangecur' option is specified. This leaves the context ready for a *show* of the first new message.

Bugs

The argument to the '−format' switch must be interpreted as a single token by the shell that invokes *inc*. Therefore, one must usually place the argument to this switch inside double−quotes.

NAME

    mark – mark messages

SYNOPSIS

    mark [+folder] [msgs] [−sequence name ...] [−add] [−delete] [−list] [−public] [−nopublic] [−zero]
        [−nozero] [−help]

DESCRIPTION

    The *mark* command manipulates message sequences by adding or deleting message numbers from folder–specific message sequences, or by listing those sequences and messages. A message sequence is a keyword, just like one of the "reserved" message names, such as "first" or "next". Unlike the "reserved" message names, which have a fixed semantics on a per–folder basis, the semantics of a message sequence may be defined, modified, and removed by the user. Message sequences are folder–specific, e.g., the sequence name "seen" in the context of folder "+inbox" need not have any relation whatsoever to the sequence of the same name in a folder of a different name.

    Three action switches direct the operation of *mark*. These switches are mutually exclusive: the last occurrence of any of them overrides any previous occurrence of the other two.

    The '−add' switch tells *mark* to add messages to sequences or to create a new sequence. For each sequence named via the '−sequence name' argument (which must occur at least once) the messages named via 'msgs' (which defaults to "cur" if no 'msgs' are given), are added to the sequence. The messages to be added need not be absent from the sequence. If the '−zero' switch is specified, the sequence will be emptied prior to adding the messages. Hence, '−add −zero' means that each sequence should be initialized to the indicated messages, while '−add −nozero' means that each sequence should be appended to by the indicated messages.

    The '−delete' switch tells *mark* to delete messages from sequences, and is the dual of '−add'. For each of the named sequences, the named messages are removed from the sequence. These messages need not be already present in the sequence. If the '−zero' switch is specified, then all messages in the folder are appended to the sequence prior to removing the messages. Hence, '−delete −zero' means that each sequence should contain all messages except those indicated, while '−delete −nozero' means that only the indicated messages should be removed from each sequence. As expected, the command 'mark −sequence seen −delete all' deletes the sequence "seen" from the current folder.

    When creating (or modifying) a sequence, the '−public' switch indicates that the sequence should be made readable for other *MH* users. In contrast, the '−nopublic' switch indicates that the sequence should be private to the user's *MH* environment.

    The '−list' switch tells *mark* to list both the sequences defined for the folder and the messages associated with those sequences. *Mark* will list the name of each sequence given by '−sequence name' and the messages associated with that sequence. If '−sequence' isn't used, all sequences will be listed, with private sequences being so indicated. The '−zero' switch does not affect the operation of '−list'.

    The current restrictions on sequences are:

        The name used to denote a message sequence must consist of an alphabetic character followed by zero or more alphanumeric characters, and cannot be one of the (reserved) message names "new", "first", "last", "all", "next", or "prev".

        Only a certain number of sequences may be defined for a given folder. This number is usually limited to 26 (10 on small systems).

        Message ranges with user–defined sequence names are restricted to the form "name:n" or "name:-

8

n'', and refer to the first or last 'n' messages of the sequence 'name', respectively. Constructs of the form ''name1−name2'' are forbidden.

Files

$HOME/.mh_profile   The user profile

Profile Components

Path: To determine the user's MH directory
Current−Folder: To find the default current folder

See Also

pick (1), mh-sequence (5)

Defaults

'+folder' defaults to the current folder
'−add' if '−sequence' is specified, '−list' otherwise
'msgs' defaults to cur (or all if '−list' is specified)
'−nopublic' if the folder is read−only, '−public' otherwise
'−nozero'

Context

If a folder is given, it will become the current folder.

Helpful Hints

Use ''pick sequence −list'' to enumerate the messages in a sequence (such as for use by a shell script).

NAME

    mhl – produce formatted listings of MH messages

SYNOPSIS

    /usr/contrib/mh-6.8/lib/mhl [–bell] [–nobell] [–clear] [–noclear] [–folder +folder] [–form formfile]
        [–length lines] [–width columns] [–moreproc program] [–nomoreproc] [files ...] [–help]

DESCRIPTION

    Mhl is a formatted message listing program. It can be used as a replacement for *more* (1) (the default
    showproc). As with *more*, each of the messages specified as arguments (or the standard input) will be
    output. If more than one message file is specified, the user will be prompted prior to each one, and a
    <RETURN> or <EOT> will begin the output, with <RETURN> clearing the screen (if appropriate), and
    <EOT> (usually CTRL–D) suppressing the screen clear. An <INTERRUPT> (usually CTRL–C) will
    abort the current message output, prompting for the next message (if there is one), and a <QUIT> (usually
    CTRL-\) will terminate the program (without core dump).

    The '–bell' option tells *mhl* to ring the terminal's bell at the end of each page, while the '–clear' option
    tells *mhl* to clear the scree at the end of each page (or output a formfeed after each message). Both of these
    switches (and their inverse counterparts) take effect only if the profile entry *moreproc* is defined but empty,
    and *mhl* is outputting to a terminal. If the *moreproc* entry is defined and non-empty, and *mhl* is outputting
    to a terminal, then *mhl* will cause the *moreproc* to be placed between the terminal and *mhl* and the switches
    are ignored. Furthermore, if the '–clear' switch is used and *mhl's* output is directed to a terminal, then *mhl*
    will consult the **$TERM** and **$TERMCAP** envariables to determine the user's terminal type in order to
    find out how to clear the screen. If the '–clear' switch is used and *mhl's* output is not directed to a terminal
    (e.g., a pipe or a file), then *mhl* will send a formfeed after each message.

    To override the default *moreproc* and the profile entry, use the '–moreproc program' switch. Note that *mhl*
    will never start a *moreproc* if invoked on a hardcopy terminal.

    The '–length length' and '–width width' switches set the screen length and width, respectively. These
    default to the values indicated by **$TERMCAP**, if appropriate, otherwise they default to 40 and 80, respec-
    tively.

    The default format file used by *mhl* is called *mhl.format* (which is first searched for in the user's *MH* direc-
    tory, and then sought in the */usr/contrib/mh-6.8/lib* directory), this can be changed by using the
    '–form formatfile' switch.

    Finally, the '–folder +folder' switch sets the *MH* folder name, which is used for the "messagename:" field
    described below. The envariable **$mhfolder** is consulted for the default value, which *show*, *next*, and *prev*
    initialize appropriately.

    Mhl operates in two phases: 1) read and parse the format file, and 2) process each message (file). During
    phase 1, an internal description of the format is produced as a structured list. In phase 2, this list is walked
    for each message, outputting message information under the format constraints from the format file.

    The "mhl.format" form file contains information controlling screen clearing, screen size, wrap–around
    control, transparent text, component ordering, and component formatting. Also, a list of components to
    ignore may be specified, and a couple of "special" components are defined to provide added functionality.
    Message output will be in the order specified by the order in the format file.

    Each line of mhl.format has one of the formats:

        ;comment
        :cleartext

8

```
variable[,variable...]
component:[variable,...]
```

A line beginning with a ';' is a comment, and is ignored. A line beginning with a ':' is clear text, and is output exactly as is. A line containing only a ':' produces a blank line in the output. A line beginning with ''component:'' defines the format for the specified component, and finally, remaining lines define the global environment.

For example, the line:

width=80,length=40,clearscreen,overflowtext="***",overflowoffset=5

defines the screen size to be 80 columns by 40 rows, specifies that the screen should be cleared prior to each page, that the overflow indentation is 5, and that overflow text should be flagged with ''***''.

Following are all of the current variables and their arguments. If they follow a component, they apply only to that component, otherwise, their affect is global. Since the whole format is parsed before any output processing, the last global switch setting for a variable applies to the whole message if that variable is used in a global context (i.e., bell, clearscreen, width, length).

variable	type	semantics
width	integer	screen width or component width
length	integer	screen length or component length
offset	integer	positions to indent ''component: ''
overflowtext	string	text to use at the beginning of an overflow line
overflowoffset	integer	positions to indent overflow lines
compwidth	integer	positions to indent component text after the first line is output
uppercase	flag	output text of this component in all upper case
nouppercase	flag	don't uppercase
clearscreen	flag/G	clear the screen prior to each page
noclearscreen	flag/G	don't clearscreen
bell	flag/G	ring the bell at the end of each page
nobell	flag/G	don't bell
component	string/L	name to use instead of ''component'' for this component
nocomponent	flag	don't output ''component: '' for this component
center	flag	center component on line (works for one−line components only)
nocenter	flag	don't center
leftadjust	flag	strip off leading whitespace on each line of text
noleftadjust	flag	don't leftadjust
compress	flag	change newlines in text to spaces
nocompress	flag	don't compress
split	flag	don't combine multiple fields into a single field
nosplit	flag	combine multiple fields into a single field
newline	flag	print newline at end of components (default)
nonewline	flag	don't print newline at end of components
formatfield	string	format string for this component (see below)
addrfield	flag	field contains addresses
datefield	flag	field contains dates

To specify the value of integer–valued and string–valued variables, follow their name with an equals–sign and the value. Integer–valued variables are given decimal values, while string–valued variables are given arbitrary text bracketed by double–quotes. If a value is suffixed by ''/G'' or ''/L'', then its value is useful in a global–only or local–only context (respectively).

A line of the form:

    ignores=component,...

specifies a list of components which are never output.

The component ''MessageName'' (case–insensitive) will output the actual message name (file name) preceded by the folder name if one is specified or found in the environment. The format is identical to that produced by the '–header' option to *show*.

The component ''Extras'' will output all of the components of the message which were not matched by explicit components, or included in the ignore list. If this component is not specified, an ignore list is not needed since all non–specified components will be ignored.

If ''nocomponent'' is NOT specified, then the component name will be output as it appears in the format file.

The default format is:

            : -- using template mhl.format --
            overflowtext=''***'',overflowoffset=5
            leftadjust,compwidth=9
            ignores=msgid,message-id,received
            Date:formatfield="%<(nodate{text})%{text}%l%(pretty{text})%>"
            To:
            cc:
            :
            From:
            Subject:
            :
            extras:nocomponent
            :
            body:nocomponent,overflowtext=,overflowoffset=0,noleftadjust

The variable ''formatfield'' specifies a format string (see *mh–format* (5)). The flag variables ''addrfield'' and ''datefield'' (which are mutually exclusive), tell *mhl* to interpret the escapes in the format string as either addresses or dates, respectively.

By default, *mhl* does not apply any formatting string to fields containing address or dates (see *mh–mail* (5) for a list of these fields). Note that this results in faster operation since *mhl* must parse both addresses and dates in order to apply a format string to them. If desired, *mhl* can be given a default format string for either address or date fields (but not both). To do this, on a global line specify: either the flag addrfield or datefield, along with the apropriate formatfield variable string.

Files

/usr/contrib/mh-6.8/lib/mhl.format	The message template
or <mh–dir>/mhl.format	Rather than the standard template
$HOME/.mh_profile	The user profile

Profile Components
>   moreproc: Program to use as interactive front–end

See Also
>   show(1), ap(8), dp(8)

Defaults
>   '–bell'
>   '–noclear'
>   '–length 40'
>   '–width 80'

Context
>   None

Bugs

There should be some way to pass 'bell' and 'clear' information to the front–end.

On hosts where *MH* was configured with the BERK option, address parsing is not enabled.

The ''nonewline'' option interacts badly with ''compress'' and ''split''.

NAME
        mhmail – send or read mail

SYNOPSIS
        mhmail [addrs ... [–body text] [–cc addrs ...] [–from addr] [–subject subject]] [–help]

DESCRIPTION

        MHmail is intended as a replacement for the standard Bell mail program (*bellmail* (1)), compatible with
        MH. When invoked without arguments, it simply invokes *inc* (1) to incorporate new messages from the
        user's maildrop. When one or more users is specified, a message is read from the standard input and
        spooled to a temporary file. *MHmail* then invokes *post* (8) with the name of the temporary file as its argu-
        ment to deliver the message to the specified user.

        The '–subject subject' switch can be used to specify the ''Subject:'' field of the message. The '–body text'
        switch can be used to specify the text of the message; if it is specified, then the standard input is not read.
        Normally, addresses appearing as arguments are put in the ''To:'' field. If the '–cc' switch is used, all
        addresses following it are placed in the ''cc:'' field.

        By using '–from addr', you can specify the ''From:'' header of the draft. Naturally, *post* will fill–in the
        ''Sender:'' header correctly.

        This program is intended for the use of programs such as *at* (1), which expect to send mail automatically
        to various users. Normally, real people (as opposed to the ''unreal'' ones) will prefer to use *comp* (1) and
        send (1) to send messages.

Files
        /usr/contrib/mh-6.8/bin/inc   Program to incorporate a maildrop into a folder
        /usr/contrib/mh-6.8/lib/post   Program to deliver a message
        /tmp/mhmail*   Temporary copy of message

Profile Components
        None

See Also
        inc(1), post(8)

Defaults
        None

Context
        If *inc* is invoked, then *inc*'s context changes occur.

NAME

    mhn – multi-media MH

SYNOPSIS

    mhn [[+folder] [msgs] | [–file file]]
            [–part number]... [–type content]...
            [–list [–headers] [–noheaders]
               [–realsize] [–norealsize]] [-nolist]
            [–show [–serialonly] [–noserialonly]
               [–form formfile] [–pause] [–nopause]] [–noshow]
            [–store [–auto] [–noauto]] [–nostore]
            [–cache] [–nocache] [–rcache policy] [–wcache policy]
            [–check] [–nocheck]
            [–ebcdicsafe] [–noebcdicsafe]
            [–rfc934mode] [–norfc934mode]
            [–verbose] [–noverbose]
            [–help]

DESCRIPTION

The *mhn* command manipulates multi-media messages as specified in RFC 1521.

Four action switches direct the operation of *mhn*, namely '–list', '–show', '–store', and '-cache'. Any of these switches may be used concurrently. Normally these action switches will operate on the content of each of the named messages. However, by using the '–part' and '–type' switches, the scope of the operation can be focused on particular subparts (of a multipart content) and/or particular content types.

A part specification consists of a series of numbers separated by dots. For example, in a multipart content containing three parts, these would be named as 1, 2, and 3, respectively. If part 2 was also a multipart content containing two parts, these would be named as 2.1 and 2.2, respectively. Note that the '–part' switch is effective for only messages containing a multipart content. If a message has some other kind of content, or if the part is itself another multipart content, the '–part' switch will not prevent the content from being acted upon.

A content specification consists of a content type and a subtype. The initial list of "standard" content types and subtypes can be found in RFC 1521. A list of commonly used contents is briefly reproduced here:

Type	Subtypes
text	plain
multipart	mixed, alternative, digest, parallel
message	rfc822, partial, external-body
application	octet-stream, postscript
image	jpeg, gif, x-pbm, x-pgm, x-ppm, x-xwd
audio	basic
video	mpeg

Subtypes are mandatory. To specify a content, regardless of its subtype, just use the name of the content, e.g., "audio". To specify a specific subtype, separate the two with a slash, e.g., "audio/basic". Note that regardless of the values given to the '–type' switch, a multipart content (of any subtype listed above) is always acted upon. Further note that if the '–type' switch is used, and it is desirable to act on a message/external-body content, then the '–type' switch must be used twice: once for message/external-body and once for the content externally referenced.

Each content may optionally have an integrity check associated with it. If present and the '-check' switch is given, then *mhn* will attempt to verify the integrity of the content.

The option '–file file' directs *mhn* to use the specified file as the source message, rather than a message from a folder. Note that the file should be a validly formatted message, just like any other *MH* message. It should **NOT** be in mail drop format (to convert a file in mail drop format to a folder of *MH* messages, see *inc* (1)).

Listing the Contents

The '–list' switch tells *mhn* to list the table of contents associated with the named messages. The '–headers' switch indicates that a one-line banner should be displayed above the listing. The '–realsize' switch tells *mhn* to evaluate the ''native'' (decoded) format of each content prior to listing. This provides an accurate count at the expense of a small delay.

Showing the Contents

The '–show' switch tells *mhn* to display the contents of the named messages. The headers of the message are displayed with the *mhlproc*, using format file *mhl.headers*. (The choice of format file can be overridden by the '–form formfile' switch.)

mhn will look for information in the user's profile to determine how the different contents should be displayed. This is accomplished by consulting a display string, and executing it under **/bin/sh**, with the standard input set to the content. The display string may contain these escapes:

    %a additional arguments
    %e exclusive execution
    %f filename containing content
    %F %e, %f, and stdin is terminal not content
    %l display listing prior to displaying content
    %p %l, and ask for confirmation
    %s subtype
    %d content description

For those display strings containing the e- or F-escape, *mhn* will execute at most one of these at any given time. Although the F-escape expands to be the filename containing the content, the e-escape has no expansion as far as the shell is concerned.

When the p-escape prompts for confirmation, typing INTR (usually control-C) will tell *mhn* not to display that content. (The p-escape can be disabled by specifying '–nopause'.) Further, when *mhn* is display a content, typing QUIT (usually control-\) will tell *mhn* to wrap things up immediately.

Note that if the content being displayed is multipart, but not one of the subtypes listed above, then the f- and F-escapes expand to multiple filenames, one for each subordinate content. Further, stdin is not redirected from the terminal to the content.

First, *mhn* will look for an entry of the form:

    mhn-show-<type>/<subtype>

to determine the command to use to display the content.

If this isn't found, *mhn* will look for an entry of the form:

    mhn-show-<type>

to determine the display command. If this isn't found, *mhn* has two default values:

    mhn-show-text/plain: %pmoreproc '%F'
    mhn-show-message/rfc822: %pshow -file '%F'

If neither apply, *mhn* will check to see if the message has a application/octet-stream content with parameter "type=tar". If so, *mhn* will use an appropriate command. If not, *mhn* will complain.

Example entries might be:

    mhn-show-audio/basic: raw2audio 2>/dev/null l play
    mhn-show-image: xv '%f'
    mhn-show-application/PostScript: lpr -Pps

Note that when using the f- or F-escape, it's a good idea to use single-quotes around the escape. This prevents misinterpretation by the shell of any funny characters that might be present in the filename.

Because the text content might be in a non-ASCII character set, when *mhn* encounters a "charset" parameter for this content, it checks to see whether the environment variable $MM_CHARSET is set and whether the value of this environment variable is equal to the value of the charset parameter. If not, then *mhn* will look for an entry of the form:

    mhn-charset-<charset>

which should contain a command creating an environment to render the character set. This command string should containing a single "%s", which will be filled-in with the command to display the content.

An example entry might be:

    mhn-charset-iso-8859-1: xterm -fn '-*-*-medium-r-normal-*-*-120-*-*-c-*-iso8859-*' -e %s

Note that many pagination programs strip off the high-order bit. However, newer releases of the *less* program have modest support for single-octet character sets. The source to *less* version 177, which has such support, is found in the MH source tree under **miscellany/less-177**. In order to view messages sent in the ISO 8859/1 character set using *less*, put these lines in your .login file:

    setenv LESSCHARSET latin1
    setenv LESS "-f"

The first line tells *less* to use 8859/1 definition for determing whether a character is "normal", "control", or "binary". The second line tells *less* not to warn you if it encounters a file that has non-ASCII characters. Then, simply set the **moreproc** profile entry to *less*, and it will get called automatically. (To handle other single-octet character sets, look at the *less* (1) manual entry for information about the **LESSCHAR-DEF** environment variable.)

Finally, *mhn* will process each message serially -- it won't start showing the next message until all the commands executed to display the current message have terminated. In the case of a multipart content (of any subtype listed above), the content contains advice indicating if the parts should be displayed serially or in parallel. Because this may cause confusion, particularly on uni-window displays, the '−serialonly' switch can be given to tell *mhn* to never display parts in parallel.

8

Storing the Contents

The '–store' switch tells *mhn* to store the contents of the named messages in ''native'' (decoded) format. Two things must be determined: the directory to store the content, and the filenames. Files are written in the directory given by the **mhn-storage** profile entry, e.g.,

      mhn-storage: /tmp

If this entry isn't present, the current working directory is used.

mhn will look for information in the user's profile to determine how the different contents should be stored. This is achieved through the use of a formatting string, which may contain these escapes:

      %m message number
      %P .part
      %p part
      %s subtype

If the content isn't part of a multipart (of any subtype listed above) content, the p-escapes are ignored. Note that if the formatting string starts with a ''+'' character, then these escapes are ignored, and the content is stored in the named folder. (A formatting string consisting solely of a ''+'' character indicates the current folder.) Further, a formatting string consisting solely of a ''-'' character indicates the standard-output.

First, *mhn* will look for an entry of the form:

      mhn-store-<type>/<subtype>

to determine the formatting string. If this isn't found, *mhn* will look for an entry of the form:

      mhn-store-<type>

to determine the formatting string. If this isn't found, *mhn* will check to see if the content is application/octet-stream with parameter ''type=tar''. If so, *mhn* will choose an appropriate filename. If the content is not application/octet-stream, then *mhn* will check to see if the content is a message. If so, *mhn* will use the value ''+''. If not, *mhn* will use the value ''%m%P.%s''.

Note that if the formatting string starts with a '/', then content will be stored in the full path given (rather than using the value of **mhn-storage** or the current working directory.) Similarly, if the formatting string starts with a 'l', then *mhn* will execute a command which should ultimately store the content. Note that before executing the command, *mhn* will change to the appropriate directory. Also note that if the formatting string starts with a 'l', then *mhn* will also honor the a-escape when processing the formatting string.

Example entries might be:

      mhn-store-text: %m%P.txt
      mhn-store-audio/basic: l raw2audio -e ulaw -s 8000 -c 1 > %m%P.au
      mhn-store-application/PostScript: %m%P.ps

Further, note that when asked to store a content containing a partial message, *mhn* will try to locate all of the portions and combine them accordingly. Thus, if someone's sent you a message in several parts, you might put them all in their own folder and do:

      mhn all -store

8

This will store exactly one message, containing the sum of the parts. Note that if *mhn* can not locate each part, it will not store anything.

Finally, if the '−auto' switch is given and the content contains information indicating the filename the content should be stored as (and if the filename doesn't begin with a '/'), then the filename from the content will be used instead.

External Access

For contents of type message/external-body, *mhn* supports these access-types:

        afs
        anon-ftp
        ftp
        local-file
        mail-server

For the "anon-ftp" and "ftp" access types, if your system supports a SOCKETs interface to TCP/IP, then *mhn* will use a built-in FTP client. Otherwise, *mhn* will look for the **mhn-access-ftp** profile entry, e.g.,

        mhn-access-ftp: myftp.sh

to determine the pathname of a program to perform the FTP retrieval. This program is invoked with these arguments:

        domain name of FTP-site
        username
        password
        remote directory
        remote filename
        local filename
        "ascii" or "binary"

The program should terminate with a zero-valued exit-status if the retrieval is successful.

The Content Cache

When *mhn* encounters an external content containing a "Content-ID:" field, and if the content allows caching, then depending on the caching behavior of *mhn*, the content might be read from or written to a cache.

The caching behavior of *mhn* is controlled with the '−rcache' and '−wcache' switches, which define the policy for reading from, and writing to, the cache, respectively. One of four policies may be specified: "public", indicating that *mhn* should make use of a publically-accessible content cache; "private", indicating that *mhn* should make use of the user's private content cache; "never", indicating that *mhn* should never make use of caching; and, "ask", indicating that *mhn* should ask the user.

There are two directories where contents may be cached: the profile entry **mhn-cache** names a directory containing world-readable contents, and, the profile entry **mhn-private-cache** names a directory containing private contents. The former should be an absolute (rooted) directory name. For example,

>   mhn-cache: /tmp

might be used if you didn't care that the cache got wiped after each reboot of the system. The latter is interpreted relative to the user's MH directory, if not rooted, e.g.,

>   mhn-private-cache: .cache

(which is the default value).

Caching the Contents

When you encounter a content of type message/external-body with access type ''mail-server'', *mhn* will ask you if may send a message to a mail-server requesting the content, e.g.,

>   % show 1
>   Retrieve content by asking mail-server@...
>
>   SEND file
>
>   ? yes
>   mhn: request sent

Regardless of your decision, *mhn* can't perform any other processing on the content.

However, if *mhn* is allowed to request the content, then when it arrives, there should be a top-level ''Content-ID:'' field which corresponds to the value in the original message/external-body content. You should now use the '-cache' switch to tell *mhn* to enter the arriving content into the content cache, e.g.,

>   % mhn -cache 2
>   caching message 2 as file ...

You can then re-process the original message/external-body content, and ''the right thing should happen'', e.g.,

>   % show 1
>   ...

Composing the Contents

The *mhn* program can also be used as a simple editor to aid in composing multi-media messages. When invoked by a *whatnow* program, *mhn* will expect the body of the draft to be formatted as an ''*mhn* composition file.''

The syntax of this is straight-forward:

```
body        ::=   1*(content I EOL)

content     ::=   directive I plaintext

directive   ::=   "#" type "/" subtype
                  0*(";" attribute "=" value)
                  [ "(" comment ")" ]
                  [ "<" id ">" ]
                  [ "[" description "]" ]
                  [ filename ]
                  EOL

                I "#@" type "/" subtype
                  0*(";" attribute "=" value)
                  [ "(" comment ")" ]
                  [ "<" id ">" ]
                  [ "[" description "]" ]
                  external-parameters
                  EOL

                I "#forw"
                  [ "<" id ">" ]
                  [ "[" description "]" ]
                  [ "+"folder ] [ 0*msg ]
                  EOL

                I "#begin"
                  [ "<" id ">" ]
                  [ "[" description "]" ]
                  [   "alternative"
                   I "parallel"
                   I something-else   ]
                  EOL
                  1*body
                 "#end" EOL

plaintext   ::=   [ "Content-Description:"
                  description EOL EOL ]
                  1*line
                  [ "#" EOL ]

                I "#<" type "/" subtype
                  0*(";" attribute "=" value)
                  [ "(" comment ")" ]
                  [ "[" description "]" ]
                  EOL
                  1*line
                  [ "#" EOL ]

line        ::=   "##" text EOL
                  -- interpreted as "#"text EOL
                I text EOL
```

Basically, the body contains one or more contents. A content consists of either a directive, indicated with a "#" as the first character of a line; or, plaintext (one or more lines of text). The continuation character, "\", may be used to enter a single directive on more than one line, e.g.,

```
#@application/octet-stream; \
   type=tar; \
   x-conversions=compress
```

There are four kinds of directives: "type" directives, which name the type and subtype of the content; "external-type" directives, which also name the type and subtype of the content; the "forw" directive, which is used to forward a digest of messages; and, the "begin" directive, which is used to create a multipart content.

For the type directives, the user may optionally specify the name of a file containing the contents in "native" (decoded) format. (If the filename starts with the "|" character, then this gives a command whose output is captured accordingly.) If a filename is not given, *mhn* will look for information in the user's profile to determine how the different contents should be composed. This is accomplished by consulting a composition string, and executing it under **/bin/sh**, with the standard output set to the content. The composition string may contain these escapes:

```
%a   additional arguments
%f   filename containing content
%F   %f, and stdout is not re-directed
%s   subtype
```

First, *mhn* will look for an entry of the form:

```
mhn-compose-<type>/<subtype>
```

to determine the command to use to compose the content. If this isn't found, *mhn* will look for an entry of the form:

```
mhn-compose-<type>
```

to determine the composition command. If this isn't found, *mhn* will complain.

An example entry might be:

```
mhn-compose-audio/basic: record | raw2audio -F
```

Because commands like these will vary, depending on the display environment used for login, composition strings for different contents should probably be put in the file specified by the **$MHN** environment variable, instead of directly in your user profile.

The external-type directives are used to provide a reference to a content, rather than enclosing the contents itself. Hence, instead of providing a filename as with the type directives, external-parameters are supplied.

These look like regular parameters, so they must be separated accordingly, e.g.,

```
#@application/octet-stream; \
    type=tar; \
    x-conversions=compress [] \
    access-type=anon-ftp; \
    name="mh-mime.tar.Z"; \
    directory="mrose/mh-mime"; \
    site="ftp.ics.uci.edu"
```

By specifying ''[]'', an empty description string is given, and the start of the external-parameters is identified. These parameters are of the form:

access-type=	usually *anon-ftp* or *mail-server*
name=	filename
permission=	read-only or read-write
site=	hostname
directory=	directoryname (optional)
mode=	usually *ascii* or *image* (optional)
size=	number of octets
server=	mailbox
subject=	subject to send
body=	command to send for retrieval

For the forw directive, the user may optionally specify the name of the folder and which messages are to be forwarded. if a folder is not given, it defaults to the current folder. Similarly, if a message is not given, it defaults to the current message. Hence, the forw directive is similar to the *forw* (1) command, except that the former uses the MIME rules for encapsulation rather than those specified in RFC 934. Usage of the '−rfc934mode' switch indicates whether *mhn* should attempt to utilize the encapsulation rules in such a way as to appear that RFC 934 is being used. If given, then RFC 934-compliant user-agents should be able to burst the message on reception -- providing that the messages being encapsulated do not contain encapsulated messages themselves. The drawback of this approach is that the encapsulations are generated by placing an extra newline at the end of the body of each message.

For the begin directive, the user must specify at least one content between the begin and end pairs.

For all of these directives, the user may include a brief description of the content between the ''['' character and the '']'' character. By default, *mhn* will generate a unique ''Content-ID:'' for each directive; however, the user may override this by defining the ID using the ''<'' and ''>'' characters. Putting this all together, here is a brief example of what a user's components file might look like:

```
To:
cc:
Subject:
--------
#audio/basic [Flint phone] \
    lraw2audio -F < /home/mrose/lib/multi-media/flint.au
#image/gif  [MTR's photo] \
                /home/mrose/lib/multi-media/mrose.gif
```

For a later example, we'll call this components file *mhncomps*.

As noted earlier, in addition to directives, plaintext can be present. Plaintext is gathered, until a directive is found or the draft is exhausted, and this is made to form a text content. If the plaintext must contain a ''#''

8

at the beginning of a line, simply double it, e.g.,

> ##when sent, this line will start with only one #

If you want to end the plaintext prior to a directive, e.g., to have two plaintext contents adjacent, simply insert a line containing a single ''#'' character, e.g.,

> this is the first content
> #
> and this is the second

Finally, if the plaintext starts with a line of the form:

> Content-Description: text

then this will be used to describe the plaintext content. **NOTE WELL:** you must follow this line with a blank line before starting your text.

By default, plaintext is captured as a text/plain content. You can override this by starting the plaintext with ''#<'' followed by a content-type specification, e.g.,

> #<text/richtext
> this content will be tagged as text/richtext
> #
> and this content will be tagged as text/plain

Note that if you use the ''#<'' plaintext-form, then the content-description must be on the same line which identifies the content type of the plaintext.

If *mhn* is successful, it renames the original draft to start with the '','' character and end with the string ''.orig'', e.g., if you are editing the file ''draft'', it will be renamed to '',draft.orig''. This allows you to easily recover the *mhn* composition file.

If the '-check' switch is given, *mhn* will associate an integrity check with each content.

Automatic Composition

Note that MH will not invoke *mhn* automatically, unless you add this line to your .mh_profile file:

> automhnproc: mhn

Otherwise, you must specifically give the command

> What now? edit mhn

prior to sending the draft.

You can easily tailor MH to help you remember to do this. Suppose you have these lines in your profile:

```
mcomp:        -editor mprompter -form mhncomps
mprompter:    -noprepend -norapid
mprompter-next: mhn
```

where *mcomp* is a link to *comp* (1), and *mprompter* is a link to *prompter* (1). Then to send a message using the *mhncomps* components file above, the sequence is:

% **mcomp**
To: **user@host**
cc:
Subject: **multi-media message**
\-\-\-\-\-\-\-\-
#audio/basic [Flint phone] \
   |raw2audio -F < /home/mrose/lib/multi-media/flint.au
#image/gif   [MTR's photo] \
              /home/mrose/lib/multi-media/mrose.gif

\-\-\-\-\-\-\-\-Enter additional text

This message contains three contents.
<CTRL-D>
\-\-\-\-\-\-\-\-

What now? **edit** (this invokes *mhn*)

What now? **send**

You have to remember to type the additional edit command, but it should be fairly obvious from the interaction.

Finally, you should consider adding this line to your profile:

lproc: show

This way, if you decide to **list** after invoking *mhn* as your editor, the command

What now? list

will work as you expect.

Sending Files via Mail

When you want to send a bunch of files to someone, you can run the *viamail* shell script, which is similar the tarmail command:

/usr/contrib/mh-6.8/lib/viamail mailpath ''subject'' files ...

viamail will archive the directories/files you name with *tar* (1), and then mail the compressed archive to the 'mailpath' with the given 'subject'. The archive will be automatically split up into as many messages as necessary in order to get past most mailers.

Sometimes you want *viamail* to pause after posting a partial message. This is usually the case when you are running *sendmail* and expect to generate a lot of partial messages. If the first argument given to *viamail* starts with a dash, then it is interpreted as the number of seconds to pause in between postings, e.g.,

            /usr/contrib/mh-6.8/lib/viamail -300 mailpath "subject" files ...

will pause 5 minutes in between each posting.

When these messages are received, invoke *mhn* once, with the list of messages, and the '−store' command. The *mhn* program will then store exactly one message containing the archive. You can then use '−show' to find out what's inside; possibly followed by '−store' to write the archive to a file where you can subsequently uncompress and untar it, e.g.,

```
% mhn -list all
msg part  type/subtype          size description
  1       message/partial       47K part 1 of 4
  2       message/partial       47K part 2 of 4
  3       message/partial       47K part 3 of 4
  4       message/partial       18K part 4 of 4
% mhn -store all
% mhn -list -verbose last
msg part  type/subtype          size description
  5       application/octet-stream 118K
          (extract with uncompress | tar xvpf -)
          type=tar
          x-conversions=compress
% mhn -show last
msg part  type/subtype          size description
  5       application/octet-stream 118K
-- headers of message, followed by tar listing appears here
% mhn -store last
% uncompress < 5.tar.Z | tar xvpf -
```

Alternately, by using the '−auto' switch, *mhn* will automatically do the extraction for you, e.g.,

```
% mhn -list all
msg part  type/subtype          size description
  1       message/partial       47K part 1 of 4
  2       message/partial       47K part 2 of 4
  3       message/partial       47K part 3 of 4
  4       message/partial       18K part 4 of 4
% mhn -store all
% mhn -list -verbose last
msg part  type/subtype          size description
  5       application/octet-stream 118K
          (extract with uncompress | tar xvpf -)
          type=tar
          x-conversions=compress
% mhn -show last
msg part  type/subtype          size description
  5       application/octet-stream 118K
-- headers of message, followed by tar listing appears here
% mhn -store -auto last
-- tar listing appears here as files are extracted
```

As the second *tar* listing is generated, the files are extracted. A prudent user will never put '−auto' in the .mh_profile file. The correct procedure is to first use '−show', to find out what will be extracted. Then *mhn* can be invoked with '−store' and '−auto' to perform the extraction.

User Environment

Because the display environment in which *mhn* operates may vary for a user, *mhn* will look for the environment variable **$MHN**. If present, this specifies the name of an additional user profile which should be read. Hence, when a user logs in on a particular display device, this environment variable should be set to refer to a file containing definitions useful for the display device. Normally, only entries of the form

    mhn-show-<type>/<subtype>
    mhn-show-<type>

need be present. Finally, *mhn* will attempt to consult one other additional user profile, e.g.,

    /usr/contrib/mh-6.8/lib/mhn_defaults

which is created automatically during MH installation.

Files

$HOME/.mh_profile	The user profile
$MHN	Additional profile entries
/usr/contrib/mh-6.8/lib/mhn_defaults	System-default profile entries
/usr/contrib/mh-6.8/lib/mhl.headers	The headers template

Profile Components

Path:	To determine the user's MH directory
Current–Folder:	To find the default current folder
mhlproc:	Default program to display message headers
mhn-access-ftp:	Program to retrieve contents via FTP
mhn-cache	Public directory to store cached external contents
mhn-charset-<charset>	Template for environment to render character sets
mhn-compose-<type>*	Template for composing contents
mhn-private-cache	Personal directory to store cached external contents
mhn-show-<type>*	Template for displaying contents
mhn-storage	Directory to store contents
mhn-store-<type>*	Template for storing contents
moreproc:	Default program to display text/plain content

See Also

mhl(1)
MIME: Mechanisms for Specifying and Describing the Format of Internet Message Bodies (RFC 1521), *Proposed Standard for Message Encapsulation* (RFC 934).

Defaults

'+folder' defaults to the current folder
'msgs' defaults to cur
'−noauto'
'−nocache'
'−nocheck'
'−noebcdicsafe'
'−form mhl.headers'
'−headers'
'−pause'
'−rcache ask'
'−realsize'
'−rfc934mode'
'−noserialonly'
'−show'
'−noverbose'
'−wcache ask'

Context

If a folder is given, it will become the current folder. The last message selected will become the current message.

Bugs

Partial messages contained within a multipart content are not reassembled with the '−store' switch.

NAME

    mhook, rcvdist, rcvpack, rcvtty – MH receive-mail hooks

SYNOPSIS

    /usr/contrib/mh-6.8/lib/rcvdist [–form formfile] [switches for *postproc*] address ... [–help]

    /usr/contrib/mh-6.8/lib/rcvpack file [–help]

    /usr/contrib/mh-6.8/lib/rcvtty [command] [–form formatfile] [–format string] [–bell] [–nobell] [–newline]
        [–nonewline] [–biff] [–help]

DESCRIPTION

    A receive–mail hook is a program that is run whenever you receive a mail message. You do **NOT** invoke
the hook yourself, rather the hook is invoked on your behalf by your system's Message Transport Agent.
See *slocal* (1) for details on how to activate receive–mail hooks on your system.

    Four programs are currently available as part of *MH*, *rcvdist* (redistribute incoming messages to additional
recipients), *rcvpack* (save incoming messages in a *packf*'d file), and *rcvtty* (notify user of incoming messages). The fourth program, *rcvstore* (1) is described separately. They all reside in the */usr/contrib/mh-
6.8/lib/* directory.

    The *rcvdist* program will resend a copy of the message to all of the addresses listed on its command line. It
uses the format string facility described in *mh–format* (5).

    The *rcvpack* program will append a copy of the message to the file listed on its command line. Its use is
obsoleted by the ''file'' action of *slocal*.

    The *rcvtty* program executes the named file with the message as its standard input, and writes the resulting
output on your terminal.

    If no file is specified, or is bogus, etc., then *rcvtty* will instead write a one–line scan listing. Either the
'–form formatfile' or '–format string' option may be used to override the default output format (see
mh–format (5)). A newline is output before the message output, and the terminal bell is rung after the output. The '–nonewline' and '–nobell' options will inhibit these functions.

    In addition to the standard *mh–format* (5) escapes, *rcvtty* also recognizes the following additional *com-
ponent* escapes:

Escape	*Returns*	*Description*
body	string	the (compressed) first part of the body
dtimenow	date	the current date
folder	string	the name of the current folder

    Normally, *rcvtty* obeys write permission as granted by *mesg* (1). With the '–biff' option, *rcvtty* will obey
the notification status set by *biff* (1) instead. If the terminal access daemon (TTYD) is available on your
system, then *rcvtty* will give its output to the daemon for output instead of writing on the user's terminal.

Files

/usr/contrib/mh-6.8/lib/mtstailor	tailor file
$HOME/.maildelivery	The file controlling local delivery
/usr/contrib/mh-6.8/lib/maildelivery	Rather than the standard file

See Also

    rcvstore (1), mh–format(5), slocal(1)

Bugs

Only two return codes are meaningful, others should be.

8

NAME

    mhparam – print MH profile components

SYNOPSIS

    mhparam [components] [-all] [-component] [-nocomponent] [–help]

DESCRIPTION

    Mhparam writes the value of the specified profile component to the standard output separated by newlines. If the profile component is not present, the default value (or nothing if there is no default) is printed.

    If more than one component is specified in the 'components' list, the component value is preceded by the component name. If '–component' is specified, the component name is displayed even when only one component is specified. If '–nocomponent' is specified, the component name is not displayed even when more than one component is specified.

    If '–all' is specified, all components if the MH profile are displayed and other arguments are ignored.

    Examples:

        % mhparam path
        Mail

        % mhparam mhlproc
        /usr/contrib/mh-6.8/lib/mhl

        % mhparam –component path
        Path: Mail

        % mhparam AliasFile rmmproc
        AliasFile: aliases
        rmmproc: rmmproc

        % mhparam –nocomponent AliasFile rmmproc
        aliases
        rmmproc

    Mhparam is also useful in back–quoted operations:

        % fgrep cornell.edu `mhpath +`/`mhparam aliasfile`

Files

    $HOME/.mh_profile   The user profile

See Also

    mh-profile (5)

Defaults

    '–nocomponent' if only one component is specified
    '–component' if more than one component is specified
    'components' defaults to none

Context

    None

8

NAME

mhpath – print full pathnames of MH messages and folders

SYNOPSIS

mhpath [+folder] [msgs] [–help]

DESCRIPTION

Mhpath expands and sorts the message list 'msgs' and writes the full pathnames of the messages to the standard output separated by newlines. If no 'msgs' are specified, *mhpath* outputs the folder pathname instead. If the only argument is '+', your MH *Path* is output; this can be useful is shell scripts.

Contrasted with other MH commands, a message argument to *mhpath* may often be intended for *writing*. Because of this:

1) the name "new" has been added to *mhpath*'s list of reserved message names (the others are "first", "last", "prev", "next", "cur", and "all"). The new message is equivalent to the message after the last message in a folder (and equivalent to 1 in a folder without messages). The "new" message may not be used as part of a message range.

2) Within a message list, the following designations may refer to messages that do not exist: a single numeric message name, the single message name "cur", and (obviously) the single message name "new". All other message designations must refer to at least one existing message.

3) An empty folder is not in itself an error.

Message numbers greater than the highest existing message in a folder as part of a range designation are replaced with the next free message number.

Examples: The current folder foo contains messages 3 5 6. Cur is 4.

```
% mhpath
/r/phyl/Mail/foo

% mhpath all
/r/phyl/Mail/foo/3
/r/phyl/Mail/foo/5
/r/phyl/Mail/foo/6

% mhpath 2001
/r/phyl/Mail/foo/7

% mhpath 1–2001
/r/phyl/Mail/foo/3
/r/phyl/Mail/foo/5
/r/phyl/Mail/foo/6

% mhpath new
/r/phyl/Mail/foo/7

% mhpath last new
/r/phyl/Mail/foo/6
/r/phyl/Mail/foo/7
```

8

```
% mhpath last–new
bad message list ''last–new''.

% mhpath cur
/r/phyl/Mail/foo/4

% mhpath 1–2
no messages in range ''1–2''.

% mhpath first:2
/r/phyl/Mail/foo/3
/r/phyl/Mail/foo/5

% mhpath 1 2
/r/phyl/Mail/foo/1
/r/phyl/Mail/foo/2
```

MHpath is also useful in back–quoted operations:

```
% cd 'mhpath +inbox'

% echo 'mhpath +'
/r/phyl/Mail
```

Files

$HOME/.mh_profile   The user profile

Profile Components

Path: To determine the user's MH directory
Current–Folder: To find the default current folder

See Also

folder(1)

Defaults

'+folder' defaults to the current folder
'msgs' defaults to none

Context

None

Bugs

Like all MH commands, *mhpath* expands and sorts [msgs]. So don't expect

```
mv 'mhpath 501 500'
```

to move 501 to 500. Quite the reverse. But

```
mv 'mhpath 501' 'mhpath 500'
```

will do the trick.

Out of range message 0 is treated far more severely than large out of range message numbers.

NAME

    msgchk – check for messages

SYNOPSIS

    msgchk [–date] [–nodate] [–notify all/mail/nomail] [–nonotify all/mail/nomail] [–host host] [–user user]
        [–apop] [–noapop] [–rpop] [–norpop] [users ...] [–help]

DESCRIPTION

    The *msgchk* program checks all known mail drops for mail waiting for you. For those drops which have mail for you, *msgchk* will indicate if it believes that you have seen the mail in question before.

    The '–notify type' switch indicates under what circumstances *msgchk* should produce a message. The default is '–notify all' which says that *msgchk* should always report the status of the users maildrop. Other values for 'type' include 'mail' which says that *msgchk* should report the status of waiting mail; and, 'nomail' which says that *msgchk* should report the status of empty maildrops. The '–nonotify type' switch has the inverted sense, so '–nonotify all' directs *msgchk* to never report the status of maildrops. This is useful if the user wishes to check *msgchk*'s exit status. A non–zero exit status indicates that mail was **not** waiting for at least one of the indicated users.

    If *msgchk* produces output, then the '–date' switch directs *msgchk* to print out the last date mail was read, if this can be determined.

    If the local host is configured as a POP client, or if the '–host host' switch is given, *msgchk* will query the POP service host as to the status of mail waiting. If the '–user user' switch is not given, then the current username is used. Normally, *msgchk* will prompt for a password to use. However, if the '–apop' switch is given, *msgchk* will generate authentication credentials to provide for origin authentication and replay protection, but which do not involve sending a password in the clear over the network. Otherwise, if the '–rpop' switch is given, then *msgchk* will try to use a "trusted" connection (ala the BSD r-commands).

Files

    $HOME/.mh_profile   The user profile
    /usr/contrib/mh-6.8/lib/mtstailor   tailor file
    /var/mail/$USER   Location of mail drop

Profile Components

    None

See Also

    Post Office Protocol - version 3 (aka RFC–1081),
    inc(1)

Defaults

    'user' defaults to the current user
    '–date'
    '–notify all'
    '–rpop'

Context

    None

NAME
      msh – MH shell (and BBoard reader)

SYNOPSIS
      msh [–prompt string] [–scan] [–noscan] [–topcur] [–notopcur] [file] [–help]

DESCRIPTION

      msh is an interactive program that implements a subset of the normal *MH* commands operating on a single
      file in *packf*'d format. That is, *msh* is used to read a file that contains a number of messages, as opposed to
      the standard *MH* style of reading a number of files, each file being a separate message in a folder. *msh*'s
      chief advantage is that the normal *MH* style does not allow a file to have more than one message in it.
      Hence, *msh* is ideal for reading *BBoards*, as these files are delivered by the transport system in this format.
      In addition, *msh* can be used on other files, such as message archives which have been *packf*ed (see
      packf (1)). Finally, *msh* is an excellent *MH* tutor. As the only commands available to the user are *MH*
      commands, this allows *MH* beginners to concentrate on how commands to *MH* are formed and (more or
      less) what they mean.

      When invoked, *msh* reads the named file, and enters a command loop. The user may type most of the nor-
      mal *MH* commands. The syntax and semantics of these commands typed to *msh* are identical to their *MH*
      counterparts. In cases where the nature of *msh* would be inconsistent (e.g., specifying a '+folder' with
      some commands), *msh* will duly inform the user. The commands that *msh* currently supports (in some
      slightly modified or restricted forms) are:

              ali
              burst
              comp
              dist
              folder
              forw
              inc
              mark
              mhmail
              mhn
              msgchk
              next
              packf
              pick
              prev
              refile
              repl
              rmm
              scan
              send
              show
              sortm
              whatnow
              whom

      In addition, *msh* has a "help" command which gives a brief overview. To terminate *msh*, type CTRL–D,
      or use the "quit" command. If *msh* is being invoked from *bbc*, then typing CTRL–D will also tell *bbc* to
      exit as well, while using the "quit" command will return control to *bbc*, and *bbc* will continue examining
      the list of BBoards that it is scanning.

8

If the file is writable and has been modified, then using "quit" will query the user if the file should be updated.

The '–prompt string' switch sets the prompting string for *msh*.

You may wish to use an alternate *MH* profile for the commands that *msh* executes; see *mh-profile* (5) for details about the **$MH** envariable.

When invoked from *bbc*, two special features are enabled: First, the '–scan' switch directs *msh* to do a 'scan unseen' on start–up if new items are present in the BBoard. This feature is best used from *bbc*, which correctly sets the stage. Second, the *mark* command in *msh* acts specially when you are reading a BBoard, since *msh* will consult the sequence "unseen" in determining what messages you have actually read. When *msh* exits, it reports this information to *bbc*. In addition, if you give the *mark* command with no arguments, *msh* will interpret it as 'mark –sequence unseen –delete –nozero all' Hence, to discard all of the messages in the current BBoard you're reading, just use the *mark* command with no arguments.

Normally, the "exit" command is identical to the "quit" command in *msh*. When run under *bbc* however, "exit" directs *msh* to mark all messages as seen and then "quit". For speedy type–in, this command is often abbreviated as just "e".

When invoked from *vmh*, another special feature is enabled: The 'topcur' switch directs *msh* to have the current message "track" the top line of the *vmh* scan window. Normally, *msh* has the current message "track" the center of the window (under '–notopcur', which is the default).

msh supports an output redirection facility. Commands may be followed by one of

> *file*　　　　write output to *file*
>> *file*　　　append output to *file*
| *command*　pipe output to UNIX *command*

If *file* starts with a '~' (tilde), then a *csh*-like expansion takes place. Note that *command* is interpreted by *sh* (1). Also note that *msh* does NOT support history substitutions, variable substitutions, or alias substitutions.

When parsing commands to the left of any redirection symbol, *msh* will honor '\' (back–slash) as the quote next–character symbol, and '"' (double–quote) as quote–word delimiters. All other input tokens are separated by whitespace (spaces and tabs).

Files

$HOME/.mh_profile　　　　　　　　　The user profile
/usr/contrib/mh-6.8/lib/mtstailor　　　tailor file

Profile Components

Path:　　　　　　　To determine the user's MH directory
Msg–Protect:　　　To set mode when creating a new 'file'
fileproc:　　　　　Program to file messages
showproc:　　　　　Program to show messages

See Also

bbc(1)

Defaults

'file' defaults to "./msgbox"
'–prompt (msh) '
'–noscan'
'–notopcur'

8

Context

None

Bugs

The argument to the '−prompt' switch must be interpreted as a single token by the shell that invokes *msh*. Therefore, one must usually place the argument to this switch inside double−quotes.

There is a strict limit of messages per file in *packf*'d format which *msh* can handle. Usually, this limit is 1000 messages.

Please remember that *msh* is not the *CShell*, and that a lot of the nice facilities provided by the latter are not present in the former.

In particular, *msh* does not understand back−quoting, so the only effective way to use *pick* inside *msh* is to always use the '−seq select' switch. Clever users of *MH* will put the line

        pick: −seq select −list

in their .mh_profile file so that *pick* works equally well from both the shell and *msh*.

sortm always uses ''−noverbose'' and if ''−textfield field'' is used, ''−limit 0''.

The *msh* program inherits most (if not all) of the bugs from the *MH* commands it implements.

NAME

next – show the next message

SYNOPSIS

next [+folder] [–header] [–noheader] [–showproc program] [–noshowproc] [switches for *showproc*]
        [–help]

DESCRIPTION

Next performs a *show* on the next message in the specified (or current) folder. Like *show*, it passes any switches on to the program *showproc*, which is called to list the message. This command is almost exactly equivalent to ''show next''. Consult the manual entry for *show* (1) for all the details.

Files

$HOME/.mh_profile   The user profile

Profile Components

Path: To determine the user's MH directory
Current–Folder: To find the default current folder
showproc: Program to show the message

See Also

show(1), prev(1)

Defaults

'+folder' defaults to the current folder
'–header'

Context

If a folder is specified, it will become the current folder. The message that is shown (i.e., the next message in sequence) will become the current message.

Bugs

next is really a link to the *show* program. As a result, if you make a link to *next* and that link is not called *next*, your link will act like *show* instead. To circumvent this, add a profile–entry for the link to your *MH* profile and add the argument *next* to the entry.

NAME

packf – compress an MH folder into a single file

SYNOPSIS

packf [+folder] [msgs] [–file name] [–help]

DESCRIPTION

Packf takes messages from a folder and copies them to a single file. Each message in the file is separated by four CTRL–A's and a newline. Messages packed can be unpacked using *inc*.

If the *name* given to the '–file name' switch exists, then the messages specified will be appended to the end of the file, otherwise the file will be created and the messages appended.

Files

$HOME/.mh_profile	The user profile
.msgbox.map	A binary index of the file

Profile Components

Path:	To determine the user's MH directory
Current–Folder:	To find the default current folder
Msg–Protect:	To set mode when creating a new 'file'

See Also

inc(1)

Defaults

'+folder' defaults to the current folder

'msgs' defaults to all

'–file ./msgbox'

Context

If a folder is given, it will become the current folder. The first message packed will become the current message.

Bugs

Packf doesn't handle the old UUCP-style ''mbox'' format (used by *SendMail*). To pack messages into this format, use the script */usr/contrib/mh-6.8/lib/packmbox*. Note that *packmbox* does not take the '–file' option of *packf*, and instead writes its output on *stdout*.

NAME

pick – select messages by content

SYNOPSIS

pick
{
 –cc
 –date
 –from
 –search
 –subject
 –to
 ––component
}
[+folder] [msgs] [–help]
[–before date] [–after date] [–datefield field]

pattern [–and ...] [–or ...] [–not ...] [–lbrace ... –rbrace]

[–sequence name ...] [–public] [–nopublic] [–zero] [–nozero]
[–list] [–nolist]

typically:
>   scan 'pick –from jones'
>   pick –to holloway –sequence select
>   show 'pick –before friday'

DESCRIPTION

Pick searches messages within a folder for the specified contents, and then identifies those messages. Two types of search primitives are available: pattern matching and date constraint operations.

A modified *grep*(1) is used to perform the matching, so the full regular expression (see *ed*(1)) facility is available within 'pattern'. With '–search', 'pattern' is used directly, and with the others, the grep pattern constructed is:

>   ''component[\t]*:.*pattern''

This means that the pattern specified for a '–search' will be found everywhere in the message, including the header and the body, while the other pattern matching requests are limited to the single specified component. The expression

>   '––component pattern'

is a shorthand for specifying

>   '–search ''component[\t]*:.*pattern'' '

It is used to pick a component which is not one of ''To:'', ''cc:'', ''Date:'', ''From:'', or ''Subject:''. An example is 'pick ––reply–to pooh'.

Pattern matching is performed on a per–line basis. Within the header of the message, each component is treated as one long line, but in the body, each line is separate. Lower–case letters in the search pattern will match either lower or upper case in the message, while upper case will match only upper case.

Note that since the '–date' switch is a pattern matching operation (as described above), to find messages sent on a certain date the pattern string must match the text of the ''Date:'' field of the message.

Independent of any pattern matching operations requested, the switches '–after date' or '–before date' may also be used to introduce date/time constraints on all of the messages. By default, the ''Date:'' field is consulted, but if another date yielding field (such as ''BB–Posted:'' or ''Delivery–Date:'') should be used, the '–datefield field' switch may be used.

With '–before' and '–after', *pick* will actually parse the date fields in each of the messages specified in 'msgs' and compare them to the date/time specified. If '–after' is given, then only those messages whose

8

"Date:" field value is chronologically after the date specified will be considered. The '–before' switch specifies the complimentary action.

Both the '–after' and '–before' switches take legal 822–style date specifications as arguments. *Pick* will default certain missing fields so that the entire date need not be specified. These fields are (in order of defaulting): timezone, time and timezone, date, date and timezone. All defaults are taken from the current date, time, and timezone.

In addition to 822–style dates, *pick* will also recognize any of the days of the week ("sunday", "monday", and so on), and the special dates "today", "yesterday" (24 hours ago), and "tomorrow" (24 hours from now). All days of the week are judged to refer to a day in the past (e.g., telling *pick* "saturday" on a "tuesday" means "last saturday" not "this saturday").

Finally, in addition to these special specifications, *pick* will also honor a specification of the form "–dd", which means "dd days ago".

Pick supports complex boolean operations on the searching primitives with the '–and', '–or', '–not', and '–lbrace ... –rbrace' switches. For example,

          pick –after yesterday –and –lbrace –from freida –or –from fear –rbrace

identifies messages recently sent by "frieda" or "fear".

The matching primitives take precedence over the '–not' switch, which in turn takes precedence over '–and' which in turn takes precedence over '–or'. To override the default precedence, the '–lbrace' and '–rbrace' switches are provided, which act just like opening and closing parentheses in logical expressions.

If no search criteria are given, all the messages specified on the command line are selected (this defaults to "all").

Once the search has been performed, if the '–list' switch is given, the message numbers of the selected messages are written to the standard output separated by newlines. This is *extremely* useful for quickly generating arguments for other *MH* programs by using the "backquoting" syntax of the shell. For example, the command

          scan `pick +todo –after "31 Mar 83 0123 PST"`

says to *scan* those messages in the indicated folder which meet the appropriate criterion. Note that since *pick* 's context changes are written out prior to *scan* 's invocation, you need not give the folder argument to *scan* as well.

Regardless of the operation of the '–list' switch, the '–sequence name' switch may be given once for each sequence the user wishes to define. For each sequence named, that sequence will be defined to mean exactly those messages selected by *pick*. For example,

          pick –from frated –seq fred

defines a new message sequence for the current folder called "fred" which contains exactly those messages that were selected.

Note that whenever *pick* processes a '–sequence name' switch, it sets '–nolist'.

By default, *pick* will zero the sequence before adding it. This action can be disabled with the '–nozero' switch, which means that the messages selected by *pick* will be added to the sequence, if it already exists, and any messages already a part of that sequence will remain so.

The '–public' and '–nopublic' switches are used by *pick* in the same way *mark* uses them.

8

Files

    $HOME/.mh_profile   The user profile

Profile Components
    Path: To determine the user's MH directory
    Current–Folder: To find the default current folder

See Also
    mark(1)

Defaults
    '+folder' defaults to the current folder
    'msgs' defaults to all
    '–datefield date'
    '–nopublic' if the folder is read–only, '–public' otherwise
    '–zero'
    '–list' is the default if no '–sequence', '–nolist' otherwise

Context
    If a folder is given, it will become the current folder.

History

In previous versions of *MH*, the *pick* command would *show*, *scan*, or *refile* the selected messages. This was rather "inverted logic" from the UNIX point of view, so *pick* was changed to define sequences and output those sequences. Hence, *pick* can be used to generate the arguments for all other *MH* commands, instead of giving *pick* endless switches for invoking those commands itself.

Also, previous versions of *pick* balked if you didn't specify a search string or a date/time constraint. The current version does not, and merely matches the messages you specify. This lets you type something like:

    show 'pick last:20 –seq fear'

instead of typing

    mark –add –nozero –seq fear last:20
    show fear

Finally, timezones used to be ignored when comparing dates: they aren't any more.

Helpful Hints

Use "pick sequence –list" to enumerate the messages in a sequence (such as for use by a shell script).

Bugs

The argument to the '–after' and '–before' switches must be interpreted as a single token by the shell that invokes *pick*. Therefore, one must usually place the argument to this switch inside double–quotes. Furthermore, any occurance of '–datefield' must occur prior to the '–after' or '–before' switch it applies to.

If *pick* is used in a back–quoted operation, such as

        scan `pick –from jones`

and *pick* selects no messages (e.g., no messages are from ''jones''), then the shell will still run the outer command (e.g., ''scan''). Since no messages were matched, *pick* produced no output, and the argument given to the outer command as a result of backquoting *pick* is empty. In the case of *MH* programs, the outer command now acts as if the default 'msg' or 'msgs' should be used (e.g., ''all'' in the case of *scan*). To prevent this unexpected behavior, if '–list' was given, and if its standard output is not a tty, then *pick* outputs the illegal message number ''0'' when it fails. This lets the outer command fail gracefully as well.

The pattern syntax ''[l-r]'' is not supported; each letter to be matched must be included within the square brackets.

NAME
>   prev – show the previous message

SYNOPSIS
>   prev [+folder] [–header] [–noheader] [–showproc program] [–noshowproc] [–switches for *showproc*]
>   [–help]

DESCRIPTION

>   *Prev* performs a *show* on the previous message in the specified (or current) folder. Like *show*, it passes any
>   switches on to the program named by *showproc*, which is called to list the message. This command is
>   almost exactly equivalent to ''show prev''. Consult the manual entry for *show* (1) for all the details.

Files

> $HOME/.mh_profile   The user profile

Profile Components

>   Path: To determine the user's MH directory
>   Current–Folder: To find the default current folder
>   showproc: Program to show the message

See Also

>   show(1), next(1)

Defaults

>   '+folder' defaults to the current folder
>   '–header'

Context

>   If a folder is specified, it will become the current folder. The message that is shown (i.e., the previous mes-
>   sage in sequence) will become the current message.

Bugs

>   *prev* is really a link to the *show* program. As a result, if you make a link to *prev* and that link is not called
>   *prev*, your link will act like *show* instead. To circumvent this, add a profile–entry for the link to your *MH*
>   profile and add the argument *prev* to the entry.

8

NAME

    prompter – prompting editor front-end for MH

SYNOPSIS

    prompter [–erase chr] [–kill chr] [–prepend] [–noprepend] [–rapid] [–norapid] [–doteof] [–nodoteof] file
        [–help]

DESCRIPTION

    This program is normally not invoked directly by users but takes the place of an editor and acts as an editor
front–end. It operates on an 822–style message draft skeleton specified by file, normally provided by
comp, dist, forw, or *repl.*

    Prompter is an editor which allows rapid composition of messages. It is particularly useful to network and
low–speed (less than 2400 baud) users of *MH.* It is an *MH* program in that it can have its own profile entry
with switches, but it is not invoked directly by the user. The commands *comp, dist, forw,* and *repl* invoke
prompter as an editor, either when invoked with '–editor prompter', or by the profile entry
''Editor: prompter'', or when given the command 'edit prompter' at ''What now?'' level.

    For each empty component *prompter* finds in the draft, the user is prompted for a response; A <RETURN>
will cause the whole component to be left out. Otherwise, a '\' preceding a <RETURN> will continue the
response on the next line, allowing for multiline components. Continuation lines **must** begin with a space
or tab.

    Each non–empty component is copied to the draft and displayed on the terminal.

    The start of the message body is denoted by a blank line or a line of dashes. If the body is non–empty, the
prompt, which isn't written to the file, is

        ''--------Enter additional text'',

or (if '–prepend' was given)

        ''--------Enter initial text''.

    Message–body typing is terminated with an end–of–file (usually CTRL–D). With the '–doteof' switch, a
period on a line all by itself also signifies end–of–file. At this point control is returned to the calling program, where the user is asked ''What now?''. See *whatnow* for the valid options to this query.

    By using the '–prepend' switch, the user can add type–in to the beginning of the message body and have
the rest of the body follow. This is useful for the *forw* command.

    By using the '–rapid' switch, if the draft already contains text in the message–body, it is not displayed on
the user's terminal. This is useful for low–speed terminals.

    The line editing characters for kill and erase may be specified by the user via the arguments '–kill chr' and
'–erase chr', where chr may be a character; or '\nnn', where ''nnn'' is the octal value for the character.

    An interrupt (usually CTRL–C) during component typing will abort *prompter* and the *MH* command that
invoked it. An interrupt during message–body typing is equivalent to CTRL–D, for historical reasons.
This means that *prompter* should finish up and exit.

    The first non–flag argument to *prompter* is taken as the name of the draft file, and subsequent non–flag
arguments are ignored.

8

Files

$HOME/.mh_profile	The user profile
/tmp/prompter*	Temporary copy of message

Profile Components

prompter–next:	To name the editor to be used on exit from *prompter*
Msg–Protect:	To set mode when creating a new draft

See Also

comp(1), dist(1), forw(1), repl(1), whatnow(1)

Defaults

'–prepend'
'–norapid'
'–nodoteof'

Context

None

Helpful Hints

The '–rapid' option is particularly useful with *forw*, and '–noprepend' is useful with *comp –use*.

The user may wish to link *prompter* under several names (e.g., ''rapid'') and give appropriate switches in the profile entries under these names (e.g., ''rapid: -rapid''). This facilitates invoking prompter differently for different *MH* commands (e.g., ''forw: -editor rapid'').

Bugs

Prompter uses *stdio* (3), so it will lose if you edit files with nulls in them.

8

NAME

    rcvstore – incorporate new mail asynchronously

SYNOPSIS

    /usr/contrib/mh-6.8/lib/rcvstore [+folder] [–create] [–nocreate] [–sequence name ...] [–public] [–nopublic]
        [–zero] [–nozero] [–help]

DESCRIPTION

    Rcvstore incorporates a message from the standard input into an *MH* folder. If '+folder' isn't specified, a
    folder in the user's *MH* directory will be used, either that specified by the ''Inbox:'' entry in the user's
    profile, or the folder named ''inbox''. The new message being incorporated is assigned the next highest
    number in the folder. If the specified (or default) folder doesn't exist, then it will be created if the '–create'
    option is specified, otherwise *rcvstore* will exit.

    If the user's profile contains a ''Msg–Protect: nnn'' entry, it will be used as the protection on the newly
    created messages, otherwise the *MH* default of 0644 will be used. During all operations on messages, this
    initially assigned protection will be preserved for each message, so *chmod*(1) may be used to set a protec-
    tion on an individual message, and its protection will be preserved thereafter.

    Rcvstore will incorporate anything except zero length messages into the user's MH folder.

    If the profile entry ''Unseen–Sequence'' is present and non–empty, then *rcvstore* will add the newly incor-
    porated message to each sequence named by the profile entry. This is similar to the ''Previous–Sequence''
    profile entry supported by all *MH* commands which take 'msgs' or 'msg' arguments. Note that *rcvstore*
    will not zero each sequence prior to adding messages.

    Furthermore, the incoming messages may be added to user-defined sequences as they arrive by appropriate
    use of the '–sequence' option. As with *pick*, use of the '–zero' and '–nozero' switches can also be used to
    zero old sequences or not. Similarly, use of the '–public' and '–nopublic' switches may be used to force
    additions to public and private sequences.

Files

    $HOME/.mh_profile   The user profile

Profile Components

    Path: To determine the user's MH directory
    Folder–Protect: To set mode when creating a new folder
    Inbox: To find the default inbox
    Msg–Protect: To set mode when creating a new message
    Unseen–Sequence: To name sequences denoting unseen messages

See Also

    inc(1), pick(1), mh–mail(5)

Defaults

    '+folder' defaults to ''inbox''
    '–create'
    '–nopublic' if the folder is read–only, '–public' otherwise
    '–nozero'

Context

    No context changes will be attempted, with the exception of sequence manipulation.

Bugs

If you use the "Unseen–Sequence" profile entry, *rcvstore* could try to update the context while another *MH* process is also trying to do so. This can cause the context to become corrupted. To avoid this, do not use *rcvstore* if you use the "Unseen–Sequence" profile entry.

NAME
     refile – file message in other folders

SYNOPSIS
     refile [msgs] [–draft] [–link] [–nolink] [–preserve] [–nopreserve] [–src +folder] [–file file] [–rmmproc pro-
          gram] [–normmproc] +folder ... [–help]

DESCRIPTION

     Refile moves (*mv* (1)) or links (*ln* (1)) messages from a source folder into one or more destination folders.
     If you think of a message as a sheet of paper, this operation is not unlike filing the sheet of paper (or
     copies) in file cabinet folders. When a message is filed, it is linked into the destination folder(s) if possible,
     and is copied otherwise. As long as the destination folders are all on the same file system, multiple filing
     causes little storage overhead. This facility provides a good way to cross–file or multiply–index messages.
     For example, if a message is received from Jones about the ARPA Map Project, the command

          refile cur +jones +Map

     would allow the message to be found in either of the two folders 'jones' or 'Map'.

     The option '–file file' directs *refile* to use the specified file as the source message to be filed, rather than a
     message from a folder. Note that the file should be a validly formatted message, just like any other *MH*
     message. It should **NOT** be in mail drop format (to convert a file in mail drop format to a folder of *MH*
     messages, see *inc* (1)).

     If a destination folder doesn't exist, *refile* will ask if you want to create it. A negative response will abort
     the file operation. If the standard input for *refile* is *not* a tty, then *refile* will not ask any questions and will
     proceed as if the user answered ''yes'' to all questions.

     The option '–link' preserves the source folder copy of the message (i.e., it does a *ln*(1) rather than a *mv*(1)),
     whereas, '–nolink' deletes the filed messages from the source folder. Normally, when a message is filed, it
     is assigned the next highest number available in each of the destination folders. Use of the '–preserve'
     switch will override this message renaming, but name conflicts may occur, so use this switch cautiously.

     If '–link' is not specified (or '–nolink' is specified), the filed messages will be removed from the source
     folder, by renaming them with a site-dependent prefix (usually a comma).

     If the user has a profile component such as

          rmmproc: /bin/rm

     then *refile* will instead call the named program to delete the message files. The user may specify
     '–rmmproc program' on the command line to override this profile specification. The `-normmproc' option
     forces the message files to be deleted by renaming them as described above.

     The '–draft' switch tells *refile* to file the <mh–dir>/draft.

Files
     $HOME/.mh_profile   The user profile

Profile Components
     Path: To determine the user's MH directory
     Current–Folder: To find the default current folder
     Folder–Protect: To set mode when creating a new folder
     rmmproc: Program to delete the message

See Also

folder(1)

Defaults

'−src +folder' defaults to the current folder
'msgs' defaults to cur
'−nolink'
'−nopreserve'

Context

If '−src +folder' is given, it will become the current folder. If neither '−link' nor 'all' is specified, the current message in the source folder will be set to the last message specified; otherwise, the current message won't be changed.

If the Previous−Sequence profile entry is set, in addition to defining the named sequences from the source folder, *refile* will also define those sequences for the destination folders. See *mh−sequence* (5) for information concerning the previous sequence.

Bugs

Since *refile* uses your *rmmproc* to delete the message, the *rmmproc* must **NOT** call *refile* without specifying '−normmproc', or you will create an infinte loop.

8

NAME
        repl – reply to a message

SYNOPSIS
        repl [+folder] [msg] [–annotate] [–noannotate] [–cc all/to/cc/me] [–nocc all/to/cc/me]
                [–draftfolder +folder] [–draftmessage msg] [–nodraftfolder] [–editor editor] [–noedit]
                [–fcc +folder] [–filter filterfile] [–form formfile] [–inplace] [–noinplace] [–query] [–noquery]
                [–width columns] [–whatnowproc program] [–nowhatnowproc] [–help]

DESCRIPTION
        Repl aids a user in producing a reply to an existing message. *Repl* uses a reply template to guide its actions
        when constructing the message draft of the reply. In its simplest form (with no arguments), it will set up a
        message–form skeleton in reply to the current message in the current folder, and invoke the whatnow shell.
        The default reply template will direct *repl* to construct the composed message as follows:

                To: <Reply–To> or <From>
                cc: <cc>, <To>, and yourself
                Subject: Re: <Subject>
                In–reply–to: Your message of <Date>.
                        <Message–Id>

        where field names enclosed in angle brackets (< >) indicate the contents of the named field from the mes-
        sage to which the reply is being made. A reply template is simply a format file. See *mh–format* (5) for the
        details.

        The '–cc type' switch takes an argument which specifies who gets placed on the ''cc:'' list of the reply.
        The '–query' switch modifies the action of '–cc type' switch by interactively asking you if each address
        that normally would be placed in the ''To:'' and ''cc:'' list should actually be sent a copy. (This is useful
        for special–purpose replies.) Note that the position of the '–cc' and '–nocc' switches, like all other
        switches which take a positive and negative form, is important.

        Lines beginning with the fields ''To:'', ''cc:'', and ''Bcc:'' will be standardized and have duplicate
        addresses removed. In addition, the '–width columns' switch will guide *repl*'s formatting of these fields.

        If the file named ''replcomps'' exists in the user's MH directory, it will be used instead of the default form.
        In either case, the file specified by '–form formfile' will be used if given.

        If the draft already exists, *repl* will ask you as to the disposition of the draft. A reply of **quit** will abort
        repl, leaving the draft intact; **replace** will replace the existing draft with a blank skeleton; and **list** will
        display the draft.

        See *comp* (1) for a description of the '–editor' and '–noedit' switches. Note that while in the editor, the
        message being replied to is available through a link named ''@'' (assuming the default *whatnowproc*). In
        addition, the actual pathname of the message is stored in the envariable **$editalt**, and the pathname of the
        folder containing the message is stored in the envariable **$mhfolder**.

        Although *repl* uses the '–form formfile' switch to direct it how to construct the beginning of the draft, the
        '–filter filterfile' switch directs *repl* as to how the message being replied–to should be formatted in the
        body of the draft. If '–filter' is not specified, then the message being replied–to is not included in the body
        of the draft. If '–filter filterfile' is specified, then the message being replied–to is filtered (re–formatted)
        prior to being output to the body of the draft. The filter file for *repl* should be a standard form file for *mhl*,
        as *repl* will invoke *mhl* to format the message being replied–to. There is no default message filter ('–filter'
        must be followed by a file name).

8

A filter file that is commonly used is:

> :
> body:nocomponent,compwidth=9,offset=9

which says to output a blank line and then the body of the message being replied–to, indented by one tab–stop. Another format popular on USENET is:

> message-id:nocomponent, nonewline, formatfield="In message %{text}, "
> from:nocomponent, formatfield="%(friendly{text}) writes:"
> body:component=">", overflowtext=">", overflowoffset=0

Which cites the Message-ID and author of the message being replied–to, and then outputs each line of the body prefaced with the ">" character.

If the '−annotate' switch is given, the message being replied–to will be annotated with the lines

> Replied: date
> Replied: addrs

where the address list contains one line for each addressee. The annotation will be done only if the message is sent directly from *repl*. If the message is not sent immediately from *repl*, "comp −use" may be used to re–edit and send the constructed message, but the annotations won't take place. The '−inplace' switch causes annotation to be done in place in order to preserve links to the annotated message.

The '−fcc +folder' switch can be used to automatically specify a folder to receive Fcc:s. More than one folder, each preceeded by '−fcc' can be named.

In addition to the standard *mh–format* (5) escapes, *repl* also recognizes the following additional *component* escape:

Escape Returns Description
fcc   string   Any folders specified with '−fcc folder'

To avoid reiteration, *repl* strips any leading 'Re: ' strings from the *subject* component.

The '−draftfolder +folder' and '−draftmessage msg' switches invoke the *MH* draft folder facility. This is an advanced (and highly useful) feature. Consult the **Advanced Features** section of the *MH* manual for more information.

Upon exiting from the editor, *repl* will invoke the *whatnow* program. See *whatnow* (1) for a discussion of available options. The invocation of this program can be inhibited by using the '−nowhatnowproc' switch. (In truth of fact, it is the *whatnow* program which starts the initial edit. Hence, '−nowhatnowproc' will prevent any edit from occurring.)

Files

/usr/contrib/mh-6.8/lib/replcomps	The reply template
or <mh–dir>/replcomps	Rather than the standard template
$HOME/.mh_profile	The user profile
<mh–dir>/draft	The draft file

Profile Components

Path:	To determine the user's MH directory
Alternate–Mailboxes:	To determine the user's mailboxes
Current–Folder:	To find the default current folder
Draft–Folder:	To find the default draft–folder
Editor:	To override the default editor
Msg–Protect:	To set mode when creating a new message (draft)
fileproc:	Program to refile the message
mhlproc:	Program to filter message being replied–to
whatnowproc:	Program to ask the ''What now?'' questions

See Also

comp(1), dist(1), forw(1), send(1), whatnow(1), mh–format(5)

Defaults

'+folder' defaults to the current folder
'msg' defaults to cur
'–nocc all' at ATHENA sites, '–cc all' otherwise
'–noannotate'
'–nodraftfolder'
'–noinplace'
'–noquery'
'–width 72'

Context

If a folder is given, it will become the current folder. The message replied–to will become the current message.

History

Prior to using the format string mechanism, '–noformat' used to cause address headers to be output as–is. Now all address fields are formatted using Internet standard guidelines.

Bugs

If any addresses occur in the reply template, addresses in the template that do not contain hosts are defaulted incorrectly. Instead of using the localhost for the default, *repl* uses the sender's host. Moral of the story: if you're going to include addresses in a reply template, include the host portion of the address.

The '–width columns' switch is only used to do address-folding; other headers are not line–wrapped.

If *whatnowproc* is *whatnow*, then *repl* uses a built–in *whatnow*, it does not actually run the *whatnow* program. Hence, if you define your own *whatnowproc*, don't call it *whatnow* since *repl* won't run it.

If your current working directory is not writable, the link named ''@'' is not available.

8

NAME
    rmf – remove an MH folder

SYNOPSIS
    rmf [+folder] [−interactive] [−nointeractive] [−help]

DESCRIPTION

    Rmf removes all of the messages (files) within the specified (or default) folder, and then removes the folder (directory) itself. If there are any files within the folder which are not a part of *MH*, they will *not* be removed, and an error will be produced. If the folder is given explicitly or the '−nointeractive' option is given, then the folder will be removed without confirmation. Otherwise, the user will be asked for confirmation. If *rmf* can't find the current folder, for some reason, the folder to be removed defaults to '+inbox' (unless overridden by user's profile entry ''Inbox'') with confirmation.

    Rmf irreversibly deletes messages that don't have other links, so use it with caution.

    If the folder being removed is a subfolder, the parent folder will become the new current folder, and *rmf* will produce a message telling the user this has happened. This provides an easy mechanism for selecting a set of messages, operating on the list, then removing the list and returning to the current folder from which the list was extracted.

    Rmf of a read−only folder will delete the private sequence and cur information (i.e., ''atr−*seq−folder*'' entries) from the profile without affecting the folder itself.

Files
    $HOME/.mh_profile   The user profile

Profile Components
Path:	To determine the user's MH directory
Current−Folder:	To find the default current folder
Inbox:	To find the default inbox

See Also
    rmm(1)

Defaults
    '+folder' defaults to the current folder, usually with confirmation
    '−interactive' if +folder' not given, '−nointeractive' otherwise

Context
    Rmf will set the current folder to the parent folder if a subfolder is removed; or if the current folder is removed, it will make ''inbox'' current. Otherwise, it doesn't change the current folder or message.

Bugs

    Although intuitively one would suspect that *rmf* works recursively, it does not. Hence if you have a sub−folder within a folder, in order to *rmf* the parent, you must first *rmf* each of the children.

8

NAME
     rmm – remove messages

SYNOPSIS
     rmm [+folder] [msgs] [–help]

DESCRIPTION

     Rmm removes the specified messages by renaming the message files with preceding commas. Many sites consider files that start with a comma to be a temporary backup, and arrange for *cron* (8) to remove such files once a day.

     If the user has a profile component such as

          rmmproc: /bin/rm

     then instead of simply renaming the message file, *rmm* will call the named program to delete the file. Note that at most installations, *cron* (8) is told to remove files that begin with a comma once a night.

     Some users of csh prefer the following:

          alias rmm 'refile +d'

     where folder +d is a folder for deleted messages, and

          alias mexp 'rm 'mhpath +d all''

     is used to ''expunge'' deleted messages.

     The current message is not changed by *rmm*, so a *next* will advance to the next message in the folder as expected.

Files
     $HOME/.mh_profile   The user profile

Profile Components
     Path: To determine the user's MH directory
     Current–Folder: To find the default current folder
     rmmproc: Program to delete the message

See Also
     rmf(1)

Defaults
     '+folder' defaults to the current folder
     'msgs' defaults to cur

Context
     If a folder is given, it will become the current folder.

Bugs
     Since *refile* uses your *rmmproc* to delete the message, the *rmmproc* must **NOT** call *refile* without specifying '–normmproc', or you will create an infinte loop.

NAME

   scan – produce a one line per message scan listing

SYNOPSIS

   scan [+folder] [msgs] [–clear] [–noclear] [–form formatfile] [–format string] [–header] [–noheader]
       [–width columns] [–reverse] [–noreverse] [–file filename] [–help]

DESCRIPTION

   Scan produces a one–line–per–message listing of the specified messages. Each *scan* line contains the message number (name), the date, the "From:" field, the "Subject" field, and, if room allows, some of the body of the message. For example:

```
15+ 7/ 5 Dcrocker  nned    ≪Last week I asked some of
16 - 7/ 5 dcrocker  message id format  ≪I recommend
18   7/ 6 Obrien    Re: Exit status from mkdir
19   7/ 7 Obrien    "scan" listing format in MH
```

   The '+' on message 15 indicates that it is the current message. The '–' on message 16 indicates that it has been replied to, as indicated by a "Replied:" component produced by an '–annotate' switch to the *repl* command.

   If there is sufficient room left on the *scan* line after the subject, the line will be filled with text from the body, preceded by <<, and terminated by >> if the body is sufficiently short. *Scan* actually reads each of the specified messages and parses them to extract the desired fields. During parsing, appropriate error messages will be produced if there are format errors in any of the messages.

   The '–header' switch produces a header line prior to the *scan* listing. Currently, the name of the folder and the current date and time are output (see the **HISTORY** section for more information).

   If the '–clear' switch is used and *scan's* output is directed to a terminal, then *scan* will consult the **$TERM** and **$TERMCAP** envariables to determine your terminal type in order to find out how to clear the screen prior to exiting. If the '–clear' switch is used and *scan's* output is not directed to a terminal (e.g., a pipe or a file), then *scan* will send a formfeed prior to exiting.

   For example, the command:

   (scan –clear –header; show all –show pr –f) I lpr

   produces a scan listing of the current folder, followed by a formfeed, followed by a formatted listing of all messages in the folder, one per page. Omitting '–show pr –f' will cause the messages to be concatenated, separated by a one–line header and two blank lines.

   If *scan* encounters a message without a "Date:" field, rather than leaving that portion of the scan listing blank, the date is filled–in with the last write date of the message, and post–fixed with a '*'. This is particularly handy for scanning a *draft folder*, as message drafts usually aren't allowed to have dates in them.

   To override the output format used by *scan*, the '–format string' or '–form file' switches are used. This permits individual fields of the scan listing to be extracted with ease. The string is simply a format string and the file is simply a format file. See *mh–format* (5) for the details.

In addition to the standard *mh–format* (5) escapes, *scan* also recognizes the following additional *component* escapes:

Escape	Returns	Description
body	string	the (compressed) first part of the body
dtimenow	date	the current date
folder	string	the name of the current folder

Also, if no date header was present in the message, the *function* escapes which operate on {*date*} will return values for the date of last modification of the message file itself.

scan will update the *MH* context prior to starting the listing, so interrupting a long *scan* listing preserves the new context. *MH* purists hate this idea.

Files

     $HOME/.mh_profile   The user profile

Profile Components

Path:	To determine the user's MH directory
Alternate–Mailboxes:	To determine the user's mailboxes
Current–Folder:	To find the default current folder

See Also

     inc(1), pick(1), show(1), mh–format(5)

Defaults

     '+folder' defaults to the folder current
     'msgs' defaults to all
     '–format' defaulted as described above
     '–noheader'
     '–width' defaulted to the width of the terminal

Context

     If a folder is given, it will become the current folder.

History

     Prior to using the format string mechanism, '–header' used to generate a heading saying what each column in the listing was. Format strings prevent this from happening.

Bugs

     The argument to the '–format' switch must be interpreted as a single token by the shell that invokes *scan*. Therefore, one must usually place the argument to this switch inside double–quotes.
     The value of each *component* escape is set by *scan* to the contents of the first message header *scan* encounters with the corresponding component name; any following headers with the same component name are ignored.

     The switch '–reverse', makes *scan* list the messages in reverse order; this should be considered a bug.

     The '–file filename' switch allows the user to obtain a *scan* listing of a maildrop file as produced by *packf*. This listing includes every message in the file. The user should use *msh* for more selective processing of the file. '–reverse' is ignored with this option.

NAME

    send – send a message

SYNOPSIS

    send [–alias aliasfile] [–draft] [–draftfolder +folder] [–draftmessage msg] [–nodraftfolder] [–filter filterfile]
    [–nofilter] [–format] [–noformat] [–forward] [–noforward] [–mime] [–nomime] [–msgid]
    [–nomsgid] [–push] [–nopush] [–split seconds] [–verbose] [–noverbose] [–watch] [–nowatch]
    [–width columns] [file ...] [–help]

DESCRIPTION

    Send will cause each of the specified files to be delivered (via *post* (8)) to each of the destinations in the
    "To:", "cc:", "Bcc:", and "Fcc:" fields of the message. If *send* is re–distributing a message, as invoked
    from *dist*, then the corresponding "Resent–xxx" fields are examined instead.

    If '–push' is specified, *send* will detach itself from the user's terminal and perform its actions in the back-
    ground. If *push* 'd and the draft can't be sent, then the '–forward' switch says that draft should be for-
    warded with the failure notice sent to the user. This differs from putting *send* in the background because
    the output is trapped and analyzed by *MH*.

    If '–verbose' is specified, *send* will indicate the interactions occurring with the transport system, prior to
    actual delivery. If '–watch' is specified *send* will monitor the delivery of local and network mail. Hence,
    by specifying both switches, a large detail of information can be gathered about each step of the message's
    entry into the transport system.

    The '–draftfolder +folder' and '–draftmessage msg' switches invoke the *MH* draft folder facility. This is
    an advanced (and highly useful) feature. Consult the **Advanced Features** section of the *MH* manual for
    more information.

    If '–split' is specified, *send* will split the draft into one or more partial messages prior to sending. This
    makes use of the multi-media content feature in MH. Note however that if *send* is invoked under *dist* (1),
    then this switch is ignored -- it makes no sense to redistribute a message in this fashion. Sometimes you
    want *send* to pause after posting a partial message. This is usually the case when you are running *sendmail*
    and expect to generate a lot of partial messages. The argument to '–split' tells it how long to pause
    between postings.

    Send with no *file* argument will query whether the draft is the intended file, whereas '–draft' will suppress
    this question. Once the transport system has successfully accepted custody of the message, the file will be
    renamed with a leading comma, which allows it to be retrieved until the next draft message is sent. If there
    are errors in the formatting of the message, *send* will abort with a (hopefully) helpful error message.

    If a "Bcc:" field is encountered, its addresses will be used for delivery, and the "Bcc:" field will be
    removed from the message sent to sighted recipients. The blind recipients will receive an entirely new
    message with a minimal set of headers. Included in the body of the message will be a copy of the message
    sent to the sighted recipients. If '–filter filterfile' is specified, then this copy is filtered (re–formatted) prior
    to being sent to the blind recipients. Otherwise, to use the MIME rules for encapsulation, specify the '-
    mime' switch.

    Prior to sending the message, the fields "From: user@local", and "Date: now" will be appended to the
    headers in the message. If the envariable **$SIGNATURE** is set, then its value is used as your personal
    name when constructing the "From:" line of the message. If this envariable is not set, then *send* will con-
    sult the profile entry "Signature" for this information. On hosts where *MH* was configured with the UCI
    option, if **$SIGNATURE** is not set and the "Signature" profile entry is not present, then the file
    $HOME/.signature is consulted. If '–msgid' is specified, then a "Message–ID:" field will also be added
    to the message.

8

If *send* is re–distributing a message (when invoked by *dist*), then ''Resent–'' will be prepended to each of these fields: ''From:'', ''Date:'', and ''Message–ID:''. If the message already contains a ''From:'' field, then a ''Sender: user@local'' field will be added as well. (An already existing ''Sender:'' field is an error!)

By using the '–format' switch, each of the entries in the ''To:'' and ''cc:'' fields will be replaced with ''standard'' format entries. This standard format is designed to be usable by all of the message handlers on the various systems around the Internet. If '–noformat' is given, then headers are output exactly as they appear in the message draft.

If an ''Fcc: folder'' is encountered, the message will be copied to the specified folder for the sender in the format in which it will appear to any non–Bcc receivers of the message. That is, it will have the appended fields and field reformatting. The ''Fcc:'' fields will be removed from all outgoing copies of the message.

By using the '–width columns' switch, the user can direct *send* as to how long it should make header lines containing addresses.

The files specified by the profile entry ''Aliasfile:'' and any additional alias files given by the '–alias aliasfile' switch will be read (more than one file, each preceeded by '–alias', can be named). See *mh–alias* (5) for more information.

Files

$HOME/.mh_profile   The user profile

Profile Components

Path: To determine the user's MH directory
Draft–Folder: To find the default draft–folder
Aliasfile: For a default alias file
Signature: To determine the user's mail signature
mailproc: Program to post failure notices
postproc: Program to post the message

See Also

comp(1), dist(1), forw(1), repl(1), mh–alias(5), post(8)

Defaults

'file' defaults to <mh–dir>/draft
'–alias /usr/contrib/mh-6.8/lib/MailAliases'
'–nodraftfolder'
'–nofilter'
'–format'
'–forward'
'–nomime'
'–nomsgid'
'–nopush'
'–noverbose'
'–nowatch'
'–width 72'

Context

None

Bugs

Under some configurations, it is not possible to monitor the mail delivery transaction; '−watch' is a no-op on those systems.

Using '−split 0' doesn't work correctly.

8

NAME

>   show – show (list) messages

SYNOPSIS

>   show [+folder] [msgs] [–draft] [–header] [–noheader] [–showproc program] [–noshowproc]
>   [switches for *showproc*] [–help]

DESCRIPTION

>   *Show* lists each of the specified messages to the standard output (typically, the terminal). Typically, the
>   messages are listed exactly as they are, with no reformatting. A program named by the *showproc* profile
>   component is invoked to do the listing, and any switches not recognized by *show* are passed along to that
>   program. The default program is known as *more* (1). To override the default and the *showproc* profile
>   component, use the '–showproc program' switch. For example, '–show pr' will cause the *pr* (1) program
>   to list the messages. The *MH* command *mhl* can be used as a *showproc* to show messages in a more uni-
>   form format. Normally, this program is specified as the *showproc* is the user's .mh_profile. See *mhl* (1)
>   for the details. If the '–noshowproc' option is specified, '/bin/cat' is used instead of *showproc*.
>
>   If you have messages with multi-media contents, the profile entry *mhnproc* defines the name of a program
>   to manipulate multi-media messages. (The *mhn* (1) program, which is suitable for this purpose, is the
>   default.) If the '–noshowproc' option is NOT specified, and if one or more named messages has a multi-
>   media content, then the program indicated by *mhnproc* will be run instead of *showproc*. The use of the
>   *mhnproc* can also be disabled if the environment variable **$NOMHNPROC** is set. Note that the *mhnproc*
>   may be invoked even for textual contents, depending on the character set involved. The environment vari-
>   able $MM_CHARSET should be set to the terminal's character set to avoid gratuitous invocations of the
>   *mhnproc*.
>
>   The '–header' switch tells *show* to display a one–line description of the message being shown. This
>   description includes the folder and the message number.
>
>   If no 'msgs' are specified, the current message is used. If more than one message is specified, *more* will
>   prompt for a <RETURN> prior to listing each message. *more* will list each message, a page at a time.
>   When the end of page is reached, *more* will ring the bell and wait for a <SPACE> or <RETURN>. If a
>   <RETURN> is entered, *more* will print the next line, whereas <SPACE> will print the next screenful. To
>   exit *more*, type ''q''.
>
>   If the standard output is not a terminal, no queries are made, and each file is listed with a one–line header
>   and two lines of separation.
>
>   ''show –draft'' will list the file <mh–dir>/draft if it exists.
>
>   If the profile entry ''Unseen–Sequence'' is present and non–empty, then *show* will remove each of the
>   messages shown from each sequence named by the profile entry. This is similar to the
>   ''Previous–Sequence'' profile entry supported by all *MH* commands which take 'msgs' or 'msg' argu-
>   ments.

Files

> $HOME/.mh_profile   The user profile

Profile Components

Path:	To determine the user's MH directory
Current–Folder:	To find the default current folder
Unseen–Sequence:	To name sequences denoting unseen messages
showproc:	Program to show messages
mhnproc:	Program to show messages with multi-media content

8

See Also

mhl(1), more(1), next(1), pick(1), prev(1), scan(1)

Defaults

'+folder' defaults to the current folder
'msgs' defaults to cur
'–header'

Context

If a folder is given, it will become the current folder. The last message shown will become the current message.

Bugs

The '–header' switch doesn't work when 'msgs' expands to more than one message. If the *showproc* is *mhl*, then is problem can be circumvented by referencing the "messagename" field in the *mhl* format file.

Show updates the user's context before showing the message. Hence *show* will mark messages as seen prior to the user actually seeing them. This is generally not a problem, unless the user relies on the "unseen" messages mechanism, and interrupts *show* while it is showing "unseen" messages.

If *showproc* is *mhl*, then *show* uses a built–in *mhl*: it does not actually run the *mhl* program. Hence, if you define your own *showproc*, don't call it *mhl* since *show* won't run it.

If *more* (1) is your showproc (the default), then avoid running *show* in the background with only its standard output piped to another process, as in

```
show | imprint &
```

Due to a bug in *more*, show will go into a "tty input" state. To avoid this problem, re–direct *show*'s diagnostic output as well. For users of *csh*:

```
show |& imprint &
```

For users of *sh*:

```
show 2>&1 | imprint &
```

NAME
     slocal – special local mail delivery

SYNOPSIS
     /usr/contrib/mh-6.8/lib/slocal [address info sender]
          [–addr address] [–info data] [–sender sender]
          [–user username] [–mailbox mbox] [–file file]
          [–maildelivery deliveryfile] [–verbose] [–noverbose] [–debug] [–help]

DESCRIPTION

     Slocal is a program designed to allow you to have your inbound mail processed according to a complex set
     of selection criteria. You do not normally invoke *slocal* yourself, rather *slocal* is invoked on your behalf
     by your system's Message Transfer Agent.

     The message selection criteria used by *slocal* is specified in the file *.maildelivery* in the user's home direc-
     tory. The format of this file is given below.

     The message delivery address and message sender are determined from the Message Transfer Agent
     envelope information, if possible. Under *SendMail*, the sender will obtained from the UUCP ''From ''
     line, if present. The user may override these values with command line arguments, or arguments to the
     '–addr' and '–sender' switches.

     The message is normally read from the standard input. The '–file' switch sets the name of the file from
     which the message should be read, instead of reading stdin. The '–user' switch tells *slocal* the name of the
     user for whom it is delivering mail. The '–mailbox' switch tells *slocal* the name of the user's maildrop file.

     The '–info' switch may be used to pass an arbitrary argument to sub-processes which *slocal* may invoke on
     your behalf. The '–verbose' switch causes *slocal* to give information on stdout about its progress. The
     '–debug' switch produces more verbose debugging output on stderr.

Message Transfer Agents

     If your MTA is *SendMail*, you should include the line

          ''| /usr/contrib/mh-6.8/lib/slocal –user username''

     in your .forward file in your home directory. This will cause *SendMail* to invoke *slocal* on your behalf.

     If your MTA is *MMDF-I*, you should (symbolically) link /usr/contrib/mh-6.8/lib/slocal to the file
     bin/rcvmail in your home directory. This will cause *MMDF-I* to invoke *slocal* on your behalf with the
     correct ''*address info sender*'' arguments.

     If your MTA is *MMDF-II*, then you should not use *slocal*. An equivalent functionality is already provided
     by *MMDF-II*; see maildelivery(5) for details.

The Maildelivery File

     The *.maildelivery* file controls how local delivery is performed. Each line of this file consists of five fields,
     separated by white-space or comma. Since double-quotes are honored, these characters may be included in
     a single argument by enclosing the entire argument in double-quotes. A double-quote can be included by
     preceding it with a backslash. Lines beginning with '#' are ignored.

8

The format of each line in the *.maildelivery* file is:

header   pattern action   result   string

header:

The name of a header field that is to be searched for a pattern. This is any field in the headers of the message that might be present. The following special fields are also defined:

source   the out-of-band sender information
addr   the address that was used to cause delivery to the recipient
default   this matches *only* if the message hasn't been delivered yet
*   this always matches

pattern:

The sequence of characters to match in the specified header field. Matching is case-insensitive, but does not use regular expressions.

action:

The action to take to deliver the message:

destroy   This action always succeeds.

file or >   Append the message to the file named by **string**. The message is appended to the file in the maildrop format which is used by your message transport system. If the message can be appended to the file, then this action succeeds. When writing to the file, a "Delivery–Date: date" header is added which indicates the date and time that message was appended to the file.

mbox   Identical to *file*, but always appends the message using the format used by *packf* (the MMDF mailbox format).

pipe or | Pipe the message as the standard input to the command named by **string**, using the Bourne shell *sh*(1) to interpret the string. Prior to giving the string to the shell, it is expanded with the following built-in variables:

$(sender)   the out-of-band sender information
$(address)   the address that was used to cause delivery to the recipient
$(size)   the size of the message in bytes
$(reply–to)   either the "Reply–To:" or "From:" field of the message
$(info)   the out-of-band information specified

qpipe or
<caret>   Similar to *pipe*, but executes the command directly, after built-in variable expansion, without assistance from the shell. This action can be used to avoid quoting special characters which your shell might interpret.

result:

Indicates how the action should be performed:

A   Perform the action. If the action succeeds, then the message is considered delivered.

R   Perform the action. Regardless of the outcome of the action, the message is not considered delivered.

8

?   Perform the action only if the message has not been delivered. If the action
                    succeeds, then the message is considered delivered.

N   Perform the action only if the message has not been delivered and the previous
                    action succeeded. If this action succeeds, then the message is considered
                    delivered.

To summarize, here's an example:

```
#field   pattern     action result   string
# lines starting with a '#' are ignored, as are blank lines
#
# file mail with mmdf2 in the ''To:'' line into file mmdf2.log
To        mmdf2       file    A       mmdf2.log
# Messages from mmdf pipe to the program err-message-archive
From      mmdf        pipe    A       /bin/err-message-archive
# Anything with the ''Sender:'' address ''mh-workers''
# file in mh.log if not filed already
Sender mh-workers file     ?       mh.log
# ''To:'' unix – put in file unix-news
To        Unix        >       A       unix-news
# if the address is jpo=ack – send an acknowledgement copy back
addr      jpo=ack     |       R       ''/bin/resend –r $(reply-to)''
# anything from steve – destroy!
From      steve       destroy A       –
# anything not matched yet – put into mailbox
default –             >       ?       mailbox
# always run rcvtty
*         –           |       R       /mh/lib/rcvtty
```

The file is always read completely, so that several matches can be made and several actions can be taken.
The *.maildelivery* file must be owned either by the user or by root, and must be writable only by the owner.
If the *.maildelivery* file cannot be found, or does not perform an action which delivers the message, then the
file /usr/contrib/mh-6.8/lib/maildelivery is read according to the same rules. This file must be owned by the
root and must be writable only by the root. If this file cannot be found or does not perform an action which
delivers the message, then standard delivery to the user's maildrop is performed.

Sub-process environment

When a process is invoked, its environment is: the user/group-ids are set to recipient's ids; the working
directory is the recipient's home directory; the umask is 0077; the process has no /dev/tty; the standard
input is set to the message; the standard output and diagnostic output are set to /dev/null; all other file-
descriptors are closed; the envariables **$USER, $HOME, $SHELL** are set appropriately, and no other
envariables exist.

The process is given a certain amount of time to execute. If the process does not exit within this limit, the
process will be terminated with extreme prejudice. The amount of time is calculated as ((size x 60) + 300)
seconds, where size is the number of bytes in the message.

The exit status of the process is consulted in determining the success of the action. An exit status of zero
means that the action succeeded. Any other exit status (or abnormal termination) means that the action
failed.

8

In order to avoid any time limitations, you might implement a process that began by *forking*. The parent would return the appropriate value immediately, and the child could continue on, doing whatever it wanted for as long as it wanted. This approach is somewhat risky if the parent is going to return an exit status of zero. If the parent is going to return a non-zero exit status, then this approach can lead to quicker delivery into your maildrop.

Files

/usr/contrib/mh-6.8/lib/mtstailor	MH tailor file
$HOME/.maildelivery	The file controlling local delivery
/usr/contrib/mh-6.8/lib/maildelivery	Rather than the standard file
/var/mail/$USER	The default maildrop

See Also

rcvstore(1), mhook(1), mh–format(5)

Defaults

‘–noverbose’
‘–maildelivery .maildelivery’
‘–mailbox /var/mail/$USER’
‘–file’ defaults to stdin
‘–user’ defaults to the current user

Context

None

History

Slocal is designed to be backward-compatible with the *maildelivery* facility provided by *MMDF-II*. Thus, the *.maildelivery* file syntax is limited, as is the functionality of *slocal*.

In addition to an exit status of zero, the *MMDF* values *RP_MOK* (32) and *RP_OK* (9) mean that the message has been fully delivered. Any other non-zero exit status, including abnormal termination, is interpreted as the *MMDF* value *RP_MECH* (200), which means ''use an alternate route'' (deliver the message to the maildrop).

Bugs

Only two return codes are meaningful, others should be.

Slocal is designed to be backwards-compatible with the *maildelivery* functionality provided by **MMDF-II**.

Versions of *MMDF* with the *maildelivery* mechanism aren't entirely backwards-compatible with earlier versions of *MMDF*. If you have an *MMDF-I* old-style hook, the best you can do is to have a one-line *.maildelivery* file:

    default – pipe A ''bin/rcvmail $(address) $(info) $(sender)''

NAME

      sortm – sort messages

SYNOPSIS

      sortm [+folder] [msgs] [–datefield field] [–textfield field] [–notextfield] [–limit days] [–nolimit] [–verbose]
           [–noverbose] [–help]

DESCRIPTION

      Sortm sorts the specified messages in the named folder according to the chronological order of the ''Date:''
field of each message.

      The '–verbose' switch directs *sortm* to tell the user the general actions that it is taking to place the folder in
sorted order.

      The '–datefield field' switch tells *sortm* the name of the field to use when making the date comparison. If
the user has a special field in each message, such as ''BB–Posted:'' or ''Delivery–Date:'', then the
'–datefield' switch can be used to direct *sortm* which field to examine.

      The '–textfield field' switch causes *sortm* to sort messages by the specified text field. If this field is ''sub-
ject'', any leading "re:" is stripped off. In any case, all characters except letters and numbers are stripped
and the resulting strings are sorted datefield–major, textfield–minor, using a case insensitive comparison.

      With '–textfield field', if '–limit days' is specified, messages with similar textfields that are dated within
'days' of each other appear together. Specifying '–nolimit' makes the limit infinity. With '–limit 0', the
sort is instead made textfield–major, date–minor.

      For example, to order a folder by date-major, subject-minor, use:

           sortm -textfield subject +folder

Files

      $HOME/.mh_profile   The user profile

Profile Components

      Path: To determine the user's MH directory
      Current–Folder: To find the default current folder

See Also

      folder (1)

Defaults

      '+folder' defaults to the current folder
      'msgs' defaults to all
      '–datefield date'
      '–notextfield'
      '–noverbose'
      '–nolimit'

Context

      If a folder is given, it will become the current folder. If the current message is moved, *sortm* will preserve
its status as current.

Timezones used to be ignored when comparing dates: they aren't any more.

Messages which were in the folder, but not specified by 'msgs', used to be moved to the end of the folder; now such messages are left untouched.

Sortm sometimes did not preserve the message numbering in a folder (e.g., messages 1, 3, and 5, might have been renumbered to 1, 2, 3 after sorting). This was a bug, and has been fixed. To compress the message numbering in a folder, use *"folder −pack"* as always.

If *sortm* encounters a message without a date−field, or if the message has a date−field that *sortm* cannot parse, then *sortm* attempts to keep the message in the same relative position. This does not always work. For instance, if the first message encountered lacks a date which can be parsed, then it will usually be placed at the end of the messages being sorted.

When *sortm* complains about a message which it can't temporally order, it complains about the message number *prior* to sorting. It should indicate what the message number will be *after* sorting.

8

NAME

> vmh – visual front-end to MH

SYNOPSIS

> vmh [–prompt string] [–vmhproc program] [–novmhproc] [switches for *vmhproc*] [–help]

DESCRIPTION

> *vmh* is a program which implements the server side of the *MH* window management protocol and uses *curses* (3) routines to maintain a split–screen interface to any program which implements the client side of the protocol. This latter program, called the *vmhproc*, is specified using the '–vmhproc program' switch.
>
> The upshot of all this is that one can run *msh* on a display terminal and get a nice visual interface. To do this, for example, just add the line
>
> > mshproc: vmh
>
> to your .mh_profile. (This takes advantage of the fact that *msh* is the default *vmhproc* for *vmh*.)
>
> In order to facilitate things, if the '–novmhproc' switch is given, and *vmh* can't run on the user's terminal, the *vmhproc* is run directly without the window management protocol.
>
> After initializing the protocol, *vmh* prompts the user for a command to be given to the client. Usually, this results in output being sent to one or more windows. If a output to a window would cause it to scroll, *vmh* prompts the user for instructions, roughly permitting the capabilities of *less* or *more* (e.g., the ability to scroll backwards and forwards):

SPACE		advance to the next windowful
RETURN	*	advance to the next line
y	*	retreat to the previous line
d	*	advance to the next ten lines
u	*	retreat to the previous ten lines
g	*	go to an arbitrary line
		(preceed g with the line number)
G	*	go to the end of the window
		(if a line number is given, this acts like 'g')
CTRL–L		refresh the entire screen
h		print a help message
q		abort the window

> (A '*' indicates that a numeric prefix is meaningful for this command.)
>
> Note that if a command resulted in more than one window's worth of information being displayed, and you allow the command which is generating information for the window to gracefully finish (i.e., you don't use the 'q' command to abort information being sent to the window), then *vmh* will give you one last change to peruse the window. This is useful for scrolling back and forth. Just type 'q' when you're done.
>
> To abnormally terminate *vmh* (without core dump), use <QUIT> (usually CTRL–\). For instance, this does the "right" thing with *bbc* and *msh*.

Files

> $HOME/.mh_profile   The user profile

Profile Components

> Path: To determine the user's MH directory

8

See Also

msh(1)

Defaults

'–prompt (vmh) '
'–vmhproc msh'

Context

None

Bugs

The argument to the '–prompt' switch must be interpreted as a single token by the shell that invokes *vmh*. Therefore, one must usually place the argument to this switch inside double–quotes.

At present, there is no way to pass signals (e.g., interrupt, quit) to the client. However, generating QUIT when *vmh* is reading a command from the terminal is sufficient to tell the client to go away quickly.

Acts strangely (loses peer or botches window management protocol with peer) on random occasions.

8

NAME

      whatnow – prompting front-end for send

SYNOPSIS

      whatnow [–draftfolder +folder] [–draftmessage msg] [–nodraftfolder] [–editor editor] [–noedit]
            [–prompt string] [file] [–help]

DESCRIPTION

      Whatnow is the default program that queries the user about the disposition of a composed draft. It is nor-
      mally invoked by one of *comp, dist, forw,* or *repl* after the initial edit.

      When started, the editor is started on the draft (unless '–noedit' is given, in which case the initial edit is
      suppressed). Then, *whatnow* repetitively prompts the user with ''What now?'' and awaits a response. The
      valid responses are:

      display   to list the message being distributed/replied–to on
                     the terminal
      edit   to re–edit using the same editor that was used on the
                     preceding round unless a profile entry
                     ''<lasteditor>–next: <editor>'' names an alternate editor
      edit <editor> to invoke <editor> for further editing
      list   to list the draft on the terminal
      push   to send the message in the background
      quit   to terminate the session and preserve the draft
      quit –delete to terminate, then delete the draft
      refile +folder to refile the draft into the given folder
      send   to send the message
      send –watch to cause the delivery process to be monitored
      whom   to list the addresses that the message will go to
      whom –check to list the addresses and verify that they are
                     acceptable to the transport service

      For the **edit** response, any valid switch to the editor is valid. Similarly, for the **send** and **whom** responses,
      any valid switch to *send* (1) and *whom* (1) commands, respectively, are valid. For the **push** response, any
      valid switch to *send* (1) is valid (as this merely invokes *send* with the '–push' option). For the *refile*
      response, any valid switch to the *fileproc* is valid. For the **display** and **list** responses, any valid argument to
      the *lproc* is valid. If any non–switch arguments are present, then the pathname of the draft will be
      excluded from the argument list given to the *lproc* (this is useful for listing another *MH* message).

      See *mh–profile* (5) for further information about how editors are used by MH. It also discusses how com-
      plex envariables can be used to direct *whatnow*'s actions.

      The '–prompt string' switch sets the prompting string for *whatnow*.

      The '–draftfolder +folder' and '–draftmessage msg' switches invoke the *MH* draft folder facility. This is
      an advanced (and highly useful) feature. Consult the **Advanced Features** section of the *MH* manual for
      more information.

Files

      $HOME/.mh_profile   The user profile
      <mh–dir>/draft   The draft file

8

Profile Components

Path:	To determine the user's MH directory
Draft–Folder:	To find the default draft–folder
Editor:	To override the default editor
<lasteditor>–next:	To name an editor to be used after exit from <lasteditor>
automhnproc:	Program to automatically run prior to sending if the draft is
an *mhn* composition file	
fileproc:	Program to refile the message
lproc:	Program to list the contents of a message
sendproc:	Program to use to send the message
whomproc:	Program to determine who a message would go to

See Also

send(1), whom(1)

Defaults

'–prompt ''What Now? '''

Context

None

Bugs

The argument to the '–prompt' switch must be interpreted as a single token by the shell that invokes *what-now*. Therefore, one must usually place the argument to this switch inside double–quotes.

If the initial edit fails, *whatnow* deletes your draft (by renaming it with a leading comma); failure of a later edit preverves the draft.

If *whatnowproc* is *whatnow*, then *comp*, *dist*, *forw*, and *repl* use a built–in *whatnow*, and do not actually run the *whatnow* program. Hence, if you define your own *whatnowproc*, don't call it *whatnow* since it won't be run.

If *sendproc* is *send*, then *whatnow* uses a built–in *send*, it does not actually run the *send* program. Hence, if you define your own *sendproc*, don't call it *send* since *whatnow* won't run it.

NAME

> whom – report to whom a message would go

SYNOPSIS

> whom [–alias aliasfile] [–check] [–nocheck] [–draft] [–draftfolder +folder] [–draftmessage msg]
>   [–nodraftfolder] [file] [–help]

DESCRIPTION

> *Whom* is used to expand the headers of a message into a set of addresses and optionally verify that those
> addresses are deliverable at that time (if '–check' is given).
>
> The '–draftfolder +folder' and '–draftmessage msg' switches invoke the *MH* draft folder facility. This is
> an advanced (and highly useful) feature. Consult the **Advanced Features** section of the *MH* manual for
> more information.
>
> The files specified by the profile entry ''Aliasfile:'' and any additional alias files given by the '–alias
> aliasfile' switch will be read (more than one file, each preceeded by '–alias', can be named). See
> *mh–alias* (5) for more information.

Files

> $HOME/.mh_profile   The user profile

Profile Components

Path:	To determine the user's MH directory
Draft–Folder:	To find the default draft–folder
Aliasfile:	For a default alias file
postproc:	Program to post the message

See Also

> mh–alias(5), post(8)

Defaults

> 'file' defaults to <mh–dir>/draft
> '–nocheck'
> '–alias /usr/contrib/mh-6.8/lib/MailAliases'

Context

> None

Bugs

> With the '–check' option, *whom* makes no guarantees that the addresses listed as being ok are really
> deliverable, rather, an address being listed as ok means that at the time that *whom* was run the address was
> thought to be deliverable by the transport service. For local addresses, this is absolute; for network ad-
> dresses, it means that the host is known; for uucp addresses, it (often) means that the *UUCP* network is
> available for use.

MORE DETAILS

This section describes some of the more intense points of the *MH* system, by expanding on topics previously discussed. The format presented conforms to the standard form for the description of UNIX documentation.

8

NAME

  mh-alias – alias file for MH message system

SYNOPSIS

  any *MH* command

DESCRIPTION

  This describes both *MH* personal alias files and the (primary) alias file for mail delivery, the file

    /usr/contrib/mh-6.8/lib/MailAliases

  It does **not** describe aliases files used by the message transport system. Each line of the alias file has the format:

      alias : address–group
  or
      alias ; address–group
  or
      < alias–file
  or
      ; comment

  where:

      address–group := address–list
                    | "<" file
                    | "=" UNIX–group
                    | "+" UNIX–group
                    | "*"

      address–list := address
                   | address–list, address

  Continuation lines in alias files end with '\' followed by the newline character.

  Alias–file and file are UNIX file names. UNIX–group is a group name (or number) from */etc/group*. An address is a "simple" Internet–style address. Throougout this file, case is ignored, except for alias–file names.

  If the line starts with a '<', then the file named after the '<' is read for more alias definitions. The reading is done recursively, so a '<' may occur in the beginning of an alias file with the expected results.

  If the address–group starts with a '<', then the file named after the '<' is read and its contents are added to the address–list for the alias.

  If the address–group starts with an '=', then the file */etc/group* is consulted for the UNIX–group named after the '='. Each login name occurring as a member of the group is added to the address–list for the alias.

  In contrast, if the address–group starts with a '+', then the file */etc/group* is consulted to determine the group–id of the UNIX–group named after the '+'. Each login name occurring in the */etc/passwd* file whose group–id is indicated by this group is added to the address–list for the alias.

  If the address–group is simply '*', then the file */etc/passwd* is consulted and all login names with a userid greater than some magic number (usually 200) are added to the address–list for the alias.

In match, a trailing * on an alias will match just about anything appropriate. (See example below.)

An approximation of the way aliases are resolved at posting time is (it's not really done this way):

1) Build a list of all addresses from the message to be delivered, eliminating duplicate addresses.

2) If this draft originated on the local host, then for those addresses in the message that have no host specified, perform alias resolution.

3) For each line in the alias file, compare ''alias'' against all of the existing addresses. If a match, remove the matched ''alias'' from the address list, and add each new address in the address–group to the address list if it is not already on the list. The alias itself is not usually output, rather the address–group that the alias maps to is output instead. If ''alias'' is terminated with a ';' instead of a ':', then both the ''alias'' and the address are output in the correct format. (This makes replies possible since *MH* aliases and personal aliases are unknown to the mail transport system.)

Since the alias file is read line by line, forward references work, but backward references are not recognized, thus, there is no recursion.

Example:
          </usr/contrib/mh-6.8/lib/BBoardAliases
          sgroup: fred, fear, freida
          b-people: Blind List: bill, betty;
          fred: frated@UCI
          UNIX–committee: <unix.aliases
          staff: =staff
          wheels: +wheel
          everyone: *
          news.*: news

The first line says that more aliases should immediately be read from the file */usr/contrib/mh-6.8/lib/BBoardAliases*. Following this, ''fred'' is defined as an alias for ''frated@UCI'', and ''sgroup'' is defined as an alias for the three names ''frated@UCI'', ''fear'', and ''freida''.

The alias ''b-people'' is a blind list which includes the addresses ''bill'' and ''betty''; the message will be delieved to those addresses, but the message header will show only ''Blind List: ;'' (not the addresses).

Next, the definition of ''UNIX–committee'' is given by reading the file *unix.aliases* in the users *MH* directory, ''staff'' is defined as all users who are listed as members of the group ''staff'' in the */etc/group* file, and ''wheels'' is defined as all users whose group–id in */etc/passwd* is equivalent to the ''wheel'' group.

Finally, ''everyone'' is defined as all users with a user–id in */etc/passwd* greater than 200, and all aliases of the form ''news.<anything>'' are defined to be ''news''.

The key thing to understand about aliasing in *MH* is that aliases in *MH* alias files are expanded into the headers of messages posted. This aliasing occurs first, at posting time, without the knowledge of the message transport system. In contrast, once the message transport system is given a message to deliver to a list of addresses, for each address that appears to be local, a system–wide alias file is consulted. These aliases are **NOT** expanded into the headers of messages delivered.

Helpful Hints

To use aliasing in *MH* quickly, do the following:

First, in your *.mh_profile*, choose a name for your alias file, say "aliases", and add the line:

Aliasfile: aliases

Second, create the file "aliases" in your *MH* directory.

Third, start adding aliases to your "aliases" file as appropriate.

Files

/usr/contrib/mh-6.8/lib/MailAliases   Primary alias file

Profile Components

Aliasfile: For a default alias file

See Also

ali(1), send(1), whom(1), group(5), passwd(5), conflict(8), post(8)

Defaults

None

Context

None

History

In previous releases of *MH*, only a single, system−wide mh−alias file was supported. This led to a number of problems, since only mail−system administrators were capable of (un)defining aliases. Hence, the semantics of mh−alias were extended to support personal alias files. Users of *MH* no longer need to bother mail−system administrators for keeping information in the system−wide alias file, as each *MH* user can create/modify/remove aliases at will from any number of personal files.

Bugs

Although the forward-referencing semantics of *mh−alias* files prevent recursion, the "< alias−file" command may defeat this. Since the number of file descriptors is finite (and very limited), such infinite recursion will terminate with a meaningless diagnostic when all the fds are used up.

Forward references do not work correctly inside blind lists.

NAME

    mh-format − format file for MH message system

SYNOPSIS

    some *MH* commands

DESCRIPTION

    Several *MH* commands utilize either a *format* string or a *format* file during their execution. For example, *scan* (1) uses a format string which directs it how to generate the scan listing for each message; *repl* (1) uses a format file which directs it how to generate the reply to a message, and so on.

    Format strings are designed to be efficiently parsed by *MH* which means they are not necessarily simple to write and understand. This means that novice, casual, or even advanced users of *MH* should not have to deal with them. Some canned scan listing formats are in /usr/contrib/mh-6.8/lib/scan.time, /usr/contrib/mh-6.8/lib/scan.size, and /usr/contrib/mh-6.8/lib/scan.timely. Look in /usr/contrib/mh-6.8/lib for other *scan* and *repl* format files which may have been written at your site.

    It suffices to have your local *MH* expert actually write new format commands or modify existing ones. This manual section explains how to do that. Note: familiarity with the C *printf* routine is assumed.

    A format string consists of ordinary text, and special multi-character *escape* sequences which begin with '%'. When specifying a format string, the usual C backslash characters are honored: '\b', '\f', '\n', '\r', and '\t'. Continuation lines in format files end with '\' followed by the newline character. There are three types of *escape* sequences: header *components*, built-in *functions*, and flow *control*.

    A *component* escape is specified as '%{*component*}', and exists for each header found in the message being processed. For example '%{date}' refers to the ''Date:'' field of the appropriate message. All component escapes have a string value. Normally, component values are compressed by converting any control characters (tab and newline included) to spaces, then eliding any leading or multiple spaces. However, commands may give different interpretations to some component escapes; be sure to refer to each command's manual entry for complete details.

    A *function* escape is specified as '%(*function*)'. All functions are built-in, and most have a string or numeric value.

Control-flow escapes

    A *control* escape is one of: '%<', '%?', '%|', or '%>'. These are combined into the conditional execution construct:

```
%<condition
        format text 1
%?condition2
        format text 2
%?condition3
        format text 3
...
%|
        format text N
%>
```

    Extra white space is shown here only for clarity. These constructs may be nested without ambiguity. They form a general **if–elseif–else–endif** block where only one of the *format text* segments is interpreted.

The '%<' and '%?' control escapes causes a condition to be evaluated. This condition may be either a *component* or a *function*. The four constructs have the following syntax:

> %<{component}
> %<(function)
> %?{component}
> %?(function)

These control escapes test whether the function or component value is non-zero (for integer-valued escapes), or non-empty (for string-valued escapes).

If this test evaulates true, then the format text up to the next corresponding control escape (one of '%|', '%?', or '%>') is interpreted normally. Next, all format text (if any) up to the corresponding '%>' control escape is skipped. The '%>' control escape is not interpreted; normal interpretation resumes after the '%>' escape.

If the test evaluates false, however, then the format text up to the next corresponding control escape (again, one of '%|', '%?', or '%>') is skipped, instead of being interpreted. If the control escape encountered was '%?', then the condition associated with that control escape is evaluated, and interpretation proceeds after that test as described in the previous paragraph. If the control escape encountered was '%|', then the format text up to the corresponding '%>' escape is interpreted normally. As above, the '%>' escape is not interpreted and normal interpretation resumes after the '%>' escape.

The '%?' control escape and its following format text is optional, and may be included zero or more times. The '%|' control escape and its following format text is also optional, and may be included zero or one times.

Function escapes

Most functions expect an argument of a particular type:

Argument	Description	Example Syntax
literal	A literal number,	%(*func* 1234)
	or string	%(*func* text string)
comp	Any header component	%(*func* {in-reply-to })
date	A date component	%(*func* {date })
addr	An address component	%(*func* {from })
expr	An optional component,	%(*func*(func2))
	function or control,	%(*func* %<{reply-to }%|%{from }%>)
	perhaps nested	%(*func*(func2 {comp }))

The types *date* and *addr* have the same syntax as *comp*, but require that the header component be a date string, or address string, respectively.

All arguments except those of type *expr* are required. For the *expr* argument type, the leading '%' must be omitted for component and function escape arguments, and must be present (with a leading space) for control escape arguments.

The evaluation of format strings is based on a simple machine with an integer register *num*, and a text string register *str*. When a function escape is processed, if it accepts an optional *expr* argument which is not present, it reads the current value of either *num* or *str* as appropriate.

Return values

Component escapes write the value of their message header in *str*. Function escapes write their return value in *num* for functions returning *integer* or *boolean* values, and in *str* for functions returning string values. (The *boolean* type is a subset of integers with usual values 0=false and 1=true.) Control escapes return a *boolean* value, and set *num*.

All component escapes, and those function escapes which return an *integer* or *string* value, pass this value back to their caller in addition to setting *str* or *num*. These escapes will print out this value unless called as part of an argument to another escape sequence. Escapes which return a *boolean* value do pass this value back to their caller in *num*, but will never print out the value.

Function	Argument	Return	Description
msg		integer	message number
cur		integer	message is current
size		integer	size of message
strlen		integer	length of *str*
width		integer	output buffer size in bytes
charleft		integer	bytes left in output buffer
timenow		integer	seconds since the UNIX epoch
me		string	the user's mailbox
eq	literal	boolean	*num* == *arg*
ne	literal	boolean	*num* != *arg*
gt	literal	boolean	*num* > *arg*
match	literal	boolean	*str* contains *arg*
amatch	literal	boolean	*str* starts with *arg*
plus	literal	integer	*arg* plus *num*
minus	literal	integer	*arg* minus *num*
divide	literal	integer	*num* divided by *arg*
modulo	literal	integer	*num* modulo *arg*
num	literal	integer	Set *num* to *arg*
lit	literal	string	Set *str* to *arg*
getenv	literal	string	Set *str* to environment value of *arg*
profile	literal	string	Set *str* to profile component *arg* value
nonzero	expr	boolean	*num* is non-zero
zero	expr	boolean	*num* is zero
null	expr	boolean	*str* is empty
nonnull	expr	boolean	*str* is non-empty
void	expr		Set *str* or *num*
comp	comp	string	Set *str* to component text
compval	comp	integer	*num* set to "**atoi**(*comp*)"
trim	expr		trim trailing white-space from *str*
putstr	expr		print *str*
putstrf	expr		print *str* in a fixed width
putnum	expr		print *num*
putnumf	expr		print *num* in a fixed width

These functions require a date component as an argument:

Function	Argument	Return	Description
sec	date	integer	seconds of the minute
min	date	integer	minutes of the hour
hour	date	integer	hours of the day (0-23)
wday	date	integer	day of the week (Sun=0)
day	date	string	day of the week (abbrev.)

8

weekday	date	string	day of the week
sday	date	integer	day of the week known?
			(0=implicit,−1=unknown)
mday	date	integer	day of the month
yday	date	integer	day of the year
mon	date	integer	month of the year
month	date	string	month of the year (abbrev.)
lmonth	date	string	month of the year
year	date	integer	year (may be > 100)
zone	date	integer	timezone in hours
tzone	date	string	timezone string
szone	date	integer	timezone explicit?
			(0=implicit,−1=unknown)
date2local	date		coerce date to local timezone
date2gmt	date		coerce date to GMT
dst	date	integer	daylight savings in effect?
clock	date	integer	seconds since the UNIX epoch
rclock	date	integer	seconds prior to current time
tws	date	string	official 822 rendering
pretty	date	string	user-friendly rendering
nodate	date	integer	*str* not a date string

These functions require an address component as an argument. The return value of functions noted with '*' pertain only to the first address present in the header component.

Function	Argument	Return	Description
proper	addr	string	official 822 rendering
friendly	addr	string	user-friendly rendering
addr	addr	string	mbox@host or host!mbox rendering*
pers	addr	string	the personal name*
note	addr	string	commentary text*
mbox	addr	string	the local mailbox*
mymbox	addr	integer	the user's addresses? (0=no,1=yes)
host	addr	string	the host domain*
nohost	addr	integer	no host was present*
type	addr	integer	host type* (0=local,1=network,
			−1=uucp,2=unknown)
path	addr	string	any leading host route*
ingrp	addr	integer	address was inside a group*
gname	addr	string	name of group*
formataddr	expr		append *arg* to *str* as a
			(comma separated) address list
putaddr	literal		print *str* address list with
			arg as optional label;
			get line width from *num*

When escapes are nested, evaluation is done from inner-most to outer-most. The outer-most escape must begin with '%'; the inner escapes must not. For example,

    %<(mymbox{from}) To: %{to}%>

writes the value of the header component "From:" to *str*; then (*mymbox*) reads *str* and writes its result to *num*; then the control escape evaluates *num*. If *num* is non-zero, the string "To: " is printed followed by the value of the header component "To:".

A minor explanation of (*mymbox{comp}*) is in order. In general, it checks each of the addresses in the header component "*comp*" against the user's mailbox name and any *Alternate-Mailboxes*. It returns true if any address matches, however, it also returns true if the "*comp*" header is not present in the message. If needed, the (*null*) function can be used to explicitly test for this condition.

When a function or component escape is interpreted and the result will be immediately printed, an optional field width can be specified to print the field in exactly a given number of characters. For example, a numeric escape like %4(*size*) will print at most 4 digits of the message size; overflow will be indicated by a '?' in the first position (like '?234'). A string escape like %4(*me*) will print the first 4 characters and truncate at the end. Short fields are padded at the right with the fill character (normally, a blank). If the field width argument begins with a leading zero, then the fill character is set to a zero.

As above, the functions (*putnumf*) and (*putstrf*) print their result in exactly the number of characters specified by their leading field width argument. For example, %06(*putnumf(size)*) will print the message size in a field six characters wide filled with leading zeros; %14(*putstrf{from}*) will print the "From:" header component in fourteen characters with trailing spaces added as needed. For *putstrf*, using a negative value for the field width causes right-justification of the string within the field, with padding on the left up to the field width. The functions (*putnum*) and (*putstr*) print their result in the minimum number of characters required, and ignore any leading field width argument.

The available output width is kept in an internal register; any output past this width will be truncated.

Comments may be inserted in most places where a function argument is not expected. A comment begins with '%;' and ends with a (non-escaped) newline.

With all this in mind, here's the default format string for *scan*. It's been divided into several pieces for readability. The first part is:

        %4(msg)%<(cur)+%| %>%<{replied}–%?{encrypted}E%| %>

which says that the message number should be printed in four digits, if the message is the current message then a '+' else a space should be printed, and if a "Replied:" field is present then a '–' else if an "Encrypted:" field is present then an 'E' otherwise a space should be printed. Next:

        %02(mon{date})/%02(mday{date})

the month and date are printed in two digits (zero filled) separated by a slash. Next,

        %<{date} %|*>

If a "Date:" field was present, then a space is printed, otherwise a '*'. Next,

        %<(mymbox{from})%<{to}To:%14(friendly{to})%>%>

if the message is from me, and there is a "To:" header, print 'To:' followed by a "user-friendly" rendering of the first address in the "To:" field. Continuing,

        %<(zero)%17(friendly{from})%>

if either of the above two tests failed, then the "From:" address is printed in a "user-friendly" format. And finally,

        %{subject}%<{body}<<%{body}%>

the subject and initial body (if any) are printed.

8

For a more complicated example, next consider the default *replcomps* format file.

        %(lit)%(formataddr %<{reply-to}

This clears *str* and formats the ''Reply-To:'' header if present. If not present, the else-if clause is executed.

        %?{from}%?{sender}%?{return-path}%>)\

This formats the ''From:'', ''Sender:'' and ''Return-Path:'' headers, stopping as soon as one of them is present. Next:

        %<(nonnull)%(void(width))%(putaddr To:)\n%>\

If the *formataddr* result is non-null, it is printed as an address (with line folding if needed) in a field *width* wide with a leading label of ''To: ''.

        %(lit)%(formataddr{to})%(formataddr{cc})%(formataddr(me))\

str is cleared, and the ''To:'' and ''Cc:'' headers, along with the user's address (depending on what was specified with the ''−cc'' switch to *repl*) are formatted.

        %<(nonnull)%(void(width))%(putaddr cc:)\n%>\

If the result is non-null, it is printed as above with a leading label of ''cc: ''.

        %<{fcc}Fcc: %{fcc}\n%>\

If a ''−fcc folder'' switch was given to *repl* (see *repl* (1) for more details about %{*fcc*}), an ''Fcc:'' header is output.

        %<{subject}Subject: Re: %{subject}\n%>\

If a subject component was present, a suitable reply subject is output.

        %<{date}In-reply-to: Your message of '\
        %<(nodate{date})%{date}%|%(pretty{date})%>."%<{message-id}
                %{message-id}%>\n%>\
        ―――――――

If a date component was present, an ''In-Reply-To:'' header is output with the preface ''Your message of ''. If the date was parseable, it is output in a user-friendly format, otherwise it is output as-is. The message-id is included if present. As with all plain-text, the row of dashes are output as-is.

This last part is a good example for a little more elaboration. Here's that part again in pseudo-code:

```
if (comp_exists(date)) then
        print (''In-reply-to: Your message of\`'')
        if (not_date_string(date.value) then
                print (date.value)
        else
                print (pretty(date.value))
        endif
        print (''\`'')
        if (comp_exists(message-id)) then
                print (''\n\t'')
```

```
                    print (message-id.value)
                    endif
                    print (''\n'')
          endif
```

Although this seems complicated, in point of fact, this method is flexible enough to extract individual fields and print them in any format the user desires.

Files

None

Profile Components

None

See Also

scan(1), repl(1), ap(8), dp(8)

Defaults

None

Context

None

History

This software was contributed for MH 6.3. Prior to this, output format specifications were much easier to write, but considerably less flexible.

Bugs

On hosts where *MH* was configured with the BERK option, address parsing is not enabled.

NAME
      mh-mail – message format for MH message system

SYNOPSIS
      any *MH* command

DESCRIPTION

      MH processes messages in a particular format. It should be noted that although neither Bell nor Berkeley
      mailers produce message files in the format that *MH* prefers, *MH* can read message files in that antiquated
      format.

      Each user possesses a mail drop box which initially receives all messages processed by *post* (8). *Inc* (1)
      will read from that drop box and incorporate the new messages found there into the user's own mail folders
      (typically '+inbox'). The mail drop box consists of one or more messages.

      Messages are expected to consist of lines of text. Graphics and binary data are not handled. No data
      compression is accepted. All text is clear ASCII 7-bit data.

      The general ''memo'' framework of RFC–822 is used. A message consists of a block of information in a
      rigid format, followed by general text with no specified format. The rigidly formatted first part of a mes-
      sage is called the header, and the free-format portion is called the body. The header must always exist, but
      the body is optional. These parts are separated by an empty line, i.e., two consecutive newline characters.
      Within *MH*, the header and body may be separated by a line consisting of dashes:

            To:
            cc:
            Subject:

      The header is composed of one or more header items. Each header item can be viewed as a single logical
      line of ASCII characters. If the text of a header item extends across several real lines, the continuation
      lines are indicated by leading spaces or tabs.

      Each header item is called a component and is composed of a keyword or name, along with associated text.
      The keyword begins at the left margin, may NOT contain spaces or tabs, may not exceed 63 characters (as
      specified by RFC–822), and is terminated by a colon (':'). Certain components (as identified by their key-
      words) must follow rigidly defined formats in their text portions.

      The text for most formatted components (e.g., ''Date:'' and ''Message–Id:'') is produced automatically.
      The only ones entered by the user are address fields such as ''To:'', ''cc:'', etc. Internet addresses are
      assigned mailbox names and host computer specifications. The rough format is ''local@domain'', such as
      ''MH@UCI'', or ''MH@UCI–ICSA.ARPA''. Multiple addresses are separated by commas. A missing
      host/domain is assumed to be the local host/domain.

      As mentioned above, a blank line (or a line of dashes) signals that all following text up to the end of the file
      is the body. No formatting is expected or enforced within the body.

      Following is a list of header components that are considered meaningful to various MH programs.

      Date:
            Added by *post* (8), contains date and time of the message's entry into the transport system.

From:
> Added by *post* (8), contains the address of the author or authors (may be more than one if a ''Sender:'' field is present). Replies are typically directed to addresses in the ''Reply–To:'' or ''From:'' field (the former has precedence if present).

Sender:
> Added by *post* (8) in the event that the message already has a ''From:'' line. This line contains the address of the actual sender. Replies are never sent to addresses in the ''Sender:'' field.

To:
> Contains addresses of primary recipients.

cc:
> Contains addresses of secondary recipients.

Bcc:
> Still more recipients. However, the ''Bcc:'' line is not copied onto the message as delivered, so these recipients are not listed. *MH* uses an encapsulation method for blind copies, see *send* (1).

Fcc:
> Causes *post* (8) to copy the message into the specified folder for the sender, if the message was successfully given to the transport system.

Message–ID:
> A unique message identifier added by *post* (8) if the '–msgid' flag is set.

Subject:
> Sender's commentary. It is displayed by *scan* (1).

In–Reply–To:
> A commentary line added by *repl* (1) when replying to a message.

Resent–Date:
> Added when redistributing a message by *post* (8).

Resent–From:
> Added when redistributing a message by *post* (8).

Resent–To:
> New recipients for a message resent by *dist* (1).

Resent–cc:
> Still more recipients. See ''cc:'' and ''Resent–To:''.

Resent–Bcc:
> Even more recipients. See ''Bcc:'' and ''Resent–To:''.

Resent–Fcc:
> Copy resent message into a folder. See ''Fcc:'' and ''Resent–To:''.

Resent–Message–Id:
> A unique identifier glued on by *post* (8) if the '–msgid' flag is set. See ''Message–Id:'' and ''Resent–To:''.

Resent:
>   Annotation for *dist* (1) under the '−annotate' option.

Forwarded:
>   Annotation for *forw* (1) under the '−annotate' option.

Replied:
>   Annotation for *repl* (1) under the '−annotate' option.

Files
>   /var/mail/$USER   Location of mail drop

Profile Components
>   None

See Also
>   *Standard for the Format of ARPA Internet Text Messages* (aka RFC−822)

Defaults
>   None

Context
>   None

NAME

mh-profile – user profile customization for MH message handler

SYNOPSIS

.mh_profile

DESCRIPTION

Each user of *MH* is expected to have a file named *.mh_profile* in his or her home directory. This file contains a set of user parameters used by some or all of the *MH* family of programs. Each line of the file is of the format

   profile–component: value

The possible profile components are exemplified below. Only 'Path:' is mandatory. The others are optional; some have default values if they are not present. In the notation used below, (profile, default) indicates whether the information is kept in the user's *MH* profile or *MH* context, and indicates what the default value is.

Path: Mail

> Locates *MH* transactions in directory ''Mail''. (profile, no default)

context: context

> Declares the location of the *MH* context file, see the **HISTORY** section below. (profile, default: <mh–dir>/context)

Current–Folder: inbox

> Keeps track of the current open folder. (context, default: folder specified by ''Inbox'')

Inbox: inbox

> Defines the name of your inbox. (profile, default: inbox)

Previous–Sequence: pseq

> Names the sequences which should be defined as the 'msgs' or 'msg' argument given to the program. If not present, or empty, no sequences are defined. Otherwise, for each name given, the sequence is first zero'd and then each message is added to the sequence. (profile, no default)

Sequence–Negation: not

> Defines the string which, when prefixed to a sequence name, negates that sequence. Hence, ''notseen'' means all those messages that are not a member of the sequence ''seen''. (profile, no default)

Unseen–Sequence: unseen

> Names the sequences which should be defined as those messages recently incorporated by *inc*. *Show* knows to remove messages from this sequence once it thinks they have been seen. If not present, or empty, no sequences are defined. Otherwise, each message is added to each sequence name given. (profile, no default)

mh–sequences: .mh_sequences

> The name of the file in each folder which defines public sequences. To disable the use of public sequences, leave the value portion of this entry blank. (profile, default: .mh_sequences)

8

atr–*seq–folder*: 172 178–181 212
> Keeps track of the private sequence called *seq* in the specified folder. (context, no default)

Editor: /usr/ucb/ex
> Defines editor to be used by *comp* (1), *dist* (1), *forw* (1), and *repl* (1). (profile, default: prompter)

Msg–Protect: 644
> Defines octal protection bits for message files. See *chmod* (1) for an explanation of the octal number. (profile, default: 0644)

Folder–Protect: 711
> Defines protection bits for folder directories. (profile, default: 0711)

program: default switches
> Sets default switches to be used whenever the mh program *program* is invoked. For example, one could override the *Editor*: profile component when replying to messages by adding a component such as:
> > repl: –editor /bin/ed
>
> (profile, no defaults)

lasteditor–next: nexteditor
> Names ''nexteditor'' to be the default editor after using ''lasteditor''. This takes effect at ''What now?'' level in *comp*, *dist*, *forw*, and *repl*. After editing the draft with ''lasteditor'', the default editor is set to be ''nexteditor''. If the user types ''edit'' without any arguments to ''What now?'', then ''nexteditor'' is used. (profile, no default)

bboards: system
> Tells *bbc* which BBoards you are interested in. (profile, default: system)

Folder–Stack: *folders*
> The contents of the folder-stack for the *folder* command. (context, no default)

mhe:

> If present, tells *inc* to compose an *MHE* auditfile in addition to its other tasks. *MHE* is Brian Reid's *Emacs* front-end for *MH*. An early version is supplied with the *mh.6* distribution. (profile, no default)

Alternate–Mailboxes: mh@uci–750a, bug-mh*
> Tells *repl* and *scan* which addresses are really yours. In this way, *repl* knows which addresses should be included in the reply, and *scan* knows if the message really originated from you. Addresses must be separated by a comma, and the hostnames listed should be the ''official'' hostnames for the mailboxes you indicate, as local nicknames for hosts are not replaced with their official site names. For each address, if a host is not given, then that address on any host is considered to be you. In addition, an asterisk ('*') may appear at either or both ends of the mailbox and host to indicate wild-card matching. (profile, default: your user-id)

Aliasfile: aliases other-alias
> Indicates aliases files for *ali*, *whom*, and *send*. This may be used instead of the '–alias file' switch. (profile, no default)

Draft–Folder: drafts
> Indicates a default draft folder for *comp*, *dist*, *forw*, and *repl*. (profile, no default)

digest–issue–*list*: 1

        Tells *forw* the last issue of the last volume sent for the digest *list*. (context, no default)

digest–volume–*list*: 1

        Tells *forw* the last volume sent for the digest *list*. (context, no default)

MailDrop: .mail

        Tells *inc* your maildrop, if different from the default. This is superseded by the **MAIL-DROP** envariable. (profile, default: /var/mail/$USER)

Signature: RAND MH System (agent: Marshall Rose)

        Tells *send* your mail signature. This is superseded by the **SIGNATURE** envariable. If **SIGNATURE** is not set and this profile entry is not present, the ''gcos'' field of the */etc/passwd* file will be used; otherwise, on hosts where *MH* was configured with the UCI option, the file $HOME/.signature is consulted. Your signature will be added to the address *send* puts in the ''From:'' header; do not include an address in the signature text. (profile, no default)

The following profile elements are used whenever an *MH* program invokes some other program such as *more* (1). The *.mh_profile* can be used to select alternate programs if the user wishes. The default values are given in the examples.

fileproc:	/usr/contrib/mh-6.8/bin/refile
incproc:	/usr/contrib/mh-6.8/bin/inc
installproc:	/usr/contrib/mh-6.8/lib/install–mh
lproc:	/usr/ucb/more
mailproc:	/usr/contrib/mh-6.8/bin/mhmail
mhlproc:	/usr/contrib/mh-6.8/lib/mhl
moreproc:	/usr/ucb/more
mshproc:	/usr/contrib/mh-6.8/bin/msh
packproc:	/usr/contrib/mh-6.8/bin/packf
postproc:	/usr/contrib/mh-6.8/lib/post
rmmproc:	none
rmfproc:	/usr/contrib/mh-6.8/bin/rmf
sendproc:	/usr/contrib/mh-6.8/bin/send
showproc:	/usr/ucb/more
whatnowproc:	/usr/contrib/mh-6.8/bin/whatnow
whomproc:	/usr/contrib/mh-6.8/bin/whom

If you define the envariable **MH**, you can specify a profile other than *.mh_profile* to be read by the *MH* programs that you invoke. If the value of **MH** is not absolute, (i.e., does not begin with a **/**), it will be presumed to start from the current working directory. This is one of the very few exceptions in *MH* where non-absolute pathnames are not considered relative to the user's *MH* directory.

Similarly, if you define the envariable **MHCONTEXT**, you can specify a context other than the normal context file (as specified in the *MH* profile). As always, unless the value of **MHCONTEXT** is absolute, it will be presumed to start from your *MH* directory.

MH programs also support other envariables:

MAILDROP : tells *inc* the default maildrop
        This supercedes the ''MailDrop:'' profile entry.

SIGNATURE : tells *send* and *post* your mail signature
        This supercedes the ''Signature:'' profile entry.

8

HOME : tells all *MH* programs your home directory

SHELL : tells *bbl* the default shell to run

TERM : tells *MH* your terminal type
> The **TERMCAP** envariable is also consulted. In particular, these tell *scan* and *mhl* how to clear your terminal, and how many columns wide your terminal is. They also tell *mhl* how many lines long your terminal screen is.

editalt : the alternate message
> This is set by *dist* and *repl* during edit sessions so you can peruse the message being distributed or replied to. The message is also available through a link called ''@'' in the current directory if your current working directory and the folder the message lives in are on the same UNIX filesystem.

mhdraft : the path to the working draft
> This is set by *comp*, *dist*, *forw*, and *repl* to tell the *whatnowproc* which file to ask ''What now?'' questions about. In addition, *dist*, *forw*, and *repl* set **mhfolder** if appropriate. Further, *dist* and *repl* set **mhaltmsg** to tell the *whatnowproc* about an alternate message associated with the draft (the message being distributed or replied to), and *dist* sets **mhdist** to tell the *whatnowproc* that message re-distribution is occurring. Also, **mheditor** is set to tell the *whatnowproc* the user's choice of editor (unless overridden by '−noedit'). Similarly, **mhuse** may be set by *comp*. Finally, **mhmessages** is set by *dist*, *forw*, and *repl* if annotations are to occur (along with **mhannotate**, and **mhinplace**). It's amazing all the information that has to get passed via envariables to make the ''What now?'' interface look squeaky clean to the *MH* user, isn't it? The reason for all this is that the *MH* user can select *any* program as the *whatnowproc*, including one of the standard shells. As a result, it's not possible to pass information via an argument list.
> If the WHATNOW option was set during *MH* configuration (type '−help' to an *MH* command to find out), and if this envariable is set, if the commands *refile*, *send*, *show*, or *whom* are not given any 'msgs' arguments, then they will default to using the file indicated by **mhdraft**. This is useful for getting the default behavior supplied by the default *whatnowproc*.

mhfolder : the folder containing the alternate message
> This is set by *dist* and *repl* during edit sessions so you can peruse other messages in the current folder besides the one being distributed or replied to. The **mhfolder** envariable is also set by *show*, *prev*, and *next* for use by *mhl*.

MHBBRC :
> If you define the envariable **MHBBRC**, you can specify a BBoards information file other than *.bbrc* to be read by *bbc*. If the value of **MHBBRC** is not absolute, (i.e., does not begin with a **/**), it will be presumed to start from the current working directory.

MHFD :
> If the OVERHEAD option was set during *MH* configuration (type '−help' to an *MH* command to find out), then if this envariable is set, *MH* considers it to be the number of a file descriptor which is opened, read-only to the *MH* profile. Similarly, if the envariable **MHCONTEXTFD** is set, this is the number of a file descriptor which is opened read-only to the *MH* context. This feature of *MH* is experimental, and is used to examine possible speed improvements for *MH* startup. Note that these envariables must be set and non-empty to enable this feature. However, if OVER-HEAD is enabled during *MH* configuration, then when *MH* programs call other *MH* programs, this scheme is used. These file descriptors are not closed throughout the execution of the *MH* program, so children may take advantage of this. This approach is thought to be completely safe and does result in some performance enhancements.

Files

$HOME/.mh_profile	The user profile
or $MH	Rather than the standard profile
<mh–dir>/context	The user context
or $CONTEXT	Rather than the standard context
<folder>/.mh_sequences	Public sequences for <folder>

Profile Components

All

See Also

mh(1), environ(5), mh-sequence(5)

Defaults

None

Context

All

History

In previous versions of *MH*, the current-message value of a writable folder was kept in a file called "cur" in the folder itself. In *mh.3*, the *.mh_profile* contained the current-message values for all folders, regardless of their writability.

In all versions of *MH* since *mh.4*, the *.mh_profile* contains only static information, which *MH* programs will **NOT** update. Changes in context are made to the *context* file kept in the users MH *directory*. This includes, but is not limited to: the "Current–Folder" entry and all private sequence information. Public sequence information is kept in a file called *.mh_sequences* in each folder.

To convert from the format used in releases of *MH* prior to the format used in the *mh.4* release, *install–mh* should be invoked with the '–compat' switch. This generally happens automatically on *MH* systems generated with the "COMPAT" option during *MH* configuration.

The *.mh_profile* may override the path of the *context* file, by specifying a "context" entry (this must be in lower-case). If the entry is not absolute (does not start with a **/**), then it is interpreted relative to the user's *MH* directory. As a result, you can actually have more than one set of private sequences by using different context files.

8

Bugs

The shell quoting conventions are not available in the .mh_profile. Each token is separated by whitespace.

There is some question as to what kind of arguments should be placed in the profile as options. In order to provide a clear answer, recall command line semantics of all *MH* programs: conflicting switches (e.g., '–header and '–noheader') may occur more than one time on the command line, with the last switch taking effect. Other arguments, such as message sequences, filenames and folders, are always remembered on the invocation line and are not superseded by following arguments of the same type. Hence, it is safe to place only switches (and their arguments) in the profile.

If one finds that an *MH* program is being invoked again and again with the same arguments, and those arguments aren't switches, then there are a few possible solutions to this problem. The first is to create a (soft) link in your *$HOME/bin* directory to the *MH* program of your choice. By giving this link a different name, you can create a new entry in your profile and use an alternate set of defaults for the *MH* command. Similarly, you could create a small shell script which called the *MH* program of your choice with an alternate set of invocation line switches (using links and an alternate profile entry is preferable to this solution).

Finally, the *csh* user could create an alias for the command of the form:

    alias cmd 'cmd arg1 arg2 ...'

In this way, the user can avoid lengthy type-in to the shell, and still give *MH* commands safely. (Recall that some *MH* commands invoke others, and that in all cases, the profile is read, meaning that aliases are disregarded beyond an initial command invocation)

NAME

    mh-sequence – sequence specification for MH message system

SYNOPSIS

    most *MH* commands

DESCRIPTION

    Most *MH* commands accept a 'msg' or 'msgs' specification, where 'msg' indicates one message and 'msgs' indicates one or more messages. To designate a message, you may use either its number (e.g., 1, 10, 234) or one of these "reserved" message names:

Name	Description
first	the first message in the folder
last	the last message in the folder
cur	the most recently accessed message
prev	the message numerically preceding "cur"
next	the message numerically following "cur"

    In commands that take a 'msg' argument, the default is "cur". As a shorthand, "." is equivalent to "cur".

    For example: In a folder containing five messages numbered 5, 10, 94, 177 and 325, "first" is 5 and "last" is 325. If "cur" is 94, then "prev" is 10 and "next" is 177.

    The word 'msgs' indicates that one or more messages may be specified. Such a specification consists of one message designation or of several message designations separated by spaces. A message designation consists either of a message name as defined above, or a message range.

    A message range is specified as "name1–name2" or "name:n", where 'name', 'name1' and 'name2' are message names, and 'n' is an integer.

    The specification "name1–name2" designates all currently-existing messages from 'name1' to 'name2' inclusive. The message name "all" is a shorthand for the message range "first–last".

    The specification "name:n" designates up to 'n' messages. These messages start with 'name' if 'name' is a message number or one of the reserved names "first" "cur", or "next", The messages end with 'name' if 'name' is "prev" or "last". The interpretation of 'n' may be overridden by preceding 'n' with a plus or minus sign; '+n' always means up to 'n' messages starting with 'name', and '–n' always means up to 'n' messages ending with 'name'.

    In commands which accept a 'msgs' argument, the default is either "cur" or "all", depending on which makes more sense for each command (see the individual man pages for details). Repeated specifications of the same message have the same effect as a single specification of the message.

User–Defined Message Sequences

    In addition to the "reserved" (pre-defined) message names given above, *MH* supports user-defined sequence names. User-defined sequences allow the *MH* user a tremendous amount of power in dealing with groups of messages in the same folder by allowing the user to bind a group of messages to a meaningful symbolic name.

    The name used to denote a message sequence must consist of an alphabetic character followed by zero or more alphanumeric characters, and can not be one of the "reserved" message names above. After defining a sequence, it can be used wherever an *MH* command expects a 'msg' or 'msgs' argument.

Some forms of message ranges are allowed with user-defined sequences. The specification ''name:n'' may be used, and it designates up to the first 'n' messages (or last 'n' messages for '–n') which are elements of the user-defined sequence 'name'.

The specifications ''name:next'' and ''name:prev'' may also be used, and they designate the next or previous message (relative to the current message) which is an element of the user-defined sequence 'name'. The specificaitions ''name:first'' and ''name:last'' are equivalent to ''name:1'' and ''name:–1'', respectively. The specification ''name:cur'' is not allowed (use just ''cur'' instead). The syntax of these message range specifcations is subject to change in the future.

User-defined sequence names are specific to each folder. They are defined using the *pick* and *mark* commands.

Public and Private User-Defined Sequences

There are two varieties of sequences: *public* sequences and *private* sequences. *Public* sequences of a folder are accessible to any *MH* user that can read that folder and are kept in the .mh_sequences file in the folder. *Private* sequences are accessible only to the *MH* user that defined those sequences and are kept in the user's *MH* context file. By default, *pick* and *mark* create *public* sequences if the folder for which the sequences are being defined is writable by the *MH* user. Otherwise, *private* sequences are created. This can be overridden with the '–public' and '–private' switches to *mark*.

Sequence Negation

MH provides the ability to select all messages not elements of a user-defined sequence. To do this, the user should define the entry ''Sequence–Negation'' in the *MH* profile file; its value may be any string. This string is then used to preface an existing user-defined sequence name. This specification then refers to those messages not elements of the specified sequence name. For example, if the profile entry is:

    Sequence–Negation: not

then anytime an *MH* command is given ''notfoo'' as a 'msg' or 'msgs' argument, it would substitute all messages that are not elements of the sequence ''foo''.

Obviously, the user should beware of defining sequences with names that begin with the value of the ''Sequence–Negation'' profile entry.

The Previous Sequence

MH provides the ability to remember the 'msgs' or 'msg' argument last given to an *MH* command. The entry ''Previous–Sequence'' should be defined in the *MH* profile; its value should be a sequence name or multiple sequence names separated by spaces. If this entry is defined, when when an *MH* command finishes, it will define the sequence(s) named in the value of this entry to be those messages that were specified to the command. Hence, a profile entry of

    Previous–Sequence: pseq

directs any *MH* command that accepts a 'msg' or 'msgs' argument to define the sequence ''pseq'' as those messages when it finishes.

Note: there can be a performance penalty in using the ''Previous–Sequence'' facility. If it is used, **all** *MH* programs have to write the sequence information to the .mh_sequences file for the folder each time they run. If the ''Previous–Sequence'' profile entry is not included, only *pick* and *mark* will write to the .mh_sequences file.

The Unseen Sequence

Finally, some users like to indicate messages which have not been previously seen by them. Both *inc* and *show* honor the profile entry ''Unseen–Sequence'' to support this activity. This entry in the .mh_profile should be defined as one or more sequence names separated by spaces. If there is a value for ''Unseen–Sequence'' in the profile, then whenever *inc* places new messages in a folder, the new messages will also be added to the sequence(s) named in the value of this entry. Hence, a profile entry of

       Unseen–Sequence: unseen

directs *inc* to add new messages to the sequence ''unseen''. Unlike the behavior of the ''Previous–Sequence'' entry in the profile, however, the sequence(s) will **not** be zeroed by *inc*.

Similarly, whenever *show* (or *next* or *prev*) displays a message, that message will be removed from any sequences named by the ''Unseen–Sequence'' entry in the profile.

Files

$HOME/.mh_profile	The user profile
<mh–dir>/context	The user context
<folder>/.mh_sequences	Public sequences for <folder>

Profile Components

Sequence–Negation:	To designate messages not in a sequence
Previous–Sequence:	The last message specification given
Unseen–Sequence:	Those messages not yet seen by the user

See Also

mh(1), mark(1), pick(1), mh-profile(5)

Defaults

None

Context

All

Bugs

User-defined sequences are stored in the .mh_sequences file as a series of message specifications separated by spaces. If a user-defined sequence contains too many individual message specifications, that line in the file may become too long for *MH* to handle. This will generate the error message ''.mh_sequences is poorly formatted''. You'll have to edit the file by hand to remove the offending line.

This can happen to users who define the ''Previous–Sequence'' entry in the *MH* profile and have a folder containing many messages with gaps in the numbering. A workaround for large folders is to minimize numbering gaps by using ''folder –pack'' often.

NAME
          ap – parse addresses 822-style

SYNOPSIS
          /usr/contrib/mh-6.8/lib/ap [–form formatfile] [–format string] [–normalize] [–nonormalize]
                    [–width columns] addrs ... [–help]

DESCRIPTION

          Ap is a program that parses addresses according to the ARPA Internet standard. It also understands many
          non–standard formats. It is useful for seeing how *MH* will interpret an address.

          The *ap* program treats each argument as one or more addresses, and prints those addresses out in the
          official 822–format. Hence, it is usually best to enclose each argument in double–quotes for the shell.

          To override the output format used by *ap*, the '–format string' or '–format file' switches are used. This
          permits individual fields of the address to be extracted with ease. The string is simply a format stringand
          thefile is simply a format file. See *mh–format* (5) for the details.

          In addition to the standard escapes, *ap* also recognizes the following additional escape:

          Escape Returns Description
          error   string   A diagnostic if the parse failed

          If the '–normalize' switch is given, *ap* will try to track down the official hostname of the address.

          Here is the default format string used by *ap*:

                    %<{error}%{error}: %{text}%|%(putstr(proper{text}))%>

          which says that if an error was detected, print the error, a ':', and the address in error. Otherwise, output
          the 822–proper format of the address.

Files
          $HOME/.mh_profile   The user profile
          /usr/contrib/mh-6.8/lib/mtstailor   tailor file

Profile Components
          None

See Also
          dp(8),
          Standard for the Format of ARPA Internet Text Messages (aka RFC–822)

Defaults
          '–format' defaults as described above
          '–normalize'
          '–width' defaults to the width of the terminal

Context
          None

8

Bugs

The argument to the '–format' switch must be interpreted as a single token by the shell that invokes *ap*. Therefore, one must usually place the argument to this switch inside double–quotes.

On hosts where *MH* was configured with the BERK option, address parsing is not enabled.

NAME

    conflict – search for alias/password conflicts

SYNOPSIS

    /usr/contrib/mh-6.8/lib/conflict [–mail name] [–search directory] [aliasfiles...] [–help]

DESCRIPTION

    Conflict is a program that checks to see if the interface between *MH* and transport system is in good shape

    Conflict also checks for maildrops in /var/mail which do not belong to a valid user. It assumes that no user name will start with '.', and thus ignores files in /var/mail which begin with '.'. It also checks for entries in the *group* (5) file which do not belong to a valid user, and for users who do not have a valid group number. In addition duplicate users and groups are noted.

    If the '–mail name' switch is used, then the results will be sent to the specified *name*. Otherwise, the results are sent to the standard output.

    The '–search directory' switch can be used to search directories other than /var/mail and to report anomalies in those directories. The '–search directory' switch can appear more than one time in an invocation to *conflict*.

    Conflict should be run under *cron* (8), or whenever system accounting takes place.

Files

/usr/contrib/mh-6.8/lib/mtstailor	tailor file
/etc/passwd	List of users
/etc/group	List of groups
/usr/contrib/mh-6.8/bin/mhmail	Program to send mail
/var/mail/	Directory of mail drop

Profile Components

    None

See Also

    mh–alias(5)

Defaults

    'aliasfiles' defaults to /usr/contrib/mh-6.8/lib/MailAliases

Context

    None

NAME

dp – parse dates 822-style

SYNOPSIS

/usr/contrib/mh-6.8/lib/dp [–form formatfile] [–format string] [–width columns] dates ... [–help]

DESCRIPTION

Dp is a program that parses dates according to the ARPA Internet standard. It also understands many non–standard formats, such as those produced by TOPS–20 sites and some UNIX sites using *ctime* (3). It is useful for seeing how *MH* will interpret a date.

The *dp* program treats each argument as a single date, and prints the date out in the official 822–format. Hence, it is usually best to enclose each argument in double–quotes for the shell.

To override the output format used by *dp*, the '–format string' or '–format file' switches are used. This permits individual fields of the address to be extracted with ease. The string is simply a format stringand thefile is simply a format file. See *mh–format* (5) for the details.

Here is the default format string used by *dp*:

%<(nodate{text})error: %{text}%|%(putstr(pretty{text}))%>

which says that if an error was detected, print the error, a ':', and the date in error. Otherwise, output the 822–proper format of the date.

Files

$HOME/.mh_profile   The user profile

Profile Components

None

See Also

ap(8)
Standard for the Format of ARPA Internet Text Messages (aka RFC–822)

Defaults

'–format' default as described above
'–width' default to the width of the terminal

Context

None

Bugs

The argument to the '–format' switch must be interpreted as a single token by the shell that invokes *dp*. Therefore, one must usually place the argument to this switch inside double–quotes.

NAME

      fmtdump – decode MH format files

SYNOPSIS

      /usr/contrib/mh-6.8/lib/fmtdump [–form formatfile] [–format string] [–help]

DESCRIPTION

      Fmtdump is a program that parses an *MH* format file and produces a pseudo-language listing of the how *MH* interprets the file.

      The '–format string' and '–form formatfile' switches may be used to specify a format string or format file to read. The string is simply a format string and the file is simply a format file. See *mh-format*(5) for the details.

Files

      $HOME/.mh_profile   The user profile
      /usr/contrib/mh-6.8/lib/scan.default   The default format file

Profile Components

      Path: To determine the user's MH directory

See Also

      mh-format(5), mh-sequences(8)

Context

      None

Bugs

      The output may not be useful unless you are familiar with the internals of the mh-format subroutines.

NAME
    install-mh – initialize the MH environment

SYNOPSIS
    /usr/contrib/mh-6.8/lib/install–mh [–auto] [–compat]

DESCRIPTION

When a user runs any *MH* program for the first time, the program will invoke *install–mh* (with the '–auto' switch) to query the user for the initial *MH* environment. The user does **NOT** invoke this program directly. The user is asked for the name of the directory that will be designated as the user's *MH* directory. If this directory does not exist, the user is asked if it should be created. Normally, this directory should be under the user's home directory, and has the default name of Mail/. After *install–mh* has written the initial .mh_profile for the user, control returns to the original *MH* program.

As with all *MH* commands, *install–mh* first consults the **$HOME** envariable to determine the user's home directory. If **$HOME** is not set, then the */etc/passwd* file is consulted.

When converting from *mh.3* to *mh.4*, *install–mh* is automatically invoked with the '–compat' switch.

Files
    $HOME/.mh_profile   The user profile

Profile Components
    Path: To set the user's MH directory

Context
    With '–auto', the current folder is changed to ''inbox''.

8

NAME
    post – deliver a message

SYNOPSIS
    /usr/contrib/mh-6.8/lib/post [−alias aliasfile] [−filter filterfile] [−nofilter] [−format] [−noformat] [−mime]
        [−nomime] [−msgid] [−nomsgid] [−verbose] [−noverbose] [−watch] [−nowatch]
        [−width columns] file [−help]

DESCRIPTION

    Post is the program called by *send* (1) to deliver the message in *file* to local and remote users. In fact, all
    of the functions attributed to *send* on its manual page are performed by *post*, with *send* acting as a rela-
    tively simple preprocessor. Thus, it is *post* which parses the various header fields, appends From: and
    Date: lines, and interacts with the *SendMail* transport system. *Post* will not normally be called directly by
    the user.

    Post searches the ''To:'', ''cc:'', ''Bcc:'', ''Fcc:'', and ''Resent−xxx:'' header lines of the specified mes-
    sage for destination addresses, checks these addresses for validity, and formats them so as to conform to
    ARPAnet Internet Message Format protocol, unless the '−noformat' flag is set. This will normally cause
    ''@*local−site*'' to be appended to each local destination address, as well as any local return addresses. The
    '−width columns' switch can be used to indicate the preferred length of the header components that contain
    addresses.

    If a ''Bcc:'' field is encountered, its addresses will be used for delivery, and the ''Bcc:'' field will be
    removed from the message sent to sighted recipients. The blind recipients will receive an entirely new
    message with a minimal set of headers. Included in the body of the message will be a copy of the message
    sent to the sighted recipients. If '−filter filterfile' is specified, then this copy is filtered (re−formatted) prior
    to being sent to the blind recipients. Otherwise, to use the MIME rules for encapsulation, specify the
    '−mime' switch.

    The '−alias aliasfile' switch can be used to specify a file that post should take aliases from. More than one
    file can be specified, each being preceded with '−alias'. In any event, the primary alias file is read first.

    The '−msgid' switch indicates that a ''Message−ID:'' or ''Resent−Message−ID:'' field should be added to
    the header.

    The '−verbose' switch indicates that the user should be informed of each step of the posting/filing process.

    The '−watch' switch indicates that the user would like to watch the transport system's handling of the mes-
    sage (e.g., local and ''fast'' delivery).

    Post consults the envariable **$SIGNATURE** to determine the sender's personal name in constructing the
    ''From:'' line of the message.

Files
    /usr/contrib/mh-6.8/lib/mtstailor   tailor file
    /usr/contrib/mh-6.8/bin/refile   Program to process Fcc:s
    /usr/contrib/mh-6.8/lib/mhl   Program to process Bcc:s
    /usr/contrib/mh-6.8/lib/MailAliases   Primary alias file

Profile Components
    post does **NOT** consult the user's .mh_profile

See Also
    Standard for the Format of ARPA Internet Text Messages (aka RFC−822),
    mhmail(1), send(1), mh−mail(5), mh−alias(5)

8

Defaults

'−alias /usr/contrib/mh-6.8/lib/MailAliases'
'−format'
'−nomime'
'−nomsgid'
'−noverbose'
'−nowatch'
'−width 72'
'−nofilter'

Context

None

Bugs

''Reply−To:'' fields are allowed to have groups in them according to the 822 specification, but *post* won't let you use them.

5. REPORTING PROBLEMS

If problems are encountered with an *MH* program, the problems should be reported to the local maintainers of *MH*. When doing this, the name of the program should be reported, along with the version information for the program. To find out what version of an *MH* program is being run, invoke the program with the '–help' switch. In addition to listing the syntax of the command, the program will list information pertaining to its version. This information includes the version of *MH*, the host it was generated on, and the date the program was loaded. A second line of information, found on versions of *MH* after #5.380 include *MH* configuration options. For example,

> version: MH 6.1 #1[UCI] (nrtc-gremlin) of Wed Nov 6 01:13:53 PST 1985
> options: [BSD42] [MHE] [NETWORK] [SENDMTS] [MMDFII] [SMTP] [POP]

The '6.1 #1[UCI]' indicates that the program is from the UCI *mh.6* version of *MH*. The program was generated on the host 'nrtc-gremlin' on 'Wed Nov 6 01:13:53 PST 1985'. It's usually a good idea to send the output of the '–help' switch along with your report.

If there is no local *MH* maintainer, try the address **Bug-MH**. If that fails, use the Internet mailbox **Bug-MH@ICS.UCI.EDU**.

6. ADVANCED FEATURES

This section describes some features of *MH* that were included strictly for advanced *MH* users. These capabilities permit *MH* to exhibit more powerful behavior for the seasoned *MH* users.

USER–DEFINED SEQUENCES

User–defined sequences allow the *MH* user a tremendous amount of power in dealing with groups of messages in the same folder by allowing the user to bind a group of messages to a meaningful symbolic name. The user may choose any name for a message sequence, as long as it consists of alphanumeric characters and does not conflict with the standard *MH* reserved message names (e.g., ''first'', etc). After defining a sequence, it can be used wherever an *MH* command expects a 'msg' or 'msgs' argument.

A restricted form of message ranges are allowed with user–defined sequences. The form ''name:n'', specifies up to the first 'n' messages which are part of the user–defined sequence 'name'. A leading plus sign is allowed on 'n', but is ignored. The interpretation of n is over-ridden if n is preceded by a minus sign; '–n' always means up to the last 'n' messages which are part of the sequence 'name'.

Although all *MH* commands expand user–defined sequences as appropriate, there are two commands that allow the user to define and manipulate them: *pick* and *mark*.

Pick and User–Defined Sequences

Most users of *MH* will use user–defined sequences only with the *pick* command. By giving the '–sequence name' switch to *pick* (which can occur more than once on the command line), each sequence named is defined as those messages which *pick* matched according the the selection criteria it was given. Hence,

        pick –from frated –seq fred

finds all those messages in the current folder which were from ''frated'', creates a sequence called ''fred'', and then adds them to the sequence. The user could then invoke

        scan fred

to get a *scan* listing of those messages. Note that by default, *pick* creates the named sequences before it adds the selected messages to the sequence. Hence, if the named sequence already existed, the sequence is destroyed prior to being re-defined (nothing happens to the messages that were a part of this sequence, they simply cease to be members of that sequence). By using the '–nozero' switch, this behavior can be inhibited, as in

        pick –from frated –seq sgroup
        pick –from fear –seq sgroup –nozero
        pick –from freida –seq sgroup –nozero

finds all those messages in the current folder which were from ''frated'', ''fear'', or ''freida'', and defines the sequence called ''sgroup'' as exactly those messages. These operations amounted to an ''inclusive–or'' of three selection criteria, using *pick*, one can also generate the ''and'' of some selection criteria as well:

        pick –from frated –seq fred

pick −before friday −seq fred fred

This example defines the sequence called "fred" as exactly those messages from "frated" that were dated prior to "friday".[1]

Pick is normally used as a back−quoted command, for example,

scan 'pick −from postmaster'

Now suppose that the user decides that another command should be issued, using exactly those messages. Since, *pick* wasn't given a '−sequence name' argument in this example, the user would end−up typing the entire back−quoted command again. A simpler way is to add a default sequence name to the .mh_profile. For example,

pick: −seq select −list

will tell *pick* to always define the sequence "select" whenever it's run. The '-list' is necessary since the '−sequence name' switch sets '−nolist' whenever the former is encountered. Hence, this profile entry makes *pick* define the "select" sequence and otherwise behave exactly as if there was no profile entry at all.

Mark and User−Defined Sequences

The *mark* command lets the user perform low−level manipulation of sequences, and also provides a well−needed debug facility to the implementors/developers/maintainers of *MH* (the *MH*−hacks). In the future, a user−friendly "front−end" for *mark* will probably be developed to give the *MH* user a way to take better advantage of the underlying facilities.

Public and Private User−Defined Sequences

There are two kinds of sequences: *public* sequences, and *private* sequences. *Public* sequences of a folder are accessible to any *MH* user that can read that folder and are kept in the .mh_sequences file in the folder. *Private* sequences are accessible only to the *MH* user that defined those sequences and are kept in the user's *MH* context file. By default, *pick* (and *mark*) create *public* sequences if the folder for which the sequences are being defined is writable by the *MH* user. Otherwise, *private* sequences are created. This can be overridden with the '−public' and '−nopublic' switches.

Sequence Negation

In addition to telling an *MH* command to use the messages in the sequence "seen", as in

refile seen +old

it would be useful to be easily able to tell an *MH* command to use all messages *except* those in the sequence. One way of doing this would be to use *mark* and define the sequence explicitly, as in

mark −delete −zero seen −seq notseen

[1] Of course, it is much easier to simply use the built−in boolean operation of *pick* to get the desired results:

pick −from frated −or −from fear −or −from freida −seq sgroup

and

pick −from frated −and −before friday −seq fred

do exactly the same thing as the five commands listed above. Hence, the '−nozero' option to *pick* is only useful to manipulate existing sequences.

8

which, owing to *mark* 's cryptic interpretation of '–delete' and '–zero', defines the sequence "notseen" to be all messages not in the sequence "seen". Naturally, anytime the sequence "seen" is changed, "notseen" will have to be updated. Another way to achieve this is to define the entry "Sequence–Negation:" in the .mh_profile. If the entry was

Sequence–Negation: not

then anytime an *MH* command was given "notseen" as a 'msg' or 'msgs' argument, it would substitute all messages that are not a member of the sequence "seen". That is,

refile notseen +new

does just that. The value of the "Sequence–Negation:" entry in the profile can be any string. Hence, experienced users of *MH* do not use a word, but rather a special character which their shell does not interpret (users of the *CShell* use a single caret or circumflex (usually shift–6), while users of the Bourne shell use an exclamation–mark). This is because there is nothing to prevent a user of *MH* from defining a sequence with this string as its prefix, if the string is nothing by letters and digits. Obviously, this could lead to confusing behavior if the "Sequence–Negation:" entry leads *MH* to believe that two sequences are opposites by virtue of their names differing by the prefix string.

The Previous Sequence

Many times users find themselves issuing a series of commands on the same sequences of messages. If the user first defined these messages as a sequence, then considerable typing may be saved. If the user doesn't have this foresight, *MH* provides a handy way of having *MH* remember the 'msgs' or 'msg' argument last given to an *MH* command. If the entry "Previous–Sequence:" is defined in the .mh_profile, then when the command finishes, it will define the sequence(s) named in the value of this entry as being exactly those messages that were specified. Hence, a profile entry of

Previous–Sequence: pseq

directs any *MH* command that accepts a 'msg' or 'msgs' argument to define the sequence "pseq" as those messages when it finishes. More than one sequence name may be placed in this entry, separated with spaces. The one disadvantage of this approach is that the *MH* progams have to update the sequence information for the folder each time they run (although most programs read this information, usually only *pick* and *mark* have to write this information out).

The Unseen Sequence

Finally, some users like to distinguish between messages which have been previously seen by them. Both *inc* and *show* honorthe profile entry "Unseen–Sequence" to support this activity. Whenever *inc* places new messages in a folder, if the entry "Unseen–Sequence" is defined in the .mh_profile, then when the command finishes, *inc* will add the new messages to the sequence(s) named in the value of this entry. Hence, a profile entry of

Unseen–Sequence: unseen

directs *inc* to add new messages to the sequence "unseen". Unlike the behavior of the "Previous–Sequence" entry in the profile however, the sequence(s) will **not** be zero'd.

Similarly, whenever *show* (or *next* or *prev*) displays a message, they remove those messages from any sequences named by the "Unseen–Sequence" entry in the profile.

8

COMPOSITION OF MAIL

There are a number of interesting advanced facilities for the composition of outgoing mail.

The Draft Folder

The *comp*, *dist*, *forw*, and *repl* commands have two switches, '–draftfolder +folder' and '–draftmessage msg'. If '–draftfolder +folder' is used, these commands are directed to construct a draft message in the indicated folder. (The ''Draft–Folder:'' profile entry may be used to declare a default draft folder for use with *comp*, *dist*, *forw*, and *repl*) If '–draftmessage msg' is not used, it defaults to 'new' (unless the user invokes *comp* with '–use', in which case the default is 'cur'). Hence, the user may have several message compositions in progress simultaneously. Now, all of the *MH* tools are available on each of the user's message drafts (e.g., *show*, *scan*, *pick*, and so on). If the folder does not exist, the user is asked if it should be created (just like with *refile*). Also, the last draft message the user was composing is known as 'cur' in the draft folder.

Furthermore, the *send* command has these switches as well. Hence, from the shell, the user can send off whatever drafts desired using the standard *MH* 'msgs' convention with '–draftmessage msgs'. If no 'msgs' are given, it defaults to 'cur'.

In addition, all five programs have a '–nodraftfolder' switch, which undoes the last occurrence of '–draftfolder folder' (useful if the latter occurs in the user's *MH* profile).

If the user does not give the '–draftfolder +folder' switch, then all these commands act ''normally''. Note that the '–draft' switch to *send* and *show* still refers to the file called 'draft' in the user's *MH* directory. In the interests of economy of expression, when using *comp* or *send*, the user needn't prefix the draft 'msg' or 'msgs' with '–draftmessage'. Both of these commands accept a 'file' or 'files' argument, and they will, if given '–draftfolder +folder' treat these arguments as 'msg' or 'msgs'.[2] Hence,

        send -draftf +drafts first

is the same as

        send -draftf +drafts -draftm first

To make all this a bit more clear, here are some examples. Let's assume that the following entries are in the *MH* profile:

        Draft–Folder: +drafts
        sendf: -draftfolder +drafts

Furthermore, let's assume that the program *sendf* is a (symbolic) link in the user's **$HOME/bin/** directory to *send*. Then, any of the commands

        comp
        dist
        forw
        repl

constructs the message draft in the 'draft' folder using the 'new' message number. Furthermore, they each define 'cur' in this folder to be that message draft. If the user were to use the

---

[2] This may appear to be inconsistent, at first, but it saves a lot of typing.

8

quit option at 'What now?' level, then later on, if no other draft composition was done, the draft could be sent with simply

sendf

Or, if more editing was required, the draft could be edited with

comp -use

Instead, if other drafts had been composed in the meantime, so that this message draft was no longer known as 'cur' in the 'draft' folder, then the user could *scan* the folder to see which message draft in the folder should be used for editing or sending. Clever users could even employ a back-quoted *pick* to do the work:

comp -use 'pick +drafts -to bug-mh'

or

sendf 'pick +drafts -to bug-mh'

Note that in the *comp* example, the output from *pick* must resolve to a single message draft (it makes no sense to talk about composing two or more drafts with one invocation of *comp*). In contrast, in the *send* example, as many message drafts as desired can appear, since *send* doesn't mind sending more than one draft at a time.

Note that the argument '–draftfolder +folder' is not included in the profile entry for *send*, since when *comp*, et. al., invoke *send* directly, they supply *send* with the UNIX pathname of the message draft, and **not** a 'draftmessage msg' argument. As far as *send* is concerned, a *draft folder* is not being used.

It is important to realize that *MH* treats the draft folder like a standard *MH* folder in nearly all respects. There are two exceptions: <u>first</u>, under no circumstancs will the '–draftfolder folder' switch cause the named folder to become the current folder.[3] <u>Second</u>, although conceptually *send* deletes the 'msgs' named in the draft folder, it does not call 'delete-prog' to perform the deletion.

What Happens if the Draft Exists

When the *comp*, *dist*, *forw*, and *repl* commands are invoked and the draft you indicated already exists, these programs will prompt the user for a reponse directing the program's action. The prompt is

Draft ''/usr/src/uci/mh/mhbox/draft'' exists (xx bytes).
Disposition?

The appropriate responses and their meanings are: <u>replace</u>: deletes the draft and starts afresh; <u>list</u>: lists the draft; <u>refile</u>: files the draft into a folder and starts afresh; and, <u>quit</u>: leaves the draft intact and exits. In addition, if you specified '–draftfolder folder' to the command, then one other response will be accepted: <u>new</u>: finds a new draft, just as if '–draftmessage new' had been given.

---

[3] Obviously, if the folder appeared in the context of a standard '+folder' argument to an *MH* program, as in

scan +drafts

it might become the current folder, depending on the context changes of the *MH* program in question.

8

Finally, the *comp* command will accept one more response: <u>use</u>: re-uses the draft, just as if '–use' had been given.

The Push Option at What now? Level

The *push* option to the "What now?" query in the *comp*, *dist*, *forw*, and *repl* commands, directs the command to *send* the draft in a special detached fashion, with all normal output discarded. If *push* is used and the draft can not be sent, then *MH* will send the user a message, indicating the name of the draft file, and an explanation of the failure.

The user can also invoke *send* from the shell with the '–push' switch, which makes *send* act like it had been *push* 'd by one of the composition commands.

By using *push*, the user can free the shell to do other things, because it appears to the shell that the *MH* command has finished. As a result the shell will immediately prompt for another command, despite the fact that the command is really still running. Note that if the user indicates that annotations are to be performed (with '–annotate' to *dist*, *forw*, or *repl*), the annotations will be performed after the message has been successfully sent. This action will appear to occur asynchronously. Obviously, if one of the messages that is to be annotated is removed before the draft has been successfully sent, then when *MH* tries to make the annotations, it won't be able to do so. In previous versions of *MH*, this resulted in an error message mysteriously appearing on the user's terminal. In *mh.5* and later versions, in this special circumstance, no error will be generated.

If send is *push* 'd, then the '–forward' switch is examined if a failure notice is generated. If given, then the draft is forwarded with the failure notice sent to the user. This allows rapid *burst* 'ing of the failure notice to retrieve the unsent draft.

Options at What now? Level

By default, the message composition programs call a program called *whatnow* before the initial draft composition. The *MH* user can specify any program for this. Following is some information about the default "What now?" level. More detailed information can be found in the *whatnow* (1) manual entry.

When using the *comp*, *dist*, *forw*, and *repl* commands at "What now?" level, the *edit*, *list*, *headers*, *refile*, and (for the *dist* and *repl* commands) the *display* options will pass on any additional arguments given them to whatever program they invoke.

In *mh.1* (the original RAND *MH*) and *mh.2* (the first UCI version of *MH*), *MH* used a complicated heuristic to determine if the draft should be deleted or preserved after an unsuccessful edit. In *mh.3*, *MH* was changed to preserve the draft always, since *comp*, et. al., could usually look at a draft, apply another set of heuristics, and decide if it was important or not. With the notion of a *draft folder*, in which one by default gets a 'new' message draft, the edit deletion/preservation algorithm was re-implemented, to keep the draft folder from being cluttered with aborted edits.

Also, note that by default, if the draft cannot be successfully sent, these commands return to "What now?" level. But, when *push* is used, this does not happen (obviously). Hence, if these commands were expected to annotate any messages, this will have to be done by hand, later on, with the *anno* command.

Finally, if the '–delete' switch is not given to the *quit* option, then these commands will inform the user of the name of the unsent draft file.

Digests

The *forw* command has the beginnings of a digestifying facility, with the '–digest list', '–issue number', and '–volume number' switches.

If *forw* is given "list" to the '–digest' switch as the name of the discussion group, and the

8

'–issue number' switch is not given, then *forw* looks for an entry in the user's *MH* context called "*digest*–issue–list" and increments its value to use as the issue number. Similarly, if the '–volume number' switch is not given, then *forw* looks for "*digest*–volume–list" (but does not increment its value) to use as the volume number.

Having calculated the name of the digest and the volume and issue numbers, *forw* will now process the components file using the same format string mechanism used by *repl*. The current '%'–escapes are:

escape	type	substitution
digest	string	digest name
msg	integer	issue number
cur	integer	volume number

In addition, to capture the current date, any of the escapes valid for *dp* (8) are also valid for *forw*.

The default components file used by *forw* when in digest mode is:

```
From:     %{digest}-Request
To:       %{digest} Distribution: dist-%{digest};
Subject:  %{digest} Digest V%(cur) #%(msg)
Reply-To: %{digest}
--------
%{digest} Digest %(weekday{date}), %2(mday{date}) %(month{date}) 19%02(year{date})
                 Volume %(cur) : Issue %(msg)

Today's Topics:
```

Hence, when the '–digest' switch is present, the first step taken by *forw* is to expand the format strings in the component file. The next step is to compose the draft using the standard digest encapsulation algorithm (even putting an "End of list Digest" trailer in the draft). Once the draft is composed by *forw*, *forw* writes out the volume and issue profile entries for the digest, and then invokes the editor.

Naturally, when composing the draft, *forw* will honor the '–filter filterfile' switch, which is given to *mhl* to filter each message being forwarded prior to encapsulation in the draft. A good filter file to use, which is called *mhl.digest*, is:

```
width=80,overflowoffset=10
leftadjust,compress,compwidth=9
Date:formatfield="%<(nodate{text})%{text}%|%(tws{text})%>"
From:
Subject:
:
body:nocomponent,overflowoffset=0,noleftadjust,nocompress
```

FOLDER HANDLING

There are two interesting facilities for manipulating folders: relative folder addressing, which allows a user to shorten the typing of long folder names; and the folder–stack, which permits a user to keep a stack of current folders.

8

Relative Folder Addressing

By default, when '+folder' is given, and the folder name is not absolute (does not start with /, ./, or ../), then the UNIX pathname of the folder is interpreted relative to the user's *MH* directory. Although this mechanism works fine for top–level folders and their immediate sub–folders, once the depth of the sub–folder tree grows, it becomes rather unwieldly:

>   scan +mh/mh.4/draft/flames

is a lot of typing. *MH* can't do anything if the current folder was "+inbox", but if the current folder was, say, "+mh/mh.4/draft", *MH* has a short–hand notation to reference a sub–folder of the current folder. Using the '@folder' notation, the *MH* user can direct any *MH* program which expects a '+folder' argument to look for the folder relative to the current folder instead of the user's *MH* directory. Hence, if the current folder *was* "+mh/mh.4/draft", then

>   scan @flames

would do the trick handily. In addition, if the current folder *was* "+mh/mh.4/draft",

>   scan @../pick

would scan the folder "+mh/mh.4/pick", since, in the UNIX fashion, it references the folder "pick" which is a sub–folder of the folder that is the parent of the current folder. Since most advanced *MH* users seem to exhibit a large degree of locality in referencing folders when they process mail, this convention should receive a wide range of uses.

The Folder–Stack

The *folder–stack* mechanism in *MH* gives the *MH* user a facility similar to the *CShell* 's directory–stack. Simply put,

>   folder –push +foo

makes "foo" the current folder, saving the folder that was previously the current folder on the *folder–stack*. As expected,

>   folder –pop

takes the top of the *folder–stack* and makes it the current folder. Each of these switches lists the *folder–stack* when they execute. It is simple to write a *pushf* command as a shell script. It's one line:

>   exec folder –push $@

Probably a better way is to link *folder* to the $HOME/bin/ directory under the name of *pushf* and then add the entry

>   pushf: –push

to the .mh_profile.

The manual page for *folder* discusses the analogy between the *CShell* directory stack commands and the switches in *folder* which manipulate the *folder–stack*. The *folder* command uses the context entry 'Folder–Stack:' to keep track of the folders in the user's stack of folders.

Appendix A
COMMAND SUMMARY

ali [–alias aliasfile] [–list] [–nolist] [–normalize] [–nonormalize] [–user] [–nouser]
    aliases ... [–help]

anno [+folder] [msgs] [–component field] [–inplace] [–noinplace] [–date] [–nodate]
    [–text body] [–help]

bbc [bboards ...] [–topics] [–check] [–read] [–quiet] [–verbose] [–archive]
    [–noarchive] [–protocol] [–noprotocol] [–mshproc program]
    [switches for *mshproc*] [–rcfile rcfile] [–norcfile] [–file BBoardsfile]
    [–user BBoardsuser] [–host host] [–help]

burst [+folder] [msgs] [–inplace] [–noinplace] [–quiet] [–noquiet] [–verbose]
    [–noverbose] [–help]

comp [+folder] [msg] [–draftfolder +folder] [–draftmessage msg] [–nodraftfolder]
    [–editor editor] [–noedit] [–file file] [–form formfile] [–use] [–nouse]
    [–whatnowproc program] [–nowhatnowproc] [–help]

dist [+folder] [msg] [–annotate] [–noannotate] [–draftfolder +folder]
    [–draftmessage msg] [–nodraftfolder] [–editor editor] [–noedit]
    [–form formfile] [–inplace] [–noinplace] [–whatnowproc program]
    [–nowhatnowproc] [–help]

/usr/contrib/mh-6.8/lib/fmtdump [–form formatfile] [–format string] [–help]

folder [+folder] [msg] [–all] [–fast] [–nofast] [–header] [–noheader] [–pack]
    [–nopack] [–recurse] [–norecurse] [–total] [–nototal] [–print] [–noprint]
    [–list] [–nolist] [–push] [–pop] [–help]

folders

forw [+folder] [msgs] [–annotate] [–noannotate] [–draftfolder +folder]
    [–draftmessage msg] [–nodraftfolder] [–editor editor] [–noedit]
    [–filter filterfile] [–form formfile] [–format] [–noformat] [–inplace]
    [–noinplace] [–mime] [–nomime] [–whatnowproc program]
    [–nowhatnowproc] [–help]

forw [+folder] [msgs] [–digest list] [–issue number] [–volume number]
    [other switches for *forw*] [–help]

8

inc [+folder] [–audit audit–file] [–noaudit] [–changecur] [–nochangecur] [–file name]
    [–form formatfile] [–format string] [–silent] [–nosilent] [–truncate]
    [–notruncate] [–width columns] [–host host] [–user user] [–apop] [–noapop]
    [–rpop] [–norpop] [–pack file] [–nopack] [–help]

mark [+folder] [msgs] [–sequence name ...] [–add] [–delete] [–list] [–public]
    [–nopublic] [–zero] [–nozero] [–help]

/usr/contrib/mh-6.8/lib/mhl [–bell] [–nobell] [–clear] [–noclear] [–folder +folder]
    [–form formfile] [–length lines] [–width columns] [–moreproc program]
    [–nomoreproc] [files ...] [–help]

mhmail [addrs ... [–body text] [–cc addrs ...] [–from addr] [–subject subject]] [–help]

mhn [[+folder] [msgs] | [–file file]]
    [–part number]... [–type content]...
    [–list [–headers] [–noheaders]
        [–realsize] [–norealsize]] [–nolist]
    [–show [–serialonly] [–noserialonly]
        [–form formfile] [–pause] [–nopause]] [–noshow]
    [–store [–auto] [–noauto]] [–nostore]
    [–cache] [–nocache] [–rcache policy] [–wcache policy]
    [–check] [–nocheck]
    [–ebcdicsafe] [–noebcdicsafe]
    [–rfc934mode] [–norfc934mode]
    [–verbose] [–noverbose]
    [–help]

mhparam [profile-components] [–components] [–nocomponents] [–all] [–help]

mhpath [+folder] [msgs] [–help]

msgchk [–date] [–nodate] [–notify all/mail/nomail] [–nonotify all/mail/nomail]
    [–host host] [–user user] [–apop] [–noapop] [–rpop] [–norpop] [users ...]
    [–help]

msh [–prompt string] [–scan] [–noscan] [–topcur] [–notopcur] [file] [–help]

next [+folder] [–header] [–noheader] [–showproc program] [–noshowproc]
    [switches for *showproc*] [–help]

packf [+folder] [msgs] [-file name] [–help]

pick   –cc   [+folder] [msgs] [–help]
         –date   [–before date] [–after date] [–datefield field]
         –from
         –search   pattern [–and ...] [–or ...] [–not ...] [–lbrace ... –rbrace]
         –subject
         –to   [–sequence name ...] [–public] [–nopublic] [–zero] [–nozero]
         ––component   [–list] [–nolist]

prev [+folder] [−header] [−noheader] [−showproc program] [−noshowproc]
        [switches for *showproc*] [−help]

prompter [−erase chr] [−kill chr] [−prepend] [−noprepend] [−rapid] [−norapid]
        [−doteof] [−nodoteof] file [−help]

/usr/contrib/mh-6.8/lib/rcvstore [+folder] [−create] [−nocreate] [−sequence name ...]
        [−public] [−nopublic] [−zero] [−nozero] [−help]

refile [msgs] [−draft] [−link] [−nolink] [−preserve] [−nopreserve] [−src +folder]
        [−file file] +folder ... [−help]

repl [+folder] [msg] [−annotate] [−noannotate] [−cc all/to/cc/me] [−nocc all/to/cc/me]
        [−draftfolder +folder] [−draftmessage msg] [−nodraftfolder] [−editor editor]
        [−noedit] [−fcc +folder] [−filter filterfile] [−form formfile] [−inplace]
        [−noinplace] [−query] [−noquery] [−whatnowproc program]
        [−nowhatnowproc] [−width columns] [−help]

rmf [+folder] [−interactive] [−nointeractive] [−help]

rmm [+folder] [msgs] [−help]

scan [+folder] [msgs] [−clear] [−noclear] [−form formatfile] [−format string]
        [−header] [−noheader] [−width columns] [−reverse] [−noreverse] [−file
        filename] [−help]

send [−alias aliasfile] [−draft] [−draftfolder +folder] [−draftmessage msg]
        [−nodraftfolder] [−filter filterfile] [−nofilter] [−format] [−noformat]
        [−forward] [−noforward] [−mime] [−nomime] [−msgid] [−nomsgid] [−push]
        [−nopush] [−split seconds] [−verbose] [−noverbose] [−watch] [−nowatch]
        [−width columns] [file ...] [−help]

show [+folder] [msgs] [−draft] [−header] [−noheader] [−showproc program]
        [−noshowproc] [switches for *showproc*] [−help]

sortm [+folder] [msgs] [−datefield field] [−textfield field] [−notextfield] [−limit days]
        [−nolimit] [−verbose] [−noverbose] [−help]

vmh [−prompt string] [−vmhproc program] [−novmhproc] [switches for *vmhproc*]
        [−help]

whatnow [−draftfolder +folder] [−draftmessage msg] [−nodraftfolder] [−editor editor]
        [−noedit] [−prompt string] [file] [−help]

whom [−alias aliasfile] [−check] [−nocheck] [−draft] [−draftfolder +folder]
        [−draftmessage msg] [−nodraftfolder] [file] [−help]

/usr/contrib/mh-6.8/lib/ap [−form formatfile] [−format string] [−normalize]
        [−nonormalize] [−width columns] addrs ... [−help]

8

/usr/contrib/mh-6.8/lib/conflict [−mail name] [−search directory] [aliasfiles ...]
      [−help]

/usr/contrib/mh-6.8/lib/dp [−form formatfile] [−format string] [−width columns]
      dates ... [−help]

/usr/contrib/mh-6.8/lib/install−mh [−auto] [−compat]

/usr/contrib/mh-6.8/lib/post [−alias aliasfile] [−filter filterfile] [−nofilter] [−format]
      [−noformat] [−mime] [−nomime] [−msgid] [−nomsgid] [−verbose]
      [−noverbose] [−watch] [−nowatch] [−width columns] file [−help]

/usr/contrib/mh-6.8/lib/slocal [address info sender] [−addr address] [−info data]
      [−sender sender] [−user username] [−mailbox mbox] [−file file]
      [−maildelivery deliveryfile] [−verbose] [−noverbose] [−debug] [−help]

8

Appendix B
MESSAGE NAME BNF

msgs	:= msgspec	|
	msgs msgspec	
msgspec	:= msg	|
	msg-range	|
	msg-sequence	|
	user-defined-sequence	
msg	:= msg-name	|
	<number>	
msg-name	:= ''first''	|
	''last''	|
	''cur''	|
	''.''	|
	''next''	|
	''prev''	
msg-range	:= msg''–''msg	|
	''all''	
msg-sequence	:= msg'':''signed-number	
signed-number	:= ''+''<number>	|
	''–''<number>	|
	<number>	
user-defined-sequence	:= <alpha>	|
	<alpha><alphanumeric>*	

Where <number> is a decimal number greater than zero.

Msg-range specifies all of the messages in the given range and must not be empty.

Msg-sequence specifies up to <number> of messages, beginning with ''msg'' (in the case of first, cur, next, or <number>), or ending with ''msg'' (in the case of prev or last). +<number> forces ''starting with msg'', and –<number> forces ''ending with number''. In all cases, ''msg'' must exist.

User–defined sequences are defined and manipulated with the *pick* and *mark* commands.

8

REFERENCES

1. Crocker, D. H., J. J. Vittal, K. T. Pogran, and D. A. Henderson, Jr., "Standard for the Format of ARPA Network Text Messages," *RFC733*, November 1977.

2. Thompson, K., and D. M. Ritchie, "The UNIX Time-sharing System," *Communications of the ACM*, Vol. 17, July 1974, pp. 365-375.

3. McCauley, E. J., and P. J. Drongowski, "KSOS–The Design of a Secure Operating System," *AFIPS Conference Proceedings*, National Computer Conference, Vol. 48, 1979, pp. 345-353.

4. Crocker, David H., *Framework and Functions of the "MS" Personal Message System*, The RAND Corporation, R-2134-ARPA, December 1977.

5. Thompson, K., and D. M. Ritchie, *UNIX Programmer's Manual*, 6th ed., Western Electric Company, May 1975 (available only to UNIX licensees).

6. Crocker, D. H., "Standard for the Format of ARPA Internet Text Messages," *RFC822*, August 1982.

8

A Tutorial Introduction to the UNIX Text Editor

Brian W. Kernighan

Murray Hill, NJ

ABSTRACT

Almost all text input on the UNIX† operating system is done with the text-editor *ed*. This memorandum is a tutorial guide to help beginners get started with text editing.

Although it does not cover everything, it does discuss enough for most users' day-to-day needs. This includes printing, appending, changing, deleting, moving and inserting entire lines of text; reading and writing files; context searching and line addressing; the substitute command; the global commands; and the use of special characters for advanced editing.

Introduction

Ed is a "text editor", that is, an interactive program for creating and modifying "text", using directions provided by a user at a terminal. The text is often a document like this one, or a program or perhaps data for a program.

This introduction is meant to simplify learning *ed*. The recommended way to learn *ed* is to read this document, simultaneously using *ed* to follow the examples, then to read the description in section I of the *UNIX Programmer's Manual,* all the while experimenting with *ed*. (Solicitation of advice from experienced users is also useful.)

Do the exercises! They cover material not completely discussed in the actual text. An appendix summarizes the commands.

Disclaimer

This is an introduction and a tutorial. For this reason, no attempt is made to cover more than a part of the facilities that *ed* offers (although this fraction includes the most useful and frequently used parts). When you have mastered the Tutorial, try *Advanced Editing on UNIX.* Also, there is not enough space to explain basic UNIX procedures. We will assume that you know how to log on to UNIX, and that you have at least a vague understanding of what a file is. For more on that, read *UNIX for Beginners.*

You must also know what character to type as the end-of-line on your particular terminal. This character is the RETURN key on most terminals. Throughout, we will refer to this character, whatever it is, as RETURN.

Getting Started

We'll assume that you have logged in to your system and it has just printed the prompt character, usually either a $ or a % . The easiest way to get *ed* is to type

    ed   (followed by a return)

You are now ready to go – *ed* is waiting for you to tell it what to do.

Creating Text – the Append command "a"

As your first problem, suppose you want to create some text starting from scratch. Perhaps you are typing the very first draft of a paper; clearly it will have to start somewhere, and undergo modifications later. This section will show how to get some text in, just to get started. Later we'll talk about how to change it.

When *ed* is first started, it is rather like working with a blank piece of paper – there is no text or information present. This must be supplied by the person using *ed;* it is usually done by typing in the text, or by reading it into *ed* from a file. We will start by typing in some text, and return shortly to how to read files.

First a bit of terminology. In *ed* jargon, the text being worked on is said to be "kept in a buffer." Think of the buffer as a work space, if you like, or simply as the information that you are going to be editing. In effect the buffer is like the piece of paper, on which we will write things, then change some of them, and finally file the whole thing away for another day.

---

† UNIX is a registered trademark of AT&T Bell Laboratories in the USA and other countries.

9

The user tells *ed* what to do to his text by typing instructions called "commands." Most commands consist of a single letter, which must be typed in lower case. Each command is typed on a separate line. (Sometimes the command is preceded by information about what line or lines of text are to be affected – we will discuss these shortly.) *Ed* makes no response to most commands – there is no prompting or typing of messages like "ready". (This silence is preferred by experienced users, but sometimes a hangup for beginners.)

The first command is *append,* written as the letter

a

all by itself. It means "append (or add) text lines to the buffer, as I type them in." Appending is rather like writing fresh material on a piece of paper.

So to enter lines of text into the buffer, just type an **a** followed by a RETURN, followed by the lines of text you want, like this:

a
Now is the time
for all good men
to come to the aid of their party.

.

The only way to stop appending is to type a line that contains only a period. The "." is used to tell *ed* that you have finished appending. (Even experienced users forget that terminating "." sometimes. If *ed* seems to be ignoring you, type an extra line with just "." on it. You may then find you've added some garbage lines to your text, which you'll have to take out later.)

After the append command has been done, the buffer will contain the three lines

Now is the time
for all good men
to come to the aid of their party.

The "**a**" and "." aren't there, because they are not text.

To add more text to what you already have, just issue another **a** command, and continue typing.

Error Messages – "?"

If at any time you make an error in the commands you type to *ed,* it will tell you by typing

?

This is about as cryptic as it can be, but with practice, you can usually figure out how you goofed.

Writing text out as a file – the Write command "w"

It's likely that you'll want to save your text for later use. To write out the contents of the buffer onto a file, use the *write* command

w

followed by the filename you want to write on. This will copy the buffer's contents onto the specified file (destroying any previous information on the file). To save the text on a file named **junk**, for example, type

w junk

Leave a space between **w** and the file name. *Ed* will respond by printing the number of characters it wrote out. In this case, *ed* would respond with

68

(Remember that blanks and the return character at the end of each line are included in the character count.) Writing a file just makes a copy of the text – the buffer's contents are not disturbed, so you can go on adding lines to it. This is an important point. *Ed* at all times works on a copy of a file, not the file itself. No change in the contents of a file takes place until you give a **w** command. (Writing out the text onto a file from time to time as it is being created is a good idea, since if the system crashes or if you make some horrible mistake, you will lose all the text in the buffer but any text that was written onto a file is relatively safe.)

Leaving ed – the Quit command "q"

To terminate a session with *ed,* save the text you're working on by writing it onto a file using the **w** command, and then type the command

q

which stands for *quit.* The system will respond with the prompt character ($ or %). At this point your buffer vanishes, with all its text, which is why you want to write it out before quitting.†

Exercise 1:

Enter *ed* and create some text using

a
. . . text . . .
.

Write it out using **w**. Then leave *ed* with the **q** command, and print the file, to see that everything worked. (To print a file, say

pr filename

or

cat filename

in response to the prompt character. Try both.)

---

† Actually, *ed* will print **?** if you try to quit without writing. At that point, write if you want; if not, another **q** will get you out regardless.

Reading text from a file – the Edit command "e"

A common way to get text into the buffer is to read it from a file in the file system. This is what you do to edit text that you saved with the **w** command in a previous session. The *edit* command **e** fetches the entire contents of a file into the buffer. So if you had saved the three lines "Now is the time", etc., with a **w** command in an earlier session, the *ed* command

    e junk

would fetch the entire contents of the file **junk** into the buffer, and respond

    68

which is the number of characters in **junk**. *If anything was already in the buffer, it is deleted first.*

If you use the **e** command to read a file into the buffer, then you need not use a file name after a subsequent **w** command; *ed* remembers the last file name used in an **e** command, and **w** will write on this file. Thus a good way to operate is

    ed
    e file
    [editing session]
    w
    q

This way, you can simply say **w** from time to time, and be secure in the knowledge that if you got the file name right at the beginning, you are writing into the proper file each time.

You can find out at any time what file name *ed* is remembering by typing the *file* command **f**. In this example, if you typed

    f

ed would reply

    junk

Reading text from a file – the Read command "r"

Sometimes you want to read a file into the buffer without destroying anything that is already there. This is done by the *read* command **r**. The command

    r junk

will read the file **junk** into the buffer; it adds it to the end of whatever is already in the buffer. So if you do a read after an edit:

    e junk
    r junk

the buffer will contain *two* copies of the text (six lines).

    Now is the time
    for all good men
    to come to the aid of their party.
    Now is the time
    for all good men
    to come to the aid of their party.

Like the **w** and **e** commands, **r** prints the number of characters read in, after the reading operation is complete.

Generally speaking, **r** is much less used than **e**.

Exercise 2:

Experiment with the **e** command – try reading and printing various files. You may get an error **?name**, where **name** is the name of a file; this means that the file doesn't exist, typically because you spelled the file name wrong, or perhaps that you are not allowed to read or write it. Try alternately reading and appending to see that they work similarly. Verify that

    ed filename

is exactly equivalent to

    ed
    e filename

What does

    f filename

do?

Printing the contents of the buffer – the Print command "p"

To *print* or list the contents of the buffer (or parts of it) on the terminal, use the print command

    p

The way this is done is as follows. Specify the lines where you want printing to begin and where you want it to end, separated by a comma, and followed by the letter **p**. Thus to print the first two lines of the buffer, for example, (that is, lines 1 through 2) say

    1,2p (starting line=1, ending line=2 p)

Ed will respond with

    Now is the time
    for all good men

Suppose you want to print *all* the lines in the buffer. You could use **1,3p** as above if you knew there were exactly 3 lines in the buffer. But in general, you don't know how many there are, so what do you use for the ending line number? *Ed* provides a shorthand symbol for "line number of last line in buffer" – the dollar sign **$**. Use it this way:

    1,$p

9

This will print *all* the lines in the buffer (line 1 to last line.) If you want to stop the printing before it is finished, push the DEL or Delete key; *ed* will type

> ?

and wait for the next command.

To print the *last* line of the buffer, you could use

> $,$p

but *ed* lets you abbreviate this to

> $p

You can print any single line by typing the line number followed by a **p**. Thus

> 1p

produces the response

> Now is the time

which is the first line of the buffer.

In fact, *ed* lets you abbreviate even further: you can print any single line by typing *just* the line number – no need to type the letter **p**. So if you say

> $

ed will print the last line of the buffer.

You can also use $ in combinations like

> $−1,$p

which prints the last two lines of the buffer. This helps when you want to see how far you got in typing.

Exercise 3:

As before, create some text using the **a** command and experiment with the **p** command. You will find, for example, that you can't print line 0 or a line beyond the end of the buffer, and that attempts to print a buffer in reverse order by saying

> 3,1p

don't work.

The current line – "Dot" or "."

Suppose your buffer still contains the six lines as above, that you have just typed

> 1,3p

and *ed* has printed the three lines for you. Try typing just

> p   (no line numbers)

This will print

> to come to the aid of their party.

which is the third line of the buffer. In fact it is the last (most recent) line that you have done anything with. (You just printed it!) You can repeat this **p** command

without line numbers, and it will continue to print line 3.

The reason is that *ed* maintains a record of the last line that you did anything to (in this case, line 3, which you just printed) so that it can be used instead of an explicit line number. This most recent line is referred to by the shorthand symbol

> .   (pronounced "dot").

Dot is a line number in the same way that $ is; it means exactly "the current line", or loosely, "the line you most recently did something to." You can use it in several ways – one possibility is to say

> .,$p

This will print all the lines from (including) the current line to the end of the buffer. In our example these are lines 3 through 6.

Some commands change the value of dot, while others do not. The **p** command sets dot to the number of the last line printed; the last command will set both . and $ to 6.

Dot is most useful when used in combinations like this one:

> .+1   (or equivalently, .+1p)

This means "print the next line" and is a handy way to step slowly through a buffer. You can also say

> .−1   (or .−1p)

which means "print the line *before* the current line." This enables you to go backwards if you wish. Another useful one is something like

> .−3,.−1p

which prints the previous three lines.

Don't forget that all of these change the value of dot. You can find out what dot is at any time by typing

> .=

Ed will respond by printing the value of dot.

Let's summarize some things about the **p** command and dot. Essentially **p** can be preceded by 0, 1, or 2 line numbers. If there is no line number given, it prints the "current line", the line that dot refers to. If there is one line number given (with or without the letter **p**), it prints that line (and dot is set there); and if there are two line numbers, it prints all the lines in that range (and sets dot to the last line printed.) If two line numbers are specified the first can't be bigger than the second (see Exercise 2.)

Typing a single return will cause printing of the next line – it's equivalent to .+1p. Try it. Try typing a −; you will find that it's equivalent to .−1p.

Deleting lines: the "d" command

Suppose you want to get rid of the three extra lines in the buffer. This is done by the *delete* command

    d

Except that **d** deletes lines instead of printing them, its action is similar to that of **p**. The lines to be deleted are specified for **d** exactly as they are for **p**:

starting line, ending line d

Thus the command

    4,$d

deletes lines 4 through the end. There are now three lines left, as you can check by using

    1,$p

And notice that **$** now is line 3! Dot is set to the next line after the last line deleted, unless the last line deleted is the last line in the buffer. In that case, dot is set to **$**.

Exercise 4:

Experiment with **a**, **e**, **r**, **w**, **p** and **d** until you are sure that you know what they do, and until you understand how dot, **$**, and line numbers are used.

If you are adventurous, try using line numbers with **a**, **r** and **w** as well. You will find that **a** will append lines *after* the line number that you specify (rather than after dot); that **r** reads a file in *after* the line number you specify (not necessarily at the end of the buffer); and that **w** will write out exactly the lines you specify, not necessarily the whole buffer. These variations are sometimes handy. For instance you can insert a file at the beginning of a buffer by saying

    Or filename

and you can enter lines at the beginning of the buffer by saying

    0a
    . . . text . . .
    .

Notice that **.w** is *very* different from

    .
    w

Modifying text: the Substitute command "s"

We are now ready to try one of the most important of all commands – the substitute command

    s

This is the command that is used to change individual words or letters within a line or group of lines. It is what you use, for example, for correcting spelling mistakes and typing errors.

Suppose that by a typing error, line 1 says

    Now is th time

– the *e* has been left off *the*. You can use **s** to fix this up as follows:

    1s/th/the/

This says: "in line 1, substitute for the characters *th* the characters *the*." To verify that it works (*ed* will not print the result automatically) say

    p

and get

    Now is the time

which is what you wanted. Notice that dot must have been set to the line where the substitution took place, since the **p** command printed that line. Dot is always set this way with the **s** command.

The general way to use the substitute command is

starting-line, ending-line s/*change this*/*to this*/

Whatever string of characters is between the first pair of slashes is replaced by whatever is between the second pair, in *all* the lines between *starting-line* and *ending-line*. Only the first occurrence on each line is changed, however. If you want to change *every* occurrence, see Exercise 5. The rules for line numbers are the same as those for **p**, except that dot is set to the last line changed. (But there is a trap for the unwary: if no substitution took place, dot is *not* changed. This causes an error **?** as a warning.)

Thus you can say

    1,$s/speling/spelling/

and correct the first spelling mistake on each line in the text. (This is useful for people who are consistent misspellers!)

If no line numbers are given, the **s** command assumes we mean "make the substitution on line dot", so it changes things only on the current line. This leads to the very common sequence

    s/something/something else/p

which makes some correction on the current line, and then prints it, to make sure it worked out right. If it didn't, you can try again. (Notice that there is a **p** on the same line as the **s** command. With few exceptions, **p** can follow any command; no other multi-command lines are legal.)

It's also legal to say

    s/ . . . //

which means "change the first string of characters to "*nothing*", i.e., remove them. This is useful for deleting extra words in a line or removing extra letters from words.

9

For instance, if you had

    Nowxx is the time

you can say

    s/xx//p

to get

    Now is the time

Notice that **//** (two adjacent slashes) means "no characters", not a blank. There *is* a difference! (See below for another meaning of **//**.)

Exercise 5:

Experiment with the substitute command. See what happens if you substitute for some word on a line with several occurrences of that word. For example, do this:

    a
    the other side of the coin
    .
    s/the/on the/p

You will get

    on the other side of the coin

A substitute command changes only the first occurrence of the first string. You can change all occurrences by adding a **g** (for "global") to the **s** command, like this:

    s/ . . . / . . . /gp

Try other characters instead of slashes to delimit the two sets of characters in the **s** command – anything should work except blanks or tabs.

(If you get funny results using any of the characters

    ^   . $ [*   \   &

read the section on "Special Characters".)

Context searching – "/ . . . /"

With the substitute command mastered, you can move on to another highly important idea of *ed* – context searching.

Suppose you have the original three line text in the buffer:

    Now is the time
    for all good men
    to come to the aid of their party.

Suppose you want to find the line that contains *their* so you can change it to *the*. Now with only three lines in the buffer, it's pretty easy to keep track of what line the word *their* is on. But if the buffer contained several hundred lines, and you'd been making changes, deleting and rearranging lines, and so on, you would no longer really know what this line number would be.

Context searching is simply a method of specifying the desired line, regardless of what its number is, by specifying some context on it.

The way to say "search for a line that contains this particular string of characters" is to type

    /*string of characters we want to find*/

For example, the *ed* command

    /their/

is a context search which is sufficient to find the desired line – it will locate the next occurrence of the characters between slashes ("their"). It also sets dot to that line and prints the line for verification:

    to come to the aid of their party.

"Next occurrence" means that *ed* starts looking for the string at line **.+1**, searches to the end of the buffer, then continues at line 1 and searches to line dot. (That is, the search "wraps around" from **$** to 1.) It scans all the lines in the buffer until it either finds the desired line or gets back to dot again. If the given string of characters can't be found in any line, *ed* types the error message

    ?

Otherwise it prints the line it found.

You can do both the search for the desired line *and* a substitution all at once, like this:

    /their/s/their/the/p

which will yield

    to come to the aid of the party.

There were three parts to that last command: context search for the desired line, make the substitution, print the line.

The expression **/their/** is a context search expression. In their simplest form, all context search expressions are like this – a string of characters surrounded by slashes. Context searches are interchangeable with line numbers, so they can be used by themselves to find and print a desired line, or as line numbers for some other command, like **s**. They were used both ways in the examples above.

Suppose the buffer contains the three familiar lines

    Now is the time
    for all good men
    to come to the aid of their party.

Then the *ed* line numbers

    /Now/+1
    /good/
    /party/−1

are all context search expressions, and they all refer to the same line (line 2).

To make a change in line 2, you could say

> /Now/+1s/good/bad/

or

> /good/s/good/bad/

or

> /party/−1s/good/bad/

The choice is dictated only by convenience. You could print all three lines by, for instance

> /Now/,/party/p

or

> /Now/,/Now/+2p

or by any number of similar combinations. The first one of these might be better if you don't know how many lines are involved. (Of course, if there were only three lines in the buffer, you'd use

> 1,$p

but not if there were several hundred.)

The basic rule is: a context search expression is *the same as* a line number, so it can be used wherever a line number is needed.

Exercise 6:

Experiment with context searching. Try a body of text with several occurrences of the same string of characters, and scan through it using the same context search.

Try using context searches as line numbers for the substitute, print and delete commands. (They can also be used with **r**, **w**, and **a**.)

Try context searching using **?text?** instead of **/text/**. This scans lines in the buffer in reverse order rather than normal. This is sometimes useful if you go too far while looking for some string of characters – it's an easy way to back up.

(If you get funny results with any of the characters

> ^   . $ [*   \   &

read the section on "Special Characters".)

Ed provides a shorthand for repeating a context search for the same string. For example, the *ed* line number

> /string/

will find the next occurrence of **string**. It often happens that this is not the desired line, so the search must be repeated. This can be done by typing merely

> //

This shorthand stands for "the most recently used context search expression." It can also be used as the first string of the substitute command, as in

> /string1/s//string2/

which will find the next occurrence of **string1** and replace it by **string2**. This can save a lot of typing. Similarly

> ??

means "scan backwards for the same expression."

Change and Insert – "c" and "i"

This section discusses the *change* command

> c

which is used to change or replace a group of one or more lines, and the *insert* command

> i

which is used for inserting a group of one or more lines.

"Change", written as

> c

is used to replace a number of lines with different lines, which are typed in at the terminal. For example, to change lines **.+1** through **$** to something else, type

> .+1,$c
> . . . *type the lines of text you want here . . .*
> .

The lines you type between the **c** command and the **.** will take the place of the original lines between start line and end line. This is most useful in replacing a line or several lines which have errors in them.

If only one line is specified in the **c** command, then just that line is replaced. (You can type in as many replacement lines as you like.) Notice the use of **.** to end the input – this works just like the **.** in the append command and must appear by itself on a new line. If no line number is given, line dot is replaced. The value of dot is set to the last line you typed in.

"Insert" is similar to append – for instance

> /string/i
> . . . *type the lines to be inserted here . . .*
> .

will insert the given text *before* the next line that contains "string". The text between **i** and **.** is *inserted before* the specified line. If no line number is specified dot is used. Dot is set to the last line inserted.

Exercise 7:

"Change" is rather like a combination of delete followed by insert.

Experiment to verify that

>   *start, end* d
>   i
>   ... *text* ...
>   .

is almost the same as

>   *start, end* c
>   ... *text* ...
>   .

These are not *precisely* the same if line $ gets deleted. Check this out. What is dot?

Experiment with **a** and **i**, to see that they are similar, but not the same. You will observe that

>   *line-number* a
>   ... *text* ...
>   .

appends *after* the given line, while

>   *line-number* i
>   ... *text* ...
>   .

inserts *before* it. Observe that if no line number is given, **i** inserts before line dot, while **a** appends after line dot.

Moving text around: the "m" command

The move command **m** is used for cutting and pasting – it lets you move a group of lines from one place to another in the buffer. Suppose you want to put the first three lines of the buffer at the end instead. You could do it by saying:

>   1,3w temp
> $r temp
>   1,3d

(Do you see why?) but you can do it a lot easier with the **m** command:

>   1,3m$

The general case is

>   *start line, end line* m *after this line*

Notice that there is a third line to be specified – the place where the moved stuff gets put. Of course the lines to be moved can be specified by context searches; if you had

>   First paragraph
>   . . .
>   end of first paragraph.
>   Second paragraph
>   . . .
>   end of second paragraph.

you could reverse the two paragraphs like this:

>   /Second/,/end of second/m/First/−1

Notice the −1: the moved text goes *after* the line mentioned. Dot gets set to the last line moved.

The global commands "g" and "v"

The *global* command **g** is used to execute one or more *ed* commands on all those lines in the buffer that match some specified string. For example

>   g/peling/p

prints all lines that contain **peling**. More usefully,

>   g/peling/s//pelling/gp

makes the substitution everywhere on the line, then prints each corrected line. Compare this to

>   1,$s/peling/pelling/gp

which only prints the last line substituted. Another subtle difference is that the **g** command does not give a **?** if **peling** is not found where the **s** command will.

There may be several commands (including **a, c, i, r, w,** but not **g**); in that case, every line except the last must end with a backslash ****:

>   g/xxx/.−1s/abc/def/\
>   .+2s/ghi/jkl/\
>   .−2,.p

makes changes in the lines before and after each line that contains **xxx**, then prints all three lines.

The **v** command is the same as **g**, except that the commands are executed on every line that does *not* match the string following **v**:

>   v/ /d

deletes every line that does not contain a blank.

Special Characters

You may have noticed that things just don't work right when you used some characters like **.**, *, $, and others in context searches and the substitute command. The reason is rather complex, although the cure is simple. Basically, *ed* treats these characters as special, with special meanings. For instance, *in a context search or the first string of the substitute command only,* . means "any character," not a period, so

>   /x.y/

means "a line with an **x**, *any character,* and a **y**," *not* just "a line with an **x**, a period, and a **y**." A complete list of the special characters that can cause trouble is the following:

>   ^   . $ [*   \

Warning: The backslash character **** is special to *ed*. For safety's sake, avoid it where possible. If you have to use one of the special characters in a substitute command, you can turn off its magic meaning temporarily by preceding it with the backslash. Thus

    s/\\\.*/backslash dot star/

will change * into "backslash dot star".

Here is a hurried synopsis of the other special characters. First, the circumflex ^ signifies the beginning of a line. Thus

    /^string/

finds **string** only if it is at the beginning of a line: it will find

    string

but not

    the string...

The dollar-sign **$** is just the opposite of the circumflex; it means the end of a line:

    /string$/

will only find an occurrence of **string** that is at the end of some line. This implies, of course, that

    /^string$/

will find only a line that contains just **string**, and

    /^.$/

finds a line containing exactly one character.

The character **.**, as we mentioned above, matches anything;

    /x.y/

matches any of

    x+y
    x−y
    x y
    x.y

This is useful in conjunction with *, which is a repetition character; **a** * is a shorthand for "any number of **a**'s," so **.** * matches any number of anythings. This is used like this:

    s/.*/stuff/

which changes an entire line, or

    s/.*,//

which deletes all characters in the line up to and including the last comma. (Since **.** * finds the longest possible match, this goes up to the last comma.)

[is used with **]** to form "character classes"; for example,

    /[0123456789]/

matches any single digit − any one of the characters inside the braces will cause a match. This can be abbreviated to **[0−9]**.

Finally, the **&** is another shorthand character − it is used only on the right-hand part of a substitute command where it means "whatever was matched on the left-hand side". It is used to save typing. Suppose the current line contained

    Now is the time

and you wanted to put parentheses around it. You could just retype the line, but this is tedious. Or you could say

    s/^/(/
    s/$/)/

using your knowledge of ^ and **$**. But the easiest way uses the **&**:

    s/.*/(&)/

This says "match the whole line, and replace it by itself surrounded by parentheses." The **&** can be used several times in a line; consider using

    s/.*/&? &!!/

to produce

    Now is the time? Now is the time!!

You don't have to match the whole line, of course: if the buffer contains

    the end of the world

you could type

    /world/s//& is at hand/

to produce

    the end of the world is at hand

Observe this expression carefully, for it illustrates how to take advantage of *ed* to save typing. The string **/world/** found the desired line; the shorthand **//** found the same word in the line; and the **&** saves you from typing it again.

The **&** is a special character only within the replacement text of a substitute command, and has no special meaning elsewhere. You can turn off the special meaning of **&** by preceding it with a ****:

    s/ampersand/\&/

will convert the word "ampersand" into the literal symbol **&** in the current line.

Summary of Commands and Line Numbers

The general form of *ed* commands is the command name, perhaps preceded by one or two line numbers, and, in the case of **e**, **r**, and **w**, followed by a file name. Only one command is allowed per line, but a **p** com-

9

mand may follow any other command (except for **e**, **r**, **w** and **q**).

a: Append, that is, add lines to the buffer (at line dot, unless a different line is specified). Appending continues until . is typed on a new line. Dot is set to the last line appended.

c: Change the specified lines to the new text which follows. The new lines are terminated by a ., as with **a**. If no lines are specified, replace line dot. Dot is set to last line changed.

d: Delete the lines specified. If none are specified, delete line dot. Dot is set to the first undeleted line, unless **$** is deleted, in which case dot is set to **$**.

e: Edit new file. Any previous contents of the buffer are thrown away, so issue a **w** beforehand.

f: Print remembered filename. If a name follows **f** the remembered name will be set to it.

g: The command

> g/---/commands

will execute the commands on those lines that contain ---, which can be any context search expression.

i: Insert lines before specified line (or dot) until a . is typed on a new line. Dot is set to last line inserted.

m: Move lines specified to after the line named after **m**. Dot is set to the last line moved.

p: Print specified lines. If none specified, print line dot. A single line number is equivalent to *line-number* **p**. A single return prints **.+1**, the next line.

q: Quit *ed*. Wipes out all text in buffer if you give it twice in a row without first giving a **w** command.

r: Read a file into buffer (at end unless specified elsewhere.) Dot set to last line read.

s: The command

> s/string1/string2/

substitutes the characters **string1** into **string2** in the specified lines. If no lines are specified, make the substitution in line dot. Dot is set to last line in which a substitution took place, which means that if no substitution took place, dot is not changed. **s** changes only the first occurrence of **string1** on a line; to change all of them, type a **g** after the final slash.

v: The command

> v/---/commands

executes **commands** on those lines that *do not* contain ---.

w: Write out buffer onto a file. Dot is not changed.

.=: Print value of dot. (= by itself prints the value of **$**.)

!: The line

> !command-line

causes **command-line** to be executed as a UNIX com-

mand.

/-----/: Context search. Search for next line which contains this string of characters. Print it. Dot is set to the line where string was found. Search starts at **.+1**, wraps around from **$** to 1, and continues to dot, if necessary.

?-----?: Context search in reverse direction. Start search at **.−1**, scan to 1, wrap around to **$**.

Advanced Editing on UNIX

Brian W. Kernighan

Murray Hill, NJ

(Updated for 4.3BSD by Mark Seiden)

10

ABSTRACT

This paper is meant to help secretaries, typists and programmers to make effective use of the UNIX† facilities for preparing and editing text. It provides explanations and examples of

- special characters, line addressing and global commands in the editor **ed**;
- commands for "cut and paste" operations on files and parts of files, including the **mv, cp, cat** and **rm** commands, and the **r, w, m** and **t** commands of the editor;
- editing scripts and editor-based programs like **grep** and **sed**.

Although the treatment is aimed at non-programmers, new UNIX users with any background should find helpful hints on how to get their jobs done more easily.

1. INTRODUCTION

Although UNIX provides remarkably effective tools for text editing, that by itself is no guarantee that everyone will automatically make the most effective use of them. In particular, people who are not computer specialists — typists, secretaries, casual users — often use the system less effectively than they might. (There is a good argument that new users would better use their time learning a display editor, like *vi,* or perhaps a version of *emacs,* like *jove,* rather than an editor as ignorant of display terminals as *ed.)*

This document is intended as a sequel to *A Tutorial Introduction to the UNIX Text Editor* [1], providing explanations and examples of how to edit using *ed* with less effort. (You should also be familiar with the material in *UNIX For Beginners* [2].) Further information on all commands discussed here can be found in section 1 of the *The UNIX User's Manual* [3].

Examples are based on observations of users and the difficulties they encounter. Topics covered include special characters in searches and substitute commands, line addressing, the global commands, and line moving and copying. There are also brief discussions of effective use of related tools, like those for file manipulation, and those based on **ed**, like **grep** and **sed**.

A word of caution. There is only one way to learn to use something, and that is to *use* it. Reading a description is no substitute for trying something. A paper like this one should give you ideas about what to try, but until you actually try something, you will not learn it.

2. SPECIAL CHARACTERS

The editor **ed** is the primary interface to the system for many people, so it is worthwhile to know how to get the most out of **ed** for the least effort.

The next few sections will discuss shortcuts and labor-saving devices. Not all of these will be instantly useful to any one person, of course, but a few will be, and the others should give you ideas to store away for future use. And as always, until you try these things, they will remain theoretical knowledge, not something you have confidence in.

The List command 'l'

ed provides two commands for printing the contents of the lines you're editing. Most people are familiar with **p**, in combinations like

l,$p

to print all the lines you're editing, or

---

† UNIX is a registered trademark of AT&T Bell Laboratories in the USA and other countries.

s/abc/def/p

to change 'abc' to 'def' on the current line. Less familiar is the *list* command l (the letter '*l*'), which gives slightly more information than **p**. In particular, l makes visible characters that are normally invisible, such as tabs and backspaces. If you list a line that contains some of these, l will print each tab as **>** and each backspace as **<**.† This makes it much easier to correct the sort of typing mistake that inserts extra spaces adjacent to tabs, or inserts a backspace followed by a space.

The l command also 'folds' long lines for printing — any line that exceeds 72 characters is printed on multiple lines; each printed line except the last is terminated by a backslash \, so you can tell it was folded. This is useful for printing long lines on short terminals.

Occasionally the l command will print in a line a string of numbers preceded by a backslash, such as \07 or \16. These combinations are used to make visible characters that normally don't print, like form feed or vertical tab or bell. Each such combination is a single character. When you see such characters, be wary — they may have surprising meanings when printed on some terminals. Often their presence means that your finger slipped while you were typing; you almost never want them.

The Substitute Command 's'

Most of the next few sections will be taken up with a discussion of the substitute command **s**. Since this is the command for changing the contents of individual lines, it probably has the most complexity of any **ed** command, and the most potential for effective use.

As the simplest place to begin, recall the meaning of a trailing **g** after a substitute command. With

s/this/that/

and

s/this/that/g

the first one replaces the *first* 'this' on the line with 'that'. If there is more than one 'this' on the line, the second form with the trailing **g** changes *all* of them.

Either form of the s command can be followed by **p** or **l** to 'print' or 'list' (as described in the previous section) the contents of the line:

s/this/that/p
s/this/that/l
s/this/that/gp
s/this/that/gl

are all legal, and mean slightly different things. Make sure you know what the differences are.

---

† These composite characters are created by overstriking a minus and a > or <, so they only appear as < or > on display terminals.

Of course, any **s** command can be preceded by one or two 'line numbers' to specify that the substitution is to take place on a group of lines. Thus

1,$s/mispell/misspell/

changes the *first* occurrence of 'mispell' to 'misspell' on every line of the file. But

1,$s/mispell/misspell/g

changes *every* occurrence in every line (and this is more likely to be what you wanted in this particular case).

You should also notice that if you add a **p** or **l** to the end of any of these substitute commands, only the last line that got changed will be printed, not all the lines. We will talk later about how to print all the lines that were modified.

The Undo Command 'u'

Occasionally you will make a substitution in a line, only to realize too late that it was a ghastly mistake. The 'undo' command **u** lets you 'undo' the last substitution: the last line that was substituted can be restored to its previous state by typing the command

u

The Metacharacter '.'

As you have undoubtedly noticed when you use **ed**, certain characters have unexpected meanings when they occur in the left side of a substitute command, or in a search for a particular line. In the next several sections, we will talk about these special characters, which are often called 'metacharacters'.

The first one is the period '**.**'. On the left side of a substitute command, or in a search with '/.../', '**.**' stands for *any* single character. Thus the search

/x**.**y/

finds any line where 'x' and 'y' occur separated by a single character, as in

x+y
x−y
x□y
x**.**y

and so on. (We will use □ to stand for a space whenever we need to make it visible.)

Since '**.**' matches a single character, that gives you a way to deal with funny characters printed by l. Suppose you have a line that, when printed with the l command, appears as

.... th\07is ....

and you want to get rid of the \07 (which represents the bell character, by the way).

The most obvious solution is to try

    s/\07//

but this will fail. (Try it.) The brute force solution, which most people would now take, is to re-type the entire line. This is guaranteed, and is actually quite a reasonable tactic if the line in question isn't too big, but for a very long line, re-typing is a bore. This is where the metacharacter '.' comes in handy. Since '\07' really represents a single character, if we say

    s/th.is/this/

the job is done. The '.' matches the mysterious character between the 'h' and the 'i', *whatever it is.*

Bear in mind that since '.' matches any single character, the command

    s/./,/

converts the first character on a line into a ',', which very often is not what you intended.

As is true of many characters in **ed**, the '.' has several meanings, depending on its context. This line shows all three:

    .s/./,/

The first '.' is a line number, the number of the line we are editing, which is called 'line dot'. (We will discuss line dot more in Section 3.) The second '.' is a metacharacter that matches any single character on that line. The third '.' is the only one that really is an honest literal period. On the *right* side of a substitution, '.' is not special. If you apply this command to the line

    Now is the time.

the result will be

    .ow is the time.

which is probably not what you intended.

The Backslash '\'

Since a period means 'any character', the question naturally arises of what to do when you really want a period. For example, how do you convert the line

    Now is the time.

into

    Now is the time?

The backslash '\' does the job. A backslash turns off any special meaning that the next character might have; in particular, '\.' converts the '.' from a 'match anything' into a period, so you can use it to replace the period in

    Now is the time.

like this:

    s/\./?/

The pair of characters '\.' is considered by **ed** to be a single real period.

The backslash can also be used when searching for lines that contain a special character. Suppose you are looking for a line that contains

    .PP

The search

    /.PP/

isn't adequate, for it will find a line like

    THE APPLICATION OF ...

because the '.' matches the letter 'A'. But if you say

    /\.PP/

you will find only lines that contain '.PP'.

The backslash can also be used to turn off special meanings for characters other than '.'. For example, consider finding a line that contains a backslash. The search

    /\/

won't work, because the '\' isn't a literal '\', but instead means that the second '/' no longer delimits the search. But by preceding a backslash with another one, you can search for a literal backslash. Thus

    /\\/

does work. Similarly, you can search for a forward slash '/' with

    /\//

The backslash turns off the meaning of the immediately following '/' so that it doesn't terminate the /.../ construction prematurely.

As an exercise, before reading further, find two substitute commands each of which will convert the line

    \x\.\y

into the line

    \x\y

Here are several solutions; verify that each works as advertised.

    s/\\\.//
    s/x..x/x/
    s/..y/y/

A couple of miscellaneous notes about backslashes and special characters. First, you can use any character to delimit the pieces of an **s** command: there is nothing sacred about slashes. (But you must use slashes for context searching.) For instance, in a line that contains a lot of slashes already, like

    //exec //sys.fort.go // etc...

you could use a colon as the delimiter — to delete all the slashes, type

    s:/::g

Second, if # and @ are your character erase and line kill characters, you have to type \# and \@; this is true whether you're talking to **ed** or any other program.

When you are adding text with **a** or **i** or **c**, backslash is not special, and you should only put in one backslash for each one you really want.

The Dollar Sign '$'

The next metacharacter, the '$', stands for 'the end of the line'. As its most obvious use, suppose you have the line

    Now is the

and you wish to add the word 'time' to the end. Use the $ like this:

    s/$/ □time/

to get

    Now is the time

Notice that a space is needed before 'time' in the substitute command, or you will get

    Now is thetime

As another example, replace the second comma in the following line with a period without altering the first:

    Now is the time, for all good men,

The command needed is

    s/,$/./

The $ sign here provides context to make specific which comma we mean. Without it, of course, the **s** command would operate on the first comma to produce

    Now is the time. for all good men,

As another example, to convert

    Now is the time.

into

    Now is the time?

as we did earlier, we can use

    s/.$/?/

Like '.', the '$' has multiple meanings depending on context. In the line

    $s/$/$/

the first '$' refers to the last line of the file, the second refers to the end of that line, and the third is a literal dollar sign, to be added to that line.

The Circumflex '^'

The circumflex (or hat or caret) '^' stands for the beginning of the line. For example, suppose you are looking for a line that begins with 'the'. If you simply say

    /the/

you will in all likelihood find several lines that contain 'the' in the middle before arriving at the one you want. But with

    /^the/

you narrow the context, and thus arrive at the desired one more easily.

The other use of '^' is of course to enable you to insert something at the beginning of a line:

    s/^/ □/

places a space at the beginning of the current line.

Metacharacters can be combined. To search for a line that contains *only* the characters

    .PP

you can use the command

    /^\.PP$/

The Star '*'

Suppose you have a line that looks like this:

    text x   y text

where *text* stands for lots of text, and there are some indeterminate number of spaces between the **x** and the **y**. Suppose the job is to replace all the spaces between **x** and **y** by a single space. The line is too long to retype, and there are too many spaces to count. What now?

This is where the metacharacter '*' comes in handy. A character followed by a star stands for as many consecutive occurrences of that character as possible. To refer to all the spaces at once, say

    s/x□*y/x□y/

The construction '□*' means 'as many spaces as possible'. Thus 'x□*y' means 'an x, as many spaces as possible, then a y'.

The star can be used with any character, not just space. If the original example was instead

    text x————y text

then all '–' signs can be replaced by a single space with

the command

    s/x–*y/x□y/

Finally, suppose that the line was

    text x················y *text*

Can you see what trap lies in wait for the unwary? If you blindly type

    s/x.*y/x□y/

what will happen? The answer, naturally, is that it depends. If there are no other x's or y's on the line, then everything works, but it's blind luck, not good management. Remember that '.' matches *any* single character? Then '.*' matches as many single characters as possible, and unless you're careful, it can eat up a lot more of the line than you expected. If the line was, for example, like this:

    text x *text* x···············y *text* y *text*

then saying

    s/x.*y/x□y/

will take everything from the *first* 'x' to the *last* 'y', which, in this example, is undoubtedly more than you wanted.

    The solution, of course, is to turn off the special meaning of '.' with '\':

    s/x\.*y/x□y/

Now everything works, for '*' means 'as many *periods* as possible'.

    There are times when the pattern '.*' is exactly what you want. For example, to change

    Now is the time for all good men ....

into

    Now is the time.

use '.*' to eat up everything after the 'for':

    s/□for.*/./

    There are a couple of additional pitfalls associated with '*' that you should be aware of. Most notable is the fact that 'as many as possible' means *zero* or more. The fact that zero is a legitimate possibility is sometimes rather surprising. For example, if our line contained

    text xy *text* x   y *text*

and we said

    s/x□*y/x□y/

the *first* 'xy' matches this pattern, for it consists of an 'x', zero spaces, and a 'y'. The result is that the substitute acts on the first 'xy', and does not touch the later one that actually contains some intervening spaces.

    The way around this, if it matters, is to specify a pattern like

    /x□□*y/

which says 'an x, a space, then as many more spaces as possible, then a y', in other words, one or more spaces.

    The other startling behavior of '*' is again related to the fact that zero is a legitimate number of occurrences of something followed by a star. The command

    s/x*/y/g

when applied to the line

    abcdef

produces

    yaybycydyeyfy

which is almost certainly not what was intended. The reason for this behavior is that zero is a legal number of matches, and there are no x's at the beginning of the line (so that gets converted into a 'y'), nor between the 'a' and the 'b' (so that gets converted into a 'y'), nor ... and so on. Make sure you really want zero matches; if not, in this case write

    s/xx*/y/g

'xx*' is one or more x's.

The Brackets '[ ]'

    Suppose that you want to delete any numbers that appear at the beginning of all lines of a file. You might first think of trying a series of commands like

    1,$s/^1*//
    1,$s/^2*//
    1,$s/^3*//

and so on, but this is clearly going to take forever if the numbers are at all long. Unless you want to repeat the commands over and over until finally all numbers are gone, you must get all the digits on one pass. This is the purpose of the brackets [and].

    The construction

    [0123456789]

matches any single digit — the whole thing is called a 'character class'. With a character class, the job is easy. The pattern '[0123456789]*' matches zero or more digits (an entire number), so

    1,$s/^[0123456789]*//

deletes all digits from the beginning of all lines.

    Any characters can appear within a character class, and just to confuse the issue there are essentially no special characters inside the brackets; even the backslash doesn't have a special meaning. To search for special characters, for example, you can say

10

/[.\$^[]/

Within [...], the '[' is not special. To get a ']' into a character class, make it the first character.

It's a nuisance to have to spell out the digits, so you can abbreviate them as [0–9]; similarly, [a–z] stands for the lower case letters, and [A–Z] for upper case.

As a final frill on character classes, you can specify a class that means 'none of the following characters'. This is done by beginning the class with a '^':

[^0–9]

stands for 'any character *except* a digit'. Thus you might find the first line that doesn't begin with a tab or space by a search like

/^[^(space)(tab)]/

Within a character class, the circumflex has a special meaning only if it occurs at the beginning. Just to convince yourself, verify that

/^[^^]/

finds a line that doesn't begin with a circumflex.

The Ampersand '&'

The ampersand '&' is used primarily to save typing. Suppose you have the line

Now is the time

and you want to make it

Now is the best time

Of course you can always say

s/the/the best/

but it seems silly to have to repeat the 'the'. The '&' is used to eliminate the repetition. On the *right* side of a substitute, the ampersand means 'whatever was just matched', so you can say

s/the/& best/

and the '&' will stand for 'the'. Of course this isn't much of a saving if the thing matched is just 'the', but if it is something truly long or awful, or if it is something like '.*' which matches a lot of text, you can save some tedious typing. There is also much less chance of making a typing error in the replacement text. For example, to parenthesize a line, regardless of its length,

s/.*/(&)/

The ampersand can occur more than once on the right side:

s/the/& best and & worst/

makes

Now is the best and the worst time

and

s/.*/&? &!!/

converts the original line into

Now is the time? Now is the time!!

To get a literal ampersand, naturally the backslash is used to turn off the special meaning:

s/ampersand/\&/

converts the word into the symbol. Notice that '&' is not special on the left side of a substitute, only on the *right* side.

Substituting Newlines

ed provides a facility for splitting a single line into two or more shorter lines by 'substituting a newline'. As the simplest example, suppose a line has gotten unmanageably long because of editing (or merely because it was unwisely typed). If it looks like

text   xy   *text*

you can break it between the 'x' and the 'y' like this:

s/xy/x\
y/

This is actually a single command, although it is typed on two lines. Bearing in mind that '\' turns off special meanings, it seems relatively intuitive that a '\' at the end of a line would make the newline there no longer special.

You can in fact make a single line into several lines with this same mechanism. As a large example, consider underlining the word 'very' in a long line by splitting 'very' onto a separate line, and preceding it by the **roff** or **nroff** formatting command '.ul'.

text a very big *text*

The command

s/□very□/\
.ul\
very\
/

converts the line into four shorter lines, preceding the word 'very' by the line '.ul', and eliminating the spaces around the 'very', all at the same time.

When a newline is substituted in, dot is left pointing at the last line created.

Joining Lines

Lines may also be joined together, but this is done with the **j** command instead of **s**. Given the lines

Now is
□the time

and supposing that dot is set to the first of them, then the command

j

joins them together. No blanks are added, which is why we carefully showed a blank at the beginning of the second line.

All by itself, a **j** command joins line dot to line dot+1, but any contiguous set of lines can be joined. Just specify the starting and ending line numbers. For example,

1,$jp

joins all the lines into one big one and prints it. (More on line numbers in Section 3.)

Rearranging a Line with \(... \)

(This section should be skipped on first reading.) Recall that '&' is a shorthand that stands for whatever was matched by the left side of an **s** command. In much the same way you can capture separate pieces of what was matched; the only difference is that you have to specify on the left side just what pieces you're interested in.

Suppose, for instance, that you have a file of lines that consist of names in the form

Smith, A. B.
Jones, C.

and so on, and you want the initials to precede the name, as in

A. B. Smith
C. Jones

It is possible to do this with a series of editing commands, but it is tedious and error-prone. (It is instructive to figure out how it is done, though.)

The alternative is to 'tag' the pieces of the pattern (in this case, the last name, and the initials), and then rearrange the pieces. On the left side of a substitution, if part of the pattern is enclosed between \(and \), whatever matched that part is remembered, and available for use on the right side. On the right side, the symbol '\1' refers to whatever matched the first \(...\) pair, '\2' to the second \(...\), and so on.

The command

1,$s/\\([^,]*\\),□*\\(.*\\)/\2□\1/

although hard to read, does the job. The first \(...\) matches the last name, which is any string up to the comma; this is referred to on the right side with '\1'. The second \(...\) is whatever follows the comma and any spaces, and is referred to as '\2'.

Of course, with any editing sequence this complicated, it's foolhardy to simply run it and hope. The global commands **g** and **v** discussed in section 4 provide a way for you to print exactly those lines which were affected by the substitute command, and thus verify that it did what you wanted in all cases.

3. LINE ADDRESSING IN THE EDITOR

The next general area we will discuss is that of line addressing in **ed**, that is, how you specify what lines are to be affected by editing commands. We have already used constructions like

1,$s/x/y/

to specify a change on all lines. And most users are long since familiar with using a single newline (or return) to print the next line, and with

/thing/

to find a line that contains 'thing'. Less familiar, surprisingly enough, is the use of

?thing?

to scan *backwards* for the previous occurrence of 'thing'. This is especially handy when you realize that the thing you want to operate on is back up the page from where you are currently editing.

The slash and question mark are the only characters you can use to delimit a context search, though you can use essentially any character in a substitute command.

Address Arithmetic

The next step is to combine the line numbers like '.', '$', '/.../' and '?...?' with '+' and '−'. Thus

$−1

is a command to print the next to last line of the current file (that is, one line before line '$'). For example, to recall how far you got in a previous editing session,

$−5,$p

prints the last six lines. (Be sure you understand why it's six, not five.) If there aren't six, of course, you'll get an error message.

As another example,

.−3,.+3p

prints from three lines before where you are now (at line dot) to three lines after, thus giving you a bit of context. By the way, the '+' can be omitted:

.−3,.3p

is absolutely identical in meaning.

Another area in which you can save typing effort in specifying lines is to use '−' and '+' as line numbers by themselves.

–

by itself is a command to move back up one line in the file. In fact, you can string several minus signs together to move back up that many lines:

———

moves up three lines, as does '–3'. Thus

    –3,+3p

is also identical to the examples above.

    Since '–' is shorter than '.–1', constructions like

    –,.s/bad/good/

are useful. This changes 'bad' to 'good' on the previous line and on the current line.

    '+' and '–' can be used in combination with searches using '/.../' and '?...?', and with '$'. The search

    /thing/––

finds the line containing 'thing', and positions you two lines before it.

Repeated Searches

    Suppose you ask for the search

    /horrible thing/

and when the line is printed you discover that it isn't the horrible thing that you wanted, so it is necessary to repeat the search again. You don't have to re-type the search, for the construction

    //

is a shorthand for 'the previous thing that was searched for', whatever it was. This can be repeated as many times as necessary. You can also go backwards:

    ??

searches for the same thing, but in the reverse direction.

    Not only can you repeat the search, but you can use '//' as the left side of a substitute command, to mean 'the most recent pattern'.

    /horrible thing/
    .... ed prints line with 'horrible thing' ...
    s//good/p

To go backwards and change a line, say

    ??s//good/

Of course, you can still use the '&' on the right hand side of a substitute to stand for whatever got matched:

    //s//& □&/p

finds the next occurrence of whatever you searched for last, replaces it by two copies of itself, then prints the line just to verify that it worked.

Default Line Numbers and the Value of Dot

    One of the most effective ways to speed up your editing is always to know what lines will be affected by a command if you don't specify the lines it is to act on, and on what line you will be positioned (i.e., the value of dot) when a command finishes. If you can edit without specifying unnecessary line numbers, you can save a lot of typing.

    As the most obvious example, if you issue a search command like

    /thing/

you are left pointing at the next line that contains 'thing'. Then no address is required with commands like **s** to make a substitution on that line, or **p** to print it, or **l** to list it, or **d** to delete it, or **a** to append text after it, or **c** to change it, or **i** to insert text before it.

    What happens if there was no 'thing'? Then you are left right where you were — dot is unchanged. This is also true if you were sitting on the only 'thing' when you issued the command. The same rules hold for searches that use '?...?'; the only difference is the direction in which you search.

    The delete command **d** leaves dot pointing at the line that followed the last deleted line. When line '$' gets deleted, however, dot points at the *new* line '$'.

    The line-changing commands **a**, **c** and **i** by default all affect the current line — if you give no line number with them, **a** appends text after the current line, **c** changes the current line, and **i** inserts text before the current line.

    a, **c**, and **i** behave identically in one respect — when you stop appending, changing or inserting, dot points at the last line entered. This is exactly what you want for typing and editing on the fly. For example, you can say

    a
    ... text ...
    ... botch ...   (minor error)
    .
    s/botch/correct/   (fix botched line)
    a
    ... more text ...

without specifying any line number for the substitute command or for the second append command. Or you can say

    a
    ... text ...
    ... horrible botch ...   (major error)
    .
    c   (replace entire line)
    ... fixed up line ...

    You should experiment to determine what happens if you add *no* lines with **a**, **c** or **i**.

The **r** command will read a file into the text being edited, either at the end if you give no address, or after the specified line if you do. In either case, dot points at the last line read in. Remember that you can even say **0r** to read a file in at the beginning of the text. (You can also say **0a** or **1i** to start adding text at the beginning.)

The **w** command writes out the entire file. If you precede the command by one line number, that line is written, while if you precede it by two line numbers, that range of lines is written. The **w** command does *not* change dot: the current line remains the same, regardless of what lines are written. This is true even if you say something like

    /⁀AB/,/⁀AE/w abstract

which involves a context search.

Since the **w** command is so easy to use, you should save what you are editing regularly as you go along just in case the system crashes, or in case you do something foolish, like clobbering what you're editing.

The least intuitive behavior, in a sense, is that of the **s** command. The rule is simple — you are left sitting on the last line that got changed. If there were no changes, then dot is unchanged.

To illustrate, suppose that there are three lines in the buffer, and you are sitting on the middle one:

    x1
    x2
    x3

Then the command

    –,+s/x/y/p

prints the third line, which is the last one changed. But if the three lines had been

    x1
    y2
    y3

and the same command had been issued while dot pointed at the second line, then the result would be to change and print only the first line, and that is where dot would be set.

Semicolon ';'

Searches with '/.../' and '?...?' start at the current line and move forward or backward respectively until they either find the pattern or get back to the current line. Sometimes this is not what is wanted. Suppose, for example, that the buffer contains lines like this:

    .
    .
    .
    ab
    .
    .
    .
    bc
    .
    .

Starting at line 1, one would expect that the command

    /a/,/b/p

prints all the lines from the 'ab' to the 'bc' inclusive. Actually this is not what happens. *Both* searches (for 'a' and for 'b') start from the same point, and thus they both find the line that contains 'ab'. The result is to print a single line. Worse, if there had been a line with a 'b' in it before the 'ab' line, then the print command would be in error, since the second line number would be less than the first, and it is illegal to try to print lines in reverse order.

This is because the comma separator for line numbers doesn't set dot as each address is processed; each search starts from the same place. In **ed**, the semicolon ';' can be used just like comma, with the single difference that use of a semicolon forces dot to be set at that point as the line numbers are being evaluated. In effect, the semicolon 'moves' dot. Thus in our example above, the command

    /a/;/b/p

prints the range of lines from 'ab' to 'bc', because after the 'a' is found, dot is set to that line, and then 'b' is searched for, starting beyond that line.

This property is most often useful in a very simple situation. Suppose you want to find the *second* occurrence of 'thing'. You could say

    /thing/
    //

but this prints the first occurrence as well as the second, and is a nuisance when you know very well that it is only the second one you're interested in. The solution is to say

    /thing/;//

This says to find the first occurrence of 'thing', set dot to that line, then find the second and print only that.

Closely related is searching for the second previous occurrence of something, as in

    ?something?;??

Printing the third or fourth or ... in either direction is left as an exercise.

Finally, bear in mind that if you want to find the first occurrence of something in a file, starting at an arbitrary place within the file, it is not sufficient to say

   1;/thing/

because this fails if 'thing' occurs on line 1. But it is possible to say

   0;/thing/

(one of the few places where 0 is a legal line number), for this starts the search at line 1.

Interrupting the Editor

   As a final note on what dot gets set to, you should be aware that if you hit the interrupt or delete or rubout or break key while **ed** is doing a command, things are put back together again and your state is restored as much as possible to what it was before the command began. Naturally, some changes are irrevocable — if you are reading or writing a file or making substitutions or deleting lines, these will be stopped in some clean but unpredictable state in the middle (which is why it is not usually wise to stop them). Dot may or may not be changed.

   Printing is more clear cut. Dot is not changed until the printing is done. Thus if you print until you see an interesting line, then hit delete, you are *not* sitting on that line or even near it. Dot is left where it was when the **p** command was started.

4. GLOBAL COMMANDS

   The global commands **g** and **v** are used to perform one or more editing commands on all lines that either contain (**g**) or don't contain (**v**) a specified pattern.

   As the simplest example, the command

   g/UNIX/p

prints all lines that contain the word 'UNIX'. The pattern that goes between the slashes can be anything that could be used in a line search or in a substitute command; exactly the same rules and limitations apply.

   As another example, then,

   g/^./p

prints all the formatting commands in a file (lines that begin with '.').

   The **v** command is identical to **g**, except that it operates on those line that do *not* contain an occurrence of the pattern. (Don't look too hard for mnemonic significance to the letter 'v'.) So

   v/^./p

prints all the lines that don't begin with '.' — the actual text lines.

   The command that follows **g** or **v** can be anything:

   g/^\./d

deletes all lines that begin with '.', and

   g/^$/d

deletes all empty lines.

   Probably the most useful command that can follow a global is the substitute command, for this can be used to make a change and print each affected line for verification. For example, we could change the word 'Unix' to 'UNIX' everywhere, and verify that it really worked, with

   g/Unix/s//UNIX/gp

Notice that we used '//' in the substitute command to mean 'the previous pattern', in this case, 'Unix'. The **p** command is done on every line that matches the pattern, not just those on which a substitution took place.

   The global command operates by making two passes over the file. On the first pass, all lines that match the pattern are marked. On the second pass, each marked line in turn is examined, dot is set to that line, and the command executed. This means that it is possible for the command that follows a **g** or **v** to use addresses, set dot, and so on, quite freely.

   g/^\.PP/+

prints the line that follows each '.PP' command (the signal for a new paragraph in some formatting packages). Remember that '+' means 'one line past dot'. And

   g/topic/?^\.SH?1

searches for each line that contains 'topic', scans backwards until it finds a line that begins '.SH' (a section heading) and prints the line that follows that, thus showing the section headings under which 'topic' is mentioned. Finally,

   g/^\.EQ/+,/^\.EN/-p

prints all the lines that lie between lines beginning with '.EQ' and '.EN' formatting commands.

   The **g** and **v** commands can also be preceded by line numbers, in which case the lines searched are only those in the range specified.

Multi-line Global Commands

   It is possible to do more than one command under the control of a global command, although the syntax for expressing the operation is not especially natural or pleasant. As an example, suppose the task is to change 'x' to 'y' and 'a' to 'b' on all lines that contain 'thing'. Then

   g/thing/s/x/y/\
   s/a/b/

is sufficient. The '\' signals the **g** command that the set

of commands continues on the next line; it terminates
on the first line that does not end with '\'. (As a minor
blemish, you can't use a substitute command to insert a
newline within a **g** command.)

You should watch out for this problem: the command

g/x/s//y/\
s/a/b/

does *not* work as you expect. The remembered pattern
is the last pattern that was actually executed, so sometimes it will be 'x' (as expected), and sometimes it will
be 'a' (not expected). You must spell it out, like this:

g/x/s/x/y/\
s/a/b/

It is also possible to execute **a**, **c** and **i** commands under a global command; as with other multi-
line constructions, all that is needed is to add a '\' at the
end of each line except the last. Thus to add a '.nf' and
'.sp' command before each '.EQ' line, type

g/\.EQ/i\
.nf\
.sp

There is no need for a final line containing a '.' to terminate the **i** command, unless there are further commands being done under the global. On the other hand,
it does no harm to put it in either.

5. CUT AND PASTE WITH UNIX COMMANDS

One editing area in which non-programmers
seem not very confident is in what might be called 'cut
and paste' operations — changing the name of a file,
making a copy of a file somewhere else, moving a few
lines from one place to another in a file, inserting one
file in the middle of another, splitting a file into pieces,
and splicing two or more files together.

Yet most of these operations are actually quite
easy, if you keep your wits about you and go cau-
tiously. The next several sections talk about cut and
paste. We will begin with the UNIX commands for
moving entire files around, then discuss **ed** commands
for operating on pieces of files.

Changing the Name of a File

You have a file named 'memo' and you want it
to be called 'paper' instead. How is it done?

The UNIX program that renames files is called
mv (for 'move'); it 'moves' the file from one name to
another, like this:

mv memo paper

That's all there is to it: **mv** from the old name to the
new name.

mv oldname newname

Warning: if there is already a file around with the new
name, its present contents will be silently clobbered by
the information from the other file. The one exception
is that you can't move a file to itself —

mv x x

is illegal.

Making a Copy of a File

Sometimes what you want is a copy of a file —
an entirely fresh version. This might be because you
want to work on a file, and yet save a copy in case
something gets fouled up, or just because you're
paranoid.

In any case, the way to do it is with the **cp** command. (**cp** stands for 'copy'; the UNIX system is big
on short command names, which are appreciated by
heavy users, but sometimes a strain for novices.) Suppose you have a file called 'good' and you want to save
a copy before you make some dramatic editing
changes. Choose a name — 'savegood' might be
acceptable — then type

cp good savegood

This copies 'good' onto 'savegood', and you now have
two identical copies of the file 'good'. (If 'savegood'
previously contained something, it gets overwritten.)

Now if you decide at some time that you want to
get back to the original state of 'good', you can say

mv savegood good

(if you're not interested in 'savegood' any more), or

cp savegood good

if you still want to retain a safe copy.

In summary, **mv** just renames a file; **cp** makes a
duplicate copy. Both of them clobber the 'target' file if
it already exists, so you had better be sure that's what
you want to do *before* you do it.

Removing a File

If you decide you are really done with a file forever, you can remove it with the **rm** command:

rm savegood

throws away (irrevocably) the file called 'savegood'.

Putting Two or More Files Together

The next step is the familiar one of collecting
two or more files into one big one. This will be needed,
for example, when the author of a paper decides that
several sections need to be combined into one. There
are several ways to do it, of which the cleanest, once
you get used to it, is a program called **cat**. (Not *all*
UNIX programs have two-letter names.) **cat** is short
for 'concatenate', which is exactly what we want to do.

Suppose the job is to combine the files 'file1' and 'file2' into a single file called 'bigfile'. If you say

    cat file

the contents of 'file' will get printed on your terminal. If you say

    cat file1 file2

the contents of 'file1' and then the contents of 'file2' will *both* be printed on your terminal, in that order. So **cat** combines the files, all right, but it's not much help to print them on the terminal — we want them in 'bigfile'.

Fortunately, there is a way. You can tell the system that instead of printing on your terminal, you want the same information put in a file. The way to do it is to add to the command line the character > and the name of the file where you want the output to go. Then you can say

    cat file1 file2 >bigfile

and the job is done. (As with **cp** and **mv**, you're putting something into 'bigfile', and anything that was already there is destroyed.)

This ability to 'capture' the output of a program is one of the most useful aspects of the UNIX system. Fortunately it's not limited to the **cat** program — you can use it with *any* program that prints on your terminal. We'll see some more uses for it in a moment.

Naturally, you can combine several files, not just two:

    cat file1 file2 file3 ... >bigfile

collects a whole bunch.

Question: is there any difference between

    cp good savegood

and

    cat good >savegood

Answer: for most purposes, no. You might reasonably ask why there are two programs in that case, since **cat** is obviously all you need. The answer is that **cp** can do some other things as well, which you can investigate for yourself by reading the manual. For now we'll stick to simple usages.

Adding Something to the End of a File

Sometimes you want to add one file to the end of another. We have enough building blocks now that you can do it; in fact before reading further it would be valuable if you figured out how. To be specific, how would you use **cp**, **mv** and/or **cat** to add the file 'good1' to the end of the file 'good'?

You could try

    cat good good1 >temp
    mv temp good

which is probably most direct. You should also understand why

    cat good good1 >good

doesn't work. (Don't practice with a good 'good'!)

The easy way is to use a variant of >, called >>. In fact, >> is identical to > except that instead of clobbering the old file, it simply tacks stuff on at the end. Thus you could say

    cat good1 >>good

and 'good1' is added to the end of 'good'. (And if 'good' didn't exist, this makes a copy of 'good1' called 'good'.)

6. CUT AND PASTE WITH THE EDITOR

Now we move on to manipulating pieces of files — individual lines or groups of lines. This is another area where new users seem unsure of themselves.

Filenames

The first step is to ensure that you know the **ed** commands for reading and writing files. Of course you can't go very far without knowing **r** and **w**. Equally useful, but less well known, is the 'edit' command **e**. Within **ed**, the command

    e newfile

says 'I want to edit a new file called *newfile,* without leaving the editor.' The **e** command discards whatever you're currently working on and starts over on *newfile.* It's exactly the same as if you had quit with the **q** command, then re-entered **ed** with a new file name, except that if you have a pattern remembered, then a command like *//* will still work.

If you enter **ed** with the command

    ed file

ed remembers the name of the file, and any subsequent **e**, **r** or **w** commands that don't contain a filename will refer to this remembered file. Thus

    ed file1
    ... (editing) ...
    w   (writes back in file1)
    e file2   (edit new file, without leaving editor)
    ... (editing on file2) ...
    w   (writes back on file2)

(and so on) does a series of edits on various files without ever leaving **ed** and without typing the name of any file more than once. (As an aside, if you examine the sequence of commands here, you can see why many UNIX systems use **e** as a synonym for **ed**.)

You can find out the remembered file name at any time with the **f** command; just type **f** without a file name. You can also change the name of the remembered file name with **f**; a useful sequence is

```
ed precious
f junk
... (editing) ...
```

which gets a copy of a precious file, then uses **f** to guarantee that a careless **w** command won't clobber the original.

Inserting One File into Another

Suppose you have a file called 'memo', and you want the file called 'table' to be inserted just after the reference to Table 1. That is, in 'memo' somewhere is a line that says

```
Table 1 shows that ...
```

and the data contained in 'table' has to go there, probably so it will be formatted properly by **nroff** or **troff**. Now what?

This one is easy. Edit 'memo', find 'Table 1', and add the file 'table' right there:

```
ed memo
/Table 1/
Table 1 shows that ... [response from ed]
.r table
```

The critical line is the last one. As we said earlier, the **r** command reads a file; here you asked for it to be read in right after line dot. An **r** command without any address adds lines at the end, so it is the same as **$r**.

Writing out Part of a File

The other side of the coin is writing out part of the document you're editing. For example, maybe you want to copy out into a separate file that table from the previous example, so it can be formatted and tested separately. Suppose that in the file being edited we have

```
.TS
...[lots of stuff]
.TE
```

which is the way a table is set up for the **tbl** program. To isolate the table in a separate file called 'table', first find the start of the table (the '.TS' line), then write out the interesting part:

```
/\.TS/
.TS [ed prints the line it found]
.//\.TE/w table
```

and the job is done. If you are confident, you can do it all at once with

```
/\.TS/;/\.TE/w table
```

and now you have two copies, one in the file you're still editing, one in the file 'table' you've just written.

The point is that the **w** command can write out a group of lines, instead of the whole file. In fact, you can write out a single line if you like; just give one line number instead of two. For example, if you have just typed a horribly complicated line and you know that it (or something like it) is going to be needed later, then save it — don't re-type it. In the editor, say

```
a
...lots of stuff...
...horrible line...
.
.w temp
a
...more stuff...
.
.r temp
a
...more stuff...
.
```

This last example is worth studying, to be sure you appreciate what's going on.

Moving Lines Around

Suppose you want to move a paragraph from its present position in a paper to the end. How would you do it? As a concrete example, suppose each paragraph in the paper begins with the formatting command '.PP'. Think about it and write down the details before reading on.

The brute force way (not necessarily bad) is to write the paragraph onto a temporary file, delete it from its current position, then read in the temporary file at the end. Assuming that you are sitting on the '.PP' command that begins the paragraph, this is the sequence of commands:

```
.,/\.PP/-w temp
.,//-d
$r temp
```

That is, from where you are now ('.') until one line before the next '.PP' ('/\.PP/-') write onto 'temp'. Then delete the same lines. Finally, read 'temp' at the end.

As we said, that's the brute force way. The easier way (often) is to use the *move* command **m** that **ed** provides — it lets you do the whole set of operations at one crack, without any temporary files.

The **m** command is like many other **ed** commands in that it takes up to two line numbers in front that tell what lines are to be affected. It is also *followed* by a line number that tells where the lines are to go. Thus

```
line1, line2 m line3
```

says to move all the lines between 'line1' and 'line2' after 'line3'. Naturally, any of 'line1' etc., can be patterns between slashes, $ signs, or other ways to specify lines.

Suppose again that you're sitting at the first line of the paragraph. Then you can say

    .,/\.PP/−m$

That's all.

As another example of a frequent operation, you can reverse the order of two adjacent lines by moving the first one to after the second. Suppose that you are positioned at the first. Then

    m+

does it. It says to move line dot to after one line after line dot. If you are positioned on the second line,

    m—

does the interchange.

As you can see, the **m** command is more succinct and direct than writing, deleting and re-reading. When is brute force better anyway? This is a matter of personal taste — do what you have most confidence in. The main difficulty with the **m** command is that if you use patterns to specify both the lines you are moving and the target, you have to take care that you specify them properly, or you may well not move the lines you thought you did. The result of a botched **m** command can be a ghastly mess. Doing the job a step at a time makes it easier for you to verify at each step that you accomplished what you wanted to. It's also a good idea to issue a **w** command before doing anything complicated; then if you goof, it's easy to back up to where you were.

Marks

ed provides a facility for marking a line with a particular name so you can later reference it by name regardless of its actual line number. This can be handy for moving lines, and for keeping track of them even after they've been moved. The *mark* command is **k**; the command

    kx

marks the current line with the name 'x'. If a line number precedes the **k**, that line is marked. (The mark name must be a single lower case letter.) Now you can refer to the marked line with the address

    'x

Marks are most useful for moving things around. Find the first line of the block to be moved, and mark it with '*a*. Then find the last line and mark it with '*b*. Now position yourself at the place where the stuff is to go and say

    'a,'bm.

Bear in mind that only one line can have a particular mark name associated with it at any given time.

Copying Lines

We mentioned earlier the idea of saving a line that was hard to type or used often, so as to cut down on typing time. Of course this could be more than one line; then the saving is presumably even greater.

ed provides another command, called **t** (for 'transfer') for making a copy of a group of one or more lines at any point. This is often easier than writing and reading.

The **t** command is identical to the **m** command, except that instead of moving lines it simply duplicates them at the place you named. Thus

    1,t

duplicates the entire contents that you are editing. A more common use for **t** is for creating a series of lines that differ only slightly. For example, you can say

    a
    .... x .... (long line)
    .
    t.   (make a copy)
    s/x/y/   (change it a bit)
    t.   (make third copy)
    s/y/z/   (change it a bit)

and so on.

The Temporary Escape '!'

Sometimes it is convenient to be able to temporarily escape from the editor to do some other UNIX command, perhaps one of the file copy or move commands discussed in section 5, without leaving the editor. The 'escape' command **!** provides a way to do this.

If you say

    !any UNIX command

your current editing state is suspended, and the UNIX command you asked for is executed. When the command finishes, **ed** will signal you by printing another **!**; at that point you can resume editing.

You can really do *any* UNIX command, including another **ed**. (This is quite common, in fact.) In this case, you can even do another **!**.

On Berkeley UNIX systems, there is an additional (and preferable) mechanism called *job control* which lets you suspend your edit session (or, for that matter, any program), return to the shell from which you invoked that program, and issue any commands, then resume the program from the point where it was stopped. See *An Introduction to the C Shell* for more details.

7. SUPPORTING TOOLS

There are several tools and techniques that go along with the editor, all of which are relatively easy once you know how **ed** works, because they are all based on the editor. In this section we will give some fairly cursory examples of these tools, more to indicate their existence than to provide a complete tutorial. More information on each can be found in [3].

Grep

Sometimes you want to find all occurrences of some word or pattern in a set of files, to edit them or perhaps just to verify their presence or absence. It may be possible to edit each file separately and look for the pattern of interest, but if there are many files this can get very tedious, and if the files are really big, it may be impossible because of limits in **ed**.

The program **grep** was invented to get around these limitations. The search patterns that we have described in the paper are often called 'regular expressions', and 'grep' stands for

g/re/p

That describes exactly what **grep** does — it prints every line in a set of files that contains a particular pattern. Thus

grep 'thing' file1 file2 file3 ...

finds 'thing' wherever it occurs in any of the files 'file1', 'file2', etc. **grep** also indicates the file in which the line was found, so you can later edit it if you like.

The pattern represented by 'thing' can be any pattern you can use in the editor, since **grep** and **ed** use exactly the same mechanism for pattern searching. It is wisest always to enclose the pattern in the single quotes '...' if it contains any non-alphabetic characters, since many such characters also mean something special to the UNIX command interpreter (the 'shell'). If you don't quote them, the command interpreter will try to interpret them before **grep** gets a chance.

There is also a way to find lines that *don't* contain a pattern:

grep −v 'thing' file1 file2 ...

finds all lines that don't contains 'thing'. The −v must occur in the position shown. Given **grep** and **grep** −v, it is possible to do things like selecting all lines that contain some combination of patterns. For example, to get all lines that contain 'x' but not 'y':

grep x file... | grep −v y

(The notation | is a 'pipe', which causes the output of the first command to be used as input to the second command; see [2].)

Editing Scripts

If a fairly complicated set of editing operations is to be done on a whole set of files, the easiest thing to do is to make up a 'script', i.e., a file that contains the operations you want to perform, then apply this script to each file in turn.

For example, suppose you want to change every 'Unix' to 'UNIX' and every 'Gcos' to 'GCOS' in a large number of files. Then put into the file 'script' the lines

g/Unix/s//UNIX/g
g/Gcos/s//GCOS/g
w
q

Now you can say

ed file1 <script
ed file2 <script
...

This causes **ed** to take its commands from the prepared script. Notice that the whole job has to be planned in advance.

And of course by using the UNIX command interpreter, you can cycle through a set of files automatically, with varying degrees of ease.

Sed

sed ('stream editor') is a version of the editor with restricted capabilities but which is capable of processing unlimited amounts of input. Basically **sed** copies its input to its output, applying one or more editing commands to each line of input.

As an example, suppose that we want to do the 'Unix' to 'UNIX' part of the example given above, but without rewriting the files. Then the command

sed 's/Unix/UNIX/g' file1 file2 ...

applies the command 's/Unix/UNIX/g' to all lines from 'file1', 'file2', etc., and copies all lines to the output. The advantage of using **sed** in such a case is that it can be used with input too large for **ed** to handle. All the output can be collected in one place, either in a file or perhaps piped into another program.

If the editing transformation is so complicated that more than one editing command is needed, commands can be supplied from a file, or on the command line, with a slightly more complex syntax. To take commands from a file, for example,

sed −f cmdfile input−files...

sed has further capabilities, including conditional testing and branching, which we cannot go into here, but which are described in detail in *Sed − A Noninteractive Text Editor.*

10

10

Acknowledgement

I am grateful to Ted Dolotta for his careful reading and valuable suggestions.

References

[1]   Brian W. Kernighan, *A Tutorial Introduction to the UNIX Text Editor,* Bell Laboratories internal memorandum.

[2]   Brian W. Kernighan, *UNIX For Beginners,* Bell Laboratories internal memorandum.

[3]   Ken L. Thompson and Dennis M. Ritchie, *The UNIX Programmer's Manual.* Bell Laboratories.

An Introduction to Display Editing with Vi

William Joy

Mark Horton

Computer Science Division
Department of Electrical Engineering and Computer Science
University of California, Berkeley
Berkeley, Ca. 94720

11

ABSTRACT

    Vi (visual) is a display oriented interactive text editor. When using *vi* the screen of your terminal acts as a window into the file which you are editing. Changes which you make to the file are reflected in what you see.

    Using *vi* you can insert new text any place in the file quite easily. Most of the commands to *vi* move the cursor around in the file. There are commands to move the cursor forward and backward in units of characters, words, sentences and paragraphs. A small set of operators, like **d** for delete and **c** for change, are combined with the motion commands to form operations such as delete word or change paragraph, in a simple and natural way. This regularity and the mnemonic assignment of commands to keys makes the editor command set easy to remember and to use.

    Vi will work on a large number of display terminals, and new terminals are easily driven after editing a terminal description file. While it is advantageous to have an intelligent terminal which can locally insert and delete lines and characters from the display, the editor will function quite well on dumb terminals over slow phone lines. The editor makes allowance for the low bandwidth in these situations and uses smaller window sizes and different display updating algorithms to make best use of the limited speed available.

    It is also possible to use the command set of *vi* on hardcopy terminals, storage tubes and ''glass tty's'' using a one line editing window; thus *vi's* command set is available on all terminals. The full command set of the more traditional, line oriented editor *ex* is available within *vi;* it is quite simple to switch between the two modes of editing.

1. Getting started

    This document provides a quick introduction to *vi*. (Pronounced *vee-eye*.) You should be running *vi* on a file you are familiar with while you are reading this. The first part of this document (sections 1 through 5) describes the basics of using *vi*. Some topics of special interest are presented in section 6, and some nitty-gritty details of how the editor functions are saved for section 7 to avoid cluttering the presentation here.

    There is also a short appendix here, which gives for each character the special meanings which this character has in *vi*. Attached to this document should be a quick reference card. This card summarizes the commands of *vi* in a very compact format. You should have the card handy while you are learning *vi*.

The financial support of an IBM Graduate Fellowship and the National Science Foundation under grants MCS74-07644-A03 and MCS78-07291 is gratefully acknowledged.

1.1. Specifying terminal type

Before you can start *vi* you must tell the system what kind of terminal you are using. Here is a (necessarily incomplete) list of terminal type codes. If your terminal does not appear here, you should consult with one of the staff members on your system to find out the code for your terminal. If your terminal does not have a code, one can be assigned and a description for the terminal can be created.

Code	Full name	Type
2621	Hewlett-Packard 2621A/P	Intelligent
2645	Hewlett-Packard 264x	Intelligent
act4	Microterm ACT-IV	Dumb
act5	Microterm ACT-V	Dumb
adm3a	Lear Siegler ADM-3a	Dumb
adm31	Lear Siegler ADM-31	Intelligent
c100	Human Design Concept 100	Intelligent
dm1520	Datamedia 1520	Dumb
dm2500	Datamedia 2500	Intelligent
dm3025	Datamedia 3025	Intelligent
fox	Perkin-Elmer Fox	Dumb
h1500	Hazeltine 1500	Intelligent
h19	Heathkit h19	Intelligent
i100	Infoton 100	Intelligent
mime	Imitating a smart act4	Intelligent
t1061	Teleray 1061	Intelligent
vt52	Dec VT-52	Dumb

Suppose for example that you have a Hewlett-Packard HP2621A terminal. The code used by the system for this terminal is '2621'. In this case you can use one of the following commands to tell the system the type of your terminal:

% **setenv TERM** 2621

This command works with the *csh* shell. If you are using the standard Bourne shell *sh* then you should give the commands

$ **TERM**=2621
$ **export TERM**

If you want to arrange to have your terminal type set up automatically when you log in, you can use the *tset* program. If you dial in on a *mime*, but often use hardwired ports, a typical line for your *.login* file (if you use csh) would be

setenv TERM `tset – –d mime`

or for your *.profile* file (if you use sh)

TERM=`tset – –d mime`

Tset knows which terminals are hardwired to each port and needs only to be told that when you dial in you are probably on a *mime*. *Tset* is usually used to change the erase and kill characters, too.

1.2. Editing a file

After telling the system which kind of terminal you have, you should make a copy of a file you are familiar with, and run *vi* on this file, giving the command

% **vi** *name*

replacing *name* with the name of the copy file you just created. The screen should clear and the text of your file should appear on the screen. If something else happens refer to the footnote.‡

---

‡ If you gave the system an incorrect terminal type code then the editor may have just made a mess out of your screen. This happens when it sends control codes for one kind of terminal to some other kind of terminal. In this case hit the keys

1.3. The editor's copy: the buffer

The editor does not directly modify the file which you are editing. Rather, the editor makes a copy of this file, in a place called the *buffer,* and remembers the file's name. You do not affect the contents of the file unless and until you write the changes you make back into the original file.

1.4. Notational conventions

In our examples, input which must be typed as is will be presented in **bold face**. Text which should be replaced with appropriate input will be given in *italics*. We will represent special characters in SMALL CAPITALS.

1.5. Arrow keys

The editor command set is independent of the terminal you are using. On most terminals with cursor positioning keys, these keys will also work within the editor. If you don't have cursor positioning keys, or even if you do, you can use the **h j k** and **l** keys as cursor positioning keys (these are labelled with arrows on an *adm3a).**

(Particular note for the HP2621: on this terminal the function keys must be *shifted* (ick) to send to the machine, otherwise they only act locally. Unshifted use will leave the cursor positioned incorrectly.)

1.6. Special characters: ESC, CR and DEL

Several of these special characters are very important, so be sure to find them right now. Look on your keyboard for a key labelled ESC or ALT. It should be near the upper left corner of your terminal. Try hitting this key a few times. The editor will ring the bell to indicate that it is in a quiescent state.‡ Partially formed commands are cancelled by ESC, and when you insert text in the file you end the text insertion with ESC. This key is a fairly harmless one to hit, so you can just hit it if you don't know what is going on until the editor rings the bell.

The CR or RETURN key is important because it is used to terminate certain commands. It is usually at the right side of the keyboard, and is the same command used at the end of each shell command.

Another very useful key is the DEL or RUB key, which generates an interrupt, telling the editor to stop what it is doing. It is a forceful way of making the editor listen to you, or to return it to the quiescent state if you don't know or don't like what is going on. Try hitting the '/' key on your terminal. This key is used when you want to specify a string to be searched for. The cursor should now be positioned at the bottom line of the terminal after a '/' printed as a prompt. You can get the cursor back to the current position by hitting the DEL or RUB key; try this now.* From now on we will simply refer to hitting the DEL or RUB key as "sending an interrupt."**

The editor often echoes your commands on the last line of the terminal. If the cursor is on the first position of this last line, then the editor is performing a computation, such as computing a new position in the file after a search or running a command to reformat part of the buffer. When this is happening you can stop the editor by sending an interrupt.

:q (colon and the q key) and then hit the RETURN key. This should get you back to the command level interpreter. Figure out what you did wrong (ask someone else if necessary) and try again.

Another thing which can go wrong is that you typed the wrong file name and the editor just printed an error diagnostic. In this case you should follow the above procedure for getting out of the editor, and try again this time spelling the file name correctly.

If the editor doesn't seem to respond to the commands which you type here, try sending an interrupt to it by hitting the DEL or RUB key on your terminal, and then hitting the **:q** command again followed by a carriage return.

* As we will see later, *h* moves back to the left (like control-h which is a backspace), *j* moves down (in the same column), *k* moves up (in the same column), and *l* moves to the right.
‡ On smart terminals where it is possible, the editor will quietly flash the screen rather than ringing the bell.
* Backspacing over the '/' will also cancel the search.
** On some systems, this interruptibility comes at a price: you cannot type ahead when the editor is computing with the cursor on the bottom line.

1.7. Getting out of the editor

After you have worked with this introduction for a while, and you wish to do something else, you can give the command **ZZ** to the editor. This will write the contents of the editor's buffer back into the file you are editing, if you made any changes, and then quit from the editor. You can also end an editor session by giving the command **:q!**CR;† this is a dangerous but occasionally essential command which ends the editor session and discards all your changes. You need to know about this command in case you change the editor's copy of a file you wish only to look at. Be very careful not to give this command when you really want to save the changes you have made.

2. Moving around in the file

2.1. Scrolling and paging

The editor has a number of commands for moving around in the file. The most useful of these is generated by hitting the control and D keys at the same time, a control-D or '^D'. We will use this two character notation for referring to these control keys from now on. You may have a key labelled '^' on your terminal. This key will be represented as '↑' in this document; '^' is exclusively used as part of the '^x' notation for control characters.‡

As you know now if you tried hitting **^D**, this command scrolls down in the file. The **D** thus stands for down. Many editor commands are mnemonic and this makes them much easier to remember. For instance the command to scroll up is **^U**. Many dumb terminals can't scroll up at all, in which case hitting **^U** clears the screen and refreshes it with a line which is farther back in the file at the top.

If you want to see more of the file below where you are, you can hit **^E** to expose one more line at the bottom of the screen, leaving the cursor where it is. The command **^Y** (which is hopelessly non-mnemonic, but next to **^U** on the keyboard) exposes one more line at the top of the screen.

There are other ways to move around in the file; the keys **^F** and **^B** move forward and backward a page, keeping a couple of lines of continuity between screens so that it is possible to read through a file using these rather than **^D** and **^U** if you wish.

Notice the difference between scrolling and paging. If you are trying to read the text in a file, hitting **^F** to move forward a page will leave you only a little context to look back at. Scrolling on the other hand leaves more context, and happens more smoothly. You can continue to read the text as scrolling is taking place.

2.2. Searching, goto, and previous context

Another way to position yourself in the file is by giving the editor a string to search for. Type the character **/** followed by a string of characters terminated by CR. The editor will position the cursor at the next occurrence of this string. Try hitting **n** to then go to the next occurrence of this string. The character **?** will search backwards from where you are, and is otherwise like **/**.†

If the search string you give the editor is not present in the file the editor will print a diagnostic on the last line of the screen, and the cursor will be returned to its initial position.

If you wish the search to match only at the beginning of a line, begin the search string with an ↑. To match only at the end of a line, end the search string with a **$**. Thus **/↑search**CR will search for the word 'search' at the beginning of a line, and **/last$**CR searches for the word 'last' at the end of a line.*

---

† All commands which read from the last display line can also be terminated with a ESC as well as an CR.

‡ If you don't have a '^' key on your terminal then there is probably a key labelled '↑'; in any case these characters are one and the same.

† These searches will normally wrap around the end of the file, and thus find the string even if it is not on a line in the direction you search provided it is anywhere else in the file. You can disable this wraparound in scans by giving the command **:se nowrapscan**CR, or more briefly **:se nows**CR.

*Actually, the string you give to search for here can be a *regular expression* in the sense of the editors *ex*(1) and *ed*(1). If you don't wish to learn about this yet, you can disable this more general facility by doing **:se nomagic**CR; by putting this command in EXINIT in your environment, you can have this always be in effect (more about *EXINIT* later.)

The command **G**, when preceded by a number will position the cursor at that line in the file. Thus **1G** will move the cursor to the first line of the file. If you give **G** no count, then it moves to the end of the file.

If you are near the end of the file, and the last line is not at the bottom of the screen, the editor will place only the character '˜' on each remaining line. This indicates that the last line in the file is on the screen; that is, the '˜' lines are past the end of the file.

You can find out the state of the file you are editing by typing a ^G. The editor will show you the name of the file you are editing, the number of the current line, the number of lines in the buffer, and the percentage of the way through the buffer which you are. Try doing this now, and remember the number of the line you are on. Give a **G** command to get to the end and then another **G** command to get back where you were.

You can also get back to a previous position by using the command `` (two back quotes). This is often more convenient than **G** because it requires no advance preparation. Try giving a **G** or a search with **/** or **?** and then a `` to get back to where you were. If you accidentally hit **n** or any command which moves you far away from a context of interest, you can quickly get back by hitting ``.

2.3. Moving around on the screen

Now try just moving the cursor around on the screen. If your terminal has arrow keys (4 or 5 keys with arrows going in each direction) try them and convince yourself that they work. If you don't have working arrow keys, you can always use **h**, **j**, **k**, and **l**. Experienced users of *vi* prefer these keys to arrow keys, because they are usually right underneath their fingers.

Hit the **+** key. Each time you do, notice that the cursor advances to the next line in the file, at the first non-white position on the line. The **–** key is like **+** but goes the other way.

These are very common keys for moving up and down lines in the file. Notice that if you go off the bottom or top with these keys then the screen will scroll down (and up if possible) to bring a line at a time into view. The RETURN key has the same effect as the **+** key.

Vi also has commands to take you to the top, middle and bottom of the screen. **H** will take you to the top (home) line on the screen. Try preceding it with a number as in **3H**. This will take you to the third line on the screen. Many *vi* commands take preceding numbers and do interesting things with them. Try **M**, which takes you to the middle line on the screen, and **L**, which takes you to the last line on the screen. **L** also takes counts, thus **5L** will take you to the fifth line from the bottom.

2.4. Moving within a line

Now try picking a word on some line on the screen, not the first word on the line. move the cursor using RETURN and **–** to be on the line where the word is. Try hitting the **w** key. This will advance the cursor to the next word on the line. Try hitting the **b** key to back up words in the line. Also try the **e** key which advances you to the end of the current word rather than to the beginning of the next word. Also try SPACE (the space bar) which moves right one character and the BS (backspace or ^H) key which moves left one character. The key **h** works as ^H does and is useful if you don't have a BS key. (Also, as noted just above, **l** will move to the right.)

If the line had punctuation in it you may have noticed that that the **w** and **b** keys stopped at each group of punctuation. You can also go back and forwards words without stopping at punctuation by using **W** and **B** rather than the lower case equivalents. Think of these as bigger words. Try these on a few lines with punctuation to see how they differ from the lower case **w** and **b**.

The word keys wrap around the end of line, rather than stopping at the end. Try moving to a word on a line below where you are by repeatedly hitting **w**.

2.5. Summary

SPACE	advance the cursor one position
^B	backwards to previous page
^D	scrolls down in the file

^E	exposes another line at the bottom
^F	forward to next page
^G	tell what is going on
^H	backspace the cursor
^N	next line, same column
^P	previous line, same column
^U	scrolls up in the file
^Y	exposes another line at the top
+	next line, at the beginning
−	previous line, at the beginning
/	scan for a following string forwards
?	scan backwards
B	back a word, ignoring punctuation
G	go to specified line, last default
H	home screen line
M	middle screen line
L	last screen line
W	forward a word, ignoring punctuation
b	back a word
e	end of current word
n	scan for next instance of **/** or **?** pattern
w	word after this word

2.6. View

If you want to use the editor to look at a file, rather than to make changes, invoke it as *view* instead of *vi*. This will set the *readonly* option which will prevent you from accidently overwriting the file.

3. Making simple changes

3.1. Inserting

One of the most useful commands is the **i** (insert) command. After you type **i**, everything you type until you hit ESC is inserted into the file. Try this now; position yourself to some word in the file and try inserting text before this word. If you are on an dumb terminal it will seem, for a minute, that some of the characters in your line have been overwritten, but they will reappear when you hit ESC.

Now try finding a word which can, but does not, end in an 's'. Position yourself at this word and type **e** (move to end of word), then **a** for append and then 'sESC' to terminate the textual insert. This sequence of commands can be used to easily pluralize a word.

Try inserting and appending a few times to make sure you understand how this works; **i** placing text to the left of the cursor, **a** to the right.

It is often the case that you want to add new lines to the file you are editing, before or after some specific line in the file. Find a line where this makes sense and then give the command **o** to create a new line after the line you are on, or the command **O** to create a new line before the line you are on. After you create a new line in this way, text you type up to an ESC is inserted on the new line.

Many related editor commands are invoked by the same letter key and differ only in that one is given by a lower case key and the other is given by an upper case key. In these cases, the upper case key often differs from the lower case key in its sense of direction, with the upper case key working backward and/or up, while the lower case key moves forward and/or down.

Whenever you are typing in text, you can give many lines of input or just a few characters. To type in more than one line of text, hit a RETURN at the middle of your input. A new line will be created for text, and you can continue to type. If you are on a slow and dumb terminal the editor may choose to wait to redraw the tail of the screen, and will let you type over the existing screen lines. This avoids the lengthy delay which would occur if the editor attempted to keep the tail of the screen always up to date. The tail of the screen will be fixed up, and the missing lines will reappear, when you hit ESC.

While you are inserting new text, you can use the characters you normally use at the system command level (usually ^H or #) to backspace over the last character which you typed, and the character which you use to kill input lines (usually @, ^X, or ^U) to erase the input you have typed on the current line.†
The character ^W will erase a whole word and leave you after the space after the previous word; it is useful for quickly backing up in an insert.

Notice that when you backspace during an insertion the characters you backspace over are not erased; the cursor moves backwards, and the characters remain on the display. This is often useful if you are planning to type in something similar. In any case the characters disappear when when you hit ESC; if you want to get rid of them immediately, hit an ESC and then **a** again.

Notice also that you can't erase characters which you didn't insert, and that you can't backspace around the end of a line. If you need to back up to the previous line to make a correction, just hit ESC and move the cursor back to the previous line. After making the correction you can return to where you were and use the insert or append command again.

3.2. Making small corrections

You can make small corrections in existing text quite easily. Find a single character which is wrong or just pick any character. Use the arrow keys to find the character, or get near the character with the word motion keys and then either backspace (hit the BS key or ^H or even just **h**) or SPACE (using the space bar) until the cursor is on the character which is wrong. If the character is not needed then hit the **x** key; this deletes the character from the file. It is analogous to the way you **x** out characters when you make mistakes on a typewriter (except it's not as messy).

If the character is incorrect, you can replace it with the correct character by giving the command **r**c, where c is replaced by the correct character. Finally if the character which is incorrect should be replaced by more than one character, give the command **s** which substitutes a string of characters, ending with ESC, for it. If there are a small number of characters which are wrong you can precede **s** with a count of the number of characters to be replaced. Counts are also useful with **x** to specify the number of characters to be deleted.

3.3. More corrections: operators

You already know almost enough to make changes at a higher level. All you need to know now is that the **d** key acts as a delete operator. Try the command **dw** to delete a word. Try hitting **.** a few times. Notice that this repeats the effect of the **dw**. The command **.** repeats the last command which made a change. You can remember it by analogy with an ellipsis '**...**'.

Now try **db**. This deletes a word backwards, namely the preceding word. Try **d**SPACE. This deletes a single character, and is equivalent to the **x** command.

Another very useful operator is **c** or change. The command **cw** thus changes the text of a single word. You follow it by the replacement text ending with an ESC. Find a word which you can change to another, and try this now. Notice that the end of the text to be changed was marked with the character '$' so that you can see this as you are typing in the new material.

3.4. Operating on lines

It is often the case that you want to operate on lines. Find a line which you want to delete, and type **dd**, the **d** operator twice. This will delete the line. If you are on a dumb terminal, the editor may just erase the line on the screen, replacing it with a line with only an @ on it. This line does not correspond to any line in your file, but only acts as a place holder. It helps to avoid a lengthy redraw of the rest of the screen

---

† In fact, the character ^H (backspace) always works to erase the last input character here, regardless of what your erase character is.

which would be necessary to close up the hole created by the deletion on a terminal without a delete line capability.

Try repeating the **c** operator twice; this will change a whole line, erasing its previous contents and replacing them with text you type up to an ESC.†

You can delete or change more than one line by preceding the **dd** or **cc** with a count, i.e. **5dd** deletes 5 lines. You can also give a command like **dL** to delete all the lines up to and including the last line on the screen, or **d3L** to delete through the third from the bottom line. Try some commands like this now.* Notice that the editor lets you know when you change a large number of lines so that you can see the extent of the change. The editor will also always tell you when a change you make affects text which you cannot see.

3.5. Undoing

Now suppose that the last change which you made was incorrect; you could use the insert, delete and append commands to put the correct material back. However, since it is often the case that we regret a change or make a change incorrectly, the editor provides a **u** (undo) command to reverse the last change which you made. Try this a few times, and give it twice in a row to notice that an **u** also undoes a **u.**

The undo command lets you reverse only a single change. After you make a number of changes to a line, you may decide that you would rather have the original state of the line back. The **U** command restores the current line to the state before you started changing it.

You can recover text which you delete, even if undo will not bring it back; see the section on recovering lost text below.

3.6. Summary

SPACE	advance the cursor one position
^H	backspace the cursor
^W	erase a word during an insert
erase	your erase (usually ^H or #), erases a character during an insert
kill	your kill (usually @, ^X, or ^U), kills the insert on this line
.	repeats the changing command
O	opens and inputs new lines, above the current
U	undoes the changes you made to the current line
a	appends text after the cursor
c	changes the object you specify to the following text
d	deletes the object you specify
i	inserts text before the cursor
o	opens and inputs new lines, below the current
u	undoes the last change

4. Moving about; rearranging and duplicating text

4.1. Low level character motions

Now move the cursor to a line where there is a punctuation or a bracketing character such as a parenthesis or a comma or period. Try the command **f**x where x is this character. This command finds the next x character to the right of the cursor in the current line. Try then hitting a **;**, which finds the next instance of the same character. By using the **f** command and then a sequence of **;**'s you can often get to a

---

† The command **S** is a convenient synonym for for **cc**, by analogy with **s**. Think of **S** as a substitute on lines, while **s** is a substitute on characters.

* One subtle point here involves using the **/** search after a **d**. This will normally delete characters from the current position to the point of the match. If what is desired is to delete whole lines including the two points, give the pattern as **/pat/+0**, a line address.

particular place in a line much faster than with a sequence of word motions or SPACEs. There is also a **F** command, which is like **f**, but searches backward. The **;** command repeats **F** also.

When you are operating on the text in a line it is often desirable to deal with the characters up to, but not including, the first instance of a character. Try **df**x for some x now and notice that the x character is deleted. Undo this with **u** and then try **dt**x; the **t** here stands for to, i.e. delete up to the next x, but not the x. The command **T** is the reverse of **t**.

When working with the text of a single line, an ↑ moves the cursor to the first non-white position on the line, and a **$** moves it to the end of the line. Thus **$a** will append new text at the end of the current line.

Your file may have tab (`^I`) characters in it. These characters are represented as a number of spaces expanding to a tab stop, where tab stops are every 8 positions.* When the cursor is at a tab, it sits on the last of the several spaces which represent that tab. Try moving the cursor back and forth over tabs so you understand how this works.

On rare occasions, your file may have nonprinting characters in it. These characters are displayed in the same way they are represented in this document, that is with a two character code, the first character of which is '^'. On the screen non-printing characters resemble a '^' character adjacent to another, but spacing or backspacing over the character will reveal that the two characters are, like the spaces representing a tab character, a single character.

The editor sometimes discards control characters, depending on the character and the setting of the *beautify* option, if you attempt to insert them in your file. You can get a control character in the file by beginning an insert and then typing a `^V` before the control character. The `^V` quotes the following character, causing it to be inserted directly into the file.

4.2. Higher level text objects

In working with a document it is often advantageous to work in terms of sentences, paragraphs, and sections. The operations (and) move to the beginning of the previous and next sentences respectively. Thus the command **d)** will delete the rest of the current sentence; likewise **d(** will delete the previous sentence if you are at the beginning of the current sentence, or the current sentence up to where you are if you are not at the beginning of the current sentence.

A sentence is defined to end at a '.', '!' or '?' which is followed by either the end of a line, or by two spaces. Any number of closing ')', ']', '"' and '' characters may appear after the '.', '!' or '?' before the spaces or end of line.

The operations **{** and **}** move over paragraphs and the operations **[[** and **]]** move over sections.†

A paragraph begins after each empty line, and also at each of a set of paragraph macros, specified by the pairs of characters in the definition of the string valued option *paragraphs*. The default setting for this option defines the paragraph macros of the −*ms* and −*mm* macro packages, i.e. the '.IP', '.LP', '.PP' and '.QP', '.P' and '.LI' macros.‡ Each paragraph boundary is also a sentence boundary. The sentence and paragraph commands can be given counts to operate over groups of sentences and paragraphs.

Sections in the editor begin after each macro in the *sections* option, normally '.NH', '.SH', '.H' and '.HU', and each line with a formfeed `^L` in the first column. Section boundaries are always line and paragraph boundaries also.

Try experimenting with the sentence and paragraph commands until you are sure how they work. If you have a large document, try looking through it using the section commands. The section commands interpret a preceding count as a different window size in which to redraw the screen at the new location,

---

* This is settable by a command of the form **:se ts=**xCR, where x is 4 to set tabstops every four columns. This has effect on the screen representation within the editor.

† The [[and]] operations require the operation character to be doubled because they can move the cursor far from where it currently is. While it is easy to get back with the command ``, these commands would still be frustrating if they were easy to hit accidentally.

‡ You can easily change or extend this set of macros by assigning a different string to the *paragraphs* option in your EXINIT. See section 6.2 for details. The '.bp' directive is also considered to start a paragraph.

and this window size is the base size for newly drawn windows until another size is specified. This is very useful if you are on a slow terminal and are looking for a particular section. You can give the first section command a small count to then see each successive section heading in a small window.

4.3. Rearranging and duplicating text

The editor has a single unnamed buffer where the last deleted or changed away text is saved, and a set of named buffers **a–z** which you can use to save copies of text and to move text around in your file and between files.

The operator **y** yanks a copy of the object which follows into the unnamed buffer. If preceded by a buffer name, **"**x**y**, where x here is replaced by a letter **a–z**, it places the text in the named buffer. The text can then be put back in the file with the commands **p** and **P; p** puts the text after or below the cursor, while **P** puts the text before or above the cursor.

If the text which you yank forms a part of a line, or is an object such as a sentence which partially spans more than one line, then when you put the text back, it will be placed after the cursor (or before if you use **P**). If the yanked text forms whole lines, they will be put back as whole lines, without changing the current line. In this case, the put acts much like a **o** or **O** command.

Try the command **YP**. This makes a copy of the current line and leaves you on this copy, which is placed before the current line. The command **Y** is a convenient abbreviation for **yy**. The command **Yp** will also make a copy of the current line, and place it after the current line. You can give **Y** a count of lines to yank, and thus duplicate several lines; try **3YP**.

To move text within the buffer, you need to delete it in one place, and put it back in another. You can precede a delete operation by the name of a buffer in which the text is to be stored as in **"a5dd** deleting 5 lines into the named buffer a. You can then move the cursor to the eventual resting place of the these lines and do a **"ap** or **"aP** to put them back. In fact, you can switch and edit another file before you put the lines back, by giving a command of the form **:e** *name*CR where *name* is the name of the other file you want to edit. You will have to write back the contents of the current editor buffer (or discard them) if you have made changes before the editor will let you switch to the other file. An ordinary delete command saves the text in the unnamed buffer, so that an ordinary put can move it elsewhere. However, the unnamed buffer is lost when you change files, so to move text from one file to another you should use an unnamed buffer.

4.4. Summary.

↑	first non-white on line
$	end of line
)	forward sentence
}	forward paragraph
]]	forward section
(	backward sentence
{	backward paragraph
[[	backward section
fx	find x forward in line
p	put text back, after cursor or below current line
y	yank operator, for copies and moves
tx	up to x forward, for operators
Fx	f backward in line
P	put text back, before cursor or above current line
Tx	t backward in line

5. High level commands

5.1. Writing, quitting, editing new files

So far we have seen how to enter *vi* and to write out our file using either **ZZ** or **:w**CR. The first exits from the editor, (writing if changes were made), the second writes and stays in the editor.

If you have changed the editor's copy of the file but do not wish to save your changes, either because you messed up the file or decided that the changes are not an improvement to the file, then you can give the command **:q!**CR to quit from the editor without writing the changes. You can also reedit the same file (starting over) by giving the command **:e!**CR. These commands should be used only rarely, and with caution, as it is not possible to recover the changes you have made after you discard them in this manner.

You can edit a different file without leaving the editor by giving the command **:e** *name*CR. If you have not written out your file before you try to do this, then the editor will tell you this, and delay editing the other file. You can then give the command **:w**CR to save your work and then the **:e** *name*CR command again, or carefully give the command **:e!** *name*CR, which edits the other file discarding the changes you have made to the current file. To have the editor automatically save changes, include *set autowrite* in your EXINIT, and use **:n** instead of **:e**.

5.2. Escaping to a shell

You can get to a shell to execute a single command by giving a *vi* command of the form **:!***cmd*CR. The system will run the single command *cmd* and when the command finishes, the editor will ask you to hit a RETURN to continue. When you have finished looking at the output on the screen, you should hit RETURN and the editor will clear the screen and redraw it. You can then continue editing. You can also give another : command when it asks you for a RETURN; in this case the screen will not be redrawn.

If you wish to execute more than one command in the shell, then you can give the command **:sh**CR. This will give you a new shell, and when you finish with the shell, ending it by typing a ^D, the editor will clear the screen and continue.

On systems which support it, ^Z will suspend the editor and return to the (top level) shell. When the editor is resumed, the screen will be redrawn.

5.3. Marking and returning

The command `` returned to the previous place after a motion of the cursor by a command such as **/**, **?** or **G**. You can also mark lines in the file with single letter tags and return to these marks later by naming the tags. Try marking the current line with the command **m***x*, where you should pick some letter for *x*, say 'a'. Then move the cursor to a different line (any way you like) and hit `a. The cursor will return to the place which you marked. Marks last only until you edit another file.

When using operators such as **d** and referring to marked lines, it is often desirable to delete whole lines rather than deleting to the exact position in the line marked by **m**. In this case you can use the form ´*x* rather than `*x*. Used without an operator, ´*x* will move to the first non-white character of the marked line; similarly ´´ moves to the first non-white character of the line containing the previous context mark ``.

5.4. Adjusting the screen

If the screen image is messed up because of a transmission error to your terminal, or because some program other than the editor wrote output to your terminal, you can hit a ^L, the ASCII form-feed character, to cause the screen to be refreshed.

On a dumb terminal, if there are @ lines in the middle of the screen as a result of line deletion, you may get rid of these lines by typing ^R to cause the editor to retype the screen, closing up these holes.

Finally, if you wish to place a certain line on the screen at the top middle or bottom of the screen, you can position the cursor to that line, and then give a **z** command. You should follow the **z** command with a RETURN if you want the line to appear at the top of the window, a **.** if you want it at the center, or a − if you want it at the bottom.

6. Special topics

6.1. Editing on slow terminals

When you are on a slow terminal, it is important to limit the amount of output which is generated to your screen so that you will not suffer long delays, waiting for the screen to be refreshed. We have already pointed out how the editor optimizes the updating of the screen during insertions on dumb terminals to limit the delays, and how the editor erases lines to @ when they are deleted on dumb terminals.

The use of the slow terminal insertion mode is controlled by the *slowopen* option. You can force the editor to use this mode even on faster terminals by giving the command **:se slow**CR. If your system is sluggish this helps lessen the amount of output coming to your terminal. You can disable this option by **:se noslow**CR.

The editor can simulate an intelligent terminal on a dumb one. Try giving the command **:se redraw**CR. This simulation generates a great deal of output and is generally tolerable only on lightly loaded systems and fast terminals. You can disable this by giving the command
:se noredrawCR.

The editor also makes editing more pleasant at low speed by starting editing in a small window, and letting the window expand as you edit. This works particularly well on intelligent terminals. The editor can expand the window easily when you insert in the middle of the screen on these terminals. If possible, try the editor on an intelligent terminal to see how this works.

You can control the size of the window which is redrawn each time the screen is cleared by giving window sizes as argument to the commands which cause large screen motions:

> **:   /   ?   [[   ]]   `   ´**

Thus if you are searching for a particular instance of a common string in a file you can precede the first search command by a small number, say 3, and the editor will draw three line windows around each instance of the string which it locates.

You can easily expand or contract the window, placing the current line as you choose, by giving a number on a **z** command, after the **z** and before the following RETURN, **.** or **−**. Thus the command **z5.** redraws the screen with the current line in the center of a five line window.†

If the editor is redrawing or otherwise updating large portions of the display, you can interrupt this updating by hitting a DEL or RUB as usual. If you do this you may partially confuse the editor about what is displayed on the screen. You can still edit the text on the screen if you wish; clear up the confusion by hitting a ˆL; or move or search again, ignoring the current state of the display.

See section 7.8 on *open* mode for another way to use the *vi* command set on slow terminals.

6.2. Options, set, and editor startup files

The editor has a set of options, some of which have been mentioned above. The most useful options are given in the following table.

The options are of three kinds: numeric options, string options, and toggle options. You can set numeric and string options by a statement of the form

> **set** *opt=val*

and toggle options can be set or unset by statements of one of the forms

> **set** *opt*
> **set no***opt*

These statements can be placed in your EXINIT in your environment, or given while you are running *vi* by preceding them with a **:** and following them with a CR.

---

† Note that the command **5z.** has an entirely different effect, placing line 5 in the center of a new window.

Name	Default	Description
autoindent	noai	Supply indentation automatically
autowrite	noaw	Automatic write before :n, :ta, ^↑, !
ignorecase	noic	Ignore case in searching
lisp	nolisp	({ }) commands deal with S-expressions
list	nolist	Tabs print as ^I; end of lines marked with $
magic	nomagic	The characters . [and * are special in scans
number	nonu	Lines are displayed prefixed with line numbers
paragraphs	para=IPLPPPQPbpP LI	Macro names which start paragraphs
redraw	nore	Simulate a smart terminal on a dumb one
sections	sect=NHSHH HU	Macro names which start new sections
shiftwidth	sw=8	Shift distance for <, > and input ^D and ^T
showmatch	nosm	Show matching (or { as) or } is typed
slowopen	slow	Postpone display updates during inserts
term	dumb	The kind of terminal you are using.

11

You can get a list of all options which you have changed by the command :setCR, or the value of a single option by the command :set *opt*?CR. A list of all possible options and their values is generated by :set allCR. Set can be abbreviated se. Multiple options can be placed on one line, e.g. :se ai aw nuCR.

Options set by the **set** command only last while you stay in the editor. It is common to want to have certain options set whenever you use the editor. This can be accomplished by creating a list of *ex* commands† which are to be run every time you start up *ex*, *edit*, or *vi*. A typical list includes a **set** command, and possibly a few **map** commands. Since it is advisable to get these commands on one line, they can be separated with the I character, for example:

> **set** ai aw terse**Imap** @ dd**Imap** # x

which sets the options *autoindent*, *autowrite*, *terse*, (the **set** command), makes @ delete a line, (the first **map**), and makes # delete a character, (the second **map**). (See section 6.9 for a description of the **map** command) This string should be placed in the variable EXINIT in your environment. If you use the shell *csh*, put this line in the file *.login* in your home directory:

> setenv EXINIT ´**set** ai aw terse**Imap** @ dd**Imap** # x´

If you use the standard shell *sh*, put these lines in the file *.profile* in your home directory:

> EXINIT=´**set** ai aw terse**Imap** @ dd**Imap** # x´
> export EXINIT

Of course, the particulars of the line would depend on which options you wanted to set.

6.3. Recovering lost lines

You might have a serious problem if you delete a number of lines and then regret that they were deleted. Despair not, the editor saves the last 9 deleted blocks of text in a set of numbered registers 1–9. You can get the *n*'th previous deleted text back in your file by the command "*n***p**. The " here says that a buffer name is to follow, *n* is the number of the buffer you wish to try (use the number 1 for now), and **p** is the put command, which puts text in the buffer after the cursor. If this doesn't bring back the text you wanted, hit **u** to undo this and then **.** (period) to repeat the put command. In general the **.** command will repeat the last change you made. As a special case, when the last command refers to a numbered text buffer, the **.** command increments the number of the buffer before repeating the command. Thus a sequence of the form

> "1pu.u.u.

will, if repeated long enough, show you all the deleted text which has been saved for you. You can omit

---

† All commands which start with : are *ex* commands.

the **u** commands here to gather up all this text in the buffer, or stop after any **.** command to keep just the then recovered text. The command **P** can also be used rather than **p** to put the recovered text before rather than after the cursor.

6.4. Recovering lost files

If the system crashes, you can recover the work you were doing to within a few changes. You will normally receive mail when you next login giving you the name of the file which has been saved for you. You should then change to the directory where you were when the system crashed and give a command of the form:

> % **vi –r** *name*

replacing *name* with the name of the file which you were editing. This will recover your work to a point near where you left off.†

You can get a listing of the files which are saved for you by giving the command:

> % **vi –r**

If there is more than one instance of a particular file saved, the editor gives you the newest instance each time you recover it. You can thus get an older saved copy back by first recovering the newer copies.

For this feature to work, *vi* must be correctly installed by a super user on your system, and the *mail* program must exist to receive mail. The invocation ''*vi -r*'' will not always list all saved files, but they can be recovered even if they are not listed.

6.5. Continuous text input

When you are typing in large amounts of text it is convenient to have lines broken near the right margin automatically. You can cause this to happen by giving the command **:se wm=10**CR. This causes all lines to be broken at a space at least 10 columns from the right hand edge of the screen.

If the editor breaks an input line and you wish to put it back together you can tell it to join the lines with **J**. You can give **J** a count of the number of lines to be joined as in **3J** to join 3 lines. The editor supplies white space, if appropriate, at the juncture of the joined lines, and leaves the cursor at this white space. You can kill the white space with **x** if you don't want it.

6.6. Features for editing programs

The editor has a number of commands for editing programs. The thing that most distinguishes editing of programs from editing of text is the desirability of maintaining an indented structure to the body of the program. The editor has a *autoindent* facility for helping you generate correctly indented programs.

To enable this facility you can give the command **:se ai**CR. Now try opening a new line with **o** and type some characters on the line after a few tabs. If you now start another line, notice that the editor supplies white space at the beginning of the line to line it up with the previous line. You cannot backspace over this indentation, but you can use ^**D** key to backtab over the supplied indentation.

Each time you type ^**D** you back up one position, normally to an 8 column boundary. This amount is settable; the editor has an option called *shiftwidth* which you can set to change this value. Try giving the command **:se sw=4**CR and then experimenting with autoindent again.

For shifting lines in the program left and right, there are operators **<** and **>**. These shift the lines you specify right or left by one *shiftwidth*. Try **<<** and **>>** which shift one line left or right, and **<L** and **>L** shifting the rest of the display left and right.

---

† In rare cases, some of the lines of the file may be lost. The editor will give you the numbers of these lines and the text of the lines will be replaced by the string 'LOST'. These lines will almost always be among the last few which you changed. You can either choose to discard the changes which you made (if they are easy to remake) or to replace the few lost lines by hand.

If you have a complicated expression and wish to see how the parentheses match, put the cursor at a left or right parenthesis and hit %. This will show you the matching parenthesis. This works also for braces { and }, and brackets [and].

If you are editing C programs, you can use the [[and]] keys to advance or retreat to a line starting with a {, i.e. a function declaration at a time. When]] is used with an operator it stops after a line which starts with }; this is sometimes useful with y]].

6.7. Filtering portions of the buffer

You can run system commands over portions of the buffer using the operator !. You can use this to sort lines in the buffer, or to reformat portions of the buffer with a pretty-printer. Try typing in a list of random words, one per line and ending them with a blank line. Back up to the beginning of the list, and then give the command !}sortCR. This says to sort the next paragraph of material, and the blank line ends a paragraph.

6.8. Commands for editing LISP

If you are editing a LISP program you should set the option *lisp* by doing :se lispCR. This changes the (and) commands to move backward and forward over s-expressions. The { and } commands are like (and) but don't stop at atoms. These can be used to skip to the next list, or through a comment quickly.

The *autoindent* option works differently for LISP, supplying indent to align at the first argument to the last open list. If there is no such argument then the indent is two spaces more than the last level.

There is another option which is useful for typing in LISP, the *showmatch* option. Try setting it with :se smCR and then try typing a '(' some words and then a ')'. Notice that the cursor shows the position of the '(' which matches the ')' briefly. This happens only if the matching '(' is on the screen, and the cursor stays there for at most one second.

The editor also has an operator to realign existing lines as though they had been typed in with *lisp* and *autoindent* set. This is the = operator. Try the command =% at the beginning of a function. This will realign all the lines of the function declaration.

When you are editing LISP,, the [[and]] advance and retreat to lines beginning with a (, and are useful for dealing with entire function definitions.

6.9. Macros

Vi has a parameterless macro facility, which lets you set it up so that when you hit a single keystroke, the editor will act as though you had hit some longer sequence of keys. You can set this up if you find yourself typing the same sequence of commands repeatedly.

Briefly, there are two flavors of macros:

a)   Ones where you put the macro body in a buffer register, say *x*. You can then type **@x** to invoke the macro. The **@** may be followed by another **@** to repeat the last macro.

b)   You can use the *map* command from *vi* (typically in your *EXINIT*) with a command of the form:

> :map *lhs rhs*CR

mapping *lhs* into *rhs*. There are restrictions: *lhs* should be one keystroke (either 1 character or one function key) since it must be entered within one second (unless *notimeout* is set, in which case you can type it as slowly as you wish, and *vi* will wait for you to finish it before it echoes anything). The *lhs* can be no longer than 10 characters, the *rhs* no longer than 100. To get a space, tab or newline into *lhs* or *rhs* you should escape them with a ^V. (It may be necessary to double the ^V if the map command is given inside *vi,* rather than in *ex.*) Spaces and tabs inside the *rhs* need not be escaped.

Thus to make the **q** key write and exit the editor, you can give the command

> :map q :wq^V^VCR CR

which means that whenever you type **q**, it will be as though you had typed the four characters **:wq**CR. A ^V's is needed because without it the CR would end the : command, rather than becoming part of the *map* definition. There are two ^V's because from within *vi*, two ^V's must be typed to get one. The first CR is part of the *rhs*, the second terminates the : command.

Macros can be deleted with

 unmap lhs

If the *lhs* of a macro is "#0" through "#9", this maps the particular function key instead of the 2 character "#" sequence. So that terminals without function keys can access such definitions, the form "#x" will mean function key *x* on all terminals (and need not be typed within one second.) The character "#" can be changed by using a macro in the usual way:

 :map ^V^V^I #

to use tab, for example. (This won't affect the *map* command, which still uses **#**, but just the invocation from visual mode.

The undo command reverses an entire macro call as a unit, if it made any changes.

Placing a '!' after the word **map** causes the mapping to apply to input mode, rather than command mode. Thus, to arrange for ^T to be the same as 4 spaces in input mode, you can type:

 :map ^T ^Vƀƀƀƀ

where ƀ is a blank. The ^V is necessary to prevent the blanks from being taken as white space between the *lhs* and *rhs*.

7. Word Abbreviations

A feature similar to macros in input mode is word abbreviation. This allows you to type a short word and have it expanded into a longer word or words. The commands are **:abbreviate** and **:unabbreviate** (**:ab** and **:una**) and have the same syntax as **:map**. For example:

 :ab eecs Electrical Engineering and Computer Sciences

causes the word 'eecs' to always be changed into the phrase 'Electrical Engineering and Computer Sciences'. Word abbreviation is different from macros in that only whole words are affected. If 'eecs' were typed as part of a larger word, it would be left alone. Also, the partial word is echoed as it is typed. There is no need for an abbreviation to be a single keystroke, as it should be with a macro.

7.1. Abbreviations

The editor has a number of short commands which abbreviate longer commands which we have introduced here. You can find these commands easily on the quick reference card. They often save a bit of typing and you can learn them as convenient.

8. Nitty-gritty details

8.1. Line representation in the display

The editor folds long logical lines onto many physical lines in the display. Commands which advance lines advance logical lines and will skip over all the segments of a line in one motion. The command | moves the cursor to a specific column, and may be useful for getting near the middle of a long line to split it in half. Try **80|** on a line which is more than 80 columns long.†

The editor only puts full lines on the display; if there is not enough room on the display to fit a logical line, the editor leaves the physical line empty, placing only an @ on the line as a place holder. When you delete lines on a dumb terminal, the editor will often just clear the lines to @ to save time (rather than rewriting the rest of the screen.) You can always maximize the information on the screen by giving the ^R command.

---

† You can make long lines very easily by using **J** to join together short lines.

If you wish, you can have the editor place line numbers before each line on the display. Give the command **:se nu**CR to enable this, and the command **:se nonu**CR to turn it off. You can have tabs represented as **^I** and the ends of lines indicated with '$' by giving the command **:se list**CR; **:se nolist**CR turns this off.

Finally, lines consisting of only the character '~' are displayed when the last line in the file is in the middle of the screen. These represent physical lines which are past the logical end of file.

8.2. Counts

Most *vi* commands will use a preceding count to affect their behavior in some way. The following table gives the common ways in which the counts are used:

new window size	**: / ? [[ ]] ` ´**
scroll amount	**^D ^U**
line/column number	**z G |**
repeat effect	most of the rest

The editor maintains a notion of the current default window size. On terminals which run at speeds greater than 1200 baud the editor uses the full terminal screen. On terminals which are slower than 1200 baud (most dialup lines are in this group) the editor uses 8 lines as the default window size. At 1200 baud the default is 16 lines.

This size is the size used when the editor clears and refills the screen after a search or other motion moves far from the edge of the current window. The commands which take a new window size as count all often cause the screen to be redrawn. If you anticipate this, but do not need as large a window as you are currently using, you may wish to change the screen size by specifying the new size before these commands. In any case, the number of lines used on the screen will expand if you move off the top with a − or similar command or off the bottom with a command such as RETURN or **^D**. The window will revert to the last specified size the next time it is cleared and refilled.†

The scroll commands **^D** and **^U** likewise remember the amount of scroll last specified, using half the basic window size initially. The simple insert commands use a count to specify a repetition of the inserted text. Thus **10a+——**ESC will insert a grid-like string of text. A few commands also use a preceding count as a line or column number.

Except for a few commands which ignore any counts (such as **^R**), the rest of the editor commands use a count to indicate a simple repetition of their effect. Thus **5w** advances five words on the current line, while **5**RETURN advances five lines. A very useful instance of a count as a repetition is a count given to the **.** command, which repeats the last changing command. If you do **dw** and then **3.**, you will delete first one and then three words. You can then delete two more words with **2.**.

8.3. More file manipulation commands

The following table lists the file manipulation commands which you can use when you are in *vi*. All of these commands are followed by a CR or ESC. The most basic commands are **:w** and **:e**. A normal editing session on a single file will end with a **ZZ** command. If you are editing for a long period of time you can give **:w** commands occasionally after major amounts of editing, and then finish with a **ZZ**. When you edit more than one file, you can finish with one with a **:w** and start editing a new file by giving a **:e** command, or set *autowrite* and use **:n** <file>.

If you make changes to the editor's copy of a file, but do not wish to write them back, then you must give an **!** after the command you would otherwise use; this forces the editor to discard any changes you have made. Use this carefully.

---

† But not by a ^L which just redraws the screen as it is.

11

:w	write back changes
:wq	write and quit
:x	write (if necessary) and quit (same as ZZ).
:e *name*	edit file *name*
:e!	reedit, discarding changes
:e + *name*	edit, starting at end
:e +*n*	edit, starting at line *n*
:e #	edit alternate file
:w *name*	write file *name*
:w! *name*	overwrite file *name*
:*x,y*w *name*	write lines *x* through *y* to *name*
:r *name*	read file *name* into buffer
:r !*cmd*	read output of *cmd* into buffer
:n	edit next file in argument list
:n!	edit next file, discarding changes to current
:n *args*	specify new argument list
:ta *tag*	edit file containing tag *tag*, at *tag*

The :e command can be given a + argument to start at the end of the file, or a +*n* argument to start at line *n*. In actuality, *n* may be any editor command not containing a space, usefully a scan like +/*pat* or +?*pat*. In forming new names to the e command, you can use the character % which is replaced by the current file name, or the character # which is replaced by the alternate file name. The alternate file name is generally the last name you typed other than the current file. Thus if you try to do a :e and get a diagnostic that you haven't written the file, you can give a :w command and then a :e # command to redo the previous :e.

You can write part of the buffer to a file by finding out the lines that bound the range to be written using ^G, and giving these numbers after the : and before the w, separated by ,'s. You can also mark these lines with **m** and then use an address of the form ´x,´y on the w command here.

You can read another file into the buffer after the current line by using the :r command. You can similarly read in the output from a command, just use !*cmd* instead of a file name.

If you wish to edit a set of files in succession, you can give all the names on the command line, and then edit each one in turn using the command :n. It is also possible to respecify the list of files to be edited by giving the :n command a list of file names, or a pattern to be expanded as you would have given it on the initial *vi* command.

If you are editing large programs, you will find the :ta command very useful. It utilizes a data base of function names and their locations, which can be created by programs such as *ctags,* to quickly find a function whose name you give. If the :ta command will require the editor to switch files, then you must :w or abandon any changes before switching. You can repeat the :ta command without any arguments to look for the same tag again.

8.4. More about searching for strings

When you are searching for strings in the file with **/** and **?**, the editor normally places you at the next or previous occurrence of the string. If you are using an operator such as **d**, **c** or **y**, then you may well wish to affect lines up to the line before the line containing the pattern. You can give a search of the form /*pat*/−*n* to refer to the *n*'th line before the next line containing *pat*, or you can use + instead of − to refer to the lines after the one containing *pat*. If you don't give a line offset, then the editor will affect characters up to the match place, rather than whole lines; thus use ''+0'' to affect to the line which matches.

You can have the editor ignore the case of words in the searches it does by giving the command :se icCR. The command :se noicCR turns this off.

Strings given to searches may actually be regular expressions. If you do not want or need this facility, you should

set nomagic

in your EXINIT. In this case, only the characters ↑ and $ are special in patterns. The character \ is also then special (as it is most everywhere in the system), and may be used to get at the an extended pattern matching facility. It is also necessary to use a \ before a / in a forward scan or a ? in a backward scan, in any case. The following table gives the extended forms when **magic** is set.

↑	at beginning of pattern, matches beginning of line
$	at end of pattern, matches end of line
.	matches any character
\<	matches the beginning of a word
\>	matches the end of a word
[*str*]	matches any single character in *str*
[↑*str*]	matches any single character not in *str*
[*x*–*y*]	matches any character between *x* and *y*
*	matches any number of the preceding pattern

11

If you use **nomagic** mode, then the . [and * primitives are given with a preceding \.

8.5. More about input mode

There are a number of characters which you can use to make corrections during input mode. These are summarized in the following table.

^H	deletes the last input character
^W	deletes the last input word, defined as by **b**
erase	your erase character, same as ^H
kill	your kill character, deletes the input on this line
\	escapes a following ^H and your erase and kill
ESC	ends an insertion
DEL	interrupts an insertion, terminating it abnormally
CR	starts a new line
^D	backtabs over *autoindent*
0^D	kills all the *autoindent*
↑^D	same as 0^D, but restores indent next line
^V	quotes the next non-printing character into the file

The most usual way of making corrections to input is by typing ^H to correct a single character, or by typing one or more ^W's to back over incorrect words. If you use # as your erase character in the normal system, it will work like ^H.

Your system kill character, normally @, ^X or ^U, will erase all the input you have given on the current line. In general, you can neither erase input back around a line boundary nor can you erase characters which you did not insert with this insertion command. To make corrections on the previous line after a new line has been started you can hit ESC to end the insertion, move over and make the correction, and then return to where you were to continue. The command **A** which appends at the end of the current line is often useful for continuing.

If you wish to type in your erase or kill character (say # or @) then you must precede it with a \, just as you would do at the normal system command level. A more general way of typing non-printing characters into the file is to precede them with a ^V. The ^V echoes as a ↑ character on which the cursor rests. This indicates that the editor expects you to type a control character. In fact you may type any character and it will be inserted into the file at that point.*

---

* This is not quite true. The implementation of the editor does not allow the NULL (^@) character to appear in files. Also the LF (linefeed or ^J) character is used by the editor to separate lines in the file, so it cannot appear in the middle of a line.

11

If you are using *autoindent* you can backtab over the indent which it supplies by typing a ˆ**D**. This backs up to a *shiftwidth* boundary. This only works immediately after the supplied *autoindent*.

When you are using *autoindent* you may wish to place a label at the left margin of a line. The way to do this easily is to type ↑ and then ˆ**D**. The editor will move the cursor to the left margin for one line, and restore the previous indent on the next. You can also type a **0** followed immediately by a ˆ**D** if you wish to kill all the indent and not have it come back on the next line.

8.6. Upper case only terminals

If your terminal has only upper case, you can still use *vi* by using the normal system convention for typing on such a terminal. Characters which you normally type are converted to lower case, and you can type upper case letters by preceding them with a \. The characters { ˜ } | ` are not available on such terminals, but you can escape them as \(\↑ \) \! \´. These characters are represented on the display in the same way they are typed.‡

8.7. Vi and ex

Vi is actually one mode of editing within the editor *ex*. When you are running *vi* you can escape to the line oriented editor of *ex* by giving the command **Q**. All of the : commands which were introduced above are available in *ex*. Likewise, most *ex* commands can be invoked from *vi* using :. Just give them without the : and follow them with a CR.

In rare instances, an internal error may occur in *vi*. In this case you will get a diagnostic and be left in the command mode of *ex*. You can then save your work and quit if you wish by giving a command **x** after the : which *ex* prompts you with, or you can reenter *vi* by giving *ex* a *vi* command.

There are a number of things which you can do more easily in *ex* than in *vi*. Systematic changes in line oriented material are particularly easy. You can read the advanced editing documents for the editor *ed* to find out a lot more about this style of editing. Experienced users often mix their use of *ex* command mode and *vi* command mode to speed the work they are doing.

8.8. Open mode: vi on hardcopy terminals and "glass tty's" ‡

If you are on a hardcopy terminal or a terminal which does not have a cursor which can move off the bottom line, you can still use the command set of *vi,* but in a different mode. When you give a *vi* command, the editor will tell you that it is using *open* mode. This name comes from the *open* command in *ex,* which is used to get into the same mode.

The only difference between *visual* mode and *open* mode is the way in which the text is displayed.

In *open* mode the editor uses a single line window into the file, and moving backward and forward in the file causes new lines to be displayed, always below the current line. Two commands of *vi* work differently in *open:* **z** and ˆ**R**. The **z** command does not take parameters, but rather draws a window of context around the current line and then returns you to the current line.

If you are on a hardcopy terminal, the ˆ**R** command will retype the current line. On such terminals, the editor normally uses two lines to represent the current line. The first line is a copy of the line as you started to edit it, and you work on the line below this line. When you delete characters, the editor types a number of \'s to show you the characters which are deleted. The editor also reprints the current line soon after such changes so that you can see what the line looks like again.

It is sometimes useful to use this mode on very slow terminals which can support *vi* in the full screen mode. You can do this by entering *ex* and using an *open* command.

You can insert any other character, however, if you wait for the editor to echo the ↑ before you type the character. In fact, the editor will treat a following letter as a request for the corresponding control character. This is the only way to type ˆS or ˆQ, since the system normally uses them to suspend and resume output and never gives them to the editor to process.

‡ The \ character you give will not echo until you type another key.

Acknowledgements

Bruce Englar encouraged the early development of this display editor. Peter Kessler helped bring sanity to version 2's command layout. Bill Joy wrote versions 1 and 2.0 through 2.7, and created the framework that users see in the present editor. Mark Horton added macros and other features and made the editor work on a large number of terminals and Unix systems.

Appendix: character functions

This appendix gives the uses the editor makes of each character. The characters are presented in their order in the ASCII character set: Control characters come first, then most special characters, then the digits, upper and then lower case characters.

For each character we tell a meaning it has as a command and any meaning it has during an insert. If it has only meaning as a command, then only this is discussed. Section numbers in parentheses indicate where the character is discussed; a 'f' after the section number means that the character is mentioned in a footnote.

^@	Not a command character. If typed as the first character of an insertion it is replaced with the last text inserted, and the insert terminates. Only 128 characters are saved from the last insert; if more characters were inserted the mechanism is not available. A **^@** cannot be part of the file due to the editor implementation (7.5f).
^A	Unused.
^B	Backward window. A count specifies repetition. Two lines of continuity are kept if possible (2.1, 6.1, 7.2).
^C	Unused.
^D	As a command, scrolls down a half-window of text. A count gives the number of (logical) lines to scroll, and is remembered for future **^D** and **^U** commands (2.1, 7.2). During an insert, backtabs over *autoindent* white space at the beginning of a line (6.6, 7.5); this white space cannot be backspaced over.
^E	Exposes one more line below the current screen in the file, leaving the cursor where it is if possible. (Version 3 only.)
^F	Forward window. A count specifies repetition. Two lines of continuity are kept if possible (2.1, 6.1, 7.2).
^G	Equivalent to **:f**CR, printing the current file, whether it has been modified, the current line number and the number of lines in the file, and the percentage of the way through the file that you are.
^H (BS)	Same as **left arrow**. (See **h**). During an insert, eliminates the last input character, backing over it but not erasing it; it remains so you can see what you typed if you wish to type something only slightly different (3.1, 7.5).
^I (TAB)	Not a command character. When inserted it prints as some number of spaces. When the cursor is at a tab character it rests at the last of the spaces which represent the tab. The spacing of tabstops is controlled by the *tabstop* option (4.1, 6.6).
^J (LF)	Same as **down arrow** (see **j**).
^K	Unused.
^L	The ASCII formfeed character, this causes the screen to be cleared and redrawn. This is useful after a transmission error, if characters typed by a program other than the editor scramble the screen, or after output is stopped by an interrupt (5.4, 7.2f).

11

^M (CR)	A carriage return advances to the next line, at the first non-white position in the line. Given a count, it advances that many lines (2.3). During an insert, a CR causes the insert to continue onto another line (3.1).
^N	Same as **down arrow** (see **j**).
^O	Unused.
^P	Same as **up arrow** (see **k**).
^Q	Not a command character. In input mode, **^Q** quotes the next character, the same as **^V**, except that some teletype drivers will eat the **^Q** so that the editor never sees it.
^R	Redraws the current screen, eliminating logical lines not corresponding to physical lines (lines with only a single @ character on them). On hardcopy terminals in *open* mode, retypes the current line (5.4, 7.2, 7.8).
^S	Unused. Some teletype drivers use **^S** to suspend output until **^Q** is
^T	Not a command character. During an insert, with *autoindent* set and at the beginning of the line, inserts *shiftwidth* white space.
^U	Scrolls the screen up, inverting **^D** which scrolls down. Counts work as they do for **^D**, and the previous scroll amount is common to both. On a dumb terminal, **^U** will often necessitate clearing and redrawing the screen further back in the file (2.1, 7.2).
^V	Not a command character. In input mode, quotes the next character so that it is possible to insert non-printing and special characters into the file (4.2, 7.5).
^W	Not a command character. During an insert, backs up as **b** would in command mode; the deleted characters remain on the display (see **^H**) (7.5).
^X	Unused.
^Y	Exposes one more line above the current screen, leaving the cursor where it is if possible. (No mnemonic value for this key; however, it is next to **^U** which scrolls up a bunch.) (Version 3 only.)
^Z	If supported by the Unix system, stops the editor, exiting to the top level shell. Same as **:stop**CR. Otherwise, unused.
^[(ESC)	Cancels a partially formed command, such as a **z** when no following character has yet been given; terminates inputs on the last line (read by commands such as **:** and **/** and **?**); ends insertions of new text into the buffer. If an ESC is given when quiescent in command state, the editor rings the bell or flashes the screen. You can thus hit ESC if you don't know what is happening till the editor rings the bell. If you don't know if you are in insert mode you can type ESC**a**, and then material to be input; the material will be inserted correctly whether or not you were in insert mode when you started (1.5, 3.1, 7.5).
^	Unused.
^]	Searches for the word which is after the cursor as a tag. Equivalent to typing **:ta**, this word, and then a CR. Mnemonically, this command is ''go right to'' (7.3).
^↑	Equivalent to **:e #**CR, returning to the previous position in the last edited file, or editing a file which you specified if you got a 'No write since last change diagnostic' and do not want to have to type the file name again (7.3). (You have to do a **:w** before **^↑** will work in this case. If you do not wish to write the file you should do **:e!** #CR instead.)
^_	Unused. Reserved as the command character for the Tektronix 4025 and 4027 terminal.
SPACE	Same as **right arrow** (see **l**).
!	An operator, which processes lines from the buffer with reformatting commands. Follow **!** with the object to be processed, and then the command name terminated by CR. Doubling **!** and preceding it by a count causes count lines to be filtered; otherwise the count is passed on to the object after the **!**. Thus 2!}*fmt*CR reformats the next two paragraphs by running them through the program *fmt*. If you are working on LISP, the

command **!%** *grind*CR,* given at the beginning of a function, will run the text of the function through the LISP grinder (6.7, 7.3). To read a file or the output of a command into the buffer use **:r** (7.3). To simply execute a command use **:!** (7.3).

"   Precedes a named buffer specification. There are named buffers **1–9** used for saving deleted text and named buffers **a–z** into which you can place text (4.3, 6.3)

The macro character which, when followed by a number, will substitute for a function key on terminals without function keys (6.9). In input mode, if this is your erase character, it will delete the last character you typed in input mode, and must be preceded with a \ to insert it, since it normally backs over the last input character you gave.

$**   Moves to the end of the current line. If you **:se list**CR, then the end of each line will be shown by printing a **$ after the end of the displayed text in the line. Given a count, advances to the count'th following end of line; thus **2$** advances to the end of the following line.

%   Moves to the parenthesis or brace **{ }** which balances the parenthesis or brace at the current cursor position.

&   A synonym for **:&**CR, by analogy with the *ex* **&** command.

´   When followed by a **´** returns to the previous context at the beginning of a line. The previous context is set whenever the current line is moved in a non-relative way. When followed by a letter **a–z**, returns to the line which was marked with this letter with a **m** command, at the first non-white character in the line. (2.2, 5.3). When used with an operator such as **d**, the operation takes place over complete lines; if you use **`**, the operation takes place from the exact marked place to the current cursor position within the line.

(Retreats to the beginning of a sentence, or to the beginning of a LISP s-expression if the *lisp* option is set. A sentence ends at a **.** ! or ? which is followed by either the end of a line or by two spaces. Any number of closing **)**] " and **´** characters may appear after the **.** ! or ?, and before the spaces or end of line. Sentences also begin at paragraph and section boundaries (see **{** and **[[** below). A count advances that many sentences (4.2, 6.8).

)   Advances to the beginning of a sentence. A count repeats the effect. See **(** above for the definition of a sentence (4.2, 6.8).

*   Unused.

+   Same as CR when used as a command.

,   Reverse of the last **f F t** or **T** command, looking the other way in the current line. Especially useful after hitting too many **;** characters. A count repeats the search.

−   Retreats to the previous line at the first non-white character. This is the inverse of + and RETURN. If the line moved to is not on the screen, the screen is scrolled, or cleared and redrawn if this is not possible. If a large amount of scrolling would be required the screen is also cleared and redrawn, with the current line at the center (2.3).

.   Repeats the last command which changed the buffer. Especially useful when deleting words or lines; you can delete some words/lines and then hit **.** to delete more and more words/lines. Given a count, it passes it on to the command being repeated. Thus after a **2dw, 3.** deletes three words (3.3, 6.3, 7.2, 7.4).

/   Reads a string from the last line on the screen, and scans forward for the next occurrence of this string. The normal input editing sequences may be used during the input on the bottom line; an returns to command state without ever searching. The search begins when you hit CR to terminate the pattern; the cursor moves to the beginning of the last line to indicate that the search is in progress; the search may then be terminated with a DEL or RUB, or by backspacing when at the beginning of the bottom line, returning the

---

*Both *fmt* and *grind* are Berkeley programs and may not be present at all installations.

11

cursor to its initial position. Searches normally wrap end-around to find a string any-where in the buffer.

When used with an operator the enclosed region is normally affected. By mentioning an offset from the line matched by the pattern you can force whole lines to be affected. To do this give a pattern with a closing a closing **/** and then an offset **+n** or **−n**.

To include the character **/** in the search string, you must escape it with a preceding ****. A ↑ at the beginning of the pattern forces the match to occur at the beginning of a line only; this speeds the search. A **$** at the end of the pattern forces the match to occur at the end of a line only. More extended pattern matching is available, see section 7.4; unless you set **nomagic** in your *.exrc* file you will have to preceed the characters **. [*** and ~ in the search pattern with a **** to get them to work as you would naively expect (1.5, 2,2, 6.1, 7.2, 7.4).

0	Moves to the first character on the current line. Also used, in forming numbers, after an initial **1–9**.
1–9	Used to form numeric arguments to commands (2.3, 7.2).
:	A prefix to a set of commands for file and option manipulation and escapes to the sys-tem. Input is given on the bottom line and terminated with an CR, and the command then executed. You can return to where you were by hitting DEL or RUB if you hit **:** acciden-tally (see primarily 6.2 and 7.3).
;	Repeats the last single character find which used **f F t** or **T**. A count iterates the basic scan (4.1).
<	An operator which shifts lines left one *shiftwidth*, normally 8 spaces. Like all operators, affects lines when repeated, as in **<<**. Counts are passed through to the basic object, thus **3<<** shifts three lines (6.6, 7.2).
=	Reindents line for LISP, as though they were typed in with *lisp* and *autoindent* set (6.8).
>	An operator which shifts lines right one *shiftwidth*, normally 8 spaces. Affects lines when repeated as in **>>**. Counts repeat the basic object (6.6, 7.2).
?	Scans backwards, the opposite of **/**. See the **/** description above for details on scanning (2.2, 6.1, 7.4).
@	A macro character (6.9). If this is your kill character, you must escape it with a **** to type it in during input mode, as it normally backs over the input you have given on the current line (3.1, 3.4, 7.5).
A	Appends at the end of line, a synonym for **$a** (7.2).
B	Backs up a word, where words are composed of non-blank sequences, placing the cursor at the beginning of the word. A count repeats the effect (2.4).
C	Changes the rest of the text on the current line; a synonym for **c$**.
D	Deletes the rest of the text on the current line; a synonym for **d$**.
E	Moves forward to the end of a word, defined as blanks and non-blanks, like **B** and **W**. A count repeats the effect.
F	Finds a single following character, backwards in the current line. A count repeats this search that many times (4.1).
G	Goes to the line number given as preceding argument, or the end of the file if no preced-ing count is given. The screen is redrawn with the new current line in the center if necessary (7.2).
H	**Home arrow**. Homes the cursor to the top line on the screen. If a count is given, then the cursor is moved to the count'th line on the screen. In any case the cursor is moved to the first non-white character on the line. If used as the target of an operator, full lines are affected (2.3, 3.2).

I   Inserts at the beginning of a line; a synonym for ↑**i**.

J   Joins together lines, supplying appropriate white space: one space between words, two spaces after a **.**, and no spaces at all if the first character of the joined on line is **)**. A count causes that many lines to be joined rather than the default two (6.5, 7.1f).

K   Unused.

L   Moves the cursor to the first non-white character of the last line on the screen. With a count, to the first non-white of the count'th line from the bottom. Operators affect whole lines when used with **L** (2.3).

M   Moves the cursor to the middle line on the screen, at the first non-white position on the line (2.3).

N   Scans for the next match of the last pattern given to **/** or **?**, but in the reverse direction; this is the reverse of **n**.

O   Opens a new line above the current line and inputs text there up to an ESC. A count can be used on dumb terminals to specify a number of lines to be opened; this is generally obsolete, as the *slowopen* option works better (3.1).

P   Puts the last deleted text back before/above the cursor. The text goes back as whole lines above the cursor if it was deleted as whole lines. Otherwise the text is inserted between the characters before and at the cursor. May be preceded by a named buffer specification "*x* to retrieve the contents of the buffer; buffers **1–9** contain deleted material, buffers **a–z** are available for general use (6.3).

Q   Quits from *vi* to *ex* command mode. In this mode, whole lines form commands, ending with a RETURN. You can give all the **:** commands; the editor supplies the **:** as a prompt (7.7).

R   Replaces characters on the screen with characters you type (overlay fashion). Terminates with an ESC.

S   Changes whole lines, a synonym for **cc**. A count substitutes for that many lines. The lines are saved in the numeric buffers, and erased on the screen before the substitution begins.

T   Takes a single following character, locates the character before the cursor in the current line, and places the cursor just after that character. A count repeats the effect. Most useful with operators such as **d** (4.1).

U   Restores the current line to its state before you started changing it (3.5).

V   Unused.

W   Moves forward to the beginning of a word in the current line, where words are defined as sequences of blank/non-blank characters. A count repeats the effect (2.4).

X   Deletes the character before the cursor. A count repeats the effect, but only characters on the current line are deleted.

Y   Yanks a copy of the current line into the unnamed buffer, to be put back by a later **p** or **P**; a very useful synonym for **yy**. A count yanks that many lines. May be preceded by a buffer name to put lines in that buffer (7.4).

ZZ   Exits the editor. (Same as **:x**CR.) If any changes have been made, the buffer is written out to the current file. Then the editor quits.

[[Backs up to the previous section boundary. A section begins at each macro in the *sections* option, normally a '.NH' or '.SH' and also at lines which which start with a formfeed ^L. Lines beginning with **{** also stop **[[**; this makes it useful for looking backwards, a function at a time, in C programs. If the option *lisp* is set, stops at each **(** at the beginning of a line, and is thus useful for moving backwards at the top level LISP objects. (4.2, 6.1, 6.6, 7.2).

11

11

\	Unused.
]]	Forward to a section boundary, see [[for a definition (4.2, 6.1, 6.6, 7.2).
↑	Moves to the first non-white position on the current line (4.4).
_	Unused.
`	When followed by a ` returns to the previous context. The previous context is set whenever the current line is moved in a non-relative way. When followed by a letter **a–z**, returns to the position which was marked with this letter with a **m** command. When used with an operator such as **d**, the operation takes place from the exact marked place to the current position within the line; if you use ´, the operation takes place over complete lines (2.2, 5.3).
a	Appends arbitrary text after the current cursor position; the insert can continue onto multiple lines by using RETURN within the insert. A count causes the inserted text to be replicated, but only if the inserted text is all on one line. The insertion terminates with an ESC (3.1, 7.2).
b	Backs up to the beginning of a word in the current line. A word is a sequence of alphanumerics, or a sequence of special characters. A count repeats the effect (2.4).
c	An operator which changes the following object, replacing it with the following input text up to an ESC. If more than part of a single line is affected, the text which is changed away is saved in the numeric named buffers. If only part of the current line is affected, then the last character to be changed away is marked with a **$**. A count causes that many objects to be affected, thus both **3c)** and **c3)** change the following three sentences (7.4).
d	An operator which deletes the following object. If more than part of a line is affected, the text is saved in the numeric buffers. A count causes that many objects to be affected; thus **3dw** is the same as **d3w** (3.3, 3.4, 4.1, 7.4).
e	Advances to the end of the next word, defined as for **b** and **w**. A count repeats the effect (2.4, 3.1).
f	Finds the first instance of the next character following the cursor on the current line. A count repeats the find (4.1).
g	Unused.
	Arrow keys **h, j, k, l,** and **H**.
h	**Left arrow.** Moves the cursor one character to the left. Like the other arrow keys, either **h**, the **left arrow** key, or one of the synonyms (^H) has the same effect. On v2 editors, arrow keys on certain kinds of terminals (those which send escape sequences, such as vt52, c100, or hp) cannot be used. A count repeats the effect (3.1, 7.5).
i	Inserts text before the cursor, otherwise like **a** (7.2).
j	**Down arrow.** Moves the cursor one line down in the same column. If the position does not exist, *vi* comes as close as possible to the same column. Synonyms include ^J (linefeed) and ^N.
k	**Up arrow.** Moves the cursor one line up. ^P is a synonym.
l	**Right arrow.** Moves the cursor one character to the right. SPACE is a synonym.
m	Marks the current position of the cursor in the mark register which is specified by the next character **a–z**. Return to this position or use with an operator using ` or ´ (5.3).
n	Repeats the last **/** or **?** scanning commands (2.2).
o	Opens new lines below the current line; otherwise like **O** (3.1).
p	Puts text after/below the cursor; otherwise like **P** (6.3).
q	Unused.

r   Replaces the single character at the cursor with a single character you type. The new character may be a RETURN; this is the easiest way to split lines. A count replaces each of the following count characters with the single character given; see **R** above which is the more usually useful iteration of **r** (3.2).

s   Changes the single character under the cursor to the text which follows up to an ESC; given a count, that many characters from the current line are changed. The last character to be changed is marked with **$** as in **c** (3.2).

t   Advances the cursor upto the character before the next character typed. Most useful with operators such as **d** and **c** to delete the characters up to a following character. You can use **.** to delete more if this doesn't delete enough the first time (4.1).

u   Undoes the last change made to the current buffer. If repeated, will alternate between these two states, thus is its own inverse. When used after an insert which inserted text on more than one line, the lines are saved in the numeric named buffers (3.5).

v   Unused.

w   Advances to the beginning of the next word, as defined by **b** (2.4).

x   Deletes the single character under the cursor. With a count deletes deletes that many characters forward from the cursor position, but only on the current line (6.5).

y   An operator, yanks the following object into the unnamed temporary buffer. If preceded by a named buffer specification, **"***x*, the text is placed in that buffer also. Text can be recovered by a later **p** or **P** (7.4).

z   Redraws the screen with the current line placed as specified by the following character: RETURN specifies the top of the screen, **.** the center of the screen, and − at the bottom of the screen. A count may be given after the **z** and before the following character to specify the new screen size for the redraw. A count before the **z** gives the number of the line to place in the center of the screen instead of the default current line. (5.4)

{   Retreats to the beginning of the beginning of the preceding paragraph. A paragraph begins at each macro in the *paragraphs* option, normally '.IP', '.LP', '.PP', '.QP' and '.bp'. A paragraph also begins after a completely empty line, and at each section boundary (see **[[** above) (4.2, 6.8, 7.6).

| Places the cursor on the character in the column specified by the count (7.1, 7.2).

}   Advances to the beginning of the next paragraph. See **{** for the definition of paragraph (4.2, 6.8, 7.6).

~   Unused.

^? (DEL)   Interrupts the editor, returning it to command accepting state (1.5, 7.5)

11

Ex Reference Manual
Version 3.7

William Joy

Mark Horton

Computer Science Division
Department of Electrical Engineering and Computer Science
University of California, Berkeley
Berkeley, Ca. 94720

ABSTRACT

   Ex a line oriented text editor, which supports both command and display oriented editing. This reference manual describes the command oriented part of *ex;* the display editing features of *ex* are described in *An Introduction to Display Editing with Vi.* Other documents about the editor include the introduction *Edit: A tutorial*, the *Ex/edit Command Summary*, and a *Vi Quick Reference* card.

1. Starting ex

   Each instance of the editor has a set of options, which can be set to tailor it to your liking. The command *edit* invokes a version of *ex* designed for more casual or beginning users by changing the default settings of some of these options. To simplify the description which follows we assume the default settings of the options.

   When invoked, *ex* determines the terminal type from the TERM variable in the environment. It there is a TERMCAP variable in the environment, and the type of the terminal described there matches the TERM variable, then that description is used. Also if the TERMCAP variable contains a pathname (beginning with a */*) then the editor will seek the description of the terminal in that file (rather than the default /etc/termcap). If there is a variable EXINIT in the environment, then the editor will execute the commands in that variable, otherwise if there is a file *.exrc* in your HOME directory *ex* reads commands from that file, simulating a *source* command. Option setting commands placed in EXINIT or *.exrc* will be executed before each editor session.

   A command to enter *ex* has the following prototype:†

   ex [−] [−**v**] [−**t** *tag*] [−**r**] [−**l**] [−**w***n*] [−**x**] [−**R**] [+*command*] name ...

The most common case edits a single file with no options, i.e.:

   ex name

The − command line option option suppresses all interactive-user feedback and is useful in processing editor scripts in command files. The −**v** option is equivalent to using *vi* rather than *ex.* The −**t** option is equivalent to an initial *tag* command, editing the file containing the *tag* and positioning the editor at its definition. The −**r** option is used in recovering after an editor or system crash, retrieving the last saved version of the named file or, if no file is specified, typing a list of saved files. The −**l** option sets up for editing LISP, setting the *showmatch* and *lisp* options. The −**w** option sets the default window size to *n,* and is

---

The financial support of an IBM Graduate Fellowship and the National Science Foundation under grants MCS74-07644-A03 and MCS78-07291 is gratefully acknowledged.
† Brackets '[' ']' surround optional parameters here.

useful on dialups to start in small windows. The −x option causes *ex* to prompt for a *key*, which is used to encrypt and decrypt the contents of the file, which should already be encrypted using the same key, see *crypt* (1). The −**R** option sets the *readonly* option at the start. *Name* arguments indicate files to be edited. An argument of the form +*command* indicates that the editor should begin by executing the specified command. If *command* is omitted, then it defaults to ''$'', positioning the editor at the last line of the first file initially. Other useful commands here are scanning patterns of the form ''/pat'' or line numbers, e.g. ''+100'' starting at line 100.

2. File manipulation

2.1. Current file

Ex is normally editing the contents of a single file, whose name is recorded in the *current* file name. *Ex* performs all editing actions in a buffer (actually a temporary file) into which the text of the file is initially read. Changes made to the buffer have no effect on the file being edited unless and until the buffer contents are written out to the file with a *write* command. After the buffer contents are written, the previous contents of the written file are no longer accessible. When a file is edited, its name becomes the current file name, and its contents are read into the buffer.

The current file is almost always considered to be *edited.* This means that the contents of the buffer are logically connected with the current file name, so that writing the current buffer contents onto that file, even if it exists, is a reasonable action. If the current file is not *edited* then *ex* will not normally write on it if it already exists.*

2.2. Alternate file

Each time a new value is given to the current file name, the previous current file name is saved as the *alternate* file name. Similarly if a file is mentioned but does not become the current file, it is saved as the alternate file name.

2.3. Filename expansion

Filenames within the editor may be specified using the normal shell expansion conventions. In addition, the character '%' in filenames is replaced by the *current* file name and the character '#' by the *alternate* file name.†

2.4. Multiple files and named buffers

If more than one file is given on the command line, then the first file is edited as described above. The remaining arguments are placed with the first file in the *argument list.* The current argument list may be displayed with the *args* command. The next file in the argument list may be edited with the *next* command. The argument list may also be respecified by specifying a list of names to the *next* command. These names are expanded, the resulting list of names becomes the new argument list, and *ex* edits the first file on the list.

For saving blocks of text while editing, and especially when editing more than one file, *ex* has a group of named buffers. These are similar to the normal buffer, except that only a limited number of operations are available on them. The buffers have names *a* through *z.*‡

2.5. Read only

It is possible to use *ex* in *read only* mode to look at files that you have no intention of modifying. This mode protects you from accidently overwriting the file. Read only mode is on when the *readonly*

---

* The *file* command will say ''[Not edited]'' if the current file is not considered edited.

† This makes it easy to deal alternately with two files and eliminates the need for retyping the name supplied on an *edit* command after a *No write since last change* diagnostic is received.

‡ It is also possible to refer to *A* through *Z;* the upper case buffers are the same as the lower but commands append to named buffers rather than replacing if upper case names are used.

option is set. It can be turned on with the –**R** command line option, by the *view* command line invocation, or by setting the *readonly* option. It can be cleared by setting *noreadonly*. It is possible to write, even while in read only mode, by indicating that you really know what you are doing. You can write to a different file, or can use the ! form of write, even while in read only mode.

3. Exceptional Conditions

3.1. Errors and interrupts

When errors occur *ex* (optionally) rings the terminal bell and, in any case, prints an error diagnostic. If the primary input is from a file, editor processing will terminate. If an interrupt signal is received, *ex* prints ''Interrupt'' and returns to its command level. If the primary input is a file, then *ex* will exit when this occurs.

3.2. Recovering from hangups and crashes

If a hangup signal is received and the buffer has been modified since it was last written out, or if the system crashes, either the editor (in the first case) or the system (after it reboots in the second) will attempt to preserve the buffer. The next time you log in you should be able to recover the work you were doing, losing at most a few lines of changes from the last point before the hangup or editor crash. To recover a file you can use the –**r** option. If you were editing the file *resume,* then you should change to the directory where you were when the crash occurred, giving the command

>   **ex –r** *resume*

After checking that the retrieved file is indeed ok, you can *write* it over the previous contents of that file.

You will normally get mail from the system telling you when a file has been saved after a crash. The command

>   **ex –r**

will print a list of the files which have been saved for you. (In the case of a hangup, the file will not appear in the list, although it can be recovered.)

4. Editing modes

Ex has five distinct modes. The primary mode is *command* mode. Commands are entered in command mode when a ':' prompt is present, and are executed each time a complete line is sent. In *text input* mode *ex* gathers input lines and places them in the file. The *append, insert,* and *change* commands use text input mode. No prompt is printed when you are in text input mode. This mode is left by typing a '.' alone at the beginning of a line, and *command* mode resumes.

The last three modes are *open* and *visual* modes, entered by the commands of the same name, and, within open and visual modes *text insertion* mode. *Open* and *visual* modes allow local editing operations to be performed on the text in the file. The *open* command displays one line at a time on any terminal while *visual* works on CRT terminals with random positioning cursors, using the screen as a (single) window for file editing changes. These modes are described (only) in *An Introduction to Display Editing with Vi.*

5. Command structure

Most command names are English words, and initial prefixes of the words are acceptable abbreviations. The ambiguity of abbreviations is resolved in favor of the more commonly used commands.*

---

* As an example, the command *substitute* can be abbreviated 's' while the shortest available abbreviation for the *set* command is 'se'.

5.1. Command parameters

Most commands accept prefix addresses specifying the lines in the file upon which they are to have effect. The forms of these addresses will be discussed below. A number of commands also may take a trailing *count* specifying the number of lines to be involved in the command.† Thus the command "10p" will print the tenth line in the buffer while "delete 5" will delete five lines from the buffer, starting with the current line.

Some commands take other information or parameters, this information always being given after the command name.‡

5.2. Command variants

A number of commands have two distinct variants. The variant form of the command is invoked by placing an '!' immediately after the command name. Some of the default variants may be controlled by options; in this case, the '!' serves to toggle the default.

5.3. Flags after commands

The characters '#', 'p' and 'l' may be placed after many commands.** In this case, the command abbreviated by these characters is executed after the command completes. Since *ex* normally prints the new current line after each change, 'p' is rarely necessary. Any number of '+' or '−' characters may also be given with these flags. If they appear, the specified offset is applied to the current line value before the printing command is executed.

5.4. Comments

It is possible to give editor commands which are ignored. This is useful when making complex editor scripts for which comments are desired. The comment character is the double quote: ". Any command line beginning with " is ignored. Comments beginning with " may also be placed at the ends of commands, except in cases where they could be confused as part of text (shell escapes and the substitute and map commands).

5.5. Multiple commands per line

More than one command may be placed on a line by separating each pair of commands by a '|' character. However the *global* commands, comments, and the shell escape '!' must be the last command on a line, as they are not terminated by a '|'.

5.6. Reporting large changes

Most commands which change the contents of the editor buffer give feedback if the scope of the change exceeds a threshold given by the *report* option. This feedback helps to detect undesirably large changes so that they may be quickly and easily reversed with an *undo.* After commands with more global effect such as *global* or *visual,* you will be informed if the net change in the number of lines in the buffer during this command exceeds this threshold.

6. Command addressing

6.1. Addressing primitives

.   The current line. Most commands leave the current line as the last line which they affect. The default address for most commands is the current line, thus '.' is rarely used alone as an address.

---

† Counts are rounded down if necessary.
‡ Examples would be option names in a *set* command i.e. "set number", a file name in an *edit* command, a regular expression in a *substitute* command, or a target address for a *copy* command, i.e. "1,5 copy 25".
** A 'p' or 'l' must be preceded by a blank or tab except in the single special case 'dp'.

n	The *n*th line in the editor's buffer, lines being numbered sequentially from 1.
$	The last line in the buffer.
%	An abbreviation for ''1,$'', the entire buffer.
+*n* −*n*	An offset relative to the current buffer line.†
/pat/ ?*pat*?	Scan forward and backward respectively for a line containing *pat*, a regular expression (as defined below). The scans normally wrap around the end of the buffer. If all that is desired is to print the next line containing *pat*, then the trailing **/** or **?** may be omitted. If *pat* is omitted or explicitly empty, then the last regular expression specified is located.‡
″ ′*x*	Before each non-relative motion of the current line '.', the previous current line is marked with a tag, subsequently referred to as '″'. This makes it easy to refer or return to this previous context. Marks may also be established by the *mark* command, using single lower case letters *x* and the marked lines referred to as '′*x*'.

6.2. Combining addressing primitives

Addresses to commands consist of a series of addressing primitives, separated by ',' or ';'. Such address lists are evaluated left-to-right. When addresses are separated by ';' the current line '.' is set to the value of the previous addressing expression before the next address is interpreted. If more addresses are given than the command requires, then all but the last one or two are ignored. If the command takes two addresses, the first addressed line must precede the second in the buffer.†

7. Command descriptions

The following form is a prototype for all *ex* commands:

> *address* **command** *! parameters count flags*

All parts are optional; the degenerate case is the empty command which prints the next line in the file. For sanity with use from within *visual* mode, *ex* ignores a '':'' preceding any command.

In the following command descriptions, the default addresses are shown in parentheses, which are *not,* however, part of the command.

abbreviate *word rhs*   abbr: **ab**

Add the named abbreviation to the current list. When in input mode in visual, if *word* is typed as a complete word, it will be changed to *rhs* .

(.) append   abbr: **a**
text
.

Reads the input text and places it after the specified line. After the command, '.' addresses the last line input or the specified line if no lines were input. If address '0' is given, text is placed at the beginning of the buffer.

a!
text
.

The variant flag to *append* toggles the setting for the *autoindent* option during the input of *text.*

---

† The forms '.+3' '+3' and '+++' are all equivalent; if the current line is line 100 they all address line 103.

‡ The forms **V** and **\?** scan using the last regular expression used in a scan; after a substitute **//** and **??** would scan using the substitute's regular expression.

† Null address specifications are permitted in a list of addresses, the default in this case is the current line '.'; thus ',100' is equivalent to '.,100'. It is an error to give a prefix address to a command which expects none.

args

> The members of the argument list are printed, with the current argument delimited by '[' and ']'.

(. , .) **change** *count*   abbr: **c**
text
.

> Replaces the specified lines with the input *text*. The current line becomes the last line input; if no lines were input it is left as for a *delete*.

c!
text
.

> The variant toggles *autoindent* during the *change*.

(. , .) **copy** *addr flags*   abbr: **co**

> A *copy* of the specified lines is placed after *addr,* which may be '0'. The current line '.' addresses the last line of the copy. The command *t* is a synonym for *copy*.

(. , .) **delete** *buffer count flags*   abbr: **d**

> Removes the specified lines from the buffer. The line after the last line deleted becomes the current line; if the lines deleted were originally at the end, the new last line becomes the current line. If a named *buffer* is specified by giving a letter, then the specified lines are saved in that buffer, or appended to it if an upper case letter is used.

edit *file*   abbr: **e**
ex *file*

> Used to begin an editing session on a new file. The editor first checks to see if the buffer has been modified since the last *write* command was issued. If it has been, a warning is issued and the command is aborted. The command otherwise deletes the entire contents of the editor buffer, makes the named file the current file and prints the new filename. After insuring that this file is sensible† the editor reads the file into its buffer.

> If the read of the file completes without error, the number of lines and characters read is typed. If there were any non-ASCII characters in the file they are stripped of their non-ASCII high bits, and any null characters in the file are discarded. If none of these errors occurred, the file is considered *edited*. If the last line of the input file is missing the trailing newline character, it will be supplied and a complaint will be issued. This command leaves the current line '.' at the last line read.‡

e! *file*

> The variant form suppresses the complaint about modifications having been made and not written from the editor buffer, thus discarding all changes which have been made before editing the new file.

e +n *file*

> Causes the editor to begin at line *n* rather than at the last line; *n* may also be an editor command containing no spaces, e.g.: "+/pat".

---

† I.e., that it is not a binary file such as a directory, a block or character special file other than */dev/tty,* a terminal, or a binary or executable file (as indicated by the first word).
‡ If executed from within *open* or *visual,* the current line is initially the first line of the file.

file   abbr: **f**

Prints the current file name, whether it has been '[Modified]' since the last *write* command, whether it is *read only*, the current line, the number of lines in the buffer, and the percentage of the way through the buffer of the current line.*

file *file*

The current file name is changed to *file* which is considered '[Not edited]'.

(1 , $) global /*pat*/ *cmds*   abbr: **g**

First marks each line among those specified which matches the given regular expression. Then the given command list is executed with '.' initially set to each marked line.

The command list consists of the remaining commands on the current input line and may continue to multiple lines by ending all but the last such line with a '\'. If *cmds* (and possibly the trailing / delimiter) is omitted, each line matching *pat* is printed. *Append, insert,* and *change* commands and associated input are permitted; the '.' terminating input may be omitted if it would be on the last line of the command list. *Open* and *visual* commands are permitted in the command list and take input from the terminal.

The *global* command itself may not appear in *cmds*. The *undo* command is also not permitted there, as *undo* instead can be used to reverse the entire *global* command. The options *autoprint* and *autoindent* are inhibited during a *global,* (and possibly the trailing / delimiter) and the value of the *report* option is temporarily infinite, in deference to a *report* for the entire global. Finally, the context mark '''' is set to the value of '.' before the global command begins and is not changed during a global command, except perhaps by an *open* or *visual* within the *global*.

g! /*pat*/ *cmds*   abbr: **v**

The variant form of *global* runs *cmds* at each line not matching *pat*.

(.) insert   abbr: **i**
text
.

Places the given text before the specified line. The current line is left at the last line input; if there were none input it is left at the line before the addressed line. This command differs from *append* only in the placement of text.

i!
text
.

The variant toggles *autoindent* during the *insert*.

(. , .+1) join *count flags*   abbr: **j**

Places the text from a specified range of lines together on one line. White space is adjusted at each junction to provide at least one blank character, two if there was a '.' at the end of the line, or none if the first following character is a ')'. If there is already white space at the end of the line, then the white space at the start of the next line will be discarded.

---

* In the rare case that the current file is '[Not edited]' this is noted also; in this case you have to use the form **w!** to write to the file, since the editor is not sure that a **write** will not destroy a file unrelated to the current contents of the buffer.

j!

> The variant causes a simpler *join* with no white space processing; the characters in the lines are simply concatenated.

(.) k *x*

> The *k* command is a synonym for *mark*. It does not require a blank or tab before the following letter.

(. , .) list *count flags*

> Prints the specified lines in a more unambiguous way: tabs are printed as '^I' and the end of each line is marked with a trailing '$'. The current line is left at the last line printed.

map *lhs rhs*

> The *map* command is used to define macros for use in *visual* mode. *Lhs* should be a single character, or the sequence ''#n'', for n a digit, referring to function key *n*. When this character or function key is typed in *visual* mode, it will be as though the corresponding *rhs* had been typed. On terminals without function keys, you can type ''#n''. See section 6.9 of the ''Introduction to Display Editing with Vi'' for more details.

(.) mark *x*

> Gives the specified line mark *x*, a single lower case letter. The *x* must be preceded by a blank or a tab. The addressing form ''x' then addresses this line. The current line is not affected by this command.

(. , .) move *addr*   abbr: **m**

> The *move* command repositions the specified lines to be after *addr*. The first of the moved lines becomes the current line.

next   abbr: **n**

> The next file from the command line argument list is edited.

n!

> The variant suppresses warnings about the modifications to the buffer not having been written out, discarding (irretrievably) any changes which may have been made.

n *filelist*
n +*command filelist*

> The specified *filelist* is expanded and the resulting list replaces the current argument list; the first file in the new list is then edited. If *command* is given (it must contain no spaces), then it is executed after editing the first such file.

(. , .) number *count flags*   abbr: **#** or **nu**

> Prints each specified line preceded by its buffer line number. The current line is left at the last line printed.

(.) open *flags*   abbr: **o**
(.) open */pat/ flags*

> Enters intraline editing *open* mode at each addressed line. If *pat* is given, then the cursor will be placed initially at the beginning of the string matched by the pattern. To exit this mode use Q. See *An Introduction to Display Editing with Vi* for more details.

preserve

The current editor buffer is saved as though the system had just crashed. This command is for use only in emergencies when a *write* command has resulted in an error and you don't know how to save your work. After a *preserve* you should seek help.

(**.** , **.**) **print** *count*   abbr: **p** or **P**

Prints the specified lines with non-printing characters printed as control characters '^x'; delete (octal 177) is represented as '^?'. The current line is left at the last line printed.

(**.**) **put** *buffer*   abbr: **pu**

Puts back previously *deleted* or *yanked* lines. Normally used with *delete* to effect movement of lines, or with *yank* to effect duplication of lines. If no *buffer* is specified, then the last *deleted* or *yanked* text is restored.* By using a named buffer, text may be restored that was saved there at any previous time.

quit   abbr: **q**

Causes *ex* to terminate. No automatic write of the editor buffer to a file is performed. However, *ex* issues a warning message if the file has changed since the last *write* command was issued, and does not *quit*.† Normally, you will wish to save your changes, and you should give a *write* command; if you wish to discard them, use the **q!** command variant.

q!

Quits from the editor, discarding changes to the buffer without complaint.

(**.**) **read** *file*   abbr: **r**

Places a copy of the text of the given file in the editing buffer after the specified line. If no *file* is given the current file name is used. The current file name is not changed unless there is none in which case *file* becomes the current name. The sensibility restrictions for the *edit* command apply here also. If the file buffer is empty and there is no current name then *ex* treats this as an *edit* command.

Address '0' is legal for this command and causes the file to be read at the beginning of the buffer. Statistics are given as for the *edit* command when the *read* successfully terminates. After a *read* the current line is the last line read.‡

(**.**) **read** !*command*

Reads the output of the command *command* into the buffer after the specified line. This is not a variant form of the command, rather a read specifying a *command* rather than a *filename;* a blank or tab before the **!** is mandatory.

recover *file*

Recovers *file* from the system save area. Used after a accidental hangup of the phone** or a system crash** or *preserve* command. Except when you use *preserve* you will be notified by mail when a file is saved.

---

* But no modifying commands may intervene between the *delete* or *yank* and the *put,* nor may lines be moved between files without using a named buffer.

† *Ex* will also issue a diagnostic if there are more files in the argument list.

‡ Within *open* and *visual* the current line is set to the first line read rather than the last.

** The system saves a copy of the file you were editing only if you have made changes to the file.

rewind   abbr: **rew**

    The argument list is rewound, and the first file in the list is edited.

rew!

    Rewinds the argument list discarding any changes made to the current buffer.

set *parameter*

    With no arguments, prints those options whose values have been changed from their defaults; with parameter *all* it prints all of the option values.

    Giving an option name followed by a '?' causes the current value of that option to be printed. The '?' is unnecessary unless the option is Boolean valued. Boolean options are given values either by the form 'set *option*' to turn them on or 'set no*option*' to turn them off; string and numeric options are assigned via the form 'set *option*=value'.

    More than one parameter may be given to *set* ; they are interpreted left-to-right.

shell   abbr: **sh**

    A new shell is created. When it terminates, editing resumes.

source *file*   abbr: **so**

    Reads and executes commands from the specified file. *Source* commands may be nested.

(. , .) **substitute** /*pat*/*repl*/ *options count flags*   abbr: **s**

    On each specified line, the first instance of pattern *pat* is replaced by replacement pattern *repl*. If the *global* indicator option character 'g' appears, then all instances are substituted; if the *confirm* indication character 'c' appears, then before each substitution the line to be substituted is typed with the string to be substituted marked with '↑' characters. By typing an 'y' one can cause the substitution to be performed, any other input causes no change to take place. After a *substitute* the current line is the last line substituted.

    Lines may be split by substituting new-line characters into them. The newline in *repl* must be escaped by preceding it with a '\'. Other metacharacters available in *pat* and *repl* are described below.

stop

    Suspends the editor, returning control to the top level shell. If *autowrite* is set and there are unsaved changes, a write is done first unless the form **stop**! is used. This commands is only available where supported by the teletype driver and operating system.

(. , .) **substitute** *options count flags*   abbr: **s**

    If *pat* and *repl* are omitted, then the last substitution is repeated. This is a synonym for the **&** command.

(. , .) **t** *addr flags*

    The *t* command is a synonym for *copy* .

ta *tag*

    The focus of editing switches to the location of *tag,* switching to a different line in the current file where it is defined, or if necessary to another file.‡

---

‡ If you have modified the current file before giving a *tag* command, you must write it out; giving another *tag* command, specifying no *tag* will reuse the previous tag.

The tags file is normally created by a program such as *ctags,* and consists of a number of lines with three fields separated by blanks or tabs. The first field gives the name of the tag, the second the name of the file where the tag resides, and the third gives an addressing form which can be used by the editor to find the tag; this field is usually a contextual scan using '*/pat/*' to be immune to minor changes in the file. Such scans are always performed as if *nomagic* was set.

The tag names in the tags file must be sorted alphabetically.

unabbreviate *word*   abbr: **una**

    Delete *word* from the list of abbreviations.

undo   abbr: **u**

    Reverses the changes made in the buffer by the last buffer editing command. Note that *global* commands are considered a single command for the purpose of *undo* (as are *open* and *visual.*) Also, the commands *write* and *edit* which interact with the file system cannot be undone. *Undo* is its own inverse.

    Undo always marks the previous value of the current line '.' as '˝'. After an *undo* the current line is the first line restored or the line before the first line deleted if no lines were restored. For commands with more global effect such as *global* and *visual* the current line regains it's pre-command value after an *undo.*

unmap *lhs*

    The macro expansion associated by *map* for *lhs* is removed.

(1 , $) **v** */pat/ cmds*

    A synonym for the *global* command variant **g!**, running the specified *cmds* on each line which does not match *pat.*

version   abbr: **ve**

    Prints the current version number of the editor as well as the date the editor was last changed.

(**.**) **visual** *type count flags*   abbr: **vi**

    Enters visual mode at the specified line. *Type* is optional and may be '−' , '↑' or '.' as in the *z* command to specify the placement of the specified line on the screen. By default, if *type* is omitted, the specified line is placed as the first on the screen. A *count* specifies an initial window size; the default is the value of the option *window.* See the document *An Introduction to Display Editing with Vi* for more details. To exit this mode, type Q.

visual file
visual +*n* file

    From visual mode, this command is the same as edit.

(1 , $) **write** *file*   abbr: **w**

    Writes changes made back to *file*, printing the number of lines and characters written. Normally *file* is omitted and the text goes back where it came from. If a *file* is specified, then text will be written to that file.* If the file does not exist it is created. The current file name is changed only if there is no current file name; the current line is never changed.

    If an error occurs while writing the current and *edited* file, the editor considers that there has been ''No write since last change'' even if the buffer had not previously been modified.

---

* The editor writes to a file only if it is the current file and is *edited* , if the file does not exist, or if the file is actually a teletype, */dev/tty, /dev/null*. Otherwise, you must give the variant form **w!** to force the write.

(1 , $) **write>>** *file*   abbr: **w>>**

    Writes the buffer contents at the end of an existing file.

w! *name*

    Overrides the checking of the normal *write* command, and will write to any file which the system permits.

(1 , $) **w** **!***command*

    Writes the specified lines into *command.* Note the difference between **w!** which overrides checks and **w** **!** which writes to a command.

wq *name*

    Like a *write* and then a *quit* command.

wq! *name*

    The variant overrides checking on the sensibility of the *write* command, as **w!** does.

xit *name*

    If any changes have been made and not written, writes the buffer out. Then, in any case, quits.

(. , .) **yank** *buffer count*   abbr: **ya**

    Places the specified lines in the named *buffer,* for later retrieval via *put.* If no buffer name is specified, the lines go to a more volatile place; see the *put* command description.

(.+1) **z** *count*

    Print the next *count* lines, default *window.*

(.) **z** *type count*

    Prints a window of text with the specified line at the top. If *type* is '−' the line is placed at the bottom; a '.' causes the line to be placed in the center.* A count gives the number of lines to be displayed rather than double the number specified by the *scroll* option. On a CRT the screen is cleared before display begins unless a count which is less than the screen size is given. The current line is left at the last line printed.

! *command*

    The remainder of the line after the '!' character is sent to a shell to be executed. Within the text of *command* the characters '%' and '#' are expanded as in filenames and the character '!' is replaced with the text of the previous command. Thus, in particular, '!!' repeats the last such shell escape. If any such expansion is performed, the expanded line will be echoed. The current line is unchanged by this command.

    If there has been ''[No write]'' of the buffer contents since the last change to the editing buffer, then a diagnostic will be printed before the command is executed as a warning. A single '!' is printed when the command completes.

---

* Forms 'z−' and 'z↑' also exist; 'z−' places the current line in the center, surrounds it with lines of '−' characters and leaves the current line at this line. The form 'z↑' prints the window before 'z−' would. The characters '+', '↑' and '−' may be repeated for cumulative effect. On some v2 editors, no *type* may be given.

(*addr* , *addr*) ! *command*

> Takes the specified address range and supplies it as standard input to *command;* the resulting output then replaces the input lines.

($) =

> Prints the line number of the addressed line. The current line is unchanged.

(. , .) > *count flags*
(. , .) < *count flags*

> Perform intelligent shifting on the specified lines; < shifts left and > shift right. The quantity of shift is determined by the *shiftwidth* option and the repetition of the specification character. Only white space (blanks and tabs) is shifted; no non-white characters are discarded in a left-shift. The current line becomes the last line which changed due to the shifting.

^D

> An end-of-file from a terminal input scrolls through the file. The *scroll* option specifies the size of the scroll, normally a half screen of text.

(.+1 , .+1)
(.+1 , .+1) |

> An address alone causes the addressed lines to be printed. A blank line prints the next line in the file.

(. , .) & *options count flags*

> Repeats the previous *substitute* command.

(. , .) ~ *options count flags*

> Replaces the previous regular expression with the previous replacement pattern from a substitution.

8. Regular expressions and substitute replacement patterns

8.1. Regular expressions

A regular expression specifies a set of strings of characters. A member of this set of strings is said to be *matched* by the regular expression. *Ex* remembers two previous regular expressions: the previous regular expression used in a *substitute* command and the previous regular expression used elsewhere (referred to as the previous *scanning* regular expression.) The previous regular expression can always be referred to by a null *re*, e.g. '//' or '??'.

8.2. Magic and nomagic

The regular expressions allowed by *ex* are constructed in one of two ways depending on the setting of the *magic* option. The *ex* and *vi* default setting of *magic* gives quick access to a powerful set of regular expression metacharacters. The disadvantage of *magic* is that the user must remember that these metacharacters are *magic* and precede them with the character '\' to use them as "ordinary" characters. With *nomagic,* the default for *edit,* regular expressions are much simpler, there being only two metacharacters. The power of the other metacharacters is still available by preceding the (now) ordinary character with a '\'. Note that '\' is thus always a metacharacter.

The remainder of the discussion of regular expressions assumes that that the setting of this option is *magic.*†

---

† To discern what is true with *nomagic* it suffices to remember that the only special characters in this case will be '↑' at the beginning of a regular expression, '$' at the end of a regular expression, and '\'. With *nomagic* the characters '~' and '&' also lose their special meanings related to the replacement pattern of a substitute.

12

8.3. Basic regular expression summary

The following basic constructs are used to construct *magic* mode regular expressions.

char　　　　An ordinary character matches itself. The characters '↑' at the beginning of a line, '$' at the end of line, '*' as any character other than the first, '.', '\', '[', and '˜' are not ordinary characters and must be escaped (preceded) by '\' to be treated as such.

↑　　　　At the beginning of a pattern forces the match to succeed only at the beginning of a line.

$　　　　At the end of a regular expression forces the match to succeed only at the end of the line.

.　　　　Matches any single character except the new-line character.

\<　　　　Forces the match to occur only at the beginning of a "variable" or "word"; that is, either at the beginning of a line, or just before a letter, digit, or underline and after a character not one of these.

\>　　　　Similar to '\<', but matching the end of a "variable" or "word", i.e. either the end of the line or before character which is neither a letter, nor a digit, nor the underline character.

[*string*]　　　　Matches any (single) character in the class defined by *string*. Most characters in *string* define themselves. A pair of characters separated by '−' in *string* defines the set of characters collating between the specified lower and upper bounds, thus '[a–z]' as a regular expression matches any (single) lower-case letter. If the first character of *string* is an '↑' then the construct matches those characters which it otherwise would not; thus '[↑a–z]' matches anything but a lower-case letter (and of course a newline). To place any of the characters '↑', '[', or '−' in *string* you must escape them with a preceding '\'.

8.4. Combining regular expression primitives

The concatenation of two regular expressions matches the leftmost and then longest string which can be divided with the first piece matching the first regular expression and the second piece matching the second. Any of the (single character matching) regular expressions mentioned above may be followed by the character '*' to form a regular expression which matches any number of adjacent occurrences (including 0) of characters matched by the regular expression it follows.

The character '˜' may be used in a regular expression, and matches the text which defined the replacement part of the last *substitute* command. A regular expression may be enclosed between the sequences '\(' and '\)' with side effects in the *substitute* replacement patterns.

8.5. Substitute replacement patterns

The basic metacharacters for the replacement pattern are '&' and '˜'; these are given as '\&' and '\˜' when *nomagic* is set. Each instance of '&' is replaced by the characters which the regular expression matched. The metacharacter '˜' stands, in the replacement pattern, for the defining text of the previous replacement pattern.

Other metasequences possible in the replacement pattern are always introduced by the escaping character '\'. The sequence '\n' is replaced by the text matched by the *n*-th regular subexpression enclosed between '\(' and '\)'.† The sequences '\u' and '\l' cause the immediately following character in the replacement to be converted to upper- or lower-case respectively if this character is a letter. The sequences '\U' and '\L' turn such conversion on, either until '\E' or '\e' is encountered, or until the end of the replacement pattern.

---

† When nested, parenthesized subexpressions are present, *n* is determined by counting occurrences of '\(' starting from the left.

9. Option descriptions

autoindent, ai   default: noai

Can be used to ease the preparation of structured program text. At the beginning of each *append*, *change* or *insert* command or when a new line is *opened* or created by an *append*, *change*, *insert*, or *substitute* operation within *open* or *visual* mode, *ex* looks at the line being appended after, the first line changed or the line inserted before and calculates the amount of white space at the start of the line. It then aligns the cursor at the level of indentation so determined.

If the user then types lines of text in, they will continue to be justified at the displayed indenting level. If more white space is typed at the beginning of a line, the following line will start aligned with the first non-white character of the previous line. To back the cursor up to the preceding tab stop one can hit **^D**. The tab stops going backwards are defined at multiples of the *shiftwidth* option. You *cannot* backspace over the indent, except by sending an end-of-file with a **^D**.

Specially processed in this mode is a line with no characters added to it, which turns into a completely blank line (the white space provided for the *autoindent* is discarded.) Also specially processed in this mode are lines beginning with an '↑' and immediately followed by a **^D**. This causes the input to be repositioned at the beginning of the line, but retaining the previous indent for the next line. Similarly, a '0' followed by a **^D** repositions at the beginning but without retaining the previous indent.

Autoindent doesn't happen in *global* commands or when the input is not a terminal.

autoprint, ap   default: ap

Causes the current line to be printed after each *delete*, *copy*, *join*, *move*, *substitute*, *t*, *undo* or shift command. This has the same effect as supplying a trailing 'p' to each such command. *Autoprint* is suppressed in globals, and only applies to the last of many commands on a line.

autowrite, aw   default: noaw

Causes the contents of the buffer to be written to the current file if you have modified it and give a *next, rewind, stop, tag,* or *!* command, or a **^↑** (switch files) or **^]** (tag goto) command in *visual*. Note, that the *edit* and *ex* commands do **not** autowrite. In each case, there is an equivalent way of switching when autowrite is set to avoid the *autowrite* (*edit* for *next*, *rewind!* for .I rewind, *stop!* for *stop*, *tag!* for *tag*, *shell* for *!*, and :e # and a :ta! command from within *visual*).

beautify, bf   default: nobeautify

Causes all control characters except tab, newline and form-feed to be discarded from the input. A complaint is registered the first time a backspace character is discarded. *Beautify* does not apply to command input.

directory, dir   default: dir=/tmp

Specifies the directory in which *ex* places its buffer file. If this directory in not writable, then the editor will exit abruptly when it fails to be able to create its buffer there.

edcompatible   default: noedcompatible

Causes the presence of absence of **g** and **c** suffixes on substitute commands to be remembered, and to be toggled by repeating the suffices. The suffix **r** makes the substitution be as in the ~ command, instead of like &.

errorbells, eb   default: noeb

Error messages are preceded by a bell.* If possible the editor always places the error message in a

---

* Bell ringing in *open* and *visual* on errors is not suppressed by setting *noeb*.

standout mode of the terminal (such as inverse video) instead of ringing the bell.

hardtabs, ht   default: ht=8

Gives the boundaries on which terminal hardware tabs are set (or on which the system expands tabs).

ignorecase, ic   default: noic

All upper case characters in the text are mapped to lower case in regular expression matching. In addition, all upper case characters in regular expressions are mapped to lower case except in character class specifications.

lisp   default: nolisp

Autoindent indents appropriately for *lisp* code, and the ( ) { } [[and]] commands in *open* and *visual* are modified to have meaning for *lisp*.

list   default: nolist

All printed lines will be displayed (more) unambiguously, showing tabs and end-of-lines as in the *list* command.

magic   default: magic for *ex* and *vi*†

If *nomagic* is set, the number of regular expression metacharacters is greatly reduced, with only '↑' and '$' having special effects. In addition the metacharacters '~' and '&' of the replacement pattern are treated as normal characters. All the normal metacharacters may be made *magic* when *nomagic* is set by preceding them with a '\'.

mesg   default: mesg

Causes write permission to be turned off to the terminal while you are in visual mode, if *nomesg* is set.

modeline   default: nomodeline

If *modeline* is set, then the first 5 lines and the last five lines of the file will be checked for ex command lines and the comands issued. To be recognized as a command line, the line must have the string **ex:** or **vi:** preceded by a tab or a space. This string may be anywhere in the line and anything after the *:* is interpeted as editor commands. This option defaults to off because of unexpected behavior when editting files such as */etc/passwd*.

number, nu   default: nonumber

Causes all output lines to be printed with their line numbers. In addition each input line will be prompted for by supplying the line number it will have.

open   default: open

If *noopen*, the commands *open* and *visual* are not permitted. This is set for *edit* to prevent confusion resulting from accidental entry to open or visual mode.

optimize, opt   default: optimize

Throughput of text is expedited by setting the terminal to not do automatic carriage returns when printing more than one (logical) line of output, greatly speeding output on terminals without addressable cursors when text with leading white space is printed.

---

† *Nomagic* for *edit*.

paragraphs, para   default: para=IPLPPPQPP LIbp

Specifies the paragraphs for the { and } operations in *open* and *visual*. The pairs of characters in the option's value are the names of the macros which start paragraphs.

prompt   default: prompt

Command mode input is prompted for with a ':'.

redraw   default: noredraw

The editor simulates (using great amounts of output), an intelligent terminal on a dumb terminal (e.g. during insertions in *visual* the characters to the right of the cursor position are refreshed as each input character is typed.) Useful only at very high speed.

remap   default: remap

If on, macros are repeatedly tried until they are unchanged. For example, if **o** is mapped to **O**, and **O** is mapped to **I**, then if *remap* is set, **o** will map to **I**, but if *noremap* is set, it will map to **O**.

report   default: report=5†

Specifies a threshold for feedback from commands. Any command which modifies more than the specified number of lines will provide feedback as to the scope of its changes. For commands such as *global*, *open*, *undo*, and *visual* which have potentially more far reaching scope, the net change in the number of lines in the buffer is presented at the end of the command, subject to this same threshold. Thus notification is suppressed during a *global* command on the individual commands performed.

scroll   default: scroll=½ window

Determines the number of logical lines scrolled when an end-of-file is received from a terminal input in command mode, and the number of lines printed by a command mode *z* command (double the value of *scroll*).

sections   default: sections=SHNHH HU

Specifies the section macros for the [[and]] operations in *open* and *visual*. The pairs of characters in the options's value are the names of the macros which start paragraphs.

shell, sh   default: sh=/bin/sh

Gives the path name of the shell forked for the shell escape command '!', and by the *shell* command. The default is taken from SHELL in the environment, if present.

shiftwidth, sw   default: sw=8

Gives the width a software tab stop, used in reverse tabbing with ^D when using *autoindent* to append text, and by the shift commands.

showmatch, sm   default: nosm

In *open* and *visual* mode, when a) or } is typed, move the cursor to the matching (or { for one second if this matching character is on the screen. Extremely useful with *lisp*.

slowopen, slow   terminal dependent

Affects the display algorithm used in *visual* mode, holding off display updating during input of new text to improve throughput when the terminal in use is both slow and unintelligent. See *An Introduction to Display Editing with Vi* for more details.

---

† 2 for *edit*.

tabstop, ts   default: ts=8

The editor expands tabs in the input file to be on *tabstop* boundaries for the purposes of display.

taglength, tl   default: tl=0

Tags are not significant beyond this many characters. A value of zero (the default) means that all characters are significant.

tags   default: tags=tags /usr/lib/tags

A path of files to be used as tag files for the *tag* command. A requested tag is searched for in the specified files, sequentially. By default, files called **tags** are searched for in the current directory and in /usr/lib (a master file for the entire system).

term   from environment TERM

The terminal type of the output device.

terse   default: noterse

Shorter error diagnostics are produced for the experienced user.

warn   default: warn

Warn if there has been '[No write since last change]' before a '!' command escape.

window   default: window=speed dependent

The number of lines in a text window in the *visual* command. The default is 8 at slow speeds (600 baud or less), 16 at medium speed (1200 baud), and the full screen (minus one line) at higher speeds.

w300, w1200, w9600

These are not true options but set **window** only if the speed is slow (300), medium (1200), or high (9600), respectively. They are suitable for an EXINIT and make it easy to change the 8/16/full screen rule.

wrapscan, ws   default: ws

Searches using the regular expressions in addressing will wrap around past the end of the file.

wrapmargin, wm   default: wm=0

Defines a margin for automatic wrapover of text during input in *open* and *visual* modes. See *An Introduction to Text Editing with Vi* for details.

writeany, wa   default: nowa

Inhibit the checks normally made before *write* commands, allowing a write to any file which the system protection mechanism will allow.

10. Acknowledgements

Chuck Haley contributed greatly to the early development of *ex*. Bruce Englar encouraged the redesign which led to *ex* version 1. Bill Joy wrote versions 1 and 2.0 through 2.7, and created the framework that users see in the present editor. Mark Horton added macros and other features and made the editor work on a large number of terminals and Unix systems.

Ex/Vi Reference Manual

Keith Bostic

Computer Science Division
Department of Electrical Engineering and Computer Science
University of California, Berkeley
Berkeley, California 94720

Abstract

This document is the reference guide for the 4.4BSD implementations of **nex/nvi**, which are reimplementations of the historic Berkeley **ex/vi** editors.

Acknowledgements

Bruce Englar encouraged the early development of the historic **ex/vi** editor. Peter Kessler helped bring sanity to version 2's command layout. Bill Joy wrote versions 1 and 2.0 through 2.7, and created the framework that users see in the present editor. Mark Horton added macros and other features and made **ex/vi** work on a large number of terminals and Unix systems.

Nvi is originally derived from software contributed to the University of California, Berkeley by Steve Kirkendall, the author of the **vi** clone **elvis**.

IEEE Standard Portable Operating System Interface for Computer Environments (POSIX) 1003.2 style Regular Expression support was done by Henry Spencer.

The curses library was originally done by Ken Arnold. Scrolling and reworking for **nvi** was done by Elan Amir.

The Institute of Electrical and Electronics Engineers has given us permission to reprint portions of their documentation. Portions of this document are reprinted and reproduced from IEEE Std 1003.2-1992, IEEE Standard Portable Operating System Interface for Computer Environments (POSIX), copyright 1992 by the Institute of Electrical and Electronics Engineers, Inc.

The financial support of UUNET Communications Services is gratefully acknowledged.

13

Table of Contents

Description 3
Startup Information 3
Recovery 3
Sizing the Screen 4
Character Display 5
Multiple Screens 5
Regular Expressions and Replacement Strings 5
General Editor Description 6
Vi Description 7
Vi Commands 10
Vi Text Input Commands 29
Ex Addressing 30
Ex Description 31
Ex Commands 32
Set Options 44
Additional Features in Nex/Nvi 51
Index 53

13

1. Description

Vi is a screen oriented text editor. **Ex** is a line-oriented text editor. **Ex** and **vi** are different interfaces to the same program, and it is possible to switch back and forth during an edit session. **View** is the equivalent of using the **–R** (read-only) option of **vi**.

This reference manual is the one provided with the **nex/nvi** versions of the **ex/vi** text editors. **Nex/nvi** are intended as bug-for-bug compatible replacements for the original Fourth Berkeley Software Distribution (4BSD) **ex/vi** programs. This reference manual is accompanied by a traditional-style manual page. That manual page describes the functionality found in **ex/vi** in far less detail than the description here. In addition, it describes the system interface to **ex/vi**, e.g. command line options, session recovery, signals, environmental variables, and similar things.

This reference is intended for users already familiar with **ex/vi**. Anyone else should almost certainly read a good tutorial on the editor first. If you're in an unfamiliar environment, and you absolutely have to get work done immediately, see the section entitled ''**Fast**''Startup in the manual page. It's probably enough to get you started.

There are a few features in **nex/nvi** that are not found in historic versions of **ex/vi**. Some of the more interesting of those features are briefly described in the section entitled ''**Additional Features**'' near the end of this document. For the rest of this document, **nex/nvi** is used only when it's necessary to distinguish it from the historic implementations of **ex/vi**.

Future versions of this software will be periodically made available by anonymous ftp, and can be retrieved from `ftp.cs.berkeley.edu`, in the directory `ucb/4bsd`.

2. Startup Information

Ex/vi interprets one of two possible environmental variables and reads up to three of five possible files during startup. The variables and files are expected to contain **ex** commands, not **vi** commands. In addition, they are interpreted *before* the file to be edited is read, and therefore many **ex** commands may not be used. Generally, any command that requires output to the screen or that needs a file upon which to operate, will cause an error if included in a startup file or environmental variable.

Because the **ex** command set supported by **nex/nvi** is a superset of the command set supported by most historical implementations of **ex**, **nex/nvi** can use the startup files created for the historical implementations, but the converse may not be true.

If the **–s** (the historic – option) is specified, or if standard input is redirected from a file, all environmental variables and startup files are ignored.

Otherwise, startup files and environmental variables are handled in the following order:

(1)   The file `/etc/vi.exrc` is read, as long as it is owned by root or the effective user ID of the user.

(2)   The environmental variable `NEXINIT` (or the variable `EXINIT`, if `NEXINIT` isn't set) is interpreted.

(3)   If neither `NEXINIT` or `EXINIT` was set, and the `HOME` environmental variable is set, the file `$HOME/.nexrc` (or the file `$HOME/.exrc`, if `$HOME/.nexrc` doesn't exist) is read, as long as the effective user ID of the user is root or is the same as the owner of the file.

(4)   If the **exrc** option was turned on by one of the previous startup information sources, the file `.nexrc` (or the file `.exrc`, if `.nexrc` doesn't exist) is read, as long as the effective user ID of the user is the same as the owner of the file.

No startup file is read if it is writable by anyone other than its owner.

It is not an error for any of the startup environmental variables or files to not exist.

Once all environmental variables are interpreted, and all startup files are read, the first file to be edited is read in (or a temporary file is created). Then, any commands specified using the **–c** option are executed, in the context of that file.

13

3. Recovery

There is no recovery program for **nvi**, nor does **nvi** run setuid. Recovery files are created readable by the owner only, therefore, users may recover any file which they can read, and the superuser may recover any edit session.

Edit sessions are backed by files in `/var/tmp/vi.recover`, and are named "**vi.XXXX**", where "**XXXX**" is a number related to the process ID. When a file is first modified, a second file, which contains an email message for the user, is created, and is named "**recover.XXXX**", where, again, "**XXXX**" is associated with the process ID. Both files are removed at the end of a normal edit session, but will remain if the edit session is abnormally terminated or the user enters the **ex** "**preserve**" command. The use of the `/var/tmp` directory may be changed by setting the **recdir** option in the user's or system startup information. (Note, however, that if a memory based file system is used as the backup directory, each system reboot will delete all of the recovery files!)

The recovery directory should be owned by root, or at least by a pseudo-user. In addition, if directory "sticky-bit" semantics are available, the directory should have the sticky-bit set so that files may only be removed by their owners. The recovery directory must be read, write, and executable by any user, i.e. mode 1777.

If the recovery directory does not exist, **ex/vi** will attempt to create it. This can result in the recovery directory being owned by a normal user, which means that that user will be able to remove other user's recovery and backup files. This is annoying, but is not be a security issue as the user cannot otherwise access or modify the files.

The recovery file has all of the necessary information in it to enable the user to recover the edit session. In addition, it has all of the necessary email headers for *sendmail*(8). When the system is rebooted, all of the files in `/var/tmp/vi.recover` named "**recover.XXXX**" should be sent to their owners, by email, using the –t option of **sendmail** (or a similar mechanism in other mailers).

A simple way to do this is to insert the following script into your `/etc/rc.local` (or other startup) file:

```
virecovery='echo /var/tmp/vi.recover/recover.*'
if [ "$virecovery" != "/var/tmp/vi.recover/recover.*" ]; then
      echo 'Recovering vi editor sessions'
      for i in $virecovery; do
            sendmail -t < $i
      done
fi
```

If **ex/vi** receives a hangup (SIGHUP) signal, or the user executes the **ex preserve** command, **ex/vi** will automatically email the recovery information to the user.

If your system doesn't have the **sendmail** utility (or a mailer program which supports its interface) the source file `nvi/recover.c` will have to be modified to use your local mail delivery programs.

4. Sizing the Screen

The size of the screen can be set in a number of ways. **Ex/vi** takes the following steps until values are obtained for both the number of rows and number of columns in the screen.

(1)   If the environmental variable `LINES` exists, it is used to specify the number of rows in the screen.

(2)   If the environmental variable `COLUMNS` exists, it is used to specify the number of columns in the screen.

(3)   The TIOCGWINSZ *ioctl*(2) is attempted on the standard error file descriptor.

(4)   The termcap entry is checked for the "li" entry (rows) and the "co" entry (columns).

(5)   The number of rows is set to 24, and the number of columns is set to 80.

If a window change size signal (SIGWINCH) is received, the new window size is retrieved using the TIOCGWINSZ *ioctl*(2) call, and all other information is ignored.

5. Character Display

In both **ex** and **vi** printable characters as defined by *isprint*(3) are displayed using the local character set.

Non-printable characters, for which *iscntrl*(3) returns true, and which are less than octal \076, are displayed as the string ``^<character>'', where `<character>` is the character that is the original character's value offset from the ``@'' character. For example, the octal character \001 is displayed as ``^A''. If *iscntrl*(3) returns true for the octal character \177, it is displayed as the string ``^?''. All other characters are displayed as either hexadecimal values, in the form ``0x<high-halfbyte> ... 0x<low-halfbyte>'', or as octal values, in the form ``\<high-one-or-two-bits> ... \<low-three-bits>''. The display of unknown characters is based on the value of the **octal** option.

In **vi** command mode, the cursor is always positioned on the last column of characters which take up more than one column on the screen. In **vi** text input mode, the cursor is positioned on the first column of characters which take up more than one column on the screen.

6. Multiple Screens

Nvi supports multiple screens by dividing the window into regions. It also supports stacks of screens by permitting the user to change the set of screens that are currently displayed.

The command **split** divides the current screen into two regions of approximately equal size. If a list of files are specified as arguments to the **split** command, the list of files to be edited is initialized as if the **next** command had been used. If no files are specified, the new screen will begin by editing the same file as the previous screen.

When more than one screen is editing a file, changes in any screen are reflected in all other screens editing the same file. Exiting any screen without saving any changes (or explicitly discarding them) is permitted until the last screen editing the file is exited.

The **resize** command permits resizing of individual screens. Screens may be grown, shrunk or set to an absolute number of rows.

The **^W** command is used to switch between screens. Each **^W** moves to the next lower screen in the window, or to the first screen in the window if there are no lower screens.

The **bg** command ``backgrounds'' the current screen. The screen disappears from the window, and the rows it occupied are taken over by a neighboring screen. It is an error to attempt to background the only screen in the window.

The **display screens** command displays the names of the files associated with the current backgrounded screens in the window.

The **fg [file]** command ``foregrounds'' the first screen in the list of backgrounded screens that is associated with its argument. If no file argument is specified, the first screen on the list is foregrounded. Foregrounding consists of backgrounding the current screen, and replacing its space in the window with the foregrounded screen.

If the last screen in the window is exited, and there are backgrounded screens, the first screen on the list of backgrounded screens takes over the window.

7. Regular Expressions and Replacement Strings

Regular expressions are used in line addresses, as the first part of **substitute**, **global**, and **vglobal** commands, and in search patterns.

The regular expressions supported by **ex/vi** are, by default, the Basic Regular Expressions (BRE's) described in the IEEE POSIX Standard 1003.2. The **extended** option causes all regular expressions to be interpreted as the Extended Regular Expressions (ERE's) described by the same standard. (See *re_format*(7) for more information.) Generally speaking, BRE's are the Regular Expressions found in *ed*(1) and *grep*(1), and ERE's are the Regular Expressions found in *egrep*(1).

13

The following is not intended to provide a description Regular Expressions. The information here only describes strings and characters which have special meanings in the **ex/vi** version of RE's, or options which change the meanings of characters that normally have special meanings in RE's.

(1) An empty RE (e.g. "//" or "??" is equivalent to the last RE used.

(2) The construct "\<" matches the beginning of a word.

(3) The construct "\>" matches the end of a word.

(4) The character "~" matches the replacement part of the last **substitute** command.

When the **magic** option is *not* set, the only characters with special meanings are a "^" character at the beginning of an RE, a "$" character at the end of an RE, and the escaping character "\". The characters ".", "*", "[" and "~" are treated as ordinary characters unless preceded by a "\"; when preceded by a "\" they regain their special meaning.

Replacement strings are the second part of a **substitute** command.

The character "&" (or "\&" if the **magic** option is *not* set) in the replacement string stands for the text matched by the RE that is being replaced. The character "~" (or "\~" if the **magic** option is *not* set) stands for the replacement part of the previous **substitute** command.

The string "\#", where "#" is an integer value from 1 to 9, stands for the text matched by the portion of the RE enclosed in the "#"'th set of escaped parentheses, e.g. "\(" and "\)". For example, "s/abc\(.*\)def/\1/" deletes the strings "abc" and "def" from the matched pattern.

The strings "\l", "\u", "\L" and "\U" can be used to modify the case of elements in the replacement string. The string "\l" causes the next character to be converted to lowercase; the string "\u" behaves similarly, but converts to uppercase. The strings "\L" causes characters up to the end of the string or the next occurrence of the strings "\e" or "\E" to be converted to lowercase; the string "\U" behaves similarly, but converts to uppercase.

If the entire replacement pattern is "%", then the last replacement pattern is used again.

In **vi**, inserting a <control-M> into the replacement string will cause the matched line to be split into two lines at that point. (The <control-M> will be discarded.)

8. General Editor Description

When **ex** or **vi** are executed, the text of a file is read (or a temporary file is created), and then all editing changes happen with the context of the copy of the file. *No changes affect the actual file until the file is written out*, either using a write command or another command which is affected by the **autowrite** option.

All files are locked (using the *flock*(2) or *fcntl*(2) interfaces) during the edit session, to avoid inadvertently making modifications to multiple copies of the file. If a lock cannot be obtained for a file because it is locked by another process, the edit session is read-only (as if the **readonly** option or the −**R** flag had been specified). If a lock cannot be obtained for other reasons, the edit session will continue, but the file status information (see the <control->G command) will reflect this fact.

Both **ex** and **vi** are modeful editors, i.e. they have two modes, "command" mode and "text input" mode. The former is intended to permit you to enter commands which modifies already existing text. The latter is intended to permit you to enter new text. When **ex** first starts running, it is in command mode, and usually displays a prompt (see the **prompt** option for more information). The prompt is a single colon (":") character. There are three commands that switch **ex** into text input mode: **append, change** and **insert**. Once in input mode, entering a line containing only a single period (".") terminates text input mode and returns to command mode, where the prompt is redisplayed.

When **vi** first starts running, it is in command mode as well. There are eleven commands that switch **vi** into text input mode: **A, a, C, c, I, i, O, o, R, S** and **s**. Once in input mode, entering an <escape> character terminates text input mode and returns to command mode.

The following words have special meanings in both the **ex** and **vi** command descriptions:

<interrupt>
   The interrupt character is used to interrupt the current operation. Normally <control-C>, whatever character is set for the current terminal is used.

<literal next>

> The literal next character is used to escape the subsequent character from any special meaning. This character is always `<control-V>`. If the terminal is not set up to do XON/XOFF flow control, then `<control-Q>` is used to mean literal next as well.

current pathname

> The pathname of the file currently being edited by vi. When the percent character ("%") appears in a file name entered as part of an **ex** command argument, it is replaced by the current pathname. (The "%" character can be escaped by preceding it with a backslash.)

alternate pathname

> The name of the last file name mentioned in an **ex** command, or, the previous current pathname if the last file mentioned becomes the current file. When the hash mark character ("#") appears in a file name entered as part of an **ex** command argument, it is replaced by the alternate pathname. (The "#" character can be escaped by preceding it with a backslash.)

buffer

> One of a number of named areas for saving copies of text. Commands that change or delete text can save the changed or deleted text into a specific buffer, for later use. Buffers are named with a single character, preceded by a double quote, e.g. `"<character>`. Historic implementations of **ex/vi** limited `<character>` to the alphanumeric characters; **nex/nvi** permits the use of any character.
>
> The buffers named by uppercase characters are the same as buffers named by the lowercase characters, e.g. the buffer named by the English character "A" is the same as the buffer named by the character "a", with the exception that, if the buffer contents are being changed (as with a text deletion or copying command), the text is *appended* to the buffer, instead of replacing the current contents.
>
> The buffers named by the numeric characters (in English, "1" through "9"), are special, in that if at least one line is changed or deleted in the file, (or a command changes or deletes a region that crosses a line boundary) a copy of the text is placed into the numeric buffer "1", regardless of the user specifying another buffer in which to save it. Before this copy is done, the previous contents of buffer "1" are moved into buffer "2", "2" into buffer "3", and so on. The contents of buffer "9" are discarded. In **vi**, text may be explicitly stored into the numeric buffers. In this case, the buffer rotation described above occurs before the replacement of the buffer's contents. (Text cannot be explicitly stored into the numeric buffers in **ex** because of ambiguities that this would cause in the **ex** command syntax.)
>
> When a **vi** command synopsis shows both a `[buffer]` and a `[count]`, they may be presented in any order.
>
> Finally, all buffers are either "line" or "character" oriented. All **ex** commands which store text into buffers are line oriented. Some **vi** commands which store text into buffers are line oriented, and some are character oriented; the description for each applicable **vi** command notes whether text copied into buffers using the command is line or character oriented. In addition, the **vi** command **display buffers** displays the current orientation for each buffer. Generally, the only importance attached to this orientation is that if the buffer is subsequently inserted into the text, line oriented buffers create new lines for each of the lines they contain, and character oriented buffers create new lines for any lines *other* than the first and last lines they contain. The first and last lines are inserted into the text at the current cursor position, becoming part of the current line. If there is more than one line in the buffer, however, the current line itself will be split.

unnamed buffer

> The unnamed buffer is a text storage area which is used by commands that take a buffer as an argument, when no buffer is specified by the user. There is no way to explicitly reference this buffer.

13

9. Vi Description

Vi takes up the entire screen to display the edited file, except for the bottom line of the screen. The bottom line of the screen is used to enter **ex** commands, and for **vi** error and informational messages. If no other information is being displayed, the default display can show the current cursor row and cursor column, an indication of whether the file has been modified, and the current mode of the editor. See the **ruler, showdirty** and **showmode** options for more information.

Empty lines do not have any special representation on the screen, but lines on the screen that would logically come after the end of the file are displayed as a single tilde (''~'') character. To differentiate between empty lines and lines consisting of only whitespace characters, use the **list** option. Historically, implementations of vi have also displayed some lines as single asterisk (''@'') characters. These were lines that were not correctly displayed, i.e. lines on the screen that did not correspond to lines in the file, or lines that did not fit on the current screen. **Nvi** never displays lines in this fashion.

Vi is a modeful editor, i.e. it has two modes, ''command'' mode and ''text input'' mode. When **vi** first starts, it is in command mode. There are several commands that change **vi** into text input mode. The `<escape>` character is used to resolve the text input into the file, and exit back into command mode. In **vi** command mode, the cursor is always positioned on the last column of characters which take up more than one column on the screen. In **vi** text insert mode, the cursor is positioned on the first column of characters which take up more than one column on the screen.

Generally, if the cursor line and cursor column are not on the screen, then the screen is scrolled (if the target cursor is close) or repainted (if the target cursor is far away) so that the cursor is on the screen. If the screen is scrolled, it is moved a minimal amount, and the cursor line will usually appear at the top or bottom of the screen. In the screen is repainted, the cursor line will appear in the center of the screen, unless the cursor is sufficiently close to the beginning or end of the file that this is not possible. If the **leftright** option is set, the screen may be scrolled or repainted in a horizontal direction as well as in a vertical one.

A major difference between the historical **vi** presentation and **nvi** is in the scrolling and screen oriented position commands, **<control-B>**, **<control-D>**, **<control-E>**, **<control-F>**, **<control-U>**, **<control-Y>**, **H**, **L** and **M**. In historical implementations of vi, these commands acted on physical (as opposed to logical, or screen) lines. For lines that were sufficiently long in relation to the size of the screen, this meant that single line scroll commands might repaint the entire screen, scrolling or screen positioning command might not change the screen or move the cursor at all, and some lines simply could not be displayed, even though **vi** would edit the file that contained them. In **nvi**, these commands act on logical, i.e. screen lines. You are unlikely to notice any difference unless you are editing files with lines significantly longer than a screen width.

Vi keeps track of the currently ''most attractive'' cursor position. Each command description (for commands that can change the current cursor position), specifies if the cursor is set to a specific location in the line, or if it is moved to the ''most attractive cursor position''. The latter means that the cursor is moved to the cursor position that is vertically as close as possible to the current cursor position. If the current line is shorter than the cursor position **vi** would select, the cursor is positioned on the last character in the line. (If the line is empty, the cursor is positioned on the first column of the line.) If a command moves the cursor to the most attractive position, it does not alter the current cursor position, and a subsequent movement will again attempt to move the cursor to that position. Therefore, although a movement to a line shorter than the currently most attractive position will cause the cursor to move to the end of that line, a subsequent movement to a longer line will cause the cursor to move back to the most attractive position.

In addition, the $ command makes the end of each line the most attractive cursor position rather than a specific column.

Each **vi** command described below notes where the cursor ends up after it is executed. This position is described in terms of characters on the line, i.e. ''the previous character'', or, ''the last character in the line''. This is to avoid needing to continually refer to on what part of the character the cursor rests.

The following words have special meaning for **vi** commands.

previous context

The position of the cursor before the command which caused the last non-relative movement was executed. Each **vi** command described in the next section that is considered a non-relative movement is so noted. In addition, specifying *any* address to an **ex** command is considered a non-relative movement.

motion

A second **vi** command can be used as an optional trailing argument to the **vi** !, <, >, **c, d, y,** and (depending on the **tildeop** option) ˜ commands. This command indicates the end of the region of text that's affected by the command. The motion command may be either the command character repeated (in which case it means the current line) or a cursor movement command. In the latter case, the region affected by the command is from the starting or stopping cursor position which comes first in the file, to immediately before the starting or stopping cursor position which comes later in the file. Commands that operate on lines instead of using beginning and ending cursor positions operate on all of the lines that are wholly or partially in the region. In addition, some other commands become line oriented depending on where in the text they are used. The command descriptions below note these special cases.

The following commands may all be used as motion components for **vi** commands:

`<control-A>`	`<control-H>`	`<control-J>`	`<control-M>`
`<control-N>`	`<control-P>`	`<space>`	`$`
`%`	`'<character>`	`(`	`)`
`+`	`,`	`-`	`/`
`0`	`;`	`?`	`B`
`E`	`F`	`G`	`H`
`L`	`M`	`N`	`T`
`W`	`[[`	`]]`	`^`
`_`	`'<character>`	`b`	`e`
`f`	`h`	`j`	`k`
`l`	`n`	`t`	`w`
`{`	`|`	`}`	

The optional count prefix available for some of the **vi** commands that take motion commands, or the count prefix available for the **vi** commands that are used as motion components, may be included and is *always* considered part of the motion argument. For example, the commands ''c2w'' and ''2cw'' are equivalent, and the region affected by the **c** command is two words of text. In addition, if the optional count prefix is specified for both the **vi** command and its motion component, the effect is multiplicative and is considered part of the motion argument. For example, the commands ''4cw'' and ''2c2w'' are equivalent, and the region affected by the **c** command is four words of text.

count

A positive number used as an optional argument to most commands, either to give a size or a position (for display or movement commands), or as a repeat count (for commands that modify text). The count argument is always optional and defaults to 1 unless otherwise noted in the command description.

When a **vi** command synopsis shows both a `[buffer]` and `[count]`, they may be presented in any order.

bigword

A set of non-whitespace characters preceded and followed by whitespace characters or the beginning or end of the file or line.

13

Groups of empty lines (or lines containing only whitespace characters) are treated as a single big-word.

word
Generally, in languages where it is applicable, **vi** recognizes two kinds of words. First, a sequence of letters, digits and underscores, delimited at both ends by: characters other than letters, digits, or underscores; the beginning or end of a line; the beginning or end of the file. Second, a sequence of characters other than letters, digits, underscores, or whitespace characters, delimited at both ends by: a letter, digit, underscore, or whitespace character; the beginning or end of a line; the beginning or end of the file.

Groups of empty lines (or lines containing only whitespace characters) are treated as a single word.

paragraph
An area of text that begins with either the beginning of a file, an empty line, or a section boundary, and continues until either an empty line, section boundary, or the end of the file.

Groups of empty lines (or lines containing only whitespace characters) are treated as a single paragraph.

Additional paragraph boundaries can be defined using the **paragraph** option.

section
An area of text that starts with the beginning of the file or a line whose first character is an open ' ace ("{") and continues until the next section or the end of the file.

lditional section boundaries can be defined using the **sections** option.

sentence
An area of text that begins with either the beginning of the file or the first nonblank character following the previous sentence, paragraph, or section boundary and continues until the end of the file or a or a period (".") exclamation point ("!") or question mark ("?") character, followed by either an end-of-line or two whitespace characters. Any number of closing parentheses (")"), brackets ("]") or double-quote (""") characters can appear between the period, exclamation point, or question mark and the whitespace characters or end-of-line.

Groups of empty lines (or lines containing only whitespace characters) are treated as a single sentence.

10. Vi Commands

The following section describes the commands available in the command mode of the **vi** editor. In each entry below, the tag line is a usage synopsis for the command character. In addition, the final line and column the cursor rests upon, and any options which affect the command are noted.

[count] <control-A>
Search forward count times for the current word. The current word begins at the current cursor position, and extends up to the next non-word character on the current line.

The **<control-A>** command is a non-relative movement. The **<control-A>** command may be used as the motion component of other **vi** commands, in which case any text copied into a buffer is character oriented.

Line: Set to the line where the word is found.
Column: Set to the first character of the word.
Options: Affected by the **extended**, **ignorecase** and **wrapscan** options.

[count] <control-B>

Page backward `count` screens. Two lines of overlap are maintained by displaying the window starting at line (`top_line - count * window_size) + 2`, where `window_size` is the value of the **window** option. (In the case of split screens, this size is corrected to the current screen size.) It is an error if the cursor is on the first line in the file.

The **<control-B>** command is a non-relative movement.

Line: Set to the last line of text displayed on the screen.
Column: Set to the first nonblank character of the line.
Options: None.

[count] <control-D>

Scroll forward `count` lines. If `count` is not specified, scroll forward the number of lines specified by the last **<control-D>** or **<control-U>** command. If this is the first **<control-D>** or **<control-U>** command, scroll forward half the number of lines in the screen. (In the case of split screens, the default scrolling distance is corrected to half the current screen size.) This is an error if the movement is past the end of the file.

The **<control-D>** command is a non-relative movement.

Line: Set to the current line plus the number of lines scrolled.
Column: Set to the first nonblank character of the line.
Options: None.

[count] <control-E>

Scroll forward `count` lines, leaving the current line and column as is, if possible. This is an e⟩ the last line in the file is already displayed on the screen.

Line: Unchanged unless the current line scrolls off the screen, in which case it is set to the line on the screen.
Column: Unchanged unless the current line scrolls off the screen, in which case it is the most attractive cursor position.
Options: None.

[count] <control-F>

Page forward `count` screens. Two lines of overlap are maintained by displaying the window starting at line `top_line + count * window_size - 2`, where `window_size` is t⟩ the **window** option. (In the case of split screens, this size is corrected to the current scre⟩ is an error if the cursor is on the last line in the file.

The **<control-F>** command is a non-relative movement.

Line: Set to the first line on the screen.
Column: Set to the first nonblank character of the current line.
Options: None.

<control-G>

Display the file information. The information includes the current pathname, the current line, the number of total lines in the file, the current line as a percentage of the total lines in the file, if the file has been modified, was able to be locked, if the file's name has been changed, and if the edit session is read-only.

Line: Unchanged.
Column: Unchanged.
Options: None.

13

<control-H>
[count] h
>Move the cursor back count characters in the current line. This is an error if the cursor is on the first character in the line.

>The **<control-H>** and **h** commands may be used as the motion component of other **vi** commands, in which case any text copied into a buffer is character oriented.

>Line: Unchanged.
>Column: Set to the previous character, or, the first character of the line if count is greater than or equal to the number of characters before the cursor in the line.
>Options: None.

[count] <control-J>
[count] <control-N>
[count] j
>Move the cursor down count lines without changing the current column. This is an error if the movement is past the end of the file.

>The **<control-J>**, **<control-N>** and **j** commands may be used as the motion component of other **vi** commands, in which case any text copied into a buffer is line oriented.

>Line: Set to the current line plus count.
>Column: The most attractive cursor position.
>Options: None.

<control-L>
<control-R>
>Repaint the screen.

>Line: Unchanged.
>Column: Unchanged.
>Options: None.

[count] <control-M>
[count] +
>Move the cursor down count lines to the first nonblank character of that line. This is an error if the movement is past the end of the file.

>The **<control-M>** and **+** commands may be used as the motion component of other **vi** commands, in which case any text copied into a buffer is line oriented.

>Line: Set to the current line plus count.
>Column: Set to the first nonblank character of the line.
>Options: None.

[count] <control-P>
[count] k
>Move the cursor up count lines, without changing the current column. This is an error if the movement is past the beginning of the file.

>The **<control-P>** and **k** commands may be used as the motion component of other **vi** commands, in which case any text copied into a buffer is line oriented.

>Line: Set to the current line minus count.
>Column: The most attractive cursor position.

Options: None.

<control-T>

Return to the most recent tag context.

Line: Set to the context of the previous tag command.
Column: Set to the context of the previous tag command.
Options: None.

<control-U>

Scroll backward `count` lines. If `count` is not specified, scroll backward the number of lines specified by the last **<control-D>** or **<control-U>** command. If this is the first **<control-D>** or **<control-U>** command, scroll backward half the number of lines in the screen. (In the case of split screens, the default scrolling distance is corrected to half the current screen size.) This is an error if the movement is past the beginning of the file.

The **<control-U>** command is a non-relative movement.

Line: Set to the current line minus the amount scrolled.
Column: Set to the first nonblank character of the line.
Options: None.

<control-W>

Switch to the next lower screen in the window, or, to the first screen if there are no lower screens in the window.

Line: Set to the previous cursor position in the window.
Column: Set to the previous cursor position in the window.
Options: None.

<control-Y>

Scroll backward `count` lines, leaving the current line and column as is, if possible. This is an error if the first line in the file is already displayed on the screen.

Line: Unchanged unless the current line scrolls off the screen, in which case it is set to the last line of text displayed on the screen.
Column: Unchanged unless the current line scrolls off the screen, in which case it is the most attractive cursor position.
Options: None.

<control-Z>

Suspend the current editor session. If the file has been modified since it was last completely written, and the **autowrite** option is set, the file is written before the editor session is suspended. If this write fails, the editor session is not suspended.

Line: Unchanged.
Column: Unchanged.
Options: Affected by the **autowrite** option.

<escape>

Execute **ex** commands or cancel partial commands. If an **ex** command is being entered (e.g. /, ?, : or !), the command is executed. If a partial command has been entered, e.g. or the command is cancelled. Otherwise, it is an error.

Line: When an **ex** command is being executed, the current line is set as described for that command. Otherwise, unchanged.

13

Column: When an **ex** command is being executed, the current column is set as described for that
          command. Otherwise, unchanged.
Options: None.

<control-]>

Push a tag reference onto the tag stack. The tags files (see the **tags** option for more information) are
searched for a tag matching the text from the current cursor position to the next non-word character
on the current line. If a matching tag is found, the current file is discarded and the file containing the
tag reference is edited.

If the current file has been modified since it was last completely written, the command will fail.

Line: Set to the line containing the matching tag string.
Column: Set to the start of the matching tag string.
Options: Affected by the **tags** and **taglength** options.

<control-^>

Switch to the most recently edited file.

If the file has been modified since it was last completely written, and the **autowrite** option is set, the
file is written out. If this write fails, the command will fail. Otherwise, if the current file has been
modified since it was last completely written, the command will fail.

Line: Set to the line the cursor was on when the file was last edited.
Column: Set to the column the cursor was on when the file was last edited.
Options: Affected by the **autowrite** option.

[count] <space>
[count] l

Move the cursor forward `count` characters without changing the current line. This is an error if the
cursor is on the last character in the line.

The <space> and l commands may be used as the motion component of other **vi** commands, in which
case any text copied into a buffer is character oriented. In addition, these commands may be used as
the motion components of other commands when the cursor is on the last character in the line,
without error.

Line: Unchanged.
Column: Set to the current character plus the next `count` characters, or to the last character on the
          line if `count` is greater than the number of characters in the line after the current charac-
          ter.
Options: None.

[count] ! motion shell-argument(s)

Replace text with results from a shell command. Pass the lines specified by the `count` and `motion`
arguments as standard input to the program named by the **shell** option, and replace those lines with
the output (both standard error and standard output) of that command.

After the motion is entered, **vi** prompts for arguments to the shell command.

Within those arguments, "%" and "#" characters are expanded to the current and alternate pathnames, respectively. The "!" character is expanded with the command text of the previous ! or :!
commands. (Therefore, the command !! repeats the previous ! command.) The special meanings of
"%", "#" and "!" can be overridden by escaping them with a backslash. If no ! or :! command
has yet been executed, it is an error to use an unescaped "!" character. The ! command does *not*
do shell expansion on the strings provided as arguments. If any of the above expansions change the
arguments the user entered, the command is redisplayed at the bottom of the screen.

Vi then executes the program named by the **shell** option, with a −c flag followed by the arguments (which are bundled into a single argument).

The **!** command is permitted in an empty file.

If the file has been modified since it was last completely written, the **!** command will warn you.

Line: The first line of the replaced text.
Column: The first column of the replaced text.
Options: Affected by the **shell** option.

[count] # +|-|#

Increment or decrement the cursor number. If the trailing character is a +, the number is incremented by `count`. If the trailing character is a -, the number is decremented by `count`. If the trailing character is a #, the previous increment or decrement is repeated.

The format of the number (decimal, hexadecimal, and octal, and leading 0's) is retained unless the new value cannot be represented in the previous format.

Line: Unchanged.
Column: Set to the first character in the cursor word.
Options: None.

[count] $

Move the cursor to the end of a line. If `count` is specified, the cursor moves down `count - 1` lines.

It is not an error to use the **$** command when the cursor is on the last character of the line or when the line is empty.

The **$** command may be used as the motion component of other **vi** commands, in which case any text copied into a buffer is character oriented, unless the cursor is at, or before the first nonblank character in the line, in which case it is line oriented. It is not an error to use the **$** command as a motion component when the cursor is on the last character of the line, although it is an error when the line is empty.

Line: Set to the current line plus `count` minus 1.
Column: Set to the last character in the line.
Options: None.

%

Move to the matching character. The cursor moves to the parenthesis or curly brace which *matches* the parenthesis or curly brace found at the current cursor position or which is the closest one to the right of the cursor on the line. It is an error to execute the **%** command on a line without a parenthesis or curly brace. Historically, any `count` specified to the **%** command was ignored.

The **%** command is a non-relative movement. The **%** command may be used as the motion component of other **vi** commands, in which case any text copied into a buffer is character oriented, unless the starting point of the region is at or before the first nonblank character on its line, and the ending point is at or after the last nonblank character on its line, in which case it is line oriented.

Line: Set to the line containing the matching character.
Column: Set to the matching character.
Options: None.

13

&

> Repeat the previous substitution command on the current line.
>
> Historically, any `count` specified to the **&** command was ignored.
>
> Line: Unchanged.
> Column: Unchanged if the cursor was on the last character of the line, otherwise, set to the first
>   nonblank character of the line.
> Options: Affected by the **edcompatible, extended, ignorecase** and **magic** options.

´<character>
`<character>

> Return to a context marked by the character `<character>`. If `<character>` is the "'" or "'"
> character, return to the previous context. If `<character>` is any other character, return to the con-
> text marked by that character (see the **m** command for more information). If the command is the ´
> command, only the line value is restored, and the cursor is placed on the first nonblank character of
> that line. If the command is the ` command, both the line and column values are restored.
>
> It is an error if the context no longer exists because of line deletion. (Contexts follow lines that are
> moved, or which are deleted and then restored.)
>
> The ´ and ` commands are both non-relative movements. They may be used as a motion component
> for other **vi** commands. For the ´ command, any text copied into a buffer is line oriented. For the `
> command, any text copied into a buffer is character oriented, unless it both starts and stops at the first
> character of the line, in which case it is line oriented. In addition, when using the ` command as a
> motion component, commands which move backward and started at the first character in the line, or
> move forward and ended at the first character in the line, are corrected to the last character of the
> starting and ending lines, respectively.
>
> Line: Set to the line from the context.
> Column: Set to the first nonblank character in the line, for the ´ command, and set to the context's
>   column for the ` command.
> Options: None.

[count] (

> Back up `count` sentences.
>
> The (command is a non-relative movement. The (command may be used as the motion component
> of other **vi** commands, in which case any text copied into a buffer is character oriented, unless the
> starting and stopping points of the region are the first column of the line, in which case it is line
> oriented. In the latter case, the stopping point of the region is adjusted to be the end of the line
> immediately before it, and not the original cursor position.
>
> Line: Set to the line containing the beginning of the sentence.
> Column: Set to the first nonblank character of the sentence.
> Options: None.

[count])

> Move forward `count` sentences.
>
> The) command is a non-relative movement. The) command may be used as the motion component
> of other **vi** commands, in which case any text copied into a buffer is character oriented, unless the
> starting point of the region is the first column of the line, in which case it is line oriented. In the
> latter case, if the stopping point of the region is also the first character in the line, it is adjusted to be
> the end of the line immediately before it.

13

Line: Set to the line containing the beginning of the sentence.
Column: Set to the first nonblank character of the sentence.
Options: None.

[count] ,

Reverse find character count times. Reverse the last **F**, **f**, **T** or **t** command, searching the other way in the line, count times.

The , command may be used as the motion component of other **vi** commands, in which case any text copied into a buffer is character oriented.

Line: Unchanged.
Column: Set to the searched-for character.
Options: None.

[count] –

Move to first nonblank of the previous line, count times.

This is an error if the movement is past the start of the file.

The - command may be used as the motion component of other **vi** commands, in which case any text copied into a buffer is line oriented.

Line: Set to the current line minus count.
Column: Set to the first nonblank character of the line.
Options: None.

[count] .

Repeat the last **vi** command that modified text. The repeated command may be a command and motion component combination. If count is specified, it replaces *both* the count specified for the repeated command, and, if applicable, for the repeated motion component. If count is not specified, the counts originally specified to the command being repeated are used again.

As a special case, if the . command is executed immediately after the **u** command, the change log is rolled forward or backward, depending on the action of the **u** command.

Line: Set as described for the repeated command.
Column: Set as described for the repeated command.
Options: None.

13

/RE<carriage-return>
/RE/ [offset]<carriage-return>
?RE<carriage-return>
?RE? [offset]<carriage-return>
N
n

Search forward or backward for a regular expression. The commands beginning with a slash ("/") character are forward searches, the commands beginning with a question mark ("?") are backward searches. **Vi** prompts with the leading character on the last line of the screen for a string. It then searches forward or backward in the file for the next occurrence of the string, which is interpreted as a Basic Regular Expression.

The **/** and **?** commands are non-relative movements. They may be used as the motion components of other **vi** commands, in which case any text copied into a buffer is character oriented, unless the search started and ended on the first column of a line, in which case it is line oriented. In addition, forward searches ending at the first column of a line, and backward searches beginning at the first column of the line, are corrected to begin or end at the last column of the previous line. (Note, forward and backward searches can occur for both **/** and **?** commands, if the **wrapscan** option is set.)

If an offset from the matched line is specified (i.e. a trailing "/" or "?" character is followed by a signed offset), the buffer will always be line oriented (e.g. "`/string/+0`" will always guarantee a line orientation).

The **n** command repeats the previous search.

The **N** command repeats the previous search, but in the reverse direction.

Missing RE's (e.g. "`//<carriage-return>`", "`/<carriage-return>`", "`??<carriage-return>`", or "`?<carriage-return>`" search for the last search RE, in the indicated direction.

Searches may be interrupted using the `<interrupt>` character.

Line: Set to the line in which the match occurred.
Column: Set to the first character of the matched string.
Options: Affected by the **edcompatible**, **extended**, **ignorecase**, **magic**, and **wrapscan** options.

0

Move to the first character in the current line. It is not an error to use the **0** command when the cursor is on the first character of the line,

The **0** command may be used as the motion component of other **vi** commands, in which case it is an error if the cursor is on the first character of the line.

Line: Unchanged.
Column: Set to the first character in the line.
Options: None.

:

Execute an ex command. **Vi** prompts for an **ex** command on the last line of the screen, using a colon (":") character. The command is terminated by a `<carriage-return>`, `<newline>` or `<escape>` character; all of these characters may be escaped by using a `<literal next>` character. The command is then executed.

If the **ex** command writes to the screen, **vi** will prompt the user for a `<carriage-return>` before continuing when the **ex** command finishes. Large amounts of output from the **ex** command will be paged for the user, and the user prompted for a `<carriage-return>` or `<space>` key to continue. In some cases, a quit (normally a "q" character) or `<interrupt>` may be entered to interrupt the **ex** command.

When the **ex** command finishes, and the user is prompted to resume visual mode, it is also possible to enter another "`:`" character followed by another **ex** command.

Line: The current line is set as described for the **ex** command.
Column: The current column is set as described for the **ex** command.
Options: None.

[count] ;

Repeat the last character find **count** times. The last character find is one of the **F**, **f**, **T** or **t** commands.

The **;** command may be used as the motion component of other **vi** commands, in which case any text copied into a buffer is character oriented.

Line: Unchanged.
Column: Set to the searched-for character.
Options: None.

[count] < motion
[count] > motion

Shift lines left or right. Shift the number of lines in the region specified by the motion component, times `count`, left (for the < command) or right (for the > command) by the number of columns specified by the **shiftwidth** option. Only whitespace characters are deleted when shifting left; once the first column of the line contains a nonblank character, the **shift** will succeed, but the line will not be modified.

Line: Unchanged.
Column: Set to the first nonblank character of the line.
Options: Affected by the **shiftwidth** option.

@ buffer

Execute a named buffer. Execute the named buffer as **vi** commands. The buffer may include **ex** commands, too, but they must be expressed as a : command. If the buffer is line oriented, `<new-line>` characters are logically appended to each line of the buffer. If the buffer is character oriented, `<newline>` characters are logically appended to all but the last line in the buffer.

If the buffer name is "@", or "*", then the last buffer executed shall be used. It is an error to specify "@@" or "**" if there were no buffer previous executions. The text of a macro may contain an **@** command, and it is possible to create infinite loops in this manner. (The `<interrupt>` character may be used to interrupt the loop.)

Line: The current line is set as described for the command(s).
Column: The current column is set as described for the command(s).
Options: None.

[count] A

Enter input mode, appending the text after the end of the line. If `count` is specified, the text is repeatedly input `count - 1` more times after input mode is exited.

Line: Set to the last line upon which characters were entered.
Column: Set to the last character entered.
Options: Affected by the **altwerase, autoindent, beautify, showmatch, ttywerase** and **wrapmargin** options.

[count] B

Move backward `count` bigwords. Move the cursor backward to the beginning of a bigword by repeating the following algorithm: if the current position is at the beginning of a bigword or the character at the current position cannot be part of a bigword, move to the first character of the preceding bigword. Otherwise, move to the first character of the bigword at the current position. If no preceding bigword exists on the current line, move to the first character of the last bigword on the first preceding line that contains a bigword.

The **B** command may be used as the motion component of other **vi** commands, in which case any text copied into a buffer is character oriented.

Line: Set to the line containing the word selected.
Column: Set to the first character of the word selected.
Options: None.

[buffer] [count] C

Change text from the current position to the end-of-line. If count is specified, the input text replaces from the current position to the end-of-line, plus count - 1 subsequent lines.

Line: Set to the last line upon which characters were entered.
Column: Set to the last character entered.
Options: Affected by the **altwerase**, **autoindent**, **beautify**, **showmatch**, **ttywerase** and **wrapmargin** options.

[buffer] D

Delete text from the current position to the end-of-line.

It is not an error to execute the **D** command on an empty line.

Line: Unchanged.
Column: Set to the character before the current character, or, column 1 if the cursor was on column 1.
Options: None.

[count] E

Move forward count end-of-bigwords. Move the cursor forward to the end of a bigword by repeating the following algorithm: if the current position is the end of a bigword or the character at that position cannot be part of a bigword, move to the last character of the following bigword. Otherwise, move to the last character of the bigword at the current position. If no succeeding bigword exists on the current line, move to the last character of the first bigword on the next following line that contains a bigword.

The **E** command may be used as the motion component of other **vi** commands, in which case any text copied into a buffer is character oriented.

Line: Set to the line containing the word selected.
Column: Set to the last character of the word selected.
Options: None.

[count] F <character>

Search count times backward through the current line for <character>.

The **F** command may be used as the motion component of other **vi** commands, in which case any text copied into a buffer is character oriented.

Line: Unchanged.
Column: Set to the searched-for character.
Options: None.

[count] G

Move to line count, or the last line of the file if count not specified.

The **G** command is a non-relative movement. The **G** command may be used as the motion component of other **vi** commands, in which case any text copied into a buffer is line oriented.

Line: Set to count, if specified, otherwise, the last line.
Column: Set to the first nonblank character of the line.
Options: None.

[count] H

Move to the screen line count - 1 lines below the top of the screen.

The **H** command is a non-relative movement. The **H** command may be used as the motion component of other **vi** commands, in which case any text copied into a buffer is line oriented.

Line: Set to the line count - 1 lines below the top of the screen.
Column: Set to the first nonblank character of the *screen* line.
Options: None.

[count] I

Enter input mode, inserting the text at the beginning of the line. If count is specified, the text input is repeatedly input count - 1 more times.

Line: Set to the last line upon which characters were entered.
Column: Set to the last character entered.
Options: None.

[count] J

Join lines. If count is specified, count lines are joined; a minimum of two lines are always joined, regardless of the value of count.

If the current line ends with a whitespace character, all whitespace is stripped from the next line. Otherwise, if the next line starts with a open parenthesis ("(") do nothing. Otherwise, if the current line ends with a question mark ("?"), period (".") or exclamation point ("!"), insert two spaces. Otherwise, insert a single space.

It is not an error to join lines past the end of the file, i.e. lines that do not exist.

Line: Unchanged.
Column: Set to the character after the last character of the next-to-last joined line.
Options: None.

[count] L

Move to the screen line count - 1 lines above the bottom of the screen.

The **L** command is a non-relative movement. The **L** command may be used as the motion component of other **vi** commands, in which case any text copied into a buffer is line oriented.

Line: Set to the line count - 1 lines above the bottom of the screen.
Column: Set to the first nonblank character of the *screen* line.
Options: None.

M

Move to the screen line in the middle of the screen.

The **M** command is a non-relative movement. The **M** command may be used as the motion component of other **vi** commands, in which case any text copied into a buffer is line oriented.

Historically, any count specified to the **M** command was ignored.

Line: Set to the line in the middle of the screen.
Column: Set to the first nonblank character of the *screen* line.
Options: None.

[count] O

Enter input mode, appending text in a new line above the current line. If count is specified, the text input is repeatedly input count - 1 more times.

Historically, any count specified to the **O** command was ignored.

13

Line: Set to the last line upon which characters were entered.
Column: Set to the last character entered.
Options: Affected by the **altwerase, autoindent, beautify, showmatch, ttywerase** and **wrapmargin** options.

[buffer] P
Insert text from a buffer. Text from the buffer (the unnamed buffer by default) is inserted before the current column or, if the buffer is line oriented, before the current line.

Line: Set to the lowest numbered line insert, if the buffer is line oriented, otherwise unchanged.
Column: Set to the first nonblank character of the appended text, if the buffer is line oriented, otherwise, the last character of the appended text.
Options: None.

Q

Exit **vi** (or visual) mode and switch to **ex** mode.

Line: Unchanged.
Column: No longer relevant.
Options: None.

[count] R
Enter input mode, replacing the characters in the current line. If count is specified, the text input is repeatedly input count - 1 more times.

If the end of the current line is reached, no more characters are replaced and any further characters input are appended to the line.

Line: Set to the last line upon which characters were entered.
Column: Set to the last character entered.
Options: Affected by the **altwerase, autoindent, beautify, showmatch, ttywerase** and **wrapmargin** options.

[buffer] [count] S
Substitute count lines.

Line: Set to the last line upon which characters were entered.
Column: Set to the last character entered.
Options: Affected by the **altwerase, autoindent, beautify, showmatch, ttywerase** and **wrapmargin** options.

[count] T <character>
Search backward, count times, through the current line for the character *after* the specified <character>.

The **T** command may be used as the motion component of other **vi** commands, in which case any text copied into a buffer is character oriented.

Line: Unchanged.
Column: Set to the character *after* the searched-for character.
Options: None.

U

Restore the current line to its state before the cursor last moved to it.

Line: Unchanged.

Column: The first character in the line.
Options: None.

[count] W

Move forward `count` bigwords. Move the cursor forward to the beginning of a bigword by repeating the following algorithm: if the current position is within a bigword or the character at that position cannot be part of a bigword, move to the first character of the next bigword. If no subsequent
bigword exists on the current line, move to the first character of the first bigword on the first following line that contains a bigword.

The **W** command may be used as the motion component of other **vi** commands, in which case any
text copied into a buffer is character oriented.

Line: The line containing the word selected.
Column: The first character of the word selected.
Options: None.

[buffer] [count] X

Delete `count` characters before the cursor. If the number of characters to be deleted is greater than
or equal to the number of characters to the beginning of the line, all of the characters before the
current cursor position, to the beginning of the line, are deleted.

Line: Unchanged.
Column: Set to the current character minus `count`, or the first character if count is greater than the
         number of characters in the line before the cursor.
Options: None.

[buffer] [count] Y

Copy (or ''yank'') `count` lines into the specified buffer.

Line: Unchanged.
Column: Unchanged.
Options: None.

ZZ

Write the file and exit **vi**. The file is only written if it has been modified since the last complete write
of the file to any file.

The **ZZ** command will exit the editor after writing the file, if there are no further files to edit. Entering two ''quit'' commands (i.e. **wq**, **quit**, **xit** or **ZZ**) in a row will override this check and the editor
will exit, ignoring any files that have not yet been edited.

Line: Unchanged.
Column: Unchanged.
Options: None.

[count] [[

Back up `count` section boundaries.

The [[command is a non-relative movement. The [[command may be used as the motion component of other **vi** commands, in which case any text copied into a buffer is character oriented, unless
the starting position is column 0, in which case it is line oriented.

This is an error if the cursor is on the first line of the file.

Line: Set to the previous line that is `count` section boundaries back, or the first line of the file
         if no more section boundaries exist preceding the current line.

Column: Set to the first nonblank character of the line.
Options: Affected by the **sections** option.

[count]]]
Move forward `count` section boundaries.

The]] command is a non-relative movement. The]] command may be used as the motion component of other **vi** commands, in which case any text copied into a buffer is character oriented, unless
the starting position is column 0, in which case it is line oriented.

This is an error if the cursor is on the first line of the file.

Line: Set to the line that is `count` section boundaries forward, or to the last line of the file if no
            more section boundaries exist following the current line.
Column: Set to the first nonblank character of the line.
Options: Affected by the **sections** option.

^
Move to first nonblank character on the current line.

The ^ command may be used as the motion component of other **vi** commands, in which case any text
copied into a buffer is character oriented.

Line: Unchanged.
Column: Set to the first nonblank character of the current line.
Options: None.

[count] _
Move down `count` - 1 lines, to the first nonblank character. The _ command may be used as the
motion component of other **vi** commands, in which case any text copied into a buffer is line oriented.

It is not an error to execute the _ command when the cursor is on the first character in the line.

Line: The current line plus `count` - 1.
Column: The first nonblank character of the line.
Options: None.

[count] a
Enter input mode, appending the text after the cursor. If `count` is specified, the text input is repeatedly input `count` - 1 more times.

Line: Set to the last line upon which characters were entered.
Column: Set to the last character entered.
Options: Affected by the **altwerase, autoindent, beautify, showmatch, ttywerase** and **wrapmar-
            gin** options.

[count] b
Move backward `count` words. Move the cursor backward to the beginning of a word by repeating
the following algorithm: if the current position is at the beginning of a word, move to the first character of the preceding word. Otherwise, the current position moves to the first character of the word at
the current position. If no preceding word exists on the current line, move to the first character of the
last word on the first preceding line that contains a word.

The **b** command may be used as the motion component of other **vi** commands, in which case any text
copied into a buffer is character oriented.

Line: Set to the line containing the word selected.
Column: Set to the first character of the word selected.
Options: None.

[buffer] [count] c motion

Change a region of text. If only part of a single line is affected, then the last character being changed is marked with a "$". Otherwise, the region of text is deleted, and input mode is entered.

If count is specified, it is applied to the motion.

Line: Set to the last line upon which characters were entered.
Column: Set to the last character entered.
Options: Affected by the **altwerase**, **autoindent**, **beautify**, **showmatch**, **ttywerase** and **wrapmargin** options.

[buffer] [count] d motion

Delete a region of text. If count is specified, it is applied to the motion.

Line: Set to the line where the region starts.
Column: Set to the first character in the line after the last character in the region. If no such character exists, set to the last character before the region.
Options: None.

[count] e

Move forward count end-of-words. Move the cursor forward to the end of a word by repeating the following algorithm: if the current position is the end of a word, move to the last character of the following word. Otherwise, move to the last character of the word at the current position. If no succeeding word exists on the current line, move to the last character of the first word on the next following line that contains a word.

The **e** command may be used as the motion component of other **vi** commands, in which case any text copied into a buffer is character oriented.

Line: Set to the line containing the word selected.
Column: Set to the last character of the word selected.
Options: None.

[count] f <character>

Search forward, count times, through the rest of the current line for <character>.

The **f** command may be used as the motion component of other **vi** commands, in which case any text copied into a buffer is character oriented.

Line: Unchanged.
Column: Set to the searched-for character.
Options: None.

[count] i

Enter input mode, inserting the text before the cursor. If count is specified, the text input is repeatedly input count - 1 more times.

Line: Set to the last line upon which characters were entered.
Column: Set to the last character entered.
Options: Affected by the **altwerase**, **autoindent**, **beautify**, **showmatch**, **ttywerase** and **wrapmargin** options.

13

m <character>

> Save the current context (line and column) as `<character>`. The exact position is referred to by "`'<character>`". The line is referred to by "`'<character>`".
>
> Historically, `<character>` was restricted to lower-case letters only, **nvi** permits the use of any character.
>
> Line: Unchanged.
> Column: Unchanged.
> Options: None.

[count] o

> Enter input mode, appending text in a new line under the current line. If `count` is specified, the text input is repeatedly input `count - 1` more times.
>
> Historically, any `count` specified to the **o** command was ignored.
>
> Line: Set to the last line upon which characters were entered.
> Column: Set to the last character entered.
> Options: Affected by the **altwerase, autoindent, beautify, showmatch, ttywerase** and **wrapmargin** options.

[buffer] p

> Append text from a buffer. Text from the buffer (the unnamed buffer by default) is appended after the current column or, if the buffer is line oriented, after the current line.
>
> Line: Set to the first line appended, if the buffer is line oriented, otherwise unchanged.
> Column: Set to the first nonblank character of the appended text if the buffer is line oriented, otherwise, the last character of the appended text.
> Options: None.

[count] r <character>

> Replace characters. The next `count` characters in the line are replaced with `<character>`. Replacing characters with `<newline>` characters results in creating new, empty lines into the file.
>
> If `<character>` is `<escape>`, the command is cancelled.
>
> Line: Unchanged unless the replacement character is a `<newline>`, in which case it is set to the current line plus `count - 1`.
> Column: Set to the last character replaced, unless the replacement character is a `<newline>`, in which case the cursor is in column 1 of the last line inserted.
> Options: None.

[buffer] [count] s

> Substitute `count` characters in the current line starting with the current character.
>
> Line: Set to the last line upon which characters were entered.
> Column: Set to the last character entered.
> Options: Affected by the **altwerase, autoindent, beautify, showmatch, ttywerase** and **wrapmargin** options.

[count] t <character>

> Search forward, `count` times, through the current line for the character immediately *before* `<character>`.
>
> The **t** command may be used as the motion component of other **vi** commands, in which case any text copied into a buffer is character oriented.

Line: Unchanged.

Column: Set to the character *before* the searched-for character.

Options: None.

u

Undo the last change made to the file. If repeated, the **u** command alternates between these two states, and is its own inverse. When used after an insert that inserted text on more than one line, the lines are saved in the numeric buffers.

The **.** command, when used immediately after the **u** command, causes the change log to be rolled forward or backward, depending on the action of the **u** command.

Line: Set to the position of the first line changed, if the reversal affects only one line or represents an addition or change; otherwise, the line preceding the deleted text.

Column: Set to the cursor position before the change was made.

Options: None.

[count] w

Move forward `count` words. Move the cursor forward to the beginning of a word by repeating the following algorithm: if the current position is at the beginning of a word, move to the first character of the next word. If no subsequent word exists on the current line, move to the first character of the first word on the first following line that contains a word.

The **w** command may be used as the motion component of other **vi** commands, in which case any text copied into a buffer is character oriented.

Line: Set to the line containing the word selected.

Column: Set to the first character of the word selected.

Options: None.

[buffer] [count] x

Delete `count` characters. The deletion is at the current character position. If the number of characters to be deleted is greater than or equal to the number of characters to the end of the line, all of the characters from the current cursor position to the end of the line are deleted.

Line: Unchanged.

Column: Unchanged unless the last character in the line is deleted and the cursor is not already on the first character in the line, in which case it is set to the previous character.

Options: None.

[buffer] [count] y motion

Copy (or "yank") a text region specified by the `count` and motion into a buffer. If `count` is specified, it is applied to the `motion`.

Line: Unchanged, unless the region covers more than a single line, in which case it is set to the line where the region starts.

Column: Unchanged, unless the region covers more than a single line, in which case it is set to the character were the region starts.

Options: None.

[count1] z [count2] -|.|+|^|<carriage-return>

Redraw, optionally repositioning and resizing the screen. Redraw the screen with a window `count2` lines long, containing line `count1` placed as specified by the following character: "+" or `<carriage-return>` specifies the top of the screen, "." specifies the center of the screen, and "−" or "^" specifies the bottom of the screen.

If `count1` is not specified, it defaults to the current line, and the action is as described above except for the ''^'' and ''+'' characters. The ''^'' character displays the screen before the current screen, and the ''+'' character displays the screen after the current screen, similarly to the **<control-B>** and **<control-L>** commands.

If count2 is not specified, it defaults to the current window size.

Line: Set to count1, if specified, otherwise unchanged.
Column: Set to the first nonblank character of the line.
Options: None.

[count] {
       Move backward count paragraphs.

The **{** command is a non-relative movement. The **{** command may be used as the motion component of other **vi** commands, in which case any text copied into a buffer is character oriented, unless the starting character is the first character on its line, in which case it is line oriented.

Line: Set to the line containing the beginning of the previous paragraph.
Column: Set to the first nonblank character of the line.
Options: Affected by the **paragraph** option.

[count] |
       Move to a specific *column* position on the current line.

The **|** command may be used as the motion component of other **vi** commands, in which case any text copied into a buffer is character oriented. It is an error to use the **|** command as a motion component and for the cursor not to move.

Line: Unchanged.
Column: Set to the character occupying the column position identified by count, if the position
           exists in the line. If the column length of the current line is less than count, the cursor is
           moved to the last character in the line.
Options: None.

[count] }
       Move forward count paragraphs.

The **}** command is a non-relative movement. The **}** command may be used as the motion component of other **vi** commands, in which case any text copied into a buffer is character oriented, unless the starting character is at or before any nonblank characters in its line, in which case it is line oriented.

Line: Set to the line containing the beginning of the next paragraph.
Column: Set to the first nonblank character of the line.
Options: Affected by the **paragraph** option.

[count] ˜
       Reverse the case of the next count character(s). This is the historic semantic for the ˜ command
       and it is only in effect if the **tildeop** option is not set.

Lowercase alphabetic characters are changed to uppercase, and uppercase characters are changed to lowercase. No other characters are affected.

Historically, the ˜ command did not take an associated count, nor did it move past the end of the current line. As it had no associated motion it was difficult to change the case of large blocks of text. In **nvi**, if the cursor is on the last character of a line, and there are more lines in the file, the cursor moves to the next line.

It is not an error to specify a count larger than the number of characters between the cursor and the end of the file.

Line: Set to the line of the character after `count` characters, or, end of file.
Column: Set to the character after `count` characters, or, end-of-file.
Options: Affected by the **tildeop** option.

[count] ˜ motion

Reverse the case of the characters in a text region specified by the `count` and `motion`. Only in effect if the **tildeop** option is set.

Lowercase characters are changed to uppercase, and uppercase characters are changed to lowercase. No other characters are affected.

Line: Set to the line of the character after the last character in the region.
Column: Set to the character after the last character in the region.
Options: Affected by the **tildeop** option.

<interrupt>

Interrupt the current operation. Many of the potentially long-running **vi** commands may be interrupted using the terminal interrupt character. These operations include searches, file reading and writing, filter operations and map character expansion. Interrupts are also enabled when running commands outside of **vi**.

If the `<interrupt>` character is used to interrupt while entering an **ex** command, the command is aborted, the cursor returns to its previous position, and **vi** remains in command mode.

Generally, if the `<interrupt>` character is used to interrupt any operation, any changes made before the interrupt are left in place.

Line: Dependent on the operation being interrupted.
Column: Dependent on the operation being interrupted.
Options: None.

11. Vi Text Input Commands

The following section describes the commands available in the text input mode of the **vi** editor.

Historically, **vi** implementations only permitted the characters inserted on the current line to be erased. In addition, only the `<control-D>` erase character and the ''0`<control-D>`'' and ''ˆ`<control-D>`'' erase strings could erase autoindent characters. This implementation permits erasure to continue past the beginning of the current line, and back to where text input mode was entered. In addition, autoindent characters may be erased using the standard erase characters. For the line and word erase characters, reaching the autoindent characters forms a ''soft'' boundary, denoting the end of the current word or line erase. Repeating the word or line erase key will erase the autoindent characters.

Historically, **vi** always used `<control-H>` and `<control-W>` as character and word erase characters, respectively, regardless of the current terminal settings. This implementation accepts, in addition to these two characters, the current terminal characters for those operations.

<nul>

If the first character of the input is a `<nul>`, the previous input is replayed, as if just entered.

<control-D>

If the previous character on the line was an autoindent character, erase it. Otherwise, if the user is entering the first character in the line, `<control-D>` is ignored. Otherwise, a literal `<control-D>` character is entered.

^<control-D>
>   If the previous character on the line was an autoindent character, erase all of the autoindent characters on the line. In addition, the autoindent level is reset to 0.

0<control-D>
>   If the previous character on the line was an autoindent character, erase all of the autoindent characters on the line.

<control-T>
>   Insert sufficient `<tab>` and `<space>` characters to move the cursor forward to a column immediately after the next column which is an even multiple of the **shiftwidth** option.
>
>   Historically, **vi** did not permit the `<control-T>` command to be used unless the cursor was at the first column of a new line or it was preceded only by autoindent characters. **Nvi** permits it to be used at any time during insert mode.

<erase>
<control-H>
>   Erase the last character.

<literal next>
>   Quote the next character. The next character will not be mapped (see the **map** command for more information) or interpreted specially. A carat ("^") character will be displayed immediately as a placeholder, but will be replaced by the next character.

<escape>
>   Resolve all text input into the file, and return to command mode.

<line erase>
>   Erase the current line.

<control-W>
<word erase>
>   Erase the last word. The definition of word is dependent on the **altwerase** and **ttywerase** options.

<control-X>[0-9A-Fa-f]*
>   Insert a character with the specified hexadecimal value into the text.

<interrupt>
>   Interrupt text input mode, returning to command mode. If the `<interrupt>` character is used to interrupt inserting text into the file, it is as if the `<escape>` character was used; all text input up to the interruption is resolved into the file.

12. Ex Addressing

Addressing in **ex** (and when **ex** commands are executed from **vi**) relates to the current line. In general, the current line is the last line affected by a command. The exact effect on the current line is discussed under the description of each command. When the file contains no lines, the current line is zero.

Addresses are constructed by one or more of the following methods:

(1)   The address ". " refers to the current line.

(2)   The address "$" refers to the last line of the file.

(3)   The address "N", where N is a positive number, refers to the N-th line of the file.

(4)   The address "`'<character>`" or "`'<character>`" refers to the line marked with the name `<character>`. (See the **k** or **m** commands for more information on how to mark lines.)

(5)   A regular expression (RE) enclosed by slashes ("`/`") is an address, and it refers to the first line found by searching forward from the line *after* the current line toward the end of the file, and stopping at the first line containing a string matching the RE. (The trailing slash can be omitted at the end of the command line.)

If no RE is specified, i.e. the pattern is "`//`", the last RE used in any command is used in the search.

If the **extended** option is set, the RE is handled as an extended RE, not a basic RE. If the **wrapscan** option is set, the search wraps around to the beginning of the file and continues up to and including the current line, so that the entire file is searched.

The form "`\/`" is accepted for historic reasons, and is identical to "`//`".

(6)   An RE enclosed in question marks ("`?`") addresses the first line found by searching backward from the line *preceding* the current line, toward the beginning of the file and stopping at the first line containing a string matching the RE. (The trailing question mark can be omitted at the end of a command line.)

If no RE is specified, i.e. the pattern is "`??`", the last RE used in any command is used in the search.

If the **extended** option is set, the RE is handled as an extended RE, not a basic RE. If the **wrapscan** option is set, the search wraps around from the beginning of the file to the end of the file and continues up to and including the current line, so that the entire file is searched.

The form "`\?`" is accepted for historic reasons, and is identical to "`??`".

(7)   An address followed by a plus sign ("`+`") or a minus sign ("`-`") followed by a number is an offset address and refers to the address plus (or minus) the indicated number of lines. If the address is omitted, the addition or subtraction is done with respect to the current line.

(8)   An address of "`+`" or "`-`" followed by a number is an offset from the current line. For example, "`-5`" is the same as "`.-5`".

(9)   An address ending with "`+`" or "`-`" has 1 added to or subtracted from the address, respectively. As a consequence of this rule and of the previous rule, the address "`-`" refers to the line preceding the current line. Moreover, trailing "`+`" and "`-`" characters have a cumulative effect. For example, "`++-++`" refers to the current line plus 3.

(10) A percent sign ("`%`") is equivalent to the address range "`1,$`".

Ex commands require zero, one, or two addresses. It is an error to specify an address to a command which requires zero addresses.

If the user provides more than the expected number of addresses to any **ex** command, the first addresses specified are discarded. For example, "`1,2,3,5`"print prints lines 3 through 5, because the **print** command only takes two addresses.

The addresses in a range are separated from each other by a comma ("`,`") or a semicolon ("`;`"). In the latter case, the current line ("`.`") is set to the first address, and only then is the second address calculated. This feature can be used to determine the starting line for forward and backward searches (see rules (5) and (6) above). The second address of any two-address sequence corresponds to a line that follows, in the file, the line corresponding to the first address. The first address must be less than or equal to the second address. The first address must be greater than or equal to the first line of the file, and the last address must be less than or equal to the last line of the file.

13

13. Ex Description

The following words have special meanings for **ex** commands.

<eof>

The end-of-file character is used to scroll the screen in the **ex** editor. This character is normally `<control-D>`, however, whatever character is set for the current terminal is used.

line

A single-line address, given in any of the forms described in the section entitled "**Ex Addressing**". The default for `line` is the current line.

range

A line, or a pair of line addresses, separated by a comma or semicolon. (See the section entitled "**Ex Addressing**" for more information.) The default for range is the current line *only*, i.e. "`.,.`". A percent sign ("`%`") stands for the range "`1,$`". The starting address must be less than, or equal to, the ending address.

count

A positive integer, specifying the number of lines to be affected by the command; the default is 1. Generally, a count past the end-of-file may be specified, e.g. the command "`p 3000`" in a 10 line file is acceptable, and will print from the current line through the last line in the file.

flags

One or more of the characters "`#`", "`p`", and "`l`". When a command that accepts these flags completes, the addressed line(s) are written out as if by the corresponding **#, l** or **p** commands. In addition, any number of "`+`" or "`−`" characters can be specified before, after, or during the flags, in which case the line written is not necessarily the one affected by the command, but rather the line addressed by the offset address specified. The default for `flags` is none.

file

A pattern used to derive a pathname; the default is the current file. File names are subjected to normal *sh*(1) word expansions.

Anywhere a file name is specified, it is also possible to use the special string "`/tmp`". This will be replaced with a temporary file name which can be used for temporary work, e.g. "`:e /tmp`" creates and edits a new file.

If both a count and a range are specified for commands that use either, the starting line for the command is the *last* line addressed by the range, and `count-` subsequent lines are affected by the command, e.g. the command "`2,3p4`" prints out lines 3, 4, 5 and 6.

When only a line or range is specified, with no command, the implied command is either a **list**, **number** or **print** command. The command used is the most recent of the three commands to have been used (including any use as a flag). If none of these commands have been used before, the **print** command is the implied command. When no range or count is specified and the command line is a blank line, the current line is incremented by 1 and then the current line is displayed.

Zero or more whitespace characters may precede or follow the addresses, count, flags, or command name. Any object following a command name (such as buffer, file, etc.), that begins with an alphabetic character, should be separated from the command name by at least one whitespace character.

Any character, including `<carriage-return>`, "`%`" and "`#`" retain their literal value when preceded by a backslash.

14. Ex Commands

The following section describes the commands available in the **ex** editor. In each entry below, the tag line is a usage synopsis for the command.

Each command can be entered as the abbreviation (those characters in the synopsis command word preceding the "[" character), the full command (all characters shown for the command word, omitting the "[" and "]" characters), or any leading subset of the full command down to the abbreviation. For example, the args command (shown as "ar[gs]" in the synopsis) can be entered as "ar", "arg" or "args".

Each **ex** command described below notes the new current line after it is executed, as well as any options that affect the command.

A comment. Command lines beginning with the double-quote character ("""") are ignored. This permits comments in editor scripts and startup files.

<end-of-file>

Scroll the screen. Write the next N lines, where N is the value of the **scroll** option. The command is the end-of-file terminal character, which may be different on different terminals. Traditionally, it is the <control-D> key.

Historically, the **eof** command ignored any preceding count, and the <end-of-file> character was ignored unless it was entered as the first character of the command. This implementation treats it as a command *only* if entered as the first character of the command line, and otherwise treats it as any other character.

Line: Set to the last line written.
Options: None.

! argument(s)
[range]! argument(s)

Execute a shell command, or filter lines through a shell command. In the first synopsis, the remainder of the line after the "!" character is passed to the program named by the **shell** option, as a single argument.

Within the rest of the line, "%" and "#" are expanded into the current and alternate pathnames, respectively. The character "!" is expanded with the command text of the previous ! command. (Therefore, the command !! repeats the previous ! command.) The special meanings of "%", "#", and "!" can be overridden by escaping them with a backslash. If no ! or :! command has yet been executed, it is an error to use an unescaped "!" character. The ! command does *not* do shell expansion on the strings provided as arguments. If any of the above expansions change the command the user entered, the command is redisplayed at the bottom of the screen.

Ex then executes the program named by the **shell** option, with a −c flag followed by the arguments (which are bundled into a single argument).

The ! command is permitted in an empty file.

If the file has been modified since it was last completely written, the command will warn you.

A single "!" character is displayed when the command completes.

In the second form of the ! command, the remainder of the line after the "!" is passed to the program named by the **shell** option, as described above. The specified lines are passed to the program as standard input, and the standard and standard error output of the program replace the original lines.

Line: Unchanged if no range was specified, otherwise set to the first line of the range.
Options: Affected by the **autowrite** and **writeany** options.

13

[range] nu[mber] [count] [flags]
[range] # [count] [flags]
> Display the selected lines, each preceded with its line number.

> The line number format is "%6d", followed by two spaces.

> Line: Set to the last line displayed.
> Options: None.

@ buffer
* buffer
> Execute a buffer. Each line in the named buffer is executed as an **ex** command. If no buffer is specified, or if the specified buffer is "@" or "*", the last buffer executed is used.

[range] <[< ...] [count] [flags]
> Shift lines left or right. The specified lines are shifted to the left (for the < command) or right (for the > command), by the number of columns specified by the **shiftwidth** option. Only leading whitespace characters are deleted when shifting left; once the first column of the line contains a nonblank character, the **shift** command will succeed, but the line will not be modified.

> If the command character < or > is repeated more than once, the command is repeated once for each additional command character.

> Line: If the current line is set to one of the lines that are affected by the command, it is unchanged. Otherwise, it is set to the first nonblank character of the lowest numbered line shifted.
> Options: Affected by the **shiftwidth** option.

[line] = [flags]
> Display the line number. Display the line number of line (which defaults to the last line in the file).

> Line: Unchanged.
> Options: None.

[range] >[> ...] [count] [flags]
> Shift right. The specified lines are shifted to the right by the number of columns specified by the **shiftwidth** option, by inserting tab and space characters. Empty lines are not changed.

> If the command character ">" is repeated more than once, the command is repeated once for each additional command character.

> Line: Set to the last line modified by the command.
> Options: None.

ab[brev] lhs rhs
> Add an abbreviation to the current abbreviation list. In **vi**, if lhs is entered such that it is preceded and followed by characters that cannot be part of a word, it is replaced by the string rhs.

> Line: Unchanged.
> Options: None.

[line] a[ppend][!]
> The input text is appended to the specified line. If line 0 is specified, the text is inserted at the beginning of the file. Set to the last line input. If no lines are input, then set to line, or to the

first line of the file if a `line` of 0 was specified. Following the command name with a "`!`" character causes the **autoindent** option to be toggled for the duration of the command.

Line: Unchanged.
Options: Affected by the **altwerase, autoindent, beautify, showmatch, ttywerase** and **wrapmargin** options.

ar[gs]

Display the argument list. The current argument is displayed inside of "`[`" and "`]`" characters. The argument list is the list of operands specified on startup, which can be replaced using the **next** command.

Line: Unchanged.
Options: None.

bg

Vi mode only. Background the current screen.

Line: Set to the current line when the screen was last edited.
Options: None.

[range] c[hange][!] [count]

Replace the lines with input text. Following the command name with a "`!`" character causes the **autoindent** option to be toggled for the duration of the command.

Line: Set to the last line input, or, if no lines were input, set to the line before the target line, or to the first line of the file if there are no lines preceding the target line.
Options: Affected by the **altwerase, autoindent, beautify, showmatch, ttywerase** and **wrapmargin** options.

chd[ir][!] [directory]
cd[!] [directory]

Change the current working directory. The `directory` argument is subjected to *sh*(1) word expansions. When invoked with no directory argument and the HOME environment variable is set, the directory named by the HOME environment variable becomes the new current directory. Otherwise, the new current directory becomes the directory returned by the *getpwent*(3) routine.

The **chdir** command will fail if the file has been modified since the last complete write of the file. You can override this check by appending a "`!`" character to the command.

Line: Unchanged.
Options: Affected by the **cdpath** option.

[range] co[py] line [flags]
[range] t line [flags]

Copy the specified lines (range) after the destination line. Line 0 may be specified to insert the lines at the beginning of the file.

Line: Unchanged.
Options: None.

[range] d[elete] [buffer] [count] [flags]

Delete the lines from the file. The deleted text is saved in the specified buffer, or, if no buffer is specified, in the unnamed buffer. If the command name is followed by a letter that could be interpreted as either a buffer name or a flag value (because neither a `count` or `flags` values were given), **ex** treats the letter as a `flags` value if the letter immediately follows the command name, without any whitespace separation. If the letter is preceded by whitespace characters, it treats it as a buffer name.

Line: Set to the line following the deleted lines, or to the last line if the deleted lines were at the end.
Options: None.

di[splay] b[uffers] | s[creens] | t[ags]

Display buffers, screens or tags. The **display** command takes one of three additional arguments, which are as follows:

b[uffers]   Display all buffers (including named, unnamed, and numeric) that contain text.
s[creens]   Display the file names of all background screens.
t[ags]   Display the tags stack.

Line: Unchanged.
Options: None.

e[dit][!] [+cmd] [file]
ex[!] [+cmd] [file]

Edit a different file. If the current buffer has been modified since the last complete write, the command will fail. You can override this by appending a ''!'' character to the command name.

If the ''+cmd'' option is specified, that **ex** command will be executed in the new file. Any **ex** command may be used, although the most common use of this feature is to specify a line number or search pattern to set the initial location in the new file.

Line: If you have previously edited the file, the current line will be set to your last position in the file. If that position does not exist, or you have not previously edited the file, the current line will be set to the first line of the file if you are in **vi** mode, and the last line of the file if you are in **ex**.
Options: Affected by the **autowrite** and **writeany** options.

exu[sage] [command]

Display usage for an **ex** command. If command is specified, a usage statement for that command is displayed. Otherwise, usage statements for all **ex** commands are displayed.

Line: Unchanged.
Options: None.

f[ile] [file]

Display and optionally change the file name. If a file name is specified, the current pathname is changed to the specified name. The current pathname, the number of lines, and the current position in the file are displayed.

Line: Unchanged.
Options: None.

fg [name]

Vi mode only. Foreground the specified screen. Swap the current screen with the specified backgrounded screen. If no screen is specified, the first background screen is foregrounded.

Line: Set to the current line when the screen was last edited.
Options: None.

13

[range] g[lobal] /pattern/ [commands]
[range] v /pattern/ [commands]

Apply commands to lines matching (or not matching) a pattern. The lines within the given range that match (''g[lobal]''), or do not match (''v'') the given pattern are selected. Then, the specified **ex** command(s) are executed with the current line (''.'') set to each selected line. If no range is specified, the entire file is searched for matching, or not matching, lines.

Multiple commands can be specified, one per line, by escaping each <newline> character with a backslash, or by separating commands with a ''|'' character. If no commands are specified, the command defaults to the **print** command.

For the **append, change** and **insert** commands, the input text must be part of the global command line. In this case, the terminating period can be omitted if it ends the commands.

The **visual** command may also be specified as one of the **ex** commands. In this mode, input is taken from the terminal. Entering a **Q** command in **vi** mode causes the next line matching the pattern to be selected and **vi** to be reentered, until the list is exhausted.

The **global, v** and **undo** commands cannot be used as part of these commands.

The editor options **autoprint, autoindent,** and **report** are turned off for the duration of the **global** and **v** commands.

Line: The last line modified.
Options: None.

he[lp]

Display a help message.

Line: Unchanged.
Options: None.

[line] i[nsert][!]

The input text is inserted before the specified line. Following the command name with a ''!'' character causes the **autoindent** option setting to be toggled for the duration of this command.

Line: Set to the last line input; if no lines were input, set to the line before the target line, or to the first line of the file if there are no lines preceding the target line.
Options: Affected by the **altwerase, autoindent, beautify, showmatch, ttywerase** and **wrapmargin** options.

[range] j[oin][!] [count] [flags]

Join lines of text together.

A count specified to the command specifies that the last line of the range plus count subsequent lines will be joined. (Note, this differs by one from the general rule where only count- subsequent lines are affected.)

If the current line ends with a whitespace character, all whitespace is stripped from the next line. Otherwise, if the next line starts with a open parenthesis (''(''), do nothing. Otherwise, if the current line ends with a question mark (''?''), period (''.'') or exclamation point (''!''), insert two spaces. Otherwise, insert a single space.

Appending a ''!'' character to the command name causes a simpler join with no white-space processing.

13

Line: Unchanged.
Options: None.

[range] l[ist] [count] [flags]
Display the lines unambiguously. Tabs are displayed as "`^I`", and the end of the line is marked with a "`$`" character.

Line: Set to the last line displayed.
Options: None.

map[!] [lhs rhs]
Define or display maps (for **vi** only).

If "`lhs`" and "`rhs`" are not specified, the current set of command mode maps are displayed. If a "`!`" character is appended to to the command, the text input mode maps are displayed.

Otherwise, when the "`lhs`" character sequence is entered in **vi**, the action is as if the corresponding "`rhs`" had been entered. If a "`!`" character is appended to the command name, the mapping is effective during text input mode, otherwise, it is effective during command mode. This allows "`lhs`" to have two different macro definitions at the same time: one for command mode and one for input mode.

Whitespace characters require escaping with a `<literal next>` character to be entered in the `lhs` string in visual mode.

Normally, keys in the `rhs` string are remapped (see the **remap** option), and it is possible to create infinite loops. However, keys which map to themselves are not further remapped, regardless of the setting of the **remap** option. For example, the command "`:map n nz.`" maps the "n" key to the **n** and **z** commands.

To exit an infinitely looping map, use the terminal `<interrupt>` character.

Line: Unchanged.
Options: None.

[line] ma[rk] <character>
[line] k <character>
Mark the line with the mark `<character>`. The expressions "`'<character>`" and "`'<character>`" can then be used as an address in any command that uses one.

Line: Unchanged.
Options: None.

[range] m[ove] line
Move the specified lines after the target line. A target line of 0 places the lines at the beginning of the file.

Line: Set to the first of the moved lines.
Options: None.

mk[exrc][!] file
Write the abbreviations, editor options and maps to the specified file. Information is written in a form which can later be read back in using the **ex source** command. If `file` already exists, the **mkexrc** command will fail. This check can be overridden by appending a "`!`" character to the command.

13

Line: Unchanged.
Options: None.

n[ext][!] [file ...]

> Edit the next file from the argument list. The **next** command will fail if the file has been modified since the last complete write. This check can be overridden by appending the ''!'' character to the command name. The argument list can optionally be replaced by specifying a new one as arguments to this command. In this case, editing starts with the first file on the new list.
>
> Line: Set as described for the **edit** command.
> Options: Affected by the options **autowrite** and **writeany**.

[line] o[pen] /pattern/ [flags]

> Enter open mode. Open mode is the same as being in **vi**, but with a one-line window. All the standard **vi** commands are available. If a match is found for the optional RE argument, the cursor is set to the start of the matching pattern.
>
> *This command is not yet implemented.*
>
> Line: Unchanged, unless the optional RE is specified, in which case it is set to the line where the matching pattern is found.
> Options: Affected by the **open** option.

pre[serve]

> Save the file in a form that can later be recovered using the **ex −r** option. When the file is preserved, an email message is sent to the user.
>
> Line: Unchanged.
> Options: None.

prev[ious][!]

> Edit the previous file from the argument list. The **previous** command will fail if the file has been modified since the last complete write. This check can be overridden by appending the ''!'' character to the command name.
>
> Line: Set as described for the **edit** command,
> Options: Affected by the options **autowrite** and **writeany**. None.

[range] p[rint] [count] [flags]

> Display the specified lines.
>
> Line: Set to the last line displayed.
> Options: None.

[line] pu[t] [buffer]

> Append buffer contents to the current line. If a buffer is specified, its contents are appended to the line, otherwise, the contents of the unnamed buffer are used.
>
> Line: Set to the line after the current line.
> Options: None.

q[uit][!]

> End the editing session. If the file has been modified since the last complete write, the **quit** command will fail. This check may be overridden by appending a ''!'' character to the command.

13

If there are more files to edit, the **quit** command will fail. Appending a ''!'' character to the command name or entering two **quit** commands (i.e. **wq, quit, xit** or **ZZ**) in a row) will override this check and the editor will exit.

Line: Unchanged.
Options: None.

[line] r[ead][!] [file]

Read a file. A copy of the specified file is appended to the line. If line is 0, the copy is inserted at the beginning of the file. If no file is specified, the current file is read; if there is no current file, then file becomes the current file. If there is no current file and no file is specified, then the **read** command will fail.

If file is preceded by a ''!'' character, file is treated as if it were a shell command, and passed to the program named by the SHELL environment variable. The standard and standard error outputs of that command are read into the file after the specified line. The special meaning of the ''!'' character can be overridden by escaping it with a backslash (''\'') character.

Line: When executed from **ex**, the current line is set to the last line read. When executed from **vi**, the current line is set to the first line read.
Options: None.

rec[over] file

Recover file if it was previously saved. If no saved file by that name exists, the **recover** command behaves similarly to the **edit** command.

Line: Set as described for the **edit** command.
Options: None.

res[ize] [+|-]size

Vi mode only. Grow or shrink the current screen. If size is a positive, signed number, the current screen is grown by that many lines. If size is a negative, signed number, the current screen is shrunk by that many lines. If size is not signed, the current screen is set to the specified size. Applicable only to split screens.

Line: Unchanged.
Options: None.

rew[ind][!]

Rewind the argument list. If the current file has been modified since the last complete write, the **rewind** command will fail. This check may be overridden by appending the ''!'' character to the command.

Otherwise, the current file is set to the first file in the argument list.

Line: Set as described for the **edit** command.
Options: Affected by the **autowrite** and **writeany** options.

se[t] [option[=[value]] ...] [nooption ...] [option? ...] [all]

Display or set editor options. When no arguments are specified, the editor option **term**, and any editor options whose values have been changed from the default settings are displayed. If the argument all is specified, the values of all of editor options are displayed.

Specifying an option name followed by the character ''?'' causes the current value of that option to be displayed. The ''?'' can be separated from the option name by whitespace characters. The ''?'' is necessary only for Boolean valued options. Boolean options can be given values by the form ''set option'' to turn them on, or ''set nooption'' to turn them off. String and numeric options can be assigned by the form "set option=value". Any whitespace characters in strings can be included literally by preceding each with a backslash. More than one option can be set or listed by a single set command, by specifying multiple arguments, each separated from the next by whitespace characters.

Line: Unchanged.
Options: None.

sh[ell]

Run a shell program. The program named by the **shell** option is run with a −i (for interactive) flag. Editing is resumed when that program exits.

Line: Unchanged.
Options: None.

so[urce] file

Read and execute **ex** commands from a file. **Source** commands may be nested.

Line: Unchanged.
Options: None.

sp[lit] [file ...]

Vi mode only. Split the screen. The current screen is split into two screens, of approximately equal size. If the cursor is in the lower half of the screen, the screen will split up, i.e. the new screen will be above the old one. If the cursor is in the upper half of the screen, the new screen will be below the old one.

If file is specified, the new screen is editing that file, otherwise, both screens are editing the same file, and changes in each will be be reflected in the other. The argument list for the new screen consists of the list of files specified as arguments to this command, or, the current pathname if no files are specified.

Line: If file is specified, set as for the **edit** command, otherwise unchanged.
Options: None.

13

[range] s[ubstitute] [/pattern/replace/] [options] [count] [flags]
[range] & [options] [count] [flags]
[range] ˜ [options] [count] [flags]

Make substitutions. Replace the first instance of pattern with the string replace on the specified line(s). If the "/pattern/repl/" argument is not specified, the "/pattern/repl/" from the previous **substitute** command is used.

If options includes the letter "c" (confirm), you will be prompted for confirmation before each replacement is done. An affirmative response (in English, a "y" character) causes the replacement to be made. A quit response (in English, a "q" character) causes the **substitute** command to be terminated. Any other response causes the replacement not to be made, and the **substitute** command continues. If options includes the letter "g" (global), all nonoverlapping instances of pattern in the line are replaced.

The **&** version of the command is the same as not specifying a pattern or replacement string to the **substitute** command, and the "&" is replaced by the pattern and replacement information from the previous substitute command.

The ˜ version of the command is the same as **&** and **s**, except that the search pattern used is the last RE used in *any* command, not necessarily the one used in the last **substitute** command.

For example, in the sequence

```
s/red/blue/
/green
~
```

the ''~'' is equivalent to ''s/green/blue/''.

The **substitute** command may be interrupted, using the terminal interrupt character. All substitutions completed before the interrupt are retained.

Line: Set to the last line upon which a substitution was made.
Options: None.

su[spend][!]
st[op][!]
<control-Z>

Suspend the edit session. Appending a ''!'' character to these commands turns off the **autowrite** option for the command.

Line: Unchanged.
Options: Affected by the **autowrite** option.

ta[g][!] tagstring

Edit the file containing the specified tag. Search for the tagstring, which can be in a different file. If the tag is in a different file, then the new file is edited. If the current file has been modified since the last complete write, the **tag** command will fail. This check can be overridden by appending the ''!'' character to the command name.

The **tag** command searches for `tagstring` in the tags file(s) specified by the option. (See *ctags*(1) for more information on tags files.)

Line: Set to the line indicated by the tag.
Options: Affected by the **autowrite, taglength, tags** and **writeany** options.

tagp[op][!] [file | number]

Pop to the specified tag in the tags stack. If neither `file` or `number` is specified, the **tagpop** command pops to the most recent entry on the tags stack. If `file` or `number` is specified, the **tagpop** command pops to the most recent entry in the tags stack for that file, or numbered entry in the tags stack, respectively. (See the **display** command for information on displaying the tags stack.)

If the file has been modified since the last complete write, the **tagpop** command will fail. This check may be overridden by appending a ''!'' character to the command name.

Line: Set to the line indicated by the tag.
Options: Affected by the **autowrite,** and **writeany** options.

tagt[op][!]

Pop to the least recent tag on the tags stack, clearing the tags stack.

If the file has been modified since the last complete write, the **tagpop** command will fail. This check may be overridden by appending a ''!'' character to the command name.

Line: Set to the line indicated by the tag.
Options: Affected by the **autowrite,** and **writeany** options.

una[bbrev] lhs

Delete an abbreviation. Delete lhs from the current list of abbreviations.

    Line: Unchanged.
    Options: None.

u[ndo]

Undo the last change made to the file. Changes made by **global, v, visual** and map sequences are considered a single command. If repeated, the **u** command alternates between these two states, and is its own inverse.

    Line: Set to the last line modified by the command.
    Options: None.

unm[ap][!] lhs

Unmap a mapped string. Delete the command mode map definition for lhs. If a "!" character is appended to the command name, delete the text input mode map definition instead.

    Line: Unchanged.
    Options: None.

ve[rsion]

Display the version of the **ex/vi** editor.

[line] vi[sual] [type] [count] [flags]

Ex mode only. Enter **vi**. The type is optional, and can be "−", "+" or "^", as in the **ex z** command, to specify the the position of the specified line in the screen window. (The default is to place the line at the top of the screen window.) A count specifies the number of lines that will initially be displayed. (The default is the value of the **window** editor option.)

    Line: Unchanged unless line is specified, in which case it is set to that line.
    Options: None.

vi[sual][!] [+cmd] [file]

Vi mode only. Edit a new file. Identical to the "edit[!] [+cmd] [file]" command.

viu[sage] [command]

Display usage for a **vi** command. If command is specified, a usage statement for that command is displayed. Otherwise, usage statements for all **vi** commands are displayed.

    Line: Unchanged.
    Options: None.

[range] w[rite][!] [>>] [file]
[range] w[rite] [!] [file]
[range] wn[!] [>>] [file]
[range] wq[!] [>>] [file]

Write the file. The specified lines (the entire file, if no range is given) is written to file. If file is not specified, the current pathname is used. If file is specified, and it exists, or if the current pathname was set using the **file** command, and the file already exists, these commands will fail. Appending a "!" character to the command name will override this check and the write will be attempted, regardless.

Specifying the optional ">>" string will cause the write to be appended to the file, in which case no tests are made for the file already existing.

If the file is preceded by a ''!'' character, the program named in the SHELL environment
variable is invoked with file as its second argument, and the specified lines are passed as standard input to that command. The ''!'' in this usage must be separated from command name
by at least one whitespace character. The special meaning of the ''!'' may be overridden by
escaping it with a backslash (''\'') character.

The **wq** version of the write command will exit the editor after writing the file, if there are no
further files to edit. Appending a ''!'' character to the command name or entering two
''quit'' commands (i.e. **wq**, **quit**, **xit** or **ZZ**) in a row) will override this check and the editor
will exit, ignoring any files that have not yet been edited.

The **wn** version of the write command will move to the next file after writing the file, unless
the write fails.

Line: Unchanged.
Options: Affected by the **readonly** and **writeany** options.

[range] x[it][!] [file]
Write the file if it has been modified. The specified lines are written to file, if the file has
been modified since the last complete write to any file. If no range is specified, the entire file
is written.

The **xit** command will exit the editor after writing the file, if there are no further files to edit.
Appending a ''!'' character to the command name or entering two ''quit'' commands (i.e.
wq, **quit**, **xit** or **ZZ**) in a row) will override this check and the editor will exit, ignoring any
files that have not yet been edited.

Line: Unchanged.
Options: Affected by the **readonly** and **writeany** options.

[range] ya[nk] [buffer] [count]
Copy the specified lines to a buffer. If no buffer is specified, the unnamed buffer is used.

Line: Unchanged.
Options: None.

[line] z [type] [count] [flags]
Adjust the window. If no type is specified, then count lines following the specified line are
displayed. The default count is the value of the **window** option. The type argument
changes the position at which line is displayed on the screen by changing the number of
lines displayed before and after line. The following type characters may be used:

−   Place line at the bottom of the screen.
+   Place line at the top of the screen.
.   Place line in the middle of the screen.
^   Write out count lines starting count * 2 lines before line; the net effect of this
         is that a ''z^'' command following a z command writes the previous page.
=   Center line on the screen with a line of hyphens displayed immediately before
         and after it. The number of preceding and following lines of text displayed are
         reduced to account for those lines.

Line: Set to the last line displayed, with the exception of the type, where the current line
            is set to the line specified by the command.
Options: Affected by the option.

15. Set Options

There are a large number of options that may be set (or unset) to change the editor's behavior. This section describes the options, their abbreviations and their default values.

In each entry below, the first part of the tag line is the full name of the option, followed by any equivalent abbreviations. (Regardless of the abbreviations, it is only necessary to use the minimum number of characters necessary to distinguish an abbreviation from all other commands for it to be accepted, in **nex/nvi**. Historically, only the full name and the official abbreviations were accepted by **ex/vi**. Using full names in your startup files and environmental variables will probably make them more portable.) The part in square brackets is the default value of the option. Most of the options are boolean, i.e. they are either on or off, and do not have an associated value.

Options apply to both **ex** and **vi** modes, unless otherwise specified.

For information on modifying the options or to display the options and their current values, see the "set" command in the section entitled "**Ex Commands**".

altwerase [off]

> **Vi** only. Change how **vi** does word erase during text input. When this option is set, text is broken up into three classes: alphabetic, numeric and underscore characters, other nonblank characters, and blank characters. Changing from one class to another marks the end of a word. In addition, the class of the first character erased is ignored (which is exactly what you want when erasing pathname components).

autoindent, ai [off]

> If this option is set, whenever you create a new line (using the **vi A, a, C, c, I, i, O, o, R, r, S,** and **s** commands, or the **ex append, change,** and **insert** commands) the new line is automatically indented to align the cursor with the first nonblank character of the line from which you created it. Lines are indented using tab characters to the extent possible (based on the value of the **tabstop** option) and then using space characters as necessary. For commands inserting text into the middle of a line, any blank characters to the right of the cursor are discarded, and the first nonblank character to the right of the cursor is aligned as described above.

> The indent characters are themselves somewhat special. If you do not enter more characters on the new line before moving to another line, or entering `<escape>`, the indent character will be deleted and the line will be empty. For example, if you enter `<carriage-return>` twice in succession, the line created by the first `<carriage-return>` will not have any characters in it, regardless of the indentation of the previous or subsequent line.

> Indent characters also require that you enter additional erase characters to delete them. For example, if you have an indented line, containing only blanks, the first `<word-erase>` character you enter will erase up to end of the indent characters, and the second will erase back to the beginning of the line. (Historically, only the **<control-D>** key would erase the indent characters. Both the **<control-D>** key and the usual erase keys work in **nvi**.) In addition, if the cursor is positioned at the end of the indent characters, the keys "0`<control-D>`" will erase all of the indent characters for the current line, resetting the indentation level to 0. Similarly, the keys "^`<control-D>`" will erase all of the indent characters for the current line, leaving the indentation level for future created lines unaffected.

> Finally, if the **autoindent** option is set, the **S** and **cc** commands change from the first nonblank of the line to the end of the line, instead of from the beginning of the line to the end of the line.

autoprint, ap [off]

> **Ex** only. Cause the current line to be automatically displayed after the **ex** commands <, >, **copy, delete, join, move, put, t, Undo,** and **undo.** This automatic display is suppressed during **global** and **vglobal** commands, and for any command where optional flags are used to explicitly display the line.

autowrite, aw [off]

If this option is set, the **vi !**, `^^`, `^]` and **<control-Z>** commands, and the **ex edit, next, rewind, stop, suspend, tag, tagpop,** and **tagtop** commands automatically write the current file back to the current file name if it has been modified since it was last written. If the write fails, the command fails and goes no further.

Appending the optional force flag character ''**!**'' to the **ex** commands **next, rewind, stop, suspend, tag, tagpop,** and **tagtop** stops the automatic write from being attempted.

(Historically, the **next** command ignored the optional force flag.) Note, the **ex** commands **edit, quit, shell,** and **xit** are *not* affected by the **autowrite** option.

beautify, bf [off]

If this option is set, all control characters that are not currently being specially interpreted, other than `<tab>`, `<newline>`, and `<form-feed>`, are discarded from commands read in by **ex** from command files, and from input text entered to **vi** (either into the file or to the colon command line). Text files read by **ex/vi** are *not* affected by the **beautify** option.

cdpath [environment variable CDPATH, or current directory]

This option is used to specify a colon separated list of directories which are used as path prefixes for any relative path names used as arguments for the **cd** command. The value of this option defaults to the value of the environmental variable CDPATH if it is set, otherwise to the current directory. For compatibility with the POSIX 1003.2 shell, the **cd** command does *not* check the current directory as a path prefix for relative path names unless it is explicitly specified. It may be so specified by entering an empty string or a ''**.**'' character into the CDPATH variable or the option value.

columns, co [80]

The number of columns in the screen. Setting this option causes **ex/vi** to set (or reset) the environmental variable COLUMNS. See the section entitled ''**Screen Sizing**'' more information.

comment [off]

Vi only. If the first non-empty line of the file begins with the string ''`/*`'', this option causes **vi** to skip to the end of that C-language comment (probably a terribly boring legal notice) before displaying the file.

directory, dir [environment variable TMPDIR, or /tmp]

The directory where temporary files are created. The environmental variable TMPDIR is used as the default value if it exists, otherwise `/tmp` is used.

edcompatible, ed [off]

Remember the values of the ''c'' and ''g'' suffices to the **substitute** commands, instead of initializing them as unset for each new command. Specifying pattern and replacement strings to the **substitute** command unsets the ''c'' and ''g'' suffices as well.

errorbells, eb [off]

Ex only. **Ex** error messages are normally presented in inverse video. If that is not possible for the terminal, setting this option causes error messages to be announced by ringing the terminal bell.

exrc, ex [off]

If this option is turned off in the system or $HOME startup files, the local startup files are never read (unless they are the same as the system or $HOME startup files). Turning it on has no effect, i.e. the normal checks for local startup files are performed, regardless. See the section entitled ''**Startup Information**'' for more information.

extended [off]

>   This option causes all regular expressions to be treated as POSIX 1003.2 Extended Regular Expressions (which are similar to historic *egrep*(1) style expressions).

flash [on]

>   This option causes the screen to flash instead of beeping the keyboard, on error, if the terminal has the capability.

hardtabs, ht [8]

>   This option defines the spacing between hardware tab settings, i.e. the tab expansion done by the operating system and/or the terminal itself. As **nex/nvi** never writes <tab> characters to the terminal, unlike historic versions of **ex/vi**, this option does not currently have any affect.

ignorecase, ic [off]

>   This option causes regular expressions, both in **ex** commands and in searches, to be evaluated in a case-insensitive manner.

keytime [6]

>   The 10th's of a second **ex/vi** waits for a subsequent key to complete a key mapping.

leftright [off]

>   **Vi** only. This option causes the screen to be scrolled left-right to view lines longer than the screen, instead of the traditional **vi** screen interface which folds long lines at the right-hand margin of the terminal.

lines, li [24]

>   **Vi** only. The number of lines in the screen. Setting this option causes **ex/vi** to set (or reset) the environmental variable LINES. See the section entitled "**Screen Sizing**" for more information.

lisp [off]

>   **Vi** only. This option changes the behavior of the **vi** (,), {, }, [[and]] commands to match the Lisp language. Also, the **autoindent** option's behavior is changed to be appropriate for Lisp.

>   *This option is not yet implemented.*

list [off]

>   This option causes lines to be displayed in an unambiguous fashion. Specifically, tabs are displayed as control characters, i.e. "^I", and the ends of lines are marked with a "$" character.

magic [on]

>   This option is on by default. Turning the **magic** option off causes all regular expression characters except for "^" and "$", to be treated as ordinary characters. To re-enable characters individually, when the **magic** option is off, precede them with a backslash "\" character. See the section entitled "**Regular Expressions and Replacement Strings**" for more information.

matchtime [7]

>   **Vi** only. The 10th's of a second **ex/vi** pauses on the matching character when the **showmatch** option is set.

mesg [on]

>   This option allows other users to contact you using the *talk*(1) and *write*(1) utilities, while you are editing. **Ex/vi** does not turn message on, i.e. if messages were turned off when the editor was invoked, they will stay turned off. This option only permits you to disallow messages for the edit session. See the *mesg*(1) utility for more information.

13

modelines, modeline [off]

If the **modelines** option is set, **ex/vi** has historically scanned the first and last five lines of each file as it is read for editing, looking for any **ex** commands that have been placed in those lines. After the startup information has been processed, and before the user starts editing the file, any commands embedded in the file are executed.

Commands were recognized by the letters ''e'' or ''v'' followed by ''x'' or ''i'', at the beginning of a line or following a tab or space character, and followed by a '':'', an **ex** command, and another '':''.

This option is a security problem of immense proportions, and should not be used under any circumstances.

This option will never be implemented.

number, nu [off]

Precede each line displayed with its current line number.

octal [off]

Display unknown characters as octal numbers, instead of the default hexadecimal.

open [on]

Ex only. If this option is not set, the **open** and **visual** commands are disallowed.

optimize, opt [on]

Vi only. Throughput of text is expedited by setting the terminal not to do automatic carriage returns when printing more than one (logical) line of output, greatly speeding output on terminals without addressable cursors when text with leading white space is printed.

This option is not yet implemented.

paragraphs, para [IPLPPPQPP LIpplpipbp]

Vi only. Define additional paragraph boundaries for the { and } commands. The value of this option must be a character string consisting of zero or more character pairs.

In the text to be edited, the character string <newline>.<char-pair>, (where <char-pair> is one of the character pairs in the option's value) defines a paragraph boundary. For example, if the option were set to LaA<space>##, then all of the following additional paragraph boundaries would be recognized:

        <newline>.La
        <newline>.A<space>
        <newline>.##

prompt [on]

Ex only. This option causes **ex** to prompt for command input with a '' : '' character; when it is not set, no prompt is displayed.

readonly, ro [off]

This option causes a force flag to be required to attempt to write the file back to the original file name. Setting this option is equivalent to using the **−R** command line option, or editing a file which lacks write permission.

recdir [/var/tmp/vi.recover]

The directory where recovery files are stored.

redraw, re [off]

> **Vi** only. The editor simulates (using great amounts of output), an intelligent terminal on a dumb terminal (e.g. during insertions in **vi** the characters to the right of the cursor are refreshed as each input character is typed).

> *This option is not yet implemented.*

remap [on]

> If this option is set, it is possible to define macros in terms of other macros. Otherwise, each key is only remapped up to one time. For example, if ''A'' is mapped to ''B'', and ''B'' is mapped to ''C'', The keystroke ''A'' will be mapped to ''C'' if the **remap** option is set, and to ''B'' if it is not set.

report [5]

> Set the threshold of the number of lines that need to be changed or yanked before a message will be displayed to the user. For everything but the yank command, the value is the largest value about which the editor is silent, i.e. by default, 6 lines must be deleted before the user is notified. However, if the number of lines yanked is greater than *or equal to* the set value, it is reported to the user.

ruler [off]

> **Vi** only. Display a row/column ruler on the colon command line.

scroll, scr [window / 2]

> Set the number of lines scrolled by the **vi <control-D>** and **<control-U>** commands.

> Historically, the **ex z** command, when specified without a count, used two times the size of the scroll value; the POSIX 1003.2 standard specified the window size, which is a better choice.

sections, sect [NHSHH HUnhsh]

> **Vi** only. Define additional section boundaries for the [[and]] commands. The **sections** option should be set to a character string consisting of zero or more character pairs. In the text to be edited, the character string `<newline>.<char-pair>`, (where `<char-pair>` is one of the character pairs in the option's value), defines a section boundary in the same manner that **paragraph** option boundaries are defined.

shell, sh [environment variable SHELL, or /bin/sh]

> Select the shell used by the editor. The specified path is the pathname of the shell invoked by the **vi** ! shell escape command and by the **ex shell** command. This program is also used to resolve any shell meta-characters in **ex** commands.

shiftwidth, sw [8]

> Set the autoindent and shift command indentation width. This width is used by the **autoindent** option and by the **<**, **>**, and **shift** commands.

showdirty [off]

> **Vi** only. Display an asterisk on the colon command line if the file has been modified.

showmatch, sm [off]

> **Vi** only. This option causes **vi**, when a '' } '' or '') '' is entered, to briefly move the cursor the matching '' { '' or '' (''. See the **matchtime** option for more information.

showmode [off]

> **Vi** only. This option causes **vi** to display a string identifying the current editor mode on the colon command line.

13

sidescroll [16]

    Vi only. Sets the number of columns that are shifted to the left or right, when **vi** is doing left-right scrolling and the left or right margin is crossed. See the **leftright** option for more information.

slowopen, slow [off]

    This option affects the display algorithm used by **vi**, holding off display updating during input of new text to improve throughput when the terminal in use is slow and unintelligent.

    This option is not yet implemented.

sourceany [off]

    If this option is turned on, **vi** historically read startup files that were owned by someone other than the editor user. See the section entitled ''**Startup Information**'' for more information. This option is a security problem of immense proportions, and should not be used under any circumstances.

    This option will never be implemented.

tabstop, ts [8]

    This option sets tab widths for the editor display.

taglength, tl [0]

    This option sets the maximum number of characters that are considered significant in a tag name. Setting the value to 0 makes all of the characters in the tag name significant.

tags, tag [tags /var/db/libc.tags /sys/kern/tags]

    Sets the list of tags files, in search order, which are used when the editor searches for a tag.

term, ttytype, tty [environment variable TERM]

    Set the terminal type. Setting this option causes **ex/vi** to set (or reset) the environmental variable TERM.

terse [off]

    This option has historically made editor messages less verbose. It has no effect in this implementation. See the **verbose** option for more information.

tildeop

    Modify the ˜ command to take an associated motion.

timeout, to [on]

    If this option is set, **ex/vi** waits for a specific period for a subsequent key to complete a key mapping (see the **keytime** option). If the option is not set, the editor waits until enough keys are entered to resolve the ambiguity, regardless of how long it takes.

ttywerase [off]

    Vi only. This option changes how **vi** does word erase during text input. If this option is set, text is broken up into two classes, blank characters and nonblank characters. Changing from one class to another marks the end of a word.

verbose [off]

    Vi only. **Vi** historically bells the terminal for many obvious mistakes, e.g. trying to move past the left-hand margin, or past the end of the file. If this option is set, an error message is displayed for all errors.

w300 [no default]
> **Vi** only. Set the window size if the baud rate is less than 1200 baud. See the **window** option for more information.

w1200 [no default]
> **Vi** only. Set the window size if the baud rate is equal to 1200 baud. See the **window** option for more information.

w9600 [no default]
> **Vi** only. Set the window size if the baud rate is greater than 1200 baud. See the **window** option for more information.

warn [on]
> **Ex** only. This option causes a warning message to the terminal if the file has been modified, since it was last written, before a **!** command.

window, w, wi [environment variable LINES]
> This option determines the default number of lines in a screenful, as written by the **z** command. It also determines the number of lines scrolled by the **vi** commands **<control-F>** and **<control-B>**. The value of window can be unrelated to the real screen size, although it starts out as the number of lines on the screen (see the section entitled "**Screen Sizing**" for more information). Setting the value of the **window** option is the same as using the −**w** command line option.
>
> If the value of the **window** option (as set by the **window, w300, w1200** or **w9600** options) is smaller than the actual size of the screen, large screen movements will result in displaying only that smaller number of lines on the screen. (Further movements in that same area will result in the screen being filled.) This can provide a performance improvement when viewing different places in one or more files over a slow link.

wrapmargin, wm [0]
> **Vi** only. If the value of the **wrapmargin** option is non-zero, **vi** will split lines so that they end at least that number of characters before the right-hand margin of the screen. (Note, the value of **wrapmargin** is *not* a text length. In a screen that is 80 columns wide, the command "`:set wrapmargin=8`" attempts to keep the lines less than or equal to 72 columns wide.)
>
> Lines are split at the previous whitespace character closest to the number. Any trailing whitespace characters before that character are deleted. If the line is split because of an inserted `<space>` or `<tab>` character, and you then enter another `<space>` character, it is discarded.
>
> If wrapmargin is set to 0, or if there is no blank character upon which to split the line, the line is not broken.

wrapscan, ws [on]
> This option causes searches to wrap around the end or the beginning of the file, and back to the starting point. Otherwise, the end or beginning of the file terminates the search.

writeany, wa [off]
> If this option is set, file-overwriting checks that would usually be made before the **write** and **xit** commands, or before an automatic write (see the **autowrite** option), are not made. This allows a write to any file, provided the file permissions allow it.

16. Additional Features in Nex/Nvi

There are a few features in **nex/nvi** that are not found in historic versions of **ex/vi**. Some of the more interesting of those features are as follows:

8-bit clean data, large lines, files

Nex/nvi will edit any format file. Line lengths are limited by available memory, and file sizes are limited by available disk space. The vi text input mode command <control-X> can insert any possible character value into the text.

Split screens

The split command divides the screen into multiple editing regions. The <control-W> command rotates between the foreground screens. The resize command can be used to grow or shrink a particular screen.

Background and foreground screens

The bg command backgrounds the current screen, and the fg command foregrounds backgrounded screens. The display command can be used to list the background screens.

Tag stacks

Tags are now maintained in a stack. The <control-T> command returns to the previous tag location. The tagpop command returns to the most recent tag location by default, or, optionally to a specific tag number in the tag stack, or the most recent tag from a specified file. The display command can be used to list the tags stack. The tagtop command returns to the top of the tag stack.

New displays

The display command can be used to display the current buffers, the backgrounded screens, and the tags stack.

Infinite undo

Changes made during an edit session may be rolled backward and forward. A . command immediately after a u command continues either forward or backward depending on whether the u command was an undo or a redo.

Usage information

The exusage and viusage commands provide usage information for all of the ex and vi commands by default, or, optionally, for a specific command or key.

Extended Regular Expressions

The extended option causes Regular Expressions to be interpreted as as Extended Regular Expressions, (i.e. egrep(1) style Regular Expressions).

Word search

The <control-A> command searches for the word referenced by the cursor.

Number increment

The # command increments or decrements the number referenced by the cursor.

Previous file

The previous command edits the previous file from the argument list.

Left-right scrolling

The leftright option causes nvi to do left-right screen scrolling, instead of the traditional vi line wrapping.

17. Index

.	17	C	20	directory	46
!	14, 33	D	20	display	36
"	33	E	20	e	25
#	15, 34	F	20	edcompatible	46
$	15	G	20	edit	36
%	15	H	20	errorbells	46
&	16, 41	I	21	exrc	46
(	16	J	21	extended	46
)	16	L	21	exusage	36
*	34	M	21	f	25
+	12	N	17	fg	36
,	17	O	21	file	32, 36
/RE/	17	P	22	flags	32
0	18	Q	22	flash	47
0<control-D>	30	R	22	global	36
:	18	S	22	hardtabs	47
;	18	T	22	help	37
<	19, 34	U	22	i	25
<control-A>	10	W	23	ignorecase	47
<control-B>	10	X	23	insert	37
<control-D>	11, 29	Y	23	j	12
<control-E>	11	ZZ	23	join	37
<control-F>	11	[[	23	k	12, 38
<control-G>	11	–	17	keytime	47
<control-H>	11, 30	]]	24	l	14
<control-J>	12	^	24	leftright	47
<control-L>	12	^<control-D>	29	line	32
<control-M>	12	_	24	lines	47
<control-N>	12	`<character>	16	lisp	47
<control-P>	12	a	24	list	38, 47
<control-R>	12	abbrev	34	m	25
<control-T>	13, 30	alternate pathname	7	magic	47
<control-U>	13	altwerase	45	map	38
<control-W>	13, 30	append	34	mark	38
<control-X>	30	args	35	matchtime	47
<control-Y>	13	autoindent	45	mesg	47
<control-Z>	13, 42	autoprint	45	mkexrc	38
<control-]>	14	autowrite	45	modelines	47
<control-^>	14	b	24	motion	9
<end-of-file>	33	beautify	46	move	38
<eof>	32	bg	35	n	17
<erase>	30	bigword	9	next	39
<escape>	13, 30	buffer	7	number	33, 48
<interrupt>	6, 29, 30	c	25	o	26
<line erase>	30	cd	35	octal	48
<literal next>	6, 30	cdpath	46	open	39, 48
<nul>	29	change	35	optimize	48
<space>	14	chdir	35	p	26
<word erase>	30	columns	46	paragraph	10
=	34	comment	46	paragraphs	48
>	19, 34	copy	35	preserve	39
?RE?	17	count	9, 32	previous	39
@	19, 34	current pathname	7	previous context	9
A	19	d	25	print	39
B	19	delete	35	prompt	48

13

put	39
quit	39
r	26
range	32
read	40
readonly	48
recdir	48
recover	40
redraw	48
remap	49
report	49
resize	40
rewind	40
ruler	49
s	26
scroll	49
section	10
sections	49
sentence	10
set	40
shell	41, 49
shiftwidth	49
showdirty	49
showmatch	49
showmode	49
sidescroll	49
slowopen	50
source	41
sourceany	50
split	41
stop	42
substitute	41
suspend	42
t	26, 35
tabstop	50
tag	42
taglength	50
tagpop	42
tags	50
tagtop	42
term	50
terse	50
tildeop	50
timeout	50
ttywerase	50
u	27
unabbrev	42
undo	43
unmap	43
unnamed buffer	7
v	37
verbose	50
version	43
visual	43
viusage	43
w	27
w1200	51

w300	51
w9600	51
warn	51
window	51
wn	43
word	10
wq	43
wrapmargin	51
wrapscan	51
write	43
writeany	51
x	27
xit	44
y	27
yank	44
z	27, 44
{	28
|	28
}	28
~	28, 29, 41

JOVE Manual for UNIX Users

Jonathan Payne
(revised for 4.3BSD by Doug Kingston and Mark Seiden)

1. Introduction

JOVE* is an advanced, self-documenting, customizable real-time display editor. It (and this tutorial introduction) are based on the original EMACS editor and user manual written at M.I.T. by Richard Stallman+.

JOVE is considered a *display* editor because normally the text being edited is visible on the screen and is updated automatically as you type your commands.

It's considered a *real-time* editor because the display is updated very frequently, usually after each character or pair of characters you type. This minimizes the amount of information you must keep in your head as you edit.

JOVE is *advanced* because it provides facilities that go beyond simple insertion and deletion: filling of text; automatic indentations of programs; view more than one file at once; and dealing in terms of characters, words, lines, sentences and paragraphs. It is much easier to type one command meaning "go to the end of the paragraph" than to find the desired spot with repetition of simpler commands.

Self-documenting means that at almost any time you can easily find out what a command does, or to find all the commands that pertain to a topic.

Customizable means that you can change the definition of JOVE commands in little ways. For example, you can rearrange the command set; if you prefer to use arrow keys for the four basic cursor motion commands (up, down, left and right), you can. Another sort of customization is writing new commands by combining built in commands.

2. The Organization of the Screen

JOVE divides the screen up into several sections. The biggest of these sections is used to display the text you are editing. The terminal's cursor shows the position of *point*, the location at which editing takes place. While the cursor appears to point *at* a character, point should be thought of as between characters; it points *before* the character that the cursor appears on top of. Terminals have only one cursor, and when output is in progress it must appear where the typing is being done. This doesn't mean that point is moving; it is only that JOVE has no way of showing you the location of point except when the terminal is idle.

The lines of the screen are usually available for displaying text but sometimes are pre-empted by typeout from certain commands (such as a listing of all the editor commands). Most of the time, output from commands like these is only desired for a short period of time, usually just long enough to glance at it. When you have finished looking at the output, you can type Space to make your text reappear. (Usually a Space that you type inserts itself, but when there is typeout on the screen, it does nothing but get rid of that). Any other command executes normally, *after* redrawing your text.

2.1. The Message Line

The bottom line on the screen, called the *message line*, is reserved for printing messages and for accepting input from the user, such as filenames or search strings. When JOVE prompts for input, the cursor will temporarily appear on the bottom line, waiting for you to type a string. When you have finished typing your input, you can type a Return to send it to JOVE. If you change your mind about running the command that is waiting for input, you can type Control-G to abort, and you can continue with your editing.

When JOVE is prompting for a filename, all the usual editing facilities can be used to fix typos and such; in addition, JOVE has the following extra functions:

^N   Insert the next filename from the argument list.

---

*JOVE stands for Jonathan's Own Version of Emacs.
+Although JOVE is meant to be compatible with EMACS, and indeed many of the basic commands are very similar, there are some major differences between the two editors, and you should not rely on their behaving identically.

^P   Insert the previous filename from the argument list.

^R   Insert the full pathname of the file in the current buffer.

Sometimes you will see **--more--** on the message line. This happens when typeout from a command is too long to fit in the screen. It means that if you type a Space the next screenful of typeout will be printed. If you are not interested, typing anything but a Space will cause the rest of the output to be discarded. Typing C-G will discard the output and print *Aborted* where the **--more--** was. Typing any other command will discard the rest of the output and also execute the command.

The message line and the list of filenames from the shell command that invoked JOVE are kept in a special buffer called *Minibuf* that can be edited like any other buffer.

2.2. The Mode Line

At the bottom of the screen, but above the message line, is the *mode line*. The mode line format looks like this:

JOVE (major minor) Buffer: bufr "file" *

major is the name of the current *major mode*. At any time, JOVE can be in only one major mode at a time. Currently there are only four major modes: *Fundamental, Text, Lisp* and *C*.

minor is a list of the minor modes that are turned on. **Abbrev** means that *Word Abbrev* mode is on; **AI** means that *Auto Indent* mode is on; **Fill** means that *Auto Fill* mode is on; **OvrWt** means that *Over Write* mode is on. **Def** means that you are in the process of defining a keyboard macro. This is not really a mode, but it's useful to be reminded about it. The meanings of these modes are described later in this document.

bufr is the name of the currently selected *buffer*. Each buffer has its own name and holds a file being edited; this is how JOVE can hold several files at once. But at any given time you are editing only one of them, the *selected* buffer. When we speak of what some command does to "the buffer", we are talking about the currently selected buffer. Multiple buffers makes it easy to switch around between several files, and then it is very useful that the mode line tells you which one you are editing at any time. (You will see later that it is possible to divide the screen into multiple *windows*, each showing a different buffer. If you do this, there is a mode line beneath each window.)

file is the name of the file that you are editing. This is the default filename for commands that expect a filename as input.

The asterisk at the end of the mode line means that there are changes in the buffer that have not been saved in the file. If the file has not been changed since it was read in or saved, there is no asterisk.

3. Command Input Conventions

3.1. Notational Conventions for ASCII Characters

In this manual, "Control" characters (that is, characters that are typed with the Control key and some other key at the same time) are represented by "C-" followed by another character. Thus, C-A is the character you get when you type A with the Control key (sometimes labeled CTRL) down. Most control characters when present in the JOVE buffer are displayed with a caret; thus, ^A for C-A. Rubout (or DEL) is displayed as ^?, escape as ^[.

3.2. Command and Filename Completion

When you are typing the name of a JOVE command, you need type only enough letters to make the name unambiguous. At any point in the course of typing the name, you can type question mark (?) to see a list of all the commands whose names begin with the characters you've already typed; you can type Space to have JOVE supply as many characters as it can; or you can type Return to complete the command if there is only one possibility. For example, if you have typed the letters "*au*" and you then type a question mark, you will see the list

        auto-execute-command
        auto-execute-macro
        auto-fill-mode
        auto-indent-mode

If you type a Return at this point, JOVE will complain by ringing the bell, because the letters you've typed do not unambiguously specify a single command. But if you type Space, JOVE will supply the characters "*to-*" because all commands that begin "*au*" also begin "*auto-*". You could then type the letter "*f*" followed by either Space or Return, and JOVE would complete the entire command.

Whenever JOVE is prompting you for a filename, say in the *find-file* command, you also need only type enough of the name to make it unambiguous with respect to files that already exist. In this case, question mark and Space work just as they do in command completion, but Return always accepts the name just as you've typed it, because you might want to create a new file with a name similar to that of an existing file.

4. Commands and Variables

JOVE is composed of *commands* which have long names such as *next-line*. Then *keys* such as C-N are connected to commands through the *command dispatch table*. When we say that C-N moves the cursor down a line, we are glossing over a distinction which is unimportant for ordinary use, but essential for simple customization: it is the command *next-line* which knows how to move a down line, and C-N moves down a line because it is connected to that command. The name for this connection is a *binding*; we say that the key C-N *is bound to* the command *next-line*.

Not all commands are bound to keys. To invoke a command that isn't bound to a key, you can type the sequence ESC X, which is bound to the command *execute-named-command*. You will then be able to type the name of whatever command you want to execute on the message line.

Sometimes the description of a command will say "to change this, set the variable *mumble–foo*". A variable is a name used to remember a value. JOVE contains variables which are there so that you can change them if you want to customize. The variable's value is examined by some command, and changing that value makes the command behave differently. Until you are interesting in customizing JOVE, you can ignore this information.

4.1. Prefix Characters

Because there are more command names than keys, JOVE provides *prefix characters* to increase the number of commands that can be invoked quickly and easily. When you type a prefix character JOVE will wait for another character before deciding what to do. If you wait more than a second or so, JOVE will print the prefix character on the message line as a reminder and leave the cursor down there until you type your next character. There are two prefix characters built into JOVE: Escape and Control-X. How the next character is interpreted depends on which prefix character you typed. For example, if you type Escape followed by B you'll run *backward-word*, but if you type Control-X followed by B you'll run *select-buffer*. Elsewhere in this manual, the Escape key is indicated as "ESC", which is also what JOVE displays on the message line for Escape.

4.2. Help

To get a list of keys and their associated commands, you type ESC X *describe-bindings*. If you want to describe a single key, ESC X *describe-key* will work. A description of an individual command is available by using ESC X *describe-command*, and descriptions of variables by using ESC X *describe-variable*. If you can't remember the name of the thing you want to know about, ESC X *apropos* will tell you if a command or variable has a given string in its name. For example, ESC X *apropos describe* will list the names of the four describe commands mentioned briefly in this section.

5. Basic Editing Commands

5.1. Inserting Text

To insert printing characters into the text you are editing, just type them. All printing characters you type are inserted into the text at the cursor (that is, at *point*), and the cursor moves forward. Any characters after the cursor move forward too. If the text in the buffer is FOOBAR, with the cursor before the B, then if you type XX, you get FOOXXBAR, with the cursor still before the B.

To correct text you have just inserted, you can use Rubout. Rubout deletes the character *before* the cursor (not the one that the cursor is on top of or under; that is the character *after* the cursor). The cursor and all characters after it move backwards. Therefore, if you typing a printing character and then type Rubout, they cancel out.

14

To end a line and start typing a new one, type Return. Return operates by inserting a *line-separator*, so if you type Return in the middle of a line, you break the line in two. Because a line-separator is just a single character, you can type Rubout at the beginning of a line to delete the line-separator and join it with the preceding line.

As a special case, if you type Return at the end of a line and there are two or more empty lines just below it, JOVE does not insert a line-separator but instead merely moves to the next (empty) line. This behavior is convenient when you want to add several lines of text in the middle of a buffer. You can use the Control-O (*newline-and-backup*) command to "open" several empty lines at once; then you can insert the new text, filling up these empty lines. The advantage is that JOVE does not have to redraw the bottom part of the screen for each Return you type, as it would ordinarily. That "redisplay" can be both slow and distracting.

If you add too many characters to one line, without breaking it with Return, the line will grow too long to display on one screen line. When this happens, JOVE puts an "!" at the extreme right margin, and doesn't bother to display the rest of the line unless the cursor happens to be in it. The "!" is not part of your text; conversely, even though you can't see the rest of your line, it's still there, and if you break the line, the "!" will go away.

Direct insertion works for printing characters and space, but other characters act as editing commands and do not insert themselves. If you need to insert a control character, Escape, or Rubout, you must first *quote* it by typing the Control-Q command first.

5.2. Moving the Cursor

To do more than insert characters, you have to know how to move the cursor. Here are a few of the commands for doing that.

C-A	Move to the beginning of the line.
C-E	Move to the end of the line.
C-F	Move forward over one character.
C-B	Move backward over one character.
C-N	Move down one line, vertically. If you start in the middle of one line, you end in the middle of the next.
C-P	Move up one line, vertically.
ESC <	Move to the beginning of the entire buffer.
ESC >	Move to the end of the entire buffer.
ESC ,	Move to the beginning of the visible window.
ESC .	Move to the end of the visible window.

5.3. Erasing Text

Rubout	Delete the character before the cursor.
C-D	Delete the character after the cursor.
C-K	Kill to the end of the line.

You already know about the Rubout command which deletes the character before the cursor. Another command, Control-D, deletes the character after the cursor, causing the rest of the text on the line to shift left. If Control-D is typed at the end of a line, that line and the next line are joined together.

To erase a larger amount of text, use the Control-K command, which kills a line at a time. If Control-K is done at the beginning or middle of a line, it kills all the text up to the end of the line. If Control-K is done at the end of a line, it joins that line and the next line. If Control-K is done twice, it kills the rest of the line and the line separator also.

5.4. Files — Saving Your Work

The commands above are sufficient for creating text in the JOVE buffer. The more advanced JOVE commands just make things easier. But to keep any text permanently you must put it in a *file*. Files are the objects which UNIX†

---

† UNIX is a registered trademark of AT&T Bell Laboratories in the USA and other countries.

uses for storing data for a length of time. To tell JOVE to read text into a file, choose a filename, such as *foo.bar*, and type C-X C-R *foo.bar*<return>. This reads the file *foo.bar* so that its contents appear on the screen for editing. You can make changes, and then save the file by typing C-X C-S (save-file). This makes the changes permanent and actually changes the file *foo.bar*. Until then, the changes are only inside JOVE, and the file *foo.bar* is not really changed. If the file *foo.bar* doesn't exist, and you want to create it, read it as if it did exist. When you save your text with C-X C-S the file will be created.

5.5. Exiting and Pausing — Leaving JOVE

The command C-X C-C (*exit-jove*) will terminate the JOVE session and return to the shell. If there are modified but unsaved buffers, JOVE will ask you for confirmation, and you can abort the command, look at what buffers are modified but unsaved using C-X C-B (*list-buffers*), save the valuable ones, and then exit. If what you want to do, on the other hand, is *preserve* the editing session but return to the shell temporarily you can (under Berkeley UNIX only) issue the command ESC S (*pause-jove*), do your UNIX work within the c-shell, then return to JOVE using the *fg* command to resume editing at the point where you paused. For this sort of situation you might consider using an *interactive shell* (that is, a shell in a JOVE window) which lets you use editor commands to manipulate your UNIX commands (and their output) while never leaving the editor. (The interactive shell feature is described below.)

5.6. Giving Numeric Arguments to JOVE Commands

Any JOVE command can be given a *numeric argument*. Some commands interpret the argument as a repetition count. For example, giving an argument of ten to the C-F command (forward-character) moves forward ten characters. With these commands, no argument is equivalent to an argument of 1.

Some commands use the value of the argument, but do something peculiar (or nothing) when there is no argument. For example, ESC G (*goto-line*) with an argument **n** goes to the beginning of the **n**'th line. But ESC G with no argument doesn't do anything. Similarly, C-K with an argument kills that many lines, including their line separators. Without an argument, C-K when there is text on the line to the right of the cursor kills that text; when there is no text after the cursor, C-K deletes the line separator.

The fundamental way of specifying an argument is to use ESC followed by the digits of the argument, for example, ESC 123 ESC G to go to line 123. Negative arguments are allowed, although not all of the commands know what to do with one.

Typing C-U means do the next command four times. Two such C-U's multiply the next command by sixteen. Thus, C-U C-U C-F moves forward sixteen characters. This is a good way to move forward quickly, since it moves about 1/4 of a line on most terminals. Other useful combinations are: C-U C-U C-N (move down a good fraction of the screen), C-U C-U C-O (make "a lot" of blank lines), and C-U C-K (kill four lines — note that typing C-K four times would kill 2 lines).

There are other, terminal-dependent ways of specifying arguments. They have the same effect but may be easier to type. If your terminal has a numeric keypad which sends something recognizably different from the ordinary digits, it is possible to program JOVE to to allow use of the numeric keypad for specifying arguments.

5.7. The Mark and the Region

In general, a command that processes an arbitrary part of the buffer must know where to start and where to stop. In JOVE, such commands usually operate on the text between point and *the mark*. This body of text is called *the region*. To specify a region, you set point to one end of it and mark at the other. It doesn't matter which one comes earlier in the text.

C-@   Set the mark where point is.

C-X C-X   Interchange mark and point.

For example, if you wish to convert part of the buffer to all upper-case, you can use the C-X C-U command, which operates on the text in the region. You can first go to the beginning of the text to be capitalized, put the mark there, move to the end, and then type C-X C-U. Or, you can set the mark at the end of the text, move to the beginning, and then type C-X C-U. C-X C-U runs the command *case-region-upper*, whose name signifies that the region, or everything between point and mark, is to be capitalized.

The way to set the mark is with the C-@ command or (on some terminals) the C-Space command. They set the mark where point is. Then you can move point away, leaving mark behind. When the mark is set, "[Point pushed]" is printed on the message line.

Since terminals have only one cursor, there is no way for JOVE to show you where the mark is located. You have to remember. The usual solution to this problem is to set the mark and then use it soon, before you forget where it is. But you can see where the mark is with the command C-X C-X which puts the mark where point was and point where mark was. The extent of the region is unchanged, but the cursor and point are now at the previous location of the mark.

5.8. The Ring of Marks

Aside from delimiting the region, the mark is also useful for remembering a spot that you may want to go back to. To make this feature more useful, JOVE remembers 16 previous locations of the mark. Most commands that set the mark push the old mark onto this stack. To return to a marked location, use C-U C-@. This moves point to where the mark was, and restores the mark from the stack of former marks. So repeated use of this command moves point to all of the old marks on the stack, one by one. Since the stack is actually a ring, enough uses of C-U C-@ bring point back to where it was originally.

Some commands whose primary purpose is to move point a great distance take advantage of the stack of marks to give you a way to undo the command. The best example is ESC <, which moves to the beginning of the buffer. If there are more than 22 lines between the beginning of the buffer and point, ESC < sets the mark first, so that you can use C-U C-@ or C-X C-X to go back to where you were. You can change the number of lines from 22 since it is kept in the variable *mark-threshold*. By setting it to 0, you can make these commands always set the mark. By setting it to a very large number you can prevent these commands from ever setting the mark. If a command decides to set the mark, it prints the message *[Point pushed]*.

5.9. Killing and Moving Text

The most common way of moving or copying text with JOVE is to kill it, and get it back again in one or more places. This is very safe because the last several pieces of killed text are all remembered, and it is versatile, because the many commands for killing syntactic units can also be used for moving those units. There are also other ways of moving text for special purposes.

5.10. Deletion and Killing

Most commands which erase text from the buffer save it so that you can get it back if you change your mind, or move or copy it to other parts of the buffer. These commands are known as *kill* commands. The rest of the commands that erase text do not save it; they are known as *delete* commands. The delete commands include C-D and Rubout, which delete only one character at a time, and those commands that delete only spaces or line separators. Commands that can destroy significant amounts of nontrivial data generally kill. A command's name and description will use the words *kill* or *delete* to say which one it does.

C-D	Delete next character.
Rubout	Delete previous character.
ESC \	Delete spaces and tabs around point.
C-X C-O	Delete blank lines around the current line.
C-K	Kill rest of line or one or more lines.
C-W	Kill region (from point to the mark).
ESC D	Kill word.
ESC Rubout	Kill word backwards.
ESC K	Kill to end of sentence.
C-X Rubout	Kill to beginning of sentence.

5.11. Deletion

The most basic delete commands are C-D and Rubout. C-D deletes the character after the cursor, the one the cursor is "on top of" or "underneath". The cursor doesn't move. Rubout deletes the character before the cursor, and moves the cursor back. Line separators act like normal characters when deleted. Actually, C-D and Rubout aren't always *delete* commands; if you give an argument, they *kill* instead. This prevents you from losing a great deal of text by typing a large argument to a C-D or Rubout.

The other delete commands are those which delete only formatting characters: spaces, tabs, and line separators. ESC \ (*delete-white-space*) deletes all the spaces and tab characters before and after point. C-X C-O (*delete-blank-lines*) deletes all blank lines after the current line, and if the current line is blank deletes all the blank lines preceding the current line as well (leaving one blank line, the current line).

5.12. Killing by Lines

The simplest kill command is the C-K command. If issued at the beginning of a line, it kills all the text on the line, leaving it blank. If given on a line containing only white space (blanks and tabs) the line disappears. As a consequence, if you go to the front of a non-blank line and type two C-K's, the line disappears completely.

More generally, C-K kills from point up to the end of the line, unless it is at the end of a line. In that case, it kills the line separator following the line, thus merging the next line into the current one. Invisible spaces and tabs at the end of the line are ignored when deciding which case applies, so if point appears to be at the end of the line, you can be sure the line separator will be killed.

C-K with an argument of zero kills all the text before point on the current line.

5.13. Other Kill Commands

A kill command which is very general is C-W (*kill-region*), which kills everything between point and the mark.* With this command, you can kill and save contiguous characters, if you first set the mark at one end of them and go to the other end.

Other syntactic units can be killed, too; words, with ESC Rubout and ESC D; and, sentences, with ESC K and C-X Rubout.

5.14. Un-killing

Un-killing (yanking) is getting back text which was killed. The usual way to move or copy text is to kill it and then un-kill it one or more times.

C-Y   Yank (re-insert) last killed text.

ESC Y   Replace re-inserted killed text with the previously killed text.

ESC W   Save region as last killed text without killing.

Killed text is pushed onto a *ring buffer* called the *kill ring* that remembers the last 10 blocks of text that were killed. (Why it is called a ring buffer will be explained below). The command C-Y (*yank*) reinserts the text of the most recent kill. It leaves the cursor at the end of the text, and puts the mark at the beginning. Thus, a single C-Y undoes the C-W.

If you wish to copy a block of text, you might want to use ESC W (*copy-region*), which copies the region into the kill ring without removing it from the buffer. This is approximately equivalent to C-W followed by C-Y, except that ESC W does not mark the buffer as "changed" and does not cause the screen to be rewritten.

There is only one kill ring shared among all the buffers. After visiting a new file, whatever was last killed in the previous file is still on top of the kill ring. This is important for moving text between files.

5.15. Appending Kills

Normally, each kill command pushes a new block onto the kill ring. However, two or more kill commands immediately in a row (without any other intervening commands) combine their text into a single entry on the ring, so that a

---

*Often users switch this binding from C-W to C-X C-K because it is too easy to hit C-W accidentally.

single C-Y command gets it all back as it was before it was killed. This means that you don't have to kill all the text in one command; you can keep killing line after line, or word after word, until you have killed it all, and you can still get it all back at once.

Commands that kill forward from *point* add onto the end of the previous killed text. Commands that kill backward from *point* add onto the beginning. This way, any sequence of mixed forward and backward kill commands puts all the killed text into one entry without needing rearrangement.

5.16. Un-killing Earlier Kills

To recover killed text that is no longer the most recent kill, you need the ESC Y (*yank-pop*) command. The ESC Y command can be used only after a C-Y (yank) command or another ESC Y. It takes the un-killed text inserted by the C-Y and replaces it with the text from an earlier kill. So, to recover the text of the next-to-the-last kill, you first use C-Y to recover the last kill, and then discard it by use of ESC Y to move back to the previous kill.

You can think of all the last few kills as living on a ring. After a C-Y command, the text at the front of the ring is also present in the buffer. ESC Y "rotates" the ring bringing the previous string of text to the front and this text replaces the other text in the buffer as well. Enough ESC Y commands can rotate any part of the ring to the front, so you can get at any killed text so long as it is recent enough to be still in the ring. Eventually the ring rotates all the way around and the most recently killed text comes to the front (and into the buffer) again. ESC Y with a negative argument rotates the ring backwards.

When the text you are looking for is brought into the buffer, you can stop doing ESC Y's and the text will stay there. It's really just a copy of what's at the front of the ring, so editing it does not change what's in the ring. And the ring, once rotated, stays rotated, so that doing another C-Y gets another copy of what you rotated to the front with ESC Y.

If you change your mind about un-killing, C-W gets rid of the un-killed text, even after any number of ESC Y's.

6. Searching

The search commands are useful for finding and moving to arbitrary positions in the buffer in one swift motion. For example, if you just ran the spell program on a paper and you want to correct some word, you can use the search commands to move directly to that word. There are two flavors of search: *string search* and *incremental search*. The former is the default flavor—if you want to use incremental search you must rearrange the key bindings (see below).

6.1. Conventional Search

C-S   Search forward.

C-R   Search backward.

To search for the string "FOO" you type "C-S FOO<return>". If JOVE finds FOO it moves point to the end of it; otherwise JOVE prints an error message and leaves point unchanged. C-S searches forward from point so only occurrences of FOO after point are found. To search in the other direction use C-R. It is exactly the same as C-S except it searches in the opposite direction, and if it finds the string, it leaves point at the beginning of it, not at the end as in C-S.

While JOVE is searching it prints the search string on the message line. This is so you know what JOVE is doing. When the system is heavily loaded and editing in exceptionally large buffers, searches can take several (sometimes many) seconds.

JOVE remembers the last search string you used, so if you want to search for the same string you can type "C-S <return>". If you mistyped the last search string, you can type C-S followed by C-R. C-R, as usual, inserts the default search string into the minibuffer, and then you can fix it up.

6.2. Incremental Search

This search command is unusual in that is is *incremental*; it begins to search before you have typed the complete search string. As you type in the search string, JOVE shows you where it would be found. When you have typed enough characters to identify the place you want, you can stop. Depending on what you will do next, you may or may not need to terminate the search explicitly with a Return first.

The command to search is C-S (*i-search-forward*). C-S reads in characters and positions the cursor at the first occurrence of the characters that you have typed so far. If you type C-S and then F, the cursor moves in the text just after the next "F". Type an "O", and see the cursor move to after the next "FO". After another "O", the cursor is after the next "FOO". At the same time, the "FOO" has echoed on the message line.

If you type a mistaken character, you can rub it out. After the FOO, typing a Rubout makes the "O" disappear from the message line, leaving only "FO". The cursor moves back in the buffer to the "FO". Rubbing out the "O" and "F" moves the cursor back to where you started the search.

When you are satisfied with the place you have reached, you can type a Return, which stops searching, leaving the cursor where the search brought it. Also, any command not specially meaningful in searches stops the searching and is then executed. Thus, typing C-A would exit the search and then move to the beginning of the line. Return is necessary only if the next character you want to type is a printing character, Rubout, Return, or another search command, since those are the characters that have special meanings inside the search.

Sometimes you search for "FOO" and find it, but not the one you hoped to find. Perhaps there is a second FOO that you forgot about, after the one you just found. Then type another C-S and the cursor will find the next FOO. This can be done any number of times. If you overshoot, you can return to previous finds by rubbing out the C-S's.

After you exit a search, you can search for the same string again by typing just C-S C-S: one C-S command to start the search and then another C-S to mean "search again for the same string".

If your string is not found at all, the message line says "Failing I-search". The cursor is after the place where JOVE found as much of your string as it could. Thus, if you search for FOOT and there is no FOOT, you might see the cursor after the FOO in FOOL. At this point there are several things you can do. If your string was mistyped, you can rub some of it out and correct it. If you like the place you have found, you can type Return or some other JOVE command to "accept what the search offered". Or you can type C-G, which undoes the search altogether and positions you back where you started the search.

You can also type C-R at any time to start searching backwards. If a search fails because the place you started was too late in the file, you should do this. Repeated C-R's keep looking backward for more occurrences of the last search string. A C-S starts going forward again. C-R's can be rubbed out just like anything else.

6.3. Searching with Regular Expressions

In addition to the searching facilities described above, JOVE can search for patterns using regular expressions. The handling of regular expressions in JOVE is like that of *ed(1)* or *vi(1)*, but with some notable additions. The extra metacharacters understood by JOVE are \<, \>, \| and \{. The first two of these match the beginnings and endings of words; Thus the search pattern, "\<Exec" would match all words beginning with the letters "Exec".

An \| signals the beginning of an alternative — that is, the pattern "foo\|bar" would match either "foo" or "bar". The "curly brace" is a way of introducing several sub-alternatives into a pattern. It parallels the [] construct of regular expressions, except it specifies a list of alternative words instead of just alternative characters. So the pattern "foo\{bar,baz\}bie" matches "foobarbie" or "foobazbie".

JOVE only regards metacharacters as special if the variable *match-regular-expressions* is set to "on". The ability to have JOVE ignore these characters is useful if you're editing a document about patterns and regular expressions or when a novice is learning JOVE.

Another variable that affects searching is *case-ignore-search*. If this variable is set to "on" then upper case and lower case letters are considered equal.

7. Replacement Commands

Global search-and-replace operations are not needed as often in JOVE as they are in other editors, but they are available. In addition to the simple Replace operation which is like that found in most editors, there is a Query Replace operation which asks, for each occurrence of the pattern, whether to replace it.

7.1. Global replacement

To replace every occurrence of FOO after point with BAR, you can do, e.g., "ESC R FOO<return>BAR" as the *replace-string* command is bound to the ESC R. Replacement takes place only between point and the end of the buffer so if you want to cover the whole buffer you must go to the beginning first.

7.2. Query Replace

If you want to change only some of the occurrences of FOO, not all, then the global *replace-string* is inappropriate; Instead, use, e.g., "ESC Q FOO<return>BAR", to run the command *query-replace-string*. This displays each occurrence of FOO and waits for you to say whether to replace it with a BAR. The things you can type when you are shown an occurrence of FOO are:

Space	to replace the FOO.
Rubout	to skip to the next FOO without replacing this one.
Return	to stop without doing any more replacements.
Period	to replace this FOO and then stop.
! or P	to replace all remaining FOO's without asking.
C-R or R	to enter a recursive editing level, in case the FOO needs to be edited rather than just replaced with a BAR. When you are done, exit the recursive editing level with C-X C-C and the next FOO will be displayed.
C-W	to delete the FOO, and then start editing the buffer. When you are finished editing whatever is to replace the FOO, exit the recursive editing level with C-X C-C and the next FOO will be displayed.
U	move to the last replacement and undo it.

Another alternative is using *replace-in-region* which is just like *replace-string* except it searches only within the region.

8. Commands for English Text

JOVE has many commands that work on the basic units of English text: words, sentences and paragraphs.

8.1. Word Commands

JOVE has commands for moving over or operating on words. By convention, they are all ESC commands.

ESC F	Move Forward over a word.
ESC B	Move Backward over a word.
ESC D	Kill forward to the end of a word.
ESC Rubout	Kill backward to the beginning of a word.

Notice how these commands form a group that parallels the character- based commands, C-F, C-B, C-D, and Rubout.

The commands ESC F and ESC B move forward and backward over words. They are thus analogous to Control-F and Control-B, which move over single characters. Like their Control- analogues, ESC F and ESC B move several words if given an argument. ESC F with a negative argument moves backward like ESC B, and ESC B with a nega- tive argument moves forward. Forward motion stops right after the last letter of the word, while backward motion stops right before the first letter.

It is easy to kill a word at a time. ESC D kills the word after point. To be precise, it kills everything from point to the place ESC F would move to. Thus, if point is in the middle of a word, only the part after point is killed. If some punctuation comes after point, and before the next word, it is killed along with the word. If you wish to kill only the next word but not the punctuation, simply do ESC F to get to the end, and kill the word backwards with ESC Rubout. ESC D takes arguments just like ESC F.

ESC Rubout kills the word before point. It kills everything from point back to where ESC B would move to. If point is after the space in "FOO, BAR", then "FOO, " is killed. If you wish to kill just "FOO", then do a ESC B and a ESC D instead of a ESC Rubout.

8.2. Sentence Commands

The JOVE commands for manipulating sentences and paragraphs are mostly ESC commands, so as to resemble the word-handling commands.

ESC A	Move back to the beginning of the sentence.
ESC E	Move forward to the end of the sentence.
ESC K	Kill forward to the end of the sentence.
C-X Rubout	Kill back to the beginning of the sentence.

The commands ESC A and ESC E move to the beginning and end of the current sentence, respectively. They were chosen to resemble Control-A and Control-E, which move to the beginning and end of a line. Unlike them, ESC A and ESC E if repeated or given numeric arguments move over successive sentences. JOVE considers a sentence to end wherever there is a ".", "?", or "!" followed by the end of a line or by one or more spaces. Neither ESC A nor ESC E moves past the end of the line or spaces which delimit the sentence.

Just as C-A and C-E have a kill command, C-K, to go with them, so ESC A and ESC E have a corresponding kill command ESC K which kills from point to the end of the sentence. With minus one as an argument it kills back to the beginning of the sentence. Positive arguments serve as a repeat count.

There is a special command, C-X Rubout for killing back to the beginning of a sentence, because this is useful when you change your mind in the middle of composing text.

8.3. Paragraph Commands

The JOVE commands for handling paragraphs are

ESC [	Move back to previous paragraph beginning.
ESC]	Move forward to next paragraph end.

ESC [moves to the beginning of the current or previous paragraph, while ESC] moves to the end of the current or next paragraph. Paragraphs are delimited by lines of differing indent, or lines with text formatter commands, or blank lines. JOVE knows how to deal with most indented paragraphs correctly, although it can get confused by one- or two-line paragraphs delimited only by indentation.

8.4. Text Indentation Commands

Tab	Indent "appropriately" in a mode-dependent fashion.
LineFeed	Is the same as Return, except it copies the indent of the line you just left.
ESC M	Moves to the line's first non-blank character.

The way to request indentation is with the Tab command. Its precise effect depends on the major mode. In *Text* mode, it indents to the next tab stop. In *C* mode, it indents to the "right" position for C programs.

To move over the indentation on a line, do ESC M (*first-non-blank*). This command, given anywhere on a line, positions the cursor at the first non-blank, non-tab character on the line.

8.5. Text Filling

Auto Fill mode causes text to be *filled* (broken up into lines that fit in a specified width) automatically as you type it in. If you alter existing text so that it is no longer properly filled, JOVE can fill it again if you ask.

Entering *Auto Fill* mode is done with ESC X *auto-fill-mode*. From then on, lines are broken automatically at spaces when they get longer than the desired width. To leave *Auto Fill* mode, once again execute ESC X *auto-fill-mode*. When *Auto Fill* mode is in effect, the word **Fill** appears in the mode line.

If you edit the middle of a paragraph, it may no longer correctly be filled. To refill a paragraph, use the command ESC J (*fill-paragraph*). It causes the paragraph that point is inside to be filled. All the line breaks are removed and new ones inserted where necessary.

The maximum line width for filling is in the variable *right-margin*. Both ESC J and auto-fill make sure that no line exceeds this width. The value of *right-margin* is initially 72.

14

Normally ESC J figures out the indent of the paragraph and uses that same indent when filling. If you want to change the indent of a paragraph you set *left-margin* to the new position and type C-U ESC J. *fill-paragraph*, when supplied a numeric argument, uses the value of *left-margin*.

If you know where you want to set the right margin but you don't know the actual value, move to where you want to set the value and use the *right-margin-here* command. *left-margin-here* does the same for the *left-margin* variable.

8.6. Case Conversion Commands

ESC L	Convert following word to lower case.
ESC U	Convert following word to upper case.
ESC C	Capitalize the following word.

The word conversion commands are most useful. ESC L converts the word after point to lower case, moving past it. Thus, successive ESC L's convert successive words. ESC U converts to all capitals instead, while ESC C puts the first letter of the word into upper case and the rest into lower case. All these commands convert several words at once if given an argument. They are especially convenient for converting a large amount of text from all upper case to mixed case, because you can move through the test using ESC L, ESC U or ESC C on each word as appropriate.

When given a negative argument, the word case conversion commands apply to the appropriate number of words before point, but do not move point. This is convenient when you have just typed a word in the wrong case. You can give the case conversion command and continue typing.

If a word case conversion command is given in the middle of a word, it applies only to the part of the word which follows the cursor, treating it as a whole word.

The other case conversion functions are *case-region-upper* and *case-region-lower*, which convert everything between point and mark to the specified case. Point and mark remain unchanged.

8.7. Commands for Fixing Typos

In this section we describe the commands that are especially useful for the times when you catch a mistake on your text after you have made it, or change your mind while composing text on line.

Rubout	Delete last character.
ESC Rubout	Kill last word.
C-X Rubout	Kill to beginning of sentence.
C-T	Transpose two characters.
C-X C-T	Transpose two lines.
ESC Minus ESC L	Convert last word to lower case.
ESC Minus ESC U	Convert last word to upper case.
ESC Minus ESC C	Convert last word to lower case with capital initial.

8.8. Killing Your Mistakes

The Rubout command is the most important correction command. When used among printing (self-inserting) characters, it can be thought of as canceling the last character typed.

When your mistake is longer than a couple of characters, it might be more convenient to use ESC Rubout or C-X Rubout. ESC Rubout kills back to the start of the last word, and C-X Rubout kills back to the start of the last sentence. C-X Rubout is particularly useful when you are thinking of what to write as you type it, in case you change your mind about phrasing. ESC Rubout and C-X Rubout save the killed text for C-Y and ESC Y to retrieve.

ESC Rubout is often useful even when you have typed only a few characters wrong, if you know you are confused in your typing and aren't sure what you typed. At such a time, you cannot correct with Rubout except by looking at the screen to see what you did. It requires less thought to kill the whole word and start over again, especially if the system is heavily loaded.

If you were typing a command or command parameters, C-G will abort the command with no further processing.

8.9. Transposition

The common error of transposing two characters can be fixed with the C-T (*transpose-characters*) command. Normally, C-T transposes the two characters on either side of the cursor and moves the cursor forward one character. Repeating the command several times "drags" a character to the right. (Remember that *point* is considered to be between two characters, even though the visible cursor in your terminal is on only one of them.) When given at the end of a line, rather than switching the last character of the line with the line separator, which would be useless, C-T transposes the last two characters on the line. So, if you catch your transposition error right away, you can fix it with just a C-T. If you don't catch it so fast, you must move the cursor back to between the two characters.

To transpose two lines, use the C-X C-T (*transpose-lines*) command. The line containing the cursor is exchanged with the line above it; the cursor is left at the beginning of the line following its original position.

8.10. Checking and Correcting Spelling

When you write a paper, you should correct its spelling at some point close to finishing it. To correct the entire buffer, do ESC X *spell-buffer*. This invokes the UNIX *spell* program, which prints a list of all the misspelled words. JOVE catches the list and places it in a JOVE buffer called **Spell**. You are given an opportunity to delete from that buffer any words that aren't really errors; then JOVE looks up each misspelled word and remembers where it is in the buffer being corrected. Then you can go forward to each misspelled word with C-X C-N (*next-error*) and backward with C-X C-P (*previous-error*). See the section entitled *Error Message Parsing*.

9. File Handling

The basic unit of stored data is the file. Each program, each paper, lives usually in its own file. To edit a program or paper, the editor must be told the name of the file that contains it. This is called *visiting* a file. To make your changes to the file permanent on disk, you must *save* the file.

9.1. Visiting Files

C-X C-V	Visit a file.
C-X C-R	Same as C-X C-V.
C-X C-S	Save the visited file.
ESC ˜	Tell JOVE to forget that the buffer has been changed.

Visiting a file means copying its contents into JOVE where you can edit them. JOVE remembers the name of the file you visited. Unless you use the multiple buffer feature of JOVE, you can only be visiting one file at a time. The name of the current selected buffer is visible in the mode line.

The changes you make with JOVE are made in a copy inside JOVE. The file itself is not changed. The changed text is not permanent until you *save* it in a file. The first time you change the text, an asterisk appears at the end of the mode line; this indicates that the text contains fresh changes which will be lost unless you save them.

To visit a file, use the command C-X C-V. Follow the command with the name of the file you wish to visit, terminated by a Return. You can abort the command by typing C-G, or edit the filename with many of the standard JOVE commands (e.g., C-A, C-E, C-F, ESC F, ESC Rubout). If the filename you wish to visit is similar to the filename in the mode line (the default filename), you can type C-R to insert the default and then edit it. If you do type a Return to finish the command, the new file's text appears on the screen, and its name appears in the mode line. In addition, its name becomes the new default filename.

If you wish to save the file and make your changes permanent, type C-X C-S. After the save is finished, C-X C-S prints the filename and the number of characters and lines that it wrote to the file. If there are no changes to save (no asterisk at the end of the mode line), the file is not saved; otherwise the changes saved and the asterisk at the end of the mode line will disappear.

What if you want to create a file? Just visit it. JOVE prints *(New file)* but aside from that behaves as if you had visited an existing empty file. If you make any changes and save them, the file is created. If you visit a nonexistent

14

file unintentionally (because you typed the wrong filename), go ahead and visit the file you meant. If you don't save the unwanted file, it is not created.

If you alter one file and then visit another in the same buffer, JOVE offers to save the old one. If you answer YES, the old file is saved; if you answer NO, all the changes you have made to it since the last save are lost. You should not type ahead after a file visiting command, because your type-ahead might answer an unexpected question in a way that you would regret.

Sometimes you will change a buffer by accident. Even if you undo the effect of the change by editing, JOVE still knows that "the buffer has been changed". You can tell JOVE to pretend that there have been no changes with the ESC ~ command (*make-buffer-unmodified*). This command simply clears the "modified" flag which says that the buffer contains changes which need to be saved. Even if the buffer really *is* changed JOVE will still act as if it were not.

If JOVE is about to save a file and sees that the date of the version on disk does not match what JOVE last read or wrote, JOVE notifies you of this fact, and asks what to do, because this probably means that something is wrong. For example, somebody else may have been editing the same file. If this is so, there is a good chance that your work or his work will be lost if you don't take the proper steps. You should first find out exactly what is going on. If you determine that somebody else has modified the file, save your file under a different filename and then DIFF the two files to merge the two sets of changes. (The "patch" command is useful for applying the results of context diffs directly). Also get in touch with the other person so that the files don't diverge any further.

9.2. How to Undo Drastic Changes to a File

If you have made several extensive changes to a file and then change your mind about them, and you haven't yet saved them, you can get rid of them by reading in the previous version of the file. You can do this with the C-X C-V command, to visit the unsaved version of the file.

9.3. Recovering from system/editor crashes

JOVE does not have *Auto Save* mode, but it does provide a way to recover your work in the event of a system or editor crash. JOVE saves information about the files you're editing every so many changes to a buffer to make recovery possible. Since a relatively small amount of information is involved it's hardly even noticeable when JOVE does this. The variable "sync-frequency" says how often to save the necessary information, and the default is every 50 changes. 50 is a very reasonable number: if you are writing a paper you will not lose more than the last 50 characters you typed, which is less than the average length of a line.

9.4. Miscellaneous File Operations

ESC X *write-file* <file><return> writes the contents of the buffer into the file <file>, and then visits that file. It can be thought of as a way of "changing the name" of the file you are visiting. Unlike C-X C-S, *write-file* saves even if the buffer has not been changed. C-X C-W is another way of getting this command.

ESC X *insert-file* <file><return> inserts the contents of <file> into the buffer at point, leaving point unchanged before the contents. You can also use C-X C-I to get this command.

ESC X *write-region* <file><return> writes the region (the text between point and mark) to the specified file. It does not set the visited filename. The buffer is not changed.

ESC X *append-region* <file><return> appends the region to <file>. The text is added to the end of <file>.

10. Using Multiple Buffers

When we speak of "the buffer", which contains the text you are editing, we have given the impression that there is only one. In fact, there may be many of them, each with its own body of text. At any time only one buffer can be *selected* and available for editing, but it isn't hard to switch to a different one. Each buffer individually remembers which file it is visiting, what modes are in effect, and whether there are any changes that need saving.

C-X B   Select or create a buffer.
C-X C-F   Visit a file in its own buffer.

C-X C-B   List the existing buffers.

C-X K   Kill a buffer.

Each buffer in JOVE has a single name, which normally doesn't change. A buffer's name can be any length. The name of the currently selected buffer and the name of the file visited in it are visible in the mode line when you are at top level. A newly started JOVE has only one buffer, named **Main**, unless you specified files to edit in the shell command that started JOVE.

10.1. Creating and Selecting Buffers

To create a new buffer, you need only think of a name for it (say, FOO) and then do C-X B FOO<return>, which is the command C-X B (*select-buffer*) followed by the name. This makes a new, empty buffer (if one by that name didn't previously exist) and selects it for editing. The new buffer is not visiting any file, so if you try to save it you will be asked for the filename to use. Each buffer has its own major mode; the new buffer's major mode is *Text* mode by default.

To return to buffer FOO later after having switched to another, the same command C-X B FOO<return> is used, since C-X B can tell whether a buffer named FOO exists already or not. C-X B Main<return> reselects the buffer Main that JOVE started out with. Just C-X B<return> reselects the previous buffer. Repeated C-X B<return>'s alternate between the last two buffers selected.

You can also read a file into its own newly created buffer, all with one command: C-X C-F (*find-file*), followed by the filename. The name of the buffer is the last element of the file's pathname. C-F stands for "Find", because if the specified file already resides in a buffer in your JOVE, that buffer is reselected. So you need not remember whether you have brought the file in already or not. A buffer created by C-X C-F can be reselected later with C-X B or C-X C-F, whichever you find more convenient. Nonexistent files can be created with C-X C-F just as they can with C-X C-V.

10.2. Using Existing Buffers

To get a list of all the buffers that exist, do C-X C-B (*list-buffers*). Each buffer's type, name, and visited filename is printed. An asterisk before the buffer name indicates a buffer which contains changes that have not been saved. The number that appears at the beginning of a line in a C-X C-B listing is that buffer's *buffer number*. You can select a buffer by typing its number in place of its name. If a buffer with that number doesn't already exist, a new buffer is created with that number as its name.

If several buffers have modified text in them, you should save some of them with C-X C-M (*write-modified-files*). This finds all the buffers that need saving and then saves them. Saving the buffers this way is much easier and more efficient (but more dangerous) than selecting each one and typing C-X C-S. If you give C-X C-M an argument, JOVE will ask for confirmation before saving each buffer.

ESC X *rename-buffer* <new name><return> changes the name of the currently selected buffer.

ESC X *erase-buffer* <buffer name><return> erases the contents of the <buffer name> without deleting the buffer entirely.

10.3. Killing Buffers

After you use a JOVE for a while, it may fill up with buffers which you no longer need. Eventually you can reach a point where trying to create any more results in an "out of memory" or "out of lines" error. When this happens you will want to kill some buffers with the C-X K (*delete-buffer*) command. You can kill the buffer FOO by doing C-X K FOO<return>. If you type C-X K <return> JOVE will kill the previously selected buffer. If you try to kill a buffer that needs saving JOVE will ask you to confirm it.

If you need to kill several buffers, use the command *kill-some-buffers*. This prompts you with the name of each buffer and asks for confirmation before killing that buffer.

11. Controlling the Display

Since only part of a large file will fit on the screen, JOVE tries to show the part that is likely to be interesting. The display control commands allow you to see a different part of the file.

14

C-L	Reposition point at a specified vertical position, OR clear and redraw the screen with point in the same place.
C-V	Scroll forwards (a screen or a few lines).
ESC V	Scroll backwards.
C-Z	Scroll forward some lines.
ESC Z	Scroll backwards some lines.

The terminal screen is rarely large enough to display all of your file. If the whole buffer doesn't fit on the screen, JOVE shows a contiguous portion of it, containing *point*. It continues to show approximately the same portion until point moves outside of what is displayed; then JOVE chooses a new portion centered around the new *point*. This is JOVE's guess as to what you are most interested in seeing, but if the guess is wrong, you can use the display control commands to see a different portion. The available screen area through which you can see part of the buffer is called *the window*, and the choice of where in the buffer to start displaying is also called *the window*. (When there is only one window, it plus the mode line and the input line take up the whole screen).

First we describe how JOVE chooses a new window position on its own. The goal is usually to place *point* half way down the window. This is controlled by the variable *scroll-step*, whose value is the number of lines above the bottom or below the top of the window that the line containing point is placed. A value of 0 (the initial value) means center *point* in the window.

The basic display control command is C-L (*redraw-display*). In its simplest form, with no argument, it tells JOVE to choose a new window position, centering point half way from the top as usual.

C-L with a positive argument chooses a new window so as to put point that many lines from the top. An argument of zero puts point on the very top line. Point does not move with respect to the text; rather, the text and point move rigidly on the screen.

If point stays on the same line, the window is first cleared and then redrawn. Thus, two C-L's in a row are guaranteed to clear the current window. ESC C-L will clear and redraw the entire screen.

The *scrolling* commands C-V, ESC V, C-Z, and ESC Z, let you move the whole display up or down a few lines. C-V (*next-page*) with an argument shows you that many more lines at the bottom of the screen, moving the text and point up together as C-L might. C-V with a negative argument shows you more lines at the top of the screen, as does ESC V (*previous-page*) with a positive argument.

To read the buffer a window at a time, use the C-V command with no argument. It takes the last line at the bottom of the window and puts it at the top, followed by nearly a whole window of lines not visible before. Point is put at the top of the window. Thus, each C-V shows the "next page of text", except for one line of overlap to provide context. To move backward, use ESC V without an argument, which moves a whole window backwards (again with a line of overlap).

C-Z and ESC Z scroll one line forward and one line backward, respectively. These are convenient for moving in units of lines without having to type a numeric argument.

11.1. Multiple Windows

JOVE allows you to split the screen into two or more *windows* and use them to display parts of different files, or different parts of the same file.

C-X 2	Divide the current window into two smaller ones.
C-X 1	Delete all windows but the current one.
C-X D	Delete current window.
C-X N	Switch to the next window.
C-X P	Switch to the previous window.
C-X O	Same as C-X P.
C-X ^	Make this window bigger.
ESC C-V	Scroll the other window.

When using *multiple window* mode, the text portion of the screen is divided into separate parts called *windows*, which can display different pieces of text. Each window can display different files, or parts of the same file. Only one of the windows is *active;* that is the window which the cursor is in. Editing normally takes place in that window alone. To edit in another window, you would give a command to move the cursor to the other window, and then edit there.

Each window displays a mode line for the buffer it's displaying. This is useful to keep track of which window corresponds with which file. In addition, the mode line serves as a separator between windows. By setting the variable *mode-line-should-standout* to "on" you can have JOVE display the mode-line in reverse video (assuming your particular terminal has the reverse video capability).

The command C-X 2 (*split-current-window*) enters multiple window mode. A new mode line appears across the middle of the screen, dividing the text display area into two halves. Both windows contain the same buffer and display the same position in it, namely where point was at the time you issued the command. The cursor moves to the second window.

To return to viewing only one window, use the command C-X 1 (*delete-other-windows*). The current window expands to fill the whole screen, and the other windows disappear until the next C-X 2. (The buffers and their contents are unaffected by any of the window operations).

While there is more than one window, you can use C-X N (*next-window*) to switch to the next window, and C-X P (*previous-window*) to switch to the previous one. If you are in the bottom window and you type C-X N, you will be placed in the top window, and the same kind of thing happens when you type C-X P in the top window, namely you will be placed in the bottom window. C-X O is the same as C-X P. It stands for "other window" because when there are only two windows, repeated use of this command will switch between the two windows.

Often you will be editing one window while using the other just for reference. Then, the command ESC C-V (*page-next-window*) is very useful. It scrolls the next window, as if you switched to the next window, typed C-V, and switched back, without your having to do all that. With a negative argument, ESC C-V will do an ESC V in the next window.

When a window splits, both halves are approximately the same size. You can redistribute the screen space between the windows with the C-X ^ (*grow-window*) command. It makes the currently selected window grow one line bigger, or as many lines as is specified with a numeric argument. Use ESC X *shrink-window* to make the current window smaller.

11.2. Multiple Windows and Multiple Buffers

Buffers can be selected independently in each window. The C-X B command selects a new buffer in whichever window contains the cursor. Other windows' buffers do not change.

You can view the same buffer in more than one window. Although the same buffer appears in both windows, they have different values of point, so you can move around in one window while the other window continues to show the same text. Then, having found one place you wish to refer to, you can go back into the other window with C-X O or C-X P to make your changes.

If you have the same buffer in both windows, you must beware of trying to visit a different file in one of the windows with C-X C-V, because if you bring a new file into this buffer, it will replaced the old file in *both* windows. To view different files in different windows, you must switch buffers in one of the windows first (with C-X B or C-X C-F, perhaps).

A convenient "combination" command for viewing something in another window is C-X 4 (*window-find*). With this command you can ask to see any specified buffer, file or tag in the other window. Follow the C-X 4 with either B and a buffer name, F and a filename, or T and a tag name. This switches to the other window and finds there what you specified. If you were previously in one-window mode, multiple-window mode is entered. C-X 4 B is similar to C-X 2 C-X B. C-X 4 F is similar to C-X 2 C-X C-F. C-X 4 T is similar to C-X 2 C-X T. The difference is one of efficiency, and also that C-X 4 works equally well if you are already using two windows.

14

12. Processes Under JOVE

Another feature in JOVE is its ability to interact with UNIX in a useful way. You can run other UNIX commands from JOVE and catch their output in JOVE buffers. In this chapter we will discuss the different ways to run and interact with UNIX commands.

12.1. Non-interactive UNIX commands

To run a UNIX command from JOVE just type "C-X !" followed by the name of the command terminated with Return. For example, to get a list of all the users on the system, you do:

        C-X ! who<return>

Then JOVE picks a reasonable buffer in which the output from the command will be placed. E.g., "who" uses a buffer called **who**; "ps alx" uses **ps**; and "fgrep -n foo *.c" uses **fgrep**. If JOVE wants to use a buffer that already exists it first erases the old contents. If the buffer it selects holds a file, not output from a previous shell command, you must first delete that buffer with C-X K.

Once JOVE has picked a buffer it puts that buffer in a window so you can see the command's output as it is running. If there is only one window JOVE will automatically make another one. Otherwise, JOVE tries to pick the most convenient window which isn't the current one.

It's not a good idea to type anything while the command is running. There are two reasons for this:

(i)   JOVE won't see the characters (thus won't execute them) until the command finishes, so you may forget what you've typed.

(ii)   Although JOVE won't know what you've typed, it *will* know that you've typed something, and then it will try to be "smart" and not update the display until it's interpreted what you've typed. But, of course, JOVE won't interpret what you type until the UNIX command completes, so you're left with the uneasy feeling you get when you don't know what the hell the computer is doing*.

If you want to interrupt the command for some reason (perhaps you mistyped it, or you changed your mind) you can type C-]. Typing this inside JOVE while a process is running is the same as typing C-C when you are outside JOVE, namely the process stops in a hurry.

When the command finishes, JOVE puts you back in the window in which you started. Then it prints a message indicating whether or not the command completed successfully in its (the command's) opinion. That is, if the command had what it considers an error (or you interrupt it with C-]) JOVE will print an appropriate message.

12.2. Limitations of Non-Interactive Processes

The reason these are called non-interactive processes is that you can't type any input to them; you can't interact with them; they can't ask you questions because there is no way for you to answer. For example, you can't run a command interpreter (a shell), or *mail* or *crypt* with C-X ! because there is no way to provide it with input. Remember that JOVE (not the process in the window) is listening to your keyboard, and JOVE waits until the process dies before it looks at what you type.

C-X ! is useful for running commands that do some output and then exit. For example, it's very useful to use with the C compiler to catch compilation error messages (see Compiling C Programs), or with the *grep* commands.

12.3. Interactive Processes — Run a Shell in a Window

Some versions of JOVE† have the capability of running interactive processes. This is more useful than non-interactive processes for certain types of jobs:

(i)   You can go off and do some editing while the command is running. This is useful for commands that do sporadic output and run for fairly long periods of time.

---

*This is a bug and should be fixed, but probably won't be for a while.
† For example, the version provided with 4.3BSD.

(ii)   Unlike non-interactive processes, you can type input to these. In addition, you can edit what you type with the power of all the JOVE commands *before* you send the input to the process. This is a really important feature, and is especially useful for running a shell in a window.

(iii) Because you can continue with normal editing while one of the processes is running, you can create a bunch of contexts and manage them (select them, delete them, or temporarily put them aside) with JOVE's window and buffer mechanisms.

Although we may have given an image of processes being attached to *windows*, in fact they are attached to *buffers*. Therefore, once an *i-process* is running you can select another buffer into that window, or if you wish you can delete the window altogether. If you reselect that buffer later it will be up to date. That is, even though the buffer wasn't visible it was still receiving output from the process. You don't have to worry about missing anything when the buffer isn't visible.

12.4. Advantages of Running Processes in JOVE Windows.

There are several advantages to running a shell in a window. What you type isn't seen immediately by the process; instead JOVE waits until you type an entire line before passing it on to the process to read. This means that before you type <return> all of JOVE's editing capabilities are available for fixing errors on your input line. If you discover an error at the beginning of the line, rather than erasing the whole line and starting over, you can simply move to the error, correct it, move back and continue typing.

Another feature is that you have the entire history of your session in a JOVE buffer. You don't have to worry about output from a command moving past the top of the screen. If you missed some output you can move back through it with ESC V and other commands. In addition, you can save yourself retyping a command (or a similar one) by sending edited versions of previous commands, or edit the output of one command to become a list of commands to be executed ("immediate shell scripts").

12.5. Differences between Normal and I-process Buffers

JOVE behaves differently in several ways when you are in an *i-process* buffer. Most obviously, <return> does different things depending on both your position in the buffer and on the state of the process. In the normal case, when point is at the end of the buffer, Return does what you'd expect: it inserts a line-separator and then sends the line to the process. If you are somewhere else in the buffer, possibly positioned at a previous command that you want to edit, Return will place a copy of that line (with the prompt discarded if there is one) at the end of the buffer and move you there. Then you can edit the line and type Return as in the normal case. If the process has died for some reason, Return does nothing. It doesn't even insert itself. If that happens unexpectedly, you should type ESC X *list-processes*<return> to get a list of each process and its state. If your process died abnormally, *list-processes* may help you figure out why.

12.6. How to Run a Shell in a Window

Type ESC X *i-shell*<return> to start up a shell. As with C-X !, JOVE will create a buffer, called **shell–1**, and select a window for this new buffer. But unlike C-X ! you will be left in the new window. Now, the shell process is said to be attached to **shell–1**, and it is considered an *i-process* buffer.

13. Directory Handling

To save having to use absolute pathnames when you want to edit a nearby file JOVE allows you to move around the UNIX filesystem just as the c-shell does. These commands are:

cd dir   Change to the specified directory.

pushd [dir]   Like *cd*, but save the old directory on the directory stack. With no directory argument, simply exchange the top two directories on the stack and *cd* to the new top.

popd   Take the current directory off the stack and *cd* to the directory now at the top.

dirs   Display the contents of the directory stack.

The names and behavior of these commands were chosen to mimic those in the c-shell.

14

14. Editing C Programs

This section details the support provided by JOVE for working on C programs.

14.1. Indentation Commands

To save having to lay out C programs "by hand", JOVE has an idea of the correct indentation of a line, based on the surrounding context. When you are in C Mode, JOVE treats tabs specially — typing a tab at the beginning of a new line means "indent to the right place". Closing braces are also handled specially, and are indented to match the corresponding open brace.

14.2. Parenthesis and Brace Matching

To check that parentheses and braces match the way you think they do, turn on *Show Match* mode (ESC X show-match-mode). Then, whenever you type a close brace or parenthesis, the cursor moves momentarily to the matching opener, if it's currently visible. If it's not visible, JOVE displays the line containing the matching opener on the message line.

14.3. C Tags

Often when you are editing a C program, especially someone else's code, you see a function call and wonder what that function does. You then search for the function within the current file and if you're lucky find the definition, finally returning to the original spot when you are done. However, if are unlucky, the function turns out to be external (defined in another file) and you have to suspend the edit, *grep* for the function name in every .c that might contain it, and finally visit the appropriate file.

To avoid this diversion or the need to remember which function is defined in which file, Berkeley UNIX has a program called *ctags(1)*, which takes a set of source files and looks for function definitions, producing a file called *tags* as its output.

JOVE has a command called C-X T (*find-tag*) that prompts you for the name of a function (a *tag*), looks up the tag reference in the previously constructed tags file, then visits the file containing that tag in a new buffer, with point positioned at the definition of the function. There is another version of this command, namely *find-tag-at-point*, that uses the identifier at *point*.

So, when you've added new functions to a module, or moved some old ones around, run the *ctags* program to regenerate the *tags* file. JOVE looks in the file specified in the *tag-file* variable. The default is "./tags", that is, the tag file in the current directory. If you wish to use an alternate tag file, you use C-U C-X T, and JOVE will prompt for a file name. If you find yourself specifying the same file again and again, you can set *tag-file* to that file, and run *find-tag* with no numeric argument.

To begin an editing session looking for a particular tag, use the *−t tag* command line option to JOVE. For example, say you wanted to look at the file containing the tag *SkipChar*, you would invoke JOVE as:

        % jove −t SkipChar

14.4. Compiling Your Program

You've typed in a program or altered an existing one and now you want to run it through the compiler to check for errors. To save having to suspend the edit, run the compiler, scribble down error messages, and then resume the edit, JOVE allows you to compile your code while in the editor. This is done with the C-X C-E (*compile-it*) command. If you run *compile-it* with no argument it runs the UNIX *make* program into a buffer; If you need a special command or want to pass arguments to *make*, run *compile-it* with any argument (C-U is good enough) and you will be prompted for the command to execute.

If any error messages are produced, they are treated specially by JOVE. That treatment is the subject of the next section.

14.5. Error Message Parsing and Spelling Checking

JOVE knows how to interpret the error messages from many UNIX commands; In particular, the messages from *cc*, *grep* and *lint* can be understood. After running the *compile-it* command, the *parse-errors* command is automatically executed, and any errors found are displayed in a new buffer. The files whose names are found in parsing the error messages are each brought into JOVE buffers and the point is positioned at the first error in the first file. The commands *current-error*, C-X C-N (*next-error*), and C-X C-P (*previous-error*) can be used to traverse the list of errors.

If you already have a file called *errs* containing, say, c compiler messages then you can get JOVE to interpret the messages by invoking it as:

> *% jove –p errs*

JOVE has a special mechanism for checking the the spelling of a document; It runs the UNIX spell program into a buffer. You then delete from this buffer all those words that are not spelling errors and then JOVE runs the *parse-spelling-errors* command to yield a list of errors just as in the last section.

15. Simple Customization

15.1. Major Modes

To help with editing particular types of file, say a paper or a C program, JOVE has several *major modes*. These are as follows:

15.1.1. Text mode

This is the default major mode. Nothing special is done.

15.1.2. C mode

This mode affects the behavior of the tab and parentheses characters. Instead of just inserting the tab, JOVE determines where the text "ought" to line up for the C language and tabs to that position instead. The same thing happens with the close brace and close parenthesis; they are tabbed to the "right" place and then inserted. Using the *auto-execute-command* command, you can make JOVE enter *C Mode* whenever you edit a file whose name ends in *.c*.

15.1.3. Lisp mode

This mode is analogous to *C Mode*, but performs the indentation needed to lay out Lisp programs properly. Note also the *grind-s-expr* command that prettyprints an *s-expression* and the *kill-mode-expression* command.

15.2. Minor Modes

In addition to the major modes, JOVE has a set of minor modes. These are as follows:

15.2.1. Auto Indent

In this mode, JOVE indents each line the same way as that above it. That is, the Return key in this mode acts as the Linefeed key ordinarily does.

15.2.2. Show Match

Move the cursor momentarily to the matching opening parenthesis when a closing parenthesis is typed.

15.2.3. Auto Fill

In *Auto Fill* mode, a newline is automatically inserted when the line length exceeds the right margin. This way, you can type a whole paper without having to use the Return key.

15.2.4. Over Write

In this mode, any text typed in will replace the previous contents. (The default is for new text to be inserted and "push" the old along.) This is useful for editing an already-formatted diagram in which you want to change some things without moving other things around on the screen.

14

15.2.5. Word Abbrev

In this mode, every word you type is compared to a list of word abbreviations; whenever you type an abbreviation, it is replaced by the text that it abbreviates. This can save typing if a particular word or phrase must be entered many times. The abbreviations and their expansions are held in a file that looks like:

> abbrev:phrase

This file can be set up in your *7. joverc* with the *read-word-abbrev-file* command. Then, whenever you are editing a buffer in *Word Abbrev* mode, JOVE checks for the abbreviations you've given. See also the commands *read-word-abbrev-file*, *write-word-abbrev-file*, *edit-word-abbrevs*, *define-global-word-abbrev*, *define-mode-word-abbrev*, and *bind-macro-to-word-abbrev*, and the variable *auto-case-abbrev*.

15.3. Variables

JOVE can be tailored to suit your needs by changing the values of variables. A JOVE variable can be given a value with the *set* command, and its value displayed with the *print* command.

The variables JOVE understands are listed along with the commands in the alphabetical list at the end of this document.

15.4. Key Re-binding

Many of the commands built into JOVE are not bound to specific keys. The command handler in JOVE is used to invoke these commands and is activated by the *execute-extended-command* command (ESC X). When the name of a command typed in is unambiguous, that command will be executed. Since it is very slow to have to type in the name of each command every time it is needed, JOVE makes it possible to *bind* commands to keys. When a command is *bound* to a key any future hits on that key will invoke that command. All the printing characters are initially bound to the command *self-insert*. Thus, typing any printing character causes it to be inserted into the text. Any of the existing commands can be bound to any key. (A *key* may actually be a *control character* or an *escape sequence* as explained previously under *Command Input Conventions*).

Since there are more commands than there are keys, two keys are treated as *prefix* commands. When a key bound to one of the prefix commands is typed, the next character typed is interpreted on the basis that it was preceded by one of the prefix keys. Initially ^X and ESC are the prefix keys and many of the built in commands are initially bound to these "two stroke" keys. (For historical reasons, the Escape key is often referred to as "Meta").

15.5. Keyboard Macros

Although JOVE has many powerful commands, you often find that you have a task that no individual command can do. JOVE allows you to define your own commands from sequences of existing ones "by example"; Such a sequence is termed a *macro*. The procedure is as follows: First you type the *start-remembering* command, usually bound to C-X (. Next you "perform" the commands which as they are being executed are also remembered, which will constitute the body of the macro. Then you give the *stop-remembering* command, usually bound to C-X). You now have a *keyboard macro*. To run this command sequence again, use the command *execute-keyboard-macro*, usually bound to C-X E. You may find this bothersome to type and re-type, so there is a way to bind the macro to a key. First, you must give the keyboard macro a name using the *name-keyboard-macro* command. Then the binding is made with the *bind-macro-to-key* command. We're still not finished because all this hard work will be lost if you leave JOVE. What you do is to save your macros into a file with the *write-macros-to-file* command. There is a corresponding *read-macros-from-file* command to retrieve your macros in the next editing session.

15.6. Initialization Files

Users will likely want to modify the default key bindings to their liking. Since it would be quite annoying to have to set up the bindings each time JOVE is started up, JOVE has the ability to read in a "startup" file. Whenever JOVE is started, it reads commands from the file *.joverc* in the user's home directory. These commands are read as if they were typed to the command handler (ESC X) during an edit. There can be only one command per line in the startup file. If there is a file */usr/lib/jove/joverc*, then this file will be read before the user's *.joverc* file. This can be used to set up a system-wide default startup mode for JOVE that is tailored to the needs of that system.

The *source* command can be used to read commands from a specified file at any time during an editing session, even from inside the *.joverc* file. This means that a macro can be used to change the key bindings, e.g., to enter a mode, by reading from a specified file which contains all the necessary bindings.

16. Alphabetical List of Commands and Variables

16.1. Prefix-1 (Escape)

This reads the next character and runs a command based on the character typed. If you wait for more than a second or so before typing the next character, the message "ESC" will be printed on the message line to remind you that JOVE is waiting for another character.

16.2. Prefix-2 (C-X)

This reads the next character and runs a command based on the character typed. If you wait for more than a second or so before typing another character, the message "C-X" will be printed on the message line to remind you that JOVE is waiting for another character.

16.3. Prefix-3 (Not Bound)

This reads the next character and runs a command based on the character typed. If you wait for more than a second or so before typing the next character, the character that invoked Prefix-3 will be printed on the message line to remind you that JOVE is waiting for another one.

16.4. allow-^S-and-^Q (variable)

This variable, when set, tells JOVE that your terminal does not need to use the characters C-S and C-Q for flow control, and that it is okay to bind things to them. This variable should be set depending upon what kind of terminal you have.

16.5. allow-bad-filenames (variable)

If set, this variable permits filenames to contain "bad" characters such as those from the set *&%!'"[]{}. These files are harder to deal with, because the characters mean something to the shell. The default value is "off".

16.6. append-region (Not Bound)

This appends the region to a specified file. If the file does not already exist it is created.

16.7. apropos (Not Bound)

This types out all the commands, variables and macros with the specific keyword in their names. For each command and macro that contains the string, the key sequence that can be used to execute the command or macro is printed; with variables, the current value is printed. So, to find all the commands that are related to windows, you type

> ESC X apropos window<Return>

16.8. auto-case-abbrev (variable)

When this variable is on (the default), word abbreviations are adjusted for case automatically. For example, if "jove" were the abbreviation for "jonathan's own version of emacs", then typing "jove" would give you "jonathan's own version of emacs", typing "Jove" would give you "Jonathan's own version of emacs", and typing "JOVE" would give you "Jonathan's Own Version of Emacs". When this variable is "off", upper and lower case are distinguished when looking for the abbreviation, i.e., in the example above, "JOVE" and "Jove" would not be expanded unless they were defined separately.

14

16.9. auto-execute-command (Not Bound)

This tells JOVE to execute a command automatically when a file whose name matches a specified pattern is visited. The first argument is the command you want executed and the second is a regular expression pattern that specifies the files that apply. For example, if you want to be in show-match-mode when you edit C source files (that is, files that end with ".c" or ".h") you can type

      ESC X auto-execute-command show-match-mode .*.[ch]$

16.10. auto-execute-macro (Not Bound)

This is like *auto-execute-command* except you use it to execute macros automatically instead of built-in commands.

16.11. auto-fill-mode (Not Bound)

This turns on Auto Fill mode (or off if it's currently on) in the selected buffer. When JOVE is in Auto Fill mode it automatically breaks lines for you when you reach the right margin so you don't have to remember to hit Return. JOVE uses 78 as the right margin but you can change that by setting the variable *right-margin* to another value. See the *set* command to learn how to do this.

16.12. auto-indent-mode (Not Bound)

This turns on Auto Indent mode (or off if it's currently on) in the selected buffer. When JOVE is in Auto Indent mode, Return indents the new line to the same position as the line you were just on. This is useful for lining up C code (or any other language (but what else is there besides C?)). This is out of date because of the new command called *newline-and-indent* but it remains because of several "requests" on the part of, uh, enthusiastic and excitable users, that it be left as it is.

16.13. backward-character (C-B)

This moves point backward over a single character. If point is at the beginning of the line it moves to the end of the previous line.

16.14. backward-paragraph (ESC [)

This moves point backward to the beginning of the current or previous paragraph. Paragraphs are bounded by lines that begin with a Period or Tab, or by blank lines; a change in indentation may also signal a break between paragraphs, except that JOVE allows the first line of a paragraph to be indented differently from the other lines.

16.15. backward-s-expression (ESC C-B)

This moves point backward over a s-expression. It is just like *forward-s-expression* with a negative argument.

16.16. backward-sentence (ESC A)

This moves point backward to the beginning of the current or previous sentence. JOVE considers the end of a sentence to be the characters ".", "!" or "?" followed by a Return or by one or more spaces.

16.17. backward-word (ESC B)

This moves point backward to the beginning of the current or previous word.

16.18. bad-filename-extensions (variable)

This contains a list of words separated by spaces which are to be considered bad filename extensions, and so will not be counted in filename completion. The default is ".o" so if you have jove.c and jove.o in the same directory, the filename completion will *not* complain of an ambiguity because it will ignore jove.o.

16.19. beginning-of-file (ESC <)

This moves point backward to the beginning of the buffer. This sometimes prints the "Point Pushed" message. If the top of the buffer isn't on the screen JOVE will set the mark so you can go back to where you were if you want.

16.20. beginning-of-line (C-A)

This moves point to the beginning of the current line.

16.21. beginning-of-window (ESC ,)

This moves point to the beginning of the current window. The sequence "ESC ," is the same as "ESC <" (beginning of file) except without the shift key on the "<", and can thus can easily be remembered.

16.22. bind-to-key (Not Bound)

This attaches a key to an internal JOVE command so that future hits on that key invoke that command. For example, to make "C-W" erase the previous word, you type "ESC X bind-to-key kill-previous-word C-W".

16.23. bind-macro-to-key (Not Bound)

This is like *bind-to-key* except you use it to attach keys to named macros.

16.24. bind-macro-to-word-abbrev (Not Bound)

This command allows you to bind a macro to a previously defined word abbreviation. Whenever you type the abbreviation, it will first be expanded as an abbreviation, and then the macro will be executed. Note that if the macro moves around, you should set the mark first (C-@) and then exchange the point and mark last (C-X C-X).

16.25. buffer-position (Not Bound)

This displays the current file name, current line number, total number of lines, percentage of the way through the file, and the position of the cursor in the current line.

16.26. c-mode (Not Bound)

This turns on C mode in the currently selected buffer. This is one of currently four possible major modes: Fundamental, Text, C, Lisp. When in C or Lisp mode, Tab, "}", and ")" behave a little differently from usual: They are indented to the "right" place for C (or Lisp) programs. In JOVE, the "right" place is simply the way the author likes it (but I've got good taste).

16.27. case-character-capitalize (Not Bound)

This capitalizes the character after point, i.e., the character undo the cursor. If a negative argument is supplied that many characters *before* point are upper cased.

16.28. case-ignore-search (variable)

This variable, when set, tells JOVE to treat upper and lower case as the same when searching. Thus "jove" and "JOVE" would match, and "JoVe" would match either. The default value of this variable is "off".

16.29. case-region-lower (Not Bound)

This changes all the upper case letters in the region to their lower case equivalent.

16.30. case-region-upper (Not Bound)

This changes all the lower case letters in the region to their upper case equivalent.

16.31. case-word-capitalize (ESC C)

This capitalizes the current word by making the current letter upper case and making the rest of the word lower case. Point is moved to the end of the word. If point is not positioned on a word it is first moved forward to the beginning of the next word. If a negative argument is supplied that many words *before* point are capitalized. This is

14

useful for correcting the word just typed without having to move point to the beginning of the word yourself.

16.32. case-word-lower (ESC L)

This lower-cases the current word and leaves point at the end of it. If point is in the middle of a word the rest of the word is converted. If point is not in a word it is first moved forward to the beginning of the next word. If a negative argument is supplied that many words *before* point are converted to lower case. This is useful for correcting the word just typed without having to move point to the beginning of the word yourself.

16.33. case-word-upper (ESC U)

This upper-cases the current word and leaves point at the end of it. If point is in the middle of a word the rest of the word is converted. If point is not in a word it is first moved forward to the beginning of the next word. If a negative argument is supplied that many words *before* point are converted to upper case. This is useful for correcting the word just typed without having to move point to the beginning of the word yourself.

16.34. character-to-octal-insert (Not Bound)

This inserts a Back-slash followed by the ascii value of the next character typed. For example, "C-G" inserts the string "\007".

16.35. cd (Not Bound)

This changes the current directory.

16.36. clear-and-redraw (ESC C-L)

This clears the entire screen and redraws all the windows. Use this when JOVE gets confused about what's on the screen, or when the screen gets filled with garbage characters or output from another program.

16.37. comment-format (variable)

This variable tells JOVE how to format your comments when you run the command *fill-comment*. Its format is this:

        <open pattern>%!<line header>%c<line trailer>%!<close pattern>

The %!, %c, and %! must appear in the format; everything else is optional. A newline (represented by %n) may appear in the open or close patterns. %% is the representation for %. The default comment format is for C comments. See *fill-comment* for more.

16.38. compile-it (C-X C-E)

This compiles your program by running the UNIX command "make" into a buffer, and automatically parsing the error messages that are created (if any). See the *parse-errors* and *parse-special-errors* commands. To compile a C program without "make", use "C-U C-X C-E" and JOVE will prompt for a command to run instead of make. (And then the command you type will become the default command.) You can use this to parse the output from the C compiler or the "grep" or "lint" programs.

16.39. continue-process (Not Bound)

This sends SIGCONT to the current interactive process, *if* the process is currently stopped.

16.40. copy-region (ESC W)

This takes all the text in the region and copies it onto the kill ring buffer. This is just like running *kill-region* followed by the *yank* command. See the *kill-region* and *yank* commands.

16.41. current-error (Not Bound)

This moves to the current error in the list of parsed errors. See the *next-error* and *previous-error* commands for more detailed information.

16.42. date (Not Bound)

This prints the date on the message line.

16.43. define-mode-word-abbrev (Not Bound)

This defines a mode-specific abbreviation.

16.44. define-global-word-abbrev (Not Bound)

This defines a global abbreviation.

16.45. delete-blank-lines (C-X C-O)

This deletes all the blank lines around point. This is useful when you previously opened many lines with "C-O" and now wish to delete the unused ones.

16.46. delete-buffer (C-X K)

This deletes a buffer and frees up all the memory associated with it. Be careful! Once a buffer has been deleted it is gone forever. JOVE will ask you to confirm if you try to delete a buffer that needs saving. This command is useful for when JOVE runs out of space to store new buffers.

16.47. delete-macro (Not Bound)

This deletes a macro from the list of named macros. It is an error to delete the keyboard-macro. Once the macro is deleted it is gone forever. If you are about to save macros to a file and decide you don't want to save a particular one, delete it.

16.48. delete-next-character (C-D)

This deletes the character that's just after point (that is, the character under the cursor). If point is at the end of a line, the line separator is deleted and the next line is joined with the current one.

16.49. delete-other-windows (C-X 1)

This deletes all the other windows except the current one. This can be thought of as going back into One Window mode.

16.50. delete-previous-character (Rubout)

This deletes the character that's just before point (that is, the character before the cursor). If point is at the beginning of the line, the line separator is deleted and that line is joined with the previous one.

16.51. delete-white-space (ESC \)

This deletes all the Tabs and Spaces around point.

16.52. delete-current-window (C-X D)

This deletes the current window and moves point into one of the remaining ones. It is an error to try to delete the only remaining window.

16.53. describe-bindings (Not Bound)

This types out a list containing each bound key and the command that gets invoked every time that key is typed. To make a wall chart of JOVE commands, set *send-typeout-to-buffer* to "on" and JOVE will store the key bindings in a buffer which you can save to a file and then print.

16.54. describe-command (Not Bound)

This prints some info on a specified command.

14

16.55. describe-key (Not Bound)

This waits for you to type a key and then tells the name of the command that gets invoked every time that key is hit. Once you have the name of the command you can use the *describe-command* command to find out exactly what it does.

16.56. describe-variable (Not Bound)

This prints some info on a specified variable.

16.57. digit (ESC [0-9])

This reads a numeric argument. When you type "ESC" followed by a number, "digit" keeps reading numbers until you type some other command. Then that command is executes with the numeric argument you specified.

16.58. digit-1 (Not Bound)

This pretends you typed "ESC 1". This is useful for terminals that have keypads that send special sequences for numbers typed on the keypad as opposed to numbers typed from the keyboard. This can save having type "ESC" when you want to specify an argument.

16.59. digit-2 (Not Bound)

This pretends you typed "ESC 2". This is useful for terminals that have keypads that send special sequences for numbers typed on the keypad as opposed to numbers typed from the keyboard. This can save having type "ESC" when you want to specify an argument.

16.60. digit-3 (Not Bound)

This pretends you typed "ESC 3". This is useful for terminals that have keypads that send special sequences for numbers typed on the keypad as opposed to numbers typed from the keyboard. This can save having type "ESC" when you want to specify an argument.

16.61. digit-4 (Not Bound)

This pretends you typed "ESC 4". This is useful for terminals that have keypads that send special sequences for numbers typed on the keypad as opposed to numbers typed from the keyboard. This can save having type "ESC" when you want to specify an argument.

16.62. digit-5 (Not Bound)

This pretends you typed "ESC 5". This is useful for terminals that have keypads that send special sequences for numbers typed on the keypad as opposed to numbers typed from the keyboard. This can save having type "ESC" when you want to specify an argument.

16.63. digit-6 (Not Bound)

This pretends you typed "ESC 6". This is useful for terminals that have keypads that send special sequences for numbers typed on the keypad as opposed to numbers typed from the keyboard. This can save having type "ESC" when you want to specify an argument.

16.64. digit-7 (Not Bound)

This pretends you typed "ESC 7". This is useful for terminals that have keypads that send special sequences for numbers typed on the keypad as opposed to numbers typed from the keyboard. This can save having type "ESC" when you want to specify an argument.

16.65. digit-8 (Not Bound)

This pretends you typed "ESC 8". This is useful for terminals that have keypads that send special sequences for numbers typed on the keypad as opposed to numbers typed from the keyboard. This can save having type "ESC" when you want to specify an argument.

14

16.66. digit-9 (Not Bound)

This pretends you typed "ESC 9". This is useful for terminals that have keypads that send special sequences for numbers typed on the keypad as opposed to numbers typed from the keyboard. This can save having type "ESC" when you want to specify an argument.

16.67. digit-0 (Not Bound)

This pretends you typed "ESC 0". This is useful for terminals that have keypads that send special sequences for numbers typed on the keypad as opposed to numbers typed from the keyboard. This can save having type "ESC" when you want to specify an argument.

16.68. dirs (Not Bound)

This prints out the directory stack. See the "cd", "pushd", "popd" commands for more info.

16.69. disable-biff (variable)

When this is set, JOVE disables biff when you're editing and enables it again when you get out of JOVE, or when you pause to the parent shell or push to a new shell. (This means arrival of new mail will not be immediately apparent but will not cause indiscriminate writing on the display). The default is "off".

16.70. dstop-process (Not Bound)

Send the "dsusp" character to the current process. This is the character that suspends a process on the next read from the terminal. Most people have it set to C-Y. This only works if you have the interactive process feature, and if you are in a buffer bound to a process.

16.71. edit-word-abbrevs (Not Bound)

This creates a buffer with a list of each abbreviation and the phrase it expands into, and enters a recursive edit to let you change the abbreviations or add some more. The format of this list is "abbreviation:phrase" so if you add some more you should follow that format. It's probably simplest just to copy some already existing abbreviations and edit them. When you are done you type "C-X C-C" to exit the recursive edit.

16.72. end-of-file (ESC >)

This moves point forward to the end of the buffer. This sometimes prints the "Point Pushed" message. If the end of the buffer isn't on the screen JOVE will set the mark so you can go back to where you were if you want.

16.73. end-of-line (C-E)

This moves point to the end of the current line. If the line is too long to fit on the screen JOVE will scroll the line to the left to make the end of the line visible. The line will slide back to its normal position when you move backward past the leftmost visible character or when you move off the line altogether.

16.74. end-of-window (ESC .)

This moves point to the last character in the window.

16.75. eof-process (Not Bound)

Sends EOF to the current interactive process. This only works on versions of JOVE which run under 4.2-3 BSD VAX UNIX. You can't send EOF to processes on the 2.9 BSD PDP-11 UNIX.

16.76. erase-buffer (Not Bound)

This erases the contents of the specified buffer. This is like *delete-buffer* except it only erases the contents of the buffer, not the buffer itself. If you try to erase a buffer that needs saving you will be asked to confirm it.

14

16.77. error-window-size (variable)

This is the percentage of the screen to use for the error-window on the screen. When you execute *compile-it*, *error-window-size* percent of the screen will go to the error window. If the window already exists and is a different size, it is made to be this size. The default value is 20%.

16.78. exchange-point-and-mark (C-X C-X)

This moves point to mark and makes mark the old point. This is for quickly moving from one end of the region to another.

16.79. execute-named-command (ESC X)

This is the way to execute a command that isn't bound to any key. When you are prompted with ": " you can type the name of the command. You don't have to type the entire name. Once the command is unambiguous you can type Space and JOVE will fill in the rest for you. If you are not sure of the name of the command, type "?" and JOVE will print a list of all the commands that you could possibly match given what you've already typed. If you don't have any idea what the command's name is but you know it has something to do with windows (for example), you can do "ESC X apropos window" and JOVE will print a list of all the commands that are related to windows. If you find yourself constantly executing the same commands this way you probably want to bind them to keys so that you can execute them more quickly. See the *bind-to-key* command.

16.80. execute-keyboard-macro (C-X E)

This executes the keyboard macro. If you supply a numeric argument the macro is executed that many times.

16.81. execute-macro (Not Bound)

This executes a specified macro. If you supply a numeric argument the macro is executed that many times.

16.82. exit-jove (C-X C-C)

This exits JOVE. If any buffers need saving JOVE will print a warning message and ask for confirmation. If you leave without saving your buffers all your work will be lost. If you made a mistake and really do want to exit then you can. If you are in a recursive editing level *exit-jove* will return you from that.

16.83. file-creation-mode (variable)

This variable has an octal value. It contains the mode (see *chmod(1)*) with which files should be created. This mode gets modified by your current umask setting (see *umask(1)*). The default value is usually *0666* or *0644*.

16.84. files-should-end-with-newline (variable)

This variable indicates that all files should always have a newline at the end. This is often necessary for line printers and the like. When set, if JOVE is writing a file whose last character is not a newline, it will add one automatically.

16.85. fill-comment (Not Bound)

This command fills in your C comments to make them pretty and readable. This filling is done according the variable *comment-format*.

```
/*
 * the default format makes comments like this.
 */
```

This can be changed by changing the format variable. Other languages may be supported by changing the format variable appropriately. The formatter looks backwards from dot for an open comment symbol. If found, all indentation is done relative the position of the first character of the open symbol. If there is a matching close symbol, the entire comment is formatted. If not, the region between dot and the open symbol is reformatted.

14

16.86. fill-paragraph (ESC J)

This rearranges words between lines so that all the lines in the current paragraph extend as close to the right margin as possible, ensuring that none of the lines will be greater than the right margin. The default value for *right-margin* is 78, but can be changed with the *set* and *right-margin-here* commands. JOVE has a complicated algorithm for determining the beginning and end of the paragraph. In the normal case JOVE will give all the lines the same indent as they currently have, but if you wish to force a new indent you can supply a numeric argument to *fill-paragraph* (e.g., by typing C-U ESC J) and JOVE will indent each line to the column specified by the *left-margin* variable. See also the *left-margin* variable and *left-margin-here* command.

16.87. fill-region (Not Bound)

This is like *fill-paragraph,* except it operates on a region instead of just a paragraph.

16.88. filter-region (Not Bound)

This sends the text in the region to a UNIX command, and replaces the region with the output from that command. For example, if you are lazy and don't like to take the time to write properly indented C code, you can put the region around your C file and *filter-region* it through *cb,* the UNIX C beautifier. If you have a file that contains a bunch of lines that need to be sorted you can do that from inside JOVE too, by filtering the region through the *sort* UNIX command. Before output from the command replaces the region JOVE stores the old text in the kill ring, so if you are unhappy with the results you can easily get back the old text with "C-Y".

16.89. find-file (C-X C-F)

This visits a file into its own buffer and then selects that buffer. If you've already visited this file in another buffer, that buffer is selected. If the file doesn't yet exist, JOVE will print "(New file)" so that you know.

16.90. find-tag (C-X T)

This finds the file that contains the specified tag. JOVE looks up tags by default in the "tags" file in the current directory. You can change the default tag name by setting the *tag-file* variable to another name. If you specify a numeric argument to this command, you will be prompted for a tag file. This is a good way to specify another tag file without changing the default. If the tag cannot be found the error is reported and point stays where it is.

16.91. find-tag-at-point (Not Bound)

This finds the file that contains the tag that point is currently on. See *find-tag.*

16.92. first-non-blank (ESC M)

This moves point back to the indent of the current line.

16.93. forward-character (C-F)

This moves forward over a single character. If point is at the end of the line it moves to the beginning of the next one.

16.94. forward-paragraph (ESC])

This moves point forward to the end of the current or next paragraph. Paragraphs are bounded by lines that begin with a Period or Tab, or by blank lines; a change in indentation may also signal a break between paragraphs, except that JOVE allows the first line of a paragraph to be indented differently from the other lines.

16.95. forward-s-expression (ESC C-F)

This moves point forward over a s-expression. If the first significant character after point is "(", this moves past the matching ")". If the character begins an identifier, this moves just past it. This is mode dependent, so this will move over atoms in LISP mode and C identifiers in C mode. JOVE also matches "{".

14

16.96. forward-sentence (ESC E)

This moves point forward to the end of the current or next sentence. JOVE considers the end of a sentence to be the characters ".", "!" or "?" followed by a Return, or one or more spaces.

16.97. forward-word (ESC F)

This moves point forward to the end of the current or next word.

16.98. fundamental-mode (Not Bound)

This sets the major mode to Fundamental. This affects what JOVE considers as characters that make up words. For instance, Single-quote is not part of a word in Fundamental mode, but is in Text mode.

16.99. goto-line (ESC G)

If a numeric argument is supplied point moves to the beginning of that line. If no argument is supplied, point remains where it is. This is so you don't lose your place unintentionally, by accidentally hitting the "G" instead of "F".

16.100. grind-s-expr (Not Bound)

When point is positioned on a "(", this re-indents that LISP expression.

16.101. grow-window (C-X ^)

This makes the current window one line bigger. This only works when there is more than one window and provided there is room to change the size.

16.102. paren-flash () }])

This handles the C mode curly brace indentation, the Lisp mode paren indentation, and the Show Match mode paren/curly brace/square bracket flashing.

16.103. handle-tab (Tab)

This handles indenting to the "right" place in C and Lisp mode, and just inserts itself in Text mode.

16.104. i-search-forward (Not Bound)

Incremental search. Like search-forward except that instead of prompting for a string and searching for that string all at once, it accepts the string one character at a time. After each character you type as part of the search string, it searches for the entire string so far. When you like what it found, type the Return key to finish the search. You can take back a character with Rubout and the search will back up to the position before that character was typed. C-G aborts the search.

16.105. i-search-reverse (Not Bound)

Incremental search. Like search-reverse except that instead of prompting for a string and searching for that string all at once, it accepts the string one character at a time. After each character you type as part of the search string, it searches for the entire string so far. When you like what it found, type the Return key to finish the search. You can take back a character with Rubout and the search will back up to the position before that character was typed. C-G aborts the search.

16.106. insert-file (C-X C-I)

This inserts a specified file into the current buffer at point. Point is positioned at the beginning of the inserted file.

16.107. internal-tabstop (variable)

The number of spaces JOVE should print when it displays a tab character. The default value is 8.

16.108. interrupt-process (Not Bound)

This sends the interrupt character (usually C-C) to the interactive process in the current buffer. This is only for versions of JOVE that have the interactive processes feature. This only works when you are inside a buffer that's attached to a process.

16.109. i-shell (Not Bound)

This starts up an interactive shell in a window. JOVE uses "shell-1" as the name of the buffer in which the interacting takes place. See the manual for information on how to use interactive processes.

16.110. i-shell-command (Not Bound)

This is like *shell-command* except it lets you continue with your editing while the command is running. This is really useful for long running commands with sporadic output. See the manual for information on how to use interactive processes.

16.111. kill-next-word (ESC D)

This kills the text from point to the end of the current or next word.

16.112. kill-previous-word (ESC Rubout)

This kills the text from point to the beginning of the current or previous word.

16.113. kill-process (Not Bound)

This command prompts for a buffer name or buffer number (just as select-buffer does) and then sends the process in that buffer a kill signal (9).

16.114. kill-region (C-W)

This deletes the text in the region and saves it on the kill ring. Commands that delete text but save it on the kill ring all have the word "kill" in their names. Type "C-Y" to yank back the most recent kill.

16.115. kill-s-expression (ESC C-K)

This kills the text from point to the end of the current or next s-expression.

16.116. kill-some-buffers (Not Bound)

This goes through all the existing buffers and asks whether or not to kill them. If you decide to kill a buffer, and it turns out that the buffer is modified, JOVE will offer to save it first. This is useful for when JOVE runs out of memory to store lines (this only happens on PDP-11's) and you have lots of buffers that you are no longer using.

16.117. kill-to-beginning-of-sentence (C-X Rubout)

This kills from point to the beginning of the current or previous sentence.

16.118. kill-to-end-of-line (C-K)

This kills from point to the end of the current line. When point is at the end of the line the line separator is deleted and the next line is joined with current one. If a numeric argument is supplied that many lines are killed; if the argument is negative that many lines *before* point are killed; if the argument is zero the text from point to the beginning of the line is killed.

16.119. kill-to-end-of-sentence (ESC K)

This kills from point to the end of the current or next sentence. If a negative numeric argument is supplied it kills from point to the beginning of the current or previous sentence.

14

16.120. left-margin (variable)

This is how far lines should be indented when auto-indent mode is on, or when the *newline-and-indent* command is run (usually by typing LineFeed). It is also used by fill-paragraph and auto-fill mode. If the value is zero (the default) then the left margin is determined from the surrounding lines.

16.121. left-margin-here (Not Bound)

This sets the *left-margin* variable to the current position of point. This is an easy way to say, "Make the left margin begin here," without having to count the number of spaces over it actually is.

16.122. lisp-mode (Not Bound)

This turns on Lisp mode. Lisp mode is one of four mutually exclusive major modes: Fundamental, Text, C, and Lisp. In Lisp mode, the characters Tab and) are treated specially, similar to the way they are treated in C mode. Also, Auto Indent mode is affected, and handled specially.

16.123. list-buffers (C-X C-B)

This types out a list containing various information about each buffer. Right now that list looks like this:

```
(* means the buffer needs saving)
NO   Lines Type       Name            File
--   ----- ----       ----            ----
1    1     File       Main            [No file]
2    1     Scratch  * Minibuf         [No file]
3    519   File     * commands.doc    commands.doc
```

The first column lists the buffer's number. When JOVE prompts for a buffer name you can either type in the full name, or you can simply type the buffer's number. The second column is the number of lines in the buffer. The third says what type of buffer. There are four types: "File", "Scratch", "Process", "I-Process". "File" is simply a buffer that holds a file; "Scratch" is for buffers that JOVE uses internally; "Process" is one that holds the output from a UNIX command; "I-Process" is one that has an interactive process attached to it. The next column contains the name of the buffer. And the last column is the name of the file that's attached to the buffer. In this case, both Minibuf and commands.doc have been changed but not yet saved. In fact Minibuf won't be saved since it's an internal JOVE buffer that I don't even care about.

16.124. list-processes (Not Bound)

This makes a list somewhat like "list-buffers" does, except its list consists of the current interactive processes. Right now the list looks like this:

```
Buffer         Status        Command name
------         ------        ------- ----
shell-1        Running       i-shell
fgrep          Done          fgrep -n Buffer *.c
```

The first column has the name of the buffer to which the process is attached. The second has the status of the process; if a process has exited normally the status is "Done" as in fgrep; if the process exited with an error the status is "Exit N" where N is the value of the exit code; if the process was killed by some signal the status is the name of the signal that was used; otherwise the process is running. The last column is the name of the command that is being run.

16.125. mailbox (variable)

Set this to the full pathname of your mailbox. JOVE will look here to decide whether or not you have any unread mail. This defaults to /usr/spool/mail/$USER, where $USER is set to your login name.

14

16.126. mail-check-frequency (variable)

This is how often (in seconds) JOVE should check your mailbox for incoming mail. See also the *mailbox* and *disable-biff* variables.

16.127. make-backup-files (variable)

If this variable is set, then whenever JOVE writes out a file, it will move the previous version of the file (if there was one) to "#filename". This is often convenient if you save a file by accident. The default value of this variable is "off". *Note:* this is an optional part of JOVE, and your guru may not have it enabled, so it may not work.

16.128. make-buffer-unmodified (ESC ˜)

This makes JOVE think the selected buffer hasn't been changed even if it has. Use this when you accidentally change the buffer but don't want it considered changed. Watch the mode line to see the * disappear when you use this command.

16.129. make-macro-interactive (Not Bound)

This command is meaningful only while you are defining a keyboard macro. Ordinarily, when a command in a macro definition requires a trailing text argument (file name, search string, etc.), the argument you supply becomes part of the macro definition. If you want to be able to supply a different argument each time the macro is used, then while you are defining it, you should give the make-macro-interactive command just before typing the argument which will be used during the definition process. Note: you must bind this command to a key in order to use it; you can't say ESC X make-macro-interactive.

16.130. mark-threshold (variable)

This variable contains the number of lines point may move by before the mark is set. If, in a search or something, point moves by more than this many lines, the mark is set so that you may return easily. The default value of this variable is 22 (one screenful, on most terminals).

16.131. marks-should-float (variable)

When this variable is "off", the position of a mark is remembered as a line number within the buffer and a character number within the line. If you add or delete text before the mark, it will no longer point to the text you marked originally because that text is no longer at the same line and character number. When this variable is "on", the position of a mark is adjusted to compensate for each insertion and deletion. This makes marks much more sensible to use, at the cost of slowing down insertion and deletion somewhat. The default value is "on".

16.132. match-regular-expressions (variable)

When set, JOVE will match regular expressions in search patterns. This makes special the characters ., *, [,], ˆ, and $, and the two-character sequences \<, \>, \{, \} and \|. See the *ed(1)* manual page, the tutorial "Advanced Editing in UNIX ", and the section above "Searching with Regular Expressions" for more information.

16.133. meta-key (variable)

You should set this variable to "on" if your terminal has a real Meta key. If your terminal has such a key, then a key sequence like ESC Y can be entered by holding down Meta and typing Y.

16.134. mode-line (variable)

The format of the mode line can be determined by setting this variable. The items in the line are specified using a printf(3) format, with the special things being marked as "%x". Digits may be used between the 'x' may be:

14

C	check for new mail, and displays "[New mail]" if there is any (see also the mail-check-interval and disable-biff variables)
F	the current file name, with leading path stripped
M	the current list of major and minor modes
b	the current buffer name
c	the fill character (-)
d	the current directory
e	end of string--this must be the last item in the string
f	the current file name
l	the current load average (updated automatically)
m	the buffer-modified symbol (*)
n	the current buffer number
s	space, but only if previous character is not a space
t	the current time (updated automatically)
[ ]	the square brackets printed when in a recursive edit
( )	items enclosed in %(... %) will only be printed on the bottom mode line, rather than copied when the window is split

In addition, any other character is simply copied into the mode line. Characters may be escaped with a backslash. To get a feel for all this, try typing "ESC X print mode-line" and compare the result with your current mode line.

16.135. mode-line-should-standout (variable)

If set, the mode line will be printed in reverse video, if your terminal supports it. The default for this variable is "off".

16.136. name-keyboard-macro (Not Bound)

This copies the keyboard macro and gives it a name freeing up the keyboard macro so you can define some more. Keyboard macros with their own names can be bound to keys just like built in commands can. See the *read-macros-file-file* and *write-macros-to-file* commands.

16.137. newline (Return)

This divides the current line at point moving all the text to the right of point down onto the newly created line. Point moves down to the beginning of the new line.

16.138. newline-and-backup (C-O)

This divides the current line at point moving all the text to the right of point down onto the newly created line. The difference between this and "newline" is that point does not move down to the beginning of the new line.

16.139. newline-and-indent (LineFeed)

This behaves the same was as Return does when in Auto Indent mode. This makes Auto Indent mode obsolete but it remains in the name of backward compatibility.

16.140. next-error (C-X C-N)

This moves to the next error in the list of errors that were parsed with *parse-errors* or *parse-special-errors*. In one window the list of errors is shown with the current one always at the top. In another window is the file that contains the error. Point is positioned in this window on the line where the error occurred.

16.141. next-line (C-N)

This moves down to the next line.

16.142. next-page (C-V)

This displays the next page of the buffer by taking the bottom line of the window and redrawing the window with it at the top. If there isn't another page in the buffer JOVE rings the bell. If a numeric argument is supplied the screen is scrolled up that many lines; if the argument is negative the screen is scrolled down.

16.143. next-window (C-X N)

This moves into the next window. Windows live in a circular list so when you're in the bottom window and you try to move to the next one you are moved to the top window. It is an error to use this command with only one window.

16.144. number-lines-in-window (Not Bound)

This displays the line numbers for each line in the buffer being displayed. The number isn't actually part of the text; it's just printed before the actual buffer line is. To turn this off you run the command again; it toggles.

16.145. over-write-mode (Not Bound)

This turns Over Write mode on (or off if it's currently on) in the selected buffer. When on, this mode changes the way the self-inserting characters work. Instead of inserting themselves and pushing the rest of the line over to the right, they replace or over-write the existing character. Also, Rubout replaces the character before point with a space instead of deleting it. When Over Write mode is on "OvrWt" is displayed on the mode line.

16.146. page-next-window (ESC C-V)

This displays the next page in the next window. This is exactly the same as "C-X N C-V C-X P".

16.147. paren-flash-delay (variable)

How long, in tenths of seconds, JOVE should pause on a matching parenthesis in *Show* mode. The default is 5.

16.148. parse-errors (Not Bound)

This takes the list of C compilation errors (or output from another program in the same format) in the current buffer and parses them for use with the *next-error* and *previous-error* and *current-error* commands. This is a very useful tool and helps with compiling C programs and when used in conjunction with the "grep" UNIX command very helpful in making changes to a bunch of files. This command understands errors produced by cc, cpp, and lint; plus any other program with the same format (e.g., "grep -n"). JOVE visits each file that has an error and remembers each line that contains an error. It doesn't matter if later you insert or delete some lines in the buffers containing errors; JOVE remembers where they are regardless. *next-error* is automatically executed after one of the parse commands, so you end up at the first error.

16.149. parse-special-errors (Not Bound)

This parses errors in an unknown format. Error parsing works with regular expression search strings with \('s around the the file name and the line number. So, you can use *parse-special-errors* to parse lines that are in a slightly different format by typing in your own search string. If you don't know how to use regular expressions you can't use this command.

16.150. parse-spelling-errors-in-buffer (Not Bound)

This parses a list of words in the current buffer and looks them up in another buffer that you specify. This will probably go away soon.

16.151. pause-jove (ESC S)

This stops JOVE and returns control to the parent shell. This only works for users using the C-shell, and on systems that have the job control facility. To return to JOVE you type "fg" to the C-shell.

14

16.152. physical-tabstop (variable)

How many spaces your terminal prints when it prints a tab character.

16.153. pop-mark (Not Bound)

This gets executed when you run *set-mark* with a numeric argument. JOVE remembers the last 16 marks and you use *pop-mark* to go backward through the ring of marks. If you execute " *pop-mark* enough times you will eventually get back to where you started.

16.154. popd (Not Bound)

This pops one entry off the directory stack. Entries are pushed with the *pushd* command. The names were stolen from the C-shell and the behavior is the same.

16.155. previous-error (C-X C-P)

This is the same as *next-error* except it goes to the previous error. See *next-error* for documentation.

16.156. previous-line (C-P)

This moves up to the previous line.

16.157. previous-page (ESC V)

This displays the previous page of the current buffer by taking the top line and redrawing the window with it at the bottom. If a numeric argument is supplied the screen is scrolled down that many lines; if the argument is negative the screen is scrolled up.

16.158. previous-window (C-X P and C-X O)

This moves into the next window. Windows live in a circular list so when you're in the top window and you try to move to the previous one you are moved to the bottom window. It is an error to use this command with only one window.

16.159. print (Not Bound)

This prints the value of a JOVE variable.

16.160. print-message (Not Bound)

This command prompts for a message, and then prints it on the bottom line where JOVE messages are printed.

16.161. process-bind-to-key (Not Bound)

This command is identical to bind-to-key, except that it only affects your bindings when you are in a buffer attached to a process. When you enter the process buffer, any keys bound with this command will automatically take their new values. When you switch to a non-process buffer, the old bindings for those keys will be restored. For example, you might want to execute

       process-bind-to-key stop-process ˆZ
       process-bind-to-key interrupt-process ˆC

Then, when you start up an interactive process and switch into that buffer, C-Z will execute stop-process and C-C will execute interrupt- process. When you switch back to a non-process buffer, C-Z will go back to executing scroll-up (or whatever you have it bound to).

16.162. process-newline (Return)

This this only gets executed when in a buffer that is attached to an interactive-process. JOVE does two different things depending on where you are when you hit Return. When you're at the end of the I-Process buffer this does what Return normally does, except it also makes the line available to the process. When point is positioned at some other position that line is copied to the end of the buffer (with the prompt stripped) and point is moved there with it, so you can then edit that line before sending it to the process. This command *must* be bound to the key you usually use to enter shell commands (Return), or else you won't be able to enter any.

16.163. process-prompt (variable)

What a prompt looks like from the i-shell and i-shell-command processes. The default is "% ", the default C-shell prompt. This is actually a regular expression search string. So you can set it to be more than one thing at once using the \| operator. For instance, for LISP hackers, the prompt can be

> "% -> <[0-9]>: ".

16.164. push-shell (Not Bound)

This spawns a child shell and relinquishes control to it. This works on any version of UNIX, but this isn't as good as *pause-jove* because it takes time to start up the new shell and you get a brand new environment every time. To return to JOVE you type "C-D".

16.165. pushd (Not Bound)

This pushes a directory onto the directory stack and cd's into it. It asks for the directory name but if you don't specify one it switches the top two entries no the stack. It purposely behaves the same as C-shell's *pushd.*

16.166. pwd (Not Bound)

This prints the working directory.

16.167. quadruple-numeric-argument (C-U)

This multiplies the numeric argument by 4. So, "C-U C-F" means forward 4 characters and "C-U C-U C-N" means down 16 lines.

16.168. query-replace-string (ESC Q)

This replaces the occurrences of a specified string with a specified replacement string. When an occurrence is found point is moved to it and then JOVE asks what to do. The options are:

Space	to replace this occurrence and go on to the next one.
Period	to replace this occurrence and then stop.
Rubout	to skip this occurrence and go on to the next one.
C-R	to enter a recursive edit. This lets you temporarily suspend the replace, do some editing, and then return to continue where you left off. To continue with the Query Replace type "C-X C-C" as if you were trying to exit JOVE. Normally you would but when you are in a recursive edit all it does is exit that recursive editing level.
C-W	to delete the matched string and then enter a recursive edit.
U	to undo the last replacement.
P or !	to go ahead and replace the remaining occurrences without asking.
Return	to stop the Query Replace.

The search for occurrences starts at point and goes to the end of the buffer, so to replace in the entire buffer you must first go to the beginning.

16.169. quit-process (Not Bound)

This is the same as typing "C-\" (the Quit character) to a normal UNIX process, except it sends it to the current process in JOVE. This is only for versions of JOVE that have the interactive processes feature. This only works when

14

you are inside a buffer that's attached to a process.

16.170. quoted-insert (C-Q)

This lets you insert characters that normally would be executed as other JOVE commands. For example, to insert "C-F" you type "C-Q C-F".

16.171. read-word-abbrev-file (Not Bound)

This reads a specified file that contains a bunch of abbreviation definitions, and makes those abbreviations available. If the selected buffer is not already in Word Abbrev mode this command puts it in that mode.

16.172. read-macros-from-file (Not Bound)

This reads the specified file that contains a bunch of macro definitions, and defines all the macros that were currently defined when the file was created. See *write-macros-to-file* to see how to save macros.

16.173. redraw-display (C-L)

This centers the line containing point in the window. If that line is already in the middle the window is first cleared and then redrawn. If a numeric argument is supplied, the line is positioned at that offset from the top of the window. For example, "ESC 0 C-L" positions the line containing point at the top of the window.

16.174. recursive-edit (Not Bound)

This enters a recursive editing level. This isn't really very useful. I don't know why it's available for public use. I think I'll delete it some day.

16.175. rename-buffer (Not Bound)

This lets you rename the current buffer.

16.176. replace-in-region (Not Bound)

This is the same as *replace-string* except that it is restricted to occurrences between Point and Mark.

16.177. replace-string (ESC R)

This replaces all occurrences of a specified string with a specified replacement string. This is just like *query-replace-string* except it replaces without asking.

16.178. right-margin (variable)

Where the right margin is for *Auto Fill* mode and the *justify-paragraph* and *justify-region* commands. The default is 78.

16.179. right-margin-here (Not Bound)

This sets the *right-margin* variable to the current position of point. This is an easy way to say, "Make the right margin begin here," without having to count the number of spaces over it actually is.

16.180. save-file (C-X C-S)

This saves the current buffer to the associated file. This makes your changes permanent so you should be sure you really want to. If the buffer has not been modified *save-file* refuses to do the save. If you really do want to write the file you can use "C-X C-W" which executes *write-file*.

16.181. scroll-down (ESC Z)

This scrolls the screen one line down. If the line containing point moves past the bottom of the window point is moved up to the center of the window. If a numeric argument is supplied that many lines are scrolled; if the argument is negative the screen is scrolled up instead.

16.182. scroll-step (variable)

How many lines should be scrolled if the *previous-line* or *next-line* commands move you off the top or bottom of the screen. You may wish to decrease this variable if you are on a slow terminal.

16.183. scroll-up (C-Z)

This scrolls the screen one line up. If the line containing point moves past the top of the window point is moved down to the center of the window. If a numeric argument is supplied that many lines are scrolled; if the argument is negative the screen is scrolled down instead.

16.184. search-exit-char (variable)

Set this to the character you want to use to exit incremental search. The default is Newline, which makes i-search compatible with normal string search.

16.185. search-forward (C-S)

This searches forward for a specified search string and positions point at the end of the string if it's found. If the string is not found point remains unchanged. This searches from point to the end of the buffer, so any matches before point will be missed.

16.186. search-reverse (C-R)

This searches backward for a specified search string and positions point at the beginning if the string if it's found. If the string is not found point remains unchanged. This searches from point to the beginning of the buffer, so any matches after point will be missed.

16.187. select-buffer (C-X B)

This selects a new or already existing buffer making it the current one. You can type either the buffer name or number. If you type in the name you need only type the name until it is unambiguous, at which point typing Escape or Space will complete it for you. If you want to create a new buffer you can type Return instead of Space, and a new empty buffer will be created.

16.188. self-insert (Most Printing Characters)

This inserts the character that invoked it into the buffer at point. Initially all but a few of the printing characters are bound to *self-insert*.

16.189. send-typeout-to-buffer (variable)

When this is set JOVE will send output that normally overwrites the screen (temporarily) to a buffer instead. This affects commands like *list-buffers*, *list-processes*, and other commands that use command completion. The default value is "off".

16.190. set (Not Bound)

This gives a specified variable a new value. Occasionally you'll see lines like "set this variable to that value to do this". Well, you use the *set* command to do that.

16.191. set-mark (C-@)

This sets the mark at the current position in the buffer. It prints the message "Point pushed" on the message line. It says that instead of "Mark set" because when you set the mark the previous mark is still remembered on a ring of 16 marks. So "Point pushed" means point is pushed onto the ring of marks and becomes the value of "the mark". To go through the ring of marks you type "C-U C-@", or execute the *pop-mark* command. If you type this enough times you will get back to where you started.

14

16.192. shell (variable)

The shell to be used with all the shell commands command. If your SHELL environment variable is set, it is used as the value of *shell;* otherwise "/bin/csh" is the default.

16.193. shell-command (C-X !)

This runs a UNIX command and places the output from that command in a buffer. JOVE creates a buffer that matches the name of the command you specify and then attaches that buffer to a window. So, when you have only one window running this command will cause JOVE to split the window and attach the new buffer to that window. Otherwise, JOVE finds the most convenient of the available windows and uses that one instead. If the buffer already exists it is first emptied, except that if it's holding a file, not some output from a previous command, JOVE prints an error message and refuses to execute the command. If you really want to execute the command you should delete that buffer (saving it first, if you like) or use *shell-command-to-buffer,* and try again.

16.194. shell-command-to-buffer (Not Bound)

This is just like *shell-command* except it lets you specify the buffer to use instead of JOVE.

16.195. shell-flags (variable)

This defines the flags that are passed to shell commands. The default is "-c". See the *shell* variable to change the default shell.

16.196. show-match-mode (Not Bound)

This turns on Show Match mode (or off if it's currently on) in the selected buffer. This changes "}" and ")" so that when they are typed the are inserted as usual, and then the cursor flashes back to the matching "{" or "(" (depending on what was typed) for about half a second, and then goes back to just after the "}" or ")" that invoked the command. This is useful for typing in complicated expressions in a program. You can change how long the cursor sits on the matching paren by setting the "paren-flash-delay" variable in tenths of a second. If the matching "{" or "(" isn't visible nothing happens.

16.197. shrink-window (Not Bound)

This makes the current window one line shorter, if possible. Windows must be at least 2 lines high, one for the text and the other for the mode line.

16.198. source (Not Bound)

This reads a bunch of JOVE commands from a file. The format of the file is the same as that in your initialization file (your ".joverc") in your main directory. There should be one command per line and it should be as though you typed "ESC X" while in JOVE. For example, here's part of my initialization file:

        bind-to-key i-search-reverse ^R
        bind-to-key i-search-forward ^S
        bind-to-key pause-jove ^[S

What they do is make "C-R" call the *i-search-reverse* command and "C-S" call *i-search-forward* and "ESC S" call *pause-jove.*

16.199. spell-buffer (Not Bound)

This runs the current buffer through the UNIX *spell* program and places the output in buffer "Spell". Then JOVE lets you edit the list of words, expecting you to delete the ones that you don't care about, i.e., the ones you know are spelled correctly. Then the *parse-spelling-errors-in-buffer* command comes along and finds all the misspelled words and sets things up so the error commands work.

16.200. split-current-window (C-X 2)

This splits the current window into two equal parts (providing the resulting windows would be big enough) and displays the selected buffer in both windows. Use "C-X 1" to go back to 1 window mode.

16.201. start-remembering (C-X ()

This starts remembering your key strokes in the Keyboard macro. To stop remembering you type "C-X)". Because of a bug in JOVE you can't stop remembering by typing "ESC X stop-remembering"; *stop-remembering* must be bound to "C-X)" in order to make things work correctly. To execute the remembered key strokes you type "C-X E" which runs the *execute-keyboard-macro* command. Sometimes you may want a macro to accept different input each time it runs. To see how to do this, see the *make-macro-interactive* command.

16.202. stop-process (Not Bound)

This sends a stop signal (C-Z, for most people) to the current process. It only works if you have the interactive process feature, and you are in a buffer attached to a process.

16.203. stop-remembering (C-X))

This stop the definition of the keyboard macro. Because of a bug in JOVE, this must be bound to "C-X)". Anything else will not work properly.

16.204. string-length (Not Bound)

This prints the number of characters in the string that point sits in. Strings are surrounded by double quotes. JOVE knows that "\007" is considered a single character, namely "C-G", and also knows about other common ones, like "\r" (Return) and "\n" (LineFeed). This is mostly useful only for C programmers.

16.205. suspend-jove (ESC S)

This is a synonym for *pause-jove*.

16.206. sync-frequency (variable)

The temporary files used by JOVE are forced out to disk every *sync-frequency* modifications. The default is 50, which really makes good sense. Unless your system is very unstable, you probably shouldn't fool with this.

16.207. tag-file (variable)

This the name of the file in which JOVE should look up tag definitions. The default value is "./tags".

16.208. text-mode (Not Bound)

This sets the major mode to Text. Currently the other modes are Fundamental, C and Lisp mode.

14

16.209. transpose-characters (C-T)

This switches the character before point with the one after point, and then moves forward one. This doesn't work at the beginning of the line, and at the end of the line it switches the two characters before point. Since point is moved forward, so that the character that was before point is still before point, you can use "C-T" to drag a character down the length of a line. This command pretty quickly becomes very useful.

16.210. transpose-lines (C-X C-T)

This switches the current line with the one above it, and then moves down one so that the line that was above point is still above point. This, like *transpose-characters*, can be used to drag a line down a page.

16.211. unbind-key (Not Bound)

Use this to unbind *any* key sequence. You can use this to unbind even a prefix command, since this command does not use "key-map completion". For example, "ESC X unbind-key ESC [" unbinds the sequence "ESC [". This is useful for "turning off" something set in the system-wide ".joverc" file.

16.212. update-time-frequency (variable)

How often the mode line is updated (and thus the time and load average, if you display them). The default is 30 seconds.

16.213. use-i/d-char (variable)

If your terminal has insert/delete character capability you can tell JOVE not to use it by setting this to "off". In my opinion it is only worth using insert/delete character at low baud rates. WARNING: if you set this to "on" when your terminal doesn't have insert/delete character capability, you will get weird (perhaps fatal) results.

16.214. version (Not Bound)

Displays the version number of this JOVE.

16.215. visible-bell (variable)

Use the terminal's visible bell instead of beeping. This is set automatically if your terminal has the capability.

16.216. visible-spaces-in-window (Not Bound)

This displays an underscore character instead of each space in the window and displays a greater-than followed by spaces for each tab in the window. The actual text in the buffer is not changed; only the screen display is affected. To turn this off you run the command again; it toggles.

16.217. visit-file (C-X C-V)

This reads a specified file into the current buffer replacing the old text. If the buffer needs saving JOVE will offer to save it for you. Sometimes you use this to start over, say if you make lots of changes and then change your mind. If that's the case you don't want JOVE to save your buffer and you answer "NO" to the question.

16.218. window-find (C-X 4)

This lets you select another buffer in another window three different ways. This waits for another character which can be one of the following:

    T   Finds a tag in the other window.
    F   Finds a file in the other window.
    B   Selects a buffer in the other window.

This is just a convenient short hand for "C-X 2" (or "C-X O" if there are already two windows) followed by the appropriate sequence for invoking each command. With this, though, there isn't the extra overhead of having to redisplay. In addition, you don't have to decide whether to type "C-X 2" or "C-X O" since "C-X 4" does the right thing.

16.219. word-abbrev-mode (Not Bound)

This turns on Word Abbrev mode (or off if it's currently on) in the selected buffer. Word Abbrev mode lets you specify a word (an abbreviation) and a phrase with which JOVE should substitute the abbreviation. You can use this to define words to expand into long phrases, e.g., "jove" can expand into "Jonathan's Own Version of Emacs"; another common use is defining words that you often misspell in the same way, e.g., "thier" => "their" or "teh" => "the". See the information on the *auto-case-abbrev* variable.

There are two kinds of abbreviations: mode specific and global. If you define a Mode specific abbreviation in C mode, it will expand only in buffers that are in C mode. This is so you can have the same abbreviation expand to different things depending on your context. Global abbreviations expand regardless of the major mode of the buffer. The way it works is this: JOVE looks first in the mode specific table, and then in the global table. Whichever it finds it in first is the one that's used in the expansion. If it doesn't find the word it is left untouched. JOVE tries to expand words as they are typed, when you type a punctuation character or Space or Return. If you are in Auto Fill mode the expansion will be filled as if you typed it yourself.

16.220. wrap-search (variable)

If set, searches will "wrap around" the ends of the buffer instead of stopping at the bottom or top. The default is "off".

16.221. write-files-on-make (variable)

When set, all modified files will be written out before calling make when the *compile-it* command is executed. The default is "on".

16.222. write-word-abbrev-file (Not Bound)

This writes the currently defined abbreviations to a specified file. They can be read back in and automatically defined with *read-word-abbrev-file*.

16.223. write-file (C-X C-W)

This saves the current buffer to a specified file, and then makes that file the default file name for this buffer. If you specify a file that already exists you are asked to confirm over-writing it.

16.224. write-macros-to-file (Not Bound)

This writes the currently defined macros to a specified file. The macros can be read back in with *read-macros-from-file* so you can define macros and still use them in other instantiations of JOVE.

16.225. write-modified-files (C-X C-M)

This saves all the buffers that need saving. If you supply a numeric argument it asks for each buffer whether you really want to save it.

16.226. write-region (Not Bound)

This writes the text in the region to a specified file. If the file already exists you are asked to confirm over-writing it.

16.227. yank (C-Y)

This undoes the last kill command. That is, it inserts the killed text at point. When you do multiple kill commands in a row, they are merged so that yanking them back with "C-Y" yanks back all of them.

16.228. yank-pop (ESC Y)

This yanks back previous killed text. JOVE has a kill ring on which the last 10 kills are stored. *Yank* yanks a copy of the text at the front of the ring. If you want one of the last ten kills you use "ESC Y" which rotates the ring so another different entry is now at the front. You can use "ESC Y" only immediately following a "C-Y" or another "ESC Y". If you supply a negative numeric argument the ring is rotated the other way. If you use this command enough times in a row you will eventually get back to where you started. Experiment with this. It's extremely useful.

14

SED — A Non-interactive Text Editor

Lee E. McMahon

AT&T Bell Laboratories
Murray Hill, New Jersey 07974

ABSTRACT

Sed is a non-interactive context editor that runs on the UNIX† operating system. *Sed* is designed to be especially useful in three cases:

    1) To edit files too large for comfortable interactive editing;

    2) To edit any size file when the sequence of editing commands is too complicated to be comfortably typed in interactive mode.

    3) To perform multiple 'global' editing functions efficiently in one pass through the input.

This memorandum constitutes a manual for users of *sed*.

Introduction

Sed is a non-interactive context editor designed to be especially useful in three cases:

    1) To edit files too large for comfortable interactive editing;

    2) To edit any size file when the sequence of editing commands is too complicated to be comfortably typed in interactive mode;

    3) To perform multiple 'global' editing functions efficiently in one pass through the input.

Since only a few lines of the input reside in core at one time, and no temporary files are used, the effective size of file that can be edited is limited only by the requirement that the input and output fit simultaneously into available secondary storage.

Complicated editing scripts can be created separately and given to *sed* as a command file. For complex edits, this saves considerable typing, and its attendant errors. *Sed* running from a command file is much more efficient than any interactive editor known to the author, even if that editor can be driven by a pre-written script.

The principal loss of functions compared to an interactive editor are lack of relative addressing (because of the line-at-a-time operation), and lack of immediate verification that a command has done what was intended.

Sed is a lineal descendant of the UNIX editor, *ed.* Because of the differences between interactive and non-interactive operation, considerable changes have been made between *ed* and *sed;* even confirmed users of *ed* will frequently be surprised (and probably chagrined), if they rashly use *sed* without reading Sections 2 and 3 of this document. The most striking family resemblance between the two editors is in the class of patterns ('regular expressions') they recognize; the code for matching patterns is copied almost verbatim from the code for *ed,* and the description of regular expressions in Section 2 is copied almost verbatim from the UNIX Programmer's Manual[1]. (Both code and description were written by Dennis M. Ritchie.)

---

† UNIX is a registered trademark of AT&T Bell Laboratories in the USA and other countries.

1. Overall Operation

Sed by default copies the standard input to the standard output, perhaps performing one or more editing commands on each line before writing it to the output. This behavior may be modified by flags on the command line; see Section 1.1 below.

The general format of an editing command is:

[address1,address2][function][arguments]

One or both addresses may be omitted; the format of addresses is given in Section 2. Any number of blanks or tabs may separate the addresses from the function. The function must be present; the available commands are discussed in Section 3. The arguments may be required or optional, according to which function is given; again, they are discussed in Section 3 under each individual function.

Tab characters and spaces at the beginning of lines are ignored.

1.1. Command-line Flags

Three flags are recognized on the command line:

-**n:** tells *sed* not to copy all lines, but only those specified by *p* functions or *p* flags after *s* functions (see Section 3.3);

-**e:** tells *sed* to take the next argument as an editing command;

-**f:** tells *sed* to take the next argument as a file name; the file should contain editing commands, one to a line.

1.2. Order of Application of Editing Commands

Before any editing is done (in fact, before any input file is even opened), all the editing commands are compiled into a form which will be moderately efficient during the execution phase (when the commands are actually applied to lines of the input file). The commands are compiled in the order in which they are encountered; this is generally the order in which they will be attempted at execution time. The commands are applied one at a time; the input to each command is the output of all preceding commands.

The default linear order of application of editing commands can be changed by the flow-of-control commands, *t* and *b* (see Section 3). Even when the order of application is changed by these commands, it is still true that the input line to any command is the output of any previously applied command.

1.3. Pattern-space

The range of pattern matches is called the pattern space. Ordinarily, the pattern space is one line of the input text, but more than one line can be read into the pattern space by using the *N* command (Section 3.6.).

1.4. Examples

Examples are scattered throughout the text. Except where otherwise noted, the examples all assume the following input text:

    In Xanadu did Kubla Khan
    A stately pleasure dome decree:
    Where Alph, the sacred river, ran
    Through caverns measureless to man
    Down to a sunless sea.

(In no case is the output of the *sed* commands to be considered an improvement on Coleridge.)

Example:

The command

    2q

will quit after copying the first two lines of the input. The output will be:

In Xanadu did Kubla Khan
A stately pleasure dome decree:

2. ADDRESSES: Selecting lines for editing

Lines in the input file(s) to which editing commands are to be applied can be selected by addresses. Addresses may be either line numbers or context addresses.

The application of a group of commands can be controlled by one address (or address-pair) by grouping the commands with curly braces ('{ }')(Sec. 3.6.).

2.1. Line-number Addresses

A line number is a decimal integer. As each line is read from the input, a line-number counter is incremented; a line-number address matches (selects) the input line which causes the internal counter to equal the address line-number. The counter runs cumulatively through multiple input files; it is not reset when a new input file is opened.

As a special case, the character $ matches the last line of the last input file.

2.2. Context Addresses

A context address is a pattern ('regular expression') enclosed in slashes ('/'). The regular expressions recognized by *sed* are constructed as follows:

1) An ordinary character (not one of those discussed below) is a regular expression, and matches that character.

2) A circumflex '^' at the beginning of a regular expression matches the null character at the beginning of a line.

3) A dollar-sign '$' at the end of a regular expression matches the null character at the end of a line.

4) The characters '\n' match an imbedded newline character, but not the newline at the end of the pattern space.

5) A period '.' matches any character except the terminal newline of the pattern space.

6) A regular expression followed by an asterisk '*' matches any number (including 0) of adjacent occurrences of the regular expression it follows.

7) A string of characters in square brackets '[ ]' matches any character in the string, and no others. If, however, the first character of the string is circumflex '^', the regular expression matches any character *except* the characters in the string and the terminal newline of the pattern space.

8) A concatenation of regular expressions is a regular expression which matches the concatenation of strings matched by the components of the regular expression.

9) A regular expression between the sequences '\(' and '\)' is identical in effect to the unadorned regular expression, but has side-effects which are described under the *s* command below and specification 10) immediately below.

10) The expression '\d' means the same string of characters matched by an expression enclosed in '\(' and '\)' earlier in the same pattern. Here *d* is a single digit; the string specified is that beginning with the *d*th occurrence of '\(' counting from the left. For example, the expression '\(.*\)\1' matches a line beginning with two repeated occurrences of the same string.

11) The null regular expression standing alone (e.g., '//') is equivalent to the last regular expression compiled.

To use one of the special characters (^ $. * [ ] \ /) as a literal (to match an occurrence of itself in the input), precede the special character by a backslash '\'.

For a context address to 'match' the input requires that the whole pattern within the address match some portion of the pattern space.

2.3. Number of Addresses

The commands in the next section can have 0, 1, or 2 addresses. Under each command the maximum number of allowed addresses is given. For a command to have more addresses than the maximum allowed is considered an error.

15

If a command has no addresses, it is applied to every line in the input.

If a command has one address, it is applied to all lines which match that address.

If a command has two addresses, it is applied to the first line which matches the first address, and to all subsequent lines until (and including) the first subsequent line which matches the second address. Then an attempt is made on subsequent lines to again match the first address, and the process is repeated.

Two addresses are separated by a comma.

Examples:

/an/	matches lines 1, 3, 4 in our sample text
/an.*an/	matches line 1
/^an/	matches no lines
/./	matches all lines
/\./	matches line 5
/r*an/	matches lines 1,3, 4 (number = zero!)
/\(an\).*\1/	matches line 1

3. FUNCTIONS

All functions are named by a single character. In the following summary, the maximum number of allowable addresses is given enclosed in parentheses, then the single character function name, possible arguments enclosed in angles (< >), an expanded English translation of the single-character name, and finally a description of what each function does. The angles around the arguments are *not* part of the argument, and should not be typed in actual editing commands.

3.1. Whole-line Oriented Functions

(2)d -- delete lines

The *d* function deletes from the file (does not write to the output) all those lines matched by its address(es).

It also has the side effect that no further commands are attempted on the corpse of a deleted line; as soon as the *d* function is executed, a new line is read from the input, and the list of editing commands is re-started from the beginning on the new line.

(2)n -- next line

The *n* function reads the next line from the input, replacing the current line. The current line is written to the output if it should be. The list of editing commands is continued following the *n* command.

(1)a\
<text> -- append lines

The *a* function causes the argument <text> to be written to the output after the line matched by its address. The *a* command is inherently multi-line; *a* must appear at the end of a line, and <text> may contain any number of lines. To preserve the one-command-to-a-line fiction, the interior newlines must be hidden by a backslash character ('\') immediately preceding the newline. The <text> argument is terminated by the first unhidden newline (the first one not immediately preceded by backslash).

Once an *a* function is successfully executed, <text> will be written to the output regardless of what later commands do to the line which triggered it. The triggering line may be deleted entirely; <text> will still be written to the output.

The <text> is not scanned for address matches, and no editing commands are attempted on it. It does not cause any change in the line-number counter.

(1)i\
<text> -- insert lines

> The *i* function behaves identically to the *a* function, except that <text> is written to the output *before* the matched line. All other comments about the *a* function apply to the *i* function as well.

(2)c\
<text> -- change lines

> The *c* function deletes the lines selected by its address(es), and replaces them with the lines in <text>. Like *a* and *i*, *c* must be followed by a newline hidden by a backslash; and interior new lines in <text> must be hidden by backslashes.

> The *c* command may have two addresses, and therefore select a range of lines. If it does, all the lines in the range are deleted, but only one copy of <text> is written to the output, *not* one copy per line deleted. As with *a* and *i*, <text> is not scanned for address matches, and no editing commands are attempted on it. It does not change the line-number counter.

> After a line has been deleted by a *c* function, no further commands are attempted on the corpse.

> If text is appended after a line by *a* or *r* functions, and the line is subsequently changed, the text inserted by the *c* function will be placed *before* the text of the *a* or *r* functions. (The *r* function is described in Section 3.4.)

Note: Within the text put in the output by these functions, leading blanks and tabs will disappear, as always in *sed* commands. To get leading blanks and tabs into the output, precede the first desired blank or tab by a backslash; the backslash will not appear in the output.

Example:

The list of editing commands:

```
n
a\
XXXX
d
```

applied to our standard input, produces:

```
In Xanadu did Kubhla Khan
XXXX
Where Alph, the sacred river, ran
XXXX
Down to a sunless sea.
```

In this particular case, the same effect would be produced by either of the two following command lists:

```
n          n
i\         c\
XXXX       XXXX
d
```

3.2. Substitute Function

One very important function changes parts of lines selected by a context search within the line.

> (2)s<pattern><replacement><flags> -- substitute

> The *s* function replaces *part* of a line (selected by <pattern>) with <replacement>. It can best be read:

>> Substitute for <pattern>, <replacement>

> The <pattern> argument contains a pattern, exactly like the patterns in addresses (see 2.2 above). The only difference between <pattern> and a context address is that the context address must be

15

delimited by slash ('/') characters; <pattern> may be delimited by any character other than space or newline.

By default, only the first string matched by <pattern> is replaced, but see the *g* flag below.

The <replacement> argument begins immediately after the second delimiting character of <pattern>, and must be followed immediately by another instance of the delimiting character. (Thus there are exactly *three* instances of the delimiting character.)

The <replacement> is not a pattern, and the characters which are special in patterns do not have special meaning in <replacement>. Instead, other characters are special:

> &   is replaced by the string matched by <pattern>
>
> \d (where *d* is a single digit) is replaced by the *d*th substring matched by parts of <pattern> enclosed in '\(' and '\)'. If nested substrings occur in <pattern>, the *d*th is determined by counting opening delimiters ('\(').
>
>> As in patterns, special characters may be made literal by preceding them with backslash ('\').

The <flags> argument may contain the following flags:

> g -- substitute <replacement> for all (non-overlapping) instances of <pattern> in the line. After a successful substitution, the scan for the next instance of <pattern> begins just after the end of the inserted characters; characters put into the line from <replacement> are not rescanned.
>
> p -- print the line if a successful replacement was done. The *p* flag causes the line to be written to the output if and only if a substitution was actually made by the *s* function. Notice that if several *s* functions, each followed by a *p* flag, successfully substitute in the same input line, multiple copies of the line will be written to the output: one for each successful substitution.
>
> w <filename> -- write the line to a file if a successful replacement was done. The *w* flag causes lines which are actually substituted by the *s* function to be written to a file named by <filename>. If <filename> exists before *sed* is run, it is overwritten; if not, it is created.
>
>> A single space must separate *w* and <filename>.
>>
>> The possibilities of multiple, somewhat different copies of one input line being written are the same as for *p*.
>>
>> A maximum of 10 different file names may be mentioned after *w* flags and *w* functions (see below), combined.

Examples:

The following command, applied to our standard input,

> s/to/by/w changes

produces, on the standard output:

> In Xanadu did Kubhla Khan
> A stately pleasure dome decree:
> Where Alph, the sacred river, ran
> Through caverns measureless by man
> Down by a sunless sea.

and, on the file 'changes':

> Through caverns measureless by man
> Down by a sunless sea.

If the nocopy option is in effect, the command:

>   s/[.,;?:]/*P&*/gp

produces:

>   A stately pleasure dome decree*P:*
>   Where Alph*P,* the sacred river*P,* ran
>   Down to a sunless sea*P.*

Finally, to illustrate the effect of the *g* flag, the command:

>   /X/s/an/AN/p

produces (assuming nocopy mode):

>   In XANadu did Kubhla Khan

and the command:

>   /X/s/an/AN/gp

produces:

>   In XANadu did Kubhla KhAN

3.3. Input-output Functions

>   (2)p -- print

>   The print function writes the addressed lines to the standard output file. They are written at the
>   time the *p* function is encountered, regardless of what succeeding editing commands may do to the
>   lines.

>   (2)w <filename> -- write on <filename>

>   The write function writes the addressed lines to the file named by <filename>. If the file previ-
>   ously existed, it is overwritten; if not, it is created. The lines are written exactly as they exist
>   when the write function is encountered for each line, regardless of what subsequent editing com-
>   mands may do to them.

>   Exactly one space must separate the *w* and <filename>.

>   A maximum of ten different files may be mentioned in write functions and *w* flags after *s* func-
>   tions, combined.

>   (1)r <filename> -- read the contents of a file

>   The read function reads the contents of <filename>, and appends them after the line matched by
>   the address. The file is read and appended regardless of what subsequent editing commands do to
>   the line which matched its address. If *r* and *a* functions are executed on the same line, the text
>   from the *a* functions and the *r* functions is written to the output in the order that the functions are
>   executed.

>   Exactly one space must separate the *r* and <filename>. If a file mentioned by a *r* function cannot
>   be opened, it is considered a null file, not an error, and no diagnostic is given.

NOTE: Since there is a limit to the number of files that can be opened simultaneously, care should be taken that no
more than ten files be mentioned in *w* functions or flags; that number is reduced by one if any *r* functions are
present. (Only one read file is open at one time.)

Examples

Assume that the file 'note1' has the following contents:

>   Note: Kubla Khan (more properly Kublai Khan; 1216-1294) was the grandson and most eminent
>   successor of Genghiz (Chingiz) Khan, and founder of the Mongol dynasty in China.

15

Then the following command:

>   /Kubla/r note1

produces:

>   In Xanadu did Kubla Khan
>>   Note: Kubla Khan (more properly Kublai Khan; 1216-1294) was the grandson and most eminent
>>   successor of Genghiz (Chingiz) Khan, and founder of the Mongol dynasty in China.
>   A stately pleasure dome decree:
>   Where Alph, the sacred river, ran
>   Through caverns measureless to man
>   Down to a sunless sea.

3.4. Multiple Input-line Functions

Three functions, all spelled with capital letters, deal specially with pattern spaces containing imbedded newlines;
they are intended principally to provide pattern matches across lines in the input.

>   (2)N -- Next line

>>   The next input line is appended to the current line in the pattern space; the two input lines are
>>   separated by an imbedded newline. Pattern matches may extend across the imbedded newline(s).

>   (2)D -- Delete first part of the pattern space

>>   Delete up to and including the first newline character in the current pattern space. If the pattern
>>   space becomes empty (the only newline was the terminal newline), read another line from the
>>   input. In any case, begin the list of editing commands again from its beginning.

>   (2)P -- Print first part of the pattern space

>>   Print up to and including the first newline in the pattern space.

The P and D functions are equivalent to their lower-case counterparts if there are no imbedded newlines in the pattern space.

3.5. Hold and Get Functions

Four functions save and retrieve part of the input for possible later use.

>   (2)h -- hold pattern space

>>   The h functions copies the contents of the pattern space into a hold area (destroying the previous
>>   contents of the hold area).

>   (2)H -- Hold pattern space

>>   The H function appends the contents of the pattern space to the contents of the hold area; the
>>   former and new contents are separated by a newline.

>   (2)g -- get contents of hold area

>>   The g function copies the contents of the hold area into the pattern space (destroying the previous
>>   contents of the pattern space).

>   (2)G -- Get contents of hold area

>>   The G function appends the contents of the hold area to the contents of the pattern space; the
>>   former and new contents are separated by a newline.

>   (2)x -- exchange

>>   The exchange command interchanges the contents of the pattern space and the hold area.

15

Example

The commands

    1h
    1s/ did.*//
    1x
    G
    s/\n/ :/

applied to our standard example, produce:

    In Xanadu did Kubla Khan :In Xanadu
    A stately pleasure dome decree: :In Xanadu
    Where Alph, the sacred river, ran :In Xanadu
    Through caverns measureless to man :In Xanadu
    Down to a sunless sea. :In Xanadu

3.6. Flow-of-Control Functions

These functions do no editing on the input lines, but control the application of functions to the lines selected by the address part.

(2)! -- Don't

The *Don't* command causes the next command (written on the same line), to be applied to all and only those input lines *not* selected by the adress part.

(2){ -- Grouping

The grouping command '{' causes the next set of commands to be applied (or not applied) as a block to the input lines selected by the addresses of the grouping command. The first of the commands under control of the grouping may appear on the same line as the '{' or on the next line.

The group of commands is terminated by a matching '}' standing on a line by itself.

Groups can be nested.

(0):<label> -- place a label

The label function marks a place in the list of editing commands which may be referred to by *b* and *t* functions. The <label> may be any sequence of eight or fewer characters; if two different colon functions have identical labels, a compile time diagnostic will be generated, and no execution attempted.

(2)b<label> -- branch to label

The branch function causes the sequence of editing commands being applied to the current input line to be restarted immediately after the place where a colon function with the same <label> was encountered. If no colon function with the same label can be found after all the editing commands have been compiled, a compile time diagnostic is produced, and no execution is attempted.

A *b* function with no <label> is taken to be a branch to the end of the list of editing commands; whatever should be done with the current input line is done, and another input line is read; the list of editing commands is restarted from the beginning on the new line.

(2)t<label> -- test substitutions

The *t* function tests whether *any* successful substitutions have been made on the current input line; if so, it branches to <label>; if not, it does nothing. The flag which indicates that a successful substitution has been executed is reset by:

    1) reading a new input line, or
    2) executing a *t* function.

15

3.7. Miscellaneous Functions

(1)= -- equals

The = function writes to the standard output the line number of the line matched by its address.

(1)q -- quit

The *q* function causes the current line to be written to the output (if it should be), any appended or read text to be written, and execution to be terminated.

Reference

[1]   Ken Thompson and Dennis M. Ritchie, *The UNIX Programmer's Manual.* Bell Laboratories, 1978.

15

Awk — A Pattern Scanning and Processing Language
(Second Edition)

Alfred V. Aho

Brian W. Kernighan

Peter J. Weinberger

AT&T Bell Laboratories
Murray Hill, New Jersey 07974

ABSTRACT

Awk is a programming language whose basic operation is to search a set of files for patterns, and to perform specified actions upon lines or fields of lines which contain instances of those patterns. *Awk* makes certain data selection and transformation operations easy to express; for example, the *awk* program

length > 72

prints all input lines whose length exceeds 72 characters; the program

NF % 2 == 0

prints all lines with an even number of fields; and the program

{ $1 = log($1); print }

replaces the first field of each line by its logarithm. .

Awk patterns may include arbitrary boolean combinations of regular expressions and of relational operators on strings, numbers, fields, variables, and array elements. Actions may include the same pattern-matching constructions as in patterns, as well as arithmetic and string expressions and assignments, **if-else**, **while**, **for** statements, and multiple output streams.

This report contains a user's guide, a discussion of the design and implementation of *awk*, and some timing statistics.

1. Introduction

Awk is a programming language designed to make many common information retrieval and text manipulation tasks easy to state and to perform.

The basic operation of *awk* is to scan a set of input lines in order, searching for lines which match any of a set of patterns which the user has specified. For each pattern, an action can be specified; this action will be performed on each line that matches the pattern.

Readers familiar with the UNIX† program *grep* [1] will

---

† UNIX is a registered trademark of AT&T Bell Laboratories in the USA and other countries.

recognize the approach, although in *awk* the patterns may be more general than in *grep*, and the actions allowed are more involved than merely printing the matching line. For example, the *awk* program

{print $3, $2}

prints the third and second columns of a table in that order. The program

$2 ~ /A |B |C/

prints all input lines with an A, B, or C in the second field.

16

The program

$1 != prev { print; prev = $1 }

prints all lines in which the first field is different from the previous first field.

1.1. Usage

The command

awk   program   [files]

executes the *awk* commands in the string **program** on the set of named files, or on the standard input if there are no files. The statements can also be placed in a file **pfile**, and executed by the command

awk   −f pfile   [files]

1.2. Program Structure

An *awk* program is a sequence of statements of the form:

        pattern   { *action* }
        pattern   { *action* }
        ...

Each line of input is matched against each of the patterns in turn. For each pattern that matches, the associated action is executed. When all the patterns have been tested, the next line is fetched and the matching starts over.

Either the pattern or the action may be left out, but not both. If there is no action for a pattern, the matching line is simply copied to the output. (Thus a line which matches several patterns can be printed several times.) If there is no pattern for an action, then the action is performed for every input line. A line which matches no pattern is ignored.

Since patterns and actions are both optional, actions must be enclosed in braces to distinguish them from patterns.

1.3. Records and Fields

Awk input is divided into "records" terminated by a record separator. The default record separator is a newline, so by default *awk* processes its input a line at a time. The number of the current record is available in a variable named **NR**.

Each input record is considered to be divided into "fields." Fields are normally separated by white space — blanks or tabs — but the input field separator may be changed, as described below. Fields are referred to as **$1**, **$2**, and so forth, where **$1** is the first field, and **$0** is the whole input record itself. Fields may be assigned to. The number of fields in the current record is available in a variable named **NF**.

The variables **FS** and **RS** refer to the input field and record separators; they may be changed at any time to any single character. The optional command-line argument −F*c* may also be used to set **FS** to the character *c* .

If the record separator is empty, an empty input line is taken as the record separator, and blanks, tabs and newlines are treated as field separators.

The variable **FILENAME** contains the name of the current input file.

1.4. Printing

An action may have no pattern, in which case the action is executed for all lines. The simplest action is to print some or all of a record; this is accomplished by the *awk* command **print**. The *awk* program

{ print }

prints each record, thus copying the input to the output intact. More useful is to print a field or fields from each record. For instance,

print $2, $1

prints the first two fields in reverse order. Items separated by a comma in the print statement will be separated by the current output field separator when output. Items not separated by commas will be concatenated, so

print $1 $2

runs the first and second fields together.

The predefined variables NF and **NR** can be used; for example

{ print NR, NF, $0 }

prints each record preceded by the record number and the number of fields.

Output may be diverted to multiple files; the program

{ print $1 >"foo1"; print $2 >"foo2" }

writes the first field, **$1**, on the file **foo1**, and the second field on file **foo2**. The >> notation can also be used:

print $1 >>"foo"

appends the output to the file **foo**. (In each case, the output files are created if necessary.) The file name can be a variable or a field as well as a constant; for example,

print $1 >$2

uses the contents of field 2 as a file name.

Naturally there is a limit on the number of output files; currently it is 10.

Similarly, output can be piped into another process (on UNIX only); for instance,

print | "mail bwk"

mails the output to **bwk**.

The variables **OFS** and **ORS** may be used to change the current output field separator and output record separator. The output record separator is appended to the output of the **print** statement.

Awk also provides the **printf** statement for output formatting:

printf format expr, expr, ...

formats the expressions in the list according to the specification in **format** and prints them. For example,

printf "%8.2f %10ld\n", $1, $2

prints **$1** as a floating point number 8 digits wide, with two after the decimal point, and **$2** as a 10-digit long decimal number, followed by a newline. No output separators are produced automatically; you must add them yourself, as in this example. The version of **printf** is identical to that used with C.[2]

2. Patterns

A pattern in front of an action acts as a selector that determines whether the action is to be executed. A variety of expressions may be used as patterns: regular expressions, arithmetic relational expressions, string-valued expressions, and arbitrary boolean combinations of these.

2.1. BEGIN and END

The special pattern **BEGIN** matches the beginning of the input, before the first record is read. The pattern **END** matches the end of the input, after the last record has been processed. **BEGIN** and **END** thus provide a way to gain control before and after processing, for initialization and wrapup.

As an example, the field separator can be set to a colon by

BEGIN   { FS = ":" }
... rest of program ...

Or the input lines may be counted by

END { print NR }

If **BEGIN** is present, it must be the first pattern; **END** must be the last if used.

2.2. Regular Expressions

The simplest regular expression is a literal string of characters enclosed in slashes, like

/smith/

This is actually a complete *awk* program which will print all lines which contain any occurrence of the name "smith". If a line contains "smith" as part of a larger word, it will also be printed, as in

blacksmithing

Awk regular expressions include the regular expression forms found in the UNIX text editor *ed*[1] and *grep* (without back-referencing). In addition, *awk* allows parentheses for grouping, | for alternatives, + for "one or more", and ? for "zero or one", all as in *lex*. Character classes may be abbreviated: **[a–zA–Z0–9]** is the set of all

letters and digits. As an example, the *awk* program

/[Aa]ho |[Ww]einberger |[Kk]ernighan/

will print all lines which contain any of the names "Aho," "Weinberger" or "Kernighan," whether capitalized or not.

Regular expressions (with the extensions listed above) must be enclosed in slashes, just as in *ed* and *sed*. Within a regular expression, blanks and the regular expression metacharacters are significant. To turn of the magic meaning of one of the regular expression characters, precede it with a backslash. An example is the pattern

/\/.*\//

which matches any string of characters enclosed in slashes.

One can also specify that any field or variable matches a regular expression (or does not match it) with the operators ~ and !~. The program

$1 ~ /[jJ]ohn/

prints all lines where the first field matches "john" or "John." Notice that this will also match "Johnson", "St. Johnsbury", and so on. To restrict it to exactly **[jJ]ohn**, use

$1 ~ /^[jJ]ohn$/

The caret ^ refers to the beginning of a line or field; the dollar sign $ refers to the end.

2.3. Relational Expressions

An *awk* pattern can be a relational expression involving the usual relational operators <, <=, ==, !=, >=, and >. An example is

$2 > $1 + 100

which selects lines where the second field is at least 100 greater than the first field. Similarly,

NF % 2 == 0

prints lines with an even number of fields.

In relational tests, if neither operand is numeric, a string comparison is made; otherwise it is numeric. Thus,

$1 >= "s"

selects lines that begin with an **s**, **t**, **u**, etc. In the absence of any other information, fields are treated as strings, so the program

$1 > $2

will perform a string comparison.

2.4. Combinations of Patterns

A pattern can be any boolean combination of patterns, using the operators || (or), && (and), and ! (not). For example,

$1 >= "s" && $1 < "t" && $1 != "smith"

selects lines where the first field begins with "s", but is not "smith". **&&** and **||** guarantee that their operands will be

16

evaluated from left to right; evaluation stops as soon as the truth or falsehood is determined.

2.5. Pattern Ranges

The "pattern" that selects an action may also consist of two patterns separated by a comma, as in

pat1, pat2 { ... }

In this case, the action is performed for each line between an occurrence of **pat1** and the next occurrence of **pat2** (inclusive). For example,

/start/, /stop/

prints all lines between **start** and **stop**, while

NR == 100, NR == 200 { ... }

does the action for lines 100 through 200 of the input.

3. Actions

An *awk* action is a sequence of action statements terminated by newlines or semicolons. These action statements can be used to do a variety of bookkeeping and string manipulating tasks.

3.1. Built-in Functions

Awk provides a "length" function to compute the length of a string of characters. This program prints each record, preceded by its length:

{print length, $0}

length by itself is a "pseudo-variable" which yields the length of the current record; **length(argument)** is a function which yields the length of its argument, as in the equivalent

{print length($0), $0}

The argument may be any expression.

Awk also provides the arithmetic functions **sqrt**, **log**, **exp**, and **int**, for square root, base *e* logarithm, exponential, and integer part of their respective arguments.

The name of one of these built-in functions, without argument or parentheses, stands for the value of the function on the whole record. The program

length < 10 || length > 20

prints lines whose length is less than 10 or greater than 20. The function **substr(s, m, n)** produces the substring of **s** that begins at position **m** (origin 1) and is at most **n** characters long. If **n** is omitted, the substring goes to the end of **s**. The function **index(s1, s2)** returns the position where the string **s2** occurs in **s1**, or zero if it does not. The function **sprintf(f, e1, e2, ...)** produces the value of the expressions e1, e2, etc., in the **printf** format specified by **f**. Thus, for example,

x = sprintf("%8.2f %10ld", $1, $2)

sets **x** to the string produced by formatting the values of **$1** and **$2**.

3.2. Variables, Expressions, and Assignments

Awk variables take on numeric (floating point) or string values according to context. For example, in

x = 1

x is clearly a number, while in

x = "smith"

it is clearly a string. Strings are converted to numbers and vice versa whenever context demands it. For instance,

x = "3" + "4"

assigns 7 to **x**. Strings which cannot be interpreted as numbers in a numerical context will generally have numeric value zero, but it is unwise to count on this behavior.

By default, variables (other than built-ins) are initialized to the null string, which has numerical value zero; this eliminates the need for most **BEGIN** sections. For example, the sums of the first two fields can be computed by

{ s1 += $1; s2 += $2 }
END { print s1, s2 }

Arithmetic is done internally in floating point. The arithmetic operators are +, −, *, /, and % (mod). The C increment ++ and decrement — operators are also available, and so are the assignment operators +=, −=, *=, /=, and %=. These operators may all be used in expressions.

3.3. Field Variables

Fields in *awk* share essentially all of the properties of variables — they may be used in arithmetic or string operations, and may be assigned to. Thus one can replace the first field with a sequence number like this:

{ $1 = NR; print }

or accumulate two fields into a third, like this:

{ $1 = $2 + $3; print $0 }

or assign a string to a field:

{ if ($3 > 1000)
** $3 = "too big"**
**   print**
}

which replaces the third field by "too big" when it is, and in any case prints the record.

Field references may be numerical expressions, as in

{ print $i, $(i+1), $(i+n) }

Whether a field is deemed numeric or string depends on context; in ambiguous cases like

if ($1 == $2) ...

fields are treated as strings.

Each input line is split into fields automatically as necessary.

16

It is also possible to split any variable or string into fields:

n = split(s, array, sep)

splits the the string **s** into **array[1]**, ..., **array[n]**. The number of elements found is returned. If the **sep** argument is provided, it is used as the field separator; otherwise **FS** is used as the separator.

3.4. String Concatenation

Strings may be concatenated. For example

length($1 $2 $3)

returns the length of the first three fields. Or in a **print** statement,

print $1 " is " $2

prints the two fields separated by " is ". Variables and numeric expressions may also appear in concatenations.

3.5. Arrays

Array elements are not declared; they spring into existence by being mentioned. Subscripts may have *any* non-null value, including non-numeric strings. As an example of a conventional numeric subscript, the statement

x[NR] = $0

assigns the current input record to the **NR**-th element of the array **x**. In fact, it is possible in principle (though perhaps slow) to process the entire input in a random order with the *awk* program

        { x[NR] = $0 }
END { ... *program* ... **}**

The first action merely records each input line in the array **x**.

Array elements may be named by non-numeric values, which gives *awk* a capability rather like the associative memory of Snobol tables. Suppose the input contains fields with values like **apple**, **orange**, etc. Then the program

```
/apple/    { x["apple"]++ }
/orange/   { x["orange"]++ }
END        { print x["apple"], x["orange"] }
```

increments counts for the named array elements, and prints them at the end of the input.

3.6. Flow-of-Control Statements

Awk provides the basic flow-of-control statements **if-else**, **while**, **for**, and statement grouping with braces, as in C. We showed the **if** statement in section 3.3 without describing it. The condition in parentheses is evaluated; if it is true, the statement following the **if** is done. The **else** part is optional.

The **while** statement is exactly like that of C. For example, to print all input fields one per line,

```
i = 1
while (i <= NF) {
        print $i
        ++i
}
```

The **for** statement is also exactly that of C:

for (i = 1; i <= NF; i++)
        print $i

does the same job as the **while** statement above.

There is an alternate form of the **for** statement which is suited for accessing the elements of an associative array:

for (i in array)
        statement

does *statement* with **i** set in turn to each element of **array**. The elements are accessed in an apparently random order. Chaos will ensue if **i** is altered, or if any new elements are accessed during the loop.

The expression in the condition part of an **if**, **while** or **for** can include relational operators like <, <=, >, >=, == ("is equal to"), and != ("not equal to"); regular expression matches with the match operators ~ and !~; the logical operators ||, &&, and !; and of course parentheses for grouping.

The **break** statement causes an immediate exit from an enclosing **while** or **for**; the **continue** statement causes the next iteration to begin.

The statement **next** causes *awk* to skip immediately to the next record and begin scanning the patterns from the top. The statement **exit** causes the program to behave as if the end of the input had occurred.

Comments may be placed in *awk* programs: they begin with the character # and end with the end of the line, as in

print x, y # this is a comment

4. Design

The UNIX system already provides several programs that operate by passing input through a selection mechanism. *Grep*, the first and simplest, merely prints all lines which match a single specified pattern. *Egrep* provides more general patterns, i.e., regular expressions in full generality; *fgrep* searches for a set of keywords with a particularly fast algorithm. *Sed*[1] provides most of the editing facilities of the editor *ed*, applied to a stream of input. None of these programs provides numeric capabilities, logical relations, or variables.

Lex[3] provides general regular expression recognition capabilities, and, by serving as a C program generator, is essentially open-ended in its capabilities. The use of *lex*, however, requires a knowledge of C programming, and a *lex* program must be compiled and loaded before use, which discourages its use for one-shot applications.

16

Awk is an attempt to fill in another part of the matrix of possibilities. It provides general regular expression capabilities and an implicit input/output loop. But it also provides convenient numeric processing, variables, more general selection, and control flow in the actions. It does not require compilation or a knowledge of C. Finally, *awk* provides a convenient way to access fields within lines; it is unique in this respect.

Awk also tries to integrate strings and numbers completely, by treating all quantities as both string and numeric, deciding which representation is appropriate as late as possible. In most cases the user can simply ignore the differences.

Most of the effort in developing *awk* went into deciding what *awk* should or should not do (for instance, it doesn't do string substitution) and what the syntax should be (no explicit operator for concatenation) rather than on writing or debugging the code. We have tried to make the syntax powerful but easy to use and well adapted to scanning files. For example, the absence of declarations and implicit initializations, while probably a bad idea for a general-purpose programming language, is desirable in a language that is meant to be used for tiny programs that may even be composed on the command line.

In practice, *awk* usage seems to fall into two broad categories. One is what might be called "report generation" — processing an input to extract counts, sums, subtotals, etc. This also includes the writing of trivial data validation programs, such as verifying that a field contains only numeric information or that certain delimiters are properly balanced. The combination of textual and numeric processing is invaluable here.

A second area of use is as a data transformer, converting data from the form produced by one program into that expected by another. The simplest examples merely select fields, perhaps with rearrangements.

5. Implementation

The actual implementation of *awk* uses the language development tools available on the UNIX operating system. The grammar is specified with *yacc*;[4] the lexical analysis is done by *lex*; the regular expression recognizers are deterministic finite automata constructed directly from the expressions. An *awk* program is translated into a parse tree which is then directly executed by a simple interpreter.

Awk was designed for ease of use rather than processing speed; the delayed evaluation of variable types and the necessity to break input into fields makes high speed difficult to achieve in any case. Nonetheless, the program has not proven to be unworkably slow.

Table I below shows the execution (user + system) time on a PDP-11/70 of the UNIX programs *wc*, *grep*, *egrep*, *fgrep*, *sed*, *lex*, and *awk* on the following simple tasks:

1. count the number of lines.

2. print all lines containing "doug".

3. print all lines containing "doug", "ken" or "dmr".

4. print the third field of each line.

5. print the third and second fields of each line, in that order.

6. append all lines containing "doug", "ken", and "dmr" to files "jdoug", "jken", and "jdmr", respectively.

7. print each line prefixed by "line-number : ".

8. sum the fourth column of a table.

The program *wc* merely counts words, lines and characters in its input; we have already mentioned the others. In all cases the input was a file containing 10,000 lines as created by the command *ls –l*; each line has the form

–rw–rw–rw– 1 ava 123 Oct 15 17:05 xxx

The total length of this input is 452,960 characters. Times for *lex* do not include compile or load.

As might be expected, *awk* is not as fast as the specialized tools *wc*, *sed*, or the programs in the *grep* family, but is faster than the more general tool *lex*. In all cases, the tasks were about as easy to express as *awk* programs as programs in these other languages; tasks involving fields were considerably easier to express as *awk* programs. Some of the test programs are shown in *awk*, *sed* and *lex*.

References

1. K. Thompson and D. M. Ritchie, *UNIX Programmer's Manual*, Bell Laboratories, May 1975. Sixth Edition

2. B. W. Kernighan and D. M. Ritchie, *The C Programming Language*, Prentice-Hall, Englewood Cliffs, New Jersey, 1978.

3. M. E. Lesk, "Lex — A Lexical Analyzer Generator," Comp. Sci. Tech. Rep. No. 39, Bell Laboratories, Murray Hill, New Jersey, October 1975 .].

4. S. C. Johnson, "Yacc — Yet Another Compiler-Compiler," Comp. Sci. Tech. Rep. No. 32, Bell Laboratories, Murray Hill, New Jersey, July 1975 .].

16

Program	Task 1	2	3	4	5	6	7	8
wc	8.6							
grep	11.7	13.1						
egrep	6.2	11.5	11.6					
fgrep	7.7	13.8	16.1					
sed	10.2	11.6	15.8	29.0	30.5	16.1		
lex	65.1	150.1	144.2	67.7	70.3	104.0	81.7	92.8
awk	15.0	25.6	29.9	33.3	38.9	46.4	71.4	31.1

Table I. Execution Times of Programs. (Times are in sec.)

The programs for some of these jobs are shown below. The *lex* programs are generally too long to show.

AWK:

1.   **END {print NR}**

2.   **/doug/**

3.   **/ken|doug|dmr/**

4.   **{print $3}**

5.   **{print $3, $2}**

6.   **/ken/ {print >"jken"}**
      /doug/   {print >"jdoug"}
      /dmr/{print >"jdmr"}

7.   **{print NR ": " $0}**

8.   **{sum = sum + $4}**
      END {print sum}

SED:

1.   **$=**

2.   **/doug/p**

3.   **/doug/p**
      /doug/d
      /ken/p
      /ken/d
      /dmr/p
      /dmr/d

4.   **/[^]* [ ]*[^]* [ ]*\([^]*\) .*/s//\1/p**

5.   **/[^]* [ ]*\([^]*\) [ ]*\([^]*\) .*/s//\2 \1/p**

6.   **/ken/w jken**
      /doug/w jdoug
      /dmr/w jdmr

LEX:

1.    ```
      %{
      int i;
      %}
      %%
      \n    i++;
      .     ;
      %%
      yywrap() {
           printf("%d\n", i);
      }
      ```

2.    ```
      %%
      ^.*doug.*$ printf("%s\n", yytext);
      .     ;
      \n    ;
      ```

16

17

Typing Documents on the UNIX System:
Using the −ms Macros with Troff and Nroff

M. E. Lesk

AT&T Bell Laboratories
Murray Hill, New Jersey 07974

ABSTRACT

This document describes a set of easy-to-use macros for preparing documents on the UNIX system. Documents may be produced on either the phototypesetter or a on a computer terminal, without changing the input.

The macros provide facilities for paragraphs, sections (optionally with automatic numbering), page titles, footnotes, equations, tables, two-column format, and cover pages for papers.

This memo includes, as an appendix, the text of the ''Guide to Preparing Documents with −ms'' which contains additional examples of features of −ms.

This manual is a revision of, and replaces, ''Typing Documents on UNIX,'' dated November 22, 1974.

Introduction. This memorandum describes a package of commands to produce papers using the *troff* and *nroff* formatting programs on the UNIX system. As with other *roff*-derived programs, text is prepared interspersed with formatting commands. However, this package, which itself is written in *troff* commands, provides higher-level commands than those provided with the basic *troff* program. The commands available in this package are listed in Appendix A.

Text. Type normally, except that instead of indenting for paragraphs, place a line reading ''.PP'' before each paragraph. This will produce indenting and extra space.

Alternatively, the command .LP that was used here will produce a left-aligned (block) paragraph. The paragraph spacing can be changed: see below under ''Registers.''

Beginning. For a document with a paper-type cover sheet, the input should start as follows:

[optional overall format .RP − see below]
.TL
Title of document (one or more lines)
.AU
Author(s) (may also be several lines)
.AI
Author's institution(s)
.AB
Abstract; to be placed on the cover sheet of a paper.
Line length is 5/6 of normal; use .ll here to change.
.AE (abstract end)
text ... (begins with .PP, which see)

To omit some of the standard headings (e.g. no abstract, or no author's institution) just omit the corresponding fields and command lines. The word ABSTRACT can be suppressed by writing ''.AB no'' for ''.AB''. Several interspersed .AU and .AI lines can be used for multiple authors. The headings are not compulsory: beginning with a .PP

17

command is perfectly OK and will just start printing an ordinary paragraph. *Warning:* You can't just begin a document with a line of text. Some −ms command must precede any text input. When in doubt, use .LP to get proper initialization, although any of the commands .PP, .LP, .TL, .SH, .NH is good enough. Figure 1 shows the legal arrangement of commands at the start of a document.

Cover Sheets and First Pages. The first line of a document signals the general format of the first page. In particular, if it is ".RP" a cover sheet with title and abstract is prepared. The default format is useful for scanning drafts.

In general −ms is arranged so that only one form of a document need be stored, containing all information; the first command gives the format, and unnecessary items for that format are ignored.

Warning: don't put extraneous material between the .TL and .AE commands. Processing of the titling items is special, and other data placed in them may not behave as you expect. Don't forget that some −ms command must precede any input text.

Page headings. The −ms macros, by default, will print a page heading containing a page number (if greater than 1). A default page footer is provided only in *nroff*, where the date is used. The user can make minor adjustments to the page headings/footings by redefining the strings LH, CH, and RH which are the left, center and right portions of the page headings, respectively; and the strings LF, CF, and RF, which are the left, center and right portions of the page footer. For more complex formats, the user can redefine the macros PT and BT, which are invoked respectively at the top and bottom of each page. The margins (taken from registers HM and FM for the top and bottom margin respectively) are normally 1 inch; the page header/footer are in the middle of that space. The user who redefines these macros should be careful not to change parameters such as point size or font without resetting them to default values.

Multi-column formats. If you place the command ".2C" in your document, the document will be printed in double column format beginning at that point. This feature is not too useful in computer terminal output, but is often desirable on the typesetter. The command ".1C" will go back to one-column format and also skip to a new page. The ".2C" command is actually a special case of the command

.MC [column width [gutter width]]

which makes multiple columns with the specified column and gutter width; as many columns as will fit across the page are used. Thus triple, quadruple, ... column pages can be printed. Whenever the number of columns is changed (except going from full width to some larger number of columns) a new page is started.

Headings. To produce a special heading, there are two commands. If you type

.NH
type section heading here
may be several lines

you will get automatically numbered section headings (1, 2, 3, ...), in boldface. For example,

.NH
Care and Feeding of Department Heads

produces

1. Care and Feeding of Department Heads

Alternatively,

.SH
Care and Feeding of Directors

will print the heading with no number added:

Care and Feeding of Directors

Every section heading, of either type, should be followed by a paragraph beginning with .PP or .LP, indicating the end of the heading. Headings may contain more than one line of text.

The .NH command also supports more complex numbering schemes. If a numerical argument is given, it is taken to be a "level" number and an appropriate sub-section number is generated. Larger level numbers indicate deeper sub-sections, as in this example:

.NH
Erie-Lackawanna
.NH 2
Morris and Essex Division
.NH 3
Gladstone Branch
.NH 3
Montclair Branch
.NH 2
Boonton Line

generates:

2. Erie-Lackawanna

2.1. Morris and Essex Division

1.1. Gladstone Branch

2.1.2. Montclair Branch

2.2. Boonton Line

An explicit ''.NH 0'' will reset the numbering of level 1 to one, as here:

```
.NH 0
Penn Central
```

1. Penn Central

Indented paragraphs. (Paragraphs with hanging numbers, e.g. references.) The sequence

```
.IP [1]
Text for first paragraph, typed
normally for as long as you would
like on as many lines as needed.
.IP [2]
Text for second paragraph, ...
```

produces

[1]   Text for first paragraph, typed normally for as long as you would like on as many lines as needed.

[2]   Text for second paragraph, ...

A series of indented paragraphs may be followed by an ordinary paragraph beginning with .PP or .LP, depending on whether you wish indenting or not. The command .LP was used here.

More sophisticated uses of .IP are also possible. If the label is omitted, for example, a plain block indent is produced.

```
.IP
This material will
just be turned into a
block indent suitable for quotations or
such matter.
.LP
```

will produce

This material will just be turned into a block indent suitable for quotations or such matter.

If a non-standard amount of indenting is required, it may be specified after the label (in character positions) and will remain in effect until the next .PP or

.LP. Thus, the general form of the .IP command contains two additional fields: the label and the indenting length. For example,

```
.IP first: 9
Notice the longer label, requiring larger
indenting for these paragraphs.
.IP second:
And so forth.
.LP
```

produces this:

first: Notice the longer label, requiring larger indenting for these paragraphs.

second: And so forth.

It is also possible to produce multiple nested indents; the command .RS indicates that the next .IP starts from the current indentation level. Each .RE will eat up one level of indenting so you should balance .RS and .RE commands. The .RS command should be thought of as ''move right'' and the .RE command as ''move left''. As an example

```
.IP 1.
Bell Laboratories
.RS
.IP 1.1
Murray Hill
.IP 1.2
Holmdel
.IP 1.3
Whippany
.RS
.IP 1.3.1
Madison
.RE
.IP 1.4
Chester
.RE
.LP
```

will result in

1.   Bell Laboratories

    1.1   Murray Hill

    1.2   Holmdel

    1.3   Whippany

        1.3.1 Madison

    1.4   Chester

All of these variations on .LP leave the right margin untouched. Sometimes, for purposes such as setting off a quotation, a paragraph indented on both right and left is required.

17

A single paragraph like this is obtained by preceding it with .QP. More complicated material (several paragraphs) should be bracketed with .QS and .QE.

Emphasis. To get italics (on the typesetter) or underlining (on the terminal) say

.I
as much text as you want
can be typed here
.R

as was done for *these three words.* The .R command restores the normal (usually Roman) font. If only one word is to be italicized, it may be just given on the line with the .I command,

.I word

and in this case no .R is needed to restore the previous font. **Boldface** can be produced by

.B
Text to be set in boldface
goes here
.R

and also will be underlined on the terminal or line printer. As with .I, a single word can be placed in boldface by placing it on the same line as the .B command.

A few size changes can be specified similarly with the commands .LG (make larger), .SM (make smaller), and .NL (return to normal size). The size change is two points; the commands may be repeated for increased effect (here one .NL canceled two .SM commands).

If actual underlining as opposed to italicizing is required on the typesetter, the command

.UL word

will underline a word. There is no way to underline multiple words on the typesetter.

Footnotes. Material placed between lines with the commands .FS (footnote) and .FE (footnote end) will be collected, remembered, and finally placed at the bottom of the current page*. By default, footnotes are 11/12th the length of normal text, but this can be changed using the FL register (see below).

Displays and Tables. To prepare displays of lines, such as tables, in which the lines should not be re-arranged, enclose them in the commands .DS and .DE

---

* Like this.

.DS
table lines, like the
examples here, are placed
between .DS and .DE
.DE

By default, lines between .DS and .DE are indented and left-adjusted. You can also center lines, or retain the left margin. Lines bracketed by .DS C and .DE commands are centered (and not re-arranged); lines bracketed by .DS L and .DE are left-adjusted, not indented, and not re-arranged. A plain .DS is equivalent to .DS I, which indents and left-adjusts. Thus,

these lines were preceded
by .DS C and followed by
a .DE command;

whereas

these lines were preceded
by .DS L and followed by
a .DE command.

Note that .DS C centers each line; there is a variant .DS B that makes the display into a left-adjusted block of text, and then centers that entire block. Normally a display is kept together, on one page. If you wish to have a long display which may be split across page boundaries, use .CD, .LD, or .ID in place of the commands .DS C, .DS L, or .DS I respectively. An extra argument to the .DS I or .DS command is taken as an amount to indent. Note: it is tempting to assume that .DS R will right adjust lines, but it doesn't work.

Boxing words or lines. To draw rectangular boxes around words the command

.BX word

will print $\boxed{\text{word}}$ as shown. The boxes will not be neat on a terminal, and this should not be used as a substitute for italics.

Longer pieces of text may be boxed by enclosing them with .B1 and .B2:

.B1
text...
.B2

as has been done here.

17

Keeping blocks together. If you wish to keep a table or other block of lines together on a page, there are "keep - release" commands. If a block of lines preceded by .KS and followed by .KE does not fit on the remainder of the current page, it will begin on a new page. Lines bracketed by .DS and .DE commands are automatically kept together this way. There is also a "keep floating" command: if the block to be kept together is preceded by .KF instead of .KS and does not fit on the current page, it will be moved down through the text until the top of the next page. Thus, no large blank space will be introduced in the document.

Nroff/Troff commands. Among the useful commands from the basic formatting programs are the following. They all work with both typesetter and computer terminal output:

.bp - begin new page.
.br - "break", stop running text
    from line to line.
.sp n - insert n blank lines.
.na - don't adjust right margins.

Date. By default, documents produced on computer terminals have the date at the bottom of each page; documents produced on the typesetter don't. To force the date, say ".DA". To force no date, say ".ND". To lie about the date, say ".DA July 4, 1776" which puts the specified date at the bottom of each page. The command

.ND May 8, 1945

in ".RP" format places the specified date on the cover sheet and nowhere else. Place this line before the title.

Signature line. You can obtain a signature line by placing the command .SG in the document. The authors' names will be output in place of the .SG line. An argument to .SG is used as a typing identification line, and placed after the signatures. The .SG command is ignored in released paper format.

Registers. Certain of the registers used by −ms can be altered to change default settings. They should be changed with .nr commands, as with

.nr PS 9

to make the default point size 9 point. If the effect is needed immediately, the normal *troff* command should be used in addition to changing the number register.

Register	Defines	Takes effect	Default
PS	point size	next para.	10

VS	line spacing	next para.	12 pts
LL	line length	next para.	6″
LT	title length	next para.	6″
PD	para. spacing	next para.	0.3 VS
PI	para. indent	next para.	5 ens
FL	footnote length	next FS	11/12 LL
CW	column width	next 2C	7/15 LL
GW	intercolumn gap	next 2C	1/15 LL
PO	page offset	next page	26/27″
HM	top margin	next page	1″
FM	bottom margin	next page	1″

You may also alter the strings LH, CH, and RH which are the left, center, and right headings respectively; and similarly LF, CF, and RF which are strings in the page footer. The page number on *output* is taken from register PN, to permit changing its output style. For more complicated headers and footers the macros PT and BT can be redefined, as explained earlier.

Accents. To simplify typing certain foreign words, strings representing common accent marks are defined. They precede the letter over which the mark is to appear. Here are the strings:

Input	Output	Input	Output
*'e	é	*~a	ã
*`e	è	*Ce	ě
*:u	ü	*,c	ç
*^e	ê		

Use. After your document is prepared and stored on a file, you can print it on a terminal with the command*

nroff −ms file

and you can print it on the typesetter with the command

troff −ms file

(many options are possible). In each case, if your document is stored in several files, just list all the filenames where we have used "file". If equations or tables are used, *eqn* and/or *tbl* must be invoked as preprocessors.

References and further study. If you have to do Greek or mathematics, see *eqn* [1] for equation setting. To aid *eqn* users, −ms provides definitions of .EQ and .EN which normally center the equation and set it off slightly. An argument on .EQ is taken to be an equation number and placed in the right margin near the equation. In addition, there are three special arguments to EQ: the letters C, I, and L indicate centered (default), indented, and left adjusted equations,

---
* If .2C was used, pipe the *nroff* output through *col;* make the first line of the input ".pi /usr/bin/col."

17

respectively. If there is both a format argument and an equation number, give the format argument first, as in

.EQ L (1.3a)

for a left-adjusted equation numbered (1.3a).

Similarly, the macros .TS and .TE are defined to separate tables (see [2]) from text with a little space. A very long table with a heading may be broken across pages by beginning it with .TS H instead of .TS, and placing the line .TH in the table data after the heading. If the table has no heading repeated from page to page, just use the ordinary .TS and .TE macros.

To learn more about *troff* see [3] for a general introduction, and [4] for the full details (experts only). Information on related UNIX commands is in [5]. For jobs that do not seem well-adapted to −ms, consider other macro packages. It is often far easier to write a specific macro packages for such tasks as imitating particular journals than to try to adapt −ms.

Acknowledgment. Many thanks are due to Brian Kernighan for his help in the design and implementation of this package, and for his assistance in preparing this manual.

References

[1]   B. W. Kernighan and L. L. Cherry, *Typesetting Mathematics — Users Guide (2nd edition),* Bell Laboratories Computing Science Report no. 17.

[2]   M. E. Lesk, *Tbl — A Program to Format Tables,* Bell Laboratories Computing Science Report no. 45.

[3]   B. W. Kernighan, *A Troff Tutorial,* Bell Laboratories, 1976.

[4]   J. F. Ossanna, *Nroff/Troff Reference Manual,* Bell Laboratories Computing Science Report no. 51.

[5]   K. Thompson and D. M. Ritchie, *UNIX Programmer's Manual,* Bell Laboratories, 1978.

17

Appendix A
List of Commands

1C	Return to single column format.	LG	Increase type size.
2C	Start double column format.	LP	Left aligned block paragraph.
AB	Begin abstract.		
AE	End abstract.		
AI	Specify author's institution.		
AU	Specify author.	ND	Change or cancel date.
B	Begin boldface.	NH	Specify numbered heading.
DA	Provide the date on each page.	NL	Return to normal type size.
DE	End display.	PP	Begin paragraph.
DS	Start display (also CD, LD, ID).		
EN	End equation.	R	Return to regular font (usually Roman).
EQ	Begin equation.	RE	End one level of relative indenting.
FE	End footnote.	RP	Use released paper format.
FS	Begin footnote.	RS	Relative indent increased one level.
		SG	Insert signature line.
I	Begin italics.	SH	Specify section heading.
		SM	Change to smaller type size.
IP	Begin indented paragraph.	TL	Specify title.
KE	Release keep.		
KF	Begin floating keep.	UL	Underline one word.
KS	Start keep.		

Register Names

The following register names are used by −ms internally. Independent use of these names in one's own macros may produce incorrect output. Note that no lower case letters are used in any −ms internal name.

Number registers used in −ms

:	DW	GW	HM	IQ	LL	NA	OJ	PO	T.	TV
#T	EF	H1	HT	IR	LT	NC	PD	PQ	TB	VS
1T	FL	H3	IK	KI	MM	NF	PF	PX	TD	YE
AV	FM	H4	IM	L1	MN	NS	PI	RO	TN	YY
CW	FP	H5	IP	LE	MO	OI	PN	ST	TQ	ZN

String registers used in −ms

'	A5	CB	DW	EZ	I	KF	MR	R1	RT	TL
`	AB	CC	DY	FA	I1	KQ	ND	R2	S0	TM
^	AE	CD	E1	FE	I2	KS	NH	R3	S1	TQ
~	AI	CF	E2	FJ	I3	LB	NL	R4	S2	TS
:	AU	CH	E3	FK	I4	LD	NP	R5	SG	TT
,	B	CM	E4	FN	I5	LG	OD	RC	SH	UL
1C	BG	CS	E5	FO	ID	LP	OK	RE	SM	WB
2C	BT	CT	EE	FQ	IE	ME	PP	RF	SN	WH
A1	C	D	EL	FS	IM	MF	PT	RH	SY	WT
A2	C1	DA	EM	FV	IP	MH	PY	RP	TA	XD
A3	C2	DE	EN	FY	IZ	MN	QF	RQ	TE	XF
A4	CA	DS	EQ	HO	KE	MO	R	RS	TH	XK

17

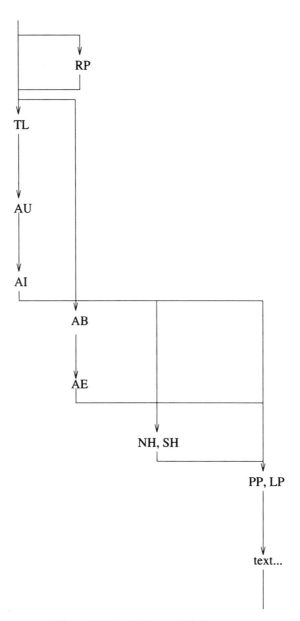

Figure 1: Order of Commands in Input

A Revised Version of −ms

Bill Tuthill

Computing Services
University of California
Berkeley, CA 94720

18

The −ms macros have been slightly revised and rearranged for the Berkeley Unix distribution. Because of the rearrangement, the new macros can be read by the computer in about half the time required by the previous version of −ms. This means that output will begin to appear between ten seconds and several minutes more quickly, depending on the system load. On long files, however, the savings in total time are not substantial. The old version of −ms is still available as −mos.

Several bugs in −ms have been fixed, including a bad problem with the .1C macro, minor difficulties with boxed text, a break induced by .EQ before initialization, the failure to set tab stops in displays, and several bothersome errors in the **refer** macros. Macros used only at Bell Laboratories have been removed. There are a few extensions to previous −ms macros, and a number of new macros, but all the documented −ms macros still work exactly as they did before, and have the same names as before. Output produced with −ms should look like output produced with −mos.

One important new feature is automatically numbered footnotes. Footnote numbers are printed by means of a pre-defined string (**), which you invoke separately from .FS and .FE. Each time it is used, this string increases the footnote number by one, whether or not you use .FS and .FE in your text. Footnote numbers will be super-scripted on the phototypesetter and on daisy-wheel terminals, but on low-resolution devices (such as the lpr and a crt), they will be bracketed. If you use ** to indicate numbered footnotes, then the .FS macro will automatically include the footnote number at the bottom of the page. This footnote, for example, was produced as follows:[1]

```
This footnote, for example, was produced as follows:\**
.FS
    ...
.FE
```

If you are using ** to number footnotes, but want a particular footnote to be marked with an asterisk or a dagger, then give that mark as the first argument to .FS: †

```
then give that mark as the first argument to .FS: \(dg
.FS  \(dg
    ...
.FE
```

Footnote numbering will be temporarily suspended, because the ** string is not used. Instead of a dagger, you could use an asterisk * or double dagger ‡, represented as \(dd.

Another new feature is a macro for printing theses according to Berkeley standards. This macro is called .TM, which stands for thesis mode. (It is much like the .th macro in −me.) It will put page numbers in the upper right-hand corner; number the first page; suppress the date; and doublespace everything except quotes, displays, and keeps. Use it at the top of each file making up your thesis. Calling .TM defines the .CT macro for chapter titles, which skips to a new page and moves the pagenumber to the center footer. The .P1 (P one) macro can be used even

---

[1] If you never use the "**" string, no footnote numbers will appear anywhere in the text, including down here. The output foot-notes will look exactly like footnotes produced with −mos.

† In the footnote, the dagger will appear where the footnote number would otherwise appear, as on the left.

18

without thesis mode to print the header on page 1, which is suppressed except in thesis mode. If you want roman numeral page numbering, use an ''.af PN i'' request.

There is a new macro especially for bibliography entries, called .XP, which stands for exdented paragraph. It will exdent the first line of the paragraph by \n(PI units, usually 5n (the same as the indent for the first line of a .PP). Most bibliographies are printed this way. Here are some examples of exdented paragraphs:

Lumley, Lyle S., *Sex in Crustaceans: Shell Fish Habits,* Harbinger Press, Tampa Bay and San Diego, October 1979. 243 pages. The pioneering work in this field.

Leffadinger, Harry A., ''Mollusk Mating Season: 52 Weeks, or All Year?'' in *Acta Biologica,* vol. 42, no. 11, November 1980. A provocative thesis, but the conclusions are wrong.

Of course, you will have to take care of italicizing the book title and journal, and quoting the title of the journal article. Indentation or exdentation can be changed by setting the value of number register PI.

If you need to produce endnotes rather than footnotes, put the references in a file of their own. This is similar to what you would do if you were typing the paper on a conventional typewriter. Note that you can use automatic footnote numbering without actually having .FS and .FE pairs in your text. If you place footnotes in a separate file, you can use .IP macros with ** as a hanging tag; this will give you numbers at the left-hand margin. With some styles of endnotes, you would want to use .PP rather then .IP macros, and specify ** before the reference begins.

There are four new macros to help produce a table of contents. Table of contents entries must be enclosed in .XS and .XE pairs, with optional .XA macros for additional entries; arguments to .XS and .XA specify the page number, to be printed at the right. A final .PX macro prints out the table of contents. Here is a sample of typical input and output text:

```
.XS ii
Introduction
.XA 1
Chapter 1: Review of the Literature
.XA 23
Chapter 2: Experimental Evidence
.XE
.PX
```

Table of Contents

Introduction ii
Chapter 1: Review of the Literature 1
Chapter 2: Experimental Evidence 23

The .XS and .XE pairs may also be used in the text, after a section header for instance, in which case page numbers are supplied automatically. However, most documents that require a table of contents are too long to produce in one run, which is necessary if this method is to work. It is recommended that you do a table of contents after finishing your document. To print out the table of contents, use the .PX macro; if you forget it, nothing will happen.

As an aid in producing text that will format correctly with both **nroff** and **troff**, there are some new string definitions that define quotation marks and dashes for each of these two formatting programs. The *− string will yield two hyphens in **nroff**, but in **troff** it will produce an em dash— like this one. The *Q and *U strings will produce '' and '' in **troff**, but " in **nroff**. (In typesetting, the double quote is traditionally considered bad form.)

There are now a large number of optional foreign accent marks defined by the −ms macros. All the accent marks available in −mos are present, and they all work just as they always did. However, there are better definitions available by placing .AM at the beginning of your document. Unlike the −mos accent marks, the accent strings should come *after* the letter being accented. Here is a list of the diacritical marks, with examples of what they look like.

name of accent	input	output
acute accent	e*´	é
grave accent	e*`	è
circumflex	o*^	ô
cedilla	c*,	ç
tilde	n*~	ñ
question	*?	¿
exclamation	*!	¡
umlaut	u*:	ü
digraph s	*8	ß
haček	c*v	č
macron	a*_	ā
underdot	s*.	ṣ
o-slash	o*/	ó
angstrom	a*o	å
yogh	knı*3t	kni₃t
Thorn	*(Th	Þ
thorn	*(th	þ
Eth	*(D-	Ð
eth	*(d-	ð
hooked o	*q	ǫ
ae ligature	*(ae	æ
AE ligature	*(Ae	Æ
oe ligature	*(oe	œ
OE ligature	*(Oe	Œ

If you want to use these new diacritical marks, don't forget the .AM at the top of your file. Without it, some will not print at all, and others will be placed on the wrong letter.

It is also possible to produce custom headers and footers that are different on even and odd pages. The .OH and .EH macros define odd and even headers, while .OF and .EF define odd and even footers. Arguments to these four macros are specified as with .tl. This document was produced with:

```
.OH \fIThe -mx Macros´`Page %\fP´
.EH \fIPage %´`The -mx Macros\fP´
```

Note that it would be a error to have an apostrophe in the header text; if you need one, you will have to use a different delimiter around the left, center, and right portions of the title. You can use any character as a delimiter, provided it doesn't appear elsewhere in the argument to .OH, .EH, .OF, or EF.

The −ms macros work in conjunction with the **tbl**, **eqn**, and **refer** preprocessors. Macros to deal with these items are read in only as needed, as are the thesis macros (.TM), the special accent mark definitions (.AM), table of contents macros (.XS and .XE), and macros to format the optional cover page. The code for the −ms package lives in /usr/lib/tmac/tmac.s, and sourced files reside in the directory /usr/ucb/lib/ms.

May 19, 1994

Writing Papers with NROFF using −me

Eric P. Allman*

Project INGRES
Electronics Research Laboratory
University of California, Berkeley
Berkeley, California 94720

19

This document describes the text processing facilities available on the UNIX† operating system via NROFF†
and the −me macro package. It is assumed that the reader already is generally familiar with the UNIX operating system and a text editor such as **ex**. This is intended to be a casual introduction, and as such not all material is covered.
In particular, many variations and additional features of the −me macro package are not explained. For a complete
discussion of this and other issues, see *The −me Reference Manual* and *The NROFF/TROFF Reference Manual*.

NROFF, a computer program that runs on the UNIX operating system, reads an input file prepared by the user
and outputs a formatted paper suitable for publication or framing. The input consists of *text*, or words to be printed,
and *requests*, which give instructions to the NROFF program telling how to format the printed copy.

Section 1 describes the basics of text processing. Section 2 describes the basic requests. Section 3 introduces
displays. Annotations, such as footnotes, are handled in section 4. The more complex requests which are not discussed in section 2 are covered in section 5. Finally, section 6 discusses things you will need to know if you want to
typeset documents. If you are a novice, you probably won't want to read beyond section 4 until you have tried some
of the basic features out.

When you have your raw text ready, call the NROFF formatter by typing as a request to the UNIX shell:

>   nroff −me −T*type files*

where *type* describes the type of terminal you are outputting to. Common values are **dtc** for a DTC 300s (daisy-
wheel type) printer and **lpr** for the line printer. If the −**T** flag is omitted, a "lowest common denominator" terminal
is assumed; this is good for previewing output on most terminals. A complete description of options to the NROFF
command can be found in *The NROFF/TROFF Reference Manual*.

The word *argument* is used in this manual to mean a word or number which appears on the same line as a
request which modifies the meaning of that request. For example, the request

>   .sp

spaces one line, but

>   .sp 4

spaces four lines. The number **4** is an *argument* to the **.sp** request which says to space four lines instead of one.
Arguments are separated from the request and from each other by spaces.

1. Basics of Text Processing

The primary function of NROFF is to *collect* words from input lines, *fill* output lines with those words, *jus-
tify* the right hand margin by inserting extra spaces in the line, and output the result. For example, the input:

---

*Author's current address: Computer Science Division, EECS, University of California, Berkeley, California 94720.
†UNIX is a trademark of AT&T Bell Laboratories

> Now is the time
> for all good men
> to come to the aid
> of their party.
> Four score and seven
> years ago,...

will be read, packed onto output lines, and justified to produce:

> Now is the time for all good men to come to the aid of their party. Four score and seven
> years ago,...

Sometimes you may want to start a new output line even though the line you are on is not yet full; for example, at the end of a paragraph. To do this you can cause a *break*, which starts a new output line. Some requests cause a break automatically, as do blank input lines and input lines beginning with a space.

Not all input lines are text to be formatted. Some of the input lines are *requests* which describe how to format the text. Requests always have a period or an apostrophe (" ' ") as the first character of the input line.

The text formatter also does more complex things, such as automatically numbering pages, skipping over page folds, putting footnotes in the correct place, and so forth.

I can offer you a few hints for preparing text for input to NROFF. First, keep the input lines short. Short input lines are easier to edit, and NROFF will pack words onto longer lines for you anyhow. In keeping with this, it is helpful to begin a new line after every period, comma, or phrase, since common corrections are to add or delete sentences or phrases. Second, do not put spaces at the end of lines, since this can sometimes confuse the NROFF processor. Third, do not hyphenate words at the end of lines (except words that should have hyphens in them, such as "mother-in-law"); NROFF is smart enough to hyphenate words for you as needed, but is not smart enough to take hyphens out and join a word back together. Also, words such as "mother-in-law" should not be broken over a line, since then you will get a space where not wanted, such as "mother- in-law".

2. Basic Requests

2.1. Paragraphs

Paragraphs are begun by using the **.pp** request. For example, the input:

```
.pp
Now is the time for all good men
to come to the aid of their party.
Four score and seven years ago,...
```

produces a blank line followed by an indented first line. The result is:

> Now is the time for all good men to come to the aid of their party. Four score and
> seven years ago,...

Notice that the sentences of the paragraphs *must not* begin with a space, since blank lines and lines beginning with spaces cause a break. For example, if I had typed:

```
.pp
Now is the time for all good men
    to come to the aid of their party.
Four score and seven years ago,...
```

The output would be:

> Now is the time for all good men
> to come to the aid of their party. Four score and seven years ago,...

A new line begins after the word "men" because the second line began with a space character.

There are many fancier types of paragraphs, which will be described later.

2.2. Headers and Footers

Arbitrary headers and footers can be put at the top and bottom of every page. Two requests of the form **.he** *title* and **.fo** *title* define the titles to put at the head and the foot of every page, respectively. The titles are called *three-part* titles, that is, there is a left-justified part, a centered part, and a right-justified part. To separate these three parts the first character of *title* (whatever it may be) is used as a delimiter. Any character may be used, but backslash and double quote marks should be avoided. The percent sign is replaced by the current page number whenever found in the title. For example, the input:

```
.he ´´%´´
.fo ´Jane Jones´´My Book´
```

results in the page number centered at the top of each page, ''Jane Jones'' in the lower left corner, and ''My Book'' in the lower right corner.

2.3. Double Spacing

NROFF will double space output text automatically if you use the request **.ls 2**, as is done in this sec-

tion. You can revert to single spaced mode by typing **.ls 1**.

2.4. Page Layout

A number of requests allow you to change the way the printed copy looks, sometimes called the *layout* of the output page. Most of these requests adjust the placing of ''white space'' (blank lines or spaces). In these explanations, characters in italics should be replaced with values you wish to use; bold characters represent characters which should actually be typed.

The **.bp** request starts a new page.

The request **.sp** *N* leaves *N* lines of blank space. *N* can be omitted (meaning skip a single line) or can be of the form *N***i** (for *N* inches) or *N***c** (for *N* centimeters). For example, the input:

```
.sp 1.5i
My thoughts on the subject
.sp
```

leaves one and a half inches of space, followed by the line ''My thoughts on the subject'', followed by a single blank line.

The **.in** +*N* request changes the amount of white space on the left of the page (the *indent*). The argument *N* can be of the form +*N* (meaning leave *N* spaces more than you are already leaving), −*N* (meaning leave less than you do now), or just *N* (meaning leave exactly *N* spaces). *N* can be of the form *N***i** or *N***c** also. For example, the input:

```
initial text
.in 5
some text
.in +1i
more text
.in −2c
final text
```

produces ''some text'' indented exactly five spaces from the left margin, ''more text'' indented five spaces plus one inch from the left margin (fifteen spaces on a pica typewriter), and ''final text'' indented five spaces plus one inch minus two centimeters from the margin. That is, the output is:

```
initial text
          some text
                        more text
              final text
```

The **.ti** +*N* (temporary indent) request is used like **.in** +*N* when the indent should apply to one line only, after which it should revert to the previous indent. For example, the input:

```
.in 1i
.ti 0
Ware, James R.  The Best of Confucius,
Halcyon House, 1950.
An excellent book containing translations of
most of Confucius´ most delightful sayings.
A definite must for anyone interested in the early foundations
of Chinese philosophy.
```

produces:

Ware, James R. The Best of Confucius, Halcyon House, 1950. An excellent book containing translations of most of Confucius' most delightful sayings. A definite must for anyone interested in the early foundations of Chinese philosophy.

Text lines can be centered by using the **.ce** request. The line after the **.ce** is centered (horizontally) on the page. To center more than one line, use **.ce** *N* (where *N* is the number of lines to center), followed by the *N* lines. If you want to center many lines but don't want to count them, type:

```
.ce 1000
lines to center
.ce 0
```

The **.ce 0** request tells NROFF to center zero more lines, in other words, stop centering.

All of these requests cause a break; that is, they always start a new line. If you want to start a new line without performing any other action, use **.br**.

2.5. Underlining

Text can be underlined using the **.ul** request. The **.ul** request causes the next input line to be underlined when output. You can underline multiple lines by stating a count of *input* lines to underline, followed by those lines (as with the **.ce** request). For example, the input:

```
.ul 2
Notice that these two input lines
are underlined.
```

will underline those eight words in NROFF. (In TROFF they will be set in italics.)

3. Displays

Displays are sections of text to be set off from the body of the paper. Major quotes, tables, and figures are types of displays, as are all the examples used in this document. All displays except centered blocks are output single spaced.

3.1. Major Quotes

Major quotes are quotes which are several lines long, and hence are set in from the rest of the text without quote marks around them. These can be generated using the commands **.(q** and **.)q** to surround the quote. For example, the input:

```
As Weizenbaum points out:
.(q
It is said that to explain is to explain away.
This maxim is nowhere so well fulfilled
as in the areas of computer programming,...
.)q
```

generates as output:

As Weizenbaum points out:

It is said that to explain is to explain away. This maxim is nowhere so well fulfilled as in the areas of computer programming,...

3.2. Lists

A *list* is an indented, single spaced, unfilled display. Lists should be used when the material to be printed should not be filled and justified like normal text, such as columns of figures or the examples used in this paper. Lists are surrounded by the requests **.(l** and **.)l**. For example, type:

```
Alternatives to avoid deadlock are:
.(l
Lock in a specified order
Detect deadlock and back out one process
Lock all resources needed before proceeding
.)l
```

will produce:
Alternatives to avoid deadlock are:

> Lock in a specified order
> Detect deadlock and back out one process
> Lock all resources needed before proceeding

3.3. Keeps

A *keep* is a display of lines which are kept on a single page if possible. An example of where you would use a keep might be a diagram. Keeps differ from lists in that lists may be broken over a page boundary whereas keeps will not.

Blocks are the basic kind of keep. They begin with the request **.(b** and end with the request **.)b**. If there is not room on the current page for everything in the block, a new page is begun. This has the unpleasant effect of leaving blank space at the bottom of the page. When this is not appropriate, you can use the alternative, called *floating keeps*.

Floating keeps move relative to the text. Hence, they are good for things which will be referred to by name, such as ''See figure 3''. A floating keep will appear at the bottom of the current page if it will fit; otherwise, it will appear at the top of the next page. Floating keeps begin with the line **.(z** and end with the line **.)z**. For an example of a floating keep, see figure 1. The **.hl** request is used to draw a horizontal line so that the figure stands out from the text.

3.4. Fancier Displays

Keeps and lists are normally collected in *nofill* mode, so that they are good for tables and such. If you want a display in fill mode (for text), type **.(l F** (Throughout this section, comments applied to **.(l** also apply to **.(b** and **.(z**. This kind of display will be indented from both margins. For example, the input:

```
.(z
.hl
Text of keep to be floated.
.sp
.ce
Figure 1. Example of a Floating Keep.
.hl
.)z
```

Figure 1. Example of a Floating Keep.

19

```
.(l F
And now boys and girls,
a newer, bigger, better toy than ever before!
Be the first on your block to have your own computer!
Yes kids, you too can have one of these modern
data processing devices.
You too can produce beautifully formatted papers
without even batting an eye!
.)l
```

will be output as:

> And now boys and girls, a newer, bigger, better toy than ever before! Be the first on your block to have your own computer! Yes kids, you too can have one of these modern data processing devices. You too can produce beautifully formatted papers without even batting an eye!

Lists and blocks are also normally indented (floating keeps are normally left justified). To get a left-justified list, type **.(l L**. To get a list centered line-for-line, type **.(l C**. For example, to get a filled, left justified list, enter:

```
.(l L F
text of block
.)l
```

The input:

```
.(l
first line of unfilled display
more lines
.)l
```

produces the indented text:

> first line of unfilled display
> more lines

Typing the character **L** after the **.(l** request produces the left justified result:

first line of unfilled display
more lines

Using **C** instead of **L** produces the line-at-a-time centered output:

first line of unfilled display
more lines

Sometimes it may be that you want to center several lines as a group, rather than centering them one line at a time. To do this use centered blocks, which are surrounded by the requests **.(c** and **.)c**. All the lines are centered as a unit, such that the longest line is centered and the rest are lined up around that line. Notice that lines do not move relative to each other using centered blocks, whereas they do using the **C** argument to keeps.

Centered blocks are *not* keeps, and may be used in conjunction with keeps. For example, to center a group of lines as a unit and keep them on one page, use:

```
.(b L
.(c
first line of unfilled display
more lines
.)c
.)b
```

to produce:

first line of unfilled display
more lines

If the block requests (**.(b** and **.)b**) had been omitted the result would have been the same, but with no guarantee that the lines of the centered block would have all been on one page. Note the use of the **L** argument to **.(b**; this causes the centered block to center within the entire line rather than within the line minus the indent. Also, the center requests must be nested *inside* the keep requests.

4. Annotations

There are a number of requests to save text for later printing. *Footnotes* are printed at the bottom of the current page. *Delayed text* is intended to be a variant form of footnote; the text is printed only when explicitly called for, such as at the end of each chapter. *Indexes* are a type of delayed text having a tag (usually the page number) attached to each entry after a row of dots. Indexes are also saved until called for explicitly.

4.1. Footnotes

Footnotes begin with the request **.(f** and end with the request **.)f**. The current footnote number is maintained automatically, and can be used by typing **, to produce a footnote number[1]. The number is automatically incremented after every footnote. For example, the input:

```
.(q
A man who is not upright
and at the same time is presumptuous;
one who is not diligent and at the same time is ignorant;
one who is untruthful and at the same time is incompetent;
such men I do not count among acquaintances.\**
.(f
\**James R. Ware,
.ul
The Best of Confucius,
Halcyon House, 1950.
Page 77.
.)f
.)q
```

generates the result:

> A man who is not upright and at the same time is presumptuous; one who is not diligent and at the same time is ignorant; one who is untruthful and at the same time is incompetent; such men I do not count among acquaintances.[2]

It is important that the footnote appears *inside* the quote, so that you can be sure that the footnote will appear on the same page as the quote.

4.2. Delayed Text

Delayed text is very similar to a footnote except that it is printed when called for explicitly. This allows a list of references to appear (for example) at the end of each chapter, as is the convention in some disciplines. Use *# on delayed text instead of ** as on footnotes.

If you are using delayed text as your standard reference mechanism, you can still use footnotes, except that you may want to reference them with special characters* rather than numbers.

---

[1]Like this.

[2]James R. Ware, *The Best of Confucius,* Halcyon House, 1950. Page 77.

*Such as an asterisk.

4.3. Indexes

An ''index'' (actually more like a table of contents, since the entries are not sorted alphabetically) resembles delayed text, in that it is saved until called for. However, each entry has the page number (or some other tag) appended to the last line of the index entry after a row of dots.

Index entries begin with the request **.(x** and end with **.)x**. The **.)x** request may have a argument, which is the value to print as the ''page number''. It defaults to the current page number. If the page number given is an underscore (''_'') no page number or line of dots is printed at all. To get the line of dots without a page number, type **.)x** "", which specifies an explicitly null page number.

The **.xp** request prints the index.

For example, the input:

```
.(x
Sealing wax
.)x
.(x
Cabbages and kings
.)x _
.(x
Why the sea is boiling hot
.)x 2.5a
.(x
Whether pigs have wings
.)x ""
.(x
This is a terribly long index entry, such as might be used
for a list of illustrations, tables, or figures; I expect it to
take at least two lines.
.)x
.xp
```

generates:

Sealing wax   8

Cabbages and kings

Why the sea is boiling hot 2.5a

Whether pigs have wings ....

This is a terribly long index entry, such as might be used for a list of illustrations, tables, or figures; I expect it to take at least two lines.   8

The **.(x** request may have a single character argument, specifying the ''name'' of the index; the normal index is **x**. Thus, several ''indices'' may be maintained simultaneously (such as a list of tables, table of contents, etc.).

Notice that the index must be printed at the *end* of the paper, rather than at the beginning where it will probably appear (as a table of contents); the pages may have to be physically rearranged after printing.

5. Fancier Features

A large number of fancier requests exist, notably requests to provide other sorts of paragraphs, numbered sections of the form **1.2.3** (such as used in this document), and multicolumn output.

5.1. More Paragraphs

Paragraphs generally start with a blank line and with the first line indented. It is possible to get left-justified block-style paragraphs by using **.lp** instead of **.pp**, as demonstrated by the next paragraph.

Sometimes you want to use paragraphs that have the *body* indented, and the first line exdented (opposite of indented) with a label. This can be done with the **.ip** request. A word specified on the same line as **.ip** is printed in the margin, and the body is lined up at a prespecified position (normally five spaces).

For example, the input:

```
.ip one
This is the first paragraph.
Notice how the first line
of the resulting paragraph lines up
with the other lines in the paragraph.
.ip two
And here we are at the second paragraph already.
You may notice that the argument to .ip
appears
in the margin.
.lp
We can continue text...
```

produces as output:

one   This is the first paragraph. Notice how the first line of the resulting paragraph lines up with the other lines in the paragraph.

two   And here we are at the second paragraph already. You may notice that the argument to **.ip** appears in the margin.

We can continue text without starting a new indented paragraph by using the **.lp** request.

If you have spaces in the label of a **.ip** request, you must use an "unpaddable space" instead of a regular space. This is typed as a backslash character (''\'') followed by a space. For example, to print the label "Part 1", enter:

```
.ip "Part\ 1"
```

If a label of an indented paragraph (that is, the argument to **.ip**) is longer than the space allocated for the label, **.ip** will begin a new line after the label. For example, the input:

```
.ip longlabel
This paragraph had a long label.
The first character of text on the first line
will not line up with the text on second and subsequent lines,
although they will line up with each other.
```

will produce:

longlabel
      This paragraph had a long label. The first character of text on the first line will not line up with the text on second and subsequent lines, although they will line up with each other.

It is possible to change the size of the label by using a second argument which is the size of the label. For example, the above example could be done correctly by saying:

```
.ip longlabel 10
```

which will make the paragraph indent 10 spaces for this paragraph only. If you have many paragraphs to indent all the same amount, use the *number register* **ii**. For example, to leave one inch of space for the label, type:

```
.nr ii 1i
```

somewhere before the first call to **.ip**. Refer to the reference manual for more information.

If **.ip** is used with no argument at all no hanging tag will be printed. For example, the input:

```
.ip [a]
This is the first paragraph of the example.
We have seen this sort of example before.
.ip
This paragraph is lined up with the previous paragraph,
but it has no tag in the margin.
```

19

produces as output:

[a]   This is the first paragraph of the example. We have seen this sort of example before.

This paragraph is lined up with the previous paragraph, but it has no tag in the margin.

A special case of **.ip** is **.np**, which automatically numbers paragraphs sequentially from 1. The numbering is reset at the next **.pp**, **.lp**, or **.sh** (to be described in the next section) request. For example, the input:

```
.np
This is the first point.
.np
This is the second point.
Points are just regular paragraphs
which are given sequence numbers automatically
by the .np request.
.pp
This paragraph will reset numbering by .np.
.np
For example,
we have reverted to numbering from one now.
```

generates:

(1)   This is the first point.

(2)   This is the second point. Points are just regular paragraphs which are given sequence numbers automatically by the .np request.

This paragraph will reset numbering by .np.

(1)   For example, we have reverted to numbering from one now.

The **.bu** request gives lists of this sort that are identified with bullets rather than numbers. The paragraphs are also crunched together. For example, the input:

```
.bu
One egg yolk
.bu
One tablespoon cream or top milk
.bu
Salt, cayenne, and lemon juice to taste
.bu
A generous two tablespoonfuls of butter
```

produces[3]:

- One egg yolk
- One tablespoon cream or top milk
- Salt, cayenne, and lemon juice to taste
- A generous two tablespoonfuls of butter

5.2. Section Headings

Section numbers (such as the ones used in this document) can be automatically generated using the **.sh** request. You must tell **.sh** the *depth* of the section number and a section title. The depth specifies how many numbers are to appear (separated by decimal points) in the section number. For example, the section number **4.2.5** has a depth of three.

---

[3]By the way, if you put the first three ingredients in a a heavy, deep pan and whisk the ingredients madly over a medium flame (never taking your hand off the handle of the pot) until the mixture reaches the consistency of custard (just a minute or two), then mix in the butter off-heat, you will have a wonderful Hollandaise sauce.

Section numbers are incremented in a fairly intuitive fashion. If you add a number (increase the depth), the new number starts out at one. If you subtract section numbers (or keep the same number) the final number is incremented. For example, the input:

```
.sh 1 "The Preprocessor"
.sh 2 "Basic Concepts"
.sh 2 "Control Inputs"
.sh 3
.sh 3
.sh 1 "Code Generation"
.sh 3
```

produces as output the result:

1. The Preprocessor
1.1. Basic Concepts
1.2. Control Inputs
1.2.1.
1.2.2.
2. Code Generation
2.1.1.

You can specify the section number to begin by placing the section number after the section title, using spaces instead of dots. For example, the request:

```
.sh 3 "Another section" 7 3 4
```

will begin the section numbered **7.3.4**; all subsequent **.sh** requests will number relative to this number.

There are more complex features which will cause each section to be indented proportionally to the depth of the section. For example, if you enter:

```
.nr si N
```

each section will be indented by an amount N. N must have a scaling factor attached, that is, it must be of the form Nx, where x is a character telling what units N is in. Common values for x are **i** for inches, **c** for centimeters, and **n** for *ens* (the width of a single character). For example, to indent each section one-half inch, type:

```
.nr si 0.5i
```

After this, sections will be indented by one-half inch per level of depth in the section number. For example, this document was produced using the request

```
.nr si 3n
```

at the beginning of the input file, giving three spaces of indent per section depth.

Section headers without automatically generated numbers can be done using:

```
.uh "Title"
```

which will do a section heading, but will put no number on the section.

5.3. Parts of the Basic Paper

There are some requests which assist in setting up papers. The **.tp** request initializes for a title page. There are no headers or footers on a title page, and unlike other pages you can space down and leave blank space at the top. For example, a typical title page might appear as:

```
.tp
.sp 2i
.(l C
THE GROWTH OF TOENAILS
IN UPPER PRIMATES
.sp
by
.sp
Frank N. Furter
.)l
.bp
```

The request **.th** sets up the environment of the NROFF processor to do a thesis, using the rules established at Berkeley. It defines the correct headers and footers (a page number in the upper right hand corner only), sets the margins correctly, and double spaces.

The **.+c** *T* request can be used to start chapters. Each chapter is automatically numbered from one, and a heading is printed at the top of each chapter with the chapter number and the chapter name *T*. For example, to begin a chapter called ''Conclusions'', use the request:

.+c "CONCLUSIONS"

which will produce, on a new page, the lines

CHAPTER 5

CONCLUSIONS

with appropriate spacing for a thesis. Also, the header is moved to the foot of the page on the first page of a chapter. Although the **.+c** request was not designed to work only with the **.th** request, it is tuned for the format acceptable for a PhD thesis at Berkeley.

If the title parameter *T* is omitted from the **.+c** request, the result is a chapter with no heading. This can also be used at the beginning of a paper; for example, **.+c** was used to generate page one of this document.

Although papers traditionally have the abstract, table of contents, and so forth at the front of the paper, it is more convenient to format and print them last when using NROFF. This is so that index entries can be collected and then printed for the table of contents (or whatever). At the end of the paper, issue the **.++ P** request, which begins the preliminary part of the paper. After issuing this request, the **.+c** request will begin a preliminary section of the paper. Most notably, this prints the page number restarted from one in lower case Roman numbers. **.+c** may be used repeatedly to begin different parts of the front material for example, the abstract, the table of contents, acknowledgments, list of illustrations, etc. The request **.++ B** may also be used to begin the bibliographic section at the end of the paper. For example, the paper might appear as outlined in figure 2. (In this figure, comments begin with the sequence \".)

5.4. Equations and Tables

Two special UNIX programs exist to format special types of material. **Eqn** and **neqn** set equations for the phototypesetter and NROFF respectively. **Tbl** arranges to print extremely pretty tables in a variety of formats. This document will only describe the embellishments to the standard features; consult the reference manuals for those processors for a description of their use.

The **eqn** and **neqn** programs are described fully in the document *Typesetting Mathematics − User's Guide* by Brian W. Kernighan and Lorinda L. Cherry. Equations are centered, and are kept on one page. They are introduced by the **.EQ** request and terminated by the **.EN** request.

The **.EQ** request may take an equation number as an optional argument, which is printed vertically centered on the right hand side of the equation. If the equation becomes too long it should be split between two lines. To do this, type:

```
.th                              \" set for thesis mode
.fo ''DRAFT''                    \" define footer for each page
.tp                              \" begin title page
.(l C                            \" center a large block
THE GROWTH OF TOENAILS
IN UPPER PRIMATES
.sp
by
.sp
Frank Furter
.)l                              \" end centered part
.+c INTRODUCTION                 \" begin chapter named "INTRODUCTION"
.(x t                            \" make an entry into index 't'
Introduction
.)x                              \" end of index entry
text of chapter one
.+c "NEXT CHAPTER"               \" begin another chapter
.(x t                            \" enter into index 't' again
Next Chapter
.)x
text of chapter two
.+c CONCLUSIONS
.(x t
Conclusions
.)x
text of chapter three
.++ B                            \" begin bibliographic information
.+c BIBLIOGRAPHY                 \" begin another 'chapter'
.(x t
Bibliography
.)x
text of bibliography
.++ P                            \" begin preliminary material
.+c "TABLE OF CONTENTS"
.xp t                            \" print index 't' collected above
.+c PREFACE                      \" begin another preliminary section
text of preface
```

19

Figure 2. Outline of a Sample Paper

```
.EQ (eq 34)
text of equation 34
.EN C
.EQ
continuation of equation 34
.EN
```

The **C** on the **.EN** request specifies that the equation will be continued.

    The **tbl** program produces tables. It is fully described (including numerous examples) in the document *Tbl – A Program to Format Tables* by M. E. Lesk. Tables begin with the **.TS** request and end with the **.TE** request. Tables are normally kept on a single page. If you have a table which is too big to fit on a single page, so that you know it will extend to several pages, begin the table with the request **.TS H** and put the request **.TH** after the part of the table which you want duplicated at the top of every page that the table is printed on. For example, a table definition for a long table might look like:

```
.TS H
c s s
n n n.
THE TABLE TITLE
.TH
text of the table
.TE
```

5.5. Two Column Output

You can get two column output automatically by using the request **.2c**. This causes everything after it to be output in two-column form. The request **.bc** will start a new column; it differs from **.bp** in that **.bp** may leave a totally blank column when it starts a new page. To revert to single column output, use **.1c**.

5.6. Defining Macros

A *macro* is a collection of requests and text which may be used by stating a simple request. Macros begin with the line **.de** *xx* (where *xx* is the name of the macro to be defined) and end with the line consisting of two dots. After defining the macro, stating the line *.xx* is the same as stating all the other lines. For example, to define a macro that spaces 3 lines and then centers the next input line, enter:

```
.de SS
.sp 3
.ce
..
```

and use it by typing:

```
.SS
Title Line
(beginning of text)
```

Macro names may be one or two characters. In order to avoid conflicts with names in −me, always use upper case letters as names. The only names to avoid are **TS**, **TH**, **TE**, **EQ**, and **EN**.

5.7. Annotations Inside Keeps

Sometimes you may want to put a footnote or index entry inside a keep. For example, if you want to maintain a ''list of figures'' you will want to do something like:

```
.(z
.(c
text of figure
.)c
.ce
Figure 5.
.(x f
Figure 5
.)x
.)z
```

which you may hope will give you a figure with a label and an entry in the index **f** (presumably a list of figures index). Unfortunately, the index entry is read and interpreted when the keep is read, not when it is printed, so the page number in the index is likely to be wrong. The solution is to use the magic string **\!** at the beginning of all the lines dealing with the index. In other words, you should use:

```
.(z
.(c
Text of figure
.)c
.ce
Figure 5.
\!.(x f
\!Figure 5
\!.)x
.)z
```

which will defer the processing of the index until the figure is output. This will guarantee that the page number in the index is correct. The same comments apply to blocks (with **.(b** and **.)b**) as well.

6. TROFF and the Photosetter

With a little care, you can prepare documents that will print nicely on either a regular terminal or when phototypeset using the TROFF formatting program.

6.1. Fonts

A *font* is a style of type. There are three fonts that are available simultaneously, Times Roman, Times Italic, and Times Bold, plus the special math font. The normal font is Roman. Text which would be underlined in NROFF with the **.ul** request is set in italics in TROFF.

There are ways of switching between fonts. The requests **.r**, **.i**, and **.b** switch to Roman, italic, and bold fonts respectively. You can set a single word in some font by typing (for example):

```
.i word
```

which will set *word* in italics but does not affect the surrounding text. In NROFF, italic and bold text is underlined.

Notice that if you are setting more than one word in whatever font, you must surround that word with double quote marks ('' '') so that it will appear to the NROFF processor as a single word. The quote marks will not appear in the formatted text. If you do want a quote mark to appear, you should quote the entire string (even if a single word), and use *two* quote marks where you want one to appear. For example, if you want to produce the text:

```
"Master Control"
```

in italics, you must type:

```
.i """"Master Control\"""""
```

The \| produces a very narrow space so that the ''l'' does not overlap the quote sign in TROFF, like this:

```
"Master Control"
```

There are also several ''pseudo-fonts'' available. The input:

```
.(b
.u underlined
.bi "bold italics"
.bx "words in a box"
.)b
```

generates

underlined
bold italics
words in a box

In NROFF these all just underline the text. Notice that pseudo font requests set only the single parameter in the pseudo font; ordinary font requests will begin setting all text in the special font if you do not provide a parameter. No more than one word should appear with these three font requests in the middle of lines. This is because of the way TROFF justifies text. For example, if you were to issue the requests:

> .bi "some bold italics"
> and
> .bx "words in a box"

in the middle of a line TROFF would produce *some***bold***italics* and |words in a box|, which I think you will agree does not look good.

The second parameter of all font requests is set in the original font. For example, the font request:

> .b bold face

generates "bold" in bold font, but sets "face" in the font of the surrounding text, resulting in:

> **bold**face.

To set the two words **bold** and **face** both in **bold face**, type:

> .b "bold face"

You can mix fonts in a word by using the special sequence **\c** at the end of a line to indicate "continue text processing"; this allows input lines to be joined together without a space between them. For example, the input:

> .u under \c
> .i italics

generates <u>under</u>*italics*, but if we had typed:

> .u under
> .i italics

the result would have been <u>under</u> *italics* as two words.

6.2. Point Sizes

The phototypesetter supports different sizes of type, measured in points. The default point size is 10 points for most text, 8 points for footnotes. To change the pointsize, type:

> .sz +*N*

where *N* is the size wanted in points. The *vertical spacing* (distance between the bottom of most letters (the *baseline*) between adjacent lines) is set to be proportional to the type size.

These pointsize changes are *temporary*!!! For example, to reset the pointsize of basic text to twelve point, use:

> .nr pp 12
> .nr sp 12
> .nr tp 12

to reset the default pointsize of paragraphs, section headers, and titles respectively. If you only want to set the names of sections in a larger pointsize, use:

> .nr sp 11

alone — this sets section titles (e.g., **Point Sizes** above) in a larger font than the default.

A single word or phrase can be set in a smaller pointsize than the surrounding text using the **.sm** request. This is especially convenient for words that are all capitals, due to the optical illusion that makes them look even larger than they actually are. For example:

> .sm UNIX

prints as UNIX rather than UNIX.

Warning: changing point sizes on the phototypesetter is a slow mechanical operation. On laser printers it may require loading new fonts. Size changes should be considered carefully.

6.3. Quotes

It is conventional when using the typesetter to use pairs of grave and acute accents to generate double quotes, rather than the double quote character (' " '). This is because it looks better to use grave and acute accents; for example, compare "quote" to ''quote''.

In order to make quotes compatible between the typesetter and terminals, you may use the sequences ***(lq** and ***(rq** to stand for the left and right quote respectively. These both appear as " on most terminals, but are typeset as '' and '' respectively. For example, use:

    *(lqSome things aren´t true
    even if they did happen.*(rq

to generate the result:

''Some things aren't true even if they did happen.''

As a shorthand, the special font request:

    .q "quoted text"

will generate ''quoted text''. Notice that you must surround the material to be quoted with double quote marks if it is more than one word.

19

Acknowledgments

I would like to thank Bob Epstein, Bill Joy, and Larry Rowe for having the courage to use the –me macros to produce non-trivial papers during the development stages; Ricki Blau, Pamela Humphrey, and Jim Joyce for their help with the documentation phase; peter kessler for numerous complaints years after I was ''done'' with this project, most accompanied by fixes (hence forcing me to fix several small bugs); and the plethora of people who have contributed ideas and have given support for the project.

This document was TROFF'ed on May 19, 1994 and applies to version 2.27 of the –me macros.

−ME REFERENCE MANUAL

Release 2.27

Eric P. Allman*

Project INGRES
Electronics Research Laboratory
University of California, Berkeley
Berkeley, California 94720

This document describes in extremely terse form the features of the **−me** macro package for version seven NROFF/TROFF. Some familiarity is assumed with those programs. Specifically, the reader should understand breaks, fonts, pointsizes, the use and definition of number registers and strings, how to define macros, and scaling factors for ens, points, **v**'s (vertical line spaces), etc.

For a more casual introduction to text processing using NROFF, refer to the document *Writing Papers with NROFF using −me*.

There are a number of macro parameters that may be adjusted. Fonts may be set to a font number only. Font 8 means bold font in TROFF; in NROFF font 8 is underlined unless the **−rb3** flag is specified to use "true bold" font (most versions of NROFF do not interpret bold font nicely). Font 0 is no font change; the font of the surrounding text is used instead. Notice that fonts 0 and 8 are "pseudo-fonts"; that is, they are simulated by the macros. This means that although it is legal to set a font register to zero or eight, it is not legal to use the escape character form, such as:

    \f8

All distances are in basic units, so it is nearly always necessary to use a scaling factor. For example, the request to set the paragraph indent to eight one-en spaces is:

    .nr pi 8n

and not

    .nr pi 8

which would set the paragraph indent to eight basic units, or about 0.02 inch. Default parameter values are given in brackets in the remainder of this document.

Registers and strings of the form **$**x may be used in expressions but should not be changed. Macros of the form **$**x perform some function (as described) and may be redefined to change this function. This may be a sensitive operation; look at the body of the original macro before changing it.

All names in −me follow a rigid naming convention. The user may define number registers, strings, and macros, provided that s/he uses single character upper case names or double character names consisting of letters and digits, with at least one upper case letter. In no case should special characters be used in user-defined names.

On daisy wheel type printers in twelve pitch, the **−rx1** flag can be stated to make lines default to one eighth inch (the normal spacing for a newline in twelve-pitch). This is normally too small for easy readability, so the default is to space one sixth inch.

---

*Author's current address: Computer Science Division, EECS, University of California, Berkeley, California 94720.
†NROFF and TROFF may be trademarks of AT&T Bell Laboratories.

The **−rv2** flag will indicates that this *is* being output on a C/A/T phototypesetter; this changes the page offset and inserts cut marks.

This documentation was TROFF'ed on May 19, 1994 and applies to version 2.27 of the −me macros.

1. Paragraphing

These macros are used to begin paragraphs. The standard paragraph macro is **.pp**; the others are all variants to be used for special purposes.

The first call to one of the paragraphing macros defined in this section or the **.sh** macro (defined in the next session) *initializes* the macro processor. After initialization it is not possible to use any of the following requests: **.sc**, **.lo**, **.th**, or **.ac**. Also, the effects of changing parameters which will have a global effect on the format of the page (notably page length and header and footer margins) are not well defined and should be avoided.

.lp   Begin left-justified paragraph. Centering and underlining are turned off if they were on, the font is set to **\n(pf** [1] the type size is set to **\n(pp** [10p], and a **\n(ps** space is inserted before the paragraph [0.35v in TROFF, 1v or 0.5v in NROFF depending on device resolution]. The indent is reset to **\n($i** [0] plus **\n(po** [0] unless the paragraph is inside a display. (see **.ba**). At least the first two lines of the paragraph are kept together on a page.

.pp   Like **.lp**, except that it puts **\n(pi** [5n] units of indent. This is the standard paragraph macro.

.ip *T I*   Indented paragraph with hanging tag. The body of the following paragraph is indented *I* spaces (or **\n(ii** [5n] spaces if *I* is not specified) more than a non-indented paragraph (such as with **.pp**) is. The title *T* is exdented (opposite of indented). The result is a paragraph with an even left edge and *T* printed in the margin. Any spaces in *T* must be unpaddable. If *T* will not fit in the space provided, **.ip** will start a new line.

.np   A variant of .ip which numbers paragraphs. Numbering is reset after a **.lp**, **.pp**, or **.sh**. The current paragraph number is in **\n($p**.

.bu   Like **.np** except that paragraphs are marked with bullets (•). Leading space is eliminated to create compact lists.

2. Section Headings

Numbered sections are similar to paragraphs except that a section number is automatically generated for each one. The section numbers are of the form **1.2.3**. The *depth* of the section is the count of numbers (separated by decimal points) in the section number.

Unnumbered section headings are similar, except that no number is attached to the heading.

.sh *+N T a b c d e f*   Begin numbered section of depth *N*. If *N* is missing the current depth (maintained in the number register **\n($0**) is used. The values of the individual parts of the section number are maintained in **\n($1** through **\n($6**. There is a **\n(ss** [1v] space before the section. *T* is printed as a section title in font **\n(sf** [8] and size **\n(sp** [10p]. The "name" of the section may be accessed via ***($n**. If **\n(si** is non-zero, the base indent is set to **\n(si** times the section depth, and the section title is exdented. (See **.ba**.) Also, an additional indent of **\n(so** [0] is added to the section title (but not to the body of the section). The font is then set to the paragraph font, so that more information may occur on the line with the section number and title. **.sh** insures that there is enough room to print the section head plus the beginning of a paragraph (about 3 lines total). If *a* through *f* are specified, the section number is set to that number rather than incremented automatically. If any of *a* through *f* are a hyphen that number is not reset. If *T* is a single underscore ("_") then the section depth and numbering is reset, but the base indent is not reset and nothing is printed out. This is useful to automatically coordinate section numbers with chapter numbers.

.sx *+N*   Go to section depth *N* [−1], but do not print the number and title, and do not increment the section number at level *N*. This has the effect of starting a new paragraph at level *N*.

.uh *T*	Unnumbered section heading. The title *T* is printed with the same rules for spacing, font, etc., as for **.sh**.
.$p *T B N*	Print section heading. May be redefined to get fancier headings. *T* is the title passed on the **.sh** or **.uh** line; *B* is the section number for this section, and *N* is the depth of this section. These parameters are not always present; in particular, **.sh** passes all three, **.uh** passes only the first, and **.sx** passes three, but the first two are null strings. Care should be taken if this macro is redefined; it is quite complex and subtle.
.$0 *T B N*	This macro is called automatically after every call to **.$p**. It is normally undefined, but may be used to automatically put every section title into the table of contents or for some similar function. *T* is the section title for the section title which was just printed, *B* is the section number, and *N* is the section depth.
.$1 – .$6	Traps called just before printing that depth section. May be defined to (for example) give variable spacing before sections. These macros are called from **.$p**, so if you redefine that macro you may lose this feature.

3. Headers and Footers

Headers and footers are put at the top and bottom of every page automatically. They are set in font \n(tf [3] and size \n(tp [10p]. Each of the definitions apply as of the *next* page. Three-part titles must be quoted if there are two blanks adjacent anywhere in the title or more than eight blanks total.

The spacing of headers and footers are controlled by three number registers. \n(hm [4v] is the distance from the top of the page to the top of the header, \n(fm [3v] is the distance from the bottom of the page to the bottom of the footer, \n(tm [7v] is the distance from the top of the page to the top of the text, and \n(bm [6v] is the distance from the bottom of the page to the bottom of the text (nominal). The macros **.m1**, **.m2**, **.m3**, and **.m4** are also supplied for compatibility with ROFF documents.

.he ´l ´m ´r´	Define three-part header, to be printed on the top of every page.
.fo ´l ´m ´r´	Define footer, to be printed at the bottom of every page.
.eh ´l ´m ´r´	Define header, to be printed at the top of every even-numbered page.
.oh ´l ´m ´r´	Define header, to be printed at the top of every odd-numbered page.
.ef ´l ´m ´r´	Define footer, to be printed at the bottom of every even-numbered page.
.of ´l ´m ´r´	Define footer, to be printed at the bottom of every odd-numbered page.
.hx	Suppress headers and footers on the next page.
.m1 +*N*	Set the space between the top of the page and the header [4v].
.m2 +*N*	Set the space between the header and the first line of text [2v].
.m3 +*N*	Set the space between the bottom of the text and the footer [2v].
.m4 +*N*	Set the space between the footer and the bottom of the page [4v].
.ep	End this page, but do not begin the next page. Useful for forcing out footnotes, but other than that hardly every used. Must be followed by a **.bp** or the end of input.
.$h	Called at every page to print the header. May be redefined to provide fancy (e.g., multi-line) headers, but doing so loses the function of the **.he**, **.fo**, **.eh**, **.oh**, **.ef**, and **.of** requests, as well as the chapter-style title feature of **.+c**.
.$f	Print footer; same comments apply as in **.$h**.
.$H	A normally undefined macro which is called at the top of each page (after putting out the header, initial saved floating keeps, etc.); in other words, this macro is called immediately before printing text on a page. It can be used for column headings and the like.

4. Displays

All displays except centered blocks and block quotes are preceded and followed by an extra \n(bs [same as \n(ps] space. Quote spacing is stored in a separate register; centered blocks have no default initial or trailing space. The vertical spacing of all displays except quotes and centered blocks is stored in register \n($R instead of \n($r.

20

.(l *m f*   Begin list. Lists are single spaced, unfilled text. If *f* is **F**, the list will be filled. If *m* **[I]** is **I** the list is indented by **\n(bi** [4m]; if **M** the list is indented to the left margin; if **L** the list is left justified with respect to the text (different from **M** only if the base indent (stored in **\n($i** and set with **.ba**) is not zero); and if **C** the list is centered on a line-by-line basis. The list is set in font **\n(df** [0]. Must be matched by a **.)l**. This macro is almost like **.(b** except that no attempt is made to keep the display on one page.

.)l   End list.

.(q   Begin major quote. These are single spaced, filled, moved in from the text on both sides by **\n(qi** [4n], preceded and followed by **\n(qs** [same as **\n(bs**] space, and are set in point size **\n(qp** [one point smaller than surrounding text].

.)q   End major quote.

.(b *m f*   Begin block. Blocks are a form of *keep*, where the text of a keep is kept together on one page if possible (keeps are useful for tables and figures which should not be broken over a page). If the block will not fit on the current page a new page is begun, *unless* that would leave more than **\n(bt** [0] white space at the bottom of the text. If **\n(bt** is zero, the threshold feature is turned off. Blocks are not filled unless *f* is **F**, when they are filled. The block will be left-justified if *m* is **L**, indented by **\n(bi** [4m] if *m* is **I** or absent, centered (line-for-line) if *m* is **C**, and left justified to the margin (not to the base indent) if *m* is **M**. The block is set in font **\n(df** [0].

.)b   End block.

.(z *m f*   Begin floating keep. Like **.(b** except that the keep is *floated* to the bottom of the page or the top of the next page. Therefore, its position relative to the text changes. The floating keep is preceded and followed by **\n(zs** [1v] space. Also, it defaults to mode **M**.

.)z   End floating keep.

.(c   Begin centered block. The next keep is centered as a block, rather than on a line-by-line basis as with **.(b C**. This call may be nested inside keeps.

.)c   End centered block.

5. Annotations

.(d   Begin delayed text. Everything in the next keep is saved for output later with **.pd**, in a manner similar to footnotes.

.)d *n*   End delayed text. The delayed text number register **\n($d** and the associated string ***#** are incremented if ***#** has been referenced.

.pd   Print delayed text. Everything diverted via **.(d** is printed and truncated. This might be used at the end of each chapter.

.(f   Begin footnote. The text of the footnote is floated to the bottom of the page and set in font **\n(ff** [1] and size **\n(fp** [8p]. Each entry is preceded by **\n(fs** [0.2v] space, is indented **\n(fi** [3n] on the first line, and is indented **\n(fu** [0] from the right margin. Footnotes line up underneath two column output. If the text of the footnote will not all fit on one page it will be carried over to the next page.

.)f *n*   End footnote. The number register **\n($f** and the associated string ****** are incremented if they have been referenced.

.$s   The macro to output the footnote separator. This macro may be redefined to give other size lines or other types of separators. Currently it draws a 1.5i line.

.(x *x*   Begin index entry. Index entries are saved in the index *x* **[x]** until called up with **.xp.** Each entry is preceded by a **\n(xs** [0.2v] space. Each entry is ''undented'' by **\n(xu** [0.5i]; this register tells how far the page number extends into the right margin.

.)x *P A*   End index entry. The index entry is finished with a row of dots with *A* [null] right justified on the last line (such as for an author's name), followed by P [**\n%**]. If *A* is specified, *P* must be specified; **\n%** can be used to print the current page number. If *P* is an underscore, no page number and no row of dots are printed.

.xp *x* Print index *x* [**x**]. The index is formatted in the font, size, and so forth in effect at the time it is printed, rather than at the time it is collected.

6. Columned Output

.2c +*S N* Enter two-column mode. The column separation is set to +*S* [4n, 0.5i in ACM mode] (saved in **\n($s)**). The column width, calculated to fill the single column line length with both columns, is stored in **\n($l)**. The current column is in **\n($c)**. You can test register **\n($m)** [1] to see if you are in single column or double column mode. Actually, the request enters *N* [2] column output.

.1c Revert to single-column mode.

.bc Begin column. This is like **.bp** except that it begins a new column on a new page only if necessary, rather than forcing a whole new page if there is another column left on the current page.

7. Fonts and Sizes

.sz +*P* The pointsize is set to *P* [10p], and the line spacing is set proportionally. The ratio of line spacing to pointsize is stored in **\n($r)**. The ratio used internally by displays and annotations is stored in **\n($R)** (although this is *not* used by **.sz**). This size is *not* sticky beyond many macros: in particular, **\n(pp** (paragraph pointsize) modifies the pointsize every time a new paragraph is begun using the **.pp**, **.lp**, **.ip**, **.np**, or **.bu** macros. Also, **\n(fp** (footnote pointsize), **\n(qp** (quote pointsize), **\n(sp** (section header pointsize), and **\n(tp** (title pointsize) may modify the pointsize.

.r *W X* Set *W* in roman font, appending *X* in the previous font. To append different font requests, use *X* = **\c**. If no parameters, change to roman font.

.i *W X* Set *W* in italics, appending *X* in the previous font. If no parameters, change to italic font. Underlines in NROFF.

.b *W X* Set *W* in bold font and append *X* in the previous font. If no parameters, switch to bold font. In NROFF, underlines.

.rb *W X* Set *W* in bold font and append *X* in the previous font. If no parameters, switch to bold font. **.rb** differs from **.b** in that **.rb** does not underline in NROFF.

.u *W X* Underline *W* and append *X*. This is a true underlining, as opposed to the **.ul** request, which changes to ''underline font'' (usually italics in TROFF). It won't work right if *W* is spread or broken (including hyphenated). In other words, it is safe in nofill mode only.

.q *W X* Quote *W* and append *X*. In NROFF this just surrounds *W* with double quote marks (' '' '), but in TROFF uses directed quotes.

.bi *W X* Set *W* in bold italics and append *X*. Actually, sets *W* in italic and overstrikes once. Underlines in NROFF. It won't work right if *W* is spread or broken (including hyphenated). In other words, it is safe in nofill mode only.

.bx *W X* Sets *W* in a box, with *X* appended. Underlines in NROFF. It won't work right if *W* is spread or broken (including hyphenated). In other words, it is safe in nofill mode only.

sm *W X* Sets *W* in a smaller pointsize, with *X* appended.

8. Roff Support

.ix +*N* Indent, no break. Equivalent to ˆin *N*.

.bl *N* Leave *N* contiguous white space, on the next page if not enough room on this page. Equivalent to a **.sp** *N* inside a block.

.pa +*N* Equivalent to **.bp**.

20

.ro	Set page number in roman numerals. Equivalent to **.af % i**.
.ar	Set page number in Arabic. Equivalent to **.af % 1**.
.n1	Number lines in margin from one on each page.
.n2 *N*	Number lines from *N*, stop if *N* = 0.
.sk	Leave the next output page blank, except for headers and footers. This is used to leave space for a full-page diagram which is produced externally and pasted in later. To get a partial-page paste-in display, say **.sv** *N*, where *N* is the amount of space to leave; this space will be output immediately if there is room, and will otherwise be output at the top of the next page. However, be warned: if *N* is greater than the amount of available space on an empty page, no space will ever be output.

9. Preprocessor Support

.EQ *m T*	Begin equation. The equation is centered if *m* is **C** or omitted, indented **\n(bi** [4m] if *m* is **I**, and left justified if *m* is **L**. *T* is a title printed on the right margin next to the equation. See *Typesetting Mathematics – User's Guide* by Brian W. Kernighan and Lorinda L. Cherry.
.EN *c*	End equation. If *c* is **C** the equation must be continued by immediately following with another **.EQ**, the text of which can be centered along with this one. Otherwise, the equation is printed, always on one page, with **\n(es** [0.5v in TROFF, 1v in NROFF] space above and below it.
.TS *h*	Table start. Tables are single spaced and kept on one page if possible. If you have a large table which will not fit on one page, use *h* = **H** and follow the header part (to be printed on every page of the table) with a **.TH**. See *Tbl – A Program to Format Tables* by M. E. Lesk.
.TH	With **.TS H**, ends the header portion of the table.
.TE	Table end. Note that this table does not float, in fact, it is not even guaranteed to stay on one page if you use requests such as **.sp** intermixed with the text of the table. If you want it to float (or if you use requests inside the table), surround the entire table (including the **.TS** and **.TE** requests) with the requests **.(z** and **.)z**.
.PS *h w*	Begin *pic* picture. *H* is the height and *w* is the width, both in basic units. *Ditroff* only.
.PE	End picture.
.IS	Begin *ideal* picture.
.IE	End *ideal* picture.
.IF	End *ideal* picture (alternate form).
GS	Begin *gremlin* picture.
GE	End *gremlin* picture.
GF	End *gremlin* picture (alternate form).

10. Miscellaneous

.re	Reset tabs. Set to every 0.5i in TROFF and every 0.8i in NROFF.
.ba +*N*	Set the base indent to +*N* [0] (saved in **\n($i**). All paragraphs, sections, and displays come out indented by this amount. Titles and footnotes are unaffected. The **.sh** request performs a **.ba** request if **\n(si** [0] is not zero, and sets the base indent to **\n(si*\n($0**.
.xl +*N*	Set the line length to *N* [6.0i]. This differs from **.ll** because it only affects the current environment.
.ll +*N*	Set line length in all environments to *N* [6.0i]. This should not be used after output has begun, and particularly not in two-column output. The current line length is stored in **\n($l**.

.hl	Draws a horizontal line the length of the page. This is useful inside floating keeps to differentiate between the text and the figure.
.lh	Print a letterhead at the current position on the page. The format of the letterhead must be defined in the file **/usr/lib/me/letterhead.me** by your local systems staff. Some environments may require *ditroff* for this macro to function properly.
.lo	This macro loads another set of macros (in **/usr/lib/me/local.me**) which is intended to be a set of locally defined macros. These macros should all be of the form **.*X**, where *X* is any letter (upper or lower case) or digit.

11. Standard Papers

.tp	Begin title page. Spacing at the top of the page can occur, and headers and footers are suppressed. Also, the page number is not incremented for this page.
.th	Set thesis mode. This defines the modes acceptable for a doctoral dissertation at Berkeley. It double spaces, defines the header to be a single page number, and changes the margins to be 1.5 inch on the left and one inch on the top. **.++** and **.+c** should be used with it. This macro must be stated before initialization, that is, before the first call of a paragraphing macro or **.sh**.
.++ *m H*	This request defines the section of the paper which we are entering. The section type is defined by *m*. **C** means that we are entering the chapter portion of the paper, **A** means that we are entering the appendix portion of the paper, **P** means that the material following should be the preliminary portion (abstract, table of contents, etc.) portion of the paper, **AB** means that we are entering the abstract (numbered independently from 1 in Arabic numerals), and **B** means that we are entering the bibliographic portion at the end of the paper. Also, the variants **RC** and **RA** are allowed, which specify renumbering of pages from one at the beginning of each chapter or appendix, respectively. The *H* parameter defines the new header. If there are any spaces in it, the entire header must be quoted. If you want the header to have the chapter number in it, Use the string \\\n(ch. For example, to number appendixes **A.1** etc., type **.++ RA** ´´\\\n(ch.%´. Each section (chapter, appendix, etc.) should be preceded by the **.+c** request. It should be mentioned that it is easier when using TROFF to put the front material at the end of the paper, so that the table of contents can be collected and put out; this material can then be physically moved to the beginning of the paper.
.+c *T*	Begin chapter with title *T*. The chapter number is maintained in **\n(ch**. This register is incremented every time **.+c** is called with a parameter. The title and chapter number are printed by **.$c**. The header is moved to the footer on the first page of each chapter. If *T* is omitted, **.$c** is not called; this is useful for doing your own ''title page'' at the beginning of papers without a title page proper. **.$c** calls **.$C** as a hook so that chapter titles can be inserted into a table of contents automatically. The footnote numbering is reset to one.
.$c *T*	Print chapter number (from **\n(ch**) and *T*. This macro can be redefined to your liking. It is defined by default to be acceptable for a PhD thesis at Berkeley. This macro calls **$C**, which can be defined to make index entries, or whatever.
.$C *K N T*	This macro is called by **.$c**. It is normally undefined, but can be used to automatically insert index entries, or whatever. *K* is a keyword, either ''Chapter'' or ''Appendix'' (depending on the **.++** mode); *N* is the chapter or appendix number, and *T* is the chapter or appendix title.
.ac *A N*	This macro (short for **.acm**) sets up the NROFF environment for camera-ready papers as used by the ACM. This format is 25% larger, and has no headers or footers. The author's name *A* is printed at the bottom of the page (but off the part which will be printed in the conference proceedings), together with the current page number and the total number of pages *N*. Additionally, this macro loads the file **/usr/lib/me/acm.me**, which may later be augmented with other macros useful for printing papers for ACM conferences. It should be noted that this macro will not work correctly in version 7

20

TROFF, since it sets the page length wider than the physical width of the C/A/T phototypesetter roll.

12. Predefined Strings

**	Footnote number, actually *[\\n($f*]. This macro is incremented after each call to .)f.
*#	Delayed text number. Actually [\\n($d].
*[	Superscript. This string gives upward movement and a change to a smaller point size if possible, otherwise it gives the left bracket character ('['). Extra space is left above the line to allow room for the superscript.
*]	Unsuperscript. Inverse to *[. For example, to produce a superscript you might type x*[2*], which will produce x^2.
*<	Subscript. Defaults to '<' if half-carriage motion not possible. Extra space is left below the line to allow for the subscript.
*>	Inverse to *<.
*(dw	The day of the week, as a word.
*(mo	The month, as a word.
*(td	Today's date, directly printable. The date is of the form May 19, 1994. Other forms of the date can be used by using \\n(dy (the day of the month; for example, 19), *(mo (as noted above) or \\n(mo (the same, but as an ordinal number; for example, May is 5), and \\n(yr (the last two digits of the current year).
*(lq	Left quote marks. Double quote in NROFF.
*(rq	Right quote.
*−	¾ em dash in TROFF; two hyphens in NROFF.

13. Special Characters and Marks

There are a number of special characters and diacritical marks (such as accents) available through −me. To reference these characters, you must call the macro .sc to define the characters before using them.

.sc   Define special characters and diacritical marks, as described in the remainder of this section. This macro must be stated before initialization. The special characters available are listed below.

Name	Usage	Example	
Acute accent	*´	a*´	á
Grave accent	*`	e*`	è
Umlat	*:	u*:	ü
Tilde	*~	n*~	ñ
Caret	*^	e*^	ê
Cedilla	*,	c*,	ç
Czech	*v	e*v	ě
Circle	*o	A*o	Å
There exists	*(qe		∃
For all	*(qa		∀

Acknowledgments

I would like to thank Bob Epstein, Bill Joy, and Larry Rowe for having the courage to use the −me macros to produce non-trivial papers during the development stages; Ricki Blau, Pamela Humphrey, and Jim Joyce for their

20

help with the documentation phase; peter kessler for numerous complaints, most accompanied by fixes; and the plethora of people who have contributed ideas and have given support for the project.

Summary

This alphabetical list summarizes all macros, strings, and number registers available in the −me macros. Selected *troff* commands, registers, and functions are included as well; those listed can generally be used with impunity.

The columns are the name of the command, macro, register, or string; the type of the object, and the description. Types are **M** for macro or builtin command (invoked with **.** or **´** in the first input column), **S** for a string (invoked with ***** or ***()**, **R** for a number register (invoked with **\\n** or **\\n()**, and **F** for a *troff* builtin function (invoked by preceding it with a single backslash).

Lines marked with § are *troff* internal codes. Lines marked with † or ‡ may be defined by the user to get special functions; ‡ indicates that these are defined by default and changing them may have unexpected side effects. Lines marked with ° are specific to *ditroff* (device-independent *troff*).

NAME	TYPE	DESCRIPTION
\\(space)	F§	unpaddable space
\\"	F§	comment (to end of line)
*#	S	optional delayed text tag string
\\$N	F§	interpolate argument N
\\n($0	R	section depth
.$0	M†	invoked after section title printed
\\n($1	R	first section number
.$1	M†	invoked before printing depth 1 section
\\n($2	R	second section number
.$2	M†	invoked before printing depth 2 section
\\n($3	R	third section number
.$3	M†	invoked before printing depth 3 section
\\n($4	R	fourth section number
.$4	M†	invoked before printing depth 4 section
\\n($5	R	fifth section number
.$5	M†	invoked before printing depth 5 section
\\n($6	R	sixth section number
.$6	M†	invoked before printing depth 6 section
.$C	M†	called at beginning of chapter
.$H	M†	text header
\\n($R	R‡	relative vertical spacing in displays
\\n($c	R	current column number
.$c	M‡	print chapter title
\\n($d	R	delayed text number
\\n($f	R	footnote number
.$f	M‡	print footer
.$h	M‡	print header
\\n($i	R	paragraph base indent
\\n($l	R	column width
\\n($m	R	number of columns in effect
*($n	S	section name
\\n($p	R	numbered paragraph number
.$p	M‡	print section heading (internal macro)
\\n($r	R‡	relative vertical spacing in text
\\n($s	R	column indent
.$s	M‡	footnote separator (from text)
\\n%	R§	current page number
\\&	F§	zero width character, useful for hiding controls
\\(xx	F§	interpolate special character xx
.(b	M	begin block

20

NAME	TYPE	DESCRIPTION
.(c	M	begin centered block
.(d	M	begin delayed text
.(f	M	begin footnote
.(l	M	begin list
.(q	M	begin quote
.(x	M	begin index entry
.(z	M	begin floating keep
.)b	M	end block
.)c	M	end centered block
.)d	M	end delayed text
.)f	M	end footnote
.)l	M	end list
.)q	M	end quote
.)x	M	end index entry
.)z	M	end floating keep
*x	F§	interpolate string x
*(xx	F§	interpolate string xx
**	S	optional footnote tag string
.++	M	set paper section type
.+c	M	begin chapter
*,	S	cedilla
\−	F§	minus sign
*−	S	3/4 em dash
\0	F§	unpaddable digit-width space
.1c	M	revert to single column output
.2c	M	begin two column output
*:	S	umlat
*<	S	begin subscript
*>	S	end subscript
.EN	M	end equation
.EQ	M	begin equation
\L´d´	F§	vertical line drawing function for distance d
.GE	M°	end *gremlin* picture
.GF	M°	end *gremlin* picture (with flyback)
.GS	M°	start *gremlin* picture
.IE	M°	end *ideal* picture
.IF	M°	end *ideal* picture (with flyback)
.IS	M°	start *ideal* picture
.PE	M°	end *pic* picture
.PF	M°	end *pic* picture (with flyback)
.PS	M°	start *pic* picture
.TE	M	end table
.TH	M	end header of table
.TS	M	begin table
*[	S	begin superscript
\n(.$	R§	number of arguments to macro
\n(.i	R§	current indent
\n(.l	R§	current line length
\n(.s	R§	current point size
*(´	S	acute accent
*(`	S	grave accent
\(´	F§	acute accent
\(`	F§	grave accent
*]	S	end superscript
\^	F§	1/12 em narrow space
*^	S	caret

NAME	TYPE	DESCRIPTION
.ac	M	ACM mode
.ad	M§	set text adjustment
.af	M§	assign format to register
.am	M§	append to macro
.ar	M	set page numbers in Arabic
.as	M§	append to string
.b	M	bold font
.ba	M	set base indent
.bc	M	begin new column
.bi	M	bold italic
\n(bi	R	display (block) indent
.bl	M	blank lines (even at top of page)
\n(bm	R	bottom title margin
.bp	M§	begin page
.br	M§	break (start new line)
\n(bs	R	display (block) pre/post spacing
\n(bt	R	block keep threshold
.bx	M	boxed
\c	F§	continue input
.ce	M§	center lines
\n(ch	R	current chapter number
.de	M§	define macro
\n(df	R	display font
.ds	M§	define string
\n(dw	R§	current day of week
*(dw	S	current day of week
\n(dy	R§	day of month
\e	F§	printable version of \
.ef	M	set footer (even numbered pages only)
.eh	M	set header (even numbered pages only)
.el	M§	else part of conditional
.ep	M	end page
\n(es	R	equation pre/post space
\f*f*	F§	inline font change to font *f*
\f(*ff*	F§	inline font change to font *ff*
.fc	M§	set field characters
\n(ff	R	footnote font
.fi	M§	fill output lines
\n(fi	R	footnote indent (first line only)
\n(fm	R	footer margin
.fo	M	set footer
\n(fp	R	footnote pointsize
\n(fs	R	footnote prespace
\n(fu	R	footnote undent (from right margin)
\h´*d*´	F§	local horizontal motion for distance *d*
.hc	M§	set hyphenation character
.he	M	set header
.hl	M	draw horizontal line
\n(hm	R	header margin
.hx	M	suppress headers and footers on next page
.hy	M§	set hyphenation mode
.i	M	italic font
.ie	M§	conditional with else
.if	M§	conditional
\n(ii	R	indented paragraph indent
.in	M§	indent (transient, use .ba for pervasive)

20

NAME	TYPE	DESCRIPTION
.ip	M	begin indented paragraph
.ix	M	indent, no break
\l´d´	F§	horizontal line drawing function for distance d
.lc	M§	set leader repetition character
.lh	M°	interpolate local letterhead
.ll	M	set line length
.lo	M	load local macros
.lp	M	begin left justified paragraph
*(lq	S	left quote marks
.ls	M§	set multi-line spacing
.m1	M	set space from top of page to header
.m2	M	set space from header to text
.m3	M	set space from text to footer
.m4	M	set space from footer to bottom of page
.mc	M§	insert margin character
.mk	M§	mark vertical position
\n(mo	R§	month of year
*(mo	S	current month
\n$x$	F§	interpolate number register x
\n(xx	F§	interpolate number register xx
.n1	M	number lines in margin
.n2	M	number lines in margin
.na	M§	turn off text adjustment
.ne	M§	need vertical space
.nf	M§	don't fill output lines
.nh	M§	turn off hyphenation
.np	M	begin numbered paragraph
.nr	M§	set number register
.ns	M§	no space mode
*o	S	circle (e.g., for Norse Å)
.of	M	set footer (odd numbered pages only)
.oh	M	set header (odd numbered pages only)
.pa	M	begin page
.pd	M	print delayed text
\n(pf	R	paragraph font
\n(pi	R	paragraph indent
.pl	M§	set page length
.pn	M§	set next page number
.po	M§	page offset
\n(po	R	simulated page offset
.pp	M	begin paragraph
\n(pp	R	paragraph pointsize
\n(ps	R	paragraph prespace
.q	M	quoted
*(qa	S	for all
*(qe	S	there exists
\n(qi	R	quote indent (also shortens line)
\n(qp	R	quote pointsize
\n(qs	R	quote pre/post space
.r	M	roman font
.rb	M	real bold font
.re	M	reset tabs
.rm	M§	remove macro or string
.rn	M§	rename macro or string
.ro	M	set page numbers in roman
*(rq	S	right quote marks

NAME	TYPE	DESCRIPTION
.rr	M§	remove register
.rs	M§	restore spacing
.rt	M§	return to vertical position
\sS	F§	inline size change to size S
.sc	M	load special characters
\n(sf	R	section title font
.sh	M	begin numbered section
\n(si	R	relative base indent per section depth
.sk	M	skip next page
.sm	M	set argument in a smaller pointsize
.so	M§	source input file
\n(so	R	additional section title offset
.sp	M§	vertical space
\n(sp	R	section title pointsize
\n(ss	R	section prespace
.sx	M	change section depth
.sz	M	set pointsize and vertical spacing
.ta	M§	set tab stops
.tc	M§	set tab repetition character
*(td	S	today's date
\n(tf	R	title font
.th	M	set thesis mode
.ti	M§	temporary indent (next line only)
.tl	M§	three part title
\n(tm	R	top title margin
.tp	M	begin title page
\n(tp	R	title pointsize
.tr	M§	translate
.u	M	underlined
.uh	M	unnumbered section
.ul	M§	underline next line
\v´d´	F§	local vertical motion for distance d
*v	S	inverted 'v' for czeck ''ě''
\w´S´	F§	return width of string S
.xl	M	set line length (local)
.xp	M	print index
\n(xs	R	index entry prespace
\n(xu	R	index undent (from right margin)
\n(yr	R§	year (last two digits only)
\n(zs	R	floating keep pre/post space
\{	F§	begin conditional group
|	F§	1/6 em narrow space
\}	F§	end conditional group
*~	S	tilde

20

NROFF/TROFF User's Manual

Joseph F. Ossanna
(updated for 4.3BSD by Mark Seiden)

Bell Laboratories
Murray Hill, New Jersey 07974

Introduction

NROFF and TROFF are text processors under the UNIX Time-Sharing System that format text for typewriter-like terminals and for a Graphic Systems phototypesetter, respectively. (Device-independent TROFF, part of the Documenter's Workbench, supports additional output devices.) They accept lines of text interspersed with lines of format control information and format the text into a printable, paginated document having a user-designed style. NROFF and TROFF offer unusual freedom in document styling, including: arbitrary style headers and footers; arbitrary style footnotes; multiple automatic sequence numbering for paragraphs, sections, etc; multiple column output; dynamic font and point-size control; arbitrary horizontal and vertical local motions at any point; and a family of automatic overstriking, bracket construction, and line drawing functions.

NROFF and TROFF are highly compatible with each other and it is almost always possible to prepare input acceptable to both. Conditional input is provided that enables the user to embed input expressly destined for either program. NROFF can prepare output directly for a variety of terminal types and is capable of utilizing the full resolution of each terminal.

Usage

The general form of invoking NROFF (or TROFF) at UNIX command level is

      nroff *options files*   (or **troff** *options files*)

where *options* represents any of a number of option arguments and *files* represents the list of files containing the document to be formatted. An argument consisting of a single minus (−) is taken to be a file name corresponding to the standard input. If no file names are given input is taken from the standard input. The options, which may appear in any order so long as they appear before the files, are:

21

Option	Effect
−**i**	Read standard input after the input files are exhausted.
−**m***name*	Prepends the macro file **/usr/lib/tmac.***name* to the input *files*.
−**n***N*	Number first generated page *N*.
−**o***list*	Print only pages whose page numbers appear in *list*, which consists of comma-separated numbers and number ranges. A number range has the form *N–M* and means pages *N* through *M;* a initial −*N* means from the beginning to page *N;* and a final *N*− means from *N* to the end.
−**q**	Invoke the simultaneous input-output mode of the **rd** request.
−**ra***N*	Number register *a* (one-character) is set to *N*.
−**s***N*	Stop every *N* pages. NROFF will halt prior to every *N* pages (default *N*=1) to allow paper loading or changing, and will resume upon receipt of a newline. TROFF will stop the phototypesetter every *N* pages, produce a trailer to allow changing cassettes, and will resume after the phototypesetter START button is pressed.
−**z**	Efficiently suppress formatted output. Only produce output to standard error (from **tm** requests or diagnostics).

NROFF Only

−T*name*   Specifies the name of the output terminal type. Currently defined names are **37** for the (default) Model 37 Teletype®, **tn300** for the GE TermiNet 300 (or any terminal without half-line capabilities), **300S** for the DASI-300S, **300** for the DASI-300, and **450** for the DASI-450 (Diablo Hyterm).

−**e**   Produce equally-spaced words in adjusted lines, using full terminal resolution.

−**h**   On output, use tabs during horizontal spacing to increase speed. Device tabs setting are assumed to be (and input tabs are initially set to) every 8 character widths.

TROFF Only

−**a**   Send a printable (ASCII) approximation of the results to the standard output.

−**b**   TROFF will report whether the phototypesetter is busy or available. No text processing is done.

−**f**   Refrain from feeding out paper and stopping phototypesetter at the end of the run.

−**t**   Direct output to the standard output instead of the phototypesetter.

−**w**   Wait until phototypesetter is available, if currently busy.

Each option is invoked as a separate argument; for example,

> **nroff** −o*4,8–10* −T*300S* −m*abc file1 file2*

requests formatting of pages 4, 8, 9, and 10 of a document contained in the files named *file1* and *file2*, specifies the output terminal as a DASI-300S, and invokes the macro package *abc*.

Various pre- and post-processors are available for use with NROFF and TROFF. These include the equation preprocessors NEQN and EQN[1] (for NROFF and TROFF respectively), and the table-construction preprocessor TBL[2]. A reverse-line postprocessor COL[3] is available for multiple-column NROFF output on terminals without reverse-line ability; COL expects the Model 37 Teletype escape sequences that NROFF produces by default. TK[3] is a 37 Teletype simulator postprocessor for printing NROFF output on a Tektronix 4014. TC[5] is a phototypesetter-simulator postprocessor for TROFF that produces an approximation of phototypesetter output on a Tektronix 4014. For example, in

> **tbl** *files* | **eqn** | **troff** −t *options* | **tc**

the first | indicates the piping of TBL's output to EQN's input; the second the piping of EQN's output to TROFF's input; and the third indicates the piping of TROFF's output to TC.

The remainder of this manual consists of: a Summary and outline; a Reference Manual keyed to the outline; and a set of Tutorial Examples. Another tutorial is [5].

References

[1]   B. W. Kernighan, L. L. Cherry, *Typesetting Mathematics — User's Guide (Second Edition)*, Bell Laboratories.

[2]   M. E. Lesk, *Tbl — A Program to Format Tables*, Bell Laboratories internal memorandum.

[3]   Internal on-line documentation (*man* pages) on UNIX.

[4]   B. W. Kernighan, *A TROFF Tutorial*, Bell Laboratories.

[5]   Your site may have similar programs for more modern displays.

21

SUMMARY OF REQUESTS AND OUTLINE OF THIS MANUAL

Request Form	Initial Value*	If No Argument	Notes#	Explanation
1. General Explanation				
2. Font and Character Size Control				
.ps ±N	10 point	previous	E	Point size; also \s±N.†
.fz F ±N	off	-	E	font F to point size ±N.
.fz S F ±N	off	-	E	Special Font characters to point size ±N.
.ss N	12/36 em	ignored	E	Space-character size set to N/36 em.†
.cs F N M	off	-	P	Constant character space (width) mode (font F).†
.bd F N	off	-	P	Embolden font F by N−1 units.†
.bd S F N	off	-	P	Embolden Special Font when current font is F.†
.ft F	Roman	previous	E	Change to font F = x, xx, or 1-4. Also \fx, \f(xx, \fN.
.fp N F	R,I,B,S	ignored	-	Font named F mounted on physical position 1≤N≤4.
3. Page Control				
.pl ±N	11 in	11 in	v	Page length.
.bp ±N	N=1	-	B‡,v	Eject current page; next page number N.
.pn ±N	N=1	ignored	-	Next page number N.
.po ±N	0; 26/27 in	previous	v	Page offset.
.ne N	-	N=1V	D,v	Need N vertical space (V = vertical spacing).
.mk R	none	internal	D	Mark current vertical place in register R.
.rt ±N	none	internal	D,v	Return (upward only) to marked vertical place.
4. Text Filling, Adjusting, and Centering				
.br	-	-	B	Break.
.fi	fill	-	B,E	Fill output lines.
.nf	fill	-	B,E	No filling or adjusting of output lines.
.ad c	adj,both	adjust	E	Adjust output lines with mode c.
.na	adjust	-	E	No output line adjusting.
.ce N	off	N=1	B,E	Center following N input text lines.
5. Vertical Spacing				
.vs N	1/6in;12pts	previous	E,p	Vertical base line spacing (V).
.ls N	N=1	previous	E	Output N−1 Vs after each text output line.
.sp N	-	N=1V	B,v	Space vertical distance N in either direction.
.sv N	-	N=1V	v	Save vertical distance N.
.os	-	-	-	Output saved vertical distance.
.ns	space	-	D	Turn no-space mode on.
.rs	-	-	D	Restore spacing; turn no-space mode off.
6. Line Length and Indenting				
.ll ±N	6.5 in	previous	E,m	Line length.
.in ±N	N=0	previous	B,E,m	Indent.
.ti ±N	-	ignored	B,E,m	Temporary indent.
7. Macros, Strings, Diversion, and Position Traps				
.de xx yy	-	.yy=..	-	Define or redefine macro xx; end at call of yy.
.am xx yy	-	.yy=..	-	Append to a macro.

*Values separated by ";" are for NROFF and TROFF respectively.

#Notes are explained at the end of this Summary and Index

†No effect in NROFF.

‡The use of " ′ " as control character (instead of ".") suppresses the break function.

21

Request Form	Initial Value	If No Argument	Notes	Explanation
.ds *xx string*	-	ignored	-	Define a string *xx* containing *string*.
.as *xx string*	-	ignored	-	Append *string* to string *xx*.
.rm *xx*	-	ignored	-	Remove request, macro, or string.
.rn *xx yy*	-	ignored	-	Rename request, macro, or string *xx* to *yy*.
.di *xx*	-	end	D	Divert output to macro *xx*.
.da *xx*	-	end	D	Divert and append to *xx*.
.wh *N xx*	-	-	v	Set location trap; negative is w.r.t. page bottom.
.ch *xx N*	-	-	v	Change trap location.
.dt *N xx*	-	off	D,v	Set a diversion trap.
.it *N xx*	-	off	E	Set an input-line count trap.
.em *xx*	none	none	-	End macro is *xx*.

8. Number Registers

.nr *R* ±*N M*	-	-	u	Define and set number register *R*; auto-increment by *M*.
.af *R c*	arabic	-	-	Assign format to register *R* (*c*=**1**, **i**, **I**, **a**, **A**).
.rr *R*	-	-	-	Remove register *R*.

9. Tabs, Leaders, and Fields

.ta *Nt* ...	0.8; 0.5in	none	E,m	Tab settings; *left* type, unless *t*=**R**(right), **C**(centered).
.tc *c*	none	none	E	Tab repetition character.
.lc *c*	.	none	E	Leader repetition character.
.fc *a b*	off	off	-	Set field delimiter *a* and pad character *b*.

10. Input and Output Conventions and Character Translations

.ec *c*	\	\	-	Set escape character.
.eo	on	-	-	Turn off escape character mechanism.
.lg *N*	-; on	on	-	Ligature mode on if *N*>0.
.ul *N*	off	*N*=1	E	Underline (italicize in TROFF) *N* input lines.
.cu *N*	off	*N*=1	E	Continuous underline in NROFF; like **ul** in TROFF.
.uf *F*	Italic	Italic	-	Underline font set to *F* (to be switched to by **ul**).
.cc *c*	.	.	E	Set control character to *c*.
.c2 *c*	'	'	E	Set nobreak control character to *c*.
.tr *abcd*....	none	-	O	Translate *a* to *b*, etc. on output.

11. Local Horizontal and Vertical Motions, and the Width Function

12. Overstrike, Bracket, Line-drawing, and Zero-width Functions

13. Hyphenation.

.nh	hyphenate	-	E	No hyphenation.
.hy *N*	hyphenate	hyphenate	E	Hyphenate; *N* = mode.
.hc *c*	\%	\%	E	Hyphenation indicator character *c*.
.hw *word1* ...		ignored	-	Exception words.

14. Three Part Titles.

.tl '*left*'*center*'*right*'		-	-	Three part title.
.pc *c*	%	off	-	Page number character.
.lt ±*N*	6.5 in	previous	E,m	Length of title.

15. Output Line Numbering.

.nm ±*N M S I*	off	E		Number mode on or off, set parameters.
.nn *N*	-	*N*=1	E	Do not number next *N* lines.

Request Form	Initial Value	If No Argument	Notes	Explanation

16. Conditional Acceptance of Input

.if *c anything* -		-		If condition *c* true, accept *anything* as input, for multi-line use \\{*anything*\\}.
.if !*c anything* -		-		If condition *c* false, accept *anything*.
.if *N anything* -		u		If expression $N > 0$, accept *anything*.
.if !*N anything*		-	u	If expression $N \le 0$, accept *anything*.
.if '*string1*' *string2*' *anything*		-		If *string1* identical to *string2*, accept *anything*.
.if ! '*string1*' *string2*' *anything*		-		If *string1* not identical to *string2*, accept *anything*.
.ie *c anything* -		u		If portion of if-else; all above forms (like **if**).
.el *anything*		-		Else portion of if-else.

17. Environment Switching.

.ev *N*	*N*=0	previous	-	Environment switched (*push down*).

18. Insertions from the Standard Input

.rd *prompt*	-	*prompt*=BEL		Read insertion.
.ex	-	-	-	Exit from NROFF/TROFF.

19. Input/Output File Switching

.so *filename*	-	-	-	Switch source file (*push down*).
.nx *filename*		end-of-file	-	Next file.
.pi *program*	-	-	-	Pipe output to *program* (NROFF only).

20. Miscellaneous

.mc *c N*	-	off	E,m	Set margin character *c* and separation *N*.
.tm *string*	-	newline	-	Print *string* on terminal (UNIX standard error output).
.ig *yy*	-	.*yy*=..	-	Ignore till call of *yy*.
.pm *t*	-	all	-	Print macro names and sizes; if *t* present, print only total of sizes.
.ab *string*	-	-	-	Print a message and abort.
.fl	-	-	B	Flush output buffer.

21. Output and Error Messages

21

Notes-

B	Request normally causes a break.
D	Mode or relevant parameters associated with current diversion level.
E	Relevant parameters are a part of the current environment.
O	Must stay in effect until logical output.
P	Mode must be still or again in effect at the time of physical output.
v,p,m,u	Default scale indicator; if not specified, scale indicators are *ignored*.

Alphabetical Request and Section Number Cross Reference

ab 20	c2 10	di 7	ex 18	hw 13	lg 10	ne 3	os 5	rd 18	ss 2	uf 10
ad 4	cc 10	ds 7	fc 9	hy 13	li 10	nf 4	pc 14	rm 7	sv 5	ul 10
af 8	ce 4	dt 7	fi 4	ie 16	ll 6	nh 13	pi 19	rn 7	ta 9	vs 5
am 7	ch 7	ec 10	fl 20	if 16	ls 5	nm 15	pl 3	rr 8	tc 9	wh 7
as 7	cs 2	el 16	fp 2	ig 20	lt 14	nn 15	pm 20	rs 5	ti 6	
bd 2	cu 10	em 7	ft 2	in 6	mc 20	nr 8	pn 3	rt 3	tl 14	
bp 3	da 7	eo 10	fz 2	it 7	mk 3	ns 5	po 3	so 19	tm 20	
br 4	de 7	ev 17	hc 13	lc 9	na 4	nx 19	ps 2	sp 5	tr 10	

Escape Sequences for Characters, Indicators, and Functions

Section Reference	Escape Sequence	Meaning
10.1	\\	\ (to prevent or delay the interpretation of \)
10.1	\e	Printable version of the *current* escape character.
2.1	\'	´ (acute accent); equivalent to \(aa
2.1	\`	` (grave accent); equivalent to \(ga
2.1	\-	– Minus sign in the *current* font
7	\.	Period (dot) (see **de**)
11.1	\(space)	Unpaddable space-size space character
11.1	\0	Digit width space
11.1	|	1/6 em narrow space character (zero width in NROFF)
11.1	\^	1/12 em half-narrow space character (zero width in NROFF)
4.1	\&	Non-printing, zero width character
10.6	\!	Transparent line indicator
10.7	\"	Beginning of comment
7.3	\$N	Interpolate argument $1 \leq N \leq 9$
13	\%	Default optional hyphenation character
2.1	\(xx	Character named xx
7.1	*x, *(xx	Interpolate string x or xx
9.1	\a	Non-interpreted leader character
12.3	\b'abc...'	Bracket building function
4.2	\c	Interrupt text processing
11.1	\d	Forward (down) 1/2 em vertical motion (1/2 line in NROFF)
2.2	\fx,\f(xx,\fN	Change to font named x or xx, or position N
11.1	\h'N'	Local horizontal motion; move right N *(negative left)*
11.3	\kx	Mark horizontal *input* place in register x
12.4	\l'Nc'	Horizontal line drawing function (optionally with c)
12.4	\L'Nc'	Vertical line drawing function (optionally with c)
8	\nx,\n(xx	Interpolate number register x or xx
12.1	\o'abc...'	Overstrike characters a, b, c, ...
4.1	\p	Break and spread output line
11.1	\r	Reverse 1 em vertical motion (reverse line in NROFF)
2.3	\sN, \s±N	Point-size change function
9.1	\t	Non-interpreted horizontal tab
11.1	\u	Reverse (up) 1/2 em vertical motion (1/2 line in NROFF)
11.1	\v'N'	Local vertical motion; move down N *(negative up)*
11.2	\w'string'	Interpolate width of *string*
5.2	\x'N'	Extra line-space function *(negative before, positive after)*
12.2	\zc	Print c with zero width (without spacing)
16	\{	Begin conditional input
16	\}	End conditional input
10.7	\(newline)	Concealed (ignored) newline
-	\X	X, any character *not* listed above

The escape sequences \\, \., \", \$, *, \a, \n, \t, and \(newline) are interpreted in *copy mode* (§7.2).

Predefined General Number Registers

Section Reference	Register Name	Description
3	%	Current page number.
19	c.	Number of *lines* read from current input file.
11.2	ct	Character type (set by *width* function).
7.4	dl	Width (maximum) of last completed diversion.
7.4	dn	Height (vertical size) of last completed diversion.
-	dw	Current day of the week (1-7).
-	dy	Current day of the month (1-31).
11.3	hp	Current horizontal place on *input* line (not in ditroff)
15	ln	Output line number.
-	mo	Current month (1-12).
4.1	nl	Vertical position of last printed text base-line.
11.2	sb	Depth of string below base line (generated by *width* function).
11.2	st	Height of string above base line (generated by *width* function).
-	yr	Last two digits of current year.

Predefined Read-Only Number Registers

Section Reference	Register Name	Description
7.3	.$	Number of arguments available at the current macro level.
-	.A	Set to 1 in TROFF, if −a option used; always 1 in NROFF.
11.1	.H	Available horizontal resolution in basic units.
5.3	.L	Set to current *line-spacing* (ls) parameter
-	.P	Set to 1 if the current page is being printed; otherwise 0.
-	.T	Set to 1 in NROFF, if −T option used; always 0 in TROFF.
11.1	.V	Available vertical resolution in basic units.
5.2	.a	Post-line extra line-space most recently utilized using \x'N'.
19	.c	Number of *lines* read from current input file.
7.4	.d	Current vertical place in current diversion; equal to **nl**, if no diversion.
2.2	.f	Current font as physical quadrant (1-4).
4	.h	Text base-line high-water mark on current page or diversion.
6	.i	Current indent.
4.2	.j	Current adjustment mode and type.
4.1	.k	Length of text portion on current partial output line.
6	.l	Current line length.
4	.n	Length of text portion on previous output line.
3	.o	Current page offset.
3	.p	Current page length.
2.3	.s	Current point size.
7.5	.t	Distance to the next trap.
4.1	.u	Equal to 1 in fill mode and 0 in nofill mode.
5.1	.v	Current vertical line spacing.
11.2	.w	Width of previous character.
-	.x	Reserved version-dependent register.
-	.y	Reserved version-dependent register.
7.4	.z	Name of current diversion.

21

REFERENCE MANUAL

1. General Explanation

1.1. Form of input. Input consists of *text lines*, which are destined to be printed, interspersed with *control lines*, which set parameters or otherwise control subsequent processing. Control lines begin with a *control character*—normally . (period) or ´ (acute accent)—followed by a one or two character name that specifies a basic *request* or the substitution of a user-defined *macro* in place of the control line. The control character ´ suppresses the *break* function—the forced output of a partially filled line—caused by certain requests. The control character may be separated from the request/macro name by white space (spaces and/or tabs) for æsthetic reasons. Names must be followed by either space or newline. Control lines with unrecognized names are ignored.

Various special functions may be introduced anywhere in the input by means of an *escape* character, normally \. For example, the function \nR causes the interpolation (insertion in place) of the contents of the *number register R* in place of the function; here *R* is either a single character name as in \nx, or left-parenthesis-introduced, two-character name as in \n(xx.

1.2. Formatter and device resolution. TROFF internally uses 432 units/inch, (for historical reasons, corresponding to the Graphic Systems phototypesetter which had a horizontal resolution of 1/432 inch and a vertical resolution of 1/144 inch.) NROFF internally uses 240 units/inch, corresponding to the least common multiple of the horizontal and vertical resolutions of various typewriter-like output devices. TROFF rounds horizontal/vertical numerical parameter input to its own internal horizontal/vertical resolution. NROFF similarly rounds numerical input to the actual resolution of the output device indicated by the −**T** option (default Model 37 Teletype).

1.3. Numerical parameter input. Both NROFF and TROFF accept numerical input with the scale indicator suffixes shown in the following table, where S is the current type size in points, V is the current vertical line spacing in basic units, and C is a *nominal character width* in basic units.

Scale Indicator	Meaning	Number of basic units TROFF	NROFF
i	Inch	432	240
c	Centimeter	432×50/127	240×50/127
P	Pica = 1/6 inch	72	240/6
m	Em = S points	6×S	C
n	En = Em/2	3×S	*C, same as Em*
p	Point = 1/72 inch	6	240/72
u	Basic unit	1	1
v	Vertical line space	V	V
none	Default, see below		

In NROFF, *both* the em and the en are taken to be equal to the C, which is output-device dependent; common values are 1/10 and 1/12 inch. Actual character widths in NROFF need not be all the same and constructed characters such as −> (→) are often extra wide. The default scaling is ems for the horizontally-oriented requests and functions **ll, in, ti, ta, lt, po, mc, \h,** and **\l**; *V*s for the vertically-oriented requests and functions **pl, wh, ch, dt, sp, sv, ne, rt, \v, \x,** and **\L; p** for the vs request; and **u** for the requests **nr, if,** and **ie.** *All* other requests ignore any scale indicators. When a number register containing an already appropriately scaled number is interpolated to provide numerical input, the unit scale indicator **u** may need to be appended to prevent an additional inappropriate default scaling. The number, N, may be specified in decimal-fraction form but the parameter finally stored is rounded to an integer number of basic units.

The *absolute position* indicator | may be prefixed to a number N to generate the distance to the vertical or horizontal place N. For vertically-oriented requests and functions, $|N$ becomes the distance in basic units from the current vertical place on the page or in a *diversion* (§7.4) to the vertical place N. For *all* other requests and functions, $|N$ becomes the distance from the current horizontal place on the *input* line to the horizontal place N. For example,

    .sp |3.2c

will space *in the required direction* to 3.2 centimeters from the top of the page.

1.4. Numerical expressions. Wherever numerical input is expected, an expression involving parentheses, the arithmetic operators +, −, /, *, % (mod), and the logical operators <, >, <=, >=, = (or ==), & (and), : (or) may be used. Except where controlled by parentheses, evaluation of expressions is left-to-right; there is no operator precedence. In the case of certain requests, an initial + or − is stripped and interpreted as an increment or decrement indicator respectively. In the presence of default scaling, the desired scale indicator must be attached to *every* number in an expression for which the desired and default scaling differ. For example, if the number register **x** contains 2 and the current point size is 10, then

> **.ll (4.25i+\nxP+3)/2u**

will set the line length to 1/2 the sum of 4.25 inches + 2 picas + 30 points.

1.5. Notation. Numerical parameters are indicated in this manual in two ways. ±*N* means that the argument may take the forms *N*, +*N*, or −*N* and that the corresponding effect is to set the affected parameter to *N*, to increment it by *N*, or to decrement it by *N* respectively. Plain *N* means that an initial algebraic sign is *not* an increment indicator, but merely the sign of *N*. Generally, unreasonable numerical input is either ignored or truncated to a reasonable value. For example, most requests expect to set parameters to non-negative values; exceptions are **sp**, **wh**, **ch**, **nr**, and **if**. The requests **ps**, **ft**, **po**, **vs**, **ls**, **ll**, **in**, and **lt** restore the *previous* parameter value in the *absence* of an argument.

Single character arguments are indicated by single lower case letters and one/two character arguments are indicated by a pair of lower case letters. Character string arguments are indicated by multi-character mnemonics.

2. Font and Character Size Control

2.1. Character set. The TROFF character set consists of a typesetter-dependent basic character set plus a Special Mathematical Font character set—each having 102 characters. An example of these character sets is shown in the Appendix Table I. All printable ASCII characters are included, with some on the Special Font. With three exceptions, these ASCII characters are input as themselves, and non-ASCII characters are input in the form \\(*xx* where *xx* is a two-character name given in the Appendix Table II. The three ASCII exceptions are mapped as follows:

ASCII Input		Printed by TROFF	
Character	Name	Character	Name
´	acute accent	'	close quote
`	grave accent	‘	open quote
−	minus	-	hyphen

21

The characters ´, `, and − may be input by \\', \\`, and \\- respectively or by their names (Table II). The ASCII characters @, #, ", ´, `, <, >, \\, {, }, ~, ^, and _ exist only on the Special Font and are printed as a 1-em space if that font is not mounted.

NROFF understands the entire TROFF character set, but can in general print only ASCII characters, additional characters as may be available on the output device, such characters as may be able to be constructed by overstriking or other combination, and those that can reasonably be mapped into other printable characters. The exact behavior is determined by a driving table prepared for each device. The characters ´, `, and _ print as themselves.

2.2. Fonts. The default mounted fonts are Times Roman (**R**), Times Italic (**I**), Times Bold (**B**), and the Special Mathematical Font (**S**) on physical typesetter positions 1, 2, 3, and 4 respectively. These fonts are used in this document. The *current* font, initially Roman, may be changed (among the mounted fonts) by use of the **ft** request, or by imbedding at any desired point either \\f*x*, \\f(*xx*, or \\f*N* where *x* and *xx* are the name of a mounted font and *N* is a numerical font position. It is *not* necessary to change to the Special Font; characters on that font are automatically handled. A request for a named but not-mounted font is *ignored*. TROFF can be informed that any particular font is mounted by use of the **fp** request. The list of known fonts is installation dependent. In the subsequent discussion of font-related requests, *F* represents either a one/two-character font name or the numerical font position, 1-4. The current font is available (as numerical position) in the read-only number register **.f**.

NROFF understands font control and normally underlines Italic characters (see §10.5).

2.3. Character size. Character point sizes available are typesetter dependent, but often include 6, 7, 8, 9, 10, 11, 12, 14, 16, 18, 20, 22, 24, 28, and 36. This is a range of 1/12 inch to 1/2 inch. The **ps** request is used to change or restore the point size. Alternatively the point size may be changed between any two characters by imbedding a \\s*N* at the desired point to set the size to *N*, or a \s±*N* (1≤*N*≤9) to increment/decrement the size by *N*; \s0 restores the *previous* size. Requested point size values that are between two valid sizes yield the larger of the two. The current size is available in the **.s** register. NROFF ignores type size control.

Request Form	Initial Value	If No Argument	Notes*	Explanation
.ps ±*N*	10 point	previous	E	Point size set to ±*N*. Alternatively imbed \s*N* or \s±*N*. Any positive size value may be requested; if invalid, the next larger valid size will result, with a maximum of 36. A paired sequence +*N*, −*N* will work because the previous requested value is also remembered. Ignored in NROFF.
.fz *F* ±*N*	off	-	E	The characters in font *F* will be adjusted to be in size ±*N*. Characters in the Special Font encountered during the use of font *F* will have the same size modification. (Use the **.fz S** request if different treatment of Special Font characters is required). **.fz** must follow any **.fp** request for the position.
.fz S *F* ±*N*	off	-	E	The characters in the Special Font will be in size ±*N* independent of previous **.fz** requests.
.ss *N*	12/36 em	ignored	E	Space-character size is set to *N*/36 ems. This size is the minimum word spacing in adjusted text. Ignored in NROFF.
.cs *F N M*	off	-	P	Constant character space (width) mode is set on for font *F* (if mounted); the width of every character will be taken to be *N*/36 ems. If *M* is absent, the em is that of the character's point size; if *M* is given, the em is *M*-points. All affected characters are centered in this space, including those with an actual width larger than this space. Special Font characters occurring while the current font is *F* are also so treated. If *N* is absent, the mode is turned off. The mode must be still or again in effect when the characters are physically printed. Ignored in NROFF.
.bd *F N*	off	-	P	The characters in font *F* will be artificially emboldened by printing each one twice, separated by *N*−1 basic units. A reasonable value for *N* is 3 when the character size is in the vicinity of 10 points. If *N* is missing the embolden mode is turned off. The column heads above were printed with **.bd I 3**. The mode must be still or again in effect when the characters are physically printed. Ignored in NROFF.
.bd S *F N*	off	-	P	The characters in the Special Font will be emboldened whenever the current font is *F*. This manual was printed with **.bd S B 3**. The mode must be still or again in effect when the characters are physically printed.
.ft *F*	Roman	previous	E	Font changed to *F*. Alternatively, imbed \f*F*. The font name **P** is reserved to mean the previous font.
.fp *N F*	R,I,B,S	ignored	-	Font position. This is a statement that a font named *F* is mounted on position *N* (1-4). It is a fatal error if *F* is not known. The phototypesetter has four fonts physically mounted. Each font consists of a film strip which can be mounted on a numbered quadrant of a wheel. The default mounting sequence assumed by TROFF is R, I, B, and S on positions 1, 2, 3 and 4.

---

*Notes are explained at the end of the Summary and Index above.

3. Page control

Top and bottom margins are *not* automatically provided; it is conventional to define two *macros* and to set *traps* for them at vertical positions 0 (top) and $-N$ (N from the bottom). See §7 and Tutorial Examples §T2. A pseudo-page transition onto the *first* page occurs either when the first *break* occurs or when the first *non-diverted* text processing occurs. Arrangements for a trap to occur at the top of the first page must be completed before this transition. In the following, references to the *current diversion* (§7.4) mean that the mechanism being described works during both ordinary and diverted output (the former considered as the top diversion level).

The usable page width on the Graphic Systems phototypesetter was about 7.54 inches, beginning about 1/27 inch from the left edge of the 8 inch wide, continuous roll paper, but these characteristics are typesetter- dependent. The physical limitations on NROFF output are output-device dependent.

Request Form	Initial Value	If No Argument	Notes	Explanation
.pl $\pm N$	11 in	11 in	v	Page length set to $\pm N$. The internal limitation is about 75 inches in TROFF and about 136 inches in NROFF. The current page length is available in the .p register.
.bp $\pm N$	$N=1$	-	B*,v	Begin page. The current page is ejected and a new page is begun. If $\pm N$ is given, the new page number will be $\pm N$. Also see request ns.
.pn $\pm N$	$N=1$	ignored	-	Page number. The next page (when it occurs) will have the page number $\pm N$. A pn must occur before the initial pseudo-page transition to affect the page number of the first page. The current page number is in the % register.
.po $\pm N$	0; 26/27 in†	previous	v	Page offset. The current *left margin* is set to $\pm N$. The TROFF initial value provides about 1 inch of paper margin including the physical typesetter margin of 1/27 inch. In TROFF the maximum (line-length)+(page-offset) is about 7.54 inches. See §6. The current page offset is available in the .o register.
.ne N	-	$N=1$ V	D,v	Need N vertical space. If the distance, D, to the next trap position (see §7.5) is less than N, a forward vertical space of size D occurs, which will spring the trap. If there are no remaining traps on the page, D is the distance to the bottom of the page. If $D < V$, another line could still be output and spring the trap. In a diversion, D is the distance to the *diversion trap*, if any, or is very large.
.mk R	none	internal	D	Mark the *current* vertical place in an internal register (both associated with the current diversion level), or in register R, if given. See rt request.
.rt $\pm N$	none	internal	D,v	Return *upward only* to a marked vertical place in the current diversion. If $\pm N$ (w.r.t. current place) is given, the place is $\pm N$ from the top of the page or diversion or, if N is absent, to a place marked by a previous mk. Note that the sp request (§5.3) may be used in all cases instead of rt by spacing to the absolute place stored in a explicit register; e. g. using the sequence .mk R ... .sp |\n$R$u.

4. Text Filling, Adjusting, and Centering

4.1. Filling and adjusting. Normally, words are collected from input text lines and assembled into a output text line until some word doesn't fit. An attempt is then made to hyphenate the word to assemble a part of it into the output

---

*The use of " ´ " as control character (instead of ".") suppresses the break function.

†Values separated by ";" are for NROFF and TROFF respectively.

line. The spaces between the words on the output line are then increased to spread out the line to the current *line length* minus any current *indent*. A *word* is any string of characters delimited by the *space* character or the beginning/end of the input line. Any adjacent pair of words that must be kept together (neither split across output lines nor spread apart in the adjustment process) can be tied together by separating them with the *unpaddable space* character '\ ' (backslash-space). The adjusted word spacings are uniform in TROFF and the minimum interword spacing can be controlled with the **ss** request (§2). In NROFF, they are normally nonuniform because of quantization to character-size spaces; however, the command line option –**e** causes uniform spacing with full output device resolution. Filling, adjustment, and hyphenation (§13) can all be prevented or controlled. The *text length* on the last line output is available in the **.n** register, and text base-line position on the page for this line is in the **nl** register. The text base-line high-water mark (lowest place) on the current page is in the **.h** register. The **.k** register (read-only) contains the horizontal size of the text portion (without indent) of the current partially-collected output line (if any) in the current environment.

An input text line ending with **.**, **?**, or **!** is taken to be the end of a *sentence*, and an additional space character is automatically provided during filling. Multiple inter-word space characters found in the input are retained, except for trailing spaces; initial spaces also cause a *break*.

When filling is in effect, a \p may be imbedded or attached to a word to cause a *break* at the *end* of the word and have the resulting output line *spread out* to fill the current line length.

A text input line that happens to begin with a control character (§10.4) can be made to not look like a control line by preceding it by the non-printing, zero-width filler character \\&. Still another way is to specify output translation of some convenient character into the control character using **tr** (§10.5).

4.2. Interrupted text. The copying of a input line in *nofill* (non-fill) mode can be *interrupted* by terminating the partial line with a \c. The *next* encountered input text line will be considered to be a continuation of the same line of input text. Similarly, a word within *filled* text may be interrupted by terminating the word (and line) with \c; the next encountered text will be taken as a continuation of the interrupted word. If the intervening control lines cause a break, any partial line will be forced out along with any partial word.

Request Form	Initial Value	If No Argument	Notes	Explanation
.br	-	-	B	Break. The filling of the line currently being collected is stopped and the line is output without adjustment. Text lines beginning with space characters and empty text lines (blank lines) also cause a break.
.fi	fill on	-	B,E	Fill subsequent output lines. The register **.u** is 1 in fill mode and 0 in nofill mode.
.nf	fill on	-	B,E	Nofill. Subsequent output lines are *neither* filled *nor* adjusted. Input text lines are copied directly to output lines *without regard* for the current line length.
.ad *c*	adj,both	adjust	E	Line adjustment is begun. If fill mode is not on, adjustment will be deferred until fill mode is back on. If the type indicator *c* is present, the adjustment type is changed as shown in the following table. The type indicator can also be a value saved from the read-only **.j** number register, which is set to contain the current adjustment mode and type.

Indicator	Adjust Type
l	adjust left margin only
r	adjust right margin only
c	center
b or **n**	adjust both margins
absent	unchanged

| .na | adjust | - | E | Noadjust. Adjustment is turned off; the right margin will be ragged. The adjustment type for **ad** is not changed. Output line filling still occurs if fill mode is on. |
| .ce *N* | off | *N*=1 | B,E | Center the next *N* input text lines within the current (line-length minus indent). If *N*=0, any residual count is cleared. A break occurs after each of the *N* input lines. If the input line is too long, it will be left adjusted. |

5. Vertical Spacing

5.1. Base-line spacing. The vertical spacing *(V)* between the base-lines of successive output lines can be set using the **vs** request with a resolution of 1/144 inch = 1/2 point in TROFF, and to the output device resolution in NROFF. *V* must be large enough to accommodate the character sizes on the affected output lines. For the common type sizes (9-12 points), usual typesetting practice is to set *V* to 2 points greater than the point size; TROFF default is 10-point type on a 12-point spacing (as in this document). The current *V* is available in the **.v** register. Multiple-*V* line separation (e. g. double spacing) may be requested with **ls**.

5.2. Extra line-space. If a word contains a vertically tall construct requiring the output line containing it to have extra vertical space before and/or after it, the *extra-line-space* function \x´*N*´ can be imbedded in or attached to that word. In this and other functions having a pair of delimiters around their parameter (here ´), the delimiter choice is arbitrary, except that it can't look like the continuation of a number expression for *N*. If *N* is negative, the output line containing the word will be preceded by *N* extra vertical space; if *N* is positive, the output line containing the word will be followed by *N* extra vertical space. If successive requests for extra space apply to the same line, the maximum values are used. The most recently utilized post-line extra line-space is available in the **.a** register.

5.3. Blocks of vertical space. A block of vertical space is ordinarily requested using **sp**, which honors the *no-space* mode and which does not space *past* a trap. A contiguous block of vertical space may be reserved using **sv**.

Request Form	Initial Value	If No Argument	Notes	Explanation
.vs *N*	1/6in;12pts	previous	E,p	Set vertical base-line spacing size *V*. Transient *extra* vertical space available with \x´*N*´ (see above).
.ls *N*	*N*=1	previous	E	*Line* spacing set to ±*N*. *N*−1 *V*s *(blank lines)* are appended to each output text line. The (read-only) number register **.L** is set to contain the current line-spacing value. Appended blank lines are omitted, if the text or previous appended blank line reached a trap position.
.sp *N*	-	*N*=1*V*	B,v	Space vertically in *either* direction. If *N* is negative, the motion is *backward* (upward) and is limited to the distance to the top of the page. Forward (downward) motion is truncated to the distance to the nearest trap. If the no-space mode is on, no spacing occurs (see **ns**, and **rs** below).
.sv *N*	-	*N*=1*V*	v	Save a contiguous vertical block of size *N*. If the distance to the next trap is greater than *N*, *N* vertical space is output. No-space mode has *no* effect. If this distance is less than *N*, no vertical space is immediately output, but *N* is remembered for later output (see **os**). Subsequent **sv** requests will overwrite any still remembered *N*.
.os	-	-	-	Output saved vertical space. No-space mode has *no* effect. Used to finally output a block of vertical space requested by an earlier **sv** request.
.ns	space	-	D	No-space mode turned on. When on, the no-space mode inhibits **sp** requests and **bp** requests *without* a next page number. The no-space mode is turned off when a line of output occurs, or with **rs**.

21

| .rs | space | - | D | Restore spacing. The no-space mode is turned off. |
| Blank text line. | | - | B | Causes a break and outputs a blank line just like **sp 1**. |

6. Line Length and Indenting

The maximum line length for fill mode may be set with **ll**. The indent may be set with **in**; an indent applicable to *only* the *next* output line may be set with **ti**. The line length includes indent space but *not* page offset space. The line-length minus the indent is the basis for centering with **ce**. The effect of **ll**, **in**, or **ti** is delayed, if a partially collected line exists, until after that line is output. In fill mode the length of text on an output line is less than or equal to the line length minus the indent. The current line length and indent are available in registers **.l** and **.i** respectively. The length of *three-part titles* produced by **tl** (see §14) is *independently* set by **lt**.

Request Form	Initial Value	If No Argument	Notes	Explanation
.ll ±N	6.5 in	previous	E,m	Line length is set to ±N. In TROFF the maximum (line-length)+(page-offset) is about 7.54 inches.
.in ±N	N=0	previous	B,E,m	Indent is set to ±N. The indent is prepended to each output line.
.ti ±N		ignored	B,E,m	Temporary indent. The *next* output text line will be indented a distance ±N with respect to the current indent. The resulting total indent may not be negative. The current indent is not changed.

7. Macros, Strings, Diversion, and Position Traps

7.1. Macros and strings. A *macro* is a named set of arbitrary *lines* that may be invoked by name or with a *trap*. A *string* is a named string of *characters*, *not* including a newline character, that may be interpolated by name at any point. Request, macro, and string names share the *same* name list. Macro and string names may be one or two characters long and may usurp previously defined request, macro, or string names. Any of these entities may be renamed with **rn** or removed with **rm**. Macros are created by **de** and **di**, and appended to by **am** and **da**; **di** and **da** cause normal output to be stored in a macro. Strings are created by **ds** and appended to by **as**. A macro is invoked in the same way as a request; a control line beginning .xx will interpolate the contents of macro xx. The remainder of the line may contain up to nine *arguments*. The strings x and xx are interpolated at any desired point with *x and *(xx respectively. String references and macro invocations may be nested.

7.2. Copy mode input interpretation. During the definition and extension of strings and macros (not by diversion) the input is read in *copy mode*. The input is copied without interpretation *except* that:

- The contents of number registers indicated by \n are interpolated.
- Strings indicated by * are interpolated.
- Arguments indicated by \$ are interpolated.
- Concealed newlines indicated by \(newline) are eliminated.
- Comments indicated by \" are eliminated.
- \t and \a are interpreted as ASCII horizontal tab and SOH respectively (§9).
- \\ is interpreted as \
- \. is interpreted as ".".

These interpretations can be suppressed by prepending a \. For example, since \\ maps into a \, \\n will copy as \n which will be interpreted as a number register indicator when the macro or string is reread.

7.3. Arguments. When a macro is invoked by name, the remainder of the line is taken to contain up to nine arguments. The argument separator is the space character, and arguments may be surrounded by double-quotes to permit imbedded space characters. Pairs of double-quotes may be imbedded in double-quoted arguments to represent a single double-quote. If the desired arguments won't fit on a line, a concealed newline may be used to continue on the next line.

When a macro is invoked the *input level* is *pushed down* and any arguments available at the previous level become unavailable until the macro is completely read and the previous level is restored. A macro's own arguments can be interpolated at *any* point within the macro with \$N, which interpolates the Nth argument (1≤N≤9). If an invoked argument doesn't exist, a null string results. For example, the macro xx may be defined by

```
.de xx          \"begin definition
Today is \\$1 the \\$2.
..              \"end definition
```

and called by

.xx Monday 14th

to produce the text

Today is Monday the 14th.

Note that the **\$** was concealed in the definition with a prepended ****. The number of currently available arguments is in the **.$** register.

No arguments are available at the top (non-macro) level in this implementation. Because string referencing is implemented as a input-level push down, no arguments are available from *within* a string. No arguments are available within a trap-invoked macro.

Arguments are copied in *copy mode* onto a stack where they are available for reference. The mechanism does not allow an argument to contain a direct reference to a *long* string (interpolated at copy time) and it is advisable to conceal string references (with an extra ****) to delay interpolation until argument reference time.

7.4. Diversions. Processed output may be diverted into a macro for purposes such as footnote processing (see Tutorial §T5) or determining the horizontal and vertical size of some text for conditional changing of pages or columns. A single diversion trap may be set at a specified vertical position. The number registers **dn** and **dl** respectively contain the vertical and horizontal size of the most recently ended diversion. Processed text that is diverted into a macro retains the vertical size of each of its lines when reread in *nofill* mode regardless of the current *V*. Constant-spaced (**cs**) or emboldened (**bd**) text that is diverted can be reread correctly only if these modes are again or still in effect at reread time. One way to do this is to imbed in the diversion the appropriate **cs** or **bd** requests with the *transparent* mechanism described in §10.6.

Diversions may be nested and certain parameters and registers are associated with the current diversion level (the top non-diversion level may be thought of as the 0th diversion level). These are the diversion trap and associated macro, no-space mode, the internally-saved marked place (see **mk** and **rt**), the current vertical place (**.d** register), the current high-water text base-line (**.h** register), and the current diversion name (**.z** register).

7.5. Traps. Three types of trap mechanisms are available—page traps, a diversion trap, and an input-line-count trap. Macro-invocation traps may be planted using **wh** at any page position including the top. This trap position may be changed using **ch**. Trap positions at or below the bottom of the page have no effect unless or until moved to within the page or rendered effective by an increase in page length. Two traps may be planted at the *same* position only by first planting them at different positions and then moving one of the traps; the first planted trap will conceal the second unless and until the first one is moved (see Tutorial Examples §T5). If the first one is moved back, it again conceals the second trap. The macro associated with a page trap is automatically invoked when a line of text is output whose vertical size *reaches* or *sweeps past* the trap position. Reaching the bottom of a page springs the top-of-page trap, if any, provided there is a next page. The distance to the next trap position is available in the **.t** register; if there are no traps between the current position and the bottom of the page, the distance returned is the distance to the page bottom.

A macro-invocation trap effective in the current diversion may be planted using **dt**. The **.t** register works in a diversion; if there is no subsequent trap a *large* distance is returned. For a description of input-line-count traps, see the **it** request below.

Request Form	Initial Value	If No Argument	Notes	Explanation
.de *xx yy*	-	*.yy=..*	-	Define or redefine the macro *xx*. The contents of the macro begin on the next input line. Input lines are copied in *copy mode* until the definition is terminated by a line beginning with *.yy*, whereupon the macro *yy* is called. In the absence of *yy*, the definition is terminated by a line beginning with "..". A macro may contain **de** requests provided the terminating macros differ

				or the contained definition terminator is concealed. ".." can be concealed as \\. which will copy as \. and be reread as "..".
.am *xx yy*	-	.*yy*=..	-	Append to macro (append version of **de**).
.ds *xx string*	-	ignored	-	Define a string *xx* containing *string*. Any initial double-quote in *string* is stripped off to permit initial blanks.
.as *xx string*	-	ignored	-	Append *string* to string *xx* (append version of **ds**).
.rm *xx*	-	ignored	-	Remove request, macro, or string. The name *xx* is removed from the name list and any related storage space is freed. Subsequent references will have no effect.
.rn *xx yy*	-	ignored	-	Rename request, macro, or string *xx* to *yy*. If *yy* exists, it is first removed.
.di *xx*	-	end	D	Divert output to macro *xx*. Normal text processing occurs during diversion except that page offsetting is not done. The diversion ends when the request **di** or **da** is encountered without an argument; extraneous requests of this type should not appear when nested diversions are being used.
.da *xx*	-	end	D	Divert, appending to *xx* (append version of **di**).
.wh *N xx*	-	-	v	Install a trap to invoke *xx* at page position *N*; a *negative N* will be interpreted with respect to the page *bottom*. Any macro previously planted at *N* is replaced by *xx*. A zero *N* refers to the *top* of a page. In the absence of *xx*, the first found trap at *N*, if any, is removed.
.ch *xx N*	-	-	v	Change the trap position for macro *xx* to be *N*. In the absence of *N*, the trap, if any, is removed.
.dt *N xx*	-	off	D,v	Install a diversion trap at position *N* in the *current* diversion to invoke macro *xx*. Another **dt** will redefine the diversion trap. If no arguments are given, the diversion trap is removed.
.it *N xx*	-	off	E	Set an input-line-count trap to invoke the macro *xx* after *N* lines of *text* input have been read (control or request lines don't count). The text may be in-line text or text interpolated by inline or trap-invoked macros.
.em *xx*	none	none	-	The macro *xx* will be invoked when all input has ended. The effect is the same as if the contents of *xx* had been at the end of the last file processed.

8. Number Registers

A variety of parameters are available to the user as predefined, named *number registers* (see Summary and Index, page 7). In addition, the user may define his own named registers. Register names are one or two characters long and *do not* conflict with request, macro, or string names. Except for certain predefined read-only registers, a number register can be read, written, automatically incremented or decremented, and interpolated into the input in a variety of formats. One common use of user-defined registers is to automatically number sections, paragraphs, lines, etc. A number register may be used any time numerical input is expected or desired and may be used in numerical *expressions* (§1.4).

Number registers are created and modified using **nr**, which specifies the name, numerical value, and the auto-increment size. Registers are also modified, if accessed with an auto-incrementing sequence. If the registers x and xx both contain N and have the auto-increment size M, the following access sequences have the effect shown:

Sequence	Effect on Register	Value Interpolated
\n*x*	none	*N*
\n(*xx*	none	*N*
\n+*x*	*x* incremented by *M*	*N+M*
\n−*x*	*x* decremented by *M*	*N−M*
\n+(*xx*	*xx* incremented by *M*	*N+M*
\n−(*xx*	*xx* decremented by *M*	*N−M*

When interpolated, a number register is converted to decimal (default), decimal with leading zeros, lower-case Roman, upper-case Roman, lower-case sequential alphabetic, or upper-case sequential alphabetic according to the format specified by **af**.

Request Form	Initial Value	If No Argument	Notes	Explanation
.nr *R ±N M*	-	-	**u**	The number register *R* is assigned the value ±*N* with respect to the previous value, if any. The increment for auto-incrementing is set to *M*.
.af *R c*	arabic	-	-	Assign format *c* to register *R*. The available formats are:

Format	Numbering Sequence
1	0,1,2,3,4,5,...
001	000,001,002,003,004,005,...
i	0,i,ii,iii,iv,v,...
I	0,I,II,III,IV,V,...
a	0,a,b,c,...,z,aa,ab,...,zz,aaa,...
A	0,A,B,C,...,Z,AA,AB,...,ZZ,AAA,...

An arabic format having *N* digits specifies a field width of *N* digits (example 2 above). The read-only registers and the *width* function (§11.2) are always arabic.

.rr *R*	-	ignored	-	Remove register *R*. If many registers are being created dynamically, it may become necessary to remove no longer used registers to recapture internal storage space for newer registers.

9. Tabs, Leaders, and Fields

9.1. Tabs and leaders. The ASCII horizontal tab character and the ASCII SOH (hereafter known as the *leader* character) can both be used to generate either horizontal motion or a string of repeated characters. The length of the generated entity is governed by internal *tab stops* specifiable with **ta**. The default difference is that tabs generate motion and leaders generate a string of periods; **tc** and **lc** offer the choice of repeated character or motion. There are three types of internal tab stops—*left* adjusting, *right* adjusting, and *centering*. In the following table: *D* is the distance from the current position on the *input* line (where a tab or leader was found) to the next tab stop; *next-string* consists of the input characters following the tab (or leader) up to the next tab (or leader) or end of line; and *W* is the width of *next-string*.

Tab type	Length of motion or repeated characters	Location of *next-string*
Left	*D*	Following *D*
Right	*D−W*	Right adjusted within *D*
Centered	*D−W/2*	Centered on right end of *D*

The length of generated motion is allowed to be negative, but that of a repeated character string cannot be.

21

Repeated character strings contain an integer number of characters, and any residual distance is prepended as motion. Tabs or leaders found after the last tab stop are ignored, but may be used as *next-string* terminators.

Tabs and leaders are not interpreted in *copy mode*. \t and \a always generate a non-interpreted tab and leader respectively, and are equivalent to actual tabs and leaders in *copy mode*.

9.2. Fields. A *field* is contained between a *pair* of *field delimiter* characters, and consists of sub-strings separated by *padding* indicator characters. The field length is the distance on the *input* line from the position where the field begins to the next tab stop. The difference between the total length of all the sub-strings and the field length is incorporated as horizontal padding space that is divided among the indicated padding places. The incorporated padding is allowed to be negative. For example, if the field delimiter is # and the padding indicator is ˆ, #ˆ*xxx*ˆ*right*# specifies a right-adjusted string with the string *xxx* centered in the remaining space.

Request Form	Initial Value	If No Argument	Notes	Explanation
.ta *Nt* ...	8n; 0.5in	none	E,m	Set tab stops and types. *t*=**R**, right adjusting; *t*=**C**, centering; *t* absent, left adjusting. TROFF tab stops are preset every 0.5in.; NROFF every 8 character widths. The stop values are separated by spaces, and a value preceded by + is treated as an increment to the previous stop value.
.tc *c*	none	none	E	The tab repetition character becomes *c*, or is removed specifying motion.
.lc *c*	.	none	E	The leader repetition character becomes *c*, or is removed specifying motion.
.fc *a b*	off	off	-	The field delimiter is set to *a*; the padding indicator is set to the *space* character or to *b*, if given. In the absence of arguments the field mechanism is turned off.

10. Input and Output Conventions and Character Translations

10.1. Input character translations. Ways of inputting the graphic character set were discussed in §2.1. The ASCII control characters horizontal tab (§9.1), SOH (§9.1), and backspace (§10.3) are discussed elsewhere. The newline delimits input lines. In addition, STX, ETX, ENQ, ACK, and BEL are accepted, and may be used as delimiters or translated into a graphic with **tr** (§10.5). *All* others are ignored.

The *escape* character \ introduces *escape sequences*—causes the following character to mean another character, or to indicate some function. A complete list of such sequences is given in the Summary and Index on page 6. \ should not be confused with the ASCII control character ESC of the same name. The escape character \ can be input with the sequence \\. The escape character can be changed with **ec**, and all that has been said about the default \ becomes true for the new escape character. \e can be used to print whatever the current escape character is. If necessary or convenient, the escape mechanism may be turned off with **eo**, and restored with **ec**.

Request Form	Initial Value	If No Argument	Notes	Explanation
.ec *c*	\	\	-	Set escape character to \, or to *c*, if given.
.eo	on	-	-	Turn escape mechanism off.

10.2. Ligatures. Five ligatures are available in the current TROFF character set — fi, fl, , , and . They may be input (even in NROFF) by \(fi, \(fl, \(ff, \(Fi, and \(Fl respectively. The ligature mode is normally on in TROFF, and *automatically* invokes ligatures during input.

Request Form	Initial Value	If No Argument	Notes	Explanation
.lg *N*	off; on	on	-	Ligature mode is turned on if *N* is absent or non-zero, and turned off if *N*=0. If *N*=2, only the two-character ligatures are automatically invoked. Ligature mode is inhibited for request, macro, string, register, or file names, and in *copy mode*. No effect in NROFF.

21

10.3. Backspacing, underlining, overstriking, etc. Unless in *copy mode*, the ASCII backspace character is replaced by a backward horizontal motion having the width of the space character. Underlining as a form of line-drawing is discussed in §12.4. A generalized overstriking function is described in §12.1.

NROFF automatically underlines characters in the *underline* font, specifiable with **uf**, normally Times Italic on font position 2 (see §2.2). In addition to **ft** and **\fF**, the underline font may be selected by **ul** and **cu**. Underlining is restricted to an output-device-dependent subset of *reasonable* characters.

Request Form	Initial Value	If No Argument	Notes	Explanation
.ul *N*	off	*N*=1	E	Underline in NROFF (italicize in TROFF) the next *N* input text lines. Actually, switch to *underline* font, saving the current font for later restoration; *other* font changes within the span of a **ul** will take effect, but the restoration will undo the last change. Output generated by **tl** (§14) *is* affected by the font change, but does *not* decrement *N*. If *N*>1, there is the risk that a trap interpolated macro may provide text lines within the span; environment switching can prevent this.
.cu *N*	off	*N*=1	E	A variant of **ul** that causes *every* character to be underlined in NROFF. Identical to **ul** in TROFF.
.uf *F*	Italic	Italic	-	Underline font set to *F*. In NROFF, *F* may *not* be on position 1 (initially Times Roman).

10.4. Control characters. Both the control character **.** and the *no-break* control character **´** may be changed, if desired. Such a change must be compatible with the design of any macros used in the span of the change, and particularly of any trap-invoked macros.

Request Form	Initial Value	If No Argument	Notes	Explanation
.cc *c*	.	.	E	The basic control character is set to *c*, or reset to ".".
.c2 *c*	´	´	E	The *nobreak* control character is set to *c*, or reset to "´".

10.5. Output translation. One character can be made a stand-in for another character using **tr**. All text processing (e. g. character comparisons) takes place with the input (stand-in) character which appears to have the width of the final character. The graphic translation occurs at the moment of output (including diversion).

Request Form	Initial Value	If No Argument	Notes	Explanation
.tr *abcd....*	none	-	O	Translate *a* into *b*, *c* into *d*, etc. If an odd number of characters is given, the last one will be mapped into the space character. To be consistent, a particular translation must stay in effect from *input* to *output* time.

10.6. Transparent throughput. An input line beginning with a **\!** is read in *copy mode* and *transparently* output (without the initial **\!**); the text processor is otherwise unaware of the line's presence. This mechanism may be used to pass control information to a post-processor or to imbed control lines in a macro created by a diversion.

10.7. Comments and concealed newlines. An uncomfortably long input line that must stay one line (e. g. a string definition, or nofilled text) can be split into many physical lines by ending all but the last one with the escape ****. The sequence ****(newline) is *always* ignored—except in a comment. Comments may be imbedded at the *end* of any line by prefacing them with **\"**. The newline at the end of a comment cannot be concealed. A line beginning with **\"** will appear as a blank line and behave like **.sp 1**; a comment can be on a line by itself by beginning the line with **.\"**.

11. Local Horizontal and Vertical Motions, and the Width Function

11.1. Local Motions. The functions **\v´N´** and **\h´N´** can be used for *local* vertical and horizontal motion respectively. The distance *N* may be negative; the *positive* directions are *rightward* and *downward*. A *local* motion is one contained *within* a line. To avoid unexpected vertical dislocations, it is necessary that the *net* vertical local motion within a word in filled text and otherwise within a line balance to zero. The above and certain other escape sequences providing local motion are summarized in the following table.

Vertical Local Motion	Effect in TROFF	NROFF	Horizontal Local Motion	Effect in TROFF	NROFF
\v´N´	Move distance N		\h´N´ \(space) \0	Move distance N Unpaddable space-size space Digit-size space	
\u \d \r	½ em up ½ em down 1 em up	½ line up ½ line down 1 line up	\\| \^	1/6 em space 1/12 em space	ignored ignored

As an example, E^2 could be generated by the sequence **E\s–2\v´–0.4m´2\v´0.4m´\s+2**; it should be noted in this example that the 0.4 em vertical motions are at the smaller size.

11.2. Width Function. The *width* function **\w´string´** generates the numerical width of *string* (in basic units). Size and font changes may be safely imbedded in *string*, and will not affect the current environment. For example, **.ti –\w´1. ´u** could be used to temporarily indent leftward a distance equal to the size of the string "**1.** ".

The width function also sets three number registers. The registers **st** and **sb** are set respectively to the highest and lowest extent of *string* relative to the baseline; then, for example, the total *height* of the string is **\n(stu–\n(sbu**. In TROFF the number register **ct** is set to a value between 0 and 3: 0 means that all of the characters in *string* were short lower case characters without descenders (like **e**); 1 means that at least one character has a descender (like **y**); 2 means that at least one character is tall (like **H**); and 3 means that both tall characters and characters with descenders are present.

11.3. Mark horizontal place. The escape sequence **\kx** will cause the *current* horizontal position in the *input line* to be stored in register *x*. As an example, the construction **\kxword\h´|\nxu+2u´word** will embolden *word* by backing up to almost its beginning and overprinting it, resulting in *word*.

12. Overstrike, Bracket, Line-drawing, and Zero-width Functions

12.1. Overstriking. Automatically centered overstriking of up to nine characters is provided by the *overstrike* function **\o´string´**. The characters in *string* are overprinted with centers aligned; the total width is that of the widest character. *string* should *not* contain local vertical motion. As examples, **\o´e\´´** produces é, and **\o´\(mo\(sl´** produces ∉.

12.2. Zero-width characters. The function **\zc** will output *c* without spacing over it, and can be used to produce left-aligned overstruck combinations. For example, **\z\(ci\h´2.2p´\v´–1p´\(pl\v´1p´** will produce ⊕. Note that tweeks to the horizontal and vertical motions are necessary to center the two symbols correctly. Unfortunately, these numbers will vary depending on the font, point size, and typesetter being used.

12.3. Large Brackets. The Special Mathematical Font contains a number of bracket construction pieces (⌈ ⌊ ⌋ ⌉ ⌞ ⌟ | ⌊ ⌋ ⌈ ⌉) that can be combined into various bracket styles. The function **\b´string´** may be used to pile up vertically the characters in *string* (the first character on top and the last at the bottom); the characters are vertically separated by 1 em and the total pile is centered 1/2 em above the current baseline (½ line in NROFF). For example, **\x´–0.5m´\x´0.5m´\b´\(lc\(lf´E\\\ \b´\(rc\(rf´** produces ⎡ E ⎤ .

12.4. Line drawing. The function **\l´Nc´** will draw a string of repeated *c*'s towards the right for a distance N. (**\l** is **\(lower case L). If *c* looks like a continuation of an expression for *N*, it may insulated from *N* with a **\&**. If *c* is not specified, the _ (baseline rule) is used (underline character in NROFF). If *N* is negative, a backward horizontal motion of size *N* is made *before* drawing the string. Any space resulting from *N*/(size of *c*) having a remainder is put at the beginning (left end) of the string. In the case of characters that are designed to be connected such as baseline-rule _, underrule _, and root-en ‾, the remainder space is covered by over-lapping. If *N* is *less* than the width of *c*, a single *c* is centered on a distance *N*. As an example, a macro to underscore a string can be written

```
.de us
\\$1\l´|0\(ul´
..
```

or one to draw a box around a string

> **.de bx**
> **\(br\|\\$1\|\(br\|l´|0\(rn´\l´|0\(ul´**
> **..**

such that

> **.us "underlined words"**

and

> **.bx "words in a box"**

yield <u>underlined words</u> and ⌐words in a box⌐.

The function \L´Nc´ will draw a vertical line consisting of the (optional) character c stacked vertically apart 1 em (1 line in NROFF), with the first two characters overlapped, if necessary, to form a continuous line. The default character is the *box rule* | (\(br); the other suitable character is the *bold vertical* | (\(bv). The line is begun without any initial motion relative to the current base line. A positive N specifies a line drawn downward and a negative N specifies a line drawn upward. After the line is drawn *no* compensating motions are made; the instantaneous baseline is at the *end* of the line.

The horizontal and vertical line drawing functions may be used in combination to produce large boxes. The zero-width *box-rule* and the ½-em wide *underrule* were *designed* to form corners when using 1-em vertical spacings. For example the macro

> **.de eb**
> **.sp −1**   \"compensate for next automatic base-line spacing
> **.nf**   \"avoid possibly overflowing word buffer
> **\h´−.5n´\L´|\\nau−1´\l´\\n(.lu+1n\(ul´\L´−|\\nau+1´\l´|0u−.5n\(ul´** \"draw box
> **.fi**
> **..**

will draw a box around some text whose beginning vertical place was saved in number register a (e. g. using **.mk a**) as done for this paragraph.

---

13. Hyphenation.

The automatic hyphenation may be switched off and on. When switched on with **hy**, several variants may be set. A *hyphenation indicator* character may be imbedded in a word to specify desired hyphenation points, or may be prepended to suppress hyphenation. In addition, the user may specify a small exception word list.

Only words that consist of a central alphabetic string surrounded by (usually null) non-alphabetic strings are considered candidates for automatic hyphenation. Words that were input containing hyphens (minus), em-dashes (\(em), or hyphenation indicator characters—such as mother-in-law—are *always* subject to splitting after those characters, whether or not automatic hyphenation is on or off.

Request Form	Initial Value	If No Argument	Notes	Explanation
.nh	hyphenate	-	E	Automatic hyphenation is turned off.
.hyN	on,N=1	on,N=1	E	Automatic hyphenation is turned on for N≥1, or off for N= 0. If N= 2, *last* lines (ones that will cause a trap) are not hyphenated. For N= 4 and 8, the last and first two characters respectively of a word are not split off. These values are additive; i. e. N= 14 will invoke all three restrictions.
.hc c	\%	\%	E	Hyphenation indicator character is set to c or to the default \%. The indicator does not appear in the output.
.hw word1 ...		ignored	-	Specify hyphenation points in words with imbedded minus signs. Versions of a word with terminal s are implied; i. e. *dig–it* implies *dig–its*. This list is examined initially *and* after each suffix stripping. The space available is small—about 128 characters.

21

14. Three Part Titles.

The titling function **tl** provides for automatic placement of three fields at the left, center, and right of a line with a title-length specifiable with **lt**. **tl** may be used anywhere, and is independent of the normal text collecting process. A common use is in header and footer macros.

Request Form	Initial Value	If No Argument	Notes	Explanation
.tl *'left 'center 'right '*	-	-	The strings *left*, *center*, and *right* are respectively left-adjusted, centered, and right-adjusted in the current title-length. Any of the strings may be empty, and overlapping is permitted. If the page-number character (initially %) is found within any of the fields it is replaced by the current page number having the format assigned to register %. Any character may be used as the string delimiter.
.pc *c*	%	off	-	The page number character is set to *c*, or removed. The page-number register remains %.
.lt ±*N*	6.5 in	previous	E,m	Length of title set to ±*N*. The line-length and the title-length are *independent*. Indents do not apply to titles; page-offsets do.

15. Output Line Numbering.

Automatic sequence numbering of output lines may be requested with **nm**. When in effect, a three-digit, arabic number plus a digit-space is prepended to output text lines. The text lines are thus offset by four digit-spaces,
3 and otherwise retain their line length; a reduction in line length may be desired to keep the right margin aligned with an earlier margin. Blank lines, other vertical spaces, and lines generated by **tl** are *not* numbered. Numbering can be temporarily suspended with **nn**, or with an **.nm** followed by a later **.nm +0**. In addition, a
6 line number indent *I*, and the number-text separation *S* may be specified in digit-spaces. Further, it can be specified that only those line numbers that are multiples of some number *M* are to be printed (the others will appear as blank number fields).

Request Form	Initial Value	If No Argument	Notes	Explanation
.nm ±*N M S I*		off	E	Line number mode. If ±*N* is given, line numbering is turned on, and the next output line numbered is numbered ±*N*. Default values are *M*=1, *S*=1, and *I*=0. Parameters corresponding to missing arguments are unaffected; a non-numeric argument is considered missing. In the absence of all arguments, numbering is turned off; the next line number is preserved for possible further use in number register **ln**.
.nn *N*	-	*N*=1	E	The next *N* text output lines are not numbered.

9 As an example, the paragraph portions of this section are numbered with *M*=3: **.nm 1 3** was placed at the beginning; **.nm** was placed at the end of the first paragraph; and **.nm +0** was placed in front of this paragraph; and **.nm** finally placed at the end. Line lengths were also changed (by **\w'0000'u**) to keep the right side
12 aligned. Another example is **.nm +5 5 x 3** which turns on numbering with the line number of the next line to be five greater than the last numbered line, with *M*=5, with spacing *S* untouched, and with the indent *I* set to 3.

16. Conditional Acceptance of Input

In the following, *c* is a one-character, built-in *condition* name, **!** signifies *not*, *N* is a numerical expression, *string1* and *string2* are strings delimited by any non-blank, non-numeric character *not* in the strings, and *anything* represents what is conditionally accepted.

Request Form	Initial Value	If No Argument	Notes	Explanation
.if c anything	-	-		If condition c true, accept anything as input; in multi-line case use \{anything \}.
.if !c anything	-	-		If condition c false, accept anything.
.if N anything	-		u	If expression N > 0, accept anything.
.if !N anything	-		u	If expression N ≤ 0, accept anything.
.if 'string1 'string2 ' anything	-		-	If string1 identical to string2, accept anything.
.if ! 'string1 'string2 ' anything	-		-	If string1 not identical to string2, accept anything.
.ie c anything	-		u	If portion of if-else; all above forms (like if).
.el anything	-	-		Else portion of if-else.

The built-in condition names are:

Condition Name	True If
o	Current page number is odd
e	Current page number is even
t	Formatter is TROFF
n	Formatter is NROFF

If the condition c is *true*, or if the number N is greater than zero, or if the strings compare identically (including motions and character size and font), *anything* is accepted as input. If a ! precedes the condition, number, or string comparison, the sense of the acceptance is reversed.

Any spaces between the condition and the beginning of *anything* are skipped over. The *anything* can be either a single input line (text, macro, or whatever) or a number of input lines. In the multi-line case, the first line must begin with a left delimiter \{ and the last line must end with a right delimiter \}.

The request ie (if-else) is identical to if except that the acceptance state is remembered. A subsequent and matching el (else) request then uses the reverse sense of that state. ie - el pairs may be nested.

Some examples are:

        .if e .tl 'Even Page %'''

which outputs a title if the page number is even; and

        .ie \n%>1 \{\
        'sp 0.5i
        .tl 'Page %'''
        'sp |1.2i \}
        .el .sp |2.5i

which treats page 1 differently from other pages.

17. Environment Switching.

A number of the parameters that control the text processing are gathered together into an *environment*, which can be switched by the user. The environment parameters are those associated with requests noting E in their *Notes* column; in addition, partially collected lines and words are in the environment. Everything else is global; examples are page-oriented parameters, diversion-oriented parameters, number registers, and macro and string definitions. All environments are initialized with default parameter values.

Request Form	Initial Value	If No Argument	Notes	Explanation
.ev N	N=0	previous	-	Environment switched to environment 0≤N≤2. Switching is done in push-down fashion so that restoring a previous environment *must* be done with .ev rather than specific reference.

18. Insertions from the Standard Input

The input can be temporarily switched to the system *standard input* with **rd**, which will switch back when *two* newlines in a row are found (the *extra* blank line is not used). This mechanism is intended for insertions in form-letter-like documentation. On UNIX, the *standard input* can be the user's keyboard, a *pipe*, or a *file*.

Request Form	Initial Value	If No Argument	Notes	Explanation
.rd *prompt*	-	*prompt*=BEL		Read insertion from the standard input until two newlines in a row are found. If the standard input is the user's keyboard, *prompt* (or a BEL) is written onto the user's terminal. **rd** behaves like a macro, and arguments may be placed after *prompt*.
.ex	-	-	-	Exit from NROFF/TROFF. Text processing is terminated exactly as if all input had ended.

If insertions are to be taken from the terminal keyboard *while* output is being printed on the terminal, the command line option −q will turn off the echoing of keyboard input and prompt only with BEL. The regular input and insertion input *cannot* simultaneously come from the standard input.

As an example, multiple copies of a form letter may be prepared by entering the insertions for all the copies in one file to be used as the standard input, and causing the file containing the letter to reinvoke itself using **nx** (§19); the process would ultimately be ended by an **ex** in the insertion file.

19. Input/Output File Switching

The (read-only) number register **.c** contains the input line number in the current input file. The number register **c.** is a general register serving the same purpose.

Request Form	Initial Value	If No Argument	Notes	Explanation
.so *filename*	-	-		Switch source file. The top input (file reading) level is switched to *filename*. The effect of an **so** encountered in a macro occurs immediately. When the new file ends, input is again taken from the original file. **so**'s may be nested.
.nx *filename*		end-of-file	-	Next file is *filename*. The current file is considered ended, and the input is immediately switched to *filename*.
.pi *program*	-	-		Pipe output to *program* (NROFF only). This request must occur *before* any printing occurs. No arguments are transmitted to *program*.

20. Miscellaneous

Request Form	Initial Value	If No Argument	Notes	Explanation
.mc *c N*	-	off	E,m	Specifies that a *margin* character *c* appear a distance *N* to the right of the right margin after each non-empty text line (except those produced by **tl**). If the output line is too-long (as can happen in nofill mode) the character will be appended to the line. If *N* is not given, the previous *N* is used; the initial *N* is 0.2 inches in NROFF and 1 em in TROFF. The margin character used with this paragraph was a 12-point box-rule.

21

.tm *string*	-	newline	-	After skipping initial blanks, *string* (rest of the line) is read in *copy mode* and written on the user's terminal. (see §21).
.ig *yy*	-	*.yy=..*	-	Ignore input lines. **ig** behaves exactly like **de** (§7) except that the input is discarded. The input is read in *copy mode*, and any auto-incremented registers will be affected.
.pm *t*	-	all	-	Print macros. The names and sizes of all of the defined macros and strings are printed on the user's terminal; if *t* is given, only the total of the sizes is printed. The sizes is given in *blocks* of 128 characters.
.ab *string*	-	-	-	Print *string* on standard error and terminate immediately. The default *string* is "User Abort". Does not cause a break. Only output preceding the last break is written.
.fl	-	-	B	Flush output buffer. Used in interactive debugging to force output.

21. Output and Error Messages.

The output from **tm**, **pm**, **ab** and the prompt from **rd**, as well as various *error* messages are written onto UNIX's *standard error* output. The latter is different from the *standard output*, where NROFF formatted output goes. By default, both are written onto the user's terminal, but they can be independently redirected.

Various *error* conditions may occur during the operation of NROFF and TROFF. Certain less serious errors having only local impact do not cause processing to terminate. Two examples are *word overflow*, caused by a word that is too large to fit into the word buffer (in fill mode), and *line overflow*, caused by an output line that grew too large to fit in the line buffer; in both cases, a message is printed, the offending excess is discarded, and the affected word or line is marked at the point of truncation with a * in NROFF and a ⇐ in TROFF. The philosophy is to continue processing, if possible, on the grounds that output useful for debugging may be produced. If a serious error occurs, processing terminates, and an appropriate message is printed. Examples are the inability to create, read, or write files, and the exceeding of certain internal limits that make future output unlikely to be useful.

21

TUTORIAL EXAMPLES

T1. Introduction

Although NROFF and TROFF have by design a syntax reminiscent of earlier text processors* with the intent of easing their use, it is almost always necessary to prepare at least a small set of macro definitions to describe most documents. Such common formatting needs as page margins and footnotes are deliberately not built into NROFF and TROFF. Instead, the macro and string definition, number register, diversion, environment switching, page-position trap, and conditional input mechanisms provide the basis for user-defined implementations.

The examples to be discussed are intended to be useful and somewhat realistic, but won't necessarily cover all relevant contingencies. Explicit numerical parameters are used in the examples to make them easier to read and to illustrate typical values. In many cases, number registers would really be used to reduce the number of places where numerical information is kept, and to concentrate conditional parameter initialization like that which depends on whether TROFF or NROFF is being used.

T2. Page Margins

As discussed in §3, *header* and *footer* macros are usually defined to describe the top and bottom page margin areas respectively. A trap is planted at page position 0 for the header, and at −*N* (*N* from the page bottom) for the footer. The simplest such definitions might be

```
.de hd          \"define header
´sp 1i
..              \"end definition
.de fo          \"define footer
´bp
..              \"end definition
.wh 0 hd
.wh −1i fo
```

which provide blank 1 inch top and bottom margins. The header will occur on the *first* page, only if the definition and trap exist prior to the initial pseudo-page transition (§3). In fill mode, the output line that springs the footer trap was typically forced out because some part or whole word didn't fit on it. If anything in the

---

*For example: P. A. Crisman, Ed., *The Compatible Time-Sharing System*, MIT Press, 1965, Section AH9.01 (Description of RUNOFF program on MIT's CTSS system).

footer and header that follows causes a *break*, that word or part word will be forced out. In this and other examples, requests like **bp** and **sp** that normally cause breaks are invoked using the *no-break* control character ´ to avoid this. When the header/footer design contains material requiring independent text processing, the environment may be switched, avoiding most interaction with the running text.

A more realistic example would be

```
.de hd          \"header
.if t .tl ´\(rn´\(rn´  \"troff cut mark
.if \\n%>1 \{\
´sp |0.5i−1     \"tl base at 0.5i
.tl ´´− % −´´   \"centered page number
.ps             \"restore size
.ft             \"restore font
.vs \}          \"restore vs
´sp |1.0i       \"space to 1.0i
.ns             \"turn on no-space mode
..
.de fo          \"footer
.ps 10          \"set footer/header size
.ft R           \"set font
.vs 12p         \"set base-line spacing
.if \\n%=1 \{\
´sp |\\n(.pu−0.5i−1 \"tl base 0.5i up
.tl ´´− % −´´\}  \"first page number
´bp
..
.wh 0 hd
.wh −1i fo
```

which sets the size, font, and base-line spacing for the header/footer material, and ultimately restores them. The material in this case is a page number at the bottom of the first page and at the top of the remaining pages. If TROFF is used, a *cut mark* is drawn in the form of *root-en*'s at each margin. The **sp**'s refer to absolute positions to avoid dependence on the base-line spacing. Another reason for this in the footer is that the footer is invoked by printing a line whose vertical spacing swept past the trap position by possibly as much as the base-line spacing. The *no-space* mode is turned on at the end of **hd** to render ineffective accidental occurrences of **sp** at the top of the running text.

The above method of restoring size, font, etc. presupposes that such requests (that set *previous* value) are *not* used in the running text. A better scheme is save and restore both the current *and* previous values as shown for size in the following:

```
.de fo
.nr s1 \\n(.s          \"current size
.ps
.nr s2 \\n(.s          \"previous size
. ---                  \"rest of footer
..
.de hd
. ---                  \"header stuff
.ps \\n(s2             \"restore previous size
.ps \\n(s1             \"restore current size
..
```

Page numbers may be printed in the bottom margin by a separate macro triggered during the footer's page ejection:

```
.de bn                 \"bottom number
.tl ''– % –''          \"centered page number
..
.wh –0.5i–1v bn \"tl base 0.5i up
```

T3. Paragraphs and Headings

The housekeeping associated with starting a new paragraph should be collected in a paragraph macro that, for example, does the desired preparagraph spacing, forces the correct font, size, base-line spacing, and indent, checks that enough space remains for *more than one* line, and requests a temporary indent.

```
.de pg                 \"paragraph
.br                    \"break
.ft R                  \"force font,
.ps 10                 \"size,
.vs 12p                \"spacing,
.in 0                  \"and indent
.sp 0.4                \"prespace
.ne 1+\\n(.Vu          \"want more than 1 line
.ti 0.2i               \"temp indent
..
```

The first break in **pg** will force out any previous partial lines, and must occur before the **vs**. The forcing of font, etc. is partly a defense against prior error and partly to permit things like section heading macros to set parameters only once. The prespacing parameter is suitable for TROFF; a larger space, at least as big as the output device vertical resolution, would be more suitable in NROFF. The choice of remaining space to test for in the **ne** is the smallest amount greater than one line (the **.V** is the available vertical resolution).

A macro to automatically number section headings might look like:

```
.de sc                 \"section
. ---                  \"force font, etc.
.sp 0.4                \"prespace
.ne 2.4+\\n(.Vu \"want 2.4+ lines
.fi
\\n+S.
..
.nr S 0 1              \"init S
```

The usage is **.sc**, followed by the section heading text, followed by **.pg**. The **ne** test value includes one line of heading, 0.4 line in the following **pg**, and one line of the paragraph text. A word consisting of the next section number and a period is produced to begin the heading line. The format of the number may be set by **af** (§8).

Another common form is the labeled, indented paragraph, where the label protrudes left into the indent space.

```
.de lp                 \"labeled paragraph
.pg
.in 0.5i               \"paragraph indent
.ta 0.2i 0.5i          \"label, paragraph
.ti 0
\t\\$1\t\c             \"flow into paragraph
..
```

The intended usage is "**.lp** *label*"; *label* will begin at 0.2 inch, and cannot exceed a length of 0.3 inch without intruding into the paragraph. The label could be right adjusted against 0.4 inch by setting the tabs instead with **.ta 0.4iR 0.5i**. The last line of **lp** ends with **\c** so that it will become a part of the first line of the text that follows.

T4. Multiple Column Output

The production of multiple column pages requires the footer macro to decide whether it was invoked by other than the last column, so that it will begin a new column rather than produce the bottom margin. The header can initialize a column register that the footer will increment and test. The following is arranged for two columns, but is easily modified for more.

```
.de hd                 \"header
. ---
.nr cl 0 1             \"init column count
.mk                    \"mark top of text
..
.de fo                 \"footer
.ie \\n+(cl<2 \{\
.po +3.4i              \"next column; 3.1+0.3
.rt                    \"back to mark
.ns \}                 \"no-space mode
.el \{\
.po \\nMu              \"restore left margin
```

21

```
.  ---
'bp \}
..
.ll 3.1i          \"column width
.nr M \\n(.o      \"save left margin
```

Typically a portion of the top of the first page contains full width text; the request for the narrower line length, as well as another **.mk** would be made where the two column output was to begin.

T5. Footnote Processing

The footnote mechanism to be described is used by imbedding the footnotes in the input text at the point of reference, demarcated by an initial **.fn** and a terminal **.ef**:

```
.fn
```
Footnote text and control lines...
```
.ef
```

In the following, footnotes are processed in a separate environment and diverted for later printing in the space immediately prior to the bottom margin. There is provision for the case where the last collected footnote doesn't completely fit in the available space.

```
.de hd           \"header
.  ---
.nr x 0 1        \"init footnote count
.nr y 0-\\nb     \"current footer place
.ch fo -\\nbu    \"reset footer trap
.if \\n(dn .fz   \"leftover footnote
..
.de fo           \"footer
.nr dn 0         \"zero last diversion size
.if \\nx \{\
.ev 1            \"expand footnotes in ev1
.nf              \"retain vertical size
.FN              \"footnotes
.rm FN           \"delete it
.if "\\n(.z"fy" .di \"end overflow diversion
.nr x 0          \"disable fx
.ev \}           \"pop environment
.  ---
'bp
..
.de fx           \"process footnote overflow
.if \\nx .di fy  \"divert overflow
..
.de fn           \"start footnote
.da FN           \"divert (append) footnote
.ev 1            \"in environment 1
.if \\n+x=1 .fs   \"if first, include separator
.fi              \"fill mode
..
.de ef           \"end footnote
.br              \"finish output
```

```
.nr z \\n(.v     \"save spacing
.ev              \"pop ev
.di              \"end diversion
.nr y -\\n(dn    \"new footer position,
.if \\nx=1 .nr y -(\\n(.v-\\nz) \
                 \"uncertainty correction
.ch fo \\nyu     \"y is negative
.if (\\n(nl+1v)>(\\n(.p+\\ny) \
.ch fo \\n(nlu+1v \"it didn't fit
..
.de fs           \"separator
\l´1i´           \"1 inch rule
.br
..
.de fz           \"get leftover footnote
.fn
.nf              \"retain vertical size
.fy              \"where fx put it
.ef
..
.nr b 1.0i       \"bottom margin size
.wh 0 hd         \"header trap
.wh 12i fo       \"footer trap, temp position
.wh -\\nbu fx    \"fx at footer position
.ch fo -\\nbu    \"conceal fx with fo
```

The header **hd** initializes a footnote count register **x**, and sets both the current footer trap position register **y** and the footer trap itself to a nominal position specified in register **b**. In addition, if the register **dn** indicates a leftover footnote, **fz** is invoked to reprocess it. The footnote start macro **fn** begins a diversion (append) in environment 1, and increments the count **x**; if the count is one, the footnote separator **fs** is interpolated. The separator is kept in a separate macro to permit user redefinition. The footnote end macro **ef** restores the previous environment and ends the diversion after saving the spacing size in register **z**. **y** is then decremented by the size of the footnote, available in **dn**; then on the first footnote, **y** is further decremented by the difference in vertical base-line spacings of the two environments, to prevent the late triggering the footer trap from causing the last line of the combined footnotes to overflow. The footer trap is then set to the lower (on the page) of **y** or the current page position (**nl**) plus one line, to allow for printing the reference line. If indicated by **x**, the footer **fo** rereads the footnotes from **FN** in nofill mode in environment 1, and deletes **FN**. If the footnotes were too large to fit, the macro **fx** will be trap-invoked to redivert the overflow into **fy**, and the register **dn** will later indicate to the header whether **fy** is empty. Both **fo** and **fx** are planted in the nominal footer trap position in an order that causes **fx** to be concealed unless the **fo** trap is moved. The footer then terminates the overflow diversion, if necessary, and zeros **x** to disable **fx**, because the uncertainty correction together with a not-too-late triggering of the footer can result in the footnote rereading finishing before reaching the **fx** trap.

A good exercise for the student is to combine the multiple-column and footnote mechanisms.

T6. The Last Page

After the last input file has ended, NROFF and TROFF invoke the *end macro* (§7), if any, and when it finishes, eject the remainder of the page. During the eject, any traps encountered are processed normally. At the *end* of this last page, processing terminates *unless* a partial line, word, or partial word remains. If it is desired that another page be started, the end-macro

```
.de en               \"end-macro
\c
'bp
..
.em en
```

will deposit a null partial word, and effect another last page.

Table I

Font Style Examples

The following fonts were originally printed in 12-point, with a vertical spacing of 14-point, and with non-alphanumeric characters separated by ¼ em space. After the photo reduction process used to produce this book, they are approximately the size of 10-point font with a vertical spacing of 12-points.

Times Roman

abcdefghijklmnopqrstuvwxyz
ABCDEFGHIJKLMNOPQRSTUVWXYZ
1234567890
! $ % & ( ) ' ' * + − . , / : ; = ? [ ] |
● □ — - _ ¼ ½ ¾ fi fl   ° † ′ ¢ ® ©

Times Italic

abcdefghijklmnopqrstuvwxyz
ABCDEFGHIJKLMNOPQRSTUVWXYZ
1234567890
*! $ % & ( ) ' ' * + − . , / : ; = ? [ ] |*
● □ — - _ ¼ ½ ¾ *fi fl*   ° † ′ ¢ ® ©

Times Bold

abcdefghijklmnopqrstuvwxyz
ABCDEFGHIJKLMNOPQRSTUVWXYZ
1234567890
! $ % & ( ) ' ' * + − . , / : ; = ? [ ] |
● □ — - _ ¼ ½ ¾ **fi fl**   ° † ′ ¢ ® ©

Special Mathematical Font

" ´ \ ^ _ ` ~ / < > { } # @ + − = *
α β γ δ ε ζ η θ ι κ λ μ ν ξ ο π ρ σ ς τ υ φ χ ψ ω
Γ Δ Θ Λ Ξ Π Σ Υ Φ Ψ Ω
√ ⁻ ≥ ≤ ≡ ~ ≈ ≠ → ← ↑ ↓ × ÷ ± ∪ ∩ ⊂ ⊃ ⊆ ⊇ ∞ ∂
§ ∇ ¬ ∫ ∝ ∅ ∈ ‡ ⇒ ⇐ | ○ ⌈ ⌋ ⌊ ⌉ | ⌊ ⌈ |

21

Table II

Input Naming Conventions for ´, `, and −
and for Non-ASCII Special Characters

Non-ASCII characters and *minus* on the standard fonts.

Char	Input Name	Character Name	Char	Input Name	Character Name
'	´	close quote	fi	\(fi	fi
`	`	open quote	fl	\(fl	fl
—	\(em	3/4 Em dash		\(ff	ff
-	–	hyphen or		\(Fi	ffi
-	\(hy	hyphen		\(Fl	ffl
–	\-	current font minus	°	\(de	degree
•	\(bu	bullet	†	\(dg	dagger
□	\(sq	square	'	\(fm	foot mark
_	\(ru	rule	¢	\(ct	cent sign
¼	\(14	1/4	®	\(rg	registered
½	\(12	1/2	©	\(co	copyright
¾	\(34	3/4			

Non-ASCII characters and ´, `, _, +, −, =, and * on the special font.

The ASCII characters @, #, ", ´, `, <, >, \, {, }, ˜, ^, and _ exist *only* on the special font and are printed as a 1-em space if that font is not mounted. The following characters exist only on the special font except for the upper case Greek letter names followed by † which are mapped into upper case English letters in whatever font is mounted on font position one (default Times Roman). The special math plus, minus, and equals are provided to insulate the appearance of equations from the choice of standard fonts.

Char	Input Name	Character Name	Char	Input Name	Character Name
+	\(pl	math plus	κ	\(*k	kappa
−	\(mi	math minus	λ	\(*l	lambda
=	\(eq	math equals	μ	\(*m	mu
*	\(**	math star	ν	\(*n	nu
§	\(sc	section	ξ	\(*c	xi
´	\(aa	acute accent	ο	\(*o	omicron
`	\(ga	grave accent	π	\(*p	pi
_	\(ul	underrule	ρ	\(*r	rho
/	\(sl	slash (matching backslash)	σ	\(*s	sigma
α	\(*a	alpha	ς	\(ts	terminal sigma
β	\(*b	beta	τ	\(*t	tau
γ	\(*g	gamma	υ	\(*u	upsilon
δ	\(*d	delta	φ	\(*f	phi
ε	\(*e	epsilon	χ	\(*x	chi
ζ	\(*z	zeta	ψ	\(*q	psi
η	\(*y	eta	ω	\(*w	omega
θ	\(*h	theta	A	\(*A	Alpha†
ι	\(*i	iota	B	\(*B	Beta†

21

Char	Input Name	Character Name
Γ	\(*G	Gamma
Δ	\(*D	Delta
E	\(*E	Epsilon†
Z	\(*Z	Zeta†
H	\(*Y	Eta†
Θ	\(*H	Theta
I	\(*I	Iota†
K	\(*K	Kappa†
Λ	\(*L	Lambda
M	\(*M	Mu†
N	\(*N	Nu†
Ξ	\(*C	Xi
O	\(*O	Omicron†
Π	\(*P	Pi
P	\(*R	Rho†
Σ	\(*S	Sigma
T	\(*T	Tau†
Y	\(*U	Upsilon
Φ	\(*F	Phi
X	\(*X	Chi†
Ψ	\(*Q	Psi
Ω	\(*W	Omega
√	\(sr	square root
‾	\(rn	root en extender
≥	\(>=	>=
≤	\(<=	<=
≡	\(==	identically equal
≈	\(~=	approx =
~	\(ap	approximates
≠	\(!=	not equal
→	\(->	right arrow
←	\(<-	left arrow
↑	\(ua	up arrow
↓	\(da	down arrow
×	\(mu	multiply
÷	\(di	divide
±	\(+-	plus-minus
∪	\(cu	cup (union)
∩	\(ca	cap (intersection)
⊂	\(sb	subset of
⊃	\(sp	superset of
⊆	\(ib	improper subset
⊇	\(ip	improper superset
∞	\(if	infinity
∂	\(pd	partial derivative
∇	\(gr	gradient
¬	\(no	not
∫	\(is	integral sign
∝	\(pt	proportional to
∅	\(es	empty set
∈	\(mo	member of
|	\(br	box vertical rule

Char	Input Name	Character Name
‡	\(dd	double dagger
⇒	\(rh	right hand
⇐	\(lh	left hand
|	\(or	or
○	\(ci	circle
⌈	\(lt	left top of big curly bracket
⌊	\(lb	left bottom
⌉	\(rt	right top
⌋	\(rb	right bot
{	\(lk	left center of big curly bracket
}	\(rk	right center of big curly bracket
|	\(bv	bold vertical
⌊	\(lf	left floor (left bottom of big square bracket)
⌋	\(rf	right floor (right bottom)
⌈	\(lc	left ceiling (left top)
⌉	\(rc	right ceiling (right top)

A TROFF Tutorial

Brian W. Kernighan
(updated for 4.3BSD by Mark Seiden)

ABSTRACT

troff is a text-formatting program for typesetting on the UNIX† operating system. This device is capable of producing high quality text; this paper is an example of **troff** output.

The phototypesetter itself normally runs with four fonts, containing roman, italic and bold letters (as on this page), a full greek alphabet, and a substantial number of special characters and mathematical symbols. Characters can be printed in a range of sizes, and placed anywhere on the page.

troff allows the user full control over fonts, sizes, and character positions, as well as the usual features of a formatter — right-margin justification, automatic hyphenation, page titling and numbering, and so on. It also provides macros, arithmetic variables and operations, and conditional testing, for complicated formatting tasks.

This document is an introduction to the most basic use of **troff**. It presents just enough information to enable the user to do simple formatting tasks like making viewgraphs, and to make incremental changes to existing packages of **troff** commands. In most respects, the UNIX formatter **nroff** and a more recent version *(device-independent* **troff**) are identical to the version described here, so this document also serves as a tutorial for them as well.

1. Introduction

troff [1] is a text-formatting program, written originally by J. F. Ossanna, for producing high-quality printed output from the phototypesetter on the UNIX operating system. This document is an example of **troff** output.

The single most important rule of using **troff** is not to use it directly, but through some intermediary. In many ways, **troff** resembles an assembly language — a remarkably powerful and flexible one — but nonetheless such that many operations must be specified at a level of detail and in a form that is too hard for most people to use effectively.

For two special applications, there are programs that provide an interface to **troff** for the majority of users. **eqn** [2] provides an easy to learn language for typesetting mathematics; the **eqn** user need know no **troff** whatsoever to typeset mathematics. **tbl** [3] provides the same convenience for producing tables of arbitrary complexity.

For producing straight text (which may well contain mathematics or tables), there are a number of 'macro pack-ages' that define formatting rules and operations for specific styles of documents, and reduce the amount of direct contact with **troff**. In particular, the '–ms' [4], PWB/MM [5], and '–me' [6] packages for internal memoranda and external papers provide most of the facilities needed for a wide range of document preparation.† (This memo was prepared with '–ms'.) There are also packages for viewgraphs, for simulating the older **roff** formatters, and for other special applications. Typically you will find these packages easier to use than **troff** once you get beyond the most trivial operations; you should always consider them first.

In the few cases where existing packages don't do the whole job, the solution is *not* to write an entirely new set of **troff** instructions from scratch, but to make small changes to adapt packages that already exist.

---

† Most Berkeley Unix sites only have –ms and –me.

In accordance with this philosophy of letting some-one else do the work, the part of **troff** described here is only a small part of the whole, although it tries to concentrate on the more useful parts. In any case, there is no attempt to be complete. Rather, the emphasis is on showing how to do simple things, and how to make incremental changes to what already exists. The contents of the remaining sections are:

2.   Point sizes and line spacing
3.   Fonts and special characters
4.   Indents and line length
5.   Tabs
6.   Local motions: Drawing lines and characters
7.   Strings
8.   Introduction to macros
9.   Titles, pages and numbering
10. Number registers and arithmetic
11. Macros with arguments
12. Conditionals
13. Environments
14. Diversions
     Appendix: Typesetter character set

The **troff** described here is the C-language version supplied with UNIX Version 7 and 32V as documented in [1].

To use **troff** you have to prepare not only the actual text you want printed, but some information that tells *how* you want it printed. (Readers who use **roff** will find the approach familiar.) For **troff** the text and the formatting information are often intertwined quite intimately. Most commands to **troff** are placed on a line separate from the text itself, beginning with a period (one command per line). For example,

> Some text.
> .ps 14
> Some more text.

will change the 'point size', that is, the size of the letters being printed, to '14 point' (one point is 1/72 inch) like this:

> Some text. Some more text.

Occasionally, though, something special occurs in the middle of a line — to produce

> Area = πr^2

you have to type

> Area = \(*p\fIr\fR\|\s8\u2\d\s0

(which we will explain shortly). The backslash character \ is used to introduce **troff** commands and special characters within a line of text.

2. Point Sizes; Line Spacing

As mentioned above, the command .ps sets the point size. One point is 1/72 inch, so 6-point characters are at most 1/12 inch high, and 36-point characters are ½ inch.

Some sample point sizes are shown below. These point sizes are selected to be approximately correct after the photo reduction process used to make this book.

6 point: Pack my box with five dozen liquor jugs.

9 point: Pack my box with five dozen liquor jugs.

10 point: Pack my box with five dozen liquor

11 point: Pack my box with five dozen

14 point: Pack my box with five

16 point 20 point

24 30 36

Not all point sizes are supported. If the number after .ps is not a legal size, it is rounded up to the next valid value, with a typical maximum of 72. If no number follows .ps, **troff** reverts to the previous size, whatever it was. **troff** begins with point size 10, which is usually fine. The original of this document (on 8.5 by 11 inch paper) is in 9 point which becomes about 7½ points after photo reduction.

The point size can also be changed in the middle of a line or even a word with the in-line command \s. To produce

> UNIX runs on a PDP-11/45

type

> \s8UNIX\s10 runs on a \s8PDP-\s1011/45

As above, \s should be followed by a legal point size, except that \s0 causes the size to revert to its previous value. Notice that \s1011 can be understood correctly as 'size 10, followed by an 11', if the size is legal, but not otherwise. Be cautious with similar constructions.

Relative size changes are also legal and useful:

> \s−2UNIX\s+2

temporarily decreases the size, whatever it is, by two points, then restores it. Relative size changes have the advantage that the size difference is independent of the starting size of the document. The amount of the relative change is restricted to a single digit.

The other parameter that determines what the type looks like is the spacing between lines, which is set independently of the point size. Vertical spacing is measured from the bottom of one line to the bottom of the next. The command to control vertical spacing is .vs. For running text, it is usually best to set the vertical spacing about 20% bigger than the character size. For example, so far in this document, we have used "9 on 11", that is,

> .ps 9
> .vs 11p

If we changed to

.ps 9
.vs 9p

the running text would look like this. After a few lines, you will agree it looks a little cramped. The right vertical spacing is partly a matter of taste, depending on how much text you want to squeeze into a given space, and partly a matter of traditional printing style. By default, **troff** uses 10 on 12.

Point size and vertical spacing make a substantial difference in the amount of text per square inch. This is 12 on 14.

Point size and vertical spacing make a substantial difference in the amount of text per square inch. For example, 10 on 12 uses about twice as much space as 7 on 8. This is 6 on 7, which is even smaller. It packs a lot more words per line, but you can go blind trying to read it.

When used without arguments, .ps and .vs revert to the previous size and vertical spacing respectively.

The command .sp is used to get extra vertical space. Unadorned, it gives you one extra blank line (one .vs, whatever that has been set to). Typically, that's more or less than you want, so .sp can be followed by information about how much space you want —

.sp 2i

means 'two inches of vertical space'.

.sp 2p

means 'two points of vertical space'; and

.sp 2

means 'two vertical spaces' — two of whatever .vs is set to (this can also be made explicit with .sp 2v); **troff** also understands decimal fractions in most places, so

.sp 1.5i

is a space of 1.5 inches. These same scale factors can be used after .vs to define line spacing, and in fact after most commands that deal with physical dimensions.

It should be noted that all size numbers are converted internally to 'machine units', which are 1/432 inch (1/6 point). For most purposes, this is enough resolution that you don't have to worry about the accuracy of the representation. The situation is not quite so good vertically, where resolution is 1/144 inch (1/2 point).

3. Fonts and Special Characters

troff and the typesetter allow four different fonts at any one time. Normally three fonts (Times roman, italic and bold) and one collection of special characters are permanently mounted.

abcdefghijklmnopqrstuvwxyz 0123456789
ABCDEFGHIJKLMNOPQRSTUVWXYZ
abcdefghijklmnopqrstuvwxyz 0123456789
ABCDEFGHIJKLMNOPQRSTUVWXYZ
abcdefghijklmnopqrstuvwxyz 0123456789
ABCDEFGHIJKLMNOPQRSTUVWXYZ

The greek, mathematical symbols and miscellany of the special font are listed in Appendix A.

troff prints in roman unless told otherwise. To switch into bold, use the .ft command

.ft B

and for italics,

.ft I

To return to roman, use .ft R; to return to the previous font, whatever it was, use either .ft P or just .ft. The 'underline' command

.ul

causes the next input line to print in italics. .ul can be followed by a count to indicate that more than one line is to be italicized.

Fonts can also be changed within a line or word with the in-line command \f:

bold*face* text

is produced by

\fBbold\fIface\fR text

If you want to do this so the previous font, whatever it was, is left undisturbed, insert extra \fP commands, like this:

\fBbold\fP\fIface\fP\fR text\fP

Because only the immediately previous font is remembered, you have to restore the previous font after each change or you can lose it. The same is true of .ps and .vs when used without an argument.

There are other fonts available besides the standard set, although you can still use only four at any given time. The command .fp tells **troff** what fonts are physically mounted on the typesetter:

.fp 3 H

says that the Helvetica font is mounted on position 3. (The complete list of font sizes and styles depends on your typesetter or laser printer.) Appropriate .fp commands should appear at the beginning of your document if you do not use the standard fonts.

It is possible to make a document relatively independent of the actual fonts used to print it by using font numbers instead of names; for example, \f3 and .ft 3 mean 'whatever font is mounted at position 3', and thus work for any setting. Normal settings are roman font on 1, italic on 2, bold on 3, and special on 4.

22

There is also a way to get 'synthetic' bold fonts by overstriking letters with a slight offset. Look at the .bd command in [1].

Special characters have four-character names beginning with \(, and they may be inserted anywhere. For example,

¼ + ½ = ¾

is produced by

\(14 + \(12 = \(34

In particular, greek letters are all of the form \(*–, where – is an upper or lower case roman letter reminiscent of the greek. Thus to get

$\Sigma(\alpha\times\beta) \to \infty$

in bare **troff** we have to type

\(*S(\(*a\(mu\(*b) \(–> \(if

That line is unscrambled as follows:

\(*S	Σ
(	(
\(*a	α
\(mu	×
\(*b	β
)	)
\(–>	→
\(if	∞

A complete list of these special names occurs in Appendix A.

In **eqn** [2] the same effect can be achieved with the input

SIGMA (alpha times beta) –> inf

which is less concise, but clearer to the uninitiated.

Notice that each four-character name is a single character as far as **troff** is concerned — the 'translate' command

.tr \(mi\(em

is perfectly clear, meaning

.tr ——

that is, to translate – into —.

Some characters are automatically translated into others: grave ` and acute ´ accents (apostrophes) become open and close single quotes ' '; the combination of ''...'' is generally preferable to the double quotes "...". Similarly a typed minus sign becomes a hyphen -. To print an explicit – sign, use \-. To get a backslash printed, use \e.

4. Indents and Line Lengths

troff starts with a line length of 6.5 inches, which some people think is too wide for 8½×11 paper. To reset the line length, use the .ll command, as in

.ll 6i

As with .sp, the actual length can be specified in several ways; inches are probably the most intuitive.

The maximum line length provided by the typesetter is 7.5 inches, by the way. To use the full width, you will have to reset the default physical left margin ("page offset"), which is normally slightly less than one inch from the left edge of the paper. This is done by the .po command.

.po 0

sets the offset as far to the left as it will go.

The indent command .in causes the left margin to be indented by some specified amount from the page offset. If we use .in to move the left margin in, and .ll to move the right margin to the left, we can make offset blocks of text:

.in 0.3i
.ll –0.3i
text to be set into a block
.ll +0.3i
.in –0.3i

will create a block that looks like this:

Pater noster qui est in caelis sanctificetur nomen tuum; adveniat regnum tuum; fiat voluntas tua, sicut in caelo, et in terra. ... Amen.

Notice the use of '+' and '–' to specify the amount of change. These change the previous setting by the specified amount, rather than just overriding it. The distinction is quite important: .ll +1i makes lines one inch longer; .ll 1i makes them one inch *long*.

With .in, .ll and .po, the previous value is used if no argument is specified.

To indent a single line, use the 'temporary indent' command .ti. For example, all paragraphs in this memo effectively begin with the command

.ti 3

Three of what? The default unit for .ti, as for most horizontally oriented commands (.ll, .in, .po), is ems; an em is roughly the width of the letter 'm' in the current point size. (Precisely, a em in size *p* is *p* points.) Although inches are usually clearer than ems to people who don't set type for a living, ems have a place: they are a measure of size that is proportional to the current point size. If you want to make text that keeps its proportions regardless of point size, you should use ems for all dimensions. Ems can be specified as scale factors directly, as in .ti 2.5m.

Lines can also be indented negatively if the indent is already positive:

.ti –0.3i

causes the next line to be moved back three tenths of an inch. Thus to make a decorative initial capital, we indent

22

the whole paragraph, then move the letter 'P' back with a .ti command:

> **P**ater noster qui est in caelis sanctificetur nomen tuum; adveniat regnum tuum; fiat voluntas tua, sicut in caelo, et in terra. ...
> Amen.

Of course, there is also some trickery to make the 'P' bigger (just a '\s36P\s0'), and to move it down from its normal position (see the section on local motions).

5. Tabs

Tabs (the ASCII 'horizontal tab' character) can be used to produce output in columns, or to set the horizontal position of output. Typically tabs are used only in unfilled text. Tab stops are set by default every half inch from the current indent, but can be changed by the .ta command. To set stops every inch, for example,

    .ta 1i 2i 3i 4i 5i 6i

Unfortunately the stops are left-justified only (as on a typewriter), so lining up columns of right-justified numbers can be painful. If you have many numbers, or if you need more complicated table layout, *don't* use **troff** directly; use the **tbl** program described in [3].

For a handful of numeric columns, you can do it this way: Precede every number by enough blanks to make it line up when typed.

    .nf
    .ta 1i 2i 3i
        1 *tab*   2 *tab*   3
       40 *tab*   50 *tab*   60
      700 *tab* 800 *tab* 900
    .fi

Then change each leading blank into the string \0. This is a character that does not print, but that has the same width as a digit. When printed, this will produce

1	2	3
40	50	60
700	800	900

It is also possible to fill up tabbed-over space with some character other than blanks by setting the 'tab replacement character' with the .tc command:

    .ta 1.5i 2.5i
    .tc \(ru   (\(ru is "_")
    Name *tab* Age *tab*

produces

    Name _____ Age _____

To reset the tab replacement character to a blank, use .tc with no argument. (Lines can also be drawn with the \l command, described in Section 6.)

troff also provides a very general mechanism called 'fields' for setting up complicated columns. (This is used by **tbl**). We will not go into it in this paper.

6. Local Motions: Drawing lines and characters

Remember 'Area = πr^2' and the big 'P' in the Paternoster. How are they done? **troff** provides a host of commands for placing characters of any size at any place. You can use them to draw special characters or to tune your output for a particular appearance. Most of these commands are straightforward, but messy to read and tough to type correctly.

If you won't use **eqn**, subscripts and superscripts are most easily done with the half-line local motions \u and \d. To go back up the page half a point-size, insert a \u at the desired place; to go down, insert a \d. (\u and \d should always be used in pairs, as explained below.) Thus

    Area = \(*pr\u2\d

produces

    Area = πr^2

To make the '2' smaller, bracket it with \s-2...\s0. Since \u and \d refer to the current point size, be sure to put them either both inside or both outside the size changes, or you will get an unbalanced vertical motion.

Sometimes the space given by \u and \d isn't the right amount. The \v command can be used to request an arbitrary amount of vertical motion. The in-line command

    \v´(amount)´

causes motion up or down the page by the amount specified in '(amount)'. For example, to move the 'P' down, we used

    .in +0.6i   (move paragraph in)
    .ll −0.3i   (shorten lines)
    .ti −0.3i   (move P back)
    \v´2´\s36P\s0\v´−2´ater noster qui est
    in caelis ...

A minus sign causes upward motion, while no sign or a plus sign means down the page. Thus \v´−2´ causes an upward vertical motion of two line spaces.

There are many other ways to specify the amount of motion —

    \v´0.1i´
    \v´3p´
    \v´−0.5m´

and so on are all legal. Notice that the scale specifier i or p or m goes inside the quotes. Any character can be used in place of the quotes; this is also true of all other **troff** commands described in this section.

Since **troff** does not take within-the-line vertical motions into account when figuring out where it is on the page, output lines can have unexpected positions if the left and right ends aren't at the same vertical position. Thus \v, like \u and \d, should always balance upward vertical motion in a line with the same amount in the downward direction.

22

Arbitrary horizontal motions are also available — \h is quite analogous to \v, except that the default scale factor is ems instead of line spaces. As an example,

    \h´−0.1i´

causes a backwards motion of a tenth of an inch. As a practical matter, consider printing the mathematical symbol '>>'. The default spacing is too wide, so **eqn** replaces this by

    >\h´−0.3m´>

to produce ≫.

Frequently \h is used with the 'width function' \w to generate motions equal to the width of some character string. The construction

    \w´thing´

is a number equal to the width of 'thing' in machine units (1/432 inch). All **troff** computations are ultimately done in these units. To move horizontally the width of an 'x', we can say

    \h´\w´x´u´

As we mentioned above, the default scale factor for all horizontal dimensions is m, ems, so here we must have the u for machine units, or the motion produced will be far too large. **troff** is quite happy with the nested quotes, by the way, so long as you don't leave any out.

As a live example of this kind of construction, all of the command names in the text, like .sp, were done by overstriking with a slight offset. The commands for .sp are

    .sp\h´−\w´.sp´u´\h´1u´.sp

That is, put out '.sp', move left by the width of '.sp', move right 1 unit, and print '.sp' again. (Of course there is a way to avoid typing that much input for each command name, which we will discuss in Section 11.)

There are also several special-purpose **troff** commands for local motion. We have already seen \0, which is an unpaddable white space of the same width as a digit. 'Unpaddable' means that it will never be widened or split across a line by line justification and filling. There is also \(blank), which is an unpaddable character the width of a space, \|, which is half that width, \ˆ, which is one quarter of the width of a space, and \&, which has zero width. (This last one is useful, for example, in entering a text line which would otherwise begin with a '.'.)

The command \o, used like

    \o´set of characters´

causes (up to 9) characters to be overstruck, centered on the widest. This is nice for accents, as in

    syst\o"e\(ga"me t\o"e\(aa"l\o"e\(aa"phonique

which makes

système téléphonique

The accents are \(ga and \(aa, or \` and \´; remember that each is just one character to **troff**.

You can make your own overstrikes with another special convention, \z, the zero-motion command. \zx suppresses the normal horizontal motion after printing the single character x, so another character can be laid on top of it. Although sizes can be changed within \o, it centers the characters on the widest, and there can be no horizontal or vertical motions, so \z may be the only way to get what you want:

is produced by

    .sp 2
    \s8\z\(sq\s14\z\(sq\s22\z\(sq\s36\(sq

The .sp is needed to leave room for the result.

As another example, an extra-heavy semicolon that looks like

; instead of ; or ;

can be constructed with a big comma and a big period above it:

    \s+6\z,\v´−0.25m´.\v´0.25m´\s0

'0.25m' is an experimentally-derived constant.

A more ornate overstrike is given by the bracketing function \b, which piles up characters vertically, centered on the current baseline. Thus we can get big brackets, constructing them with piled-up smaller pieces:

$$\left\{ \left[\ x \ \right] \right\}$$

by typing in only this:

    .sp
    \b´\(lt\(lk\(lb´ \b´\(lc\(lf´ x \b´\(rc\(rf´ \b´\(rt\(rk\(rb´

troff also provides a convenient facility for drawing horizontal and vertical lines of arbitrary length with arbitrary characters. \l´1i´ draws a line one inch long, like this: _____ . The length can be followed by the character to use if the _ isn't appropriate; \l´0.5i.´ draws a half-inch line of dots: .... The construction \L is entirely analogous, except that it draws a vertical line instead of horizontal.

7. Strings

Obviously if a paper contains a large number of occurrences of an acute accent over a letter 'e', typing \o"e\´" for each é would be a great nuisance.

Fortunately, **troff** provides a way in which you can store an arbitrary collection of text in a 'string', and thereafter use the string name as a shorthand for its contents. Strings are one of several **troff** mechanisms whose judicious use lets you type a document with less effort and organize it so that extensive format changes can be made with few editing changes.

A reference to a string is replaced by whatever text the string was defined as. Strings are defined with the command .ds. The line

.ds e \o"e\'"

defines the string e to have the value \o"e\'"

String names may be either one or two characters long, and are referred to by *x for one character names or *(xy for two character names. Thus to get téléphone, given the definition of the string e as above, we can say t*el*ephone.

If a string must begin with blanks, define it as

.ds xx "   text

The double quote signals the beginning of the definition. There is no trailing quote; the end of the line terminates the string.

A string may actually be several lines long; if **troff** encounters a \ at the end of *any* line, it is thrown away and the next line added to the current one. So you can make a long string simply by ending each line but the last with a backslash:

.ds xx this \
is a very \
long string

Strings may be defined in terms of other strings, or even in terms of themselves; we will discuss some of these possibilities later.

8. Introduction to Macros

Before we can go much further in **troff**, we need to learn a bit about the macro facility. In its simplest form, a macro is just a shorthand notation quite similar to a string. Suppose we want every paragraph to start in exactly the same way — with a space and a temporary indent of two ems:

.sp
.ti +2m

Then to save typing, we would like to collapse these into one shorthand line, a **troff** 'command' like

.PP

that would be treated by **troff** exactly as

.sp
.ti +2m

.PP is called a *macro*. The way we tell **troff** what .PP means is to *define* it with the .de command:

.de PP
.sp
.ti +2m
..

The first line names the macro (we used '.PP' for 'paragraph', and upper case so it wouldn't conflict with any name that **troff** might already know about). The last line .. marks the end of the definition. In between is the text, which is simply inserted whenever **troff** sees the 'command' or macro call

.PP

A macro can contain any mixture of text and formatting commands.

The definition of .PP has to precede its first use; undefined macros are simply ignored. Names are restricted to one or two characters.

Using macros for commonly occurring sequences of commands is critically important. Not only does it save typing, but it makes later changes much easier. Suppose we decide that the paragraph indent is too small, the vertical space is much too big, and roman font should be forced. Instead of changing the whole document, we need only change the definition of .PP to something like

.de PP   \" paragraph macro
.sp 2p
.ti +3m
.ft R
..

and the change takes effect everywhere we used .PP.

\" is a **troff** command that causes the rest of the line to be ignored. We use it here to add comments to the macro definition (a wise idea once definitions get complicated).

As another example of macros, consider these two which start and end a block of offset, unfilled text, like most of the examples in this paper:

.de BS   \" start indented block
.sp
.nf
.in +0.3i
..
.de BE   \" end indented block
.sp
.fi
.in −0.3i
..

Now we can surround text like

Copy to
John Doe
Richard Roberts
Stanley Smith

by the commands .BS and .BE, and it will come out as it did above.

Notice that we indented by .in +0.3i instead of .in 0.3i. This way we can nest our uses of .BS and BE to get blocks within blocks.

If later on we decide that the indent should be 0.5i, then it is only necessary to change the definitions of .BS and .BE, not the whole paper.

9. Titles, Pages and Numbering

This is an area where things get tougher, because nothing is done for you automatically. Of necessity, some of this section is a cookbook, to be copied literally until you get some experience.

Suppose you want a title at the top of each page, saying just

left top   center top   right top

In **roff**, one can say

```
.he 'left top'center top'right top'
.fo 'left bottom'center bottom'right bottom'
```

to get headers and footers automatically on every page. Alas, this doesn't work so easily in **troff**, a serious hardship for the novice. Instead you have to do a lot of specification (or use a macro package, which makes it effortless).

You have to say what the actual title is (easy); when to print it (easy enough); and what to do at and around the title line (harder). Taking these in reverse order, first we define a macro .NP (for 'new page') to process titles and the like at the end of one page and the beginning of the next:

```
.de NP
'bp
'sp 0.5i
.tl 'left top'center top'right top'
'sp 0.3i
..
```

To make sure we're at the top of a page, we issue a 'begin page' command 'bp, which causes a skip to top-of-page (we'll explain the ' shortly). Then we space down half an inch, print the title (the use of .tl should be self explanatory; later we will discuss parameterizing the titles), space another 0.3 inches, and we're done.

To ask for .NP at the bottom of each page, we have to say something like 'when the text is within an inch of the bottom of the page, start the processing for a new page.' This is done with a 'when' command .wh:

```
.wh −1i NP
```

(No '.' is used before NP; this is simply the name of a macro, not a macro call.) The minus sign means 'measure up from the bottom of the page', so '−1i' means 'one inch from the bottom'.

The .wh command appears in the input outside the definition of .NP; typically the input would be

```
.de NP
...
..
.wh −1i NP
```

Now what happens? As text is actually being output, **troff** keeps track of its vertical position on the page, and after a line is printed within one inch from the bottom, the .NP macro is activated. (In the jargon, the .wh command sets a *trap* at the specified place, which is 'sprung' when that point is passed.) .NP causes a skip to the top of the next page (that's what the 'bp was for), then prints the title with the appropriate margins.

Why 'bp and 'sp instead of .bp and .sp? The answer is that .sp and .bp, like several other commands, cause a *break* to take place. That is, all the input text collected but not yet printed is flushed out as soon as possible, and the next input line is guaranteed to start a new line of output. If we had used .sp or .bp in the .NP macro, this would cause a break in the middle of the current output line when a new page is started. The effect would be to print the left-over part of that line at the top of the page, followed by the next input line on a new output line. This is *not* what we want. Using ' instead of . for a command tells **troff** that no break is to take place — the output line currently being filled should *not* be forced out before the space or new page.

The list of commands that cause a break is short and natural:

```
.bp .br .ce .fi .nf .sp .in .ti
```

All others cause *no* break, regardless of whether you use a . or a '. If you really need a break, add a .br command at the appropriate place.

One other thing to beware of — if you're changing fonts or point sizes a lot, you may find that if you cross a page boundary in an unexpected font or size, your titles come out in that size and font instead of what you intended. Furthermore, the length of a title is independent of the current line length, so titles will come out at the default length of 6.5 inches unless you change it, which is done with the .lt command.

There are several ways to fix the problems of point sizes and fonts in titles. For the simplest applications, we can change .NP to set the proper size and font for the title, then restore the previous values, like this:

```
.de NP
'bp
'sp 0.5i
.ft R            \" set title font to roman
.ps 10           \" and size to 10 point
.lt 6i           \" and length to 6 inches
.tl 'left'center'right'
.ps              \" revert to previous size
.ft P            \" and to previous font
'sp 0.3i
..
```

This version of .NP does *not* work if the fields in the .tl command contain size or font changes. To cope with that requires **troff**'s 'environment' mechanism, which we will discuss in Section 13.

To get a footer at the bottom of a page, you can modify .NP so it does some processing before the 'bp command, or split the job into a footer macro invoked at the bottom margin and a header macro invoked at the top of the page. These variations are left as exercises.

Output page numbers are computed automatically as each page is produced (starting at 1), but no numbers are printed unless you ask for them explicitly. To get page numbers printed, include the character % in the .tl line at the position where you want the number to appear. For example

```
.tl ''- % -''
```

centers the page number inside hyphens, as on this page. You can set the page number at any time with either .bp n, which immediately starts a new page numbered n, or with .pn n, which sets the page number for the next page but doesn't cause a skip to the new page. Again, .bp +n sets the page number to n more than its current value; .bp means .bp +1.

10. Number Registers and Arithmetic

troff has a facility for doing arithmetic, and for defining and using variables with numeric values, called *number registers*. Number registers, like strings and macros, can be useful in setting up a document so it is easy to change later. And of course they serve for any sort of arithmetic computation.

Like strings, number registers have one or two character names. They are set by the .nr command, and are referenced anywhere by \nx (one character name) or \n(xy (two character name).

There are quite a few pre-defined number registers maintained by **troff**, among them % for the current page number; nl for the current vertical position on the page; dy, mo and yr for the current day, month and year; and .s and .f for the current size and font. (The font is a number from 1 to 4.) Any of these can be used in computations like any other register, but some, like .s and .f, cannot be changed with .nr.

As an example of the use of number registers, in the −ms macro package [4], most significant parameters are defined in terms of the values of a handful of number registers. These include the point size for text, the vertical spacing, and the line and title lengths. To set the point size and vertical spacing for the following paragraphs, for example, a user may say

```
.nr PS 9
.nr VS 11
```

The paragraph macro .PP is defined (roughly) as follows:

```
.de PP
.ps \\n(PS          \" reset size
.vs \\n(VSp         \" spacing
.ft R               \" font
.sp 0.5v            \" half a line
.ti +3m
..
```

This sets the font to Roman and the point size and line spacing to whatever values are stored in the number registers PS and VS.

Why are there two backslashes? This is the eternal problem of how to quote a quote. When **troff** originally reads the macro definition, it peels off one backslash to see what's coming next. To ensure that another is left in the definition when the macro is *used,* we have to put in two backslashes in the definition. If only one backslash is used, point size and vertical spacing will be frozen at the time the macro is defined, not when it is used.

Protecting by an extra layer of backslashes is only needed for \n, *, \$ (which we haven't come to yet), and \ itself. Things like \s, \f, \h, \v, and so on do not need an extra backslash, since they are converted by **troff** to an internal code immediately upon being seen.

Arithmetic expressions can appear anywhere that a number is expected. As a trivial example,

```
.nr PS \\n(PS−2
```

decrements PS by 2. Expressions can use the arithmetic operators +, −, *, /, % (mod), the relational operators >, >=, <, <=, =, and != (not equal), and parentheses.

Although the arithmetic we have done so far has been straightforward, more complicated things are somewhat tricky. First, number registers hold only integers. **troff** arithmetic uses truncating integer division, just like Fortran. Second, in the absence of parentheses, evaluation is done left-to-right without any operator precedence (including relational operators). Thus

```
7*−4+3/13
```

becomes '−1'. Number registers can occur anywhere in an expression, and so can scale indicators like p, i, m, and so on (but no spaces). Although integer division causes truncation, each number and its scale indicator is converted to machine units (1/432 inch) before any arithmetic is done, so 1i/2u evaluates to 0.5i correctly.

The scale indicator u often has to appear when you wouldn't expect it — in particular, when arithmetic is being done in a context that implies horizontal or vertical dimensions. For example,

```
.ll 7/2i
```

would seem obvious enough — 3½ inches. Sorry. Remember that the default units for horizontal parameters like .ll are ems. That's really '7 ems / 2 inches', and when translated into machine units, it becomes zero.

22

How about

.ll 7i/2

Sorry, still no good — the '2' is '2 ems', so '7i/2' is small, although not zero. You *must* use

.ll 7i/2u

So again, a safe rule is to attach a scale indicator to every number, even constants.

For arithmetic done within a .nr command, there is no implication of horizontal or vertical dimension, so the default units are 'units', and 7i/2 and 7i/2u mean the same thing. Thus

.nr ll 7i/2
.ll \\n(llu

does just what you want, so long as you don't forget the u on the .ll command.

11. Macros with arguments

The next step is to define macros that can change from one use to the next according to parameters supplied as arguments. To make this work, we need two things: first, when we define the macro, we have to indicate that some parts of it will be provided as arguments when the macro is called. Then when the macro is called we have to provide actual arguments to be plugged into the definition.

Let us illustrate by defining a macro .SM that will print its argument two points smaller than the surrounding text. That is, the macro call

.SM TROFF

will produce TROFF.

The definition of .SM is

.de SM
\s-2\\$1\s+2
..

Within a macro definition, the symbol \\$n refers to the nth argument that the macro was called with. Thus \\$1 is the string to be placed in a smaller point size when .SM is called.

As a slightly more complicated version, the following definition of .SM permits optional second and third arguments that will be printed in the normal size:

.de SM
\\$3\s-2\\$1\s+2\\$2
..

Arguments not provided when the macro is called are treated as empty, so

.SM TROFF),

produces TROFF), while

.SM TROFF). (

produces (TROFF). It is convenient to reverse the order of

arguments because trailing punctuation is much more common than leading.

By the way, the number of arguments that a macro was called with is available in number register .$.

The following macro .BD is the one used to make the 'bold roman' we have been using for **troff** command names in text. It combines horizontal motions, width computations, and argument rearrangement.

.de BD
\&\\$3\fI\\$1\h´-\w \\$1´u+1u \\$1\fP\\$2
..

The \h and \w commands need no extra backslash, as we discussed above. The \& is there in case the argument begins with a period.

Two backslashes are needed with the \\$n commands, though, to protect one of them when the macro is being defined. Perhaps a second example will make this clearer. Consider a macro called .SH which produces section headings rather like those in this paper, with the sections numbered automatically, and the title in bold in a smaller size. The use is

.SH "Section title ..."

(If the argument to a macro is to contain blanks, then it must be *surrounded* by double quotes, unlike a string, where only one leading quote is permitted.)

Here is the definition of the .SH macro:

.nr SH 0   \" initialize section number
.de SH
.sp 0.3i
.ft B
.nr SH \\n(SH+1   \" increment number
.ps \\n(PS-1   \" decrease PS
\\n(SH. \\$1   \" number. title
.ps \\n(PS   \" restore PS
.sp 0.3i
.ft R
..

The section number is kept in number register SH, which is incremented each time just before it is used. (A number register may have the same name as a macro without conflict but a string may not.)

We used \\n(SH instead of \n(SH and \\n(PS instead of \n(PS. If we had used \n(SH, we would get the value of the register at the time the macro was *defined*, not at the time it was *used*. If that's what you want, fine, but not here. Similarly, by using \\n(PS, we get the point size at the time the macro is called.

As an example that does not involve numbers, recall our .NP macro which had a

.tl ´left´center´right´

We could make these into parameters by using instead

    .tl *(LT´*(CT´*(RT´

so the title comes from three strings called LT, CT and RT.
If these are empty, then the title will be a blank line. Normally CT would be set with something like

    .ds CT - % -

to give just the page number between hyphens (as on the top
of this page), but a user could supply private definitions for
any of the strings.

12. Conditionals

Suppose we want the .SH macro to leave two extra
inches of space just before section 1, but nowhere else. The
cleanest way to do that is to test inside the .SH macro
whether the section number is 1, and add some space if it is.
The .if command provides the conditional test that we can
add just before the heading line is output:

    .if \\n(SH=1 .sp 2i   \" first section only

The condition after the .if can be any arithmetic or
logical expression. If the condition is logically true, or
arithmetically greater than zero, the rest of the line is treated
as if it were text — here a command. If the condition is
false, or zero or negative, the rest of the line is skipped.

It is possible to do more than one command if a condition is true. Suppose several operations are to be done
before section 1. One possibility is to define a macro .S1
and invoke it if we are about to do section 1 (as determined
by an .if).

    .de S1
    --- processing for section 1 ---
    ..
    .de SH
    ...
    .if \\n(SH=1 .S1
    ...
    ..

An alternate way is to use the extended form of the
.if, like this:

    .if \\n(SH=1 \{--- processing
    for section 1 ----\}

The braces \{ and \} must occur in the positions shown or
you will get unexpected extra lines in your output. **troff**
also provides an 'if-else' construction, which we will not go
into here.

A condition can be negated by preceding it with !;
we get the same effect as above (but less clearly) by using

    .if !\\n(SH>1 .S1

There are a handful of other conditions that can be
tested with .if. For example, is the current page even or
odd?

    .if o .tl ´odd page title´´- % -´
    .if e .tl ´- % -´´even page title´

gives facing pages different titles and page numbers on the
outside edge when used inside an appropriate new page
macro.

Two other conditions are t and n, which tell you
whether the formatter is **troff** or **nroff**.

    .if t troff stuff ...
    .if n nroff stuff ...

Finally, string comparisons may be made in an .if:

    .if ´string1´string2´ stuff

does 'stuff' if *string1* is the same as *string2*. The character
separating the strings can be anything reasonable that is not
contained in either string. The strings themselves can reference strings with *, arguments with \$, and so on.

13. Environments

As we mentioned, there is a potential problem when
going across a page boundary: parameters like size and font
for a page title may well be different from those in effect in
the text when the page boundary occurs. **troff** provides a
very general way to deal with this and similar situations.
There are three 'environments', each of which has independently settable versions of many of the parameters associated with processing, including size, font, line and title
lengths, fill/nofill mode, tab stops, and even partially collected lines. Thus the titling problem may be readily solved
by processing the main text in one environment and titles in
a separate one with its own suitable parameters.

The command .ev n shifts to environment n; n must
be 0, 1 or 2. The command .ev with no argument returns to
the previous environment. Environment names are maintained in a stack, so calls for different environments may be
nested and unwound consistently.

Suppose we say that the main text is processed in
environment 0, which is where **troff** begins by default.
Then we can modify the new page macro .NP to process
titles in environment 1 like this:

    .de NP
    .ev 1   \" shift to new environment
    .lt 6i   \" set parameters here
    .ft R
    .ps 10
    ... any other processing ...
    .ev   \" return to previous environment
    ..

It is also possible to initialize the parameters for an environment outside the .NP macro, but the version shown keeps all
the processing in one place and is thus easier to understand
and change.

22

14. Diversions

There are numerous occasions in page layout when it is necessary to store some text for a period of time without actually printing it. Footnotes are the most obvious example: the text of the footnote usually appears in the input well before the place on the page where it is to be printed is reached. In fact, the place where it is output normally depends on how big it is, which implies that there must be a way to process the footnote at least enough to decide its size without printing it.

troff provides a mechanism called a diversion for doing this processing. Any part of the output may be diverted into a macro instead of being printed, and then at some convenient time the macro may be put back into the input.

The command .di xy begins a diversion — all subsequent output is collected into the macro xy until the command .di with no arguments is encountered. This terminates the diversion. The processed text is available at any time thereafter, simply by giving the command

        .xy

The vertical size of the last finished diversion is contained in the built-in number register dn.

As a simple example, suppose we want to implement a 'keep-release' operation, so that text between the commands .KS and .KE will not be split across a page boundary (as for a figure or table). Clearly, when a .KS is encountered, we have to begin diverting the output so we can find out how big it is. Then when a .KE is seen, we decide whether the diverted text will fit on the current page, and print it either there if it fits, or at the top of the next page if it doesn't. So:

```
.de KS      \" start keep
.br         \" start fresh line
.ev 1       \" collect in new environment
.fi         \" make it filled text
.di XX      \" collect in XX
..

.de KE      \" end keep
.br         \" get last partial line
.di         \" end diversion
.if \\n(dn>=\\n(.t .bp  \" bp if doesn´t fit
.nf         \" bring it back in no-fill
.XX         \" text
.ev         \" return to normal environment
..
```

Recall that number register nl is the current position on the output page. Since output was being diverted, this remains at its value when the diversion started. dn is the amount of text in the diversion; .t (another built-in register) is the distance to the next trap, which we assume is at the bottom margin of the page. If the diversion is large enough to go past the trap, the .if is satisfied, and a .bp is issued. In either case, the diverted output is then brought back with .XX. It is essential to bring it back in no-fill mode so **troff** will do no

further processing on it.

This is not the most general keep-release, nor is it robust in the face of all conceivable inputs, but it would require more space than we have here to write it in full generality. This section is not intended to teach everything about diversions, but to sketch out enough that you can read existing macro packages with some comprehension.

Acknowledgements

I am deeply indebted to J. F. Ossanna, the author of **troff**, for his repeated patient explanations of fine points, and for his continuing willingness to adapt **troff** to make other uses easier. I am also grateful to Jim Blinn, Ted Dolotta, Doug McIlroy, Mike Lesk and Joel Sturman for helpful comments on this paper.

References

[1] J. F. Ossanna, *NROFF/TROFF* User's Manual, Bell Laboratories Computing Science Technical Report 54, 1976.

[2] B. W. Kernighan, *A System for Typesetting Mathematics — User's Guide (Second Edition),* Bell Laboratories Computing Science Technical Report 17, 1977.

[3] M. E. Lesk, *TBL — A Program to Format Tables,* Bell Laboratories Computing Science Technical Report 49, 1976.

[4] M. E. Lesk, *Typing Documents on UNIX,* Bell Laboratories, 1978.

[5] J. R. Mashey and D. W. Smith, *PWB/MM — Programmer's Workbench Memorandum Macros,* Bell Laboratories internal memorandum.

[6] Eric P. Allman, *Writing Papers with NROFF using -me,* University of California, Berkeley.

22

Appendix A: Phototypesetter Character Set (APS-5)

These characters exist in roman, italic, and bold. To get the one on the left, type the four-character name on the right.

	\\(ff	fi	\\(fi	fl	\\(fl		\\(Fi		\\(Fl
_	\\(ru	—	\\(em	¼	\\(14	½	\\(12	¾	\\(34
©	\\(co	°	\\(de	†	\\(dg	′	\\(fm	¢	\\(ct
®	\\(rg	•	\\(bu	□	\\(sq	-	\\(hy		

(In bold, \\(sq is ■.)

The following are special-font characters:

+	\\(pl	−	\\(mi	×	\\(mu	÷	\\(di
=	\\(eq	≡	\\(==	≥	\\(>=	≤	\\(<=
≠	\\(!=	±	\\(+-	¬	\\(no	/	\\(sl
~	\\(ap	≈	\\(~=	∝	\\(pt	∇	\\(gr
→	\\(->	←	\\(<-	↑	\\(ua	↓	\\(da
∫	\\(is	∂	\\(pd	∞	\\(if	√	\\(sr
⊂	\\(sb	⊃	\\(sp	∪	\\(cu	∩	\\(ca
⊆	\\(ib	⊇	\\(ip	∈	\\(mo	∅	\\(es
´	\\(aa	`	\\(ga	○	\\(ci	♥	\\(bs
§	\\(sc	‡	\\(dd	⇐	\\(lh	⇒	\\(rh
⌈	\\(lt	⌉	\\(rt	⌈	\\(lc	⌉	\\(rc
⌊	\\(lb	⌋	\\(rb	⌊	\\(lf	⌋	\\(rf
{	\\(lk	}	\\(rk	|	\\(bv	ς	\\(ts
|	\\(br	|	\\(or	_	\\(ul		\\(rn
*	\\(**						

These four characters also have two-character names. The ´ is the apostrophe on terminals; the ` is the other quote mark.

    ´   \\´   `   \\`   –   \\-   _   _

These characters exist only on the special font, but they do not have four-character names:

    "   {   }   <   >   ~   ^   \\   #   @

For greek, precede the roman letter by \\(* to get the corresponding greek; for example, \\(*a is α.

a b g d e z y h i k l m n c o p r s t u f x q w
α β γ δ ε ζ η θ ι κ λ μ ν ξ ο π ρ σ τ υ φ χ ψ ω

A B G D E Z Y H I K L M N C O P R S T U F X Q W
Α Β Γ Δ Ε Ζ Η Θ Ι Κ Λ Μ Ν Ξ Ο Π Ρ Σ Τ Υ Φ Χ Ψ Ω

22

Index

! (negating conditionals) 17
#$ (macro argument) 16
#*x, #(xy (invoke string macro) 14
#b (bracketing function) 13
#d (subscript) 11
#f (font change) 5
#h (horizontal motion) 12
#nx, #n(xy (number register) 15
#o (overstrike) 13
#s (size change) 3
#u (superscript) 11
#v (vertical motion) 11
#w (width function) 12
#z (zero motion) 13
'command instead of ^command 9
% (page number register) 10,15
^^ (end of macro definition) 7
^bp 9,10
^br (break) 9
^ce (center) 2
^ds (define string macro) 7,14
^fi (fill) 2
^ft (change font) 5
^if (conditional test) 16
^in (indent) 6
^lg (set ligatures) 5
^ll (line length) 6
^nf (nofill) 2
^nr (set number register) 14
^pn (page number) 10
^ps (change point size) 1,3
^sp (space) 4
^ss (set space size) 10
^ta (set tab stops) 11
^tc (set tab character) 10
^tl (title) 9
^tr (translate characters) 2,6
^ul (italicize) 6
^vs (vertical spacing) 3
^wh (when conditional) 9,17
accents 6,13
apostrophes 6
arithmetic 15
backslash 1,3,5,14,16
begin page (^bp) 9
block macros (B1,B2) 8
bold font (.ft B) 5
boustrophedon 12
bracketing function (##b) 13
break (^br) 9
break-causing commmands 9
centering (^ce) 2
changing fonts (^ft, #f) 5
changing macros 15
character set 4,5,19
character translation (^tr) 2,6
columnated output 10
commands 1
commands that cause break 9
conditionals (^if) 16
constant proportion 7
default break list 9
define macro (^de) 7
define string macro (^ds) 14
drawing lines 11
em 7,11
end of macro (^^) 7
even page test (e) 17
fill (^fi) 2
fonts (^ft) 4,19
Greek (#(*-) 5,19

hanging indent (^ti) 12
hints 20
horizontal motion (#h) 12
hp (horizontal position register) 15
hyphen 6
i scale indicator 4
indent (^in) 6
index 21
italic font (.ft I) 4
italicize (^ul) 6
legal point sizes 3
ligatures (ff,fi,fl; ^lg) 5
line length (^ll) 6
line spacing (^vs) 3
local motions (#u,#d,#v,#h,#w,#o,#z,#b) 11 ff
m scale indicator 7
machine units 4,12
macro arguments 15
macros 7
macros that change 15
multiple backslashes 14
negating conditionals (!) 17
new page macro (NP) 8
nl (current vertical position register) 15
nofill (^nf) 2
NROFF test (n) 17
nested quotes 12
number registers (^nr,#n) 14
numbered paragraphs 12
odd page test (o) 17
order of evaluation 14
overstrike (#o) 13
p scale indicator 3
page number register (%) 10
page numbers (^pn, ^bp) 10
paragraph macro (PG) 7
Paternoster 6
point size (^ps) 1,3
previous font (#fP, ^ft P) 5
previous point size (#s0,^ps) 3
quotes 6
relative change (±) 6
ROFF 1
ROFF header and footer 8
Roman font (.ft R) 4
scale indicator i 4
scale indicator m 7
scale indicator p 3
scale indicator u 12
scale indicators in arithmetic 15
section heading macro (SC) 15
set space size (^ss) 10
size _ see point size
space (^sp) 4
space between lines (^vs) 3
special characters (#(xx) 5,19
string macros (^ds,#*) 14
subscripts (#d) 11
superscripts (#u) 11
tab character (^tc) 11
tabs (^ta) 10
temporary indent (^ti) 7
titles (^tl) 8
translate (^tr) 2,6,12
TROFF examples 19
TROFF test (t) 17
truncating division 15
type faces _ see fonts
u scale indicator 12
underline (^ul) 6
valid point sizes 3
vertical motion (#v) 11

22

vertical position on page 9
vertical spacing (ˇvs) 3
when (ˇwh) 9,17
width function (#w) 12
width of digits 10
zero motion (#z) 13

22

A System for Typesetting Mathematics

Brian W. Kernighan and Lorinda L. Cherry

AT&T Bell Laboratories
Murray Hill, New Jersey 07974

ABSTRACT

This paper describes the design and implementation of a system for typesetting mathematics. The language has been designed to be easy to learn and to use by people (for example, secretaries and mathematical typists) who know neither mathematics nor typesetting. Experience indicates that the language can be learned in an hour or so, for it has few rules and fewer exceptions. For typical expressions, the size and font changes, positioning, line drawing, and the like necessary to print according to mathematical conventions are all done automatically. For example, the input

sum from i=0 to infinity x sub i = pi over 2

produces

$$\sum_{i=0}^{\infty} x_i = \frac{\pi}{2}$$

The syntax of the language is specified by a small context-free grammar; a compiler-compiler is used to make a compiler that translates this language into typesetting commands. Output may be produced on either a phototypesetter or on a terminal with forward and reverse half-line motions. The system interfaces directly with text formatting programs, so mixtures of text and mathematics may be handled simply.

This paper is a revision of a paper originally published in CACM, March, 1975.

1. Introduction

"Mathematics is known in the trade as *difficult, or penalty, copy* because it is slower, more difficult, and more expensive to set in type than any other kind of copy normally occurring in books and journals." [1]

One difficulty with mathematical text is the multiplicity of characters, sizes, and fonts. An expression such as

$$\lim_{x \to \pi/2} (\tan x)^{\sin 2x} = 1$$

requires an intimate mixture of roman, italic and greek letters, in three sizes, and a special character or two. ("Requires" is perhaps the wrong word, but mathematics has its own typographical conventions which are quite different from those of ordinary text.) Typesetting such an expression by traditional methods is still an essentially manual operation.

A second difficulty is the two dimensional character of mathematics, which the superscript and limits in the preceding example showed in its simplest form. This is carried further by

$$a_0 + \cfrac{b_1}{a_1 + \cfrac{b_2}{a_2 + \cfrac{b_3}{a_3 + \cdots}}}$$

and still further by

$$\int \frac{dx}{ae^{mx} - be^{-mx}} = \begin{cases} \dfrac{1}{2m\sqrt{ab}} \log \dfrac{\sqrt{a}\,e^{mx} - \sqrt{b}}{\sqrt{a}\,e^{mx} + \sqrt{b}} \\ \dfrac{1}{m\sqrt{ab}} \tanh^{-1}(\dfrac{\sqrt{a}}{\sqrt{b}} e^{mx}) \\ \dfrac{-1}{m\sqrt{ab}} \coth^{-1}(\dfrac{\sqrt{a}}{\sqrt{b}} e^{mx}) \end{cases}$$

These examples also show line-drawing, built-up characters like braces and radicals, and a spectrum of positioning problems. (Section 6 shows what a user has to type to produce these on our system.)

2. Photocomposition

Photocomposition techniques can be used to solve some of the problems of typesetting mathematics. A phototypesetter is a device which exposes a piece of photographic paper or film, placing characters wherever they are wanted. The Graphic Systems phototypesetter[2] on the UNIX operating system[3] works by shining light through a character stencil. The character is made the right size by lenses, and the light beam directed by fiber optics to the desired

23

place on a piece of photographic paper. The exposed paper is developed and typically used in some form of photo-offset reproduction.

On UNIX, the phototypesetter is driven by a formatting program called TROFF [4]. TROFF was designed for setting running text. It also provides all of the facilities that one needs for doing mathematics, such as arbitrary horizontal and vertical motions, line-drawing, size changing, but the syntax for describing these special operations is difficult to learn, and difficult even for experienced users to type correctly.

For this reason we decided to use TROFF as an "assembly language," by designing a language for describing mathematical expressions, and compiling it into TROFF.

3. Language Design

The fundamental principle upon which we based our language design is that the language should be easy to use by people (for example, secretaries) who know neither mathematics nor typesetting.

This principle implies several things. First, "normal" mathematical conventions about operator precedence, parentheses, and the like cannot be used, for to give special meaning to such characters means that the user has to understand what he or she is typing. Thus the language should not assume, for instance, that parentheses are always balanced, for they are not in the half-open interval $(a,b]$. Nor should it assume that that $\sqrt{a+b}$ can be replaced by $(a+b)^{1/2}$, or that $1/(1-x)$ is better written as $\frac{1}{1-x}$ (or vice versa).

Second, there should be relatively few rules, keywords, special symbols and operators, and the like. This keeps the language easy to learn and remember. Furthermore, there should be few exceptions to the rules that do exist: if something works in one situation, it should work everywhere. If a variable can have a subscript, then a subscript can have a subscript, and so on without limit.

Third, "standard" things should happen automatically. Someone who types "x=y+z+1" should get "$x=y+z+1$". Subscripts and superscripts should automatically be printed in an appropriately smaller size, with no special intervention. Fraction bars have to be made the right length and positioned at the right height. And so on. Indeed a mechanism for overriding default actions has to exist, but its application is the exception, not the rule.

We assume that the typist has a reasonable picture (a two-dimensional representation) of the desired final form, as might be handwritten by the author of a paper. We also assume that the input is typed on a computer terminal much like an ordinary typewriter. This implies an input alphabet of perhaps 100 characters, none of them special.

A secondary, but still important, goal in our design was that the system should be easy to implement, since neither of the authors had any desire to make a long-term project of it. Since our design was not firm, it was also necessary that the program be easy to change at any time.

To make the program easy to build and to change, and to guarantee regularity ("it should work everywhere"), the language is defined by a context-free grammar, described in Section 5. The compiler for the language was built using a compiler-compiler.

A priori, the grammar/compiler-compiler approach seemed the right thing to do. Our subsequent experience leads us to believe that any other course would have been folly. The original language was designed in a few days. Construction of a working system sufficient to try significant examples required perhaps a person-month. Since then, we have spent a modest amount of additional time over several years tuning, adding facilities, and occasionally changing the language as users make criticisms and suggestions.

We also decided quite early that we would let TROFF do our work for us whenever possible. TROFF is quite a powerful program, with a macro facility, text and arithmetic variables, numerical computation and testing, and conditional branching. Thus we have been able to avoid writing a lot of mundane but tricky software. For example, we store no text strings, but simply pass them on to TROFF. Thus we avoid having to write a storage management package. Furthermore, we have been able to isolate ourselves from most details of the particular device and character set currently in use. For example, we let TROFF compute the widths of all strings of characters; we need know nothing about them.

A third design goal is special to our environment. Since our program is only useful for typesetting mathematics, it is necessary that it interface cleanly with the underlying typesetting language for the benefit of users who want to set intermingled mathematics and text (the usual case). The standard mode of operation is that when a document is typed, mathematical expressions are input as part of the text, but marked by user settable delimiters. The program reads this input and treats as comments those things which are not mathematics, simply passing them through untouched. At the same time it converts the mathematical input into the necessary TROFF commands. The resulting ioutput is passed directly to TROFF where the comments and the mathematical parts both become text and/or TROFF commands.

4. The Language

We will not try to describe the language precisely here; interested readers may refer to the appendix for more details. Throughout this section, we will write expressions exactly as they are handed to the typesetting program (hereinafter called "EQN"), except that we won't show the delimiters that the user types to mark the beginning and end of the expression. The interface between EQN and TROFF is described at the end of this section.

As we said, typing x=y+z+1 should produce $x=y+z+1$, and indeed it does. Variables are made italic, operators and digits become roman, and normal spacings between letters and operators are altered slightly to give a more pleasing appearance.

Input is free-form. Spaces and new lines in the input are used by EQN to separate pieces of the input; they are not used to create space in the output. Thus

```
x   =   y
  + z + 1
```

also gives $x=y+z+1$. Free-form input is easier to type initially; subsequent editing is also easier, for an expression may be typed as many short lines.

Extra white space can be forced into the output by several characters of various sizes. A tilde "~" gives a space equal to the normal word spacing in text; a circumflex gives half this much, and a tab charcter spaces to the next tab stop.

Spaces (or tildes, etc.) also serve to delimit pieces of the input. For example, to get

$$f(t)=2\pi\int\sin(\omega t)dt$$

we write

```
f(t) = 2 pi int sin ( omega t )dt
```

Here spaces are *necessary* in the input to indicate that *sin, pi, int,* and *omega* are special, and potentially worth special treatment. EQN looks up each such string of characters in a table, and if appropriate gives it a translation. In this case, *pi* and *omega* become their greek equivalents, *int* becomes the integral sign (which must be moved down and enlarged so it looks "right"), and *sin* is made roman, following conventional mathematical practice. Parentheses, digits and operators are automatically made roman wherever found.

Fractions are specified with the keyword *over:*

```
a+b over c+d+e = 1
```

produces

$$\frac{a+b}{c+d+e}=1$$

Similarly, subscripts and superscripts are introduced by the keywords *sub* and *sup:*

$$x^2+y^2=z^2$$

is produced by

```
x sup 2 + y sup 2 = z sup 2
```

The spaces after the 2's are necessary to mark the end of the superscripts; similarly the keyword *sup* has to be marked off by spaces or some equivalent delimiter. The return to the proper baseline is automatic. Multiple levels of subscripts or superscripts are of course allowed: "x sup y sup z" is x^{y^z}. The construct "something *sub* something *sup* something" is recognized as a special case, so "x sub i sup 2" is x_i^2 instead of $x_i{}^2$.

More complicated expressions can now be formed with these primitives:

$$\frac{\partial^2 f}{\partial x^2}=\frac{x^2}{a^2}+\frac{y^2}{b^2}$$

is produced by

```
{partial sup 2 f} over {partial x sup 2} =
x sup 2 over a sup 2 + y sup 2 over b sup 2
```

Braces {} are used to group objects together; in this case they indicate unambiguously what goes over what on the left-hand side of the expression. The language defines the precedence of *sup* to be higher than that of *over,* so no braces are needed to get the correct association on the right side. Braces can always be used when in doubt about precedence.

The braces convention is an example of the power of using a recursive grammar to define the language. It is part of the language that if a construct can appear in some context, then *any expression* in braces can also occur in that context.

There is a *sqrt* operator for making square roots of the appropriate size: "sqrt a+b" produces $\sqrt{a+b}$, and

```
x = {-b +- sqrt{b sup 2 -4ac}} over 2a
```

is

$$x=\frac{-b\pm\sqrt{b^2-4ac}}{2a}$$

Since large radicals look poor on our typesetter, *sqrt* is not useful for tall expressions.

Limits on summations, integrals and similar constructions are specified with the keywords *from* and *to.* To get

$$\sum_{i=0}^{\infty}x_i\rightarrow 0$$

we need only type

```
sum from i=0 to inf x sub i -> 0
```

Centering and making the Σ big enough and the limits smaller are all automatic. The *from* and *to* parts are both optional, and the central part (e.g., the Σ) can in fact be anything:

```
lim from {x -> pi /2} ( tan~x) = inf
```

is

$$\lim_{x\rightarrow\pi/2}(\tan x)=\infty$$

Again, the braces indicate just what goes into the *from* part.

There is a facility for making braces, brackets, parentheses, and vertical bars of the right height, using the keywords *left* and *right:*

```
left [ x+y over 2a right ]~=~1
```

makes

$$\left[\frac{x+y}{2a}\right]=1$$

A *left* need not have a corresponding *right,* as we shall see in the next example. Any characters may follow *left* and *right,* but generally only various parentheses and bars are meaningful.

Big brackets, etc., are often used with another facility, called *piles,* which make vertical piles of objects. For example, to get

$$sign(x) \equiv \begin{cases} 1 & \text{if } x>0 \\ 0 & \text{if } x=0 \\ -1 & \text{if } x<0 \end{cases}$$

we can type

```
sign (x) ~==~ left {
   rpile {1 above 0 above −1}
   ~lpile {if above if above if}
   ~lpile {x>0 above x=0 above x<0}
```

The construction "left {" makes a left brace big enough to enclose the "rpile {...}", which is a right-justified pile of "above ... above ...". "lpile" makes a left-justified pile. There are also centered piles. Because of the recursive language definition, a pile can contain any number of elements; any element of a pile can of course contain piles.

Although EQN makes a valiant attempt to use the right sizes and fonts, there are times when the default assumptions are simply not what is wanted. For instance the italic *sign* in the previous example would conventionally be in roman. Slides and transparencies often require larger characters than normal text. Thus we also provide size and font changing commands: "size 12 bold {A~x~=~y}" will produce $\mathbf{A\ x = y}$. *Size* is followed by a number representing a character size in points. (One point is 1/72 inch; this paper is set in 9 point type.)

If necessary, an input string can be quoted in "...", which turns off grammatical significance, and any font or spacing changes that might otherwise be done on it. Thus we can say

```
lim~ roman "sup" ~x sub n = 0
```

to ensure that the supremum doesn't become a superscript:

$$\lim \sup x_n = 0$$

Diacritical marks, long a problem in traditional typesetting, are straightforward:

$$\dot{x} + \hat{x} + \tilde{y} + \hat{X} + \ddot{Y} = \overline{z+Z}$$

is made by typing

```
x dot under + x hat + y tilde
+ X hat + Y dotdot = z+Z bar
```

There are also facilities for globally changing default sizes and fonts, for example for making viewgraphs or for setting chemical equations. The language allows for matrices, and for lining up equations at the same horizontal position.

Finally, there is a definition facility, so a user can say

```
define name "..."
```

at any time in the document; henceforth, any occurrence of

the token "name" in an expression will be expanded into whatever was inside the double quotes in its definition. This lets users tailor the language to their own specifications, for it is quite possible to redefine keywords like *sup* or *over.* Section 6 shows an example of definitions.

The EQN preprocessor reads intermixed text and equations, and passes its output to TROFF. Since TROFF uses lines beginning with a period as control words (e.g., ".ce" means "center the next output line"), EQN uses the sequence ".EQ" to mark the beginning of an equation and ".EN" to mark the end. The ".EQ" and ".EN" are passed through to TROFF untouched, so they can also be used by a knowledgeable user to center equations, number them automatically, etc. By default, however, ".EQ" and ".EN" are simply ignored by TROFF, so by default equations are printed in-line.

".EQ" and ".EN" can be supplemented by TROFF commands as desired; for example, a centered display equation can be produced with the input:

```
.ce
.EQ
x sub i = y sub i ...
.EN
```

Since it is tedious to type ".EQ" and ".EN" around very short expressions (single letters, for instance), the user can also define two characters to serve as the left and right delimiters of expressions. These characters are recognized anywhere in subsequent text. For example if the left and right delimiters have both been set to "#", the input:

Let #x sub i#, #y# and #alpha# be positive

produces:

Let x_i, y and α be positive

Running a preprocessor is strikingly easy on UNIX. To typeset text stored in file "f", one issues the command:

```
eqn f| troff
```

The vertical bar connects the output of one process (EQN) to the input of another (TROFF).

5. Language Theory

The basic structure of the language is not a particularly original one. Equations are pictured as a set of "boxes," pieced together in various ways. For example, something with a subscript is just a box followed by another box moved downward and shrunk by an appropriate amount. A fraction is just a box centered above another box, at the right altitude, with a line of correct length drawn between them.

The grammar for the language is shown below. For purposes of exposition, we have collapsed some productions. In the original grammar, there are about 70 productions, but many of these are simple ones used only to guarantee that some keyword is recognized early enough in the parsing process. Symbols in capital letters are terminal symbols; lower case symbols are non-terminals, i.e., syntactic categories. The vertical bar | indicates an alternative; the brackets [ ] indicate optional material. A TEXT is a string of non-blank characters or any string inside double quotes; the other terminal symbols represent literal occurrences of the corresponding keyword.

eqn   : box | eqn box

box   : text
      | { eqn }
      | box OVER box
      | SQRT box
      | box SUB box | box SUP box
      | [L | C | R]PILE { list }
      | LEFT text eqn [RIGHT text]
      | box [FROM box] [TO box]
      | SIZE text box
      | [ROMAN | BOLD | ITALIC] box
      | box [HAT | BAR | DOT | DOTDOT | TILDE]
      | DEFINE text text

list : eqn | list ABOVE eqn

text : TEXT

The grammar makes it obvious why there are few exceptions. For example, the observation that something can be replaced by a more complicated something in braces is implicit in the productions:

eqn   : box | eqn box
box   : text | { eqn }

Anywhere a single character could be used, *any* legal construction can be used.

Clearly, our grammar is highly ambiguous. What, for instance, do we do with the input

a over b over c ?

Is it

{a over b} over c

or is it

a over {b over c} ?

To answer questions like this, the grammar is supplemented with a small set of rules that describe the precedence and associativity of operators. In particular, we specify (more or less arbitrarily) that *over* associates to the left, so the first alternative above is the one chosen. On the other hand, *sub* and *sup* bind to the right, because this is closer to standard mathematical practice. That is, we assume x^{a^*} is $x^{(a^*)}$, not $(x^a)^b$.

The precedence rules resolve the ambiguity in a construction like

a sup 2 over b

We define *sup* to have a higher precedence than *over*, so this construction is parsed as $\dfrac{a^2}{b}$ instead of $a^{\frac{2}{b}}$.

Naturally, a user can always force a particular parsing by placing braces around expressions.

The ambiguous grammar approach seems to be quite useful. The grammar we use is small enough to be easily understood, for it contains none of the productions that would be normally used for resolving ambiguity. Instead the supplemental information about precedence and associativity (also small enough to be understood) provides the compiler-compiler with the information it needs to make a fast, deterministic parser for the specific language we want. When the language is supplemented by the disambiguating rules, it is in fact LR(1) and thus easy to parse[5].

The output code is generated as the input is scanned. Any time a production of the grammar is recognized, (potentially) some TROFF commands are output. For example, when the lexical analyzer reports that it has found a TEXT (i.e., a string of contiguous characters), we have recognized the production:

text : TEXT

The translation of this is simple. We generate a local name for the string, then hand the name and the string to TROFF, and let TROFF perform the storage management. All we save is the name of the string, its height, and its baseline.

As another example, the translation associated with the production

box   : box OVER box

is:

Width of output box =
  slightly more than largest input width
Height of output box =
  slightly more than sum of input heights
Base of output box =
  slightly more than height of bottom input box
String describing output box =
  move down;
  move right enough to center bottom box;
  draw bottom box (i.e., copy string for bottom box);
  move up; move left enough to center top box;
  draw top box (i.e., copy string for top box);
  move down and left; draw line full width;
  return to proper base line.

Most of the other productions have equally simple semantic actions. Picturing the output as a set of properly placed boxes makes the right sequence of positioning commands quite obvious. The main difficulty is in finding the right numbers to use for esthetically pleasing positioning.

With a grammar, it is usually clear how to extend the language. For instance, one of our users suggested a TENSOR operator, to make constructions like

$$\underset{m\;\,n\;i}{\overset{\;\,k\;\,j}{l\;\mathbf{T}}}$$

Grammatically, this is easy: it is sufficient to add a production like

23

box   : TENSOR { list }

Semantically, we need only juggle the boxes to the right places.

6. Experience

There are really three aspects of interest—how well EQN sets mathematics, how well it satisfies its goal of being "easy to use," and how easy it was to build.

The first question is easily addressed. This entire paper has been set by the program. Readers can judge for themselves whether it is good enough for their purposes. One of our users commented that although the output is not as good as the best hand-set material, it is still better than average, and much better than the worst. In any case, who cares? Printed books cannot compete with the birds and flowers of illuminated manuscripts on esthetic grounds, either, but they have some clear economic advantages.

Some of the deficiencies in the output could be cleaned up with more work on our part. For example, we sometimes leave too much space between a roman letter and an italic one. If we were willing to keep track of the fonts involved, we could do this better more of the time.

Some other weaknesses are inherent in our output device. It is hard, for instance, to draw a line of an arbitrary length without getting a perceptible overstrike at one end.

As to ease of use, at the time of writing, the system has been used by two distinct groups. One user population consists of mathematicians, chemists, physicists, and computer scientists. Their typical reaction has been something like:

(1)   It's easy to write, although I make the following mistakes...

(2)   How do I do...?

(3)   It botches the following things.... Why don't you fix them?

(4)   You really need the following features...

The learning time is short. A few minutes gives the general flavor, and typing a page or two of a paper generally uncovers most of the misconceptions about how it works.

The second user group is much larger, the secretaries and mathematical typists who were the original target of the system. They tend to be enthusiastic converts. They find the language easy to learn (most are largely self-taught), and have little trouble producing the output they want. They are of course less critical of the esthetics of their output than users trained in mathematics. After a transition period, most find using a computer more interesting than a regular typewriter.

The main difficulty that users have seems to be remembering that a blank is a delimiter; even experienced users use blanks where they shouldn't and omit them when they are needed. A common instance is typing

f(x sub i)

which produces

$$f(x_{i)}$$

instead of

$$f(x_i)$$

Since the EQN language knows no mathematics, it cannot deduce that the right parenthesis is not part of the subscript.

The language is somewhat prolix, but this doesn't seem excessive considering how much is being done, and it is certainly more compact than the corresponding TROFF commands. For example, here is the source for the continued fraction expression in Section 1 of this paper:

```
a sub 0 + b sub 1 over
  {a sub 1 + b sub 2 over
    {a sub 2 + b sub 3 over
      {a sub 3 + ... }}}
```

This is the input for the large integral of Section 1; notice the use of definitions:

```
define emx "{e sup mx}"
define mab "{m sqrt ab}"
define sa "{sqrt a}"
define sb "{sqrt b}"
int dx over {a emx – be sup –mx} ˜=˜
left { lpile {
   1 over {2 mab} ˜log˜
      {sa emx – sb} over {sa emx + sb}
  above
   1 over mab ˜ tanh sup –1 ( sa over sb emx )
  above
   –1 over mab ˜ coth sup –1 ( sa over sb emx )
}
```

As to ease of construction, we have already mentioned that there are really only a few person-months invested. Much of this time has gone into two things—fine-tuning (what is the most esthetically pleasing space to use between the numerator and denominator of a fraction?), and changing things found deficient by our users (shouldn't a tilde be a delimiter?).

The program consists of a number of small, essentially unconnected modules for code generation, a simple lexical analyzer, a canned parser which we did not have to write, and some miscellany associated with input files and the macro facility. The program is now about 1600 lines of C [6], a high-level language reminiscent of BCPL. About 20 percent of these lines are "print" statements, generating the output code.

The semantic routines that generate the actual TROFF commands can be changed to accommodate other formatting languages and devices. For example, in less than 24 hours, one of us changed the entire semantic package to drive NROFF, a variant of TROFF, for typesetting mathematics on teletypewriter devices capable of reverse line motions. Since many potential users do not have access to a typesetter, but still have to type mathematics, this provides a way to get a typed version of the final output which is close enough for debugging purposes, and sometimes even for ultimate use.

7. Conclusions

We think we have shown that it is possible to do acceptably good typesetting of mathematics on a photo-typesetter, with an input language that is easy to learn and use and that satisfies many users' demands. Such a package can be implemented in short order, given a compiler-compiler and a decent typesetting program underneath.

Defining a language, and building a compiler for it with a compiler-compiler seems like the only sensible way to do business. Our experience with the use of a grammar and a compiler-compiler has been uniformly favorable. If we had written everything into code directly, we would have been locked into our original design. Furthermore, we would have never been sure where the exceptions and special cases were. But because we have a grammar, we can change our minds readily and still be reasonably sure that if a construction works in one place it will work everywhere.

Acknowledgements

We are deeply indebted to J. F. Ossanna, the author of TROFF, for his willingness to modify TROFF to make our task easier and for his continuous assistance during the development of our program. We are also grateful to A. V. Aho for help with language theory, to S. C. Johnson for aid with the compiler-compiler, and to our early users A. V. Aho, S. I. Feldman, S. C. Johnson, R. W. Hamming, and M. D. McIlroy for their constructive criticisms.

References

[1]   *A Manual of Style,* 12th Edition. University of Chicago Press, 1969. p 295.

[2]   *Model C/A/T Phototypesetter.* Graphic Systems, Inc., Hudson, N. H.

[3]   Ritchie, D. M., and Thompson, K. L., ''The UNIX time-sharing system.'' *Comm. ACM 17,* 7 (July 1974), 365-375.

[4]   Ossanna, J. F., TROFF User's Manual. Bell Laboratories Computing Science Technical Report 54, 1977.

[5]   Aho, A. V., and Johnson, S. C., ''LR Parsing.'' *Comp. Surv. 6,* 2 (June 1974), 99-124.

[6]   B. W. Kernighan and D. M. Ritchie, *The C Programming Language.* Prentice-Hall, Inc., 1978.

23

Typesetting Mathematics — User's Guide   (Second Edition)

Brian W. Kernighan and Lorinda L. Cherry

AT&T Bell Laboratories
Murray Hill, NJ

ABSTRACT

This is the user's guide for a system for typesetting mathematics, using the photo-typesetters on the UNIX® operating system.

Mathematical expressions are described in a language designed to be easy to use by people who know neither mathematics nor typesetting. Enough of the language to set in-line expressions like $\lim_{x \to \pi/2} (\tan x)^{\sin 2x} = 1$ or display equations like

$$G(z) = e^{\ln G(z)} = \exp\left(\sum_{k \geq 1} \frac{S_k z^k}{k}\right) = \prod_{k \geq 1} e^{S_k z^k / k}$$

$$= \left(1 + S_1 z + \frac{S_1^2 z^2}{2!} + \cdots\right)\left(1 + \frac{S_2 z^2}{2} + \frac{S_2^2 z^4}{2^2 \cdot 2!} + \cdots\right)\cdots$$

$$= \sum_{m \geq 0} \left(\sum_{\substack{k_1, k_2, \ldots, k_m \geq 0 \\ k_1 + 2k_2 + \cdots + mk_m = m}} \frac{S_1^{k_1}}{1^{k_1} k_1!} \frac{S_2^{k_2}}{2^{k_2} k_2!} \cdots \frac{S_m^{k_m}}{m^{k_m} k_m!} \right) z^m$$

can be learned in an hour or so.

The language interfaces directly with the phototypesetting language TROFF, so mathematical expressions can be embedded in the running text of a manuscript, and the entire document produced in one process. This user's guide is an example of its output.

The same language may be used with the UNIX formatter NROFF to set mathematical expressions on DASI and GSI terminals and Model 37 teletypes.

1. Introduction

EQN is a program for typesetting mathematics on the Graphics Systems phototypesetters on the UNIX operating system. The EQN language was designed to be easy to use by people who know neither mathematics nor typesetting. Thus EQN knows relatively little about mathematics. In particular, mathematical symbols like +, −, ×, parentheses, and so on have no special meanings. EQN is quite happy to set garbage (but it will look good).

EQN works as a preprocessor for the type-setter formatter, TROFF[1], so the normal mode of operation is to prepare a document with both mathematics and ordinary text interspersed, and let EQN set the mathematics while TROFF does the body of the text.

On UNIX, EQN will also produce mathematics on DASI and GSI terminals and on Model 37 teletypes. The input is identical, but you have to use the programs NEQN and NROFF instead of EQN and TROFF. Of course, some things won't look as good because terminals don't provide the variety of characters, sizes and fonts that a typesetter does, but the output is usually adequate for proof-reading.

To use EQN on UNIX,

```
eqn files | troff
```

24

2. Displayed Equations

To tell EQN where a mathematical expression begins and ends, we mark it with lines beginning .EQ and .EN. Thus if you type the lines

```
.EQ
x=y+z
.EN
```

your output will look like

$$x = y + z$$

The .EQ and .EN are copied through untouched; they are not otherwise processed by EQN. This means that you have to take care of things like centering, numbering, and so on yourself. The most common way is to use the TROFF and NROFF macro package package '−ms' developed by M. E. Lesk[3], which allows you to center, indent, left-justify and number equations.

With the '−ms' package, equations are centered by default. To left-justify an equation, use .EQ L instead of .EQ. To indent it, use .EQ I. Any of these can be followed by an arbitrary 'equation number' which will be placed at the right margin. For example, the input

```
.EQ I (3.1a)
x = f(y/2) + y/2
.EN
```

produces the output

$$x = f(y/2) + y/2 \qquad (3.1a)$$

There is also a shorthand notation so in-line expressions like π_i^2 can be entered without .EQ and .EN. We will talk about it in section 19.

3. Input spaces

Spaces and newlines within an expression are thrown away by EQN. (Normal text is left absolutely alone.) Thus between .EQ and .EN,

```
x=y+z
```

and

```
x = y + z
```

and

```
x   =   y
    + z
```

and so on all produce the same output

$$x = y + z$$

You should use spaces and newlines freely to make your input equations readable and easy to edit. In particular, very long lines are a bad idea, since they are often hard to fix if you make a mistake.

4. Output spaces

To force extra spaces into the *output,* use a tilde " ~ " for each space you want:

```
x~=~y~+~z
```

gives

$$x = y + z$$

You can also use a circumflex "^", which gives a space half the width of a tilde. It is mainly useful for fine-tuning. Tabs may also be used to position pieces of an expression, but the tab stops must be set by TROFF commands.

5. Symbols, Special Names, Greek

EQN knows some mathematical symbols, some mathematical names, and the Greek alphabet. For example,

```
x=2 pi int sin ( omega t)dt
```

produces

$$x = 2\pi \int \sin(\omega t)dt$$

Here the spaces in the input are **necessary** to tell EQN that *int, pi, sin* and *omega* are separate entities that should get special treatment. The *sin,* digit 2, and parentheses are set in roman type instead of italic; *pi* and *omega* are made Greek; and *int* becomes the integral sign.

When in doubt, leave spaces around separate parts of the input. A *very* common error is to type *f(pi)* without leaving spaces on both sides of the *pi.* As a result, EQN does not recognize *pi* as a special word, and it appears as $f(pi)$ instead of $f(\pi)$.

A complete list of EQN names appears in section 23. Knowledgeable users can also use TROFF four-character names for anything EQN doesn't know about.

6. Spaces, Again

The only way EQN can deduce that some sequence of letters might be special is if that sequence is separated from the letters on either side of it. This can be done by surrounding a special word by ordinary spaces (or tabs or newlines), as we did in the previous section.

24

You can also make special words stand out by surrounding them with tildes or circumflexes:

x~=~2~pi~int~sin~(~omega~t~)~dt

is much the same as the last example, except that the tildes not only separate the magic words like *sin, omega,* and so on, but also add extra spaces, one space per tilde:

$$x = 2\,\pi \int \sin (\omega\, t\,)\, dt$$

Special words can also be separated by braces { } and double quotes "...", which have special meanings that we will see soon.

7. Subscripts and Superscripts

Subscripts and superscripts are obtained with the words *sub* and *sup*.

x sup 2 + y sub k

gives

$$x^2 + y_k$$

EQN takes care of all the size changes and vertical motions needed to make the output look right. The words *sub* and *sup* must be surrounded by spaces; *x sub2* will give you *xsub2* instead of x_2. Furthermore, don't forget to leave a space (or a tilde, etc.) to mark the end of a subscript or superscript. A common error is to say something like

y = (x sup 2)+1

which causes

$$y = (x^{2)+1}$$

instead of the intended

$$y = (x^2) + 1$$

Subscripted subscripts and superscripted superscripts also work:

x sub i sub 1

is

$$x_{i_1}$$

A subscript and superscript on the same thing are printed one above the other if the subscript comes *first:*

x sub i sup 2

is

$$x_i^2$$

Other than this special case, *sub* and *sup* group to the right, so *x sup y sub z* means x^{y_z}, not $x^y{}_z$.

8. Braces for Grouping

Normally, the end of a subscript or superscript is marked simply by a blank (or tab or tilde, etc.) What if the subscript or superscript is something that has to be typed with blanks in it? In that case, you can use the braces { and } to mark the beginning and end of the subscript or superscript:

e sup {i omega t}

is

$$e^{i\omega t}$$

Rule: Braces can *always* be used to force EQN to treat something as a unit, or just to make your intent perfectly clear. Thus:

x sub {i sub 1} sup 2

is

$$x_{i_1}^2$$

with braces, but

x sub i sub 1 sup 2

is

$$x_{i_1^2}$$

which is rather different.

Braces can occur within braces if necessary:

e sup {i pi sup {rho +1}}

is

$$e^{i\pi^{\rho+1}}$$

The general rule is that anywhere you could use some single thing like *x,* you can use an arbitrarily complicated thing if you enclose it in braces. EQN will look after all the details of positioning it and making it the right size.

In all cases, make sure you have the right number of braces. Leaving one out or adding an extra will cause EQN to complain bitterly.

Occasionally you will have to print braces. To do this, enclose them in double quotes, like "{". Quoting is discussed in more detail in section 14.

24

9. Fractions

To make a fraction, use the word *over:*

a+b over 2c =1

gives

$$\frac{a+b}{2c} = 1$$

The line is made the right length and positioned automatically. Braces can be used to make clear what goes over what:

{alpha + beta} over {sin (x)}

is

$$\frac{\alpha + \beta}{\sin(x)}$$

What happens when there is both an *over* and a *sup* in the same expression? In such an apparently ambiguous case, EQN does the *sup* before the *over,* so

−b sup 2 over pi

is $\dfrac{-b^2}{\pi}$ instead of $-b^{\frac{2}{\pi}}$ The rules which decide which operation is done first in cases like this are summarized in section 23. When in doubt, however, *use braces* to make clear what goes with what.

10. Square Roots

To draw a square root, use *sqrt:*

sqrt a+b + 1 over sqrt {ax sup 2 +bx+c}

is

$$\sqrt{a+b} + \frac{1}{\sqrt{ax^2 + bx + c}}$$

Warning — square roots of tall quantities look lousy, because a root-sign big enough to cover the quantity is too dark and heavy:

sqrt {a sup 2 over b sub 2}

is

$$\sqrt{\frac{a^2}{b_2}}$$

Big square roots are generally better written as something to the power ½:

$$(a^2/b_2)^{\frac{1}{2}}$$

which is

(a sup 2 /b sub 2) sup half

11. Summation, Integral, Etc.

Summations, integrals, and similar constructions are easy:

sum from i=0 to {i= inf} x sup i

produces

$$\sum_{i=0}^{i=\infty} x^i$$

Notice that we used braces to indicate where the upper part $i = \infty$ begins and ends. No braces were necessary for the lower part $i = 0$, because it contained no blanks. The braces will never hurt, and if the *from* and *to* parts contain any blanks, you must use braces around them.

The *from* and *to* parts are both optional, but if both are used, they have to occur in that order.

Other useful characters can replace the *sum* in our example:

int   prod   union   inter

become, respectively,

$$\int \quad \Pi \quad \cup \quad \cap$$

Since the thing before the *from* can be anything, even something in braces, *from-to* can often be used in unexpected ways:

lim from {n −> inf} x sub n =0

is

$$\lim_{n->\infty} x_n = 0$$

12. Size and Font Changes

By default, equations are set in 10-point type (the same size as this guide), with standard mathematical conventions to determine what characters are in roman and what in italic. Although EQN makes a valiant attempt to use esthetically pleasing sizes and fonts, it is not perfect. To change sizes and fonts, use *size n* and *roman, italic, bold* and *fat.* Like *sub* and *sup,* size and font changes affect only the thing that follows them, and revert to the normal situation at the end of it. Thus

bold x y

is

$$\mathbf{x}y$$

and

$$\text{size 14 bold x = y +}$$
$$\text{size 14 \{alpha + beta\}}$$

gives

$$\mathbf{X} = y + \alpha + \beta$$

As always, you can use braces if you want to affect something more complicated than a single letter. For example, you can change the size of an entire equation by

$$\text{size 12 \{ ... \}}$$

Legal sizes which may follow *size* are 6, 7, 8, 9, 10, 11, 12, 14, 16, 18, 20, 22, 24, 28, 36. You can also change the size *by* a given amount; for example, you can say *size +2* to make it three two points bigger, or *size −3* to make it three points smaller. This has the advantage that you don't have to know what the current size is.

If you are using fonts other than roman, italic and bold, you can say *font X* where *X* is a one character TROFF name or number for the font. Since EQN is tuned for roman, italic and bold, other fonts may not give quite as good an appearance.

The *fat* operation takes the current font and widens it by overstriking: *fat grad* is ∇ and *fat {x sub i}* is x_i.

If an entire document is to be in a non-standard size or font, it is a severe nuisance to have to write out a size and font change for each equation. Accordingly, you can set a "global" size or font which thereafter affects all equations. At the beginning of any equation, you might say, for instance,

```
.EQ
gsize 16
gfont R
   ...
.EN
```

to set the size to 16 and the font to roman thereafter. In place of R, you can use any of the TROFF font names. The size after *gsize* can be a relative change with + or −.

Generally, *gsize* and *gfont* will appear at the beginning of a document but they can also appear thoughout a document: the global font and size can be changed as often as needed. For example, in a footnote‡ you will typically want the size of

‡Like this one, in which we have a few random

equations to match the size of the footnote text, which is two points smaller than the main text. Don't forget to reset the global size at the end of the footnote.

13. Diacritical Marks

To get funny marks on top of letters, there are several words:

x dot	$\dot{x}$
x dotdot	$\ddot{x}$
x hat	$\hat{x}$
x tilde	$\tilde{x}$
x vec	$\vec{x}$
x dyad	$\overleftrightarrow{x}$
x bar	$\bar{x}$
x under	$\underline{x}$

The diacritical mark is placed at the right height. The *bar* and *under* are made the right length for the entire construct, as in $\overline{x + y + z}$; other marks are centered.

14. Quoted Text

Any input entirely within quotes ("...") is not subject to any of the font changes and spacing adjustments normally done by the equation setter. This provides a way to do your own spacing and adjusting if needed:

$$\text{italic "sin(x)" + sin (x)}$$

is

$$sin(x) + \sin(x)$$

Quotes are also used to get braces and other EQN keywords printed:

$$\text{"\{ size alpha \}"}$$

is

$$\{ \ size \ alpha \ \}$$

and

$$\text{roman "\{ size alpha \}"}$$

is

$$\{ \ \text{size alpha} \ \}$$

The construction "" is often used as a place-holder when grammatically EQN needs something, but you don't actually want anything in your output. For example, to make ^{2}He, you can't just type *sup 2 roman He* because a *sup* has to be a

expressions like x_i and π^2. The sizes for these were set by the command *gsize −2*.

superscript *on* something. Thus you must say

    "" sup 2 roman He

To get a literal quote use "\"". TROFF characters like *bs* can appear unquoted, but more complicated things like horizontal and vertical motions with \h and \v should always be quoted. (If you've never heard of \h and \v, ignore this section.)

15. Lining Up Equations

Sometimes it's necessary to line up a series of equations at some horizontal position, often at an equals sign. This is done with two operations called *mark* and *lineup*.

The word *mark* may appear once at any place in an equation. It remembers the horizontal position where it appeared. Successive equations can contain one occurrence of the word *lineup*. The place where *lineup* appears is made to line up with the place marked by the previous *mark* if at all possible. Thus, for example, you can say

```
.EQ I
x+y mark = z
.EN
.EQ I
x lineup = 1
.EN
```

to produce

$$x + y = z$$

$$x = 1$$

For reasons too complicated to talk about, when you use EQN and '−ms', use either .EQ I or .EQ L. mark and *lineup* don't work with centered equations. Also bear in mind that *mark* doesn't look ahead;

    x mark =1
    ...
    x+y lineup =z

isn't going to work, because there isn't room for the *x+y* part after the *mark* remembers where the *x* is.

16. Big Brackets, Etc.

To get big brackets [ ], braces { }, parentheses ( ), and bars | | around things, use the *left* and *right* commands:

```
left { a over b + 1 right }
~=~ left ( c over d right )
+ left [ e right ]
```

is

$$\left\{ \frac{a}{b} + 1 \right\} = \left(\frac{c}{d} \right) + [e]$$

The resulting brackets are made big enough to cover whatever they enclose. Other characters can be used besides these, but the are not likely to look very good. One exception is the *floor* and *ceiling* characters:

```
left floor x over y right floor
<= left ceiling a over b right ceiling
```

produces

$$\left\lfloor \frac{x}{y} \right\rfloor \le \left\lceil \frac{a}{b} \right\rceil$$

Several warnings about brackets are in order. First, braces are typically bigger than brackets and parentheses, because they are made up of three, five, seven, etc., pieces, while brackets can be made up of two, three, etc. Second, big left and right parentheses often look poor, because the character set is poorly designed.

The *right* part may be omitted: a "left something" need not have a corresponding "right something". If the *right* part is omitted, put braces around the thing you want the left bracket to encompass. Otherwise, the resulting brackets may be too large.

If you want to omit the *left* part, things are more complicated, because technically you can't have a *right* without a corresponding *left*. Instead you have to say

    left "" ..... right)

for example. The *left* "" means a "left nothing". This satisfies the rules without hurting your output.

17. Piles

There is a general facility for making vertical piles of things; it comes in several flavors. For example:

```
A ~=~ left [
   pile { a above b above c }
   ~ pile { x above y above z }
right ]
```

will make

$$A = \begin{bmatrix} a & x \\ b & y \\ c & z \end{bmatrix}$$

The elements of the pile (there can be as many as you want) are centered one above another, at the right height for most purposes. The keyword *above* is used to separate the pieces; braces are used around the entire list. The elements of a pile can be as complicated as needed, even containing more piles.

Three other forms of pile exist: *lpile* makes a pile with the elements left-justified; *rpile* makes a right-justified pile; and *cpile* makes a centered pile, just like *pile.* The vertical spacing between the pieces is somewhat larger for *l-, r-* and *cpiles* than it is for ordinary piles.

```
roman sign (x)~=~
left {
   lpile {1 above 0 above −1}
   ~ lpile
   {if~x>0 above if~x=0 above if~x<0}
```

makes

$$\text{sign}(x) = \begin{cases} 1 & \text{if } x > 0 \\ 0 & \text{if } x = 0 \\ -1 & \text{if } x < 0 \end{cases}$$

Notice the left brace without a matching right one.

18. Matrices

It is also possible to make matrices. For example, to make a neat array like

$$\begin{matrix} x_i & x^2 \\ y_i & y^2 \end{matrix}$$

you have to type

```
matrix {
   ccol { x sub i above y sub i }
   ccol { x sup 2 above y sup 2 }
}
```

This produces a matrix with two centered columns. The elements of the columns are then listed just as for a pile, each element separated by the word *above.* You can also use *lcol* or *rcol* to left or right adjust columns. Each column can be separately adjusted, and there can be as many columns as you like.

The reason for using a matrix instead of two adjacent piles, by the way, is that if the elements of the piles don't all have the same height,

they won't line up properly. A matrix forces them to line up, because it looks at the entire structure before deciding what spacing to use.

A word of warning about matrices — *each column must have the same number of elements in it.* The world will end if you get this wrong.

19. Shorthand for In-line Equations

In a mathematical document, it is necessary to follow mathematical conventions not just in display equations, but also in the body of the text, for example by making variable names like x italic. Although this could be done by surrounding the appropriate parts with .EQ and .EN, the continual repetition of .EQ and .EN is a nuisance. Furthermore, with '−ms', .EQ and .EN imply a displayed equation.

EQN provides a shorthand for short in-line expressions. You can define two characters to mark the left and right ends of an in-line equation, and then type expressions right in the middle of text lines. To set both the left and right characters to dollar signs, for example, add to the beginning of your document the three lines

```
.EQ
delim $$
.EN
```

Having done this, you can then say things like

Let $alpha sub i$ be the primary variable, and let $beta$ be zero. Then we can show that $x sub 1$ is $>=0$.

This works as you might expect — spaces, newlines, and so on are significant in the text, but not in the equation part itself. Multiple equations can occur in a single input line.

Enough room is left before and after a line that contains in-line expressions that something like $\sum_{i=1}^{n} x_i$ does not interfere with the lines surrounding it.

To turn off the delimiters,

```
.EQ
delim off
.EN
```

Warning: don't use braces, tildes, circumflexes, or double quotes as delimiters — chaos will result.

20. Definitions

EQN provides a facility so you can give a frequently-used string of characters a name, and

24

thereafter just type the name instead of the whole string. For example, if the sequence

x sub i sub 1 + y sub i sub 1

appears repeatedly throughout a paper, you can save re-typing it each time by defining it like this:

define xy 'x sub i sub 1 + y sub i sub 1'

This makes *xy* a shorthand for whatever characters occur between the single quotes in the definition. You can use any character instead of quote to mark the ends of the definition, so long as it doesn't appear inside the definition.

Now you can use *xy* like this:

.EQ
f(x) = xy ...
.EN

and so on. Each occurrence of *xy* will expand into what it was defined as. Be careful to leave spaces or their equivalent around the name when you actually use it, so EQN will be able to identify it as special.

There are several things to watch out for. First, although definitions can use previous definitions, as in

.EQ
define xi ' x sub i '
define xi1 ' xi sub 1 '
.EN

don't define something in terms of itself' A favorite error is to say

define X ' roman X '

This is a guaranteed disaster, since X *is* now defined in terms of itself. If you say

define X ' roman "X" '

however, the quotes protect the second X, and everything works fine.

EQN keywords can be redefined. You can make / mean *over* by saying

define / ' over '

or redefine *over* as / with

define over ' / '

If you need different things to print on a terminal and on the typesetter, it is sometimes worth defining a symbol differently in NEQN and EQN. This can be done with *ndefine* and *tdefine*. A definition made with *ndefine* only takes effect if you

are running NEQN; if you use *tdefine,* the definition only applies for EQN. Names defined with plain *define* apply to both EQN and NEQN.

21. Local Motions

Although EQN tries to get most things at the right place on the paper, it isn't perfect, and occasionally you will need to tune the output to make it just right. Small extra horizontal spaces can be obtained with tilde and circumflex. You can also say *back n* and *fwd n* to move small amounts horizontally. *n* is how far to move in 1/100's of an em (an em is about the width of the letter 'm'.) Thus *back 50* moves back about half the width of an m. Similarly you can move things up or down with *up n* and *down n.* As with *sub* or *sup,* the local motions affect the next thing in the input, and this can be something arbitrarily complicated if it is enclosed in braces.

22. A Large Example

Here is the complete source for the three display equations in the abstract of this guide.

```
.EQ I
G(z)~mark =~ e sup { ln ~ G(z) }
~=~ exp left (
sum from k>=1 {S sub k z sup k} over k right )
~=~ prod from k>=1 e sup {S sub k z sup k /k}
.EN
.EQ I
lineup = left ( 1 + S sub 1 z +
{ S sub 1 sup 2 z sup 2 } over 2! + ... right )
left ( 1+ { S sub 2 z sup 2 } over 2
+ { S sub 2 sup 2 z sup 4 } over { 2 sup 2 cdot 2! }
+ ... right ) ...
.EN
.EQ I
lineup =  sum from m>=0 left (
sum from
pile { k sub 1 ,k sub 2 ,..., k sub m  >=0
above
k sub 1 +2k sub 2 + ... +mk sub m =m}
{ S sub 1 sup {k sub 1} } over {1 sup k sub 1 k sub 1 ! } ~
{ S sub 2 sup {k sub 2} } over {2 sup k sub 2 k sub 2 ! } ~
...
{ S sub m sup {k sub m} } over {m sup k sub m k sub m ! }
right ) z sup m
.EN
```

23. Keywords, Precedences, Etc.

If you don't use braces, EQN will do operations in the order shown in this list.

24

dyad vec under bar tilde hat dot dotdot
fwd back down up
fat roman italic bold size
sub sup sqrt over
from to

These operations group to the left:

over sqrt left right

All others group to the right.

Digits, parentheses, brackets, punctuation marks, and these mathematical words are converted to Roman font when encountered:

sin cos tan sinh cosh tanh arc
max min lim log ln exp
Re Im and if for det

These character sequences are recognized and translated as shown.

>=	$\geq$
<=	$\leq$
==	$\equiv$
!=	$\neq$
+-	$\pm$
->	$\rightarrow$
<-	$\leftarrow$
<<	$\ll$
>>	$\gg$
inf	∞
partial	∂
half	$\frac{1}{2}$
prime	$\prime$
approx	$\approx$
nothing	
cdot	$\cdot$
times	$\times$
del	∇
grad	∇
...	$\cdots$
,...,	$,\cdots,$
sum	Σ
int	$\int$
prod	Π
union	$\cup$
inter	$\cap$

To obtain Greek letters, simply spell them out in whatever case you want:

DELTA	Δ	iota	ι
GAMMA	Γ	kappa	κ
LAMBDA	Λ	lambda	λ

OMEGA	Ω	mu	μ
PHI	Φ	nu	ν
PI	Π	omega	ω
PSI	Ψ	omicron	o
SIGMA	Σ	phi	ϕ
THETA	Θ	pi	π
UPSILON	Υ	psi	ψ
XI	Ξ	rho	ρ
alpha	α	sigma	σ
beta	β	tau	τ
chi	χ	theta	θ
delta	δ	upsilon	υ
epsilon	ε	xi	ξ
eta	η	zeta	ζ
gamma	γ		

These are all the words known to EQN (except for characters with names), together with the section where they are discussed.

above	17, 18	lpile	17
back	21	mark	15
bar	13	matrix	18
bold	12	ndefine	20
ccol	18	over	9
col	18	pile	17
cpile	17	rcol	18
define	20	right	16
delim	19	roman	12
dot	13	rpile	17
dotdot	13	size	12
down	21	sqrt	10
dyad	13	sub	7
fat	12	sup	7
font	12	tdefine	20
from	11	tilde	13
fwd	21	to	11
gfont	12	under	13
gsize	12	up	21
hat	13	vec	13
italic	12	~, ^	4, 6
lcol	18	{ }	8
left	16	"..."	8, 14
lineup	15		

24. Troubleshooting

If you make a mistake in an equation, like leaving out a brace (very common) or having one too many (very common) or having a *sup* with nothing before it (common), EQN will tell you with the message

24

syntax error between lines x and y, file z

where *x* and *y* are approximately the lines between which the trouble occurred, and *z* is the name of the file in question. The line numbers are approximate — look nearby as well. There are also self-explanatory messages that arise if you leave out a quote or try to run EQN on a non-existent file.

If you want to check a document before actually printing it (on UNIX only),

    eqn files >/dev/null

will throw away the output but print the messages.

If you use something like dollar signs as delimiters, it is easy to leave one out. This causes very strange troubles. The program *checkeq* checks for misplaced or missing dollar signs and similar troubles.

In-line equations can only be so big because of an internal buffer in TROFF. If you get a message "word overflow", you have exceeded this limit. If you print the equation as a displayed equation this message will usually go away. The message "line overflow" indicates you have exceeded an even bigger buffer. The only cure for this is to break the equation into two separate ones.

On a related topic, EQN does not break equations by itself — you must split long equations up across multiple lines by yourself, marking each by a separate .EQ ... .EN sequence. EQN does warn about equations that are too long to fit on one line.

25. Use on UNIX

To print a document that contains mathematics on the UNIX typesetter,

    eqn files | troff

If there are any TROFF options, they go after the TROFF part of the command. For example,

    eqn files | troff −ms

A compatible version of EQN can be used on devices like teletypes and DASI and GSI terminals which have half-line forward and reverse capabilities. To print equations on a Model 37 teletype, for example, use

    neqn files | nroff

The language for equations recognized by NEQN is identical to that of EQN, although of course the output is more restricted.

To use a GSI or DASI terminal as the output device,

    neqn files | nroff −T*x*

where *x* is the terminal type you are using, such as *300* or *300S*.

EQN and NEQN can be used with the TBL program[2] for setting tables that contain mathematics. Use TBL before [N]EQN, like this:

    tbl files | eqn | troff
    tbl files | neqn | nroff

26. Acknowledgments

We are deeply indebted to J. F. Ossanna, the author of TROFF, for his willingness to extend TROFF to make our task easier, and for his continuous assistance during the development and evolution of EQN. We are also grateful to A. V. Aho for advice on language design, to S. C. Johnson for assistance with the YACC compiler-compiler, and to all the EQN users who have made helpful suggestions and criticisms.

References

[1] J. F. Ossanna, "NROFF/TROFF User's Manual", Bell Laboratories Computing Science Technical Report #54, 1976.

[2] M. E. Lesk, "Typing Documents on UNIX", Bell Laboratories, 1976.

[3] M. E. Lesk, "TBL — A Program for Setting Tables", Bell Laboratories Computing Science Technical Report #49, 1976.

Tbl — A Program to Format Tables

M. E. Lesk

AT&T Bell Laboratories
Murray Hill, Nwe Jersey 07974

ABSTRACT

Tbl is a document formatting preprocessor for *troff* or *nroff* which makes even fairly complex tables easy to specify and enter. It is available on the UNIX® system and on Honeywell 6000 GCOS. Tables are made up of columns which may be independently centered, right-adjusted, left-adjusted, or aligned by decimal points. Headings may be placed over single columns or groups of columns. A table entry may contain equations, or may consist of several rows of text. Horizontal or vertical lines may be drawn as desired in the table, and any table or element may be enclosed in a box. For example:

1970 Federal Budget Transfers (in billions of dollars)			
State	Taxes collected	Money spent	Net
New York	22.91	21.35	−1.56
New Jersey	8.33	6.96	−1.37
Connecticut	4.12	3.10	−1.02
Maine	0.74	0.67	−0.07
California	22.29	22.42	+0.13
New Mexico	0.70	1.49	+0.79
Georgia	3.30	4.28	+0.98
Mississippi	1.15	2.32	+1.17
Texas	9.33	11.13	+1.80

Introduction.

Tbl turns a simple description of a table into a *troff* or *nroff* [1] program (list of commands) that prints the table. *Tbl* may be used on the UNIX [2] system and on the Honeywell 6000 GCOS system. It attempts to isolate a portion of a job that it can successfully handle and leave the remainder for other programs. Thus *tbl* may be used with the equation formatting program *eqn* [3] or various layout macro packages [4,5,6], but does not duplicate their functions.

This memorandum is divided into two parts. First we give the rules for preparing *tbl* input; then some examples are shown. The description of rules is precise but technical, and the beginning user may prefer to read the examples first, as they show some common table arrangements. A section explaining how to invoke *tbl* precedes the examples. To avoid repetition, henceforth read *troff* as *"troff or nroff."*

The input to *tbl* is text for a document, with tables preceded by a ".TS" (table start) command and followed by a ".TE" (table end) command. *Tbl* processes the tables, generating *troff* formatting commands, and leaves the remainder of the text unchanged. The ".TS" and ".TE" lines are copied, too, so that *troff* page layout macros (such as the memo formatting macros [4]) can use these lines to delimit and place tables as they see fit. In particular, any arguments on the ".TS" or ".TE" lines are copied but otherwise ignored, and may be used by document layout macro commands.

25

The format of the input is as follows:

```
text
.TS
table
.TE
text
.TS
table
.TE
text
. . .
```

where the format of each table is as follows:

```
.TS
options ;
format .
data
.TE
```

Each table is independent, and must contain formatting information followed by the data to be entered in the table. The formatting information, which describes the individual columns and rows of the table, may be preceded by a few options that affect the entire table. A detailed description of tables is given in the next section.

Input commands.

As indicated above, a table contains, first, global options, then a format section describing the layout of the table entries, and then the data to be printed. The format and data are always required, but not the options. The various parts of the table are entered as follows:

1) OPTIONS. There may be a single line of options affecting the whole table. If present, this line must follow the .TS line immediately and must contain a list of option names separated by spaces, tabs, or commas, and must be terminated by a semicolon. The allowable options are:

center	— center the table (default is left-adjust);
expand	— make the table as wide as the current line length;
box	— enclose the table in a box;
allbox	— enclose each item in the table in a box;
doublebox	— enclose the table in two boxes;
tab (x)	— use x instead of tab to separate data items.
linesize (n)	— set lines or rules (e.g. from **box**) in n point type;
delim (xy)	— recognize x and y as the *eqn* delimiters.

The *tbl* program tries to keep boxed tables on one page by issuing appropriate "need" (*.ne*) commands. These requests are calculated from the number of lines in the tables, and if there are spacing commands embedded in the input, these requests may be inaccurate; use normal *troff* procedures, such as keep-release macros, in that case. The user who must have a multi-page boxed table should use macros designed for this purpose, as explained below under 'Usage.'

2) FORMAT. The format section of the table specifies the layout of the columns. Each line in this section corresponds to one line of the table (except that the last line corresponds to all following lines up to the next .T&, if any — see below), and each line contains a key-letter for each column of the table. It is good practice to separate the key letters for each column by spaces or tabs. Each key-letter is one of the following:

L or **l**	to indicate a left-adjusted column entry;
R or **r**	to indicate a right-adjusted column entry;
C or **c**	to indicate a centered column entry;
N or **n**	to indicate a numerical column entry, to be aligned with other numerical entries so that the units digits of numbers line up;
A or **a**	to indicate an alphabetic subcolumn; all corresponding entries are aligned on the left, and positioned so that the widest is centered within the column (see example on page 12);
S ori **s**	to indicate a spanned heading, i.e. to indicate that the entry from the previous column continues across this column (not allowed for the first column, obviously); or
^	to indicate a vertically spanned heading, i.e. to indicate that the entry from the previous row continues down through this row. (Not allowed for the first row of the table, obviously).

When numerical alignment is specified, a location for the decimal point is sought. The rightmost dot (.) adjacent to a digit is used as a decimal point; if there is no dot adjoining a digit, the rightmost digit is used as a units digit; if no alignment is indicated, the item is centered in the column. However, the special non-printing character string \& may be used to override unconditionally dots and digits, or to align alphabetic data; this string lines up where a dot normally would, and then disappears from the final output. In the example below, the items shown at the left will be aligned (in a numerical column) as shown on the right:

```
13              13
4.2             4.2
26.4.12         26.4.12
abc             abc
abc\&           abc
43\&3.22        433.22
749.12          749.12
```

Note: If numerical data are used in the same column with wider **L** or **r** type table entries, the widest *number* is centered relative to the wider **L** or **r** items (**L** is used instead of **l** for readability; they have the same meaning as key-letters). Alignment within the numerical items is preserved. This is similar to the behavior of **a** type data, as explained above. However, alphabetic subcolumns (requested by the **a** key-letter) are always slightly indented relative to **L** items; if necessary, the column width is increased to force this. This is not true for **n** type entries.

Warning: the **n** and **a** items should not be used in the same column.

For readability, the key-letters describing each column should be separated by spaces. The end of the format section is indicated by a period. The layout of the key-letters in the format section resembles the layout of the actual data in the table. Thus a simple format might appear as:

```
c s s
l n n .
```

which specifies a table of three columns. The first line of the table contains a heading centered across all three columns; each remaining line contains a left-adjusted item in the first column followed by two columns of numerical data. A sample table in this format might be:

	Overall title	
Item-a	34.22	9.1
Item-b	12.65	.02
Items: c,d,e	23	5.8
Total	69.87	14.92

There are some additional features of the key-letter system:

25

Horizontal lines

— A key-letter may be replaced by '_' (underscore) to indicate a horizontal line in place of the corresponding column entry, or by '=' to indicate a double horizontal line. If an adjacent column contains a horizontal line, or if there are vertical lines adjoining this column, this horizontal line is extended to meet the nearby lines. If any data entry is provided for this column, it is ignored and a warning message is printed.

Vertical lines

— A vertical bar may be placed between column key-letters. This will cause a vertical line between the corresponding columns of the table. A vertical bar to the left of the first key-letter or to the right of the last one produces a line at the edge of the table. If two vertical bars appear between key-letters, a double vertical line is drawn.

Space between columns

— A number may follow the key-letter. This indicates the amount of separation between this column and the next column. The number normally specifies the separation in *ens* (one en is about the width of the letter 'n').* If the "expand" option is used, then these numbers are multiplied by a constant such that the table is as wide as the current line length. The default column separation number is 3. If the separation is changed the worst case (largest space requested) governs.

Vertical spanning

— Normally, vertically spanned items extending over several rows of the table are centered in their vertical range. If a key-letter is followed by **t** or **T**, any corresponding vertically spanned item will begin at the top line of its range.

Font changes

— A key-letter may be followed by a string containing a font name or number preceded by the letter **f** or **F**. This indicates that the corresponding column should be in a different font from the default font (usually Roman). All font names are one or two letters; a one-letter font name should be separated from whatever follows by a space or tab. The single letters **B**, **b**, **I**, and **i** are shorter synonyms for **fB** and **fI**. Font change commands given with the table entries override these specifications.

Point size changes

— A key-letter may be followed by the letter **p** or **P** and a number to indicate the point size of the corresponding table entries. The number may be a signed digit, in which case it is taken as an increment or decrement from the current point size. If both a point size and a column separation value are given, one or more blanks must separate them.

Vertical spacing changes

— A key-letter may be followed by the letter **v** or **V** and a number to indicate the vertical line spacing to be used within a multi-line corresponding table entry. The number may be a signed digit, in which case it is taken as an increment or decrement from the current vertical spacing. A column separation value must be separated by blanks or some other specification from a vertical spacing request. This request has no effect unless the corresponding table entry is a text block (see below).

Column width indication

— A key-letter may be followed by the letter **w** or **W** and a width value in parentheses. This width is used as a minimum column width. If the largest element in the column is not as wide as the width value given after the **w**, the largest element is assumed to be that wide. If the largest element in the column is wider than the specified value, its width is used. The width is also used as a default line length for included text blocks. Normal *troff* units can be used to scale the width value; if none are used, the default is ens. If the width specification is a unitless integer the parentheses may be omitted. If the width value is changed in a column, the *last* one given controls.

---

* More precisely, an en is a number of points (1 point = 1/72 inch) equal to half the current type size.

Equal width columns

— A key-letter may be followed by the letter **e** or **E** to indicate equal width columns. All columns whose key-letters are followed by **e** or **E** are made the same width. This permits the user to get a group of regularly spaced columns.

Note:

The order of the above features is immaterial; they need not be separated by spaces, except as indicated above to avoid ambiguities involving point size and font changes. Thus a numerical column entry in italic font and 12 point type with a minimum width of 2.5 inches and separated by 6 ens from the next column could be specified as

np12w(2.5i)fI 6

Alternative notation

— Instead of listing the format of successive lines of a table on consecutive lines of the format section, successive line formats may be given on the same line, separated by commas, so that the format for the example above might have been written:

c s s, l n n .

Default

— Column descriptors missing from the end of a format line are assumed to be **L**. The longest line in the format section, however, defines the number of columns in the table; extra columns in the data are ignored silently.

3)   DATA. The data for the table are typed after the format. Normally, each table line is typed as one line of data. Very long input lines can be broken: any line whose last character is \ is combined with the following line (and the \ vanishes). The data for different columns (the table entries) are separated by tabs, or by whatever character has been specified in the option *tabs* option. There are a few special cases:

Troff commands within tables

— An input line beginning with a '.' followed by anything but a number is assumed to be a command to *troff* and is passed through unchanged, retaining its position in the table. So, for example, space within a table may be produced by ".sp" commands in the data.

Full width horizontal lines

— An input *line* containing only the character _ (underscore) or = (equal sign) is taken to be a single or double line, respectively, extending the full width of the *table.*

Single column horizontal lines

— An input table *entry* containing only the character _ or = is taken to be a single or double line extending the full width of the *column.* Such lines are extended to meet horizontal or vertical lines adjoining this column. To obtain these characters explicitly in a column, either precede them by \& or follow them by a space before the usual tab or newline.

Short horizontal lines

— An input table *entry* containing only the string _ is taken to be a single line as wide as the contents of the column. It is not extended to meet adjoining lines.

Vertically spanned items

— An input table entry containing only the character string \^ indicates that the table entry immediately above spans downward over this row. It is equivalent to a table format key-letter of '^'.

Text blocks

— In order to include a block of text as a table entry, precede it by **T{** and follow it by **T}**. Thus the sequence

. . . **T{**
block of
text
T} . . .

is the way to enter, as a single entry in the table, something that cannot conveniently be typed

25

as a simple string between tabs. Note that the **T}** end delimiter must begin a line; additional columns of data may follow after a tab on the same line. See the example on page 11 for an illustration of included text blocks in a table. If more than twenty or thirty text blocks are used in a table, various limits in the *troff* program are likely to be exceeded, producing diagnostics such as 'too many string/macro names' or 'too many number registers.'

Text blocks are pulled out from the table, processed separately by *troff,* and replaced in the table as a solid block. If no line length is specified in the *block of text* itself, or in the table format, the default is to use $L \times C/(N+1)$ where L is the current line length, C is the number of table columns spanned by the text, and N is the total number of columns in the table. The other parameters (point size, font, etc.) used in setting the *block of text* are those in effect at the beginning of the table (including the effect of the ".TS" macro) and any table format specifications of size, spacing and font, using the **p**, **v** and **f** modifiers to the column key-letters. Commands within the text block itself are also recognized, of course. However, *troff* commands within the table data but not within the text block do not affect that block.

Warnings:

— Although any number of lines may be present in a table, only the first 200 lines are used in calculating the widths of the various columns. A multi-page table, of course, may be arranged as several single-page tables if this proves to be a problem. Other difficulties with formatting may arise because, in the calculation of column widths all table entries are assumed to be in the font and size being used when the ".TS" command was encountered, except for font and size changes indicated (a) in the table format section and (b) within the table data (as in the entry \s+3\fIdata\fP\s0). Therefore, although arbitrary *troff* requests may be sprinkled in a table, care must be taken to avoid confusing the width calculations; use requests such as '.ps' with care.

4)   ADDITIONAL COMMAND LINES. If the format of a table must be changed after many similar lines, as with sub-headings or summarizations, the ".T&" (table continue) command can be used to change column parameters. The outline of such a table input is:

```
.TS
options ;
format .
data
. . .
.T&
format .
data
.T&
format .
data
.TE
```

as in the examples on pages 10 and 13. Using this procedure, each table line can be close to its corresponding format line.

Warning: it is not possible to change the number of columns, the space between columns, the global options such as *box,* or the selection of columns to be made equal width.

Usage.

On UNIX, *tbl* can be run on a simple table with the command

    tbl input-file I troff

but for more complicated use, where there are several input files, and they contain equations and *ms* memorandum layout commands as well as tables, the normal command would be

25

    tbl file-1 file-2 . . . I eqn I troff −ms

and, of course, the usual options may be used on the *troff* and *eqn* commands. The usage for *nroff* is similar to that for *troff,* but only TELETYPE® Model 37 and Diablo-mechanism (DASI or GSI) terminals can print boxed tables directly.

    For the convenience of users employing line printers without adequate driving tables or post-filters, there is a special −*TX* command line option to *tbl* which produces output that does not have fractional line motions in it. The only other command line options recognized by *tbl* are −*ms* and −*mm* which are turned into commands to fetch the corresponding macro files; usually it is more convenient to place these arguments on the *troff* part of the command line, but they are accepted by *tbl* as well.

    Note that when *eqn* and *tbl* are used together on the same file *tbl* should be used first. If there are no equations within tables, either order works, but it is usually faster to run *tbl* first, since *eqn* normally produces a larger expansion of the input than *tbl.* However, if there are equations within tables (using the *delim* mechanism in *eqn*), *tbl* must be first or the output will be scrambled. Users must also beware of using equations in **n**-style columns; this is nearly always wrong, since *tbl* attempts to split numerical format items into two parts and this is not possible with equations. The user can defend against this by giving the *delim(xx)* table option; this prevents splitting of numerical columns within the delimiters. For example, if the *eqn* delimiters are *$$*, giving *delim($$)* a numerical column such as "1245 $+- 16$" will be divided after 1245, not after 16.

    Tbl limits tables to twenty columns; however, use of more than 16 numerical columns may fail because of limits in *troff,* producing the 'too many number registers' message. *Troff* number registers used by *tbl* must be avoided by the user within tables; these include two-digit names from 31 to 99, and names of the forms #*x*, *x*+, *x* I, ^*x*, and *x*−, where *x* is any lower case letter. The names ##, #−, and #^ are also used in certain circumstances. To conserve number register names, the **n** and **a** formats share a register; hence the restriction above that they may not be used in the same column.

    For aid in writing layout macros, *tbl* defines a number register TW which is the table width; it is defined by the time that the ".TE" macro is invoked and may be used in the expansion of that macro. More importantly, to assist in laying out multi-page boxed tables the macro T# is defined to produce the bottom lines and side lines of a boxed table, and then invoked at its end. By use of this macro in the page footer a multi-page table can be boxed. In particular, the *ms* macros can be used to print a multi-page boxed table with a repeated heading by giving the argument H to the ".TS" macro. If the table start macro is written
    .TS H
a line of the form
    .TH
must be given in the table after any table heading (or at the start if none). Material up to the ".TH" is placed at the top of each page of table; the remaining lines in the table are placed on several pages as required. Note that this is *not* a feature of *tbl,* but of the *ms* layout macros.

Examples.

    Here are some examples illustrating features of *tbl.* The symbol Ⓣ in the input represents a tab character.

25

Input:

```
.TS
box;
c c c
l l l.
Language ⊕ Authors ⊕ Runs on

Fortran ⊕ Many ⊕ Almost anything
PL/1 ⊕ IBM ⊕ 360/370
C ⊕ BTL ⊕ 11/45,H6000,370
BLISS ⊕ Carnegie-Mellon ⊕ PDP-10,11
IDS ⊕ Honeywell ⊕ H6000
Pascal ⊕ Stanford ⊕ 370
.TE
```

Output:

Language	Authors	Runs on
Fortran	Many	Almost anything
PL/1	IBM	360/370
C	BTL	11/45,H6000,370
BLISS	Carnegie-Mellon	PDP-10,11
IDS	Honeywell	H6000
Pascal	Stanford	370

Input:

```
.TS
allbox;
c s s
c c c
n n n.
AT&T Common Stock
Year ⊕ Price ⊕ Dividend
1971 ⊕ 41-54 ⊕ $2.60
2 ⊕ 41-54 ⊕ 2.70
3 ⊕ 46-55 ⊕ 2.87
4 ⊕ 40-53 ⊕ 3.24
5 ⊕ 45-52 ⊕ 3.40
6 ⊕ 51-59 ⊕ .95*
.TE
* (first quarter only)
```

Output:

AT&T Common Stock		
Year	Price	Dividend
1971	41-54	$2.60
2	41-54	2.70
3	46-55	2.87
4	40-53	3.24
5	45-52	3.40
6	51-59	.95*

* (first quarter only)

25

Input:

```
.TS
box;
c s s
c | c | c
l | l | l | n.
Major New York Bridges
=
Bridge ⊕ Designer ⊕ Length

_
Brooklyn ⊕ J. A. Roebling ⊕ 1595
Manhattan ⊕ G. Lindenthal ⊕ 1470
Williamsburg ⊕ L. L. Buck ⊕ 1600

_
Queensborough ⊕ Palmer & ⊕ 1182
⊕    Hornbostel

_
⊕ ⊕ 1380
Triborough ⊕ O. H. Ammann ⊕ _
⊕ ⊕ 383

_
Bronx Whitestone ⊕ O. H. Ammann ⊕ 2300
Throgs Neck ⊕ O. H. Ammann ⊕ 1800

_
George Washington ⊕ O. H. Ammann ⊕ 3500
.TE
```

Output:

Major New York Bridges		
Bridge	Designer	Length
Brooklyn	J. A. Roebling	1595
Manhattan	G. Lindenthal	1470
Williamsburg	L. L. Buck	1600
Queensborough	Palmer & Hornbostel	1182
Triborough	O. H. Ammann	1380
		383
Bronx Whitestone	O. H. Ammann	2300
Throgs Neck	O. H. Ammann	1800
George Washington	O. H. Ammann	3500

Input:

```
.TS
c c
n p-2 | n | .
⊕ Stack
⊕ _
1 ⊕ 46
⊕ _
2 ⊕ 23
⊕ _
3 ⊕ 15
⊕ _
4 ⊕ 6.5
⊕ _
5 ⊕ 2.1
⊕ _
.TE
```

Output:

	Stack
1	46
2	23
3	15
4	6.5
5	2.1

25

Input:

```
.TS
box;
L L L
L L _
L L | LB
L L _
L L L.
january ⓣ february ⓣ march
april ⓣ may
june ⓣ july ⓣ Months
august ⓣ september
october ⓣ november ⓣ december
.TE
```

Output:

january	february	march
april	may	
june	july	**Months**
august	september	
october	november	december

Input:

```
.TS
box;
cfB s s s.
Composition of Foods
_
.T&
c | c s s
c | c s s
c | c | c | c.
Food ⓣ Percent by Weight
\^ ⓣ _
\^ ⓣ Protein ⓣ Fat ⓣ Carbo-
\^ ⓣ \^ ⓣ \^ ⓣ hydrate
_
.T&
l | n | n | n.
Apples ⓣ .4 ⓣ .5 ⓣ 13.0
Halibut ⓣ 18.4 ⓣ 5.2 ⓣ . . .
Lima beans ⓣ 7.5 ⓣ .8 ⓣ 22.0
Milk ⓣ 3.3 ⓣ 4.0 ⓣ 5.0
Mushrooms ⓣ 3.5 ⓣ .4 ⓣ 6.0
Rye bread ⓣ 9.0 ⓣ .6 ⓣ 52.7
.TE
```

Output:

Composition of Foods			
Food	Percent by Weight		
	Protein	Fat	Carbo-hydrate
Apples	.4	.5	13.0
Halibut	18.4	5.2	...
Lima beans	7.5	.8	22.0
Milk	3.3	4.0	5.0
Mushrooms	3.5	.4	6.0
Rye bread	9.0	.6	52.7

Input:

```
.TS
allbox;
cfI s s
c   cw(1i)  cw(1i)
lp9 lp9 lp9.
New York Area Rocks
Era ⊕ Formation ⊕ Age (years)
Precambrian ⊕ Reading Prong ⊕ >1 billion
Paleozoic ⊕ Manhattan Prong ⊕ 400 million
Mesozoic ⊕ T{
.na
Newark Basin, incl.
Stockton, Lockatong, and Brunswick
formations; also Watchungs
and Palisades.
T} ⊕ 200 million
Cenozoic ⊕ Coastal Plain ⊕ T{
On Long Island 30,000 years;
Cretaceous sediments redeposited
by recent glaciation.
.ad
T}
.TE
```

Output:

New York Area Rocks		
Era	Formation	Age (years)
Precambrian	Reading Prong	>1 billion
Paleozoic	Manhattan Prong	400 million
Mesozoic	Newark Basin, incl. Stockton, Lockatong, and Brunswick formations; also Watchungs and Palisades.	200 million
Cenozoic	Coastal Plain	On Long Island 30,000 years; Cretaceous sediments redeposited by recent glaciation.

Input:

```
.EQ
delim $$
.EN

. . .

.TS
doublebox;
c c
l l.
Name ⊕ Definition
.sp
.vs +2p
Gamma ⊕ $GAMMA (z) = int sub 0 sup inf  t sup {z-1} e sup -t dt$
Sine ⊕ $sin (x) = 1 over 2i ( e sup ix - e sup -ix )$
Error ⊕ $ roman erf (z) = 2 over sqrt pi int sub 0 sup z e sup {-t sup 2} dt$
Bessel ⊕ $ J sub 0 (z) = 1 over pi int sub 0 sup pi cos ( z sin theta ) d theta $
Zeta ⊕ $ zeta (s) = sum from k=1 to inf k sup -s ~( Re~s > 1)$
.vs -2p
.TE
```

Output:

Name	Definition
Gamma	$\Gamma(z) = \int_0^\infty t^{z-1} e^{-t} dt$
Sine	$\sin(x) = \dfrac{1}{2i} (e^{ix} - e^{-ix})$
Error	$\mathrm{erf}(z) = \dfrac{2}{\sqrt{\pi}} \int_0^z e^{-t^2} dt$
Bessel	$J_0(z) = \dfrac{1}{\pi} \int_0^\pi \cos(z \sin \theta) d\theta$
Zeta	$\zeta(s) = \sum_{k=1}^{\infty} k^{-s} \ \ (\mathrm{Re}\ s > 1)$

25

Input:

```
.TS
box, tab( : );
cb s s s s
cp-2 s s s s
c | | c | c | c | c
c | | c | c | c | c
r2 | | n2 | n2 | n2 | n.
Readability of Text
Line Width and Leading for 10-Point Type
=
Line : Set : 1-Point : 2-Point : 4-Point
Width : Solid : Leading : Leading : Leading
_
9 Pica : \-9.3 : \-6.0 : \-5.3 : \-7.1
14 Pica : \-4.5 : \-0.6 : \-0.3 : \-1.7
19 Pica : \-5.0 : \-5.1 :  0.0 : \-2.0
31 Pica : \-3.7 : \-3.8 : \-2.4 : \-3.6
43 Pica : \-9.1 : \-9.0 : \-5.9 : \-8.8
.TE
```

Output:

| Readability of Text | | | | |
Line Width and Leading for 10-Point Type				
Line Width	Set Solid	1-Point Leading	2-Point Leading	4-Point Leading
9 Pica	−9.3	−6.0	−5.3	−7.1
14 Pica	−4.5	−0.6	−0.3	−1.7
19 Pica	−5.0	−5.1	0.0	−2.0
31 Pica	−3.7	−3.8	−2.4	−3.6
43 Pica	−9.1	−9.0	−5.9	−8.8

25

Input:

```
.TS
c s
cip-2 s
l n
a n.
Some London Transport Statistics
(Year 1964)
Railway route miles ⊕ 244
Tube ⊕ 66
Sub-surface ⊕ 22
Surface ⊕ 156
.sp .5
.T&
l r
a r.
Passenger traffic \- railway
Journeys ⊕ 674 million
Average length ⊕ 4.55 miles
Passenger miles ⊕ 3,066 million
.T&
l r
a r.
Passenger traffic \- road
Journeys ⊕ 2,252 million
Average length ⊕ 2.26 miles
Passenger miles ⊕ 5,094 million
.T&
l n
a n.
.sp .5
Vehicles ⊕ 12,521
Railway motor cars ⊕ 2,905
Railway trailer cars ⊕ 1,269
Total railway ⊕ 4,174
Omnibuses ⊕ 8,347
.T&
l n
a n.
.sp .5
Staff ⊕ 73,739
Administrative, etc. ⊕ 5,582
Civil engineering ⊕ 5,134
Electrical eng. ⊕ 1,714
Mech. eng. \- railway ⊕ 4,310
Mech. eng. \- road ⊕ 9,152
Railway operations ⊕ 8,930
Road operations ⊕ 35,946
Other ⊕ 2,971
.TE
```

Output:

Some London Transport Statistics
(Year 1964)

Railway route miles	244
Tube	66
Sub-surface	22
Surface	156
Passenger traffic – railway	
Journeys	674 million
Average length	4.55 miles
Passenger miles	3,066 million
Passenger traffic – road	
Journeys	2,252 million
Average length	2.26 miles
Passenger miles	5,094 million
Vehicles	12,521
Railway motor cars	2,905
Railway trailer cars	1,269
Total railway	4,174
Omnibuses	8,347
Staff	73,739
Administrative, etc.	5,582
Civil engineering	5,134
Electrical eng.	1,714
Mech. eng. – railway	4,310
Mech. eng. – road	9,152
Railway operations	8,930
Road operations	35,946
Other	2,971

Input:

```
.ps 8
.vs 10p
.TS
center box;
c s s
ci s s
c c c
lB l n.
New Jersey Representatives
(Democrats)
.sp .5
Name ⊕ Office address ⊕ Phone
.sp .5
James J. Florio ⊕ 23 S. White Horse Pike, Somerdale 08083 ⊕ 609-627-8222
William J. Hughes ⊕ 2920 Atlantic Ave., Atlantic City 08401 ⊕ 609-345-4844
James J. Howard ⊕ 801 Bangs Ave., Asbury Park 07712 ⊕ 201-774-1600
Frank Thompson, Jr. ⊕ 10 Rutgers Pl., Trenton 08618 ⊕ 609-599-1619
Andrew Maguire ⊕ 115 W. Passaic St., Rochelle Park 07662 ⊕ 201-843-0240
Robert A. Roe ⊕ U.S.P.O., 194 Ward St., Paterson 07510 ⊕ 201-523-5152
Henry Helstoski ⊕ 666 Paterson Ave., East Rutherford 07073 ⊕ 201-939-9090
Peter W. Rodino, Jr. ⊕ Suite 1435A, 970 Broad St., Newark 07102 ⊕ 201-645-3213
Joseph G. Minish ⊕ 308 Main St., Orange 07050 ⊕ 201-645-6363
Helen S. Meyner ⊕ 32 Bridge St., Lambertville 08530 ⊕ 609-397-1830
Dominick V. Daniels ⊕ 895 Bergen Ave., Jersey City 07306 ⊕ 201-659-7700
Edward J. Patten ⊕ Natl. Bank Bldg., Perth Amboy 08861 ⊕ 201-826-4610
.sp .5
.T&
ci s s
lB l n.
(Republicans)
.sp .5v
Millicent Fenwick ⊕ 41 N. Bridge St., Somerville 08876 ⊕ 201-722-8200
Edwin B. Forsythe ⊕ 301 Mill St., Moorestown 08057 ⊕ 609-235-6622
Matthew J. Rinaldo ⊕ 1961 Morris Ave., Union 07083 ⊕ 201-687-4235
.TE
.ps 10
.vs 12p
```

Output:

New Jersey Representatives *(Democrats)*		
Name	Office address	Phone
James J. Florio	23 S. White Horse Pike, Somerdale 08083	609-627-8222
William J. Hughes	2920 Atlantic Ave., Atlantic City 08401	609-345-4844
James J. Howard	801 Bangs Ave., Asbury Park 07712	201-774-1600
Frank Thompson, Jr.	10 Rutgers Pl., Trenton 08618	609-599-1619
Andrew Maguire	115 W. Passaic St., Rochelle Park 07662	201-843-0240
Robert A. Roe	U.S.P.O., 194 Ward St., Paterson 07510	201-523-5152
Henry Helstoski	666 Paterson Ave., East Rutherford 07073	201-939-9090
Peter W. Rodino, Jr.	Suite 1435A, 970 Broad St., Newark 07102	201-645-3213
Joseph G. Minish	308 Main St., Orange 07050	201-645-6363
Helen S. Meyner	32 Bridge St., Lambertville 08530	609-397-1830
Dominick V. Daniels	895 Bergen Ave., Jersey City 07306	201-659-7700
Edward J. Patten	Natl. Bank Bldg., Perth Amboy 08861	201-826-4610
(Republicans)		
Millicent Fenwick	41 N. Bridge St., Somerville 08876	201-722-8200
Edwin B. Forsythe	301 Mill St., Moorestown 08057	609-235-6622
Matthew J. Rinaldo	1961 Morris Ave., Union 07083	201-687-4235

This is a paragraph of normal text placed here only to indicate where the left and right margins are. In this way the reader can judge the appearance of centered tables or expanded tables, and observe how such tables are formatted.

Input:

```
.TS
expand;
c s s s
c c c c
l l n n.
Bell Labs Locations
Name ⊕ Address ⊕ Area Code ⊕ Phone
Holmdel ⊕ Holmdel, N. J. 07733 ⊕ 201 ⊕ 949-3000
Murray Hill ⊕ Murray Hill, N. J. 07974 ⊕ 201 ⊕ 582-6377
Whippany ⊕ Whippany, N. J. 07981 ⊕ 201 ⊕ 386-3000
Indian Hill ⊕ Naperville, Illinois 60540 ⊕ 312 ⊕ 690-2000
.TE
```

Output:

	Bell Labs Locations		
Name	Address	Area Code	Phone
Holmdel	Holmdel, N. J. 07733	201	949-3000
Murray Hill	Murray Hill, N. J. 07974	201	582-6377
Whippany	Whippany, N. J. 07981	201	386-3000
Indian Hill	Naperville, Illinois 60540	312	690-2000

25

Input:

```
.TS
box;
cb  s  s  s
c | c | c  s
ltiw(1i) | ltw(2i) | lp8 | lw(1.5i)p8.
Some Interesting Places
_
Name ① Description ① Practical Information
_
T{
American Museum of Natural History
T} ① T{
The collections fill 11.5 acres (Michelin) or 25 acres (MTA)
of exhibition halls on four floors.  There is a full-sized replica
of a blue whale and the world's largest star sapphire (stolen in 1964).
T} ① Hours ① 10-5, ex. Sun 11-5, Wed. to 9
\^ ① \^ ① Location ① T{
Central Park West & 79th St.
T}
\^ ① \^ ① Admission ① Donation: $1.00 asked
\^ ① \^ ① Subway ① AA to 81st St.
\^ ① \^ ① Telephone ① 212-873-4225
_
Bronx Zoo ① T{
About a mile long and .6 mile wide, this is the largest zoo in America.
A lion eats 18 pounds
of meat a day while a sea lion eats 15 pounds of fish.
T} ① Hours ① T{
10-4:30 winter, to 5:00 summer
T}
\^ ① \^ ① Location ① T{
185th St. & Southern Blvd, the Bronx.
T}
\^ ① \^ ① Admission ① $1.00, but Tu,We,Th free
\^ ① \^ ① Subway ① 2, 5 to East Tremont Ave.
\^ ① \^ ① Telephone ① 212-933-1759
_
Brooklyn Museum ① T{
Five floors of galleries contain American and ancient art.
There are American period rooms and architectural ornaments saved
from wreckers, such as a classical figure from Pennsylvania Station.
T} ① Hours ① Wed-Sat, 10-5, Sun 12-5
\^ ① \^ ① Location ① T{
Eastern Parkway & Washington Ave., Brooklyn.
T}
\^ ① \^ ① Admission ① Free
\^ ① \^ ① Subway ① 2,3 to Eastern Parkway.
\^ ① \^ ① Telephone ① 718-638-5000
_
T{
New-York Historical Society
T} ① T{
All the original paintings for Audubon's
.I
Birds of America
.R
are here, as are exhibits of American decorative arts, New York history,
Hudson River school paintings, carriages, and glass paperweights.
T} ① Hours ① T{
Tues-Fri & Sun, 1-5; Sat 10-5
T}
\^ ① \^ ① Location ① T{
Central Park West & 77th St.
T}
\^ ① \^ ① Admission ① Free
\^ ① \^ ① Subway ① AA to 81st St.
\^ ① \^ ① Telephone ① 212-873-3400
.TE
```

25

Output:

Some Interesting Places			
Name	Description	Practical Information	
American Muse-um of Natural History	The collections fill 11.5 acres (Michelin) or 25 acres (MTA) of exhibition halls on four floors. There is a full-sized replica of a blue whale and the world's largest star sapphire (stolen in 1964).	Hours Location Admission Subway Telephone	10-5, ex. Sun 11-5, Wed. to 9 Central Park West & 79th St. Donation: $1.00 asked AA to 81st St. 212-873-4225
Bronx Zoo	About a mile long and .6 mile wide, this is the largest zoo in America. A lion eats 18 pounds of meat a day while a sea lion eats 15 pounds of fish.	Hours Location Admission Subway Telephone	10-4:30 winter, to 5:00 summer 185th St. & Southern Blvd, the Bronx. $1.00, but Tu,We,Th free 2, 5 to East Tremont Ave. 212-933-1759
Brooklyn Museum	Five floors of galleries contain American and ancient art. There are American period rooms and architectural ornaments saved from wreckers, such as a classical figure from Pennsylvania Station.	Hours Location Admission Subway Telephone	Wed-Sat, 10-5, Sun 12-5 Eastern Parkway & Washington Ave., Brooklyn. Free 2,3 to Eastern Parkway. 718-638-5000
New-York Histor-ical Society	All the original paintings for Audubon's *Birds of America* are here, as are exhibits of American decorative arts, New York history, Hudson River school paintings, carriages, and glass paperweights.	Hours Location Admission Subway Telephone	Tues-Fri & Sun, 1-5; Sat 10-5 Central Park West & 77th St. Free AA to 81st St. 212-873-3400

Acknowledgments.

Many thanks are due to J. C. Blinn, who has done a large amount of testing and assisted with the design of the program. He has also written many of the more intelligible sentences in this document and helped edit all of it. All phototypesetting programs on UNIX are dependent on the work of J. F. Ossanna, whose assistance with this program in particular has been most helpful. This program is patterned on a table formatter originally written by J. F. Gimpel. The assistance of T. A. Dolotta, B. W. Kernighan, and J. N. Sturman is gratefully acknowledged.

References.

[1]   J. F. Ossanna, *NROFF/TROFF User's Manual,* Computing Science Technical Report No. 54, Bell Laboratories, 1976.

[2]   K. Thompson and D. M. Ritchie, ''The UNIX Time-Sharing System,'' *Comm. ACM.* **17**, pp. 365–75 (1974).

[3]   B. W. Kernighan and L. L. Cherry, ''A System for Typesetting Mathematics,'' *Comm. ACM.* **18**, pp. 151–57 (1975).

[4]   M. E. Lesk, *Typing Documents on UNIX,* Bell Laboratories internal memorandum.

[5]   M. E. Lesk and B. W. Kernighan, *Computer Typesetting of Technical Journals on UNIX,* Computing Science Technical Report No. 44, Bell Laboratories, July 1976.

[6]   J. R. Mashey and D. W. Smith, *PWB/MM — Programmer's Workbench Memorandum Macros,* Bell Laboratories memorandum.

25

List of Tbl Command Characters and Words

Command	Meaning	Section
a A	Alphabetic subcolumn	2
allbox	Draw box around all items	1
b B	Boldface item	2
box	Draw box around table	1
c C	Centered column	2
center	Center table in page	1
doublebox	Doubled box around table	1
e E	Equal width columns	2
expand	Make table full line width	1
f F	Font change	2
i I	Italic item	2
l L	Left adjusted column	2
n N	Numerical column	2
nnn	Column separation	2
p P	Point size change	2
r R	Right adjusted column	2
s S	Spanned item	2
t T	Vertical spanning at top	2
tab (*x*)	Change data separator character	1
T{ T}	Text block	3
v V	Vertical spacing change	2
w W	Minimum width value	2
.*xx*	Included *troff* command	3
|	Vertical line	2
| |	Double vertical line	2
^	Vertical span	2
\^	Vertical span	3
=	Double horizontal line	2,3
_	Horizontal line	2,3
_	Short horizontal line	3

Refer — A Bibliography System

Bill Tuthill

Computing Services
University of California
Berkeley, CA 94720

26

ABSTRACT

Refer is a bibliography system that supports data entry, indexing, retrieval, sorting, runoff, convenient citations, and footnote or endnote numbering. This document assumes you know how to use some Unix editor, and that you are familiar with the **nroff/troff** text formatters.

The **refer** program is a preprocessor for **nroff/troff,** like **eqn** and **tbl,** except that it is used for literature citations, rather than for equations and tables. Given incomplete but sufficiently precise citations, **refer** finds references in a bibliographic database. The complete references are formatted as footnotes, numbered, and placed either at the bottom of the page, or at the end of a chapter.

A number of ancillary programs make **refer** easier to use. The **addbib** program is for creating and extending the bibliographic database; **sortbib** sorts the bibliography by author and date, or other selected criteria; and **roffbib** runs off the entire database, formatting it not as footnotes, but as a bibliography or annotated bibliography.

Once a full bibliography has been created, access time can be improved by making an index to the references with **indxbib**. Then, the **lookbib** program can be used to quickly retrieve individual citations or groups of citations. Creating this inverted index will speed up **refer,** and **lookbib** will allow you to verify that a citation is sufficiently precise to deliver just one reference.

Introduction

Taken together, the **refer** programs constitute a database system for use with variable-length information. To distinguish various types of bibliographic material, the system uses labels composed of upper case letters, preceded by a percent sign and followed by a space. For example, one document might be given this entry:

```
%A   Joel Kies
%T   Document Formatting on Unix Using the -ms Macros
%I   Computing Services
%C   Berkeley
%D   1980
```

Each line is called a field, and lines grouped together are called a record; records are separated from each other by a blank line. Bibliographic information follows the labels, containing data to be used by the **refer** system. The order of fields is not important, except that authors should be entered in the same order as they are listed on the document. Fields can be as long as necessary, and may even be continued on the following line(s).

The labels are meaningful to **nroff/troff** macros, and, with a few exceptions, the **refer** program itself does not pay attention to them. This implies that you can change the label codes, if you also change the macros used by **nroff/troff** . The macro package takes care of details like proper ordering, underlining the book title or journal name, and quoting the article's title. Here are the labels used by **refer,** with an indication of what they represent:

%H   Header commentary, printed before reference
%A   Author's name
%Q   Corporate or foreign author (unreversed)
%T   Title of article or book
%S   Series title
%J   Journal containing article
%B   Book containing article
%R   Report, paper, or thesis (for unpublished material)
%V   Volume
%N   Number within volume
%E   Editor of book containing article
%P   Page number(s)
%I   Issuer (publisher)
%C   City where published
%D   Date of publication
%O   Other commentary, printed at end of reference
%K   Keywords used to locate reference
%L   Label used by –k option of **refer**
%X   Abstract (used by **roffbib,** not by **refer**)

Only relevant fields should be supplied. Except for %A, each field should be given only once; in the case of multiple authors, the senior author should come first. The %Q is for organizational authors, or authors with Japanese or Arabic names, in which cases the order of names should be preserved. Books should be labeled with the %T, not with the %B, which is reserved for books containing articles. The %J and %B fields should never appear together, although if they do, the %J will override the %B. If there is no author, just an editor, it is best to type the editor in the %A field, as in this example:

%A   Bertrand Bronson, ed.

The %E field is used for the editor of a book (%B) containing an article, which has its own author. For unpublished material such as theses, use the %R field; the title in the %T field will be quoted, but the contents of the %R field will not be underlined. Unlike other fields, %H, %O, and %X should contain their own punctuation. Here is a modest example:

%A   Mike E. Lesk
%T   Some Applications of Inverted Indexes on the Unix System
%B   Unix Programmer's Manual
%I   Bell Laboratories
%C   Murray Hill, NJ
%D   1978
%V   2a
%K   refer mkey inv hunt
%X   Difficult to read paper that dwells on indexing strategies,
giving little practical advice about using \fBrefer\fP.

Note that the author's name is given in normal order, without inverting the surname; inversion is done automatically, except when %Q is used instead of %A. We use %X rather than %O for the commentary because we do not want the comment printed all the time. The %O and %H fields are printed by both **refer** and **roffbib;** the %X field is printed only by **roffbib,** as a detached annotation paragraph.

Data Entry with Addbib

The **addbib** program is for creating and extending bibliographic databases. You must give it the filename of your bibliography:

% **addbib database**

Every time you enter **addbib**, it asks if you want instructions. To get them, type **y** ; to skip them, type RETURN.

Addbib prompts for various fields, reads from the keyboard, and writes records containing the **refer** codes to the database. After finishing a field entry, you should end it by typing RETURN. If a field is too long to fit on a line, type a backslash (\) at the end of the line, and you will be able to continue on the following line. Note: the backslash works in this capacity only inside **addbib**.

A field will not be written to the database if nothing is entered into it. Typing a minus sign as the first character of any field will cause **addbib** to back up one field at a time. Backing up is the best way to add multiple authors, and it really helps if you forget to add something important. Fields not contained in the prompting skeleton may be entered by typing a backslash as the last character before RETURN. The following line will be sent verbatim to the database and **addbib** will resume with the next field. This is identical to the procedure for dealing with long fields, but with new fields, don't forget the % key-letter.

Finally, you will be asked for an abstract (or annotation), which will be preserved as the %X field. Type in as many lines as you need, and end with a control-D (hold down the CTRL button, then press the ''d'' key). This prompting for an abstract can be suppressed with the −a command line option.

After one bibliographic record has been completed, **addbib** will ask if you want to continue. If you do, type RETURN; to quit, type **q** or **n** (quit or no). It is also possible to use one of the system editors to correct mistakes made while entering data. After the ''Continue?'' prompt, type any of the following: **edit, ex, vi,** or **ed** — you will be placed inside the corresponding editor, and returned to **addbib** afterwards, from where you can either quit or add more data.

If the prompts normally supplied by **addbib** are not enough, are in the wrong order, or are too numerous, you can redefine the skeleton by constructing a promptfile. Create some file, to be named after the −p command line option. Place the prompts you want on the left side, followed by a single TAB (control-I), then the **refer** code that is to appear in the bibliographic database. **Addbib** will send the left side to the screen, and the right side, along with data entered, to the database.

Printing the Bibliography

Sortbib is for sorting the bibliography by author (%A) and date (%D), or by data in other fields. It is quite useful for producing bibliographies and annotated bibliographies, which are seldom entered in strict alphabetical order. It takes as arguments the names of up to 16 bibliography files, and sends the sorted records to standard output (the terminal screen), which may be redirected through a pipe or into a file.

The −s*KEYS* flag to **sortbib** will sort by fields whose key-letters are in the *KEYS* string, rather than merely by author and date. Key-letters in *KEYS* may be followed by a '+' to indicate that all such fields are to be used. The default is to sort by senior author and date (printing the senior author last name first), but −sA+D will sort by all authors and then date, and −sATD will sort on senior author, then title, and then date.

Roffbib is for running off the (probably sorted) bibliography. It can handle annotated bibliographies — annotations are entered in the %X (abstract) field. **Roffbib** is a shell script that calls **refer** −**B** and **nroff** −**mbib**. It uses the macro definitions that reside in /usr/lib/tmac/tmac.bib, which you can redefine if you know **nroff** and **troff**. Note that **refer** will print the %H and %O commentaries, but will ignore abstracts in the %X field; **roffbib** will print both fields, unless annotations are suppressed with the −x option.

The following command sequence will lineprint the entire bibliography, organized alphabetically by author and date:

    % **sortbib database | roffbib | lpr**

This is a good way to proofread the bibliography, or to produce a stand-alone bibliography at the end of a paper. Incidentally, **roffbib** accepts all flags used with **nroff**. For example:

    % **sortbib database | roffbib** −**Tdtc** −**s1**

will make accent marks work on a DTC daisy-wheel printer, and stop at the bottom of every page for changing paper. The −n and −o flags may also be quite useful, to start page numbering at a selected point, or to produce only specific pages.

26

Roffbib understands four command-line number registers, which are something like the two-letter number registers in −ms. The −rN1 argument will number references beginning at one (1); use another number to start somewhere besides one. The −rV2 flag will double-space the entire bibliography, while −rV1 will double-space the references, but single-space the annotation paragraphs. Finally, specifying −rL6i changes the line length from 6.5 inches to 6 inches, and saying −rO1i sets the page offset to one inch, instead of zero. (That's a capital O after −r, not a zero.)

Citing Papers with Refer

The **refer** program normally copies input to output, except when it encounters an item of the form:

    .[
    partial citation
    .]

The partial citation may be just an author's name and a date, or perhaps a title and a keyword, or maybe just a document number. **Refer** looks up the citation in the bibliographic database, and transforms it into a full, properly formatted reference. If the partial citation does not correctly identify a single work (either finding nothing, or more than one reference), a diagnostic message is given. If nothing is found, it will say "No such paper." If more than one reference is found, it will say "Too many hits." Other diagnostic messages can be quite cryptic; if you are in doubt, use **checknr** to verify that all your .['s have matching .]'s.

When everything goes well, the reference will be brought in from the database, numbered, and placed at the bottom of the page. This citation,[1] for example, was produced by:

    This citation,
    .[
    lesk inverted indexes
    .]
    for example, was produced by

The .[and .] markers, in essence, replace the .FS and .FE of the −ms macros, and also provide a numbering mechanism. Footnote numbers will be bracketed on the the the lineprinter, but superscripted on daisy-wheel terminals and in **troff**. In the reference itself, articles will be quoted, and books and journals will be underlined in **nroff,** and italicized in **troff.**

Sometimes you need to cite a specific page number along with more general bibliographic material. You may have, for instance, a single document that you refer to several times, each time giving a different page citation. This is how you could get "p. 10" in the reference:

    .[
    kies document formatting
    %P   10
    .]

The first line, a partial citation, will find the reference in your bibliography. The second line will insert the page number into the final citation. Ranges of pages may be specified as "%P 56-78".

When the time comes to run off a paper, you will need to have two files: the bibliographic database, and the paper to format. Use a command line something like one of these:

    % refer −p database paper | nroff −ms
    % refer −p database paper | tbl | nroff −ms
    % refer −p database paper | tbl | neqn | nroff −ms

If other preprocessors are used, **refer** should precede **tbl,** which must in turn precede **eqn** or **neqn**. The −p option specifies a "private" database, which most bibliographies are.

---

[1] Mike E. Lesk, "Some Applications of Inverted Indexes on the Unix System," *Unix Programmer's Manual*, vol. 2a, Bell Laboratories, Murray Hill, NJ, 1978.

Refer's Command-line Options

Many people like to place references at the end of a chapter, rather than at the bottom of the page. The −e option will accumulate references until a macro sequence of the form

```
.[
$LIST$
.]
```

is encountered (or until the end of file). **Refer** will then write out all references collected up to that point, collapsing identical references. Warning: there is a limit (currently 200) on the number of references that can be accumulated at one time.

It is also possible to sort references that appear at the end of text. The −s*KEYS* flag will sort references by fields whose key-letters are in the *KEYS* string, and permute reference numbers in the text accordingly. It is unnecessary to use −e with it, since −s implies −e. Key-letters in *KEYS* may be followed by a '+' to indicate that all such fields are to be used. The default is to sort by senior author and date, but −sA+D will sort on all authors and then date, and −sA+T will sort by authors and then title.

Refer can also make citations in what is known as the Social or Natural Sciences format. Instead of number- ing references, the −l (letter ell) flag makes labels from the senior author's last name and the year of publication. For example, a reference to the paper on Inverted Indexes cited above might appear as [Lesk1978a]. It is possible to control the number of characters in the last name, and the number of digits in the date. For instance, the com- mand line argument −l6,2 might produce a reference such as [Kernig78c].

Some bibliography standards shun both footnote numbers and labels composed of author and date, requiring some keyword to identify the reference. The −k flag indicates that, instead of numbering references, key labels specified on the %L line should be used to mark references.

The −n flag means to not search the default reference file, located in /usr/dict/papers/Rv7man. Using this flag may make **refer** marginally faster. The −a*n* flag will reverse the first *n* author names, printing Jones, J. A. instead of J. A. Jones. Often −a1 is enough; this will reverse the names of only the senior author. In some versions of **refer** there is also the −f flag to set the footnote number to some predetermined value; for example, −f23 would start numbering with footnote 23.

Making an Index

Once your database is large and relatively stable, it is a good idea to make an index to it, so that references can be found quickly and efficiently. The **indxbib** program makes an inverted index to the bibliographic database (this program is called **pubindex** in the Bell Labs manual). An inverted index could be compared to the thumb cuts of a dictionary — instead of going all the way through your bibliography, programs can move to the exact location where a citation is found.

Indxbib itself takes a while to run, and you will need sufficient disk space to store the indexes. But once it has been run, access time will improve dramatically. Furthermore, large databases of several million characters can be indexed with no problem. The program is exceedingly simple to use:

% **indxbib database**

Be aware that changing your database will require that you run **indxbib** over again. If you don't, you may fail to find a reference that really is in the database.

Once you have built an inverted index, you can use **lookbib** to find references in the database. **Lookbib** can- not be used until you have run **indxbib**. When editing a paper, **lookbib** is very useful to make sure that a citation can be found as specified. It takes one argument, the name of the bibliography, and then reads partial citations from the terminal, returning references that match, or nothing if none match. Its prompt is the greater-than sign.

26

```
% lookbib  database
> lesk inverted indexes
%A    Mike E. Lesk
%T    Some Applications of Inverted Indexes on the Unix System
%J    Unix Programmer's Manual
%I    Bell Laboratories
%C    Murray Hill, NJ
%D    1978
%V    2a
%X    Difficult to read paper that dwells on indexing strategies,
giving little practical advice about using \fBrefer\fP.
>
```

If more than one reference comes back, you will have to give a more precise citation for **refer**. Experiment until you find something that works; remember that it is harmless to overspecify. To get out of the **lookbib** program, type a control-D alone on a line; **lookbib** then exits with an "EOT" message.

    Lookbib can also be used to extract groups of related citations. For example, to find all the papers by Brian Kernighan found in the system database, and send the output to a file, type:

```
% lookbib /usr/dict/papers/Ind  >  kern.refs
> kernighan
> EOT
% cat  kern.refs
```

Your file, "kern.refs", will be full of references. A similar procedure can be used to pull out all papers of some date, all papers from a given journal, all papers containing a certain group of keywords, etc.

Refer Bugs and Some Solutions

    The **refer** program will mess up if there are blanks at the end of lines, especially the %A author line. **Addbib** carefully removes trailing blanks, but they may creep in again during editing. Use an editor command — g/ *$/s/// — to remove trailing blanks from your bibliography.

    Having bibliographic fields passed through as string definitions implies that interpolated strings (such as accent marks) must have two backslashes, so they can pass through copy mode intact. For instance, the word "téléphone" would have to be represented:

    te*´le*´phone

in order to come out correctly. In the %X field, by contrast, you will have to use single backslashes instead. This is because the %X field is not passed through as a string, but as the body of a paragraph macro.

    Another problem arises from authors with foreign names. When a name like "Valéry Giscard d'Estaing" is turned around by the −a option of **refer,** it will appear as "d'Estaing, Valéry Giscard," rather than as "Giscard d'Estaing, Valéry." To prevent this, enter names as follows:

    %A   Vale*´ry Giscard\0d'Estaing
    %A   Alexander Csoma\0de\0Ko*:ro*:s

(The second is the name of a famous Hungarian linguist.) The backslash-zero is an **nroff/troff** request meaning to insert a digit-width space. It will protect against faulty name reversal, and also against mis-sorting.

    Footnote numbers are placed at the end of the line before the .[macro. This line should be a line of text, not a macro. As an example, if the line before the .[is a .R macro, then the .R will eat the footnote number. (The .R is an −ms request meaning change to Roman font.) In cases where the font needs changing, it is necessary to do the following:

```
\fIet al.\fR
.[
awk  aho  kernighan  weinberger
.]
```

Now the reference will be to Aho *et al.*[2] The \fI changes to italics, and the \fR changes back to Roman font. Both these requests are **nroff/troff** requests, not part of −ms. If and when a footnote number is added after this sequence, it will indeed appear in the output.

Internal Details of Refer

You have already read everything you need to know in order to use the **refer** bibliography system. The remaining sections are provided only for extra information, and in case you need to change the way **refer** works.

The output of **refer** is a stream of string definitions, one for each field in a reference. To create string names, percent signs are simply changed to an open bracket, and an [F string is added, containing the footnote number. The %X, %Y and %Z fields are ignored; however, the **annobib** program changes the %X to an .AP (annotation paragraph) macro. The citation used above yields this intermediate output:

```
.ds [F  1
.]-
.ds [A  Mike E. Lesk
.ds [T  Some Applications of Inverted Indexes on the Unix System
.ds [J  Unix Programmer's Manual
.ds [I  Bell Laboratories
.ds [C  Murray Hill, NJ
.ds [D  1978
.ds [V  2a
.nr [T  0
.nr [A  0
.nr [O  0
.][  1  journal-article
```

These string definitions are sent to **nroff**, which can use the −ms macros defined in /usr/lib/mx/tmac.xref to take care of formatting things properly. The initializing macro .]− precedes the string definitions, and the labeled macro .][follows. These are changed from the input .[and .] so that running a file twice through **refer** is harmless.

The .][macro, used to print the reference, is given a type-number argument, which is a numeric label indicating the type of reference involved. Here is a list of the various kinds of references:

Field	Value	Kind of Reference
%J	1	Journal Article
%B	3	Article in Book
%R %G	4	Report, Government Report
%I	2	Book
%M	5	Bell Labs Memorandum (undefined)
none	0	Other

The order listed above is indicative of the precedence of the various fields. In other words, a reference that has both the %J and %B fields will be classified as a journal article. If none of the fields listed is present, then the reference will be classified as "other."

---

[2] Alfred V. Aho, Brian W. Kernighan, and Peter J. Weinberger, "Awk — A Pattern Scanning and Processing Language," *Unix Programmer's Manual*, vol. 2a, Bell Laboratories, Murray Hill, NJ, 1978.

26

The footnote number is flagged in the text with the following sequence, where *number* is the footnote number:

*([.*number**(.]

The *([. and *(.] stand for bracketing or superscripting. In **nroff** with low-resolution devices such as the lpr and a crt, footnote numbers will be bracketed. In **troff,** or on daisy-wheel printers, footnote numbers will be superscripted. Punctuation normally comes before the reference number; this can be changed by using the −P (postpunctuation) option of **refer**.

In some cases, it is necessary to override certain fields in a reference. For instance, each time a work is cited, you may want to specify different page numbers, and you may want to change certain fields. This citation will find the Lesk reference, but will add specific page numbers to the output, even though no page numbers appeared in the original reference.

```
.[
lesk  inverted  indexes
%P   7-13
%I   Computing Services
%O   UNX 12.2.2.
.]
```

The %I line will also override any previous publisher information, and the %O line will append some commentary. The **refer** program simply adds the new %P, %I, and %O strings to the output, and later strings definitions cancel earlier ones.

It is also possible to insert an entire citation that does not appear in the bibliographic database. This reference, for example, could be added as follows:

```
.[
%A   Brian Kernighan
%T   A Troff Tutorial
%I   Bell Laboratories
%D   1978
.]
```

This will cause **refer** to interpret the fields exactly as given, without searching the bibliographic database. This practice is not recommended, however, because it's better to add new references to the database, so they can be used again later.

If you want to change the way footnote numbers are printed, signals can be given on the **.[** and **.]** lines. For example, to say ''See reference (2),'' the citation should appear as:

```
See reference
.[(
partial citation
.]),
```

Note that blanks are significant on these signal lines. If a permanent change in the footnote format is desired, it's best to redefine the **[.** and **.]** strings.

Changing the Refer Macros

This section is provided for those who wish to rewrite or modify the **refer** macros. This is necessary in order to make output correspond to specific journal requirements, or departmental standards. First there is an explanation of how new macros can be substituted for the old ones. Then several alterations are given as examples. Finally, there is an annotated copy of the **refer** macros used by **roffbib** .

The **refer** macros for **nroff/troff** supplied by the −ms macro package reside in /usr/lib/mx/tmac.xref; they are reference macros, for producing footnotes or endnotes. The **refer** macros used by **roffbib,** on the other hand, reside in /usr/lib/tmac/tmac.bib; they are for producing a stand-alone bibliography.

To change the macros used by **roffbib,** you will need to get your own version of this shell script into the directory where you are working. These two commands will get you a copy of **roffbib** and the macros it uses: †

   % **cp /usr/lib/tmac/tmac.bib bibmac**

You can proceed to change bibmac as much as you like. Then when you use **roffbib**, you should specify your own version of the macros, which will be substituted for the normal ones

   % **roffbib −m bibmac** *filename*

where *filename* is the name of your bibliography file. Make sure there's a space between −m and **bibmac**.

If you want to modify the **refer** macros for use with **nroff** and the −ms macros, you will need to get a copy of ''tmac.xref'':

   % **cp /usr/lib/ms/s.ref refmac**

These macros are much like ''bibmac'', except they have .FS and .FE requests, to be used in conjunction with the −ms macros, rather than independently defined .XP and .AP requests. Now you can put this line at the top of the paper to be formatted:

   .so refmac

Your new **refer** macros will override the definitions previously read in by the −ms package. This method works only if ''refmac'' is in the working directory.

Suppose you didn't like the way dates are printed, and wanted them to be parenthesized, with no comma before. There are five identical lines you will have to change. The first line below is the old way, while the second is the new way:

```
.if !"\\*([D"" , \\*([D\c
.if !"\\*([D"" \& (\\*([D)\c
```

In the first line, there is a comma and a space, but no parentheses. The ''\c'' at the end of each line indicates to **nroff** that it should continue, leaving no extra space in the output. The ''\&'' in the second line is the do-nothing character; when followed by a space, a space is sent to the output.

If you need to format a reference in the style favored by the Modern Language Association or Chicago University Press, in the form (city: publisher, date), then you will have to change the middle of the book macro [2 as follows:

```
\& (\c
.if !"\\*([C"" \\*([C:
\\*([I\c
.if !"\\*([D"" , \\*([D\c
)\c
```

This would print (Berkeley: Computing Services, 1982) if all three strings were present. The first line prints a space and a parenthesis; the second prints the city (and a colon) if present; the third always prints the publisher (books must have a publisher, or else they're classified as other); the fourth line prints a comma and the date if present; and the fifth line closes the parentheses. You would need to make similar changes to the other macros as well.

Acknowledgements

Mike Lesk of Bell Laboratories wrote the original **refer** software, including the indexing programs. Al Stangenberger of the Forestry Department wrote the first version of **addbib**, then called **bibin**. Greg Shenaut of the Linguistics Department wrote the original versions of **sortbib** and **roffbib**. All these contributions are greatly appreciated.

Commented Refer Macros

```
.\" refer macros for citations
.de []
.][ \\$1                                  # mysterious synonym for .][
..
.de ][                                    # changes .][ according to argument
.if \\$1>4 .tm %M undefined (Bell Labs)   # no macros defined above [4
.[\\$1                                    # call one of the macros below
..
.if \n(.V>19 .ds [. \f1[                  # open bracket for nroff
.if \n(.V<20 .ds [. \f1\s-2\v'-0.4m'      # superscripting for troff/daisy-wheel
.if \n(.V>19 .ds .] ]\fP                  # close bracket for nroff
.if \n(.V<20 .ds .] \v'0.4m'\s+2\fP       # end troff/daisy-wheel superscripting
.if n .ds [o \&"                          # open quote for nroff
.if n .ds [c \&"                          # close quote for nroff
.if t .ds [o ''                           # open quote for troff
.if t .ds [c ''                           # close quote for troff
.ds <. .                                  # period before citation number
.ds <, ,                                  # comma before citation number
.\" [0 - other type of citation
.de [0
.FS                                       # start -ms footnote
.nr [: 0                                  # has anything been printed?
.if !"\\*([F"" .FP \\*([F                 # number for footnote paragraph
.if !"\\*([Q"" \{\
.nr [: 1                                  # if there's a corporate author,
\\*([Q\c                                  # set [: to 1 and print [Q
.\}
.if !"\\*([A"" \{\                        # if there's an author,
.nr [: 1                                  # set [: to 1,
\\*([A\c                                  # print the author and continue
.\}
.if !"\\*([T"" \{\                        # if there's a title,
.if \\n([:>0 ,                            # print comma if there was author,
.nr [: 1                                  # set [: to 1,
\f2\\*([T\f1\c                            # and print the title in italics
.\}
.if !"\\*([S"" , \\*([S\c                 # series title, not in italics
.if !"\\*([V"" , \\*([V\c                 # if there's a volume, print it
.if !"\\*([P"" \{\
.ie \\n([P>0 , pp. \\*([P\c               # if multiple pages, use pp.
.el , p. \\*([P\c                         # if only one page, use p.
.\}
.if !"\\*([C"" , \\*([C\c                 # if there's a city, print it
.if !"\\*([D"" , \\*([D\c                 # if there's a date, print it
.if \\n([:>0 \&.                          # if [Q [A or [T, print period
.if !"\\*([O"" \\*([O                     # print the other field if present
.FE                                       # end -ms footnote
..
.\" [1 - journal article
.de [1
.FS                                       # start -ms footnote
.if !"\\*([F"" .FP \\*([F                 # number for footnote paragraph
```

```
.if !"\\*([Q""  \\*([Q,              # if corporate author, print it
.if !"\\*([A""  \\*([A,              # if author, print with comma
.if !"\\*([T""  \\*([o\\*([T,\\*([c  # if title, print with quotes
\f2\\*([J\f1\c                       # always a journal, in italics
.if !"\\*([V""  , vol. \\*([V\c      # if volume, print after "vol."
.if !"\\*([N""  , no. \\*([N\c       # if number, print after "no."
.if !"\\*([P""  \{\
.ie \\n([P>0 , pp. \\*([P\c          # if multiple pages, use pp.
.el , p. \\*([P\c                    # if only one page, use p.
.\}
.if !"\\*([I""  , \\*([I\c           # if there's a publisher, print it
.if !"\\*([C""  , \\*([C\c           # if there's a city, print it
.if !"\\*([D""  , \\*([D\c           # if there's a date, print it
\&.                                  # end reference with period
.if !"\\*([O""  \\*([O               # if other information, print it
.FE                                  # end -ms footnote
..
.\" [2 - book
.de [2
.FS                                  # start -ms footnote
.if !"\\*([F""  .FP \\*([F           # number for footnote paragraph
.if !"\\*([Q""  \\*([Q,              # if corporate author, print it
.if !"\\*([A""  \\*([A,              # if author, print with comma
.if !"\\*([T""  \f2\\*([T,\f1        # title and comma in italics
.if !"\\*([S""  \\*([S,              # series title, not in italics
.if !"\\*([V""  \\*([V,              # perhaps [V says "4 vols."
.if !"\\*([P""  \{\
.ie \\n([P>0 pp. \\*([P,             # if multiple pages, use pp.
.el p. \\*([P,                       # if only one page, use p.
.\}
\\*([I\c                             # always a publisher with book
.if !"\\*([C""  , \\*([C\c           # if there's a city, print it
.if !"\\*([D""  , \\*([D\c           # if there's a date, print it
\&.                                  # end reference with period
.if !"\\*([O""  \\*([O               # if other information, print it
.FE                                  # end -ms footnote
..
.\" [3 - article in book
.de [3
.FS                                  # start -ms footnote
.if !"\\*([F""  .FP \\*([F           # number for footnote paragraph
.if !"\\*([Q""  \\*([Q,              # if corporate author, print it
.if !"\\*([A""  \\*([A,              # if author, print with comma
.if !"\\*([T""  \\*([o\\*([T,\\*([c  # title and comma in quotes
in \f2\\*([B\f1\c                    # always "in" book, italicized
.if !"\\*([E""  , ed. \\*([E\c       # if an editor, should follow book
.if !"\\*([S""  , \\*([S\c           # series title, not in italics
.if !"\\*([V""  , vol. \\*([V\c      # if volume, print after "vol."
.if !"\\*([P""  \{\
.ie \\n([P>0 , pp. \\*([P\c          # if multiple pages, use pp.
.el , p. \\*([P\c                    # if only one page, use p.
.\}
.if !"\\*([I""  , \\*([I\c           # if there's a publisher, print it
.if !"\\*([C""  , \\*([C\c           # if there's a city, print it
```

26

```
.if !"\\*([D"" , \\*([D\c            # if there's a date, print it
\&.                                  # end reference with period
.if !"\\*([O"" \\*([O                # if other information, print it
.FE                                  # end -ms footnote
..
.\" [4 - report
.de [4
.FS                                  # start -ms footnote
.if !"\\*([F"" .FP \\*([F            # number for footnote paragraph
.if !"\\*([Q"" \\*([Q,               # if corporate author, print it
.if !"\\*([A"" \\*([A,               # if author, print with comma
.if !"\\*([T"" \\*([o\\*([T,\\*([c   # title and comma in quotes
.if !"\\*([R"" \\*([R\c              # if a report number, print it
.if !"\\*([G"" \& (\\*([G)\c         # put [G string in parentheses
.if !"\\*([P"" \{\
.ie \\n([P>0 , pp. \\*([P\c          # if multiple pages, use pp.
.el , p. \\*([P\c                    # if only one page, use p.
.\}
.if !"\\*([I"" , \\*([I\c            # if there's a publisher, print it
.if !"\\*([C"" , \\*([C\c            # if there's a city, print it
.if !"\\*([D"" , \\*([D\c            # if there's a date, print it
\&.                                  # end reference with period
.if !"\\*([O"" \\*([O                # if other information, print it
.FE                                  # end -ms footnote
..
.de ]<                               # mysterious synonym for [<
.[<
..
.de [<                               # For footnotes at end of text,
.SH                                  # with the -e or -s $LIST$ options.
References                           # Print References section heading.
.LP                                  # Initialize; IP references printed,
.rn IP FP                            # because FP is replaced by IP,
.rm FS FE                            # and footnote macros are removed.
..
.de [>                               # mysterious synonym for ]>
.]>
..
.de ]>                               # with the -e or -s $LIST$ options,
.sp                                  # put a space between references
..
.de ]-                               # mysterious synonym for [-
.[-
..
.de [-                               # Appears at start of references,
.rm [Q [A [T [J [B [E [S [V          # to remove old string definitions--
.rm [N [P [I [C [D [O [R [G          # if you add new field strings,
..                                   # they should be removed as well.
.de ]]
.\" circumvent EOF bug in troff      # mysterious fix for .MC output
..
```

Note that the double quotes in string comparisons are in fact control-g characters; this allows fields to contain double quotes.

Some Applications of Inverted Indexes on the UNIX System

M. E. Lesk

1. Introduction.

The UNIX† system has many utilities (e.g. *grep, awk, lex, egrep, fgrep,* ...) to search through files of text, but most of them are based on a linear scan through the entire file, using some deterministic automaton. This memorandum discusses a program which uses inverted indexes[1] and can thus be used on much larger data bases.

As with any indexing system, of course, there are some disadvantages; once an index is made, the files that have been indexed can not be changed without remaking the index. Thus applications are restricted to those making many searches of relatively stable data. Furthermore, these programs depend on hashing, and can only search for exact matches of whole keywords. It is not possible to look for arithmetic or logical expressions (e.g. "date greater than 1970") or for regular expression searching such as that in *lex.*[2]

Currently there are two uses of this software, the *refer* preprocessor to format references, and the *lookall* command to search through all text files on the UNIX system.‡

The remaining sections of this memorandum discuss the searching programs and their uses. Section 2 explains the operation of the searching algorithm and describes the data collected for use with the *lookall* command. The more important application, *refer* has a user's description in section 3. Section 4 goes into more detail on reference files for the benefit of those who wish to add references to data bases or write new *troff* macros for use with *refer*. The options to make *refer* collect identical citations, or otherwise relocate and adjust references, are described in section 5.

2. Searching.

The indexing and searching process is divided into two phases, each made of two parts. These are shown below.

A.   Construct the index.

    (1)   Find keys — turn the input files into a sequence of tags and keys, where each tag identifies a distinct item in the input and the keys for each such item are the strings under which it is to be indexed.

    (2)   Hash and sort — prepare a set of inverted indexes from which, given a set of keys, the appropriate item tags can be found quickly.

B.   Retrieve an item in response to a query.

    (3)   Search — Given some keys, look through the files prepared by the hashing and sorting facility and derive the appropriate tags.

    (4)   Deliver — Given the tags, find the original items. This completes the searching process.

The first phase, making the index, is presumably done relatively infrequently. It should, of course, be done whenever the data being indexed change. In contrast, the second phase, retrieving items, is presumably done often, and must be rapid.

An effort is made to separate code which depends on the data being handled from code which depends on the searching procedure. The search algorithm is involved only in programs (2) and (3), while knowledge of the actual data files is needed only by programs (1) and (4). Thus it is easy to adapt to different data files or different search algorithms.

---

† UNIX is a registered trademark of AT&T Bell Laboratories in the USA and other countries.

‡ *lookall* is not part of the Berkeley UNIX distribution.

To start with, it is necessary to have some way of selecting or generating keys from input files. For dealing with files that are basically English, we have a key-making program which automatically selects words and passes them to the hashing and sorting program (step 2). The format used has one line for each input item, arranged as follows:

> name:start,length (tab) key1 key2 key3 ...

where *name* is the file name, *start* is the starting byte number, and *length* is the number of bytes in the entry.

These lines are the only input used to make the index. The first field (the file name, byte position, and byte count) is the tag of the item and can be used to retrieve it quickly. Normally, an item is either a whole file or a section of a file delimited by blank lines. After the tab, the second field contains the keys. The keys, if selected by the automatic program, are any alphanumeric strings which are not among the 100 most frequent words in English and which are not entirely numeric (except for four-digit numbers beginning 19, which are accepted as dates). Keys are truncated to six characters and converted to lower case. Some selection is needed if the original items are very large. We normally just take the first *n* keys, with *n* less than 100 or so; this replaces any attempt at intelligent selection. One file in our system is a complete English dictionary; it would presumably be retrieved for all queries.

To generate an inverted index to the list of record tags and keys, the keys are hashed and sorted to produce an index. What is wanted, ideally, is a series of lists showing the tags associated with each key. To condense this, what is actually produced is a list showing the tags associated with each hash code, and thus with some set of keys. To speed up access and further save space, a set of three or possibly four files is produced. These files are:

File	Contents
entry	Pointers to posting file for each hash code
posting	Lists of tag pointers for each hash code
tag	Tags for each item
key	Keys for each item (optional)

The posting file comprises the real data: it contains a sequence of lists of items posted under each hash code. To speed up searching, the entry file is an array of pointers into the posting file, one per potential hash code. Furthermore, the items in the lists in the posting file are not referred to by their complete tag, but just by an address in the tag file, which gives the complete tags. The key file is optional and contains a copy of the keys used in the indexing.

The searching process starts with a query, containing several keys. The goal is to obtain all items which were indexed under these keys. The query keys are hashed, and the pointers in the entry file used to access the lists in the posting file. These lists are addresses in the tag file of documents posted under the hash codes derived from the query. The common items from all lists are determined; this must include the items indexed by every key, but may also contain some items which are false drops, since items referenced by the correct hash codes need not actually have contained the correct keys. Normally, if there are several keys in the query, there are not likely to be many false drops in the final combined list even though each hash code is somewhat ambiguous. The actual tags are then obtained from the tag file, and to guard against the possibility that an item has false-dropped on some hash code in the query, the original items are normally obtained from the delivery program (4) and the query keys checked against them by string comparison.

Usually, therefore, the check for bad drops is made against the original file. However, if the key derivation procedure is complex, it may be preferable to check against the keys fed to program (2). In this case the optional key file which contains the keys associated with each item is generated, and the item tag is supplemented by a string

> ;start,length

which indicates the starting byte number in the key file and the length of the string of keys for each item. This file is not usually necessary with the present key-selection program, since the keys always appear in the original document.

There is also an option (-C*n*) for coordination level searching. This retrieves items which match all but *n* of the query keys. The items are retrieved in the order of the number of keys that they match. Of course, *n* must be less than the number of query keys (nothing is retrieved unless it matches at least one key).

As an example, consider one set of 4377 references, comprising 660,000 bytes. This included 51,000 keys, of which 5,900 were distinct keys. The hash table is kept full to save space (at the expense of time); 995 of 997 possible hash codes were used. The total set of index files (no key file) included 171,000 bytes, about 26% of the original file size. It took 8 minutes of processor time to hash, sort, and write the index. To search for a single query with the resulting index took 1.9 seconds of processor time, while to find the same paper with a sequential linear search using *grep* (reading all of the tags and keys) took 12.3 seconds of processor time.

We have also used this software to index all of the English stored on our UNIX system. This is the index searched by the *lookall* command. On a typical day there were 29,000 files in our user file system, containing about 152,000,000 bytes. Of these 5,300 files, containing 32,000,000 bytes (about 21%) were English text. The total number of 'words' (determined mechanically) was 5,100,000. Of these 227,000 were selected as keys; 19,000 were distinct, hashing to 4,900 (of 5,000 possible) different hash codes. The resulting inverted file indexes used 845,000 bytes, or about 2.6% of the size of the original files. The particularly small indexes are caused by the fact that keys are taken from only the first 50 non-common words of some very long input files.

Even this large *lookall* index can be searched quickly. For example, to find this document by looking for the keys "lesk inverted indexes" required 1.7 seconds of processor time and system time. By comparison, just to search the 800,000 byte dictionary (smaller than even the inverted indexes, let alone the 27,000,000 bytes of text files) with *grep* takes 29 seconds of processor time. The *lookall* program is thus useful when looking for a document which you believe is stored on-line, but do not know where. For example, many memos from our center are in the file system, but it is often difficult to guess where a particular memo might be (it might have several authors, each with many directories, and have been worked on by a secretary with yet more directories). Instructions for the use of the *lookall* command are given in the manual section, shown in the appendix to this memorandum.

The only indexes maintained routinely are those of publication lists and all English files. To make other indexes, the programs for making keys, sorting them, searching the indexes, and delivering answers must be used. Since they are usually invoked as parts of higher-level commands, they are not in the default command directory, but are available to any user in the directory */usr/lib/refer*. Three programs are of interest: *mkey*, which isolates keys from input files; *inv*, which makes an index from a set of keys; and *hunt*, which searches the index and delivers the items. Note that the two parts of the retrieval phase are combined into one program, to avoid the excessive system work and delay which would result from running these as separate processes.

These three commands have a large number of options to adapt to different kinds of input. The user not interested in the detailed description that now follows may skip to section 3, which describes the *refer* program, a packaged-up version of these tools specifically oriented towards formatting references.

Make Keys. The program *mkey* is the key-making program corresponding to step (1) in phase A. Normally, it reads its input from the file names given as arguments, and if there are no arguments it reads from the standard input. It assumes that blank lines in the input delimit separate items, for each of which a different line of keys should be generated. The lines of keys are written on the standard output. Keys are any alphanumeric string in the input not among the most frequent words in English and not entirely numeric (except that all-numeric strings are acceptable if they are between 1900 and 1999). In the output, keys are translated to lower case, and truncated to six characters in length; any associated punctuation is removed. The following flag arguments are recognized by *mkey:*

−**c** *name*	Name of file of common words; default is */usr/lib/eign*.
−**f** *name*	Read a list of files from *name* and take each as an input argument.
−**i** *chars*	Ignore all lines which begin with '%' followed by any character in *chars* .
−**k***n*	Use at most *n* keys per input item.
−**l***n*	Ignore items shorter than *n* letters long.
−**n***m*	Ignore as a key any word in the first *m* words of the list of common English words. The default is 100.
−**s**	Remove the labels *(file:start,length)* from the output; just give the keys. Used when searching rather than indexing.
−**w**	Each whole file is a separate item; blank lines in files are irrelevant.

The normal arguments for indexing references are the defaults, which are −*c /usr/lib/eign*, −*n100*, and −*l3* . For searching, the −*s* option is also needed. When the big *lookall* index of all English files is run, the options are −*w*, −*k50*, and −*f (filelist)*. When running on textual input, the *mkey* program processes about 1000 English words per processor second. Unless the −k option is used (and the input files are long enough for it to take effect) the output of *mkey* is comparable in size to its input.

Hash and invert. The *inv* program computes the hash codes and writes the inverted files. It reads the output of *mkey* and writes the set of files described earlier in this section. It expects one argument, which is used as the base name for the three (or four) files to be written. Assuming an argument of *Index* (the default) the entry file is named *Index.ia*, the posting file *Index.ib*, the tag file *Index.ic*, and the key file (if present) *Index.id*. The *inv* program recognizes the following options:

−a	Append the new keys to a previous set of inverted files, making new files if there is no old set using the same base name.
−d	Write the optional key file. This is needed when you can not check for false drops by looking for the keys in the original inputs, i.e. when the key derivation procedure is complicated and the output keys are not words from the input files.
−h*n*	The hash table size is *n* (default 997); *n* should be prime. Making *n* bigger saves search time and spends disk space.
−i[**u**] *name*	Take input from file *name*, instead of the standard input; if **u** is present *name* is unlinked when the sort is started. Using this option permits the sort scratch space to overlap the disk space used for input keys.
−n	Make a completely new set of inverted files, ignoring previous files.
−p	Pipe into the sort program, rather than writing a temporary input file. This saves disk space and spends processor time.
−v	Verbose mode; print a summary of the number of keys which finished indexing.

About half the time used in *inv* is in the contained sort. Assuming the sort is roughly linear, however, a guess at the total timing for *inv* is 250 keys per second. The space used is usually of more importance: the entry file uses four bytes per possible hash (note the −**h** option), and the tag file around 15-20 bytes per item indexed. Roughly, the posting file contains one item for each key instance and one item for each possible hash code; the items are two bytes long if the tag file is less than 65336 bytes long, and the items are four bytes wide if the tag file is greater than 65536 bytes long. Note that to minimize storage, the hash tables should be over-full; for most of the files indexed in this way, there is no other real choice, since the *entry* file must fit in memory.

Searching and Retrieving. The *hunt* program retrieves items from an index. It combines, as mentioned above, the two parts of phase (B): search and delivery. The reason why it is efficient to combine delivery and search is partly to avoid starting unnecessary processes, and partly because the delivery operation must be a part of the search operation in any case. Because of the hashing, the search part takes place in two stages: first items are retrieved which have the right hash codes associated with them, and then the actual items are inspected to determine false drops, i.e. to determine if anything with the right hash codes doesn't really have the right keys. Since the original item is retrieved to check on false drops, it is efficient to present it immediately, rather than only giving the tag as output and later retrieving the item again. If there were a separate key file, this argument would not apply, but separate key files are not common.

Input to *hunt* is taken from the standard input, one query per line. Each query should be in *mkey* −*s* output format; all lower case, no punctuation. The *hunt* program takes one argument which specifies the base name of the index files to be searched. Only one set of index files can be searched at a time, although many text files may be indexed as a group, of course. If one of the text files has been changed since the index, that file is searched with *fgrep*; this may occasionally slow down the searching, and care should be taken to avoid having many out of date files. The following option arguments are recognized by *hunt*:

−a	Give all output; ignore checking for false drops.
−C*n*	Coordination level *n*; retrieve items with not more than *n* terms of the input missing; default *C0*, implying that each search term must be in the output items.

−F[yn_d_ **]**	"−Fy" gives the text of all the items found; "−Fn" suppresses them. "−F_d_" where _d_ is an integer gives the text of the first _d_ items. The default is −_Fy_.
−g	Do not use _fgrep_ to search files changed since the index was made; print an error comment instead.
−i _string_	Take _string_ as input, instead of reading the standard input.
−l _n_	The maximum length of internal lists of candidate items is _n;_ default 1000.
−o _string_	Put text output ("−Fy") in _string;_ of use _only_ when invoked from another program.
−p	Print hash code frequencies; mostly for use in optimizing hash table sizes.
−T[yn_d_ **]**	"−Ty" gives the tags of the items found; "−Tn" suppresses them. "−T_d_" where _d_ is an integer gives the first _d_ tags. The default is −_Tn_.
−t _string_	Put tag output ("−Ty") in _string;_ of use _only_ when invoked from another program.

27

The timing of _hunt_ is complex. Normally the hash table is overfull, so that there will be many false drops on any single term; but a multi-term query will have few false drops on all terms. Thus if a query is underspecified (one search term) many potential items will be examined and discarded as false drops, wasting time. If the query is overspecified (a dozen search terms) many keys will be examined only to verify that the single item under consideration has that key posted. The variation of search time with number of keys is shown in the table below. Queries of varying length were constructed to retrieve a particular document from the file of references. In the sequence to the left, search terms were chosen so as to select the desired paper as quickly as possible. In the sequence on the right, terms were chosen inefficiently, so that the query did not uniquely select the desired document until four keys had been used. The same document was the target in each case, and the final set of eight keys are also identical; the differences at five, six and seven keys are produced by measurement error, not by the slightly different key lists.

	Efficient Keys				Inefficient Keys		
No. keys	Total drops (incl. false)	Retrieved Documents	Search time (seconds)	No. keys	Total drops (incl. false)	Retrieved Documents	Search time (seconds)
1	15	3	1.27	1	68	55	5.96
2	1	1	0.11	2	29	29	2.72
3	1	1	0.14	3	8	8	0.95
4	1	1	0.17	4	1	1	0.18
5	1	1	0.19	5	1	1	0.21
6	1	1	0.23	6	1	1	0.22
7	1	1	0.27	7	1	1	0.26
8	1	1	0.29	8	1	1	0.29

As would be expected, the optimal search is achieved when the query just specifies the answer; however, overspecification is quite cheap. Roughly, the time required by _hunt_ can be approximated as 30 milliseconds per search key plus 75 milliseconds per dropped document (whether it is a false drop or a real answer). In general, overspecification can be recommended; it protects the user against additions to the data base which turn previously uniquely-answered queries into ambiguous queries.

The careful reader will have noted an enormous discrepancy between these times and the earlier quoted time of around 1.9 seconds for a search. The times here are purely for the search and retrieval: they are measured by running many searches through a single invocation of the _hunt_ program alone. The normal retrieval operation involves using the shell to set up a pipeline through _mkey_ to _hunt_ and starting both processes; this adds a fixed overhead of about 1.7 seconds of processor time to any single search. Furthermore, remember that all these times are processor times: on a typical morning on our PDP 11/70 system, with about one dozen people logged on, to obtain 1 second of processor time for the search program took between 2 and 12 seconds of real time, with a median of 3.9 seconds and a mean of 4.8 seconds. Thus, although the work involved in a single search may be only 200 milliseconds, after you add the 1.7 seconds of startup processor time and then assume a 4:1 elapsed/processor time ratio, it will be 8 seconds before any response is printed.

3. Selecting and Formatting References for TROFF

The major application of the retrieval software is *refer,* which is a *troff* preprocessor like *eqn*.[3] It scans its input looking for items of the form

    .[
    imprecise citation
    .]

where an imprecise citation is merely a string of words found in the relevant bibliographic citation. This is translated into a properly formatted reference. If the imprecise citation does not correctly identify a single paper (either selecting no papers or too many) a message is given. The data base of citations searched may be tailored to each system, and individual users may specify their own citation files. On our system, the default data base is accumulated from the publication lists of the members of our organization, plus about half a dozen personal bibliographies that were collected. The present total is about 4300 citations, but this increases steadily. Even now, the data base covers a large fraction of local citations.

For example, the reference for the *eqn* paper above was specified as

    ...
    preprocessor like
    .I eqn.
    .[
    kernighan cherry acm 1975
    .]
    It scans its input looking for items
    ...

This paper was itself printed using *refer.* The above input text was processed by *refer* as well as *tbl* and *troff* by the command

    refer memo-file | tbl | troff –ms

and the reference was automatically translated into a correct citation to the ACM paper on mathematical typesetting.

The procedure to use to place a reference in a paper using *refer* is as follows. First, use the *lookbib* command to check that the paper is in the data base and to find out what keys are necessary to retrieve it. This is done by typing *lookbib* and then typing some potential queries until a suitable query is found. For example, had one started to find the *eqn* paper shown above by presenting the query

    $ lookbib
    kernighan cherry
    (EOT)

lookbib would have found several items; experimentation would quickly have shown that the query given above is adequate. Overspecifying the query is of course harmless. A particularly careful reader may have noticed that "acm" does not appear in the printed citation; we have supplemented some of the data base items with common extra keywords, such as common abbreviations for journals or other sources, to aid in searching.

If the reference is in the data base, the query that retrieved it can be inserted in the text, between .[and .] brackets. If it is not in the data base, it can be typed into a private file of references, using the format discussed in the next section, and then the –**p** option used to search this private file. Such a command might read (if the private references are called *myfile*)

    refer –p myfile document | tbl | eqn | troff –ms . . .

where *tbl* and/or *eqn* could be omitted if not needed. The use of the *–ms* macros[4] or some other macro package, however, is essential. *Refer* only generates the data for the references; exact formatting is done by some macro package, and if none is supplied the references will not be printed.

By default, the references are numbered sequentially, and the *—ms* macros format references as footnotes at the bottom of the page. This memorandum is an example of that style. Other possibilities are discussed in section 5 below.

4. Reference Files.

A reference file is a set of bibliographic references usable with *refer*. It can be indexed using the software described in section 2 for fast searching. What *refer* does is to read the input document stream, looking for imprecise citation references. It then searches through reference files to find the full citations, and inserts them into the document. The format of the full citation is arranged to make it convenient for a macro package, such as the *—ms* macros, to format the reference for printing. Since the format of the final reference is determined by the desired style of output, which is determined by the macros used, *refer* avoids forcing any kind of reference appearance. All it does is define a set of string registers which contain the basic information about the reference; and provide a macro call which is expanded by the macro package to format the reference. It is the responsibility of the final macro package to see that the reference is actually printed; if no macros are used, and the output of *refer* fed untranslated to *troff,* nothing at all will be printed.

The strings defined by *refer* are taken directly from the files of references, which are in the following format. The references should be separated by blank lines. Each reference is a sequence of lines beginning with % and followed by a key-letter. The remainder of that line, and successive lines until the next line beginning with %, contain the information specified by the key-letter. In general, *refer* does not interpret the information, but merely presents it to the macro package for final formatting. A user with a separate macro package, for example, can add new key-letters or use the existing ones for other purposes without bothering *refer.*

The meaning of the key-letters given below, in particular, is that assigned by the *—ms* macros. Not all information, obviously, is used with each citation. For example, if a document is both an internal memorandum and a journal article, the macros ignore the memorandum version and cite only the journal article. Some kinds of information are not used at all in printing the reference; if a user does not like finding references by specifying title or author keywords, and prefers to add specific keywords to the citation, a field is available which is searched but not printed (**K**).

The key letters currently recognized by *refer* and *—ms,* with the kind of information implied, are:

Key	Information specified	Key	Information specified
A	Author's name	N	Issue number
B	Title of book containing item	O	Other information
C	City of publication	P	Page(s) of article
D	Date	R	Technical report reference
E	Editor of book containing item	T	Title
G	Government (NTIS) ordering number	V	Volume number
I	Issuer (publisher)		
J	Journal name		
K	Keys (for searching)	X	or
L	Label	Y	or
M	Memorandum label	Z	Information not used by *refer*

For example, a sample reference could be typed as:

27

```
%T Bounds on the Complexity of the Maximal
Common Subsequence Problem
%Z ctr127
%A A. V. Aho
%A D. S. Hirschberg
%A J. D. Ullman
%J J. ACM
%V 23
%N 1
%P 1-12
%M abcd-78
%D Jan. 1976
```

Order is irrelevant, except that authors are shown in the order given. The output of *refer* is a stream of string definitions, one for each of the fields of each reference, as shown below.

```
.]-
.ds [A authors' names ...
.ds [T title ...
.ds [J journal ...
...
.][ type-number
```

The special macro **.]−** precedes the string definitions and the special macro **.][** follows. These are changed from the input **.[** and **.]** so that running the same file through *refer* again is harmless. The **.]−** macro can be used by the macro package to initialize. The **.][** macro, which should be used to print the reference, is given an argument *type-number* to indicate the kind of reference, as follows:

Value	Kind of reference
1	Journal article
2	Book
3	Article within book
4	Technical report
5	Bell Labs technical memorandum
0	Other

The reference is flagged in the text with the sequence

```
\* ([.number\* (.]
```

where *number* is the footnote number. The strings **[.** and **.]** should be used by the macro package to format the reference flag in the text. These strings can be replaced for a particular footnote, as described in section 5. The footnote number (or other signal) is available to the reference macro **.][** as the string register **[F**.

In some cases users wish to suspend the searching, and merely use the reference macro formatting. That is, the user doesn't want to provide a search key between **.[** and **.]** brackets, but merely the reference lines for the appropriate document. Alternatively, the user can wish to add a few fields to those in the reference as in the standard file, or override some fields. Altering or replacing fields, or supplying whole references, is easily done by inserting lines beginning with %; any such line is taken as direct input to the reference processor rather than keys to be searched. Thus

```
.[
key1 key2 key3 ...
%Q New format item
%R Override report name
.]
```

makes the indicated changes to the result of searching for the keys. All of the search keys must be given before the first % line.

If no search keys are provided, an entire citation can be provided in-line in the text. For example, if the *eqn* paper citation were to be inserted in this way, rather than by searching for it in the data base, the input would read

```
    ...
    preprocessor like
    .I eqn.
    .[
    %A B. W. Kernighan
    %A L. L. Cherry
    %T A System for Typesetting Mathematics
    %J Comm. ACM
    %V 18
    %N 3
    %P 151-157
    %D March 1975
    .]
    It scans its input looking for items
    ...
```

This would produce a citation of the same appearance as that resulting from the file search.

As shown, fields are normally turned into *troff* strings. Sometimes users would rather have them defined as macros, so that other *troff* commands can be placed into the data. When this is necessary, simply double the control character % in the data. Thus the input

```
    .[
    %V 23
    %%M
    Bell Laboratories,
    Murray Hill, N.J. 07974
    .]
```

is processed by *refer* into

```
    .ds [V 23
    .de [M
    Bell Laboratories,
    Murray Hill, N.J. 07974
    ..
```

The information after %%M is defined as a macro to be invoked by .[M while the information after %V is turned into a string to be invoked by *([V. At present −*ms* expects all information as strings.

5. Collecting References and other Refer Options

Normally, the combination of *refer* and −*ms* formats output as *troff* footnotes which are consecutively numbered and placed at the bottom of the page. However, options exist to place the references at the end; to arrange references alphabetically by senior author; and to indicate references by strings in the text of the form [Name1975a] rather than by number. Whenever references are not placed at the bottom of a page identical references are coalesced.

For example, the −e option to *refer* specifies that references are to be collected; in this case they are output whenever the sequence

```
    .[
    $LIST$
    .]
```

is encountered. Thus, to place references at the end of a paper, the user would run *refer* with the −e option and place the above $LIST$ commands after the last line of the text. *Refer* will then move all the references to that point. To aid in formatting the collected references, *refer* writes the references preceded by the line

```
.]<
```

and followed by the line

```
.]>
```

to invoke special macros before and after the references.

Another possible option to *refer* is the −s option to specify sorting of references. The default, of course, is to list references in the order presented. The −s option implies the −e option, and thus requires a

```
.[
$LIST$
.]
```

entry to call out the reference list. The −s option may be followed by a string of letters, numbers, and '+' signs indicating how the references are to be sorted. The sort is done using the fields whose key-letters are in the string as sorting keys; the numbers indicate how many of the fields are to be considered, with '+' taken as a large number. Thus the default is −s**AD** meaning ''Sort on senior author, then date.'' To sort on all authors and then title, specify −s**A+T**. And to sort on two authors and then the journal, write −s**A2J**.

Other options to *refer* change the signal or label inserted in the text for each reference. Normally these are just sequential numbers, and their exact placement (within brackets, as superscripts, etc.) is determined by the macro package. The −l option replaces reference numbers by strings composed of the senior author's last name, the date, and a disambiguating letter. If a number follows the **l** as in −l3 only that many letters of the last name are used in the label string. To abbreviate the date as well the form −l*m,n* shortens the last name to the first *m* letters and the date to the last *n* digits. For example, the option −l3,2 would refer to the *eqn* paper (reference 3) by the signal *Ker75a*, since it is the first cited reference by Kernighan in 1975.

A user wishing to specify particular labels for a private bibliography may use the −k option. Specifying −k*x* causes the field *x* to be used as a label. The default is **L**. If this field ends in −, that character is replaced by a sequence letter; otherwise the field is used exactly as given.

If none of the *refer*-produced signals are desired, the −b option entirely suppresses automatic text signals.

If the user wishes to override the −*ms* treatment of the reference signal (which is normally to enclose the number in brackets in *nroff* and make it a superscript in *troff*) this can be done easily. If the lines .**[** or .**]** contain anything following these characters, the remainders of these lines are used to surround the reference signal, instead of the default. Thus, for example, to say ''See reference (2).'' and avoid ''See reference.[2]'' the input might appear

```
See reference
.[ (
imprecise citation ...
.]).
```

Note that blanks are significant in this construction. If a permanent change is desired in the style of reference signals, however, it is probably easier to redefine the strings **[.** and **.]** (which are used to bracket each signal) than to change each citation.

Although normally *refer* limits itself to retrieving the data for the reference, and leaves to a macro package the job of arranging that data as required by the local format, there are two special options for rearrangements that can not be done by macro packages. The −c option puts fields into all upper case (CAPS-SMALL CAPS in *troff* output). The key-letters indicated what information is to be translated to upper case follow the **c**, so that −c**AJ** means that authors' names and journals are to be in caps. The −a option writes the names of authors last name first, that is *A. D. Hall, Jr.* is written as *Hall, A. D. Jr*. The citation form of the *Journal of the ACM* , for example, would require both −c**A** and −a options. This produces authors' names in the style KERNIGHAN, B. W. AND CHERRY, L. L. for the previous example. The −a option may be followed by a number to indicate how many author names should be reversed; −a1 (without any −c option) would produce *Kernighan, B. W. and L. L. Cherry*, for example.

Finally, there is also the previously-mentioned −p option to let the user specify a private file of references to be searched before the public files. Note that *refer* does not insist on a previously made index for these files. If a file is named which contains reference data but is not indexed, it will be searched (more slowly) by *refer* using *fgrep.* In this way it is easy for users to keep small files of new references, which can later be added to the public data bases.

References

1.   D. Knuth, *The Art of Computer Programming: Vol. 3, Sorting and Searching,* Addison-Wesley, Reading, Mass., 1977. See section 6.5.

2.   M. E. Lesk, ''Lex — A Lexical Analyzer Generator,'' Comp. Sci. Tech. Rep. No. 39, Bell Laboratories, Murray Hill, New Jersey, October 1975 .].

3.   B. W. Kernighan and L. L. Cherry, ''A System for Typesetting Mathematics,'' *Comm. Assoc. Comp. Mach.,* vol. 18, pp. 151-157, Bell Laboratories, Murray Hill, New Jersey, March 1975 .].

4.   M. E. Lesk, *Typing Documents on UNIX and GCOS: The -ms Macros for Troff,* 1977.

27

BIB – A Program for Formatting Bibliographies

Timothy A. Budd
revised by A. Dain Samples,

Bib is a program for collecting and formatting reference lists in documents. It is a preprocessor to the nroff/troff typesetting systems, (much like the *tbl* [7] and *eqn* [3] programs) and an alternative to the *refer* [6] and *tib* [2] bibliography programs. *Bib* takes two inputs: a document to be formatted and a library of references. Imprecise citations in the source document are replaced by more conventional citation strings, the appropriate references are selected from the reference file, and commands are generated to format both citation and the referenced item in the bibliography.

Bib has been enhanced to promote sharing of bibliographic references from the *refer*, *bib*, and Tib tools. *Bib* now accepts the Tib style of macro invocation, i.e. surrounding names that are to be expanded with vertical bars. If you or your group are not contemplating moving to the TeX or LaTeX [4,5] text processors, then you need not worry about any of the references to Tib in this document. However, if you are considering such a move, and are worried about how you will convert your bibliographic databases to the BibTeX format, then the current version of *bib*, in conjunction with the existing Tib software[1] will make life a lot easier for you.

28

Description

An imprecise citation is a list of words surrounded by the characters [. and .]. Words (which are truncated to six letters) in the imprecise citation are matched against entries in the reference file, and if an entry is found that matches all words, that reference is used. For example:

> In Brooks' interesting book [. brooks mythical.] various reasons ...

Multiple citations are indicated by simply placing a comma in the imprecise citation:

> In [.kernig tools, kernig elements.], Kernighan and Plauger have ...

Embedded newlines, tabs and extra blanks within the imprecise citation are ignored.

Judicious use of the K (keyword) field in references in the database can simplify citations considerably. Also additional information can be placed into citations by surrounding text with curly braces. The additional information is inserted verbatim into the citation, e.g. [1, Chapter 6]. Note that it may be desirable to use non-breakable spaces, in order that the citation not be split across a line boundary by *troff*, for example:

> For a description of LR parsing, see [.dragon {,\ Chapter 6}.] by Aho and Ullman.

The angle brackets can be used as alternatives to the curly braces.

> For a description of LR parsing, see [.dragon <,\ Chapter 6>.] by Aho and Ullman.

---

1. Tib is available, for a handling charge, from James C. Alexander at the Dept. of Mathematics, University of Maryland, College Park, MD 20742. It is also available from **eneevax.umd.edu:pub/tib** via *ftp*.

An alternative citation style can be used by surrounding the imprecise citation with {. and .}. Most document styles just give the raw citation, without the braces, in this case. This is useful, for example, to refer to citations in running text.

> For a discussion of this point, see reference {.dragon.}.

The algorithm used by *bib* scans the source input in two passes. In the first pass, references are collected and the location of citations marked. In the second pass, these marks are replaced by the appropriate citation, and the entire list of references is dumped following a call on the macro .[]. This macro is left untouched. However, this can be altered to achieve other typographic effects.

An exception to this process is made in those instances where references are indicated in footnotes. In this case the macro that generates the reference is placed immediately after each line in which the reference is cited.

Creating the Database

Reference files are prepared for *bib* using *invert*. By default *invert* places an inverted index for the reference list in the file INDEX. Unless the user specifies an alternative (see the –p switch described below), this is the first file searched by *bib* in attempting to locate a reference. If the entry is not found in the user's file, a standard system-wide index is searched. If the entry is still not found in the system file, a warning message is produced and a blank citation is generated.

The format for entries in the reference file is described more fully in the section 'Reference File Formats'.

Since the user's index is searched before the system index, if the user wants to alter a specific entry in the system index (say to change the name W. E. Howden to William E. Howden, for example) it is a simple matter to copy the system information into a private database and make the changes locally. *Bib* issues messages warning the user if there are multiple entries in a reference file that match an imprecise reference, or if there are multiple index files that match an imprecise reference. (Note that previous versions of *bib* stopped searching after the first match was found. Current users of *bib* may see warning messages now that they did not receive before.) The 'duplicate matches' warning message can be controlled by making the citations more precise.

Citation formats are either determined by explicit switch settings or, more generally, by using a predefined formatting style. In the latter form, usage looks something like:

bib –tstyle [files]

where *style* is a citation style. Currently the following citation styles are available:

astro	astrophysical journal style references
compsurv	Computing Surveys style references
foot	footnoted references.
hnf	Hanson Normal Form
jrnl	lists references in alphabetical and date order by journal; see Miscellaneous Tools section.
lib	useful for printing the entire bibliography; see Miscellaneous Tools section
list	a useful format for listrefs, which see.
llist	another useful format for printing everything about your bibliography database; see Miscellaneous Tools section
opena	same as stda, but using an open format.
openn	same as stdsn, only using an open reference format (each major entry is on a new line[1]).
spe	format used by the journal *Software—Practice and Experience.*

---

1. The open reference format is adapted from *A Handbook for Scholars*, by Mary-Claire van Leunen, published by Knopf, 1978.

spe2	a second format for *Software—Practice and Experience*.
stda	standard alphabetic format, where citations are three letters followed by the last two digits of the date; for papers with a single author, the letters are the first three letters of the authors last name (e.g. Knu); in papers with two authors the first two letters are from the first author followed by one letter from the second (e.g. HoU); etc. (see the section **Citation Templates** under **Reference Format Desiner's Guide** for more details).
stdafull	standard alphabetic format, with full references.
stdn	standard numeric citation; reference entries are listed in order of mention.
stdsn	same as stdn, but references are sorted by senior author followed by date.
supn	same as stdn, but using superscripts.

It is possible to alter slightly the format of standard styles. For example, to generate references in standard numeric style with first names abbreviated:

$$\text{bib } -\text{tstdn } -\text{aa } ...$$

If two reference items create the same citation string (this can happen if two works by the same authors published in a single year are referred to in one paper) a disambiguating final letter is added to the citation (i.e., Knu79 becomes Knu79a and Knu79b). This can be altered by using the F field (see the section on Reference File Formats).

For the purposes of sorting by author, the last name is taken to be the last word of the name field. This means some care must be taken when names contain embedded blanks, such as in 'Hartley Rogers, Jr.' or 'Mary-Claire van Leunen'. In these cases a concealed space (\ ) should be used, as in 'Hartley Rogers,\ Jr.'.

bib knows very little about *troff* usage or syntax. This can sometimes be useful. For example, to cause an entry to appear in a reference list without having it explicitly cited in the text the citation can be placed in a *troff* comment.

    .\" [.imprecise citation.]

It is also possible to embed *troff* commands within a reference definition. See 'Abbreviations' in the section 'Reference Format Designer's Guide' for an example. However, be aware that unbridled use of such embedded processor-specific commands makes it more difficult to convert to other processors later. In the section on Miscellaneous Tools, we discuss ways to avoid such specificity.

In some styles (superscripts) periods and commas should precede the citation while spaces follow. In other styles (brackets) these rules are reversed. If a period, comma or space immediately precedes a citation, it will be moved to the appropriate location for the particular reference style being used. This movement is not done for citations given in the alternative style (i.e. {.dragon.}).

The following is a complete list of options for *bib*:

−aa	reduce author's first names to abbreviations.
−ar*num*	reverse the first *num* author's names. If *num* is omitted all names are reversed.
−ax	print authors last names in Caps-Small Caps style. For example Budd becomes BUDD.
−c*str*	build citations according to the template *str*; see the section **Citation Templates** under **Reference Format Desiner's Guide** for the format of the string and its effect.
−d *dir*	
−d*dir*	change the base directory in which files are sought. It is initially /usr/new/lib/bmac.
−ea	abbreviate editors' names
−ex	places editors' names in Caps-Small Caps style. (see −x)
−er*num*	reverse the first *num* editors' names. If *num* is omitted all editors' names are reversed.
−f	instead of dumping references following the call on .[], dump each reference immediately following the line on which the citation is placed (used for footnoted references).

−h   hyphenate runs of three or more contiguous references in the citation string. (eg 2,3,4,5 becomes 2-5). This is most useful for numeric citation styles, but works generally. The −h option implies the −o option.

−i file

−ifile   include and process the indicated file. This is useful for including a private file of string definitions.

−n*str*   turn off the indicated options. *str* must be composed of the characters *afhoRrvx*.

−o   sort contiguous citations according to the order given by the reference list. (This option defaults on).

−p *file*

−p*file*   instead of searching the file INDEX, search the indicated reference file(s) before searching the system file. Multiple files are separated by commas.

−R   print a warning each time there is an attempt to redefine a name. (No warning is the default.)

−r*num*   synonym for −ar.

−s*str*   sort references according to the template *str*.

−t *type*

−t*type*   use the standard macros and switch settings to generate citations and references in the indicated style.

−Tib   use the Tib macro conventions. See the discussion in the Reference Format Designer's Guide.

−Tibx   creates the file .bib.m4.in in the current directory. This file contains macro definitions that when applied to a database file, converts calls on macros to the form expected by the Tib bibliography preprocessor; more information is in the section Miscellaneous Tools.

−v   **[[I'm not sure what this does; it is related to the −f option, but it apparently suppresses the printing of certain information.]]**

−x   synonym for −ax.

When a file is to be included during normal *bib* processing (options −i and −t, and the style file command I) *bib* searches a specific set of directories and filenames. For example, if **-i myfile** is specified on the invocation line, *bib* attempts to open, in order, the following files until one is found.

1.   *./myfile*

2.   **BMACLIB**/*myfile*, where **BMACLIB** is defined by the −d option (default: /usr/new/lib/bmac).

3.   **BMACLIB**/*tibmacs*/*myfile* if −Tib was specified, otherwise **BMACLIB**/*bibmacs*/*myfile*

4.   *./bib.myfile*

5.   **BMACLIB**/*bib.myfile*.

If none are found, an error message is issued, and execution halts.

Reference File Formats

A reference file contains any number of reference items. Reference items are separated by one or more blank lines. There are no restrictions placed on the order of reference items in a file, although the user will find that imposing some order simplifies updates.

A reference item is a collection of field tags and values. A field tag is a percent sign followed by a single letter. Currently, the following field tags are recognized:

A	Author's name †
B	Title of book containing item
C	City of publication
D	Date
E	Editor(s) of book containing item †
F	Caption
G	Government (NTIS) ordering number
I	Issuer (publisher)
J	Journal name
K	Keys for searching § †
N	Issue number
O	Other information § †
P	Page(s) of article
R	Technical report number
S	Series title
T	Title
V	Volume number
W	Where the item can be found locally § †
X	Annotations § †

Fields marked with † are *accumulated* fields and can be repeated as necessary, but for all others only the last occurence of the field in any reference will be used. Those fields marked with § are ignored by most styles designed for publication, but can have additional information and are available to database listing styles and other software tools. A field can be as long as necessary and can extend onto new lines. No continuation characters are necessary: lines that do not begin with a percent sign or a period and are not blank are treated as continuations of the previous line. The order of fields is irrelevant, except that accumulated fields are listed in the order of occurrence.

The format of the reference file for *bib* is similar to that used by *refer* except that *bib* has the following additional capabilities:

1. An F field, if present, overrides whatever citation string would otherwise be constructed.

2. Certain defined names can be used, and will be expanded differently by different document styles. For example, the string CACM is expanded into 'Communications of the ACM' by some document styles, 'Comm. ACM' by others, and 'Comm. of the Assoc. of Comp. Mach.' by yet others. Appendix 1 lists some of the currently recognized names.

3. The program automatically abbreviates names, reverses names, and hyphenates strings of contiguous references, if requested.

4. A reference can have more than one editor field, and editor's names can be abbreviated, reversed, and/or printed in cap/small caps style, independent of any processing done to authors names.

5. Comments (lines with '#' in the first column) can be interspersed throughout the reference file. They are not used as sources of keywords (use the %O or %X fields for that).

The format of the reference file for *bib* is also similar to that used by *tib*, which shares a lot of source code with *bib*, with the following exceptions:

1. *Bib* does not recognize field tags *M, Z, a* through *z* and \, while *tib* does.

2. *Tib* currently does not recognize field tag *X*, and *bib* does.

3. *Tib* currently does not have any form of comment lines in the reference file, while *bib* marks comment lines with a '#' at the beginning of a line.

4. *Troff* commands may be inserted verbatim into *bib* references. In *tib* the '%\' field tag is used to insert TeX commands.

There may be (and probably are) other differences between *bib*, *tib*, and *refer* not documented here.

Generally a reference falls into one of several basic categories: book, journal article, conference paper, article in a book, compilations, technical report, PhD thesis, etc. An example of each and a brief comment is given below. With less standard references (Archival Sources, Correspondence, Government Documents, Newspapers) generally some experimentation is necessary.

Books

A book is something with a publisher that isn't a journal article or a technical report. Generally, books also have authors and titles and dates of publication (although some don't). For books not published by a major publishing house it is also helpful to give a city for the publisher. Some government documents also qualify as books, so a book may have a government ordering number.

It is conventional that the authors names appear in the reference in the same form as on the title page of the book. Note also that string definitions are provided for most of the major publishing houses (PRHALL for Prentice-Hall, for example). The string definition may include the city as part of the definition, depending on the database in use.

```
%A    R. E. Griswold
%A    J. F. Poage
%A    I. P. Polonsky
%T    The SNOBOL4 Programming Language
%I    PRHALL
%D    second edition 1971
```

Sometimes a book (particularly old books) will have no listed publisher. The reference entry must still have an I field.

```
%A    R. Colt Hoare
%T    A Tour through the Island of Elba
%I    (no listed publisher)
%C    London
%D    1814
```

If a reference database contains entries from many people (such as a departmental-wide database), the W field can be used to indicate where the referenced item can be found; using the initials of the owner, for example. Any entry style can take a W field, since this field is not used in formatting the reference.

The K field is used to define general subject categories for an entry. This is useful in locating all entries pertaining to a specific subject area. Note the use of the backslash to indicate the last name is Van Tassel, and not simply Tassel.

```
%A    Dennie Van\ Tassel
%T    Program Style, Design, Efficiency,
Debugging and Testing
%I    PRHALL
%D    1978
%W    tab
%K    testing debugging
```

Journal article

The only requirement for a journal article is that it have a journal name and a volume number. Usually journal articles also have authors, titles, page numbers, and a date of publication. They may also have numbers, and, less frequently, a publisher. (Generally, publishers are only listed for obscure journals).

Note that string names (such as CACM for *Communications of the ACM*) are defined for most major journals. There are also string names for the months of the year, so that months can be abbreviated to the first three (capital) letters. Note also in this example the use of the %K field to define a short name (hru) that can be used as a shorthand in an imprecise citation. (This is to be contrasted with BibTeX which not only *requires* user selected abbreviations, but also requires that they all be distinct from one another.)

```
%A    M. A. Harrison
%A    W. L. Ruzzo
%A    J. D. Ullman
%T    Protection in Operating Systems
%J    CACM
%V    19
%N    8
%P    461-471
%D    AUG 1976
%K    hru
```

Article in conference proceedings

An article from a conference is printed as though it were a journal article and the journal name was the name of the conference. Note that string names (SOSP, The Symposium on Operating System Principles) are also defined for the major conferences.

```
%A    M. Bishop
%A    L. Snyder
%T    The Transfer of Information and Authority
in a Protection System
%J    Proceedings of the 7th SOSP
%P    45-54
%D    1979
```

Article in book

An article in a book has two titles, the title of the article and the title of the book. The first goes into the T field and the second into the B field. Similarly the author of the article goes into the A field and the editor of the book goes into the E field.

```
%A    John B. Goodenough
%T    A Survey of Program Testing Issues
%B    Research Directions in Software Technology
%E    Peter Wegner
%I    MIT Press
%P    316-340
%D    1979
```

If a work as more than one editor, they each get their own %E field.

```
%A    R. J. Lipton
%A    L. Snyder
%T    On Synchronization and Security
%E    Richard A. DeMillo
%E    David P. Dobkin
```

```
%E    Anita K. Jones
%E    Richard J. Lipton
%B    Foundations of Secure Computation
%P    367-388
%I    ACPRESS
%D    1978
```

Sometimes the book is part of a multi-volume series, and hence may contain a volume field and/or a series name.

```
%A    C.A.R. Hoare
%T    Procedures and parameters: An axiomatic approach
%B    Symposium on semantics of algorithmic languages
%E    E. Engeler
%P    102-116
%S    Lecture Notes in Mathematics
%V    188
%I    Springer-Verlag
%C    Berlin-Heidelberg-New York
%D    1971
```

In any reference format, the O field can be used to give additional information. This is frequently used, for example, for secondary references.

```
%A    A. Girard
%A    J-C Rault
%T    A Programming Technique for Software Reliability
%B    Symposium on Software Reliability
%I    IEEE
%C    Montvale, New Jersey
%D    1977
%O    (Discussed in Glib [32])
```

Compilations

A compilation is the work of several authors gathered together by an editor into a book. The reference format is the same as for a book, with the editor(s) taking the place of the author.

```
%E    R. A. DeMillo
%E    D. P. Dobkin
%E    A. K. Jones
%E    R. J. Lipton
%T    Foundations of Secure Computation
%I    ACPRESS
%D    1978
```

Technical Reports

A technical report must have a report number. They usually have authors, titles, dates and an issuing institution (the I field is used for this). They may also have a city and a government issue number. Again string values (UATR for 'University of Arizona Technical Report') will frequently simplify typing references.

```
%A    T. A. Budd
%T    An APL Complier
%R    UATR 81-17
%C    Tucson, Arizona
%D    1981
```

If the institution name is not part of the technical report number, then the institution should be given separately.

```
%A    Douglas Baldwin
%A    Frederick Sayward
%T    Heuristics for Determining Equivalence of Program Mutations
%R    Technical Report Number 161
%I    Yale University
%D    1979
```

PhD Thesis

A PhD thesis is listed as if it were a book, and the institution granting the degree the publisher.

```
%A    Martin Brooks
%T    Automatic Generation of Test Data for
Recursive Programs Having Simple Errors
%I    PhD Thesis, Stanford University
%D    1980
```

Some authors prefer to treat Master's and Bachelor theses similarly, although most references on style instruct say to treat a Master's degree as an article or as a report.

```
%A    A. Snyder
%T    A Portable Compiler for the Language C
%R    Master's Thesis
%I    M.I.T.
%D    1974
```

28

Miscellaneous

A miscellaneous object is something that does not fit into any other form. It can have any of the the following fields; an author, a title, a date, page numbers, and, most generally, other information (the O field).

Any reference item can contain an F field, and the corresponding text will override whatever citation would otherwise be constructed.

```
%F    BHS--
%A    Timothy A. Budd
%A    Robert Hess
%A    Frederick G. Sayward
%T    User's Guide for the EXPER Mutation Analysis system
%O    (Yale university, memo)
```

Reference Format Designer's Guide

This section need only be read by those users who wish to write their own formatting macro packages.

The information necessary for generating citations and references of a particular style is contained in a *format file*. A format file consists of two parts; a sequence of format commands, which are read and interpreted by *bib*, and a sequence of text lines (usually *troff* macro definitions) which are merely copied to output. The format file name is always prefixed by 'bib.'. Thus the format file for a standard document type, such as stdn, is found in a file called bib.stdn.

Each formatting command is distinguished by a single letter, which must be the first character on a line. The formatting commands in a database file are similar to the command line options for *bib*. The legal commands, and their arguments, are as follows:

#*text*	A line beginning with a sharp sign is a comment, and all remaining text on the line is ignored.
A	The A command controls how authors' names are to be formatted. It can be followed by the following character sequences:

	A	Authors' names are to be abbreviated (see the section **Abbreviations**, below).
	R*num*	The first *num* authors' names are to be reversed. If *num* is omitted, all authors' names are reversed.
	X	Authors' names are to be printed in Caps-Small Caps style.

E	The E command is equivalent to the A command, except that it controls the formatting of editors' names.
F	The F command indicates that references are to be dumped immediately after a line containing a citation, such as when the references are to be placed in footnotes.
S *template*	The S command indicates references are to be sorted before being dumped. The comparison used in sorting is based on the *template*. See the discussion in the section **Sort Template** for an explanation of templates.
C *template*	The *template* is used as a model in constructing citations. See the discussion below in the section **Citation Templates**.
D *word definition*	The word-definition pair is placed into a table. Before each reference is dumped it is examined for the occurrence of these words. Any occurrence of a word from this table is replaced by the definition, which is then rescanned for other words. Words are limited to alphanumeric characters, ampersand and underscore. Definitions can extend over multiple lines by ending lines with a backslash (\). The backslash will be removed, and the definition, including the newline and the next line, will be entered into the table. This is useful for including several fields as part of a single definition (city names can be included as part of a definition for a publishing house, for example). *Bib* has been enhanced to recognize macro calls where the macro name is surrounded by vertical bars. This enhancement was implemented to to provide a little more compatibility between *bib* and Tib, a preprocessor that uses a database format very similar to *bib*'s. To have *bib* recognize only macro names surrounded by vertical bars, invoke the −Tib option.
I *filename*	The indicated file is included at the current point. The included file may contain other formatting commands.
H	Three or more contiguous citations that refer to adjacent items in the reference list are replaced by a hyphenated string. For example, the citation 2,3,4,5 would be replaced by 2-5. This is most useful with numeric citations. The H option implies the O option.
O	Contiguous citations are sorted according to the order given by the reference list.
R *number*	The first *number* author's names are reversed on output (i.e. T. A. Budd becomes Budd, T. A.). If number is omitted all names are reversed.

T *str* The *str* is a list of field names. Each time a definition string for a named field is produced, a second string containing just the last character will also be generated. See the section **Trailing Characters** below.

X Authors' last names are to be printed in Caps/Small Caps format (i.e., Budd becomes Budd).

** NOTE ** The first line encountered in the format input that does not match a format command causes that line, and all subsequent lines, to be immediately copied to the output without further processing.

File Naming Conventions

Standard database format files are kept in a standard library area. The string BMACLIB in bib.h points to this directory (/usr/new/lib/bmac in the distribution). In addition, this name is always defined when reading format files, and is defined with the l] macro when processing with *troff*. The first command output by *bib* defines the string l] to be this standard macro database directory. This allows macro files to be independent of where they are actually stored. There are three types of files:

bib.xxx These files contain bib commands to format documents in the xxx style.

bmac.xxx These files are the *troff* macros to actually implement a style. They are generally not examined by *bib* at all, but are processed by troff in response to a .so command.

bibinc.xxx These files contain information (such as definitions) used by more than one style database. The two usual files are bibinc.fullnames and bibinc.shortnames. Both of these include files bibinc.Xlocal (where X is full or short, respectively). Due to the way *bib* searches for files, if the user has these in his local directory, they will be read just before the contents of bibinc.Xnames are processed.

Troff Naming Conventions

There is a simple naming convention for strings, registers and macros used by *bib* during processing by *trof*. All strings, registers and macros are denoted by two character names containing either a left or right brace. The following are general rules:

[*x* If *x* is alphanumeric, the string contains the value of a reference field. If *x* is nonalphanumeric, this is a formatting string preceding a citation.

]*x* If *x* is alphanumeric, this is the final character from a reference field. If *x* is nonalphanumeric, the string is formatting information within a citation.

x[Strings in this format, where *x* is can be any character, are defined by the specific macro package in use and are not specified by *bib*.

x] If *x* is nonalphanumeric these strings represent formatting commands following citations (the inverse of [*x* commands). Other strings represent miscellaneous formatting commands, such as the space between leading letters in abbreviated names.

There are two such macro names to be particularly aware of: .s[and .e[. The first is called at the beginning of formatting a reference and the latter is called at the end of the formatting. The user can have some control over the formatting of references by redefining these macros.

It might be noted here that the best way to understand this stuff is to look at some existing definition files, and start making small changes here and there.

Sort Templates

The sort template is used in comparing two references to generate the sorted reference list. The sort template is a sequence of sort objects. Each sort object consists of an optional negative sign, followed by a field character, followed by an optional signed size. The leading negative sign, if present, specifies the sort is to be in decreasing order, rather than increasing. The field character indicates which field in the reference is to be compared. The entire field is used, except in the case of the 'A' field, in which case only the senior author's last name is used. A positive number following the field character indicates that only the first n characters are to be examined in the comparison. The negative value indicates only the last *n* characters. Thus, for example, the template AD−2 indicates that sorting is to be done by the senior author followed by the last two characters of the date.

The sort algorithm is stable, so that two documents which compare equally will be listed in citation order.

Note that in sorting, citation construction, and elsewhere, if an author field is not present the senior editor will be used. If neither author nor editor fields are present the institution name will be used.

Citation Templates

A citation template is similar to a sort template, with the following additions:

0   suppresses all printing. [[**True? can anyone tell me what this does?**]]

1   refers to the number which represents the position of the reference in the reference list (after sorting).

2   generates a three character sequence: if the paper being referenced has only one author, this is the first three characters of the author's last name; for two author papers, this is the first two characters of the senior author, followed by the first character of the second author; for papers with three or more authors the first letter of the first three authors is used.

3   used to specify a format consisting of the authors' last names, or the senior author followed by the text 'et al' if more than four authors are listed. This is the Astrophysical Journal style of citation.

4   the Computing Surveys style of citation.

8   full alphabetic.

9   last name of senior author.

Each object can be followed by either of the letters 'u' or 'l' and the field will be printed in all upper or all lower case, respectively.

If necessary for disambiguating, the character '@' can be used as a separator between objects in the citation template. Any text which should be inserted into the citation uninterpreted should be surrounded by either '{..}' or '<..>' pairs.

Citation Formatting in Troff

In the output, each citation is surrounded by the strings *([[and *(]] (or in the alternative style *([{ and *(}]). Multiple citations are separated by the string *(],. The text portion of a format file should contain *troff* definitions for these strings to achieve the appropriate typographic effect.

Citations that are preceded by a period, comma, space or other punctuation are surrounded by string values for formatting the punctuation in the appropriate location. Again, *troff* commands should be given to insure the appropriate values are produced.

The following table summarizes the string values that must be defined to handle citations.

[[	]]	Standard citation beginning and ending
{[	}]	Alternate citation beginning and ending
[.	.]	Period before and after citation
[,	,]	Comma before and after citation
[?	?]	Question mark before and after citation
[!	!]	Exclamation Point before and after citation
[:	:]	Colon before and after citation
[;	;]	Semi-Colon before and after citation
["	"]	Double Quote before and after citation
['	']	Single Quote before and after citation
[<	>]	Space before and after citation
],		Multiple citation separator
]-		Separator for a range of citations

Name Formatting in Troff

Authors' (and editors') names can be abbreviated, reversed, and/or printed in Caps-small Caps format. In producing the string values for an author, formatting strings are inserted to give the macro writer greater flexibility in producing the final output. Currently the following strings are used:

a]   gap between successive initials
b]   comma between last name and initial in reversed text
c]   comma between authors
n]   *and* between two authors
m]   *and* between last two authors
p]   period following initial

For example, suppose the name 'William E. Howden' is abbreviated and reversed. It will come out looking like

Howden*(b]W*(p]*(a]E*(p]

Reference Formatting in Troff

The particular style used in printing references is decided by macros passed to *troff*. Basically, for each reference, *bib* generates a sequence of string definitions, one for each field in the reference, followed by a call on the formatting macro. For example an entry which in the reference file looks like:

```
%A    M. A. Harrison
%A    W. L. Ruzzo
%A    J. D. Ullman
%T    Protection in Operating Systems
%J    CACM
%V    19
%N    8
%P    461-471
%D    1976
%K    hru
```

is converted into the following sequence of *troff* commands

```
.[−
.ds [F 1
.ds [A M\*(p]\*(a]A\*(p] Harrison
.as [A \*(c]W\*(p]\*(a]L\*(p] Ruzzo
.as [A \*(m]J\*(p]\*(a]D\*(p] Ullman
.ds [T Protection in Operating Systems
.ds [J Communications of the ACM
.ds [V 19
.ds [N 8
.nr [P 1
.ds [P 461-471
.ds [D 1976
.ds [K hru
.][
```

Note that the commands are preceded by a call on the macro '.[−'. This can be used by the macro routines for initialization, for example to delete old string values. (For some reason, the ending macro .e[also calls .PP The string [F is the citation string used in the document. Note that the string CACM has been expanded.

The strings c], n] and m] are used to separate authors. c] separates the initial authors in multi-author documents (it is usually a comma with some space before and after), n] separates authors in two author documents (usually ' and '), and m] separates the last two authors in multi-author documents (either ' and ' or ', and ').

If abbreviation is specified, the string a] is used to separate initials in the author's first name, and the string p] determines the punctuation to use (usually a period).

The *bib* system provides minimal assistance in deciding format types. For example note that the number register [P has been set of 1, to indicate that the article is on more than one page. Similarly, in documents with editors, the register [E is set to the number of editors.

Trailing Characters

There is a problem with fields that end with punctuation characters causing multiple occurrences of those characters to be printed. For example, suppose author fields are terminated with a period, as in T. A. Budd. If names are reversed, this could be printed as Budd, T. A.. Even if names are not reversed, abbreviations, such as in Jr. can cause problems.

To avoid this problem *bib*, if instructed, generates the last character from a particular field as a separate string. The string name is a right brace followed by the field character (e.g.]A for the author field). Macro packages should test this value before generating punctuation.

Abbreviations

The algorithm used to generate abbreviations from first names is fairly simple: Each word in the first name field that begins with a capital is reduced to that capital letter followed by a period. In some cases, this may not be sufficient. For example, suppose Ole-Johan Dahl should be abbreviated 'O–J. Dahl'. The only way to achieve this (short of editing the output) is to include *troff* commands in the reference file that alter the strings produced by *bib*, as in the following

```
...
%A Ole-Johan Dahl
.ds [A O–J. Dahl
...
```

In fact, if absolutely necessary, any *troff* commands can be entered in the middle of a reference entry, and the commands are copied uninterpreted to the output. For example, the user may wish to have a switch indicating whether the name is to be abbreviated or not:

```
...
%A Ole-Johan Dahl
.if \n(i[ .ds [A O–J. Dahl
...
```

However, keep in mind the restrictions this imposes on the portability and convertibility of the database.

An Example

Figure 1 shows the format file for the standard alphabetic format. The I command includes a file of definitions for common strings, such as dates and journal names. A portion of this file is shown in figure 2. The sort command indicates that sorting is to be done by senior author, followed by the last two digits of the date. The citation template indicates that citations will be a three character sequence followed by the last two characters of the date (e.g. AHU79) (described in the section on citations above). Author and editor names will be abbreviated. The .so command causes *troff* to read a basic set of macro definitions for formatting the references; the beginning of this file is shown in figure 3; note that a no-op has been inserted into the definition string for BIT in order to avoid further expansion when the definition is rescanned. Finally, the *troff* macro s[is redefined to turn off hyphenation across line-boundaries, and to make sure the citation is put in the bibliography list indented 10 ens and surrounded by square brackets.

```
# standard alphabetic format
I bibinc.shortnames
SAD–2
C2D–2
AA
EA
.so \*(l]/bmac.std
.de s[\" start reference by turning off hyphenation
.nh
.IP [\\*([F] 10n    \" indent the citation
..
```

Figure 1

```
D ACTA Acta Informatica
D BIT B\&IT
D CACM Communications of the ACM
...
D JAN Jan.
...
D DEC Dec.
```

Figure 2

```
.\" standard format troff commands
.\" citation formatting strings
.ds [[ [
.ds ]] ]
.ds ], ,\
.ds ]- -
.ds [. " \&
.ds .] .
.ds [, " \&
.ds ,] ,
 ...
.\" reference formating strings
.ds a] " \&
.ds b] , \&
.ds c] , \&
.ds n] '\& and \&
.ds m] '\& and \&
.ds e] \\fIet al.\\fP
.ds p] .
 ...
.\" reference formating macros
.de s[   \" start reference
.nh
.IP "[\*([F]" 5m
..
.de e[   \" end reference
.[–
..
.de []   \" start to display collected references
.LP
..
```

Figure 3

```
.de ][   \" choose format
.ie !'\\*([J'"' \{\
.   ie !'\\*([V'"' .nr t[ 1   \" journal
.   el          .nr t[ 5   \" conference paper
.\}
.el .ie !'\\*([B'"' .nr t[ 3   \" article in book
.el .ie !'\\*([R'"' .nr t[ 4   \" technical report
.el .ie !'\\*([I'"' .nr t[ 2   \" book
.el          .nr t[ 0   \" other
.\\n(t[[
..
```

Figure 4

On the basis of some simple rules (the presence or absence of certain fields) the document is identified as one of five different types, and a call made on a different macro for each type. This is shown in figure 4. Note that how the reference is printed (as a book, a journal article reference, etc.) is not determined by *bib*, but by the .][macro invoked by *troff*.

Finally figure 5 shows the macro for one of those different types, in this case the formatting macro for references to books.

```
.de 2[ \" book
.s[
.ie !"\\*([A'"" \\*([A,
.el .if !"\\*([E'"" \{\
.    ie \\n([E-1 \\*([E, eds.,
.    el \\*([E, ed.,\}
.if !"\\*([T'"" \\fI\\*([T\fP,
.rm a[
.if !"\\*([I'"" .ds a[ \\*([I
.if !"\\*([S'"" , \\*([S\c      \" book in a series
.if !"\\*([C'"" \{\
.    if !"\\*(a['"" .as a[ , \\&
.    as a[ \\*([C\}
.if !"\\*([D'"" \{\
.    if !"\\*(a['"" .as a[ , \\&
.    as a[ \\*([D\}
\\*(a[.
.if !"\\*([G'"" Gov. ordering no. \\*([G.
.if !"\\*([O'"" \\*([O.
.e[
..
```

Figure 5

Miscellaneous Tools

Bibinc

Some editors require journal names in a reference to be spelled out completely, while other journals expect a standardized shortened version. *Bib* is able to accomodate these requirements by reading different different definition files. For example, standard open alphabetic format (see **BMACLIB**/*bib.opena*) expects a definition file called *bibinc.fullnames*, while **BMACLIB**/*bib.spe* reads *bibinc.shortnames*. Maintaining these two files and making sure they are consistent with one another can be tedious. A program is included with *bib* to ease this problem. It allows the user to keep a single file with all definitions, and to have those definitions sent to the appropriate file(s). In what follows we assume that the name of this common file, the input file to *bibinc*, is called *bibinc.names*.

The format of the lines in *bibinc.names* is formally:

```
<inputline> ::= '+'<char1> <filename>
          | '+'<char1> '+'<char2> '+'<char3> ...
          | '+'<char> <name> <stuff>
          | '+'<char><stuff>
          | '?'<name>
```

In all cases the '+' or '?' must be the first character of a line to be recognized, and there can be no spaces between it and the following character. Continuation lines are all lines from the preceding '+' to the following '+'. Any and all whitespace at the beginning of a continuation line is discarded.

The first form defines <char1> to be the character that denotes an outputfile named <filename>. It must be the first occurence of <char1> following a '+' in the file.

The second form defines <char1> to be the character that denotes several previously defined outputfiles. It must be the first occurence of '+'<char1> in the file.

The third form says that the following line is to be written to the file or files denoted by <char> as:

D <name> <stuff>

The fourth form allows the inclusion of arbitrary stuff into the file. Note that there is no space between the <stuff> and <char> in the fourth form.

The fifth form is used to provide some mechanism to select lines to be processed according to whether one is intending to use *tib* or *bib*, and whether one is intending to use the TeX or the *troff* processors. The problem to be solved is that we want to be able to create files for three possibilities:

(1)   the user is using bib-style macros with troff,

(2)   the user is using tib-style macros with troff,

(3)   the user is using tib-style macros with TeX or LaTeX.

Therefore, the user can type the invocation line as:

```
bibinc bib troff  <bibinc.names
bibinc bib        <bibinc.names   (troff implied)
bibinc tib troff  <bibinc.names
bibinc tib tex    <bibinc.names
bibinc tex        <bibinc.names   (tib implied)
```

(Note that 'bibinc bib tex' is illegal: not a supported combination.) If a line of the form "?tib" is encountered in *bibinc.names*, then the lines following that line are processed only if "tib" was specified or implied on the invocation line. This restriction remains true until a line beginning "?bib" or "?" is encountered. Likewise, "?troff" will permit the processing of the following lines only if troff was specified or implied on the invocation line, and this remains true until "?tex" or "?" is encountered.

More on Tib style macro invocation

  Tib macro mechanism is quite different from the *bib* macro style. In *bib*, you define and use a macro as follows:

```
D macro expansion text
     :
%A A. Nonymous
%T macro on macro
```

The title will be expanded to 'expansion text on expansion text'. In *tib*, macro calls are always enclosed in vertical bars:

```
D macro expansion text
     :
%A A. Nonymous
%T The macro as macro
```

The title will be expanded to 'The macro as expansion text', therewith demonstrating a major benefit of using the vertical bars. Here is another benefit of the bars:

```
D u_um \"{u}
D Karlsruhe Karlsru_umhe
```

It's easy now to get the diacritical marks right, and still have a recognizable word to act as a key in the INDEX. It is possible to acheive this same effect with *bib*-style macros by using the non-printing space '\&'.

```
D u_um \*(:u
D Karlsruhe Karlsr\&u_um\&he
```

A Bibinc Example

  The Karlsruhe example has a problem if your database is being used for both TeX and ditroff: bib/tib macros have no conditionals, and you have to choose either the TeX code or the troff code for special characters. Bibinc has a mechanism to solve this. Let's assume you have the following in a file called bibinc.names:

```
━━━━━━━━━━━━━━━━━━━━━━━━━━━━━━━ bibinc.names
# first line of bibinc.names
#
# first use of a letter after '+' constitutes its definition
#
# define the letter F to mean 'write this line into the fullnames file'
?bib
?troff
+F bibinc.fullnames
+S bibinc.shortnames
+B +F +S      # both
?tib
?troff
+F bibinc-t.fullnames
+S bibinc-t.shortnames
?tex
+F tibinc.fullnames
+S tibinc.shortnames
?          # turns off specialization
+B +F +S      # both
#
?tex
+B a_um \"{a}
```

28

```
+B o_sl \o
+B o_um \"{o}
+B u_um \"{u}
+B TCOLADA $\mbox{TCOL}_\mbox{Ada}$
+B dash --
+B Rn  $\mbox{R}^\mbox{n}$
+B AMP \\&
?troff        # either bib or tib
+B a_um \*(:a
+B o_sl \*(/o
+B o_um \*(:o
+B u_um \*(:u
+B TCOLADA TCOL\dAda\u
+B dash \(hy
+B Rn  \*(Rn
+B AMP &
?
+B fuer f|u_um|r
#
+B IFI   Institut |fuer| Informatik
+B Universitat Universit|a_um|t
+B KARLSRUHE Karlsr|u_um|he
+F Karlsruhe |IFI|, |Universitat| KARLSRUHE|
   %C |KARLSRUHE|, West Germany       # note that leading blanks are removed
+S Karlsruhe |IFI|, |Universitat| KARLSRUHE|
+F SIGPLAN SIG\&PLAN Notices
+S SIGPLAN SIG\&PLAN
+B GUNS Smith |AMP| Wesson
# last line of bibinc.names
=================================== bibinc.names
```

This input to bibinc will select the correct expansion for u_um depending on whether -Tib was specified on its invocation line or not. That is, with the following invocation:

% bibinc troff tib <bibinc.names

two files will be written, bibinc-t.fullnames and bibinc-t.shortnames:

```
=================================== bibinc-t.fullnames
D a_um \*(:a
D o_sl \*(/o
D o_um \*(:o
D u_um \*(:u
D TCOLADA TCOL\dAda\u
D dash \(hy
D Rn  \*(Rn
D AMP &
D fuer f|u_um|r
D IFI   Institut |fuer| Informatik
D Universitat Universit|a_um|t
D KARLSRUHE Karlsr|u_um|he
D Karlsruhe |IFI|, |Universitat| KARLSRUHE\
%C |KARLSRUHE|, West Germany
D SIGPLAN SIGPLAN Notices
=================================== bibinc-t.fullnames
```

and

```
============================== bibinc-t.shortnames
D a_um \*(:a
D o_sl \*(/o
D o_um \*(:o
D u_um \*(:u
D TCOLADA TCOL\dAda\u
D dash \(hy
D Rn \*(Rn
D AMP &
D fuer f\u_um\r
D IFI   Institut fuer Informatik
D Universitat Universita_um\t
D KARLSRUHE Karlsru_um\he
D Karlsruhe  IFI, Universitat KARLSRUHE
D SIGPLAN SIGPLAN
============================== bibinc-t.shortnames
```

Users of bib/ditroff will have to specify -Tib on their invocations of bib to use these files.

The command:

%bibinc bib troff <bibinc.names

produces

```
============================== bibinc.fullnames
D a_um \*(:a
D o_sl \*(/o
D o_um \*(:o
D u_um \*(:u
D TCOLADA TCOL\dAda\u
D dash \(hy
D Rn \*(Rn
D AMP &
D fuer f\&u_um\&r
D IFI   Institut fuer Informatik
D Universitat Universit\&a_um\&t
D KARLSRUHE Karlsr\&u_um\&he
D Karlsruhe  IFI, Universitat KARLSRUHE\
%C KARLSRUHE, West Germany
D SIGPLAN SIG\&PLAN Notices
============================== bibinc.fullnames
```

and

```
============================== bibinc.shortnames
D a_um \*(:a
D o_sl \*(/o
D o_um \*(:o
D u_um \*(:u
D TCOLADA TCOL\dAda\u
D dash \(hy
D Rn \*(Rn
D AMP &
D fuer f\&u_um\&r
D IFI   Institut fuer Informatik
D Universitat Universit\&a_um\&t
D KARLSRUHE Karlsr\&u_um\&he
```

D Karlsruhe IFI, Universitat KARLSRUHE
D SIGPLAN SIG\&PLAN
================================= bibinc.shortnames

   In this mode, users of bib/ditroff will have to be very careful that their macro names do not conflict with anything in normal text.

   The command:

%bibinc tex tib <bibinc.names

produces:

================================= tibinc.fullnames
D a_um \"{a}
D o_sl \o
D o_um \"{o}
D u_um \"{u}
D TCOLADA $\mbox{TCOL}_\mbox{Ada}$
D dash --
D Rn $\mbox{R}^\mbox{n}$
D AMP \&
D fuer \fu_um\r
D IFI   Institut \fuer\ Informatik
D Universitat Universit\a_um\t
D KARLSRUHE Karlsr\u_um\he
D Karlsruhe \IFI\, \Universitat\ \KARLSRUHE\
%C \KARLSRUHE\, West Germany
D SIGPLAN SIGPLAN Notices
================================= tibinc.fullnames

and

================================= tibinc.shortnames
D a_um \"{a}
D o_sl \o
D o_um \"{o}
D u_um \"{u}
D TCOLADA $\mbox{TCOL}_\mbox{Ada}$
D dash --
D Rn $\mbox{R}^\mbox{n}$
D AMP \&
D fuer \fu_um\r
D IFI   Institut \fuer\ Informatik
D Universitat Universit\a_um\t
D KARLSRUHE Karlsr\u_um\he
D Karlsruhe \IFI\, \Universitat\ \KARLSRUHE\
D SIGPLAN SIGPLAN
================================= tibinc.shortnames

   Notice how bibinc handles the bib/troff use of the special character sequence \& in the above definitions of
the SIGPLAN macro. I.e., bibinc removes all user inserted \&'s when tib/tex is specified. NOTICE that when
tib/tex is specified, any other \<char> is passed through exactly as is, unless <char> is \, in which case bibinc
reduces it to a single \. Otherwise, all other \<char> are passed through as is.

An Example Makefile

Included with the distribution of *bib* is an example makefile that provides some hints on how to print out one's bibliographic database. The file is **BMACLIB**/Makefile.e.g., with a final period. For example, by typing

make -f Makefile.e.g. KEYWORD=cache print

you will get a listing of all entries in your database that have the keyword *cache* in them. Typing

make -f Makefile.e.g. bib

a complete listing of the database is produced. And finally,

make -f Makefile.e.g. KEYWORD=Ineed2read journals

will list all entries which have the keyword *Ineed2read*, presumably put in the %K field of references the user wants to read. Moreover, the listing is then sorted by the %J (journal) field, which is a convenient ordering for organizing your trips to the library.

Converting a database to a database

If at any point in the future you intend to begin using the TeX or LaTeX text processors, you will face the problem of converting your existing database files either to BibTeX format or to Tib format. Use of the -Tibx option to *bib* can simplify the conversion to *tib*. There is a public domain program called *tr2tex* which may also help convert existing documents; however, it is not included with the distribution of *bib*. Try contacting Kamal Al-Yahya at kamal@hanauma.stanford.edu. If that doesn't work try kamal%hanauma@score.stanford.edu.

To convert a database, run your usual sequence of commands to create your document using *bib*, except add the option -Tibx to *bib*'s command line. After the creation of your document, will also find the file *bib.m4.in which contains a set of m4 macro definitions. For each database file INDEX you wish to convert, type*

% bib2tib INDEX

and that's it! Well, almost. At this point your database files have had almost all macro calls converted to the vertical bar style. The ones that have not been caught are those that have ampersands in them: bib allows ampersands in macro names, but the m4 macro processor does not. Therefore, you will need to chase those down by hand.

Also, this has done nothing to remove any *troff* specific commands that may be embedded in you source files: they, too, will need to be changed *but only if you are converting to TeX.* If you are staying with *troff* for a while, or even for a long time, there is nothing more you need do.

28

Acknowledgements

bib was inspired by *refer*, written by M. Lesk. Enhancements to support *tib* style macros were discussed in depth with Michael van De Vanter and Ethan Munson. However, they did not do the implementation: blame that on Dain Samples.

1.   A. V. Aho and J. D. Ullman, *Principles of Compiler Design*, Addison-Wesley, 1977.

2.   J. C. Alexander, *Tib: A TeX bibliographic preprocessor*, (draft), 1987.

3.   B. W. Kernighan and L. L. Cherry, A System for Typesetting Mathematics, *CACM 18*, 3 (MAR 1978), 151-156.

4.   D. Knuth, *The TeXbook*, ADDISON, 1984.

5.   L. Lamport, *LaTeX: A Document Preparation System*, ADDISON, 1986.

6.   M. E. Lesk, Some Applications of Inverted Indexes on the UNIX System, Bell Laboratories Computing Science Technical Report 69, JUN 1978.

7.   M. E. Lesk, Tbl - A Program to Format Tables, *Unix Programmer's Manual, Vol 2A*, .

28

APPENDIX 1

Standard Names

The following list gives some of the standard names recognized in most citation styles. Various different forms for the output are used by the different styles. In the longer reference style, the conference proceedings will also refer to the date (%D), city (%C), and when the proceedings are published as a journal, the journal name (%J), volume (%V) and number (%N). Not all names are listed here. See BMACLIB/bibmacs/bibinc.fullnames for a complete list.

Miscellaneous Names

a_um	ä
o_um	ö
u_um	ü
A_um	Ä
O_um	Ö
U_um	Ü
o_sl	ø
AMP	&
dash	-
ARCH	Architecture
COMP	Computer
COMPs	Computers
COMPg	Computing
CONF	Conference
CORP	Corporation
CS	Computer Science
CSD	Computer Science Department
DCS	Department of Computer Science
DEPT	Department
DISS	Dissertation
ENG	Engineering
EE	Electrical Engineering
fuer	für
INTL	International
JOUR	Journal
LANG	Language
LANGs	Languages
NATL	National
PHD	PhD Dissertation
PROC	Proceedings
PROG	Program
PRing	Programming
PROCSIGPLAN	Proceedings of the ACM-SIGPLAN
SCI	Science
SCIs	Sciences
SOFT	Software
SYMP	Symposium
SYS	System
SYSs	Systems
TRANS	Transactions
TR	Technical Report
UNIV	University
UNIVCA	University of California

Journal Names

ACMCS	ACM Computing Surveys
ACTA	Acta Informatica
AT&TTJ	AT&T Technical Journal

28

28

BIT	BIT
BSTJ	Bell System Technical Journal
CACM	Communications of the ACM
CAN	Computer Architecture News
COMPJOUR	The Computer Journal
COMPLANG	Journal of Computer Languages
COMPSUR	ACM Computing Surveys
HCI	Human-Computer Interaction
HUMFACT	Human Factors
I&C	Information and Control
IBMJRD	IBM Journal of Research and Development
IBMSJ	IBM Systems Journal
IEEEC	IEEE Computer
IEEEIT	IEEE Transactions on Information Theory
IEEEM	IEEE Micro
IEEESW	IEEE Softare
IEEETC	IEEE Transactions on Computers
IEEETIT	IEEE Transactions on Information Theory
IEEETSE	IEEE Transactions on Softare Engineering
IEEETSMC	IEEE Transactions on Systems, Man, and Information Sciences
IJCAI	International Joint Conference on Artificial Intelligence
IJCIS	International Journal of Computer and Information Sciences
IJCM	International Journal of Computer Mathematics
IJMMS	International Journal of Man-Machine Studies
IPL	Information Processing Letters
JACM	Journal of the ACM
JALG	Journal of Algorithms
JCSS	Journal of Computer and System Sciences
JPhil	Journal of Philosophy
JS&S	Journal of Systems and Softare
MATHST	Mathematics Systems Theory
NMATH	Numerical Mathematics
PerfEv	Performance Evaluation
SIAMJAM	SIAM Journal on Applied Mathematics
SIAMJC	SIAM Journal on Computing
SIAMJNA	SIAM Journal on Numerical Analysis
SIGACT	SIGACT News
SIGCHI	ACM SIGCHI Bulletin
SIGPLAN	SIGPLAN Notices
SIGSOFT	Softare Engineering Notes
SP&E	Softare–Practice & Experience
TIPSJ	Transactions of the Information Processing Society of Japan (Japanese)
TOCS	ACM Transactions on Computer Systems
TODS	ACM Transactions on Database Systems
TOMS	ACM Transactions on Mathematical Softare
TOOIS	ACM Transactions on Office Information Systems
TOPLAS	ACM Transactions on Programming Languages and Systems
TSE	IEEE Transactions on Softare Engineering

Selected Conferences

ADA80	PROC of the ACM-SIGPLAN Symposium on the Ada Programming Language, SIGPLAN
ASPLOS82	PROC of the SYMP on Architectural Support for Programming Languages and Operating Systems, SIGPLAN
CCC79	PROC of the SIGPLAN 1979 SYMP on Compiler Construction, SIGPLAN
CCC82	PROC of the SIGPLAN 1982 SYMP on Compiler Construction, SIGPLAN
CCC84	PROC of the SIGPLAN 1984 SYMP on Compiler Construction, SIGPLAN
CONF	Conference
FJCC	Fall Joint Computer Conference
FOCS	Annual SYMP on Foundations of Computer Science

HICSS	Hawaii International CONF on System Science
ICSE	International CONF on Software Engineering
JER3	PROC Third Jerusalem CONF on Information Technology
JICAI	Joint International CONF on Artificial Intelligence
PLISS83	PROC SIGPLAN 1983 SYMP on Programming Language Issues in Software Systems, SIGPLAN
POPL	ACM SYMP on Principles of Programming Languages
POPL5	Conference Record of the Fifth POPL
POPL6	Conference Record of the Sixth POPL
POPL7	Conference Record of the Seventh POPL
POPL8	Conference Record of the Eighth POPL
POPL9	Conference Record of the Ninth POPL
POPL10	Conference Record of the Tenth POPL
POPL11	Conference Record of the Eleventh POPL
PROC	Proceedings
SOSP	SYMP on Operating System Principles
STOC	Annual ACM SYMP on Theory of Computing
SYMP	Symposium
WJCC	PROC Western Joint Computer CONF

Place Names

BTLHO	Bell Laboratories
BTLMH	Bell Laboratories
CMU	Carnegie-Mellon University
CMUCS	Computer Science Department, Carnegie-Mellon University
DG	Data General
MITAI	MIT Artificial Intelligence Laboratory
MITLCS	MIT Laboratory for Computer Science
SUCS	Computer Science Department, Stanford University
SUCSL	Computer Systems Lab., Stanford Electronics Lab., Dept. of Electrical Engineering and Computer Science
SUEE	Department of Electrical Engineering, Stanford University
TUM	Technische Universität München
UCB	University of California, Berkeley
UCBCS	Computer Science Division, EECS, UCB
UCBERL	ERL, EECS, UCB

28

Months of the year

JAN	January
FEB	February
MAR	March
APR	April
MAY	May
JUN	June
JUL	July
AUG	August
SEP	September
OCT	October
NOV	November
DEC	December

Publishers

ACADEMIC	Academic Press
ACPRESS	Academic Press
ADDISON	Addison Wesley
ANSI	American National Standards Institute
CSPRESS	Computer Science Press
DIGITAL	Digital Press

ELSEVIER	American Elsevier
FREEMAN	W. H. Freeman and Company
GPO	U. S. Government Printing Office
HOLT	Holt, Rinehart, and Winston
IEEEP	IEEE Press
MCGRAW	McGraw-Hill
MGHILL	McGraw-Hill
MITP	MIT Press
NHOLL	North-Holland
NYC	New York, NY
PRENTICE	Prentice Hall
PRHALL	Prentice Hall
SPRINGER	Springer Verlag
SRA	Science Research Associates
WILEY	John Wiley & Sons
WINTH	Winthrop Publishers

28

Writing Tools - The STYLE and DICTION Programs

L. L. Cherry

W. Vesterman

Livingston College
Rutgers University

ABSTRACT

Text processing systems are now in heavy use in many companies to format documents. With many documents stored on line, it has become possible to use computers to study writing style itself and to help writers produce better written and more readable prose. The system of programs described here is an initial step toward such help. It includes programs and a data base designed to produce a stylistic profile of writing at the word and sentence level. The system measures readability, sentence and word length, sentence type, word usage, and sentence openers. It also locates common examples of wordy phrasing and bad diction. The system is useful for evaluating a document's style, locating sentences that may be difficult to read or excessively wordy, and determining a particular writer's style over several documents.

1. Introduction

Computers have become important in the document preparation process, with programs to check for spelling errors and to format documents. As the amount of text stored on line increases, it becomes feasible and attractive to study writing style and to attempt to help the writer in producing readable documents. The system of writing tools described here is a first step toward such help. The system includes programs and a data base to analyze writing style at the word and sentence level. We use the term "style" in this paper to describe the results of a writer's particular choices among individual words and sentence forms. Although many judgements of style are subjective, particularly those of word choice, there are some objective measures that experts agree lead to good style. Three programs have been written to measure some of the objectively definable characteristics of writing style and to identify some commonly misused or unnecessary phrases. Although a document that conforms to the stylistic rules is not guaranteed to be coherent and readable, one that violates all of the rules is likely to be difficult or tedious to read. The program STYLE calculates readability, sentence length variability, sentence type, word usage and sentence openers at a rate of about 400 words per second on a PDP11/70 running the UNIX† Operating System. It assumes that the sentences are well-formed, i. e. that each sentence has a verb and that the subject and verb agree in number. DICTION identifies phrases that are either bad usage or unnecessarily wordy. EXPLAIN acts as a thesaurus for the phrases found by DICTION. Sections 2, 3, and 4 describe the programs; Section 5 gives the results on a cross-section of technical documents; Section 6 discusses accuracy and problems; Section 7 gives implementation details.

---

† UNIX is a registered trademark of AT&T Bell Laboratories in the USA and other countries.

2. STYLE

The program STYLE reads a document and prints a summary of readability indices, sentence length and type, word usage, and sentence openers. It may also be used to locate all sentences in a document longer than a given length, of readability index higher than a given number, those containing a passive verb, or those beginning with an expletive. STYLE is based on the system for finding English word classes or parts of speech, PARTS [1]. PARTS is a set of programs that uses a small dictionary (about 350 words) and suffix rules to partially assign word classes to English text. It then uses experimentally derived rules of word order to assign word classes to all words in the text with an accuracy of about 95%. Because PARTS uses only a small dictionary and general rules, it works on text about any subject, from physics to psychology. Style measures have been built into the output phase of the programs that make up PARTS. Some of the measures are simple counters of the word classes found by PARTS; many are more complicated. For example, the verb count is the total number of verb phrases. This includes phrases like:

> has been going
> was only going
> to go

each of which each counts as one verb. Figure 1 shows the output of STYLE run on a paper by Kernighan and Mashey about the UNIX programming environment [2].

```
programming environment
readability grades:
                        (Kincaid) 12.3  (auto) 12.8  (Coleman-Liau) 11.8  (Flesch) 13.5 (46.3)
sentence info:
                        no. sent 335 no. wds 7419
                        av sent leng 22.1 av word leng 4.91
                        no. questions 0 no. imperatives 0
                        no. nonfunc wds 4362  58.8%  av leng 6.38
                        short sent (<17) 35% (118) long sent (>32)  16% (55)
                        longest sent 82 wds at sent 174; shortest sent 1 wds at sent 117
sentence types:
                        simple  34% (114) complex  32% (108)
                        compound  12% (41) compound-complex  21% (72)
word usage:
                        verb types as % of total verbs
                        tobe  45% (373) aux  16% (133) inf  14% (114)
                        passives as % of non-inf verbs  20% (144)
                        types as % of total
                        prep 10.8% (804) conj 3.5% (262) adv 4.8% (354)
                        noun 26.7% (1983) adj 18.7% (1388) pron 5.3% (393)
                        nominalizations  2 % (155)
sentence beginnings:
                        subject opener: noun (63) pron (43) pos (0) adj (58) art (62) tot  67%
                        prep  12% (39) adv  9% (31)
                        verb  0% (1) sub_conj  6% (20) conj  1% (5)
                        expletives  4% (13)
```

Figure 1

As the example shows, STYLE output is in five parts. After a brief discussion of sentences, we will describe the parts in order.

2.1. What is a sentence?

Readers of documents have little trouble deciding where the sentences end. People don't even have to stop and think about uses of the character ''.'' in constructions like 1.25, A. J. Jones, Ph.D., i. e., or etc. . When a computer reads a document, finding the end of sentences is not as easy. First we must throw away the printer's marks and formatting commands that litter the text in computer form. Then STYLE defines a sentence as a string of words ending in one of:

> . ! ? /.

The end marker ''/.'' may be used to indicate an imperative sentence. Imperative sentences that are not so marked are not identified as imperative. STYLE properly handles numbers with embedded decimal points and commas, strings of letters and numbers with embedded decimal points used for naming computer file names, and the common abbreviations listed in Appendix 1. Numbers that end sentences, like the preceding sentence, cause a sentence break if the next word begins with a capital letter. Initials only cause a sentence break if the next word begins with a capital and is found in the dictionary of function words used by PARTS. So the string

> J. D. JONES

does not cause a break, but the string

> ... system H. The ...

does. With these rules most sentences are broken at the proper place, although occasionally either two sentences are called one or a fragment is called a sentence. More on this later.

2.2. Readability Grades

The first section of STYLE output consists of four readability indices. As Klare points out in [3] readability indices may be used to estimate the reading skills needed by the reader to understand a document. The readability indices reported by STYLE are based on measures of sentence and word lengths. Although the indices may not measure whether the document is coherent and well organized, experience has shown that high indices seem to be indicators of stylistic difficulty. Documents with short sentences and short words have low scores; those with long sentences and many polysyllabic words have high scores. The 4 formulae reported are Kincaid Formula [4], Automated Readability Index [5], Coleman-Liau Formula [6] and a normalized version of Flesch Reading Ease Score [7]. The formulae differ because they were experimentally derived using different texts and subject groups. We will discuss each of the formulae briefly; for a more detailed discussion the reader should see [3].

The Kincaid Formula, given by:

$$Reading\_Grade = 11.8*syl\_per\_wd + .39*wds\_per\_sent - 15.59$$

was based on Navy training manuals that ranged in difficulty from 5.5 to 16.3 in reading grade level. The score reported by this formula tends to be in the mid-range of the 4 scores. Because it is based on adult training manuals rather than school book text, this formula is probably the best one to apply to technical documents.

The Automated Readability Index (ARI), based on text from grades 0 to 7, was derived to be easy to automate. The formula is:

$$Reading\_Grade = 4.71*let\_per\_wd + .5*wds\_per\_sent - 21.43$$

ARI tends to produce scores that are higher than Kincaid and Coleman-Liau but are usually slightly lower than Flesch.

The Coleman-Liau Formula, based on text ranging in difficulty from .4 to 16.3, is:

$$Reading\_Grade = 5.89*let\_per\_wd - .3*sent\_per\_100\_wds - 15.8$$

Of the four formulae this one usually gives the lowest grade when applied to technical documents.

29

The last formula, the Flesch Reading Ease Score, is based on grade school text covering grades 3 to 12. The formula, given by:

$$Reading\_Score = 206.835 - 84.6*syl\_per\_wd - 1.015*wds\_per\_sent$$

is usually reported in the range 0 (very difficult) to 100 (very easy). The score reported by STYLE is scaled to be comparable to the other formulas, except that the maximum grade level reported is set to 17. The Flesch score is usually the highest of the 4 scores on technical documents.

Coke [8] found that the Kincaid Formula is probably the best predictor for technical documents; both ARI and Flesch tend to overestimate the difficulty; Coleman-Liau tend to underestimate. On text in the range of grades 7 to 9 the four formulas tend to be about the same. On easy text the Coleman-Liau formula is probably preferred since it is reasonably accurate at the lower grades and it is safer to present text that is a little too easy than a little too hard.

If a document has particularly difficult technical content, especially if it includes a lot of mathematics, it is probably best to make the text very easy to read, i.e. a lower readability index by shortening the sentences and words. This will allow the reader to concentrate on the technical content and not the long sentences. The user should remember that these indices are estimators; they should not be taken as absolute numbers. STYLE called with ''–r number'' will print all sentences with an Automated Readability Index equal to or greater than ''number''.

2.3. Sentence length and structure

The next two sections of STYLE output deal with sentence length and structure. Almost all books on writing style or effective writing emphasize the importance of variety in sentence length and structure for good writing. Ewing's first rule in discussing style in the book *Writing for Results* [9] is:

''Vary the sentence structure and length of your sentences.''

Leggett, Mead and Charvat break this rule into 3 in *Prentice-Hall Handbook for Writers* [10] as follows:

''34a. Avoid the overuse of short simple sentences.''
''34b. Avoid the overuse of long compound sentences.''
''34c. Use various sentence structures to avoid monotony and increase effectiveness.''

Although experts agree that these rules are important, not all writers follow them. Sample technical documents have been found with almost no sentence length or type variability. One document had 90% of its sentences about the same length as the average; another was made up almost entirely of simple sentences (80%).

The output sections labeled ''sentence info'' and ''sentence types'' give both length and structure measures. STYLE reports on the number and average length of both sentences and words, and number of questions and imperative sentences (those ending in ''/.''). The measures of non-function words are an attempt to look at the content words in the document. In English non-function words are nouns, adjectives, adverbs, and non-auxiliary verbs; function words are prepositions, conjunctions, articles, and auxiliary verbs. Since most function words are short, they tend to lower the average word length. The average length of non-function words may be a more useful measure for comparing word choice of different writers than the total average word length. The percentages of short and long sentences measure sentence length variability. Short sentences are those at least 5 words less than the average; long sentences are those at least 10 words longer than the average. Last in the sentence information section is the length and location of the longest and shortest sentences. If the flag ''–l number'' is used, STYLE will print all sentences longer than ''number''.

Because of the difficulties in dealing with the many uses of commas and conjunctions in English, sentence type definitions vary slightly from those of standard textbooks, but still measure the same constructional activity.

1. A simple sentence has one verb and no dependent clause.

2. A complex sentence has one independent clause and one dependent clause, each with one verb. Complex sentences are found by identifying sentences that contain either a subordinate conjunction

or a clause beginning with words like ''that'' or ''who''. The preceding sentence has such a clause.

3.   A compound sentence has more than one verb and no dependent clause. Sentences joined by '';'' are also counted as compound.

4.   A compound-complex sentence has either several dependent clauses or one dependent clause and a compound verb in either the dependent or independent clause.

Even using these broader definitions, simple sentences dominate many of the technical documents that have been tested, but the example in Figure 1 shows variety in both sentence structure and sentence length.

2.4. Word Usage

The word usage measures are an attempt to identify some other constructional features of writing style. There are many different ways in English to say the same thing. The constructions differ from one another in the form of the words used. The following sentences all convey approximately the same meaning but differ in word usage:

> The cxio program is used to perform all communication between the systems.
> The cxio program performs all communications between the systems.
> The cxio program is used to communicate between the systems.
> The cxio program communicates between the systems.
> All communication between the systems is performed by the cxio program.

The distribution of the parts of speech and verb constructions helps identify overuse of particular constructions. Although the measures used by STYLE are crude, they do point out problem areas. For each category, STYLE reports a percentage and a raw count. In addition to looking at the percentage, the user may find it useful to compare the raw count with the number of sentences. If, for example, the number of infinitives is almost equal to the number of sentences, then many of the sentences in the document are constructed like the first and third in the preceding example. The user may want to transform some of these sentences into another form. Some of the implications of the word usage measures are discussed below.

Verbs are measured in several different ways to try to determine what types of verb constructions are most frequent in the document. Technical writing tends to contain many passive verb constructions and other usage of the verb ''to be''. The category of verbs labeled ''tobe'' measures both passives and sentences of the form:

> *subject tobe predicate*

In counting verbs, whole verb phrases are counted as one verb. Verb phrases containing auxiliary verbs are counted in the category ''aux''. The verb phrases counted here are those whose tense is not simple present or simple past. It might eventually be useful to do more detailed measures of verb tense or mood. Infinitives are listed as ''inf''. The percentages reported for these three categories are based on the total number of verb phrases found. These categories are not mutually exclusive; they cannot be added, since, for example, ''to be going'' counts as both ''tobe'' and ''inf''. Use of these three types of verb constructions varies significantly among authors.

29

STYLE reports passive verbs as a percentage of the finite verbs in the document. Most style books warn against the overuse of passive verbs. Coleman [11] has shown that sentences with active verbs are easier to learn than those with passive verbs. Although the inverted object-subject order of the passive voice seems to emphasize the object, Coleman's experiments showed that there is little difference in retention by word position. He also showed that the direct object of an active verb is retained better than the subject of a passive verb. These experiments support the advice of the style books suggesting that writers should try to use active verbs wherever possible. The flag ''−p'' causes STYLE to print all sentences containing passive verbs.

Pronouns

add cohesiveness and connectivity to a document by providing back-reference. They are often a short-hand notation for something previously mentioned, and therefore connect the sentence containing the pronoun with the word to which the pronoun refers. Although there are other mechanisms for such connections, documents with no pronouns tend to be wordy and to have little connectivity.

Adverbs

can provide transition between sentences and order in time and space. In performing these functions, adverbs, like pronouns, provide connectivity and cohesiveness.

Conjunctions

provide parallelism in a document by connecting two or more equal units. These units may be whole sentences, verb phrases, nouns, adjectives, or prepositional phrases. The compound and compound-complex sentences reported under sentence type are parallel structures. Other uses of parallel structures are indicated by the degree that the number of conjunctions reported under word usage exceeds the compound sentence measures.

Nouns and Adjectives.

A ratio of nouns to adjectives near unity may indicate the over-use of modifiers. Some technical writers qualify every noun with one or more adjectives. Qualifiers in phrases like "simple linear single-link network model" often lend more obscurity than precision to a text.

Nominalizations

are verbs that are changed to nouns by adding one of the suffixes "ment", "ance", "ence", or "ion". Examples are accomplishment, admittance, adherence, and abbreviation. When a writer transforms a nominalized sentence to a non-nominalized sentence, she/he increases the effectiveness of the sentence in several ways. The noun becomes an active verb and frequently one complicated clause becomes two shorter clauses. For example,

> Their inclusion of this provision is admission of the importance of the system.
> When they included this provision, they admitted the importance of the system.

Coleman found that the transformed sentences were easier to learn, even when the transformation produced sentences that were slightly longer, provided the transformation broke one clause into two. Writers who find their document contains many nominalizations may want to transform some of the sentences to use active verbs.

2.5. Sentence openers

Another agreed upon principle of style is variety in sentence openers. Because STYLE determines the type of sentence opener by looking at the part of speech of the first word in the sentence, the sentences counted under the heading "subject opener" may not all really begin with the subject. However, a large percentage of sentences in this category still indicates lack of variety in sentence openers. Other sentence opener measures help the user determine if there are transitions between sentences and where the subordination occurs. Adverbs and conjunctions at the beginning of sentences are mechanisms for transition between sentences. A pronoun at the beginning shows a link to something previously mentioned and indicates connectivity.

The location of subordination can be determined by comparing the number of sentences that begin with a subordinator with the number of sentences with complex clauses. If few sentences start with subordinate conjunctions then the subordination is embedded or at the end of the complex sentences. For variety the writer may want to transform some sentences to have leading subordination.

The last category of openers, expletives, is commonly overworked in technical writing. Expletives are the words "it" and "there", usually with the verb "to be", in constructions where the subject follows the verb. For example,

> There are three streets used by the traffic.
> There are too many users on this system.

This construction tends to emphasize the object rather than the subject of the sentence. The flag ''−e'' will cause STYLE to print all sentences that begin with an expletive.

3. DICTION

The program DICTION prints all sentences in a document containing phrases that are either frequently misused or indicate wordiness. The program, an extension of Aho's FGREP [12] string matching program, takes as input a file of phrases or patterns to be matched and a file of text to be searched. A data base of about 450 phrases has been compiled as a default pattern file for DICTION. Before attempting to locate phrases, the program maps upper case letters to lower case and substitutes blanks for punctuation. Sentence boundaries were deemed less critical in DICTION than in STYLE, so abbreviations and other uses of the character ''.'' are not treated specially. DICTION brackets all pattern matches in a sentence with the characters ''['' '']'' . Although many of the phrases in the default data base are correct in some contexts, in others they indicate wordiness. Some examples of the phrases and suggested alternatives are:

Phrase	Alternative
a large number of	many
arrive at a decision	decide
collect together	collect
for this reason	so
pertaining to	about
through the use of	by or with
utilize	use
with the exception of	except

Appendix 2 contains a complete list of the default file. Some of the entries are short forms of problem phrases. For example, the phrase ''the fact'' is found in all of the following and is sufficient to point out the wordiness to the user:

Phrase	Alternative
accounted for by the fact that	caused by
an example of this is the fact that	thus
based on the fact that	because
despite the fact that	although
due to the fact that	because
in light of the fact that	because
in view of the fact that	since
notwithstanding the fact that	although

Entries in Appendix 2 preceded by ''~'' are not matched. See Section 7 for details on the use of ''~''.

The user may supply her/his own pattern file with the flag ''−f patfile''. In this case the default file will be loaded first, followed by the user file. This mechanism allows users to suppress patterns contained in the default file or to include their own pet peeves that are not in the default file. The flag ''−n'' will exclude the default file altogether. In constructing a pattern file, blanks should be used before and after each phrase to avoid matching substrings in words. For example, to find all occurrences of the word ''the'', the pattern '' the '' should be used. The blanks cause only the word ''the'' to be matched and not the string ''the'' in words like there, other, and therefore. One side effect of surrounding the words with blanks is that when two phrases occur without intervening words, only the first will be matched.

4. EXPLAIN

The last program, EXPLAIN, is an interactive thesaurus for phrases found by DICTION. The user types one of the phrases bracketed by DICTION and EXPLAIN responds with suggested substitutions for the phrase that will improve the diction of the document.

Table 1
Text Statistics on 20 Technical Documents

	variable	minimum	maximum	mean	standard deviation
Readability	Kincaid	9.5	16.9	13.3	2.2
	automated	9.0	17.4	13.3	2.5
	Cole-Liau	10.0	16.0	12.7	1.8
	Flesch	8.9	17.0	14.4	2.2
sentence info.	av sent length	15.5	30.3	21.6	4.0
	av word length	4.61	5.63	5.08	.29
	av nonfunction length	5.72	7.30	6.52	.45
	short sent	23%	46%	33%	5.9
	long sent	7%	20%	14%	2.9
sentence types	simple	31%	71%	49%	11.4
	complex	19%	50%	33%	8.3
	compound	2%	14%	7%	3.3
	compound-complex	2%	19%	10%	4.8
verb types	tobe	26%	64%	44.7%	10.3
	auxiliary	10%	40%	21%	8.7
	infinitives	8%	24%	15.1%	4.8
	passives	12%	50%	29%	9.3
word usage	prepositions	10.1%	15.0%	12.3%	1.6
	conjunction	1.8%	4.8%	3.4%	.9
	adverbs	1.2%	5.0%	3.4%	1.0
	nouns	23.6%	31.6%	27.8%	1.7
	adjectives	15.4%	27.1%	21.1%	3.4
	pronouns	1.2%	8.4%	2.5%	1.1
	nominalizations	2%	5%	3.3%	.8
sentence openers	prepositions	6%	19%	12%	3.4
	adverbs	0%	20%	9%	4.6
	subject	56%	85%	70%	8.0
	verbs	0%	4%	1%	1.0
	subordinating conj	1%	12%	5%	2.7
	conjunctions	0%	4%	0%	1.5
	expletives	0%	6%	2%	1.7

5. Results

5.1. STYLE

To get baseline statistics and check the program's accuracy, we ran STYLE on 20 technical documents. There were a total of 3287 sentences in the sample. The shortest document was 67 sentences long; the longest 339 sentences. The documents covered a wide range of subject matter, including theoretical computing, physics, psychology, engineering, and affirmative action. Table 1 gives the range, median, and standard deviation of the various style measures. As you will note most of the measurements have a fairly wide range of values across the sample documents.

As a comparison, Table 2 gives the median results for two different technical authors, a sample of instructional material, and a sample of the Federalist Papers. The two authors show similar styles, although author 2 uses somewhat shorter sentences and longer words than author 1. Author 1 uses all types of sentences, while author 2 prefers simple and complex sentences, using few compound or compound-complex sentences. The other major difference in the styles of these authors is the location of subordination. Author 1 seems to prefer embedded or trailing subordination, while author 2 begins many sentences with the subordinate clause. The documents tested for both authors 1 and 2 were technical documents, written for a technical audience. The instructional documents, which are written for craftspeople, vary surprisingly little from the two technical samples. The sentences and words are a little longer, and they contain many passive and auxiliary verbs, few adverbs, and almost no pronouns. The instructional documents contain many imperative sentences, so there are many sentence with verb openers. The sample of Federalist Papers contrasts with the other samples in almost every way.

Table 2
Text Statistics on Single Authors

	variable	author 1	author 2	inst.	FED
readability	Kincaid	11.0	10.3	10.8	16.3
	automated	11.0	10.3	11.9	17.8
	Coleman-Liau	9.3	10.1	10.2	12.3
	Flesch	10.3	10.7	10.1	15.0
sentence info	av sent length	22.64	19.61	22.78	31.85
	av word length	4.47	4.66	4.65	4.95
	av nonfunction length	5.64	5.92	6.04	6.87
	short sent	35%	43%	35%	40%
	long sent	18%	15%	16%	21%
sentence types	simple	36%	43%	40%	31%
	complex	34%	41%	37%	34%
	compound	13%	7%	4%	10%
	compound-complex	16%	8%	14%	25%
verb type	tobe	42%	43%	45%	37%
	auxiliary	17%	19%	32%	32%
	infinitives	17%	15%	12%	21%
	passives	20%	19%	36%	20%
word usage	prepositions	10.0%	10.8%	12.3%	15.9%
	conjunctions	3.2%	2.4%	3.9%	3.4%
	adverbs	5.05%	4.6%	3.5%	3.7%
	nouns	27.7%	26.5%	29.1%	24.9%
	adjectives	17.0%	19.0%	15.4%	12.4%
	pronouns	5.3%	4.3%	2.1%	6.5%
	nominalizations	1%	2%	2%	3%
sentence openers	prepositions	11%	14%	6%	5%
	adverbs	9%	9%	6%	4%
	subject	65%	59%	54%	66%
	verb	3%	2%	14%	2%
	subordinating conj	8%	14%	11%	3%
	conjunction	1%	0%	0%	3%
	expletives	3%	3%	0%	3%

5.2. DICTION

In the few weeks that DICTION has been available to users about 35,000 sentences have been run with about 5,000 string matches. The authors using the program seem to make the suggested changes about 50-75% of the time. To date, almost 200 of the 450 strings in the default file have been matched. Although most of these phrases are valid and correct in some contexts, the 50-75% change rate seems to show that the phrases are used much more often than concise diction warrants.

6. Accuracy

6.1. Sentence Identification

The correctness of the STYLE output on the 20 document sample was checked in detail. STYLE misidentified 129 sentence fragments as sentences and incorrectly joined two or more sentences 75 times in the 3287 sentence sample. The problems were usually because of nonstandard formatting commands, unknown abbreviations, or lists of non-sentences. An impossibly long sentence found as the longest sentence in the document usually is the result of a long list of non-sentences.

6.2. Sentence Types

Style correctly identified sentence type on 86.5% of the sentences in the sample. The type distribution of the sentences was 52.5% simple, 29.9% complex, 8.5% compound and 9% compound-complex. The program reported 49.5% simple, 31.9% complex, 8% compound and 10.4% compound-complex. Looking at the errors on the individual documents, the number of simple sentences was under-reported by about 4% and the complex and compound-complex were over-reported by 3% and 2%, respectively. The following matrix shows the programs output vs. the actual sentence type.

		Program Results			
		simple	complex	compound	comp-complex
Actual	simple	1566	132	49	17
Sentence	complex	47	892	6	65
Type	compound	40	6	207	23
	comp-complex	0	52	5	249

The system's inability to find imperative sentences seems to have little effect on most of the style statistics. A document with half of its sentences imperative was run, with and without the imperative end marker. The results were identical except for the expected errors of not finding verbs as sentence openers, not counting the imperative sentences, and a slight difference (1%) in the number of nouns and adjectives reported.

6.3. Word Usage

The accuracy of identifying word types reflects that of PARTS, which is about 95% correct. The largest source of confusion is between nouns and adjectives. The verb counts were checked on about 20 sentences from each document and found to be about 98% correct.

7. Technical Details

7.1. Finding Sentences

The formatting commands embedded in the text increase the difficulty of finding sentences. Not all text in a document is in sentence form; there are headings, tables, equations and lists, for example. Headings like "Finding Sentences" above should be discarded, not attached to the next sentence. However, since many of the documents are formatted to be phototypeset, and contain font changes, which usually operate on the most important words in the document, discarding all formatting commands is not correct. To improve the programs' ability to find sentence boundaries, the deformatting program, DEROFF [13], has been given some knowledge of the formatting packages used on the UNIX operating system. DEROFF will now do the following:

1. Suppress all formatting macros that are used for titles, headings, author's name, etc.

2. Suppress the arguments to the macros for titles, headings, author's name, etc.

3. Suppress displays, tables, footnotes and text that is centered or in no-fill mode.

4. Substitute a place holder for equations and check for hidden end markers. The place holder is necessary because many typists and authors use the equation setter to change fonts on important words. For this reason, header files containing the definition of the EQN delimiters must also be included as

input to STYLE. End markers are often hidden when an equation ends a sentence and the period is typed inside the EQN delimiters.

5.   Add a "." after lists. If the flag −ml is also used, all lists are suppressed. This is a separate flag because of the variety of ways the list macros are used. Often, lists are sentences that should be included in the analysis. The user must determine how lists are used in the document to be analyzed.

Both STYLE and DICTION call DEROFF before they look at the text. The user should supply the −ml flag if the document contains many lists of non-sentences that should be skipped.

7.2. Details of DICTION

The program DICTION is based on the string matching program FGREP. FGREP takes as input a file of patterns to be matched and a file to be searched and outputs each line that contains any of the patterns with no indication of which pattern was matched. The following changes have been added to FGREP:

1.   The basic unit that DICTION operates on is a sentence rather than a line. Each sentence that contains one of the patterns is output.

2.   Upper case letters are mapped to lower case.

3.   Punctuation is replaced by blanks.

4   All pattern matches in the sentence are found and surrounded with ''['' '']'' .

5.   A method for suppressing a string match has been added. Any pattern that begins with ''˜'' will not be matched. Because the matching algorithm finds the longest substring, the suppression of a match allows words in some correct contexts not to be matched while allowing the word in another context to be found. For example, the word ''which'' is often incorrectly used instead of ''that'' in restrictive clauses. However, ''which'' is usually correct when preceded by a preposition or '',''. The default pattern file suppresses the match of the common prepositions or a double blank followed by ''which'' and therefore matches only the suspect uses. The double blank accounts for the replaced comma.

8. Conclusions

A system of writing tools that measure some of the objective characteristics of writing style has been developed. The tools are sufficiently general that they may be applied to documents on any subject with equal accuracy. Although the measurements are only of the surface structure of the text, they do point out problem areas. In addition to helping writers produce better documents, these programs may be useful for studying the writing process and finding other formulae for measuring readability.

29

References

1. L. L. Cherry, ''PARTS - A System for Assigning Word Classes to English Text,'' submitted *Communications of the ACM.*

2. B. W. Kernighan and J. R. Mashey, ''The UNIX Programming Environment,'' *Software – Practice & Experience ,* **9**, 1-15 (1979).

3. G. R. Klare, ''Assessing Readability,'' *Reading Research Quarterly,* 1974-1975, **10** , 62-102.

4. E. A. Smith and P. Kincaid, ''Derivation and validation of the automated readability index for use with technical materials,'' *Human Factors,* 1970, 12, 457-464.

5. J. P. Kincaid, R. P. Fishburne, R. L. Rogers, and B. S. Chissom, ''Derivation of new readability formulas (Automated Readability Index, Fog count, and Flesch Reading Ease Formula) for Navy enlisted personnel,'' Navy Training Command Research Branch Report 8-75, Feb., 1975.

6. M. Coleman and T. L. Liau, ''A Computer Readability Formula Designed for Machine Scoring,'' *Journal of Applied Psychology,* 1975, 60, 283-284.

7. R. Flesch, ''A New Readability Yardstick,'' *Journal of Applied Psychology,* 1948, 32, 221-233.

8. E. U. Coke, private communication.

9. D. W. Ewing, *Writing for Results,* John Wiley & Sons, Inc., New York, N. Y. (1974).

10. G. Leggett, C. D. Mead and W. Charvat, *Prentice-Hall Handbook for Writers,* Seventh Edition, Prentice-Hall Inc., Englewood Cliffs, N. J. (1978).

11. E. B. Coleman, ''Learning of Prose Written in Four Grammatical Transformations,'' *Journal of Applied Psychology,* 1965, vol. 49, no. 5, pp. 332-341.

12 A. V. Aho and M. J. Corasick, ''Efficient String Matching: an aid to Bibliographic Search,'' *Communications of the ACM,* **18**, (6), 333-340, June 1975.

13. Bell Laboratories, *''UNIX TIME-SHARING SYSTEM: UNIX PROGRAMMER'S MANUAL,''* Seventh Edition, Vol. 1 (January 1979).

29

Appendix 1

STYLE Abbreviations

a. d.
A. M.
a. m.
b. c.
Ch.
ch.
ckts.
dB.
Dept.
dept.
Depts.
depts.
Dr.
Drs.
e. g.
Eq.
eq.
et al.
etc.
Fig.
fig.
Figs.
figs.
ft.
i. e.
in.
Inc.
Jr.
jr.
mi.
Mr.
Mrs.
Ms.
No.
no.
Nos.
nos.
P. M.
p. m.
Ph. D.
Ph. d.
Ref.
ref.
Refs.
refs.
St.
vs.
yr.

29

Appendix 2

Default DICTION Patterns

a great deal of
a large number of
a lot of
a majority of
a need for
a number of
a particular preference for
a preference for
a small number of
a tendency to
abovementioned
absolutely complete
absolutely essential
accomplished
accordingly
activate
actual
added increments
adequate enough
advent
afford an opportunity
aggregate
all of
all throughout
along the line
an indication of
analyzation
and etc
and or
another additional
any and all
arrive at a
as a matter of fact
as a method of
as good or better than
as of now
as per
as regards
as related to
as to
assistance
assistance to
assistance to
assuming that
at a later date
at about
at above
at all times
at an early date
at below

at the present
at the time when
at this point in time
at this time
at which time
at your earliest convenience
authorization
awful
basic fundamentals
basically
be cognizant of
being as
being that
brief in duration
bring to a conclusion
but that
but what
by means of
by the use of
carry out experiments
center about
center around
center portion
check into
check on
check up on
circle around
close proximity
collaborate together
collect together
combine together
come to an end
commence
common accord
compensation
completely eliminated
comprise
concerning
conduct an investigation of
conjecture
connect up
consensus of opinion
consequent result
consolidate together
construct
contemplate
continue on
continue to remain
could of
count up

couple together
debate about
decide on
deleterious effect
demean
demonstrate
depreciate in value
deserving of
desirable benefits
desirous of
different than
discontinue
disutility
divide up
doubt but
due to
duly noted
during the time that
each and every
early beginnings
effectuate
emotional feelings
empty out
enclosed herein
enclosed herewith
end result
end up
endeavor
enter in
enter into
enthused
entirely complete
equally good as
essentially
eventuate
every now and then
exactly identical
experiencing difficulty
fabricate
face up to
facilitate
facts and figures
fast in action
fearful of
fearful that
few in number
file away
final completion
final ending
final outcome

final result
finalize
find it interesting to know
first and foremost
first beginnings
first initiated
firstly
follow after
following after
for the purpose of
for the reason that
for the simple reason that
for this reason
for your information
from the point of view of
full and complete
generally agreed
good and
got to
gratuitous
greatly minimize
head up
help but
helps in the production of
hopeful
if and when
if at all possible
impact
implement
important essentials
importantly
in a large measure
in a position to
in accordance
in advance of
in agreement with
in all cases
in back of
in behalf of
in behind
in between
in case
in close proximity
in conflict with
in conjunction with
in connection with
in fact
in large measure
in many cases
in most cases
in my opinion I think
in order to
in rare cases
in reference to

in regard to
in regards to
in relation with
in short supply
in size
in terms of
in the amount of
in the case of
in the course of
in the event
in the field of
in the form of
in the instance of
in the interim
in the last analysis
in the matter of
in the near future
in the neighborhood of
in the not too distant future
in the proximity of
in the range of
in the same way as described
in the shape of
in the vicinity of
in this case
in view of the
in violation of
inasmuch as
indicate
indicative of
initialize
initiate
injurious to
inquire
inside of
institute a
intents and purposes
intermingle
irregardless
is defined as
is used to control
is when
is where
it is incumbent
it stands to reason
it was noted that if
joint cooperation
joint partnership
just exactly
kind of
know about
last but not least
later on
leaving out of consideration

liable
link up
literally
little doubt that
lose out on
lots of
main essentials
make a
make adjustments to
make an
make application to
make contact with
make mention of
make out a list of
make the acquaintance of
make the adjustment
manner
maximum possible
meaningful
meet up with
melt down
melt up
methodology
might of
minimize as far as possible
minor importance
miss out on
modification
more preferable
most unique
must of
mutual cooperation
necessary requisite
necessitate
need for
nice
not be un
not in a position to
not of a high order of accuracy
not un
notwithstanding
of considerable magnitude
of that
of the opinion that
off of
on a few occasions
on account of
on behalf of
on the grounds that
on the occasion
on the part of
one of the
open up
operates to correct

29

29

outside of
over with
overall
past history
perceptive of
perform a measurement
perform the measurement
permits the reduction of
personalize
pertaining to
physical size
plan ahead
plan for the future
plan in advance
plan on
present a conclusion
present a report
presently
prior to
prioritize
proceed to
procure
productive of
prolong the duration
protrude out from
provided that
pursuant to
put to use in
range all the way from
reason is because
reason why
recur again
reduce down
refer back
reference to this
reflective of
regarding
regretful
reinitiate
relative to
repeat again
representative of
resultant effect
resume again
retreat back
return again
return back
revert back
seal off
seems apparent
send a communication

short space of time
should of
single unit
situation
so as to
sort of
spell out
still continue
still remain
subsequent
substantially in agreement
succeed in
suggestive of
superior than
surrounding circumstances
take appropriate
take cognizance of
take into consideration
termed as
terminate
termination
the author
the authors
the case that
the fact
the foregoing
the foreseeable future
the fullest possible extent
the majority of
the nature
the necessity of
the only difference being that
the order of
the point that
the truth is
there are not many
through the medium of
through the use of
throughout the entire
time interval
to summarize the above
total effect of all this
totality
transpire
true facts
try and
ultimate end
under a separate cover
under date of
under separate cover
under the necessity to

underlying purpose
undertake a study
uniformly consistent
unique
until such time as
up to this time
upshot
utilize
very
very complete
very unique
vital
which
with a view to
with reference to
with regard to
with the exception of
with the object of
with the result that
with this in mind, it is clear that
within the realm of possibility
without further delay
worth while
would of
ing behavior
wise
~which
~about which
~after which
~at which
~between which
~by which
~for which
~from which
~in which
~into which
~of which
~on which
~on which
~over which
~through which
~to which
~under which
~upon which
~with which
~without which
~clockwise
~likewise
~otherwise

A Guide to the Dungeons of Doom

Michael C. Toy
Kenneth C. R. C. Arnold

Computer Systems Research Group
Department of Electrical Engineering and Computer Science
University of California
Berkeley, California 94720

ABSTRACT

Rogue is a visual CRT based fantasy game which runs under the UNIX† timesharing system. This paper describes how to play rogue, and gives a few hints for those who might otherwise get lost in the Dungeons of Doom.

1. Introduction

You have just finished your years as a student at the local fighter's guild. After much practice and sweat you have finally completed your training and are ready to embark upon a perilous adventure. As a test of your skills, the local guildmasters have sent you into the Dungeons of Doom. Your task is to return with the Amulet of Yendor. Your reward for the completion of this task will be a full membership in the local guild. In addition, you are allowed to keep all the loot you bring back from the dungeons.

In preparation for your journey, you are given an enchanted mace, a bow, and a quiver of arrows taken from a dragon's hoard in the far off Dark Mountains. You are also outfitted with elf-crafted armor and given enough food to reach the dungeons. You say goodbye to family and friends for what may be the last time and head up the road.

You set out on your way to the dungeons and after several days of uneventful travel, you see the ancient ruins that mark the entrance to the Dungeons of Doom. It is late at night, so you make camp at the entrance and spend the night sleeping under the open skies. In the morning you gather your weapons, put on your armor, eat what is almost your last food, and enter the dungeons.

2. What is going on here?

You have just begun a game of rogue. Your goal is to grab as much treasure as you can, find the Amulet of Yendor, and get out of the Dungeons of Doom alive. On the screen, a map of where you have been and what you have seen on the current dungeon level is kept. As you explore more of the level, it appears on the screen in front of you.

Rogue differs from most computer fantasy games in that it is screen oriented. Commands are all one or two keystrokes[1] and the results of your commands are displayed graphically on the screen rather than being explained in words.[2]

---

†UNIX is a trademark of Bell Laboratories

[1] As opposed to pseudo English sentences.

[2] A minimum screen size of 24 lines by 80 columns is required. If the screen is larger, only the 24x80 section will be used for the map.

Another major difference between rogue and other computer fantasy games is that once you have solved all the puzzles in a standard fantasy game, it has lost most of its excitement and it ceases to be fun. Rogue, on the other hand, generates a new dungeon every time you play it and even the author finds it an entertaining and exciting game.

3. What do all those things on the screen mean?

In order to understand what is going on in rogue you have to first get some grasp of what rogue is doing with the screen. The rogue screen is intended to replace the ''You can see ...'' descriptions of standard fantasy games. Figure 1 is a sample of what a rogue screen might look like.

3.1. The bottom line

At the bottom line of the screen are a few pieces of cryptic information describing your current status. Here is an explanation of what these things mean:

Level This number indicates how deep you have gone in the dungeon. It starts at one and goes up as you go deeper into the dungeon.

Gold The number of gold pieces you have managed to find and keep with you so far.

Hp Your current and maximum health points. Health points indicate how much damage you can take before you die. The more you get hit in a fight, the lower they get. You can regain health points by resting. The number in parentheses is the maximum number your health points can reach.

Str Your current strength and maximum ever strength. This can be any integer less than or equal to 99, or greater than or equal to 1. The higher the number, the stronger you are. The number in the parentheses is the maximum strength you have attained so far this game.

Arm Your current armor protection. This number indicates how effective your armor is in stopping blows from unfriendly creatures. The higher this number is, the more effective the armor.

Exp These two numbers give your current experience level and experience points. As you do things, you gain experience points. At certain experience point totals, you gain an experience level. The more experienced you are, the better you are able to fight and to withstand magical attacks.

3.2. The top line

The top line of the screen is reserved for printing messages that describe things that are impossible to represent visually. If you see a ''--More--'' on the top line, this means that rogue wants to print another message on the screen, but it wants to make certain that you have read the one that is there first. To read the next message, just type a space.

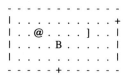

Level: 1 Gold: 0   Hp: 12(12) Str: 16(16) Arm: 4 Exp: 1/0

Figure 1

3.3. The rest of the screen

The rest of the screen is the map of the level as you have explored it so far. Each symbol on the screen represents something. Here is a list of what the various symbols mean:

@   This symbol represents you, the adventurer.

-| These symbols represent the walls of rooms.

+   A door to/from a room.

.   The floor of a room.

The floor of a passage between rooms.

*   A pile or pot of gold.

)   A weapon of some sort.

]   A piece of armor.

!   A flask containing a magic potion.

?   A piece of paper, usually a magic scroll.

=   A ring with magic properties

/   A magical staff or wand

^   A trap, watch out for these.

%   A staircase to other levels

:   A piece of food.

A-Z The uppercase letters represent the various inhabitants of the Dungeons of Doom. Watch out, they can be nasty and vicious.

4. Commands

Commands are given to rogue by typing one or two characters. Most commands can be preceded by a count to repeat them (e.g. typing ''10s'' will do ten searches). Commands for which counts make no sense have the count ignored. To cancel a count or a prefix, type <ESCAPE>. The list of commands is rather long, but it can be read at any time during the game with the ''?'' command. Here it is for reference, with a short explanation of each command.

?   The help command. Asks for a character to give help on. If you type a ''*'', it will list all the commands, otherwise it will explain what the character you typed does.

/   This is the ''What is that on the screen?'' command. A ''/'' followed by any character that you see on the level, will tell you what that character is. For instance, typing ''/@'' will tell you that the ''@'' symbol represents you, the player.

h, H, ^H
     Move left. You move one space to the left. If you use upper case ''h'', you will continue to move left until you run into something. This works for all movement commands (e.g. ''L'' means run in direction ''l'') If you use the ''control'' ''h'', you will continue moving in the specified direction until you pass something interesting or run into a wall. You should experiment with this, since it is a very useful command, but very difficult to describe. This also works for all movement commands.

j   Move down.

k   Move up.

l   Move right.

y   Move diagonally up and left.

u   Move diagonally up and right.

b   Move diagonally down and left.

n   Move diagonally down and right.

30

t   Throw an object. This is a prefix command. When followed with a direction it throws an object in
       the specified direction. (e.g. type ''th'' to throw something to the left.)

f   Fight until someone dies. When followed with a direction this will force you to fight the creature in
       that direction until either you or it bites the big one.

m   Move onto something without picking it up. This will move you one space in the direction you
       specify and, if there is an object there you can pick up, it won't do it.

z   Zap prefix. Point a staff or wand in a given direction and fire it. Even non-directional staves must be
       pointed in some direction to be used.

˄   Identify trap command. If a trap is on your map and you can't remember what type it is, you can get
       rogue to remind you by getting next to it and typing ''˄'' followed by the direction that would move
       you on top of it.

s   Search for traps and secret doors. Examine each space immediately adjacent to you for the existence
       of a trap or secret door. There is a large chance that even if there is something there, you won't find
       it, so you might have to search a while before you find something.

>   Climb down a staircase to the next level. Not surprisingly, this can only be done if you are standing
       on staircase.

<   Climb up a staircase to the level above. This can't be done without the Amulet of Yendor in your
       possession.

.   Rest. This is the ''do nothing'' command. This is good for waiting and healing.

,   Pick up something. This picks up whatever you are currently standing on, if you are standing on
       anything at all.

i   Inventory. List what you are carrying in your pack.

I   Selective inventory. Tells you what a single item in your pack is.

q   Quaff one of the potions you are carrying.

r   Read one of the scrolls in your pack.

e   Eat food from your pack.

w   Wield a weapon. Take a weapon out of your pack and carry it for use in combat, replacing the one
       you are currently using (if any).

W   Wear armor. You can only wear one suit of armor at a time. This takes extra time.

T   Take armor off. You can't remove armor that is cursed. This takes extra time.

P   Put on a ring. You can wear only two rings at a time (one on each hand). If you aren't wearing any
       rings, this command will ask you which hand you want to wear it on, otherwise, it will place it on the
       unused hand. The program assumes that you wield your sword in your right hand.

R   Remove a ring. If you are only wearing one ring, this command takes it off. If you are wearing two,
       it will ask you which one you wish to remove,

d   Drop an object. Take something out of your pack and leave it lying on the floor. Only one object
       can occupy each space. You cannot drop a cursed object at all if you are wielding or wearing it.

c   Call an object something. If you have a type of object in your pack which you wish to remember
       something about, you can use the call command to give a name to that type of object. This is usually
       used when you figure out what a potion, scroll, ring, or staff is after you pick it up but before it is
       truly identified. Each type of scroll and potion will become identified after its first use.

o   Examine and set options. This command is further explained in the section on options.

˄R   Redraws the screen. Useful if spurious messages or transmission errors have messed up the display.

˄P   Print last message. Useful when a message disappears before you can read it. Consecutive repeti-
       tions of this command will reveal the last five messages.

<ESCAPE>
       Cancel a command, prefix, or count.

!   Escape to a shell for some commands.

Q   Quit. Leave the game.

S   Save the current game in a file. It will ask you whether you wish to use the default save file. *Caveat*: Rogue won't let you start up a copy of a saved game, and it removes the save file as soon as you start up a restored game. This is to prevent people from saving a game just before a dangerous position and then restarting it if they die. To restore a saved game, give the file name as an argument to rogue. As in

% rogue save_file

v   Prints the program version number.

)   Print the weapon you are currently wielding

]   Print the armor you are currently wearing

=   Print the rings you are currently wearing

5. Rooms

Rooms in the dungeons are lit as you enter them. Upon leaving a room, all monsters inside the room are erased from the screen. In the darkness of a corridor, you can only see one space in all directions around you.

6. Fighting

If you see a monster and you wish to fight it, just attempt to run into it. Many times a monster you find will mind its own business unless you attack it. It is often the case that discretion is the better part of valor.

7. Objects you can find

When you find something in the dungeon, it is common to want to pick the object up. This is accomplished in rogue by walking over the object (unless you use the "m" prefix, see above). If you are carrying too many things, the program will tell you and it won't pick up the object, otherwise it will add it to your pack and tell you what you just picked up.

Many of the commands that operate on objects must prompt you to find out which object you want to use. If you change your mind and don't want to do that command after all, just type an <ESCAPE> and the command will be aborted.

Some objects, like armor and weapons, are easily differentiated. Others, like scrolls and potions, are given labels which vary according to type. During a game, any two of the same kind of object with the same label are the same type. However, the labels will vary from game to game.

When you use one of these labeled objects, if its effect may be obvious. Potions or scrolls will become identified at this point, but not other items. You may want to call these other items something so you will recognize it later, you can use the "call" command (see above).

7.1. Weapons

Some weapons, like arrows, come in bunches, but most come one at a time. In order to use a weapon, you must wield it. To fire an arrow out of a bow, you must first wield the bow, then throw the arrow. You can only wield one weapon at a time, but you can't change weapons if the one you are currently wielding is cursed. The commands to use weapons are "w" (wield) and "t" (throw).

7.2. Armor

There are various sorts of armor lying around in the dungeon. Some of it is enchanted, some is cursed, and some is just normal. Different armor types have different armor protection. The higher the armor protection, the more protection the armor affords against the blows of monsters. Here is a list of the various armor types and their normal armor protection:

Type	Protection
None	0
Leather armor	2
Studded leather / Ring mail	3
Scale mail	4
Chain mail	5
Banded mail / Splint mail	6
Plate mail	7

If a piece of armor is enchanted, its armor protection will be higher than normal. If a suit of armor is cursed, its armor protection will be lower, and you will not be able to remove it. However, not all armor with a protection that is lower than normal is cursed.

The commands to use weapons are "W" (wear) and "T" (take off).

7.3. Scrolls

Scrolls come with titles in an unknown tongue[3]. After you read a scroll, it disappears from your pack. The command to use a scroll is "r" (read).

7.4. Potions

Potions are labeled by the color of the liquid inside the flask. They disappear after being quaffed. The command to use a scroll is "q" (quaff).

7.5. Staves and Wands

Staves and wands do the same kinds of things. Staves are identified by a type of wood; wands by a type of metal or bone. They are generally things you want to do to something over a long distance, so you must point them at what you wish to affect to use them. Some staves are not affected by the direction they are pointed, though. Staves come with multiple magic charges, the number being random, and when they are used up, the staff is just a piece of wood or metal.

The command to use a wand or staff is "z" (zap)

7.6. Rings

Rings are very useful items, since they are relatively permanent magic, unlike the usually fleeting effects of potions, scrolls, and staves. Of course, the bad rings are also more powerful. Most rings also cause you to use up food more rapidly, the rate varying with the type of ring. Rings are differentiated by their stone settings. The commands to use rings are "P" (put on) and "R" (remove).

7.7. Food

Food is necessary to keep you going. If you go too long without eating you will faint, and eventually die of starvation. The command to use food is "e" (eat).

8. Options

Due to variations in personal tastes and conceptions of the way rogue should do things, there are a set of options you can set that cause rogue to behave in various different ways.

---

[3] Actually, it's a dialect spoken only by the twenty-seven members of a tribe in Outer Mongolia, but you're not supposed to *know* that.

8.1. Setting the options

There are two ways to set the options. The first is with the ''o'' command of rogue; the second is with the ''ROGUEOPTS'' environment variable[4].

8.1.1. Using the 'o' command

When you type ''o'' in rogue, it clears the screen and displays the current settings for all the options. It then places the cursor by the value of the first option and waits for you to type. You can type a <RETURN> which means to go to the next option, a ''−'' which means to go to the previous option, an <ESCAPE> which means to return to the game, or you can give the option a value. For boolean options this merely involves typing ''t'' for true or ''f'' for false. For string options, type the new value followed by a <RETURN>.

8.1.2. Using the ROGUEOPTS variable

The ROGUEOPTS variable is a string containing a comma separated list of initial values for the various options. Boolean variables can be turned on by listing their name or turned off by putting a ''no'' in front of the name. Thus to set up an environment variable so that **jump** is on, **passgo** is off, and the **name** is set to ''Blue Meanie'', use the command

    % setenv ROGUEOPTS "jump,nopassgo,name=Blue Meanie"[5]

8.2. Option list

Here is a list of the options and an explanation of what each one is for. The default value for each is enclosed in square brackets. For character string options, input over forty characters will be ignored.

jump [*nojump*]

If this option is set, running moves will not be displayed until you reach the end of the move. This saves considerable cpu and display time. This option defaults to *jump* if you are using a slow terminal.

passgo [*nopassgo*]

Follow turnings in passageways. If you run in a passage and you run into stone or a wall, rogue will see if it can turn to the right or left. If it can only turn one way, it will turn that way. If it can turn either or neither, it will stop. This algorithm can sometimes lead to slightly confusing occurrences which is why it defaults to *nopassgo*.

skull [*skull*]

Print out the skull at the end if you get killed. This is nice but slow, so you can turn it off if you like.

name [account name]

This is the name of your character. It is used if you get on the top ten scorer's list.

fruit [*slime-mold*]

This should hold the name of a fruit that you enjoy eating. It is basically a whimsey that rogue uses in a couple of places.

file [~/*rogue.save*]

The default file name for saving the game. If your phone is hung up by accident, rogue will automatically save the game in this file. The file name may start with the special character ''~'' which expands to be your home directory.

30

---

[4] On Version 6 systems, there is no equivalent of the ROGUEOPTS feature.

[5] For those of you who use the Bourne shell sh (1), the commands would be
$ ROGUEOPTS="jump,nopassgo,name=Blue Meanie"
$ export ROGUEOPTS

9. Scoring

Rogue maintains a list of the top scoring people or scores on your machine. If you score higher than someone else on this list, or better your previous score on the list, you will be inserted in the proper place under your current name.

If you quit the game, you get out with all of your gold intact. If, however, you get killed in the Dungeons of Doom, your body is forwarded to your next-of-kin, along with 90% of your gold; ten percent of your gold is kept by the Dungeons' wizard as a fee[6]. This should make you consider whether you want to take one last hit at that monster and possibly live, or quit and thus stop with whatever you have. If you quit, you do get all your gold, but if you swing and live, you might find more.

If you just want to see what the current top players/games list is, you can type
        % rogue −s

10. Acknowledgements

Rogue was originally conceived of by Glenn Wichman and Michael Toy. Ken Arnold and Michael Toy then smoothed out the user interface, and added jillions of new features. We would like to thank Bob Arnold, Michelle Busch, Andy Hatcher, Kipp Hickman, Mark Horton, Daniel Jensen, Bill Joy, Joe Kalash, Steve Maurer, Marty McNary, Jan Miller, and Scott Nelson for their ideas and assistance; and also the teeming multitudes who graciously ignored work, school, and social life to play rogue and send us bugs, complaints, suggestions, and just plain flames. And also Mom.

The public domain version of rogue now distributed with Berkeley UNIX was written by Timothy Stoehr.

30

---

[6] The Dungeon's wizard is named Wally the Wonder Badger. Invocations should be accompanied by a sizable donation.

STAR

TREK

by

Eric Allman
University of California
Berkeley

INTRODUCTION

Well, the federation is once again at war with the Klingon empire. It is up to you, as captain of the U.S.S. Enterprise, to wipe out the invasion fleet and save the Federation.

For the purposes of the game the galaxy is divided into 64 quadrants on an eight by eight grid, with quadrant 0,0 in the upper left hand corner. Each quadrant is divided into 100 sectors on a ten by ten grid. Each sector contains one object (e.g., the Enterprise, a Klingon, or a star).

Navigation is handled in degrees, with zero being straight up and ninety being to the right. Distances are measured in quadrants. One tenth quadrant is one sector.

The galaxy contains starbases, at which you can dock to refuel, repair damages, etc. The galaxy also contains stars. Stars usually have a knack for getting in your way, but they can be triggered into going nova by shooting a photon torpedo at one, thereby (hopefully) destroying any adjacent Klingons. This is not a good practice however, because you are penalized for destroying stars. Also, a star will sometimes go supernova, which obliterates an entire quadrant. You must never stop in a supernova quadrant, although you may "jump over" one.

Some starsystems have inhabited planets. Klingons can attack inhabited planets and enslave the populace, which they then put to work building more Klingon battle cruisers.

STARTING UP THE GAME

To request the game, issue the command

/usr/games/trek

31

from the shell. If a filename is supplied, a log of the game is written onto that file. (Otherwise, no file is written.) If the "−a" flag is stated before the filename, the log of the game is appended to the file.

The game will ask you what length game you would like. Valid responses are "short", "medium", and "long". You may also type "restart", which restarts a previously saved game. Ideally, the length of the game does not affect the difficulty, but currently the shorter games tend to be harder than the longer ones.

You will then be prompted for the skill, to which you must respond "novice", "fair", "good", "expert", "commodore", or "impossible". You should start out with a novice and work up, but if you really want to see how fast you can be slaughtered, start out with an impossible game.

In general, throughout the game, if you forget what is appropriate the game will tell you what it expects if you just type in a question mark.

ISSUING COMMANDS

If the game expects you to enter a command, it will say "Command: " and wait for your response. Most commands can be abbreviated.

At almost any time you can type more than one thing on a line. For example, to move straight up one quadrant, you can type
                        move 0 1
or you could just type
                        move
and the game would prompt you with
                        Course:
to which you could type
                        0 1
The "1" is the distance, which could be put on still another line. Also, the "move" command could have been abbreviated "mov", "mo", or just "m".

If you are partway through a command and you change your mind, you can usually type "-1" to cancel the command.

Klingons generally cannot hit you if you don't consume anything (e.g., time or energy), so some commands are considered "free". As soon as you consume anything though -- POW!

31

THE COMMANDS

Short Range Scan

> Mnemonic: srscan
> Shortest Abbreviation: s
> Full Commands: srscan
> > srscan yes/no
>
> Consumes: nothing

The short range scan gives you a picture of the quadrant you are in, and (if you say "yes") a status report which tells you a whole bunch of interesting stuff. You can get a status report alone by using the *status* command. An example follows:

```
Short range sensor scan
    0 1 2 3 4 5 6 7 8 9
0   . . . . . . * . * 0      stardate      3702.16
1   . . E . . . . . . 1      condition     RED
2   . . . . . . . . * 2      position      0,3/1,2
3   * . . . . # . . . 3      warp factor   5.0
4   . . . . . . . . . 4      total energy  4376
5   . . * . * . . . . 5      torpedoes     9
6   . . . @ . . . . . 6      shields       down, 78%
7   . . . . . . . . . 7      Klingons left 3
8   . . . K . . . . . 8      time left     6.43
9   . . . . . . * . . 9      life support  damaged, reserves = 2.4
    0 1 2 3 4 5 6 7 8 9
Distressed Starsystem Marcus XII
```

The cast of characters is as follows:

> E the hero
> K the villain
> # the starbase
> * stars
> @ inhabited starsystem
> . empty space
>   a black hole

The name of the starsystem is listed underneath the short range scan. The word "distressed", if present, means that the starsystem is under attack.

Short range scans are absolutely free. They use no time, no energy, and they don't give the Klingons another chance to hit you.

31

Status Report

> Mnemonic: status
> Shortest Abbreviation: st

Consumes: nothing

This command gives you information about the current status of the game and your ship, as follows:

Stardate -- The current stardate.

Condition -- as follows:

RED -- in battle
YELLOW -- low on energy
GREEN -- normal state
DOCKED -- docked at starbase
CLOAKED -- the cloaking device is activated

Position -- Your current quadrant and sector.

Warp Factor -- The speed you will move at when you move under warp power (with the *move* command).

Total Energy -- Your energy reserves. If they drop to zero, you die. Energy regenerates, but the higher the skill of the game, the slower it regenerates.

Torpedoes -- How many photon torpedoes you have left.

Shields -- Whether your shields are up or down, and how effective they are if up (what percentage of a hit they will absorb).

Klingons Left -- Guess.

Time Left -- How long the Federation can hold out if you sit on your fat ass and do nothing. If you kill Klingons quickly, this number goes up, otherwise, it goes down. If it hits zero, the Federation is conquered.

Life Support -- If "active", everything is fine. If "damaged", your reserves tell you how long you have to repair your life support or get to a starbase before you starve, suffocate, or something equally unpleasant.

Current Crew -- The number of crew members left. This figures does not include officers.

Brig Space -- The space left in your brig for Klingon captives.

Klingon Power -- The number of units needed to kill a Klingon. Remember, as Klingons fire at you they use up their own energy, so you probably need somewhat less than this.

Skill, Length -- The skill and length of the game you are playing.

Status information is absolutely free.

Long Range Scan

Mnemonic: lrscan

Shortest Abbreviation: l
Consumes: nothing

Long range scan gives you information about the eight quadrants that surround the quadrant you're in. A sample long range scan follows:

Long range scan for quadrant 0,3

	2	3	4
	! * !	* !	* !
0	! 108 !	6 !	19 !
1	! 9 !	/// !	8 !

The three digit numbers tell the number of objects in the quadrants. The units digit tells the number of stars, the tens digit the number of starbases, and the hundreds digit is the number of Klingons. "*" indicates the negative energy barrier at the edge of the galaxy, which you cannot enter. "///" means that that is a supernova quadrant and must not be entered.

Damage Report

Mnemonic: damages
Shortest Abbreviation: da
Consumes: nothing

A damage report tells you what devices are damaged and how long it will take to repair them. Repairs proceed faster when you are docked at a starbase.

Set Warp Factor

Mnemonic: warp
Shortest Abbreviation: w
Full Command: warp factor
Consumes: nothing

The warp factor tells the speed of your starship when you move under warp power (with the *move* command). The higher the warp factor, the faster you go, and the more energy you use.

The minimum warp factor is 1.0 and the maximum is 10.0. At speeds above warp 6 there is danger of the warp engines being damaged. The probability of this increases at higher warp speeds. Above warp 9.0 there is a chance of entering a time warp.

31

Move Under Warp Power

Mnemonic: move
Shortest Abbreviation: m
Full Command: move course distance

Consumes: time and energy

This is the usual way of moving. The course is in degrees and the distance is in quadrants. To move one sector specify a distance of 0.1.

Time is consumed proportionately to the inverse of the warp factor squared, and directly to the distance. Energy is consumed as the warp factor cubed, and directly to the distance. If you move with your shields up it doubles the amount of energy consumed.

When you move in a quadrant containing Klingons, they get a chance to attack you.

The computer detects navigation errors. If the computer is out, you run the risk of running into things.

The course is determined by the Space Inertial Navigation System [SINS]. As described in Star Fleet Technical Order TO:02:06:12, the SINS is calibrated, after which it becomes the base for navigation. If damaged, navigation becomes inaccurate. When it is fixed, Spock recalibrates it, however, it cannot be calibrated extremely accurately until you dock at starbase.

Move Under Impulse Power

Mnemonic: impulse
Shortest Abbreviation: i
Full Command: impulse course distance
Consumes: time and energy

The impulse engines give you a chance to maneuver when your warp engines are damaged; however, they are incredibly slow (0.095 quadrants/stardate). They require 20 units of energy to engage, and ten units per sector to move.

The same comments about the computer and the SINS apply as above.

There is no penalty to move under impulse power with shields up.

Deflector Shields

Mnemonic: shields
Shortest Abbreviation: sh
Full Command: shields up/down
Consumes: energy

Shields protect you from Klingon attack and nearby novas. As they protect you, they weaken. A shield which is 78% effective will absorb 78% of a hit and let 22% in to hurt you.

31

The Klingons have a chance to attack you every time you raise or lower shields. Shields do not rise and lower instantaneously, so the hit you receive will be computed with the shields at an intermediate effectiveness.

It takes energy to raise shields, but not to drop them.

Cloaking Device

> Mnemonic: cloak
> Shortest Abbreviation: cl
> Full Command: cloak up/down
> Consumes: energy

When you are cloaked, Klingons cannot see you, and hence they do not fire at you. They are useful for entering a quadrant and selecting a good position, however, weapons cannot be fired through the cloak due to the huge energy drain that it requires.

The cloak up command only starts the cloaking process; Klingons will continue to fire at you until you do something which consumes time.

Fire Phasers

> Mnemonic: phasers
> Shortest Abbreviation: p
> Full Commands: phasers automatic amount
>   phasers manual amt1 course1 spread1 ...
> Consumes: energy

Phasers are energy weapons; the energy comes from your ship's reserves ("total energy" on a srscan). It takes about 250 units of hits to kill a Klingon. Hits are cumulative as long as you stay in the quadrant.

Phasers become less effective the further from a Klingon you are. Adjacent Klingons receive about 90% of what you fire, at five sectors about 60%, and at ten sectors about 35%. They have no effect outside of the quadrant.

Phasers cannot be fired while shields are up; to do so would fry you. They have no effect on starbases or stars.

31

In automatic mode the computer decides how to divide up the energy among the Klingons present; in manual mode you do that yourself.

In manual mode firing you specify a direction, amount (number of units to fire) and spread (0 -> 1.0) for each of the six phaser banks. A zero amount terminates the manual input.

Fire Photon Torpedoes

>   Mnemonic: torpedo
>   Shortest Abbreviation: t
>   Full Command: torpedo course [yes/no] [burst angle]
>   Consumes: torpedoes

Torpedoes are projectile weapons -- there are no partial hits. You either hit your target or you don't. A hit on a Klingon destroys him. A hit on a starbase destroys that starbase (woops!). Hitting a star usually causes it to go nova, and occasionally supernova.

Photon torpedoes cannot be aimed precisely. They can be fired with shields up, but they get even more random as they pass through the shields.

Torpedoes may be fired in bursts of three. If this is desired, the burst angle is the angle between the three shots, which may vary from one to fifteen. The word "no" says that a burst is not wanted; the word "yes" (which may be omitted if stated on the same line as the course) says that a burst is wanted.

Photon torpedoes have no effect outside the quadrant.

Onboard Computer Request

>   Mnemonic: computer
>   Shortest Abbreviation: c
>   Full Command: computer request; request;...
>   Consumes: nothing

The computer command gives you access to the facilities of the onboard computer, which allows you to do all sorts of fascinating stuff. Computer requests are:

score -- Shows your current score.

course quad/sect -- Computes the course and distance from wherever you are to the given location. If you type "course /x,y" you will be given the course to sector x,y in the current quadrant.

move quad/sect -- Identical to the course request, except that the move is executed.

chart -- prints a chart of the known galaxy, i.e., everything that you have seen with a long range scan. The format is the same as on a long range scan, except that "..." means that you don't yet know what is there, and ".1." means that you know that a starbase exists, but you don't know anything else. "$$$" mans the quadrant that you are currently in.

trajectory -- prints the course and distance to all the Klingons in the quadrant.

warpcost dist warp_factor -- computes the cost in time and energy to move 'dist' quadrants at warp 'warp_factor'.

31

impcost dist -- same as warpcost for impulse engines.

pheff range -- tells how effective your phasers are at a given range.

distresslist -- gives a list of currently distressed starbases and starsystems.

More than one request may be stated on a line by separating them with semicolons.

Dock at Starbase

> Mnemonic: dock
> Shortest Abbreviation: do
> Consumes: nothing

You may dock at a starbase when you are in one of the eight adjacent sectors.

When you dock you are resupplied with energy, photon torpedoes, and life support reserves. Repairs are also done faster at starbase. Any prisoners you have taken are unloaded. You do not receive points for taking prisoners until this time.

Starbases have their own deflector shields, so you are safe from attack while docked.

Undock from Starbase

> Mnemonic: undock
> Shortest Abbreviation: u
> Consumes: nothing

This just allows you to leave starbase so that you may proceed on your way.

Rest

> Mnemonic: rest
> Shortest Abbreviation: r
> Full Command: rest time
> Consumes: time

This command allows you to rest to repair damages. It is not advisable to rest while under attack.

Call Starbase For Help

> Mnemonic: help
> Shortest Abbreviation: help
> Consumes: nothing

31

You may call starbase for help via your subspace radio. Starbase has long range transporter beams to get you. Problem is, they can't always rematerialize you.

You should avoid using this command unless absolutely necessary, for the above reason and because it counts heavily against you in the scoring.

Capture Klingon

> Mnemonic: capture
> Shortest Abbreviation: ca
> Consumes: time

You may request that a Klingon surrender to you. If he accepts, you get to take captives (but only as many as your brig can hold). It is good if you do this, because you get points for captives. Also, if you ever get captured, you want to be sure that the Federation has prisoners to exchange for you.

You must go to a starbase to turn over your prisoners to Federation authorities.

Visual Scan

> Mnemonic: visual
> Shortest Abbreviation: v
> Full Command: visual course
> Consumes: time

When your short range scanners are out, you can still see what is out "there" by doing a visual scan. Unfortunately, you can only see three sectors at one time, and it takes 0.005 stardates to perform.

The three sectors in the general direction of the course specified are examined and displayed.

Abandon Ship

> Mnemonic: abandon
> Shortest Abbreviation: abandon
> Consumes: nothing

The officers escape the Enterprise in the shuttlecraft. If the transporter is working and there is an inhabitable starsystem in the area, the crew beams down, otherwise you leave them to die. You are given an old but still usable ship, the Faire Queene.

Ram

> Mnemonic: ram
> Shortest Abbreviation: ram
> Full Command: ram course distance
> Consumes: time and energy

This command is identical to "move", except that the computer doesn't stop you from making navigation errors.

You get very nearly slaughtered if you ram anything.

Self Destruct

> Mnemonic: destruct
> Shortest Abbreviation: destruct
> Consumes: everything

Your starship is self-destructed. Chances are you will destroy any Klingons (and stars, and starbases) left in your quadrant.

Terminate the Game

> Mnemonic: terminate
> Shortest Abbreviation: terminate
> Full Command: terminate yes/no

Cancels the current game. No score is computed. If you answer yes, a new game will be started, otherwise trek exits.

Call the Shell

> Mnemonic: shell
> Shortest Abbreviation: shell

Temporarily escapes to the shell. When you exit the shell you will return to the game.

SCORING

The scoring algorithm is rather complicated. Basically, you get points for each Klingon you kill, for your Klingon per stardate kill rate, and a bonus if you win the game. You lose points for the number of Klingons left in the galaxy at the end of the game, for getting killed, for each star, starbase, or inhabited starsystem you destroy, for calling for help, and for each casualty you incur.

You will be promoted if you play very well. You will never get a promotion if you call for help, abandon the Enterprise, get killed, destroy a starbase or inhabited starsystem, or destroy too many stars.

31

COMMAND SUMMARY

Command	Requires	Consumes
abandon	shuttlecraft, transporter	-
capture	subspace radio	time
cloak **up/down**	cloaking device	energy
computer request; ...	computer	-
damages	-	-
destruct	computer	-
dock	-	-
help	subspace radio	-
impulse course distance	impulse engines, computer, SINS	time, energy
lrscan	L.R. sensors	-
move course distance	warp engines, computer, SINS	time, energy
phasers automatic amount amt1 course1 spread1 ...	phasers, computer phasers	energy phasers manual energy
torpedo course [yes] angle/**no**	torpedo tubes	torpedoes
ram course distance	warp engines, computer, SINS	time, energy
rest time	-	time
shell	-	-
shields **up/down**	shields	energy
srscan [yes/no]	S.R. sensors	-
status	-	-
terminate yes/no	-	-
undock	-	-
visual course	-	time
warp warp_factor	-	-

31

BERKELEY 4.4 SOFTWARE DISTRIBUTION

4.4BSD is the final release of what may be one of the most significant research projects in the history of computing. When Bell Labs originally released UNIX source code to the R&D community, brilliant researchers wrote their own software and added it to UNIX in a spree of creative anarchy that hasn't been equaled since. The Berkeley Software Distribution became the repository of much of that work.

In those years of creative ferment, source code was widely available, so programmers could build on the work of others. As UNIX became commercialized, access to source became increasingly curtailed and original development more difficult.

With this release of 4.4BSD-Lite, you need no longer work at a university or UNIX system development house to have access to UNIX source. The source code included on the 4.4BSD-Lite CD-ROM Companion will provide invaluable information on the design of any modern UNIX or UNIX-like system, and the source code for the utilities and support libraries will greatly enhance any programmer's toolkit. (Note that the 4.4BSD-Lite distribution does not include sources for the complete 4.4BSD system.

The source code for a small number of utilities and files, including a few from the operating system, were removed so that the system could be freely distributed.)

In addition to source code, the CD includes the manual pages, other documentation, and research papers from the University of California, Berkeley's 4.4BSD-Lite distribution.

This documentation is also available in printed form as a five-volume set.

—Tim O'Reilly

4.4BSD-Lite CD Companion

112 pages plus CD-ROM
CD Domestic ISBN 1-56592-081-3
CD International ISBN 1-56592-092-9

This CD is a copy of the University of California, Berkeley's 4.4BSD-Lite release, with additional documentation and enhancements. Access to the source code included here will provide invaluable information on the design of a modern UNIX-like system, and the source code for the utilities and support libraries will greatly enhance any programmer's toolkit. The CD is a source distribution, and does not contain program binaries for any architecture. It will not be possible to compile or run this software without a pre-existing system that is already installed and running. The 4.4BSD-Lite distribution did not include sources for the complete 4.4BSD system. The source code for a small number of utilities and files (including a few from the operating system) were removed so that the system could be freely distributed.

4.4BSD System Manager's Manual

646(est.) pages, ISBN 1-56592-080-5

Man pages for system administration commands and files, plus papers on system administration.

4.4BSD User's Reference Manual

909 pages, ISBN 1-56592-075-9

The famous "man pages" for over 500 utilities.

4.4BSD User's Supplementary Documents

686(est.) pages, ISBN 1-56592-076-7

Papers providing in-depth documentation of complex programs such as the shell, editors, and word processing utilities.

4.4BSD Programmer's Reference Manual

884 pages, ISBN 1-56592-078-3

Man pages for system calls, libraries, and file formats.

4.4BSD Programmer's Supplementary Documents

606(est.) pages, ISBN 1-56592-079-1

The original Bell and BSD research papers providing in-depth documentation of the programming environment.

GLOBAL NETWORK NAVIGATOR

The Global Network Navigator™ (GNN) is a unique kind of information service that makes the Internet easy and enjoyable to use. We organize access to the vast information resources of the Internet so that you can find what you want. We also help you understand the Internet and the many ways you can explore it.

Charting the Internet, the Ultimate Online Service

In GNN you'll find:

- **The Online Whole Internet Catalog**, an interactive card catalog for Internet resources that expands on the catalog in Ed Krol's bestselling book, *The Whole Internet User's Guide & Catalog.*

- **Newsnet**, a news service that keeps you up to date on what's happening on the Net.

- **The Netheads department**, which features profiles of interesting people on the Internet and commentary by Internet experts.

- **GNN Metacenters**, special-interest online magazines aimed at serving the needs of particular audiences. GNN Metacenters not only gather the best Internet resources together in one convenient place, they also introduce new material from a variety of sources. Each Metacenter contains new feature articles, as well as columns, subject-oriented reference guides for using the Internet, and topic-oriented discussion groups. Travel, music, education, and computers are some of the areas that we cover.

All in all, GNN helps you get more value for the time you spend on the Internet.

Subscribe Today

GNN is available over the Internet as a subscription service. To get complete information about subscribing to GNN, send email to **info@gnn.com**. If you have access to a World Wide Web browser such as Mosaic or Lynx, you can use the following URL to register online: `http://gnn.com/`

If you use a browser that does not support online forms, you can retrieve an email version of the registration form automatically by sending email to **form@gnn.com**. Fill this form out and send it back to us by email, and we will confirm your registration.

BOOK INFORMATION
AT YOUR FINGERTIPS

O'Reilly & Associates offers extensive online information through a Gopher server (*gopher.ora.com*). Here you can find detailed information on our entire catalog of books, tapes, and much more.

The O'Reilly Online Catalog

Gopher is basically a hierarchy of menus and files that can easily lead you to a wealth of information. Gopher is also easy to navigate; helpful instructions appear at the bottom of each screen (notice the three prompts in the sample screen below). Another nice feature is that Gopher files can be downloaded, saved, or printed out for future reference. You can also search Gopher files and even email them.

To give you an idea of our Gopher, here's a look at the top, or root, menu:

```
O'Reilly & Associates (The public gopher server)

    1.  News Flash! -- New Products and Projects/

    2.  Feature Articles/

    3.  Product Descriptions/

    4.  Ordering Information/

    5.  Complete Listing of Titles

    6.  Errata for "Learning Perl"

    7.  FTP Archive and Email Information/

    8.  Bibliographies/


Press ? for Help, q to Quit, u to go up a menu
```

The heart of the O'Reilly Gopher service is the extensive information provided on all ORA products in menu item three, "Product Descriptions." For most books this usually includes title information, a long description, a short author bio, the table of contents, quotes and reviews, a gif image of the book's cover, and even some interesting information about the animal featured on the cover (one of the benefits of a Gopher database is the ability to pack a lot of information in an organized, easy-to-find place).

How to Order

Another important listing is "Ordering Information," where we supply information to those interested in buying our books. Here, you'll find instructions and an application for ordering O'Reilly products online, a listing of distributors (local and international), a listing of bookstores that carry our titles, and much more.

The item that follows, "Complete Listing of Titles," is helpful when it's time to order. This single file, with short one-line listings of all ORA products, quickly provides the essentials for easy ordering: title, ISBN, and price.

And More

One of the most widely read areas of the O'Reilly Gopher is "News Flash!," which focuses on important new products and projects of ORA. Here, you'll find entries on newly published books and audiotapes; announcements of exciting new projects and product lines from ORA; upcoming tradeshows, conferences, and exhibitions of interest; author appearances; contest winners; job openings; and anything else that's timely and topical.

"Feature Articles" contains just that—many of the articles and interviews found here are excerpted from the O'Reilly magazine/catalog *ora.com*.

The "Bibliographies" entries are also very popular with readers, providing critical, objective reviews on the important literature in the field.

"FTP Archive and Email Information" contains helpful ORA email addresses, information about our "ora-news" listproc server, and detailed instructions on how to download ORA book examples via FTP.

Other menu listings are often available. "Errata for 'Learning Perl,'" for example, apprised readers of errata found in the first edition of our book, and responses to this file greatly aided our campaign to ferret out errors and typos for the upcoming corrected edition (a nice example of the mutual benefits of online interactivity).

Come and Explore

Our Gopher is vibrant and constantly in flux. By the time you actually log onto this Gopher, the root menu may well have changed. The goal is to always improve, and to that end we welcome your input (email: **gopher@ora.com**). We invite you to come and explore.

Here are four basic ways to call up our Gopher online.

1) If you have a local Gopher client, type:
   ```
   gopher gopher.ora.com
   ```

2) For Xgopher:
   ```
   xgopher -xrm "xgopher.root\
   Server: gopher.ora.com"
   ```

3) To use telnet (for those without a Gopher client):
   ```
   telnet gopher.ora.com
   ```
   login: **gopher** (no password)

4) For a World Wide Web browser, use this URL:
   ```
   http://gopher.ora.com:70/
   ```

COMPLETE LISTING OF TITLES

from O'Reilly & Associates, Inc.

INTERNET
The Whole Internet User's Guide & Catalog
Connecting to the Internet: An O'Reilly Buyer's Guide
!%@:: A Directory of Electronic Mail Addressing & Networks
Smileys

USING UNIX AND X
UNIX Power Tools (with CD-ROM)
UNIX in a Nutshell: System V Edition
UNIX in a Nutshell: Berkeley Edition
SCO UNIX in a Nutshell
Learning the UNIX Operating System
Learning the vi Editor
Learning GNU Emacs
Learning the Korn Shell
Making TeX Work
sed & awk
MH & xmh: E-mail for Users & Programmers
Using UUCP and Usenet
X Window System User's Guide: Volume 3
X Window System User's Guide, Motif Edition: Volume 3M

SYSTEM ADMINISTRATION
Essential System Administration
sendmail
Computer Security Basics
Practical UNIX Security
System Performance Tuning
TCP/IP Network Administration
Learning Perl
Programming perl
Managing NFS and NIS
Managing UUCP and Usenet
DNS and BIND
termcap & terminfo
X Window System Administrator's Guide: Volume 8
    (available with or without CD-ROM)

UNIX AND C PROGRAMMING
ORACLE Performance Tuning
High Performance Computing
lex & yacc
POSIX Programmer's Guide
Power Programming with RPC
Programming with curses
Managing Projects with make
Software Portability with imake
Understanding and Using COFF
Migrating to Fortran 90
UNIX for FORTRAN Programmers
Using C on the UNIX System
Checking C Programs with lint
Practical C Programming
Understanding Japanese Information Processing

DCE (DISTRIBUTED COMPUTING ENVIRONMENT)
Distributing Applications Across DCE and Windows NT
Guide to Writing DCE Applications
Understanding DCE

BERKELEY 4.4 SOFTWARE DISTRIBUTION
4.4BSD System Manager's Manual
4.4BSD User's Reference Manual
4.4BSD User's Supplementary Documents
4.4BSD Programmer's Reference Manual
4.4BSD Programmer's Supplementary Documents
4.4BSD-Lite CD Companion

X PROGRAMMING
The X Window System in a Nutshell
X Protocol Reference Manual: Volume 0
Xlib Programming Manual: Volume 1
Xlib Reference Manual: Volume 2
X Toolkit Intrinsics Programming Manual: Volume 4
X Toolkit Intrinsics Programming Manual, Motif Edition: Volume 4M
X Toolkit Intrinsics Reference Manual: Volume 5
Motif Programming Manual: Volume 6A
Motif Reference Manual: Volume 6B
XView Programming Manual: Volume 7A
XView Reference Manual: Volume 7B
PEXlib Programming Manual
PEXlib Reference Manual
PHIGS Programming Manual (softcover or hardcover)
PHIGS Reference Manual
Programmer's Supplement for R5 of the X Window System

THE X RESOURCE
A quarterly working journal for X programmers
The X Resource: Issues 0 through 10

OTHER
Building a Successful Software Business
Love Your Job!

TRAVEL
Travelers' Tales Thailand

AUDIOTAPES
Internet Talk Radio's "Geek of the Week" Interviews
The Future of the Internet Protocol, 4 hours
Global Network Operations, 2 hours
Mobile IP Networking, 1 hour
Networked Information and Online Libraries, 1 hour
Security and Networks, 1 hour
European Networking, 1 hour

Notable Speeches of the Information Age
John Perry Barlow, 1.5 hours

INTERNATIONAL DISTRIBUTORS

Customers outside North America can now order O'Reilly & Associates' books through the following distributors. They offer our international customers faster order processing, more bookstores, increased representation at tradeshows worldwide, and the high-quality, responsive service our customers have come to expect.

EUROPE, MIDDLE EAST, AND AFRICA
except Germany, Switzerland, and Austria

INQUIRIES
International Thomson Publishing Europe
Berkshire House
168-173 High Holborn
London WC1V 7AA
United Kingdom
Telephone: 44-71-497-1422
Fax: 44-71-497-1426
Email: danni.dolbear@itpuk.co.uk

ORDERS
International Thomson Publishing Services, Ltd.
Cheriton House, North Way
Andover, Hampshire SP10 5BE
United Kingdom
Telephone: 44-264-342-832 (UK orders)
Telephone: 44-264-342-806 (outside UK)
Fax: 44-264-364418 (UK orders)
Fax: 44-264-342761 (outside UK)

GERMANY, SWITZERLAND, AND AUSTRIA

International Thomson Publishing GmbH
O'Reilly-International Thomson Verlag
Königswinterer Strasse 418
53227 Bonn
Germany
Telephone: 49-228-445171
Fax: 49-228-441342
Email (CompuServe): 100272,2422
Email (Internet): 100272.2422@compuserve.com

ASIA
except Japan

INQUIRIES
International Thomson Publishing Asia
221 Henderson Road
#05 10 Henderson Building
Singapore 0315
Telephone: 65-272-6496
Fax: 65-272-6498

ORDERS
Telephone: 65-268-7867
Fax: 65-268-6727

AUSTRALIA

WoodsLane Pty. Ltd.
Unit 8, 101 Darley Street (P.O. Box 935)
Mona Vale NSW 2103
Australia
Telephone: 61-2-9795944
Fax: 61-2-9973348
Email: woods@tmx.mhs.oz.au

NEW ZEALAND

WoodsLane New Zealand Ltd.
7 Purnell Street (P.O. Box 575)
Wanganui, New Zealand
Telephone: 64-6-3476543
Fax: 64-6-3454840
Email: woods@tmx.mhs.oz.au

THE AMERICAS, JAPAN, AND OCEANIA

O'Reilly & Associates, Inc.
103A Morris Street
Sebastopol, CA 95472 U.S.A.
Telephone: 707-829-0515
Telephone: 800-998-9938 (U.S. & Canada)
Fax: 707-829-0104
Email: order@ora.com